THE TIME-LIFE BOOK OF THE
FAMILY CAR

TIME
LIFE
BOOKS ®

LIFE WORLD LIBRARY
LIFE NATURE LIBRARY
TIME READING PROGRAM
THE LIFE HISTORY OF THE UNITED STATES
LIFE SCIENCE LIBRARY
GREAT AGES OF MAN
TIME-LIFE LIBRARY OF ART
TIME-LIFE LIBRARY OF AMERICA
FOODS OF THE WORLD
THIS FABULOUS CENTURY
LIFE LIBRARY OF PHOTOGRAPHY
THE TIME-LIFE ENCYCLOPEDIA OF GARDENING
THE AMERICAN WILDERNESS
THE EMERGENCE OF MAN
THE OLD WEST
THE ART OF SEWING

·

FAMILY LIBRARY:

    THE TIME-LIFE BOOK OF FAMILY FINANCE
    THE TIME-LIFE FAMILY LEGAL GUIDE
    THE TIME-LIFE BOOK OF THE FAMILY CAR

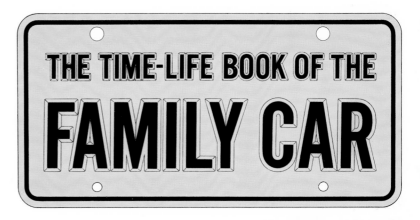

THE TIME-LIFE BOOK OF THE FAMILY CAR

BY THE EDITORS OF TIME-LIFE BOOKS

TIME-LIFE BOOKS, NEW YORK

TIME-LIFE BOOKS

FOUNDER: Henry R. Luce 1898–1967

Editor-in-Chief: Hedley Donovan
Chairman of the Board: Andrew Heiskell
President: James R. Shepley
Chairman, Executive Committee: James A. Linen
Group Vice President: Rhett Austell
Vice Chairman: Roy E. Larsen

MANAGING EDITOR: Jerry Korn
Assistant Managing Editors: David Maness,
Martin Mann, A. B. C. Whipple
Planning Director: Oliver E. Allen
Art Director: Sheldon Cotler
Chief of Research: Beatrice T. Dobie
Director of Photography: Melvin L. Scott
Senior Text Editors: Diana Hirsh, Ogden Tanner
Assistant Art Director: Arnold C. Holeywell

PUBLISHER: Joan D. Manley
General Manager: John D. McSweeney
Business Manager: John Steven Maxwell
Sales Director: Carl G. Jaeger
Promotion Director: Paul R. Stewart
Public Relations Director: Nicholas Benton

EDITORIAL STAFF FOR "THE FAMILY CAR"

EDITOR: John Paul Porter
Text Editors: George Constable, Frank K. Kappler,
Geraldine Schremp
Designer: Edward Frank
Staff Writers: Lee Greene, Don Nelson,
John von Hartz
Chief Researcher: Myra Mangan
Researchers: Gail Cruikshank, Marilyn Daley,
Michael Drons, Lee Hassig, Michael Luftman,
Mary Carroll Marden, Joyce Pelto
Art Assistants: Marion Flynn, Anne B. Landry,
Frank Pagnato

Editorial Production
Production Editor: Douglas B. Graham
Assistant: Gennaro C. Esposito
Quality Director: Robert L. Young
Assistant: James J. Cox
Copy Staff: Rosalind Stubenberg (chief),
Heidi Sanford, Florence Keith
Picture Department: Dolores A. Littles,
Marianne Dowell

*Valuable assistance was given by the following
departments and individuals of Time Inc.:
MONEY Senior Editor Robert Klein; Editorial
Production, Norman Airey, Nicholas Costino
Jr.; Library, Benjamin Lightman; Picture
Collection, Doris O'Neil; Photographic Library,
George Karas; TIME-LIFE News Service,
Murray J. Gart; Correspondents Bonnie
Angelo and Jerry Hannifin (Washington), Jane
Rieker (Miami), Ed Thomas (San Diego).*

CONTENTS

CONSULTANTS

DOUGLAS W. TOMS, as general consultant, has read and commented on all parts of this book. He is a former head of the National Highway Traffic Safety Administration, an agency of the U.S. Department of Transportation, and prior to his federal service was Director of the Department of Motor Vehicles for the state of Washington. Mr. Toms holds a master's degree in Traffic Administration from Michigan State University. At present he is in private industry.

I. ROBERT EHRLICH was chief consultant to the editors on automotive engineering principles and theory. Dr. Ehrlich is Research Associate Professor of Mechanical Engineering and manager of the Transportation Research Group at Stevens Institute of Technology, Hoboken, New Jersey. He received his doctorate in Mechanical Engineering at the University of Michigan.

HAROLD H. ALTMAN and **ANTHONY J. ZEME** were chief consultants for the chapters on practical maintenance and repairs. Both Mr. Altman and Mr. Zeme have been engaged in automotive repair work for more than 40 years. They jointly own and operate a repair service in New York City.

ARTISTS

ARTHUR DALE GUSTAFSON executed all the illustrations that show how the automobile works, as well as the drawings that accompany the chapters on maintenance and repairs and on tuning an engine. Mr. Gustafson has worked as a stylist and illustrator with two major automobile-manufacturing companies and is presently a freelance artist specializing in automotive subjects.

George V. Kelvin, Syd Mead and Dan Todd also contributed major illustrations to this book. A complete list of credits will be found on page 348.

WRITERS

Charles G. Burck, Kim Chapin, Tony Chiu, Henry Moscow, Morton J. Schultz, Carlton Smith, Peter Vanderwicken and Paul Weissler have contributed to the text of this book.

INTRODUCTION

Good relationships, with cars as with all else, are based on understanding. If you know how cars are sold, what sort of financing and insurance is available, how your car works, how to get the most out of it under all conditions, how to take care of it and how to deal with mechanics, you're bound to be a happier owner. Yet car ownership in all of its aspects is today so formidably complicated that practically all owners sooner or later make some bad decisions—usually because they lacked or ignored relatively basic and easy-to-come-by facts. Perhaps they reject inexpensive options that would add immeasurably to their driving pleasure or they take out too little insurance or they permit themselves to be cheated by a garage. Even the little mistakes often exact a high price in money and inconvenience. Long gone is that forgiving era when you could replace a front fender on a Model T for only $2.50.

This book is designed to promote the best possible relationship between you and your car by removing the mysteries that can cause grief. It is a reference book and should be used as such whenever you face a decision or a problem. At the back of the book are a glossary of automotive terms and an extensive index; they are designed to direct you to the information you need when you need it.

Several chapters deal with the mechanical workings of a car—and what you can do to keep the car working right. In an age of soaring repair costs, you can save a great deal of money by personally taking on some of the upkeep and repair chores. However, this ambition should be approached in stages. First get acquainted with how a car operates *(Chapter 1)*; then try your hand at simple upkeep tasks; and as your skill and confidence grow, move up to more demanding maintenance and repairs. Any of the jobs described in this book can be competently performed by an amateur who has the proper tools. But you must follow the instructions to the letter, for the work must be done meticulously and it can be hazardous. The degree to which you choose to be your own mechanic is, of course, a personal judgment; certainly some jobs (so indicated) are better left to professional experts. But it pays off—and not just in money or in convenience—to become as expert as you can. The more you know about your car, the more you will appreciate and enjoy it.

The Editors

THE CAR

WHY IT'S MADE THE WAY IT IS, AND HOW IT WORKS

1

No individual invented the automobile you drive today. The car—a word derived from an ancient Celtic term for cart or wagon—has evolved, bit by bit, from the inspirations, creations and tinkerings of hundreds of men dating back to the 13th Century, when English scientist-philosopher Roger Bacon wrote that "cars can be made so that without animals they will move with unbelievable rapidity."

Bacon, who was convinced that such vehicles had actually existed in ancient times, unfortunately had not the foggiest notion of what would make them go. It was a problem that apparently also stumped the brilliant Leonardo da Vinci two centuries later. Leonardo drew sketches of a tanklike self-propelled vehicle but provided no clues to its power source.

The development of the steam engine in the 18th Century triggered the first crude attempts to build a self-propelled vehicle. Actually, the idea of a steam-powered carriage had been put forward by physicist Isaac Newton as early as 1680. But it was another hundred years before a Scotsman, James Watt, created an engine that eventually would make a steam car feasible. Watt's engine applied steam to a piston enclosed within a sealed cylinder to drive a power-providing crankshaft. His invention triggered the Industrial Revolution as English industry adopted steam-powered machinery.

While England pioneered stationary steam engines, it was a Frenchman, Captain Nicholas Cugnot, who constructed the first steam car (overleaf). Its performance in 1769 left much to be desired. At a top speed of three miles an hour—half the speed of a normal walk—it lumbered 100 yards on a head of steam.

For all practical purposes, Cugnot's car was

a failure. And although the steam car continued to intrigue engineers and mechanics, as it does to this day (pages 330, 331), it had become obvious by the middle of the 19th Century that something better than a steam engine was needed to fulfill Bacon's prophecy. By that time the bulky fireboxes and boilers of the early steam engines had been adapted, with great success and far-reaching consequences, to steamships and railroad locomotives. These engines, however, were too heavy and inefficient for use in a road vehicle. In fact, the development of steam cars in England stopped altogether after 1865, when the Red Flag Law was passed. The law, which remained in effect until 1896, forbade any self-propelled vehicle from traveling on a public road unless preceded by a man on foot carrying a red warning flag.

But even as the railroad was being hailed as the ultimate form of land transportation in Europe and the United States, a handful of men were beginning to tinker with a completely new concept: a gas-powered car. They were inspired by the compactness and efficiency of a new type of engine that was being developed in the second half of the 19th Century. Like the steam engine, it was designed to provide power by moving a piston inside a cylinder. But where the steam engine used fuel to boil water outside the cylinder in order to produce steam pressure, the new internal-combustion engine was able to convert fuel directly into power by burning it inside the cylinder. The fuel could be any flammable gas, and many of the early internal-combustion engines ran on coal-derived illuminating gas, the kind that was used in the street lamps of the period.

One of the early experimenters with the new internal-combustion engine was a versatile Viennese engineer-chemist named Siegfried Marcus. In 1860 he devised a way to create a superior flammable gas by mixing liquid fuel and air. He called the mixture "carbureted air," using the chemical term for adding carbon to air and indirectly contributing the word carburetor to the automotive lexicon.

In 1864, Marcus tested his new fuel in an internal-combustion engine of his own design. Mounting the engine on a four-wheeled wagon, he ran it at night on a road alongside a Vienna cemetery. The unearthly racket didn't wake the dead, but it aroused the living and Marcus was forced to halt his test runs.

Marcus contented himself by experimenting indoors with stationary engines until he read of a new development in internal-combustion engines that led him to think about building another car. Until the 1860s, the only practical gas engines operated on the same two-cycle basis as the steam engine, with one small explosion required for every up-and-down piston stroke. While the two-cycle gas engine produced more power than a steam engine of the same size, it was noisier and used a lot of fuel.

By 1862 a French engineer, Alphonse Beau de Rochas, had come up with a better idea. He patented the design for a four-cycle internal-combustion engine. This design called for a single large explosion for every two up-and-down piston strokes (page 23), providing the power of a two-cycle engine with far less fuel.

Beau de Rochas never built the engine he patented, but his description of it was so clear and logical that a number of European engineers immediately began working on their own models. One of them was Siegfried Marcus.

In 1875, using a four-cycle engine, Marcus had developed an improved vehicle that many historians identify as the first practical motorcar. Its four sturdy wagon wheels were linked by belts and pulleys to a crude one-cylinder engine. Since the vehicle had no gearshift, it was restricted to a single forward speed of about 10 miles an hour. But Marcus was far ahead of

THE OLDEST ANCESTOR OF THE AUTOMOBILE

History's first self-propelled vehicle was this steam tractor designed and built in 1769 by Captain Nicholas Cugnot of the French Army. The copper boiler in front was heated by an internal fire pot and transmitted steam through a pipe at the top to a pair of cylinders. The steam pressure inside the cylinders forced down pistons that turned the single front wheel. The wheel's rotation then lifted the pistons for the next stroke. The springless vehicle was steered by a tiller that swiveled the front end.

Clumsy and inefficient—it had to stop every 100 yards to get up steam again—the steam tractor came to an ignominious end in 1770 by running off the road and hitting a stone wall. The French War Ministry, embarrassed at having financed such an improbable project, ordered Captain Cugnot to cease work on his invention.

his time in devising an efficient carburetor with a manual throttle, an electric-spark ignition system, a small steering wheel that turned the entire front axle on a pivot, and a convenient cranking system that allowed the engine to be started from the driver's seat.

Unfortunately, Marcus regarded his car as nothing more than an interesting experiment and decided not to develop it any further. By the time he got around to patenting the car's original features, almost a decade later, his achievement had been all but forgotten. Today his 1875 car is a museum curiosity in Vienna, while credit for patenting the first car is shared by a pair of German engineers, Gottlieb Daimler and Karl Benz.

Daimler and Benz, whose names were later commercially linked in the corporate name of Germany's most prestigious automobile manufacturer, were relentless rivals who never once spoke to each other. Part of their mutual ill feeling was due to the fact that each claimed to be the first to have built a practical motorcar with an internal-combustion engine—completely ignoring the earlier Marcus car.

Daimler's claim was based on the help he gave a German manufacturer, Nikolaus Otto, in the development of a remarkable four-cycle internal-combustion engine that came to be called the Silent Otto. As Otto's chief engineer, Daimler had helped design the stationary engine. Compact, quiet and economical, the Otto was intended for use with light industrial machinery. But Daimler, feeling it could be easily adapted for transportation, opened his own workshop in 1882 to make the modifications.

Within a year Daimler had come up with an engine not only much lighter than the Otto but able to turn a crankshaft at 900 revolutions per

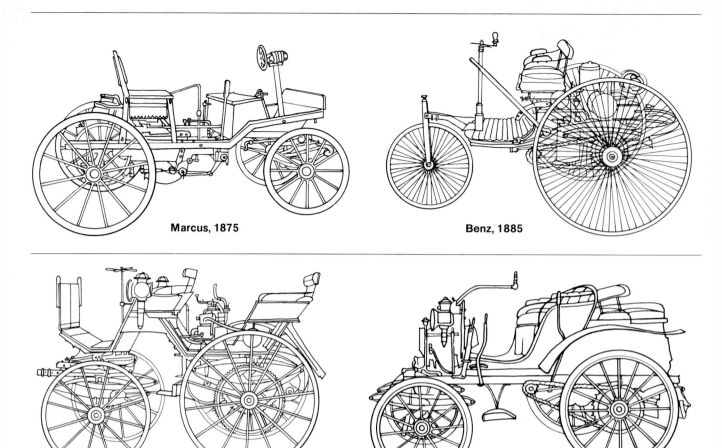

Marcus, 1875

Benz, 1885

Daimler, 1886

Panhard, 1894

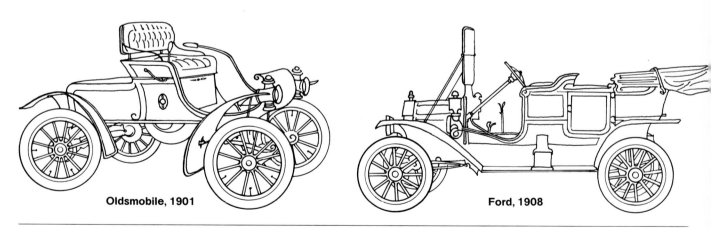

Oldsmobile, 1901

Ford, 1908

These six quaint vehicles, whose origins are discussed in the accompanying chapter, are among the most important ancestors of today's cars. The Marcus motorized wagon was the first vehicle to be effectively powered by an internal-combustion engine. The first motorcars developed for production were the Benz three-wheeler and the Daimler motorized carriage. The Panhard, generally considered to be the prototype of the modern car, was the first to be designed with an engine in the front, drive wheels in the rear and a passenger area in between. Oldsmobile's sprightly curved-dash runabout was the world's first mass-produced automobile; 18,500 were made in five years. That record was soon dwarfed by Ford's fabulous Model T; 15 million were manufactured before the T's 15-year run ended in 1927.

minute compared to the Otto's 200. The secret behind the engine's superior performance was a new fuel formula that combined 91 parts of gasoline—previously a little-used petroleum by-product—with 9 parts of air. Daimler boasted that with his new engine, "I have created the basis for an entirely new industry!"

Daimler felt that his engine would be ideal for motorboats and all sorts of land vehicles. His pet project was a motorized bicycle that was successfully tested and patented in 1885. Not until late in 1886 did Daimler get around to patenting his motor vehicle, a simple conversion of a horse-drawn carriage utilizing a one-cylinder, one-and-one-half-horsepower engine mounted in the rear. A crude transmission system allowed the engine to be run in two forward speeds and in neutral. Satisfied that he had created the first real car with an internal-combustion engine, Daimler then tried his hand at boats, streetcars and fire engines.

But Daimler hadn't been the only one to realize the potential of the Otto engine. Before the Otto came along, Karl Benz had developed a two-cycle engine. Impressed by the greater efficiency of the new Otto design, Benz—like Daimler—began modifying the Otto, but with the single thought of using it in a motor vehicle. The vehicle turned out to be a specially built tricycle that Benz successfully tested in 1885 and patented early in 1886—*after* Daimler's two-wheeler but *before* Daimler's four-wheeler. Benz then claimed the honor of having built the first true car with an internal-combustion engine.

With both prestige and future sales at stake, Daimler and Benz hotly disputed each other's claim. Daimler pointed out that he had successfully tested his engine on a bicycle before Benz had patented his tricycle and that, in any event, he was the first to patent a four-wheeled car. Benz was willing to concede that Daimler

was the inventor of the motorcycle but insisted that his tricycle was the first motorcar.

The claims are argued to this day, with historians giving both men a good share of the credit: Daimler for an engine superior to Benz's that ran at less than one horsepower and had a speed of about 300 revolutions per minute; Benz for such features as water cooling, electric ignition and differential gears.

Although both Daimler and Benz went on to become successful independent automobile manufacturers, it was in France (rather than Germany) during the last decade of the 19th Century that the automobile began to assume its present form and popularity. The wide, level boulevards of Paris, and the fine paved roads radiating out of the French capital, were ideal settings for rich sportsmen to display their noisy new playthings. By 1895 there were so many self-propelled vehicles puttering about that the French Academy formally added a new word to the French language to describe them. The word was automobile, from the Greek word for self (*auto*) and the Latin word for moving (*mobilis*).

One of the first vehicles to become officially designated as an automobile was a car generally considered to be the prototype of the modern automobile. It was a Daimler-powered vehicle built in 1892 by the Parisian carriage-making firm of Panhard & Levassor. The Panhard marked the initial appearance of the automobile in what was to be its classic design: the engine in front, supplying power to a gearbox behind it; the gearbox was connected by a chain drive to the rear drive wheels. The Panhard had four forward speeds as well as a reverse, and an 1894 model made headlines when it covered the 750-mile distance from Paris to Rouen in 48 hours at an average speed of 15 miles an hour.

THE CAR'S DEBT TO THE BICYCLE

While early automobiles were called horse-less carriages—and indeed the first ones were little more than motorized versions of horse-drawn vehicles—the automobile surprisingly owes more to the bicycle than to the buggy. In fact, the booming American bicycle industry of the 1890s can be considered the parent of the infant automobile industry.

Many automobile pioneers were men with extensive experience in manufacturing and repairing bicycles. Charles Duryea, who designed the first American car in 1893, was a skilled bicycle mechanic. Alexander Winton, a bicycle manufacturer, produced the first American high-performance car in 1897, a 12-horsepower model that recorded an astounding speed of 33.7 miles an hour. Henry Ford, an inveterate tinkerer, made extensive use of bicycle parts, including a saddle, in the construction of his first car in 1896. Appropriately, it was called a quadricycle.

In all there were 27 American bicycle manufacturers in 1890, and many of them were, like Winton, to play important roles in automobile development. For example, the Pope Manufacturing Company opened a motor-carriage department in 1897 that produced Columbia cars, capitalizing on the popularity of its Columbia bicycles. The makers of the rival Rambler bike were so successful with the Rambler automobile they introduced in 1902 that they decided to stop making bicycles entirely and concentrate on cars.

For struggling auto makers, bicycle firms were among the chief suppliers of lightweight steel tubing, gears, chain drives, ball and roller bearings, wire wheels, pneumatic tires, tools—and occasionally even factory space.

Finally, it was from the ranks of bicycle dealers that many of the first automobile dealers were recruited. And so, as it turned out, the place to buy your first horseless carriage at the turn of the century was at your neighborhood bicycle shop.

But even as the automobile was becoming an increasingly familiar sight on European roads in the 1890s, it was still considered a freakish contraption in the United States. Americans relied on railroads, bicycles and horse-drawn carriages to get them about in a nation where only 200 miles of paved roads existed outside the cities as late as 1900. There was relatively little interest in European cars and engine developments until almost a decade after Daimler and Benz had patented their cars. By the early 1890s, when American automotive pioneers began assembling crude horseless carriages, they had a lot of catching up to do.

According to Hiram Maxim, a young engineer who began working on a car of his own design in 1892, there were at least 50 other people in the United States doing the same thing at the same time—with hardly any of them aware of the others' existence.

The first of these cars to be completed and successfully tested was the modest motor carriage assembled from existing odds and ends by the Duryea brothers, Frank and Charles, in 1893. The Duryeas, both skilled mechanics, put together a simple car that consisted of a one-cylinder, four-horsepower engine fixed underneath the seat of a secondhand buggy and connected to the drive wheels by a belt. The carburetor was constructed from a perfume atomizer and an alcohol burner.

Hard on the heels of the Duryea brothers came a flood of American cars. It was estimated that some 300 different pilot models were produced by Americans during the 1890s. By 1900 there were at least 57 American automobile plants producing about 4,000 cars annually. Most of them were assembled from purchased parts and required no heavy initial investment. A typical automobile plant might consist of a dozen mechanics working out of a converted barn.

The first of these early cars to catch the public's fancy was a sprightly little open roadster immortalized in song as the Merry Oldsmobile.

Designed as an economy car by automotive pioneer Ransom E. Olds after his earlier steam cars and electric cars failed to sell, the curved-dash runabout had two seats and a dependable one-cylinder engine that delivered three horsepower. The car sold for $650, about half the price of its competitors, and sales zoomed from 425 in 1901, the year it was introduced, to a then-phenomenal 6,500 in 1905, its last year.

Olds discontinued the little car to concentrate on larger, more expensive designs. But other manufacturers quickly moved in to fill the need for an inexpensive family car. One of them was Henry Ford, a self-trained engineer who founded the Ford Motor Company in 1903. Ford believed it was possible to produce a no-frills "car for the great multitude" for $500. The car that was to prove him right, and put a nation on wheels, was the Model T.

Adapted from an earlier version called the Model N, the Model T was solidly constructed, and easy to operate and repair. Its chassis was mounted high to provide clearance on rutted country roads, and a peppy four-cylinder engine produced 20 horsepower in two forward speeds and reverse. When it was introduced, the 1909 Model T came in five body styles and the least expensive version cost $825—much higher than Ford's $500 goal.

But the car was so superior in its price range to any being made by other manufacturers that Ford discontinued all other models in 1909 to concentrate on the Model T. By 1911 the T was the most popular car in America, selling at a rate of 50,000 per year.

In 1914, when Ford opened the world's first moving assembly line for automobiles, production—and sales—jumped to an astounding 472,000. Ford's assembly line could turn out a complete car in 90 minutes, and by 1920, when Ford sold nearly a million cars, one of every two automobiles being made was a Model T. By 1927, when the last Model T rolled off the assembly line, more than 15 million had been made and the price had dropped to $320— almost half the original target point.

The 18-year supremacy of the Model T saw the disappearance of many of the smaller manufacturers and the consolidation of others. One of those consolidations was to become the General Motors Corporation, today the world's largest automobile manufacturer.

General Motors was the brainchild of a colorful entrepreneur named William C. Durant. Originally a successful carriage maker in Flint, Michigan, Durant had purchased the financially ailing Buick Motor Car Company in 1904. By 1907 Durant had conceived the idea of combining Buick and other major automobile companies into a single large corporation that would sell a variety of cars and manufacture many of its own parts. Under Durant's leadership General Motors was incorporated in 1908 and quickly merged Buick, Cadillac, Oldsmobile and Oakland (later Pontiac) under a single management. Henry Ford was willing to join the new group, but Durant couldn't meet his price—eight million dollars in cash.

But Ford's virtual monopoly of the low-priced automobile market ended shortly after World War I, as other manufacturers began to produce more attractive cars than the Model T at prices well under $1,000. The Chevrolet Motor Company put out a popular four-cylinder model priced at $490 in 1916, the year before the company was acquired by General Motors. As the lowest-priced car in the General Motors line, Chevrolet eventually was to pass Ford as the best-selling car in America.

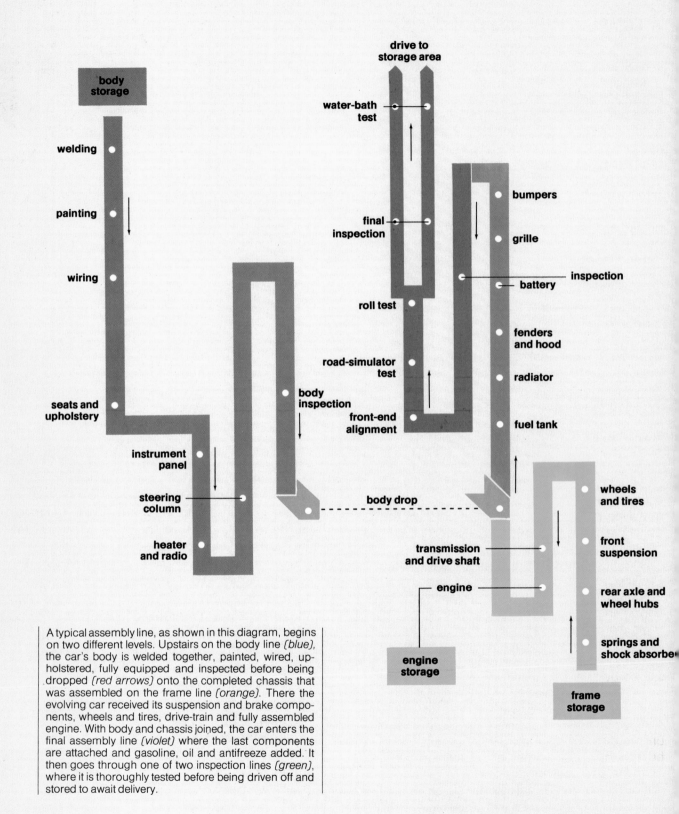

body storage

welding

painting

wiring

seats and upholstery

instrument panel

steering column

heater and radio

body inspection

body drop

drive to storage area

water-bath test

final inspection

roll test

road-simulator test

front-end alignment

bumpers

grille

inspection

battery

fenders and hood

radiator

fuel tank

wheels and tires

front suspension

transmission and drive shaft

engine

rear axle and wheel hubs

springs and shock absorbers

engine storage

frame storage

A typical assembly line, as shown in this diagram, begins on two different levels. Upstairs on the body line *(blue)*, the car's body is welded together, painted, wired, upholstered, fully equipped and inspected before being dropped *(red arrows)* onto the completed chassis that was assembled on the frame line *(orange)*. There the evolving car received its suspension and brake components, wheels and tires, drive-train and fully assembled engine. With body and chassis joined, the car enters the final assembly line *(violet)* where the last components are attached and gasoline, oil and antifreeze added. It then goes through one of two inspection lines *(green)*, where it is thoroughly tested before being driven off and stored to await delivery.

A COMPUTERIZED ASSEMBLY LINE

When Henry Ford envisioned the world's first automobile assembly line, his plan was to make 500 Model Ts a day, each as alike as "one pin is like another pin." Today, a single automobile-assembly operation like the typical one diagrammed here can produce as many as 1,000 cars a day, and only rarely are any two of the vehicles exactly alike. Because most assembly lines are equipped to produce several different models with a wide choice of colors, optional equipment and accessories, the variations are almost endless. It is not unusual to see a red station wagon following a beige sedan following a yellow taxicab off the line.

This kind of variety is made possible by computer-monitored assembly lines that are far more complex and precise than any of the early automobile makers could have imagined. An assembly line is actually an interlocking complex of overhead and surface conveyors that provide a constant flow of components from storage areas to assembly points. At these points they join other components, until at the end of the line all have been combined into a single unit—a complete automobile. It is the computer's job to establish and monitor a schedule so exact that every component arrives at its assembly point just as the previously assembled components roll slowly by on the moving line.

Although a new car rolls off an assembly line about once a minute, it takes about 18 to 24 hours from the time that the first components—the body and frame—begin their journeys along separate routes, until the fully assembled car is driven off under its own power. During that time the components, delivered by about 10 miles of conveyors, will have been assembled by several thousand workers and inspected over 1,000 times. The end result makes possible the greatest triumph of the system: a mass-produced car built to the special order of its new owner, from the size of its engine to the color of its upholstery to its optional dashboard clock.

Another strong competitor of the Model T was the tough four-cylinder Dodge. Manufactured by John and Horace Dodge, who had formerly built engines for Ford, by 1924 the Dodge cars were being assembled at a rate of about 1,000 a day. Four years later the company was purchased for what was then a world's record sale price of $175 million by Walter P. Chrysler, a former General Motors executive.

Chrysler, who had earlier bought control of the company that manufactured the popular Maxwell car, used the Dodge acquisition to launch the Chrysler Corporation. In 1928, the year that Presidential candidate Herbert Hoover promised Americans "two cars in every garage," the Chrysler Corporation began selling Dodges, DeSotos, Plymouths and Chryslers.

By then, the pressure of competition among manufacturers had added a number of refinements to the typical American car. Such things as roll-up windows, electric horns, speedometers, headlamps, temperature gauges, windshield wipers and four-wheel brakes all had become standard equipment. Most important of the innovations was the self-starter; invented in 1911, it was the one accessory, more than any other, that put women behind the steering wheel. The car itself had undergone a gradual transformation from a wood-bodied open vehicle to a steel, fully enclosed sedan that could be used year round.

The modern automobile was mechanically complete by 1929, when 4,587,400 cars were sold in the United States—a record not surpassed for another 20 years. All of the major mechanical developments since then—including automatic transmission, power steering and power brakes—simply have been improvements or refinements of existing systems.

And so, the genius of many men—contributing to a common pool of knowledge—created the institution we know as the family car.

THE ESSENTIAL SYSTEMS OF THE FAMILY CAR

This see-through version of a V8 sedan, the most typical of American cars, shows the location of major components and serves as a guide to their interrelationships in the detailed studies that follow. Individual parts are much the same from car to car; and though the positioning of some of them varies, they are integrated into nine basic systems used on almost every make and model.

Several hundred million times every day American motorists slide into the driver's seat of an automobile, slip a shining key into a slot and, with a flick of a wrist, activate an electrical switch. In seconds—usually—the car transforms itself: the inert conglomeration of materials that were originally extracted from the earth and the air begins to purr, pulse and throb. Now, a well-trained genie, it awaits only the next command of its master to take him wherever he desires, as fast as he is likely to want to go whether his destination is across town or across the continent.

But rare is the driver who understands in more than the vaguest way why his car moves at all. Still rarer is the driver who ponders—or even gives a casual thought to—the complex magic that he is employing. His vehicle represents the union of 15,000 separate parts. Those parts, most of them dependent on the others for their proper functioning, are contrived from 2,300 pounds of steel, 600 pounds of cast iron, 110 pounds of aluminum, 85 pounds of zinc, 23 pounds of copper, 16 pounds of lead, 185 pounds of rubber, 75 pounds of plastic and 87 pounds of glass—plus varying quantities of antimony, asbestos, cadmium, carbon, chromium, cork, cotton, jute, linseed oil, manganese, mercury, mica, molybdenum, nickel, paper and cardboard, platinum, silver, soybeans, tin, tungsten and wool. (In explanation of the more surprising components: the cork is for gaskets, the paper and cardboard for ceiling and door liners, the platinum for the voltage regulator and the turn-signal contacts, the soybeans for paint, and the wool for insulation.) The car's wiring alone, stretched in a straight line, would extend 1,100 feet or the length of 60 full-sized cars lined up bumper to bumper.

Except for the relatively few parts that merely add to the driver's ego or the passengers' comfort, the components function in a relationship to each other almost as intricate as that of the organs, nerves and glands of the human body. The heart of the car is its engine. But just as the human heart requires the supportive systems of the rest of the body, the engine depends on other mechanisms within the car. The engine must be fed. It must be kept at a steady temperature. It must be lubricated constantly if it is to avoid automotive arthritis. It must have a waste-disposal system. It must have a system that directs its movements and mechanisms that enable it to employ its power. And the car as a whole must have the means to change direction quickly, to stop in a matter of seconds, to smooth the ride on rough roads for its passengers and to light the way during the night for its brain—the driver.

To fill these needs, the car has nine separate systems, which are shown in the cutaway view (right) of a V8 sedan. Each system is distinguished by a different color and the color code at the far right of the opposite page indicates each system's identity. How these systems operate as a unit and some of the individual functions that they perform are explained in detail with illustrations on the pages that follow.

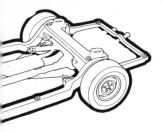

For combining maximum power and minimum weight with low cost and high durability, the modern internal-combustion engine has no equal. The engine shown here is used in most large American cars. Called a V8 because its eight cylinders are angled in two banks of four cylinders each and form a V, engines of this design range from 150 to 450 horsepower. The most popular model, in terms of sales volume, is designed to develop

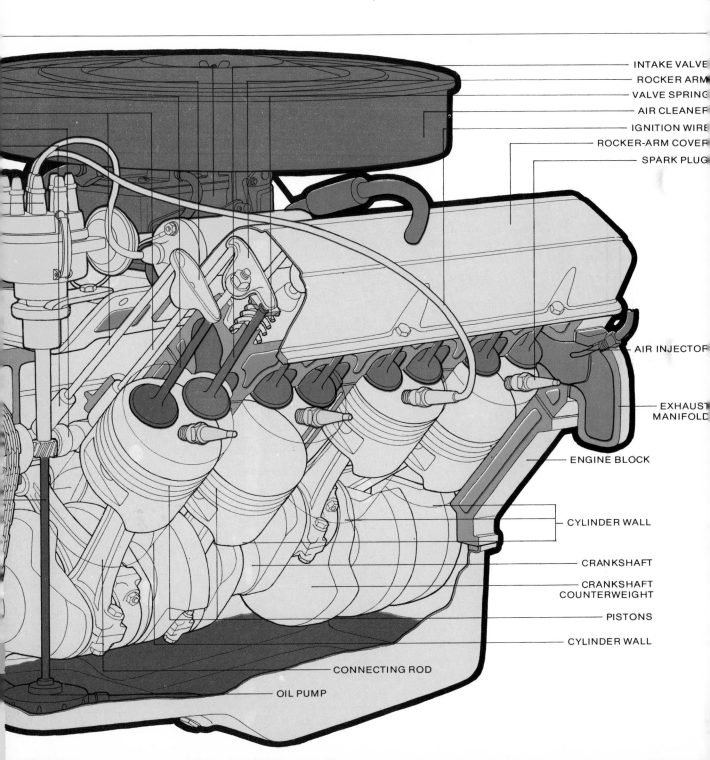

- INTAKE VALVE
- ROCKER ARM
- VALVE SPRING
- AIR CLEANER
- IGNITION WIRE
- ROCKER-ARM COVER
- SPARK PLUG
- AIR INJECTOR
- EXHAUST MANIFOLD
- ENGINE BLOCK
- CYLINDER WALL
- CRANKSHAFT
- CRANKSHAFT COUNTERWEIGHT
- PISTONS
- CYLINDER WALL
- CONNECTING ROD
- OIL PUMP

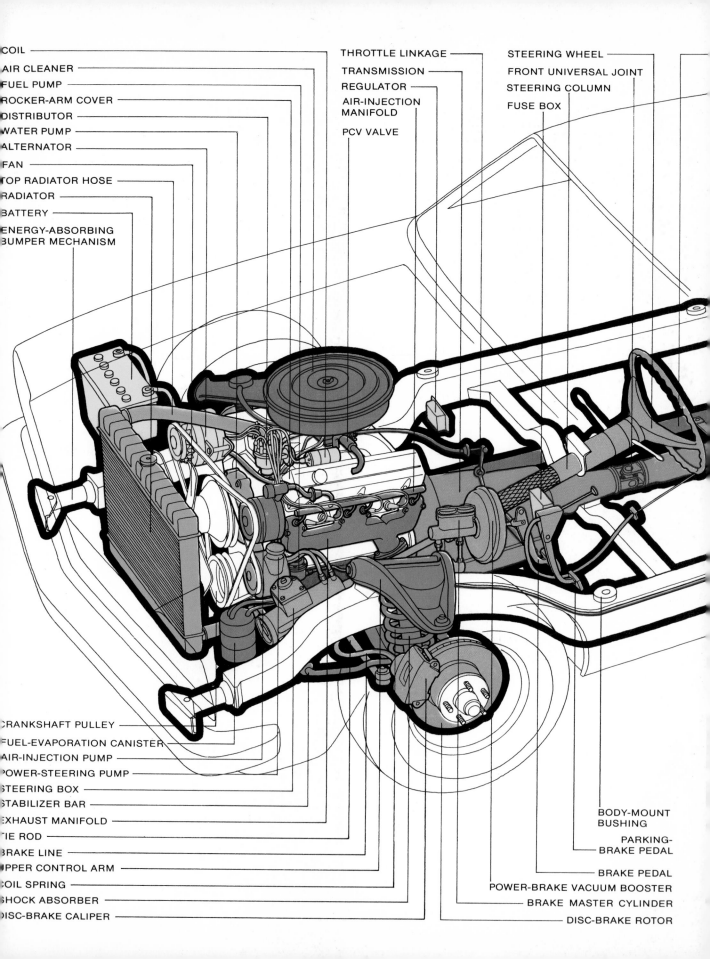

COIL
AIR CLEANER
FUEL PUMP
ROCKER-ARM COVER
DISTRIBUTOR
WATER PUMP
ALTERNATOR
FAN
TOP RADIATOR HOSE
RADIATOR
BATTERY
ENERGY-ABSORBING
BUMPER MECHANISM

THROTTLE LINKAGE
TRANSMISSION
REGULATOR
AIR-INJECTION
MANIFOLD
PCV VALVE

STEERING WHEEL
FRONT UNIVERSAL JOINT
STEERING COLUMN
FUSE BOX

CRANKSHAFT PULLEY
FUEL-EVAPORATION CANISTER
AIR-INJECTION PUMP
POWER-STEERING PUMP
STEERING BOX
STABILIZER BAR
EXHAUST MANIFOLD
TIE ROD
BRAKE LINE
UPPER CONTROL ARM
COIL SPRING
SHOCK ABSORBER
DISC-BRAKE CALIPER

BODY-MOUNT
BUSHING
PARKING-
BRAKE PEDAL
BRAKE PEDAL
POWER-BRAKE VACUUM BOOSTER
BRAKE MASTER CYLINDER
DISC-BRAKE ROTOR

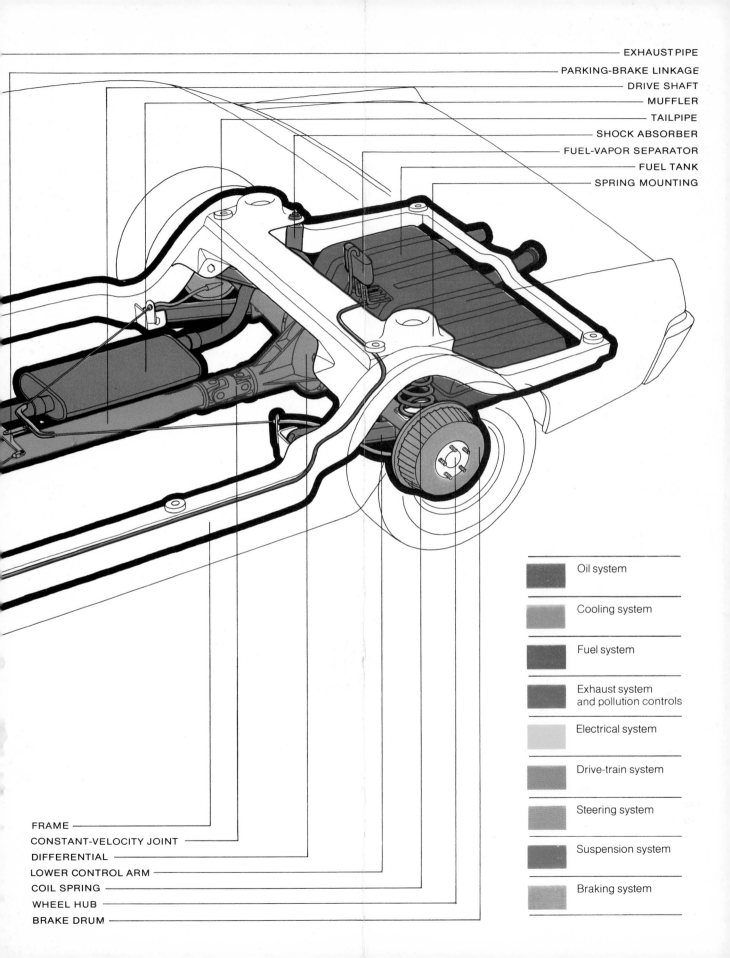

EXHAUST PIPE
PARKING-BRAKE LINKAGE
DRIVE SHAFT
MUFFLER
TAILPIPE
SHOCK ABSORBER
FUEL-VAPOR SEPARATOR
FUEL TANK
SPRING MOUNTING

Oil system

Cooling system

Fuel system

Exhaust system
and pollution controls

Electrical system

Drive-train system

Steering system

Suspension system

Braking system

FRAME
CONSTANT-VELOCITY JOINT
DIFFERENTIAL
LOWER CONTROL ARM
COIL SPRING
WHEEL HUB
BRAKE DRUM

THE INTERNAL COMBUSTION ENGINE

CYLINDERS AND PISTONS

In this cutaway view of a standard V8 engine, four of the eight cylinders are visible. Each of the pistons shown is in one of the four strokes of its combustion cycle. They operate in close synchronization with the other four cylinders on the opposite side of the engine. All eight are linked by connecting rods to the crankshaft. These rods translate the up-and-down (reciprocating) motion of the pistons into rotary motion by turning the crankshaft.

Only in the ignition stroke is the piston powered by fuel (opposite). During the intake, compression and exhaust strokes, the piston is moved by the crankshaft rotation. Counterweights help keep the crankshaft spinning evenly and without vibration as it supplies power, directly or indirectly, to every other drive shaft and to most of the mechanical devices in the engine. The water pump, alternator and fan all work off a belt and pulleys driven by the crankshaft. So do the power-steering pump and the air-conditioning compressor—in cars that have these options.

Through a chain and gears, the crankshaft drives the smaller camshaft above it. Rotating at half the speed of the crankshaft, the camshaft opens and closes the cylinder valves through a system of valve lifters, pushrods and rocker arms. The camshaft also turns the vertical shaft whose upper end drives the distributor and lower end spins the rotors in the oil pump.

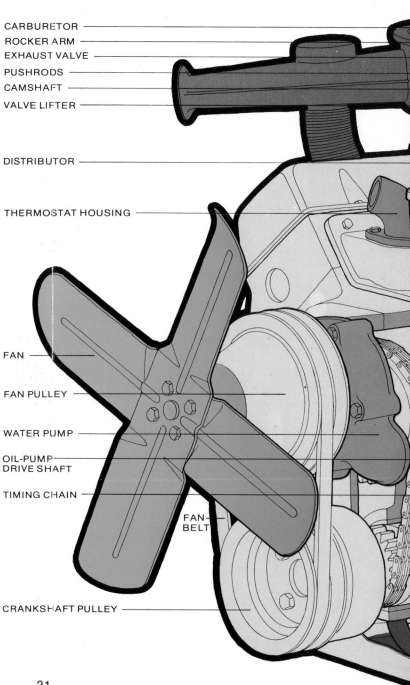

CARBURETOR
ROCKER ARM
EXHAUST VALVE
PUSHRODS
CAMSHAFT
VALVE LIFTER

DISTRIBUTOR

THERMOSTAT HOUSING

FAN

FAN PULLEY

WATER PUMP

OIL-PUMP
DRIVE SHAFT

TIMING CHAIN

FAN
BELT

CRANKSHAFT PULLEY

about 170 horsepower and to do so efficiently enough to move a two-ton car between 10 and 15 miles at 60 mph on one gallon of gasoline.

Each of the engine's eight cylinders is a combustion chamber in which a compressed mixture of gasoline and air is ignited every 160th of a second at 60 mph. The resulting explosions drive pistons up and down inside the cylinders, each piston going through 20 complete power-producing cycles *(below, right)* in a single second. The object of all this speed and power is to turn the crankshaft at the bottom of the engine. At 60 mph the crankshaft revolves about 2,500 times per minute.

Smaller cars use engines with four or six cylinders, working on the same principles as the V8. However, a new internal-combustion engine that needs no pistons at all *(overleaf)* is proving to be a husky competitor to the traditional design.

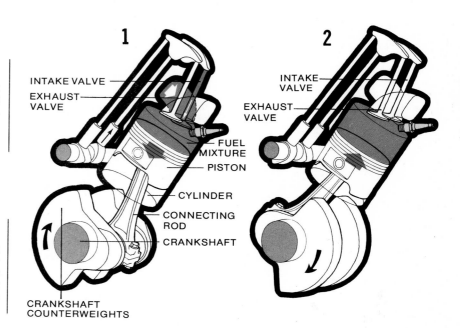

1 INTAKE

The piston begins its four-stroke cycle at the top of the cylinder. With the exhaust valve closed and the intake valve open, a partial vacuum is created as the piston moves downward, drawing a vaporized fuel mixture into the cylinder.

2 COMPRESSION

After sucking in the fuel mixture the piston is forced upward by the crankshaft; the intake valve is closed by the linkage of valve lifters, pushrods and rocker arms driven by the camshaft. The piston compresses the mixture to an eighth of its original volume.

3 IGNITION

Combustion takes place when the compressed fuel-air mixture is ignited by the spark plug. Suddenly heated to more than 4,000° F., the fuel expands rapidly, exerting enormous pressure on the piston and forcing it down to turn the crankshaft.

4 EXHAUST

The exhaust valve is opened as the piston reaches bottom and moves upward again, forcing the burned gases out of the cylinder. At the top of the stroke the exhaust valve closes and the intake valve opens to begin a new combustion cycle.

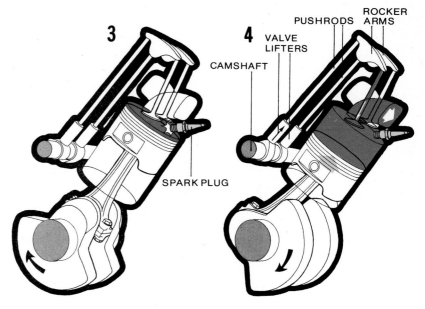

THE ROTARY ENGINE

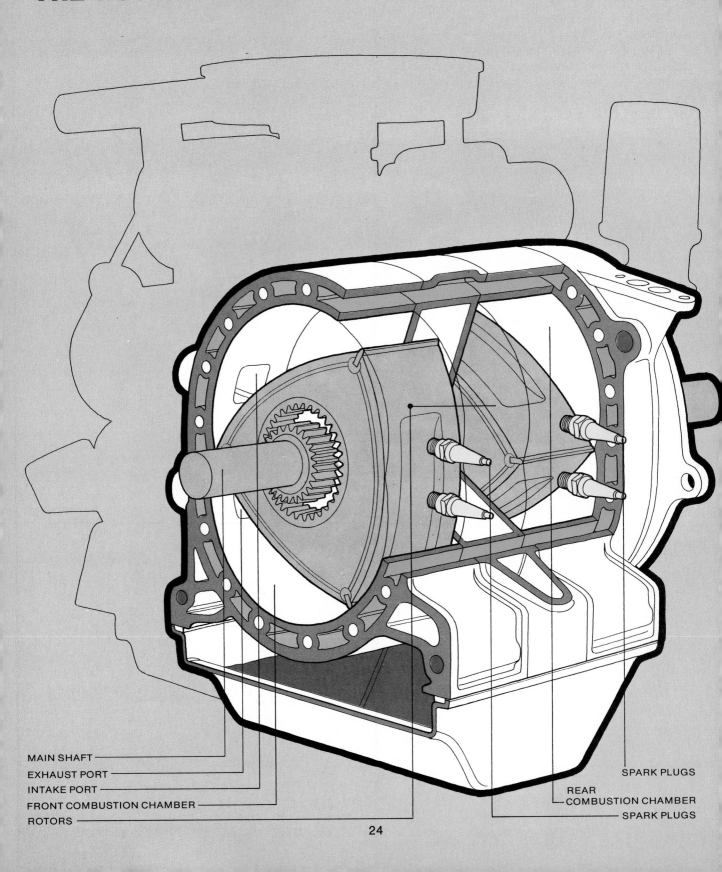

MAIN SHAFT

EXHAUST PORT

INTAKE PORT

FRONT COMBUSTION CHAMBER

ROTORS

SPARK PLUGS

REAR
COMBUSTION CHAMBER

SPARK PLUGS

An increasingly attractive alternative to the conventional automobile power plant is the rotary engine—also called the Wankel engine after Felix Wankel, the German engineer who developed and patented the first successful version. Dispensing with separate cylinders, pistons, valves and crankshaft, the rotary applies power directly to the transmission. Its ingenious construction allows it to provide the power of a conventional engine that is twice its size and weight and that has twice as many parts. The Wankel burns as much as 20 per cent more fuel than a conventional engine and is potentially a high polluter. But its reduced size means that bulky emission-control devices can be added more conveniently than to a piston engine.

The basic unit of the rotary engine is a large combustion chamber in the form of a pinched oval called an epitrochoid. Within this chamber all four functions of a piston take place simultaneously in the three pockets that are formed between the rotor and the chamber wall *(right)*.

A main shaft, linked to the transmission, runs through the center of the chamber. It forms an axis for the three-sided rotor, which is geared to spin eccentrically along the chamber walls. As a result of this eccentric spinning, pockets are formed between the rotor's three surfaces and the chamber wall. Each pocket changes size four times in a single sweep of the rotor, and each change signals a new step in the continuous combustion cycle. In effect, each face of the rotor is performing the work of a piston inside a cylinder.

Just as the addition of cylinders increases the horsepower of a piston-powered engine, so the addition of combustion chambers increases the power of a rotary engine. The engine at left is similar to the two-chamber version being used in compact cars. Larger cars eventually may use rotaries with three or four chambers.

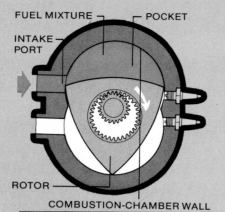

INTAKE

As the rotor whirls in a clockwise direction, it creates a partial vacuum in a crescent-shaped pocket formed by one of its faces and the wall of the combustion chamber. This vacuum draws the fuel mixture from the carburetor (not shown) into the pocket through a valveless intake port.

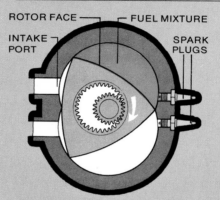

COMPRESSION

The rotor face passes the intake port, sealing the fuel mixture in the pocket. As the rotor continues to revolve the pocket shrinks, compressing the trapped fuel. The revolving motion carries the compressed fuel mixture toward the spark plugs.

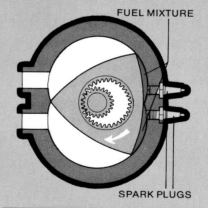

IGNITION

With the pocket reduced to about a tenth of its original size, the tightly compressed fuel mixture is ignited by a pair of spark plugs. The lower plug fires almost instantaneously after the upper to assure complete combustion in the narrowed pocket.

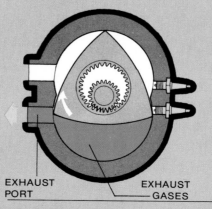

EXHAUST

The force of the combustion drives the rotor along its clockwise orbit. The pocket now widens to absorb some of the power of the explosion. The waste gases remaining in the pocket are swept out as the rotor whirls past a valveless exhaust port, clearing the pocket for the next cycle. The same continuous process is also taking place in the two pockets formed by the other two sides of the rotor during its eccentric orbit.

THE OIL SYSTEM

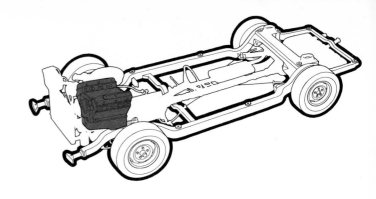

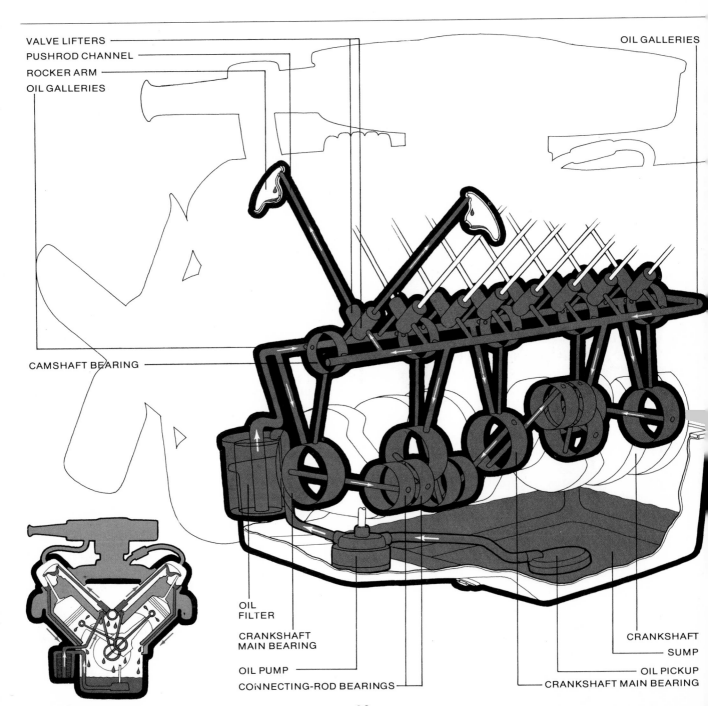

VALVE LIFTERS

PUSHROD CHANNEL

ROCKER ARM

OIL GALLERIES

OIL GALLERIES

CAMSHAFT BEARING

OIL
FILTER

CRANKSHAFT
MAIN BEARING

OIL PUMP

CONNECTING-ROD BEARINGS

CRANKSHAFT

SUMP

OIL PICKUP

CRANKSHAFT MAIN BEARING

The oil that circulates through an engine performs four important functions. Its primary task is to provide a slippery film between fast-moving parts in order to reduce friction that can cause excessive wear or even binding. The oil also acts as a sealant in the cylinders, placing a fluid bond between the pistons and the cylinder walls. In its other two functions oil serves as a coolant, absorbing and carrying away some of the engine heat, and as a cleanser, picking up such contaminants as water, gasoline, dust, dirt and metal particles.

Pumped upward from its oil-pan reservoir, or sump, the oil passes through a filter and specially bored passages called galleries to reach the engine's critical moving parts—crankshaft and camshaft bearings, connecting-rod bearings, valve lifters, rocker arms and pistons. Then it drips back to the oil pan to be used again.

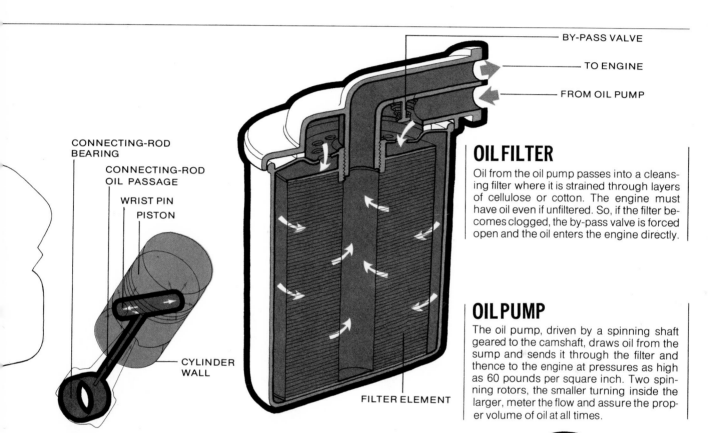

CONNECTING-ROD BEARING
CONNECTING-ROD OIL PASSAGE
WRIST PIN
PISTON
CYLINDER WALL

BY-PASS VALVE
TO ENGINE
FROM OIL PUMP

FILTER ELEMENT

OIL FILTER

Oil from the oil pump passes into a cleansing filter where it is strained through layers of cellulose or cotton. The engine must have oil even if unfiltered. So, if the filter becomes clogged, the by-pass valve is forced open and the oil enters the engine directly.

OIL PUMP

The oil pump, driven by a spinning shaft geared to the camshaft, draws oil from the sump and sends it through the filter and thence to the engine at pressures as high as 60 pounds per square inch. Two spinning rotors, the smaller turning inside the larger, meter the flow and assure the proper volume of oil at all times.

PATTERN OF FLOW

The routes that oil travels to reach the engine's important moving parts are shown at left. Sucked up through the oil pickup from the sump, oil is pumped through the filter into two main systems of oil galleries. From there the oil travels in several directions (arrows). Some moves downward to the crankshaft main bearings and the connecting-rod bearings. The cylinder walls are lubricated (above) by oil passing through the connecting rods and spraying from either end of the wrist pin. Other oil is pumped upward into the camshaft bearings, through the valve lifters and pushrod channels to the rocker arms.

A front view of the oil system, at far left, shows how the oil returns to the crankcase through specially bored channels.

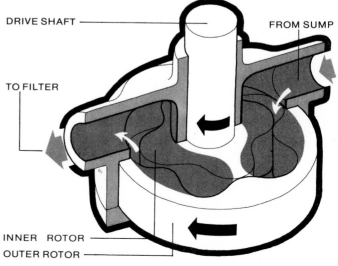

DRIVE SHAFT
FROM SUMP
TO FILTER
INNER ROTOR
OUTER ROTOR

THE COOLING SYSTEM

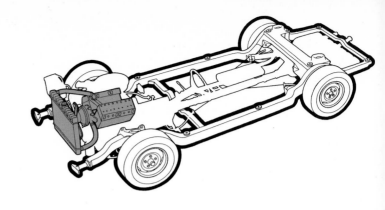

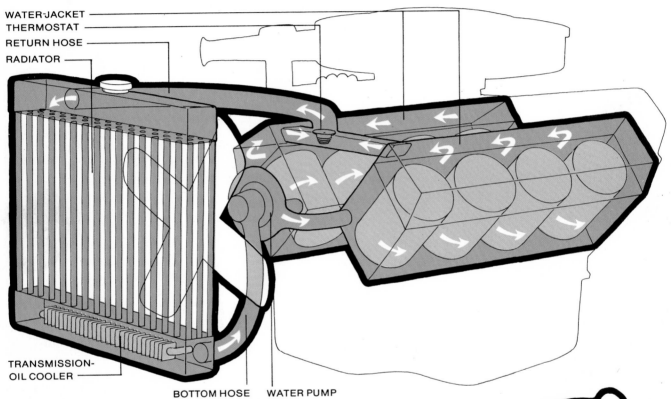

WATER-JACKET
THERMOSTAT
RETURN HOSE
RADIATOR

TRANSMISSION-OIL COOLER

BOTTOM HOSE   WATER PUMP

PATTERN OF FLOW

Water, or a chemical solution, is pumped from the bottom of the radiator through a hose into the water jacket surrounding the cylinders. As the water circulates, it absorbs engine heat before returning to the radiator. Then it descends through a series of copper tubes and is cooled by inflowing air, drawn by the car's forward motion and the radiator fan.

A thermostat controls a valve that remains closed when the engine is cold, so that the water recirculates within the jacket. When the engine has warmed, the thermostat opens the valve so that the hot water can be cooled by the radiator before it is recirculated. A separate unit at the bottom of the radiator cools automatic transmission oil.

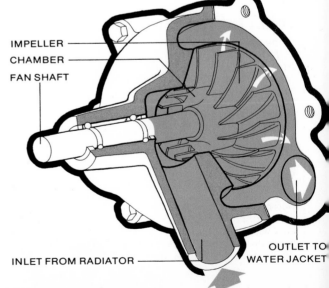

IMPELLER
CHAMBER
FAN SHAFT

INLET FROM RADIATOR

OUTLET TO WATER JACKET

A car is designed to perform most efficiently when its engine temperature is around 180° F. Below that temperature, the oil is sluggish and circulates too slowly to be fully effective; above it, the oil tends to thin and its protective film begins to break down. The twofold task of the cooling system is to help bring the engine up to its best operating temperature as quickly as possible and then to maintain that temperature by removing heat.

Most cooling systems use both water and air to do the job. The water—in modern automobiles it is mixed with a year-round chemical solution that helps prevent both winter freezing and summer boiling—first circulates around the engine to absorb and distribute warming cylinder heat. When the proper temperature is reached, a thermostat opens a valve that shunts water through the radiator to be air-cooled before being recirculated.

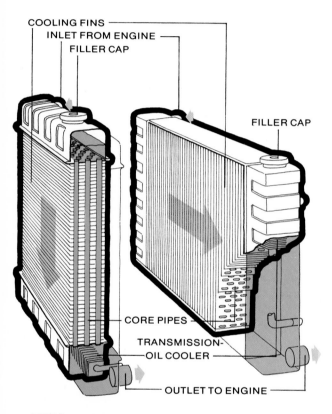

TWO TYPES OF RADIATORS

In the downflow type of radiator *(above, left)*, hot water flows vertically through core pipes surrounded by thin, heat-dissipating cooling fins. In the lower, wider crossflow type of radiator *(right)* used in some cars, the water flows from side to side in order to give it the same cooling exposure as in the downflow type, but in less space.

◄ WATER PUMP

Powered by the spinning fan shaft, the pump draws water into its chamber from the bottom of the radiator. There the impeller, a whirling series of vanes, forces out the water by centrifugal force to circulate under pressure through the water jacket.

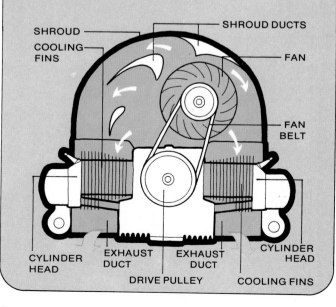

AIR-COOLED ENGINE

Pioneered by European manufacturers, the air-cooled engine has proved to be a reliable and inexpensive alternative to the water-cooled engine in some small cars and sport models. In the rear-engine cooling system illustrated below, air enters the compartment through ducts in a shroud covering the engine. A fan, powered by a belt and drive pulley attached to the crankshaft, sends air across the top of the engine. The air passes through a series of cooling fins cast into the engine block around each cylinder head. The engine heat, which has been absorbed by the fins, is picked up by the passing air. The fan then vents the hot air through ducts at the bottom of the engine.

THE FUEL SYSTEM

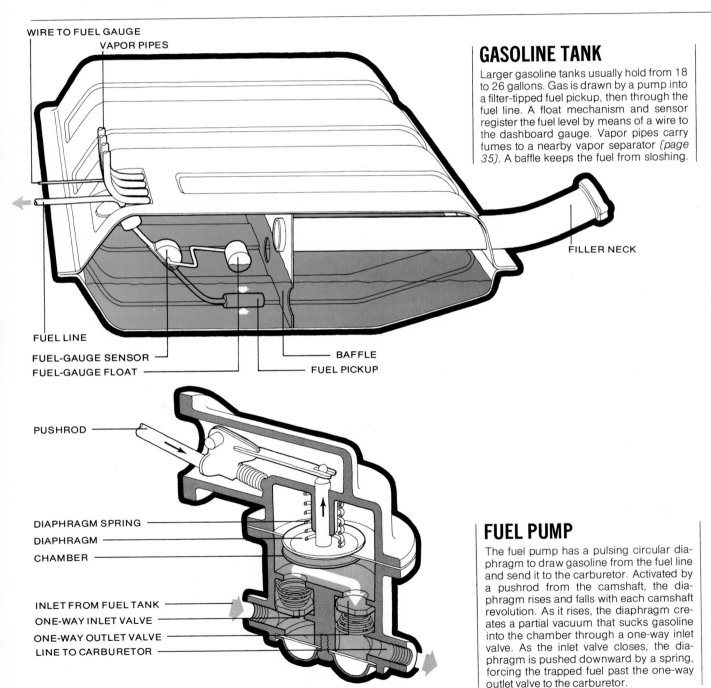

WIRE TO FUEL GAUGE

VAPOR PIPES

GASOLINE TANK

Larger gasoline tanks usually hold from 18 to 26 gallons. Gas is drawn by a pump into a filter-tipped fuel pickup, then through the fuel line. A float mechanism and sensor register the fuel level by means of a wire to the dashboard gauge. Vapor pipes carry fumes to a nearby vapor separator *(page 35)*. A baffle keeps the fuel from sloshing.

FILLER NECK

FUEL LINE

FUEL-GAUGE SENSOR

FUEL-GAUGE FLOAT

BAFFLE

FUEL PICKUP

PUSHROD

DIAPHRAGM SPRING

DIAPHRAGM

CHAMBER

INLET FROM FUEL TANK

ONE-WAY INLET VALVE

ONE-WAY OUTLET VALVE

LINE TO CARBURETOR

FUEL PUMP

The fuel pump has a pulsing circular diaphragm to draw gasoline from the fuel line and send it to the carburetor. Activated by a pushrod from the camshaft, the diaphragm rises and falls with each camshaft revolution. As it rises, the diaphragm creates a partial vacuum that sucks gasoline into the chamber through a one-way inlet valve. As the inlet valve closes, the diaphragm is pushed downward by a spring, forcing the trapped fuel past the one-way outlet valve to the carburetor.

The fuel that eventually reaches the cylinders is a misty vapor usually composed of about 15 parts of air for every part of gasoline. It is the job of the fuel system to supply the correct mixture of the two ingredients at all times regardless of the engine's speed, load and temperature.

By different routes gasoline and air enter the carburetor where fuel mixing takes place *(overleaf)*. The gasoline is drawn by a fuel pump from a stor-age tank in the rear. It passes through at least two filters before it reaches the carburetor. The air enters the engine compartment through the radiator at the front of the car, after cooling the engine's water supply *(pages 28-29),* and is scooped by an intake snorkel into an air cleaner. There it is filtered before being drawn downward from the center of the air cleaner, becoming part of the fuel mixture in the carburetor.

FILTER

CIRCULAR CHAMBER

CARBURETOR

INTAKE SNORKEL

AIR CLEANER

For every gallon of gasoline consumed, the equivalent of 9,000 gallons of air is sucked through the air cleaner and into the carburetor by the vacuum power of the running engine. The air enters through an intake snorkel, goes into a circular chamber and then is drawn through a ring-shaped filter —the one shown is made of cellulose fibers—that removes dirt and dust particles.

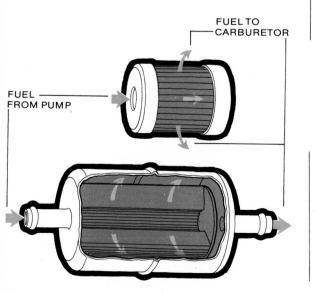

FUEL TO CARBURETOR

FUEL FROM PUMP

TWO TYPES OF FILTERS

Two general types of filters are used to remove foreign matter from gasoline as it passes from the pump to the carburetor. One type *(left)* fits into the gas line, usually about midway between where the line enters the engine compartment and the carburetor; it is called, logically, an in-line filter. The other type *(left, above)* fits into a housing in the carburetor itself.

THE FUEL SYSTEM: The carburetor

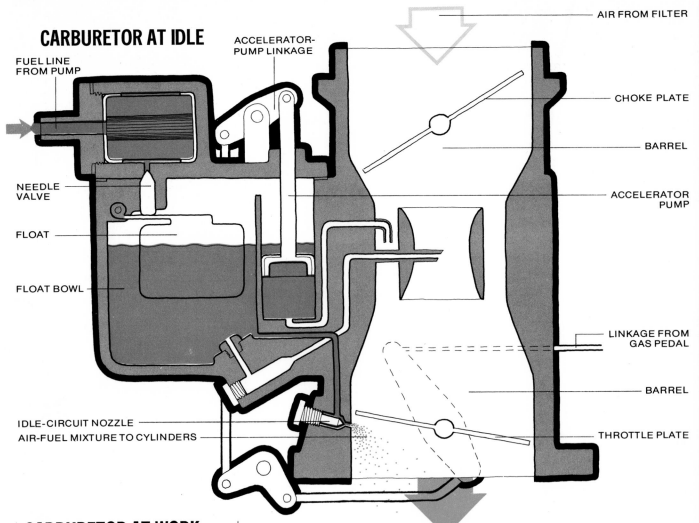

CARBURETOR AT IDLE

FUEL LINE FROM PUMP

ACCELERATOR-PUMP LINKAGE

AIR FROM FILTER

CHOKE PLATE

BARREL

NEEDLE VALVE

ACCELERATOR PUMP

FLOAT

FLOAT BOWL

LINKAGE FROM GAS PEDAL

BARREL

IDLE-CIRCUIT NOZZLE

AIR-FUEL MIXTURE TO CYLINDERS

THROTTLE PLATE

CARBURETOR AT WORK

The carburetor supplies a small amount of a very rich fuel mixture when the engine is cold and running at idle *(above)*. With the throttle plate closed and air from the air cleaner restricted by the closed choke plate, engine suction is amplified at the idle-circuit nozzle. This vacuum draws a thick spray of gasoline through the nozzle from the full float bowl, whose fuel line is closed by the float-supported needle valve.

Maximum fuel is provided when the gas pedal is depressed for acceleration *(right)*. The pedal linkage opens the throttle plate and the choke plate to send air rushing through the barrel. The linkage also depresses the accelerator pump, providing added gasoline through the accelerator-circuit nozzle. As air passes through the narrow center of the barrel, called the venturi, it produces suction that draws spray from the cruising-circuit nozzle. The float-bowl level drops, causing the float to tip and the needle valve to open the fuel line.

CARBURETOR UNDER ACCELERATION

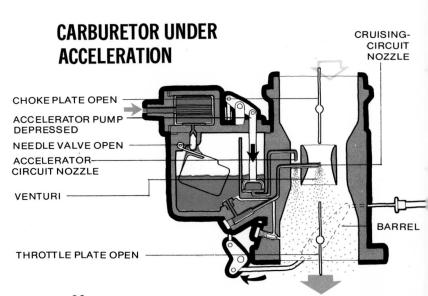

CRUISING-CIRCUIT NOZZLE

CHOKE PLATE OPEN

ACCELERATOR PUMP DEPRESSED

NEEDLE VALVE OPEN

ACCELERATOR-CIRCUIT NOZZLE

VENTURI

BARREL

THROTTLE PLATE OPEN

THE FUEL-INJECTION SYSTEM

Some engines dispense with the carburetor and substitute a compact computer to provide more precise fuel mixtures. In the fuel-injection system shown here, the computer decides how much fuel is needed and meters the proper amount into a series of injector nozzles *(below)*. The nozzles, on further command from the computer, provide individual sprays for each cylinder instead of the carburetor's single spray for all cylinders at once. The separate mixings of air and gasoline take place at the top of the intake manifold just above the intake valves of the individual cylinders *(right)*.

Every time the driver steps on the gas pedal he triggers a new series of computer calculations. The pedal opens a valve, comparable to the carburetor's choke, that increases the volume of air entering the engine's intake manifold. The computer instantly reacts to the increased air flow in the intake manifold, comparing it to the engine speed and power required, as well as to the temperatures of both the engine and the incoming air. It then calculates the proper fuel mixture and directs a spray of gasoline toward each cylinder. The result is efficient combustion with a minimum of wasted fuel.

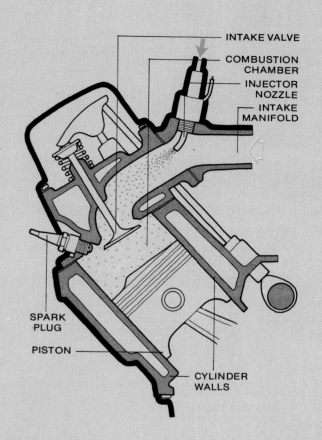

INTAKE VALVE
COMBUSTION CHAMBER
INJECTOR NOZZLE
INTAKE MANIFOLD
SPARK PLUG
PISTON
CYLINDER WALLS

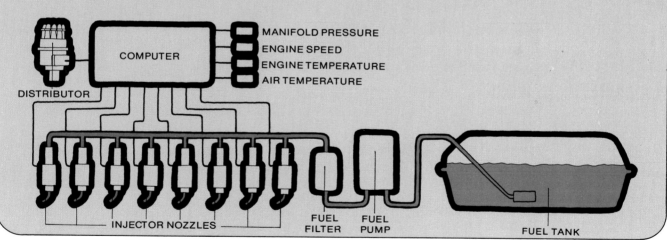

COMPUTER
DISTRIBUTOR
MANIFOLD PRESSURE
ENGINE SPEED
ENGINE TEMPERATURE
AIR TEMPERATURE
INJECTOR NOZZLES
FUEL FILTER
FUEL PUMP
FUEL TANK

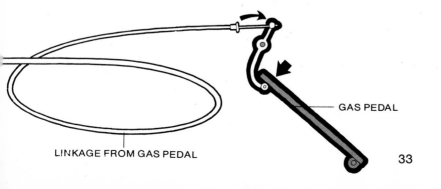

LINKAGE FROM GAS PEDAL
GAS PEDAL

33

THE EXHAUST SYSTEM AND POLLUTION CONTROLS

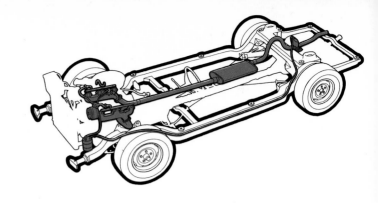

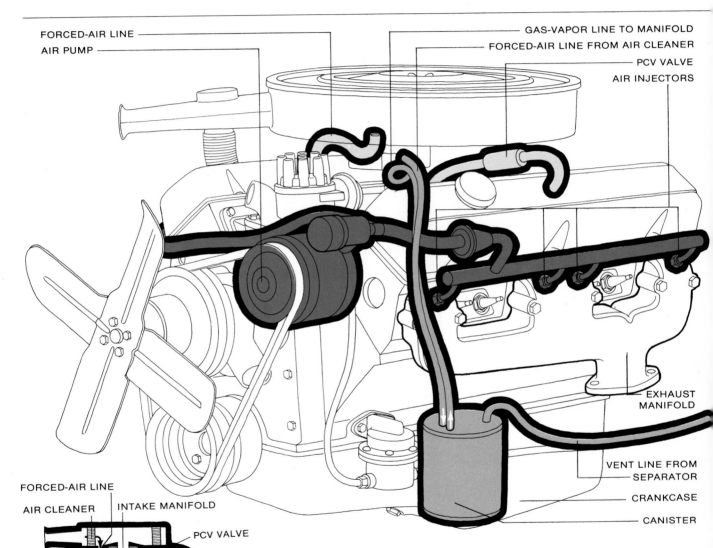

FORCED-AIR LINE

AIR PUMP

GAS-VAPOR LINE TO MANIFOLD

FORCED-AIR LINE FROM AIR CLEANER

PCV VALVE

AIR INJECTORS

EXHAUST MANIFOLD

VENT LINE FROM SEPARATOR

CRANKCASE

CANISTER

FORCED-AIR LINE

AIR CLEANER

INTAKE MANIFOLD

PCV VALVE

CRANKCASE GASES

POLLUTION CONTROLS

Three separate pollution-control devices are shown above. An air-injection device *(dark blue)* employs a pump to send air through injectors set in the exhaust manifold. The oxygen in the air combines with hot exhaust gases in the manifold, creating an afterburn that completes combustion.

An evaporation-control device *(medium blue)* uses a vapor separator to collect fuel-tank fumes. Some fumes are condensed to liquid and returned to the tank; the rest enter a canister and are carried by forced air into the intake manifold.

A positive crankcase-ventilation, or PCV, circuit *(light blue, above and left)* uses forced air from the air cleaner and engine suction to flush gases out of the crankcase and into the intake manifold for burning *(arrows)*. The PCV valve controls the flow so that the basic fuel mixture is unchanged.

If every drop of gasoline were completely consumed in the cylinders, the exhaust system would release only harmless water vapor, carbon dioxide and nitrogen into the air. But a few drops of every gallon never reach the cylinders, and a few more that do get there are not fully consumed. These unused drops produce two types of harmful emission: hydrocarbons and carbon monoxide. Another, oxides of nitrogen, is caused by the high temperature of combustion. All of these accumulate to cause atmospheric pollution. While the exhaust system effectively cools and vents gases (and also muffles the natural engine noises), a number of different pollution-control systems are needed to remove harmful emissions from the engine, crankcase and fuel line. Some of the systems now being used are shown here. For a look at a new system, catalytic converters, see page 318.

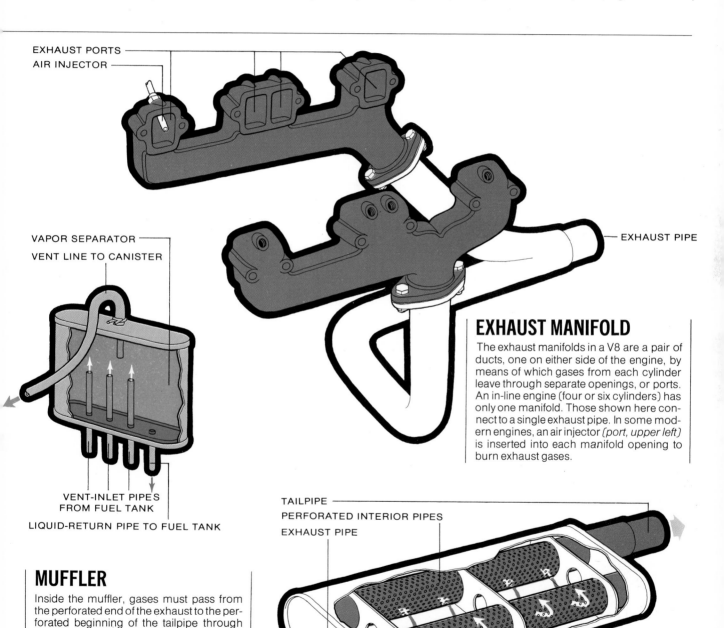

EXHAUST PORTS
AIR INJECTOR

VAPOR SEPARATOR
VENT LINE TO CANISTER

EXHAUST PIPE

VENT-INLET PIPES
FROM FUEL TANK

LIQUID-RETURN PIPE TO FUEL TANK

EXHAUST MANIFOLD

The exhaust manifolds in a V8 are a pair of ducts, one on either side of the engine, by means of which gases from each cylinder leave through separate openings, or ports. An in-line engine (four or six cylinders) has only one manifold. Those shown here connect to a single exhaust pipe. In some modern engines, an air injector *(port, upper left)* is inserted into each manifold opening to burn exhaust gases.

TAILPIPE
PERFORATED INTERIOR PIPES
EXHAUST PIPE

MUFFLER

Inside the muffler, gases must pass from the perforated end of the exhaust to the perforated beginning of the tailpipe through layers of sound-deadening material such as glass wool. Thus, the muffler sharply reduces the explosive sound of engine combustion that travels down the exhaust pipe with the escaping gases. This process also cools the gases before expelling them.

THE ELECTRICAL SYSTEM

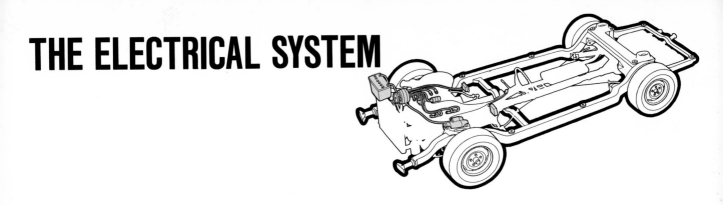

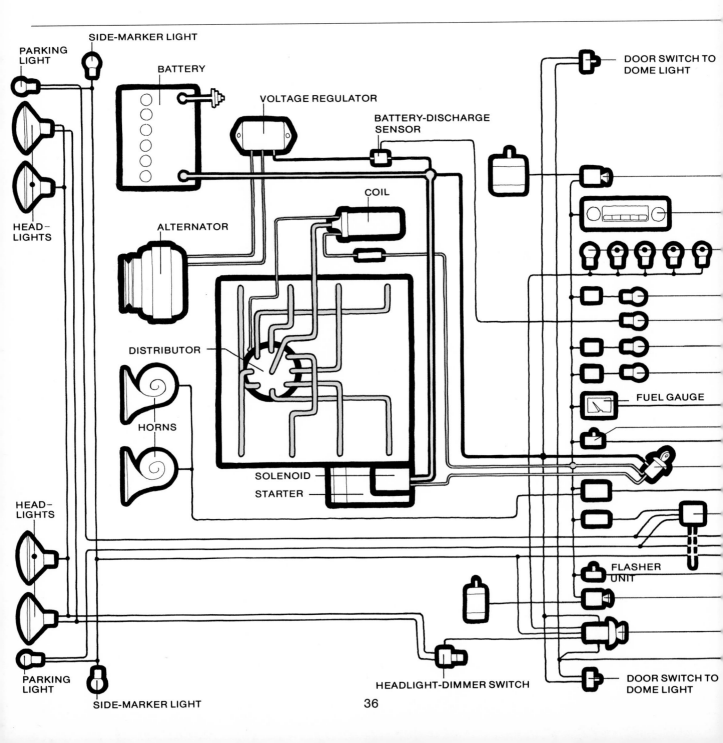

PARKING LIGHT

SIDE-MARKER LIGHT

BATTERY

VOLTAGE REGULATOR

BATTERY-DISCHARGE SENSOR

DOOR SWITCH TO DOME LIGHT

COIL

HEAD-LIGHTS

ALTERNATOR

DISTRIBUTOR

HORNS

FUEL GAUGE

HEAD-LIGHTS

SOLENOID

STARTER

FLASHER UNIT

PARKING LIGHT

HEADLIGHT-DIMMER SWITCH

DOOR SWITCH TO DOME LIGHT

SIDE-MARKER LIGHT

36

When the automobile was in its infancy, it used electricity only to ignite the fuel inside the engine. By the late 1920s, however, the electric starter replaced the hand crank, electric headlights made acetylene lamps obsolete and the braying of the electric horn drowned out the squeak of the hand-squeezed air horn. Today an automobile requires an elaborate system to produce, store and distribute all the electricity it requires simply for everyday operation *(below)*.

The car's basic source of electricity is a battery, whose most important job is to start the engine. Once the engine is running, an alternator takes over to supply the car's electrical needs and to recharge the battery. So versatile is the standard 12-volt electrical system that it can serve dozens of auxiliary accessories and instruments while it is simultaneously producing a continuous series of 20,000-volt sparks to ignite the fuel mixture in the cylinders *(page 40)*.

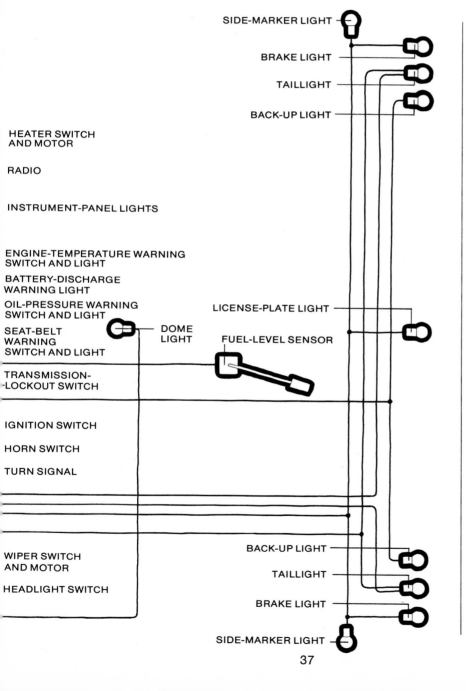

BASIC CIRCUITS

This schematic diagram of a basic automobile electrical system shows the many different devices that draw electrical power from the battery and alternator. More than 1,000 feet of wire and cable are required for the car's various circuits and subcircuits. To be completed, most electrical circuits, such as the one in a house, need two wires. One carries the current from the source and the other returns it to the source. A car's system has only one wire, the one that brings power from the source. The circuit is completed by attaching a short wire to a near point on the car frame. This allows the electricity to flow back through the frame to the battery's ground terminal, symbolized by a triangular line-cluster.

The most important circuits, examined individually on the pages that follow, are: the starting circuit *(light yellow lines)*, which feeds large amounts of current to the starter; the charging circuit *(dark yellow)*, which supplies electricity from the alternator to the battery; and the ignition circuit *(medium yellow)*, by which the coil and distributor deliver the high-voltage sparks that ignite the fuel mixture.

Most of the other circuits (indicated by single black lines) are controlled by the ignition switch. The same key that controls the circuits that start the car also controls a master circuit through which electricity reaches the horns, lights, gauges, windshield wipers, radio and heater. In some cases a second switch also must be used; the heater fan, for example, works only when both the ignition and heater switches are turned on to open its circuit.

Several subcircuits may be necessary for multiple-switch components such as the parking and taillights, which also are used as turn signals and emergency flashers. Others, like the fuel gauge and battery-discharge warning light, rely on sensors to transmit electrical impulses that vary with the quantity of gasoline or electricity.

THE ELECTRICAL SYSTEM: Starting and charging

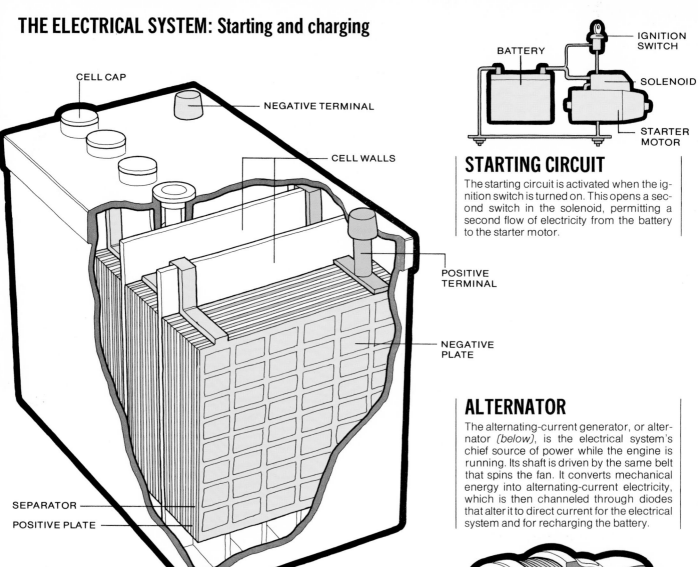

CELL CAP

NEGATIVE TERMINAL

CELL WALLS

POSITIVE TERMINAL

NEGATIVE PLATE

SEPARATOR

POSITIVE PLATE

BATTERY

IGNITION SWITCH

SOLENOID

STARTER MOTOR

STARTING CIRCUIT

The starting circuit is activated when the ignition switch is turned on. This opens a second switch in the solenoid, permitting a second flow of electricity from the battery to the starter motor.

ALTERNATOR

The alternating-current generator, or alternator *(below)*, is the electrical system's chief source of power while the engine is running. Its shaft is driven by the same belt that spins the fan. It converts mechanical energy into alternating-current electricity, which is then channeled through diodes that alter it to direct current for the electrical system and for recharging the battery.

BATTERY

This cutaway view of a 12-volt storage battery reveals the layers of positively and negatively charged lead plates that, together with their insulated separators, make up each of six two-volt cells. The cells are filled with an electricity-conducting liquid electrolyte that is usually two thirds distilled water and one third sulfuric acid. Spaces between the immersed plates provide maximum exposure to the electrolyte. The interaction of the plates and the electrolyte produces chemical energy that becomes electricity when a circuit is formed between the negative and positive battery terminals.

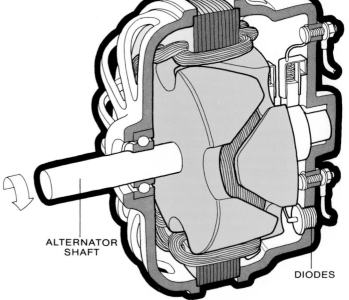

ALTERNATOR SHAFT

DIODES

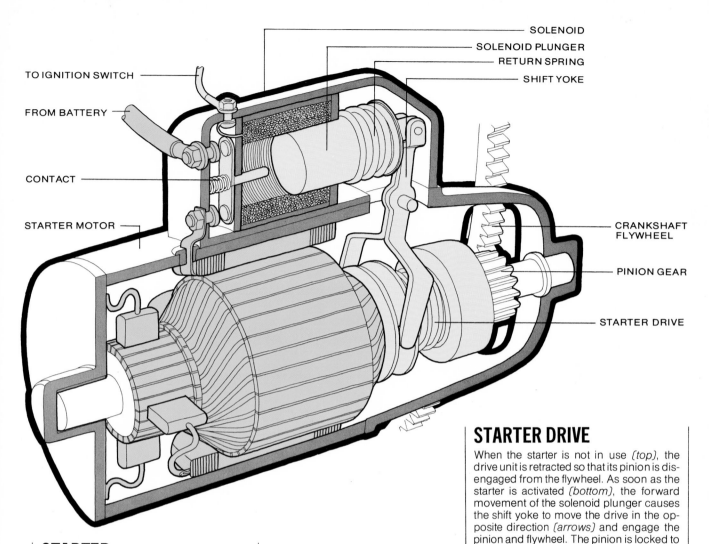

SOLENOID
SOLENOID PLUNGER
RETURN SPRING
SHIFT YOKE

TO IGNITION SWITCH

FROM BATTERY

CONTACT

STARTER MOTOR

CRANKSHAFT
FLYWHEEL

PINION GEAR

STARTER DRIVE

STARTER

The starter converts electricity to mechanical energy in two stages. Turning on the ignition switch releases a small amount of power from the battery to the solenoid above the starter. This creates a magnetic field that pulls the solenoid plunger forward *(arrow)*, forcing the attached shift yoke to move the starter drive *(lower right)* so that its pinion gear meshes with the engine's crankshaft flywheel.

When the plunger completes its travels, it strikes a contact that permits a greater amount of current to flow from the battery to the starter motor. The motor then spins the drive and turns the meshed gears to provide power to the crankshaft, which prepares each cylinder for ignition *(overleaf)*. After the engine starts, the ignition key is released to break the starting circuit. The solenoid's magnetic field collapses and the return spring pulls the plunger back, automatically shutting off the starter motor and disengaging the starter drive.

STARTER DRIVE

When the starter is not in use *(top)*, the drive unit is retracted so that its pinion is disengaged from the flywheel. As soon as the starter is activated *(bottom)*, the forward movement of the solenoid plunger causes the shift yoke to move the drive in the opposite direction *(arrows)* and engage the pinion and flywheel. The pinion is locked to its shaft by a clutch that unlocks if the engine starts up and the flywheel begins turning the pinion faster than its normal speed. By allowing the pinion to spin freely for a moment, the clutch protects the motor from damage until the drive is retracted.

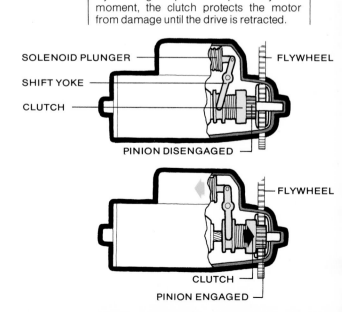

SOLENOID PLUNGER

SHIFT YOKE

CLUTCH

FLYWHEEL

PINION DISENGAGED

FLYWHEEL

CLUTCH

PINION ENGAGED

THE ELECTRICAL SYSTEM: Ignition

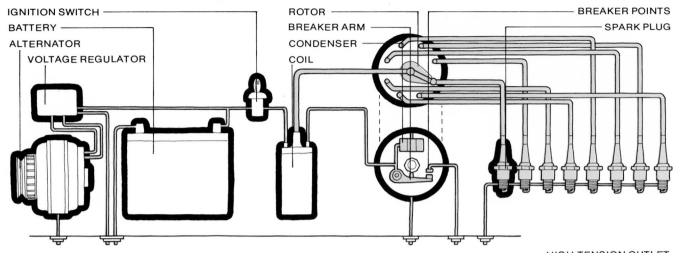

IGNITION SWITCH
BATTERY
ALTERNATOR
VOLTAGE REGULATOR
ROTOR
BREAKER ARM
CONDENSER
COIL
BREAKER POINTS
SPARK PLUG

IGNITION CIRCUIT

The ignition circuit consists of two subcircuits: the primary, which carries low voltage; and the secondary, which carries high voltage. The primary circuit, controlled by the ignition key, releases 12 volts of electricity from the battery or alternator through the coil to a set of breaker points in the lower part of the distributor.

The breaker points open and close with great rapidity. When they are closed, current flows through a ground wire and thence back to the battery, thus completing the circuit. When the points are open the flow stops, causing high-voltage current to pass from the coil through a rotor in the top of the distributor to the spark plugs.

Once the car has started, the voltage regulator protects the battery from being overcharged by the alternator. The condenser absorbs part of the low-voltage current when the points are open.

COIL

The coil is a compact electrical transformer that boosts the battery's 12 volts to as high as 20,000 volts. The incoming 12 volts of electricity pass through a primary winding of about 200 turns of copper wire that raises the power to about 250 volts. Inside the distributor *(opposite, top),* this low-voltage circuit is continuously broken by the opening and closing of the points, each interruption causing a breakdown in the coil's electromagnetic field. Each time the field collapses, a surge of electricity passes to a secondary winding made up of more than a mile of hairlike wire twisted into 25,000 turns. Here the current is boosted to the high voltage needed for ignition and is then relayed to the rotor.

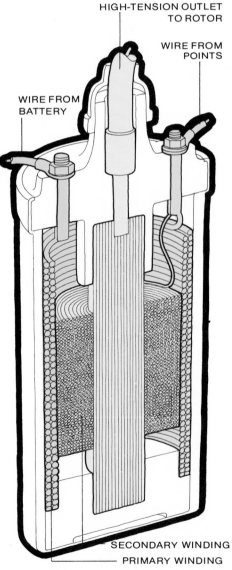

HIGH-TENSION OUTLET TO ROTOR
WIRE FROM POINTS
WIRE FROM BATTERY
SECONDARY WINDING
PRIMARY WINDING

40

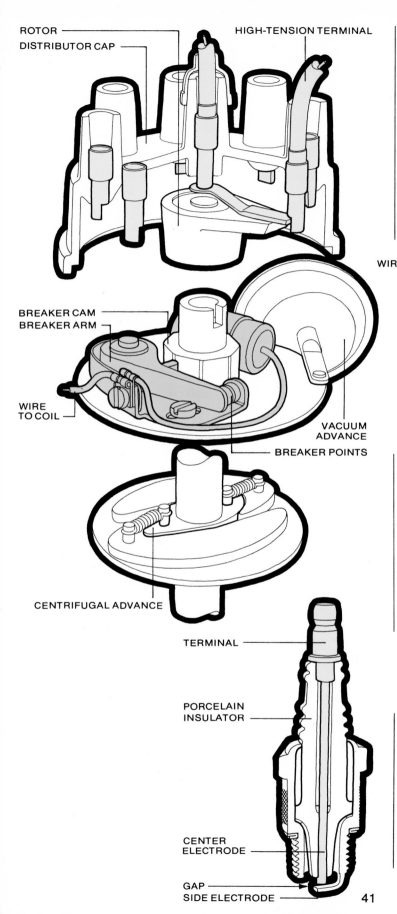

ROTOR
DISTRIBUTOR CAP
HIGH-TENSION TERMINAL

BREAKER CAM
BREAKER ARM

WIRE
TO COIL

VACUUM
ADVANCE

BREAKER POINTS

CENTRIFUGAL ADVANCE

TERMINAL

PORCELAIN
INSULATOR

CENTER
ELECTRODE

GAP
SIDE ELECTRODE

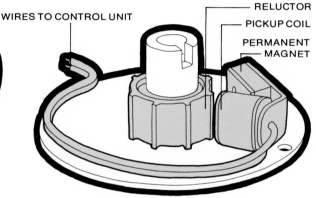

WIRES TO CONTROL UNIT

RELUCTOR
PICKUP COIL
PERMANENT
MAGNET

DISTRIBUTOR

At left, the distributor is shown separated into its three sections—upper, middle and lower. In the middle section the corners of the spinning breaker cam strike the breaker arm and separate the points some 160 times per second when the car is going 60 miles an hour. High-voltage surges thus generated in the coil travel to the rotor that whirls inside a circle of high-tension terminals in the distributor cap. At each terminal, current is transferred to wires that lead to the spark plugs. Two other devices—the vacuum advance and the centrifugal advance—precisely coordinate the functions of the points and the rotor assembly as engine requirements vary.

ELECTRONIC IGNITION

A rotating reluctor and magnetic-pickup coil replace the traditional cam, breaker points and condenser in the distributors of cars equipped for electronic ignition. This system reduces the time between tune-ups. The high spots of the reluctor interrupt the magnetic field of the pickup coil and the permanent magnet. These interruptions, or pulses, are transmitted from the pickup to a nearby electronic control unit. There the pulses signal a transistor to break the low-voltage subcircuit and release high voltage from the coil to the spark plugs.

SPARK PLUG

The high-voltage burst from the distributor is received at the spark plug's terminal and conducted down a center electrode protected by a porcelain insulator. At the bottom of the plug, which projects into the cylinder, the voltage must be powerful enough to jump a gap of about 35/1,000 of an inch between the center and side electrodes through a thick atmosphere of fuel mixture. When the spark bridges the gap it fires the fuel in the cylinder.

41

THE DRIVE-TRAIN SYSTEM

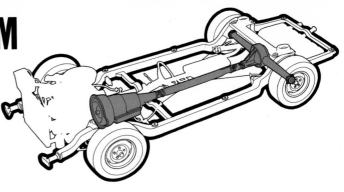

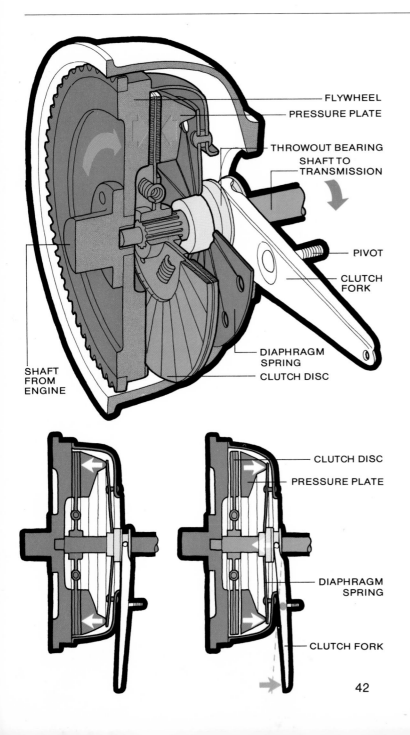

FLYWHEEL

PRESSURE PLATE

THROWOUT BEARING

SHAFT TO TRANSMISSION

PIVOT

CLUTCH FORK

DIAPHRAGM SPRING

CLUTCH DISC

SHAFT FROM ENGINE

CLUTCH DISC

PRESSURE PLATE

DIAPHRAGM SPRING

CLUTCH FORK

MANUAL CLUTCH

In a car that has a manual transmission a clutch is used to disconnect the engine from the transmission when shifting gears. When the clutch is engaged *(left and bottom left)* the clutch disc is sandwiched tightly between the flywheel and pressure plate by a flexible steel diaphragm spring. When the driver depresses the clutch pedal, pressure is transmitted to the spring through the clutch fork and throwout bearing. As it bends at the center, the spring relaxes the pressure on its edges. The disc then disengages itself from the flywheel *(diagram, bottom right)* and prevents engine power from reaching the transmission.

MANUAL TRANSMISSION

Manual transmissions in all modern automobiles are synchromeshed *(right)*. In this system all gears are constantly in contact. Through the gearshift the driver manipulates the selector forks—shown withdrawn from the mechanism—that control the synchronizer sleeves. Each sleeve slides forward or backward to lock or unlock the various gear combinations.

Engine power enters the gearbox through the shaft from the clutch, but it is not passed directly to the output shaft except in third gear *(lower right)*. For lower speeds, the engine torque is multiplied and the speed reduced by passing it through the first set of gears into the countershaft. The gears on the countershaft turn those on the output shaft, which simply spin on the shaft until locked to it by a synchronizer sleeve.

The two-stage contact that occurs when the gearshift locks in a new gear—in this case second gear—is shown in the three small drawings *(near right)*. Starting from a neutral position *(top)*, the sleeve moves the cone clutch into an initial contact that synchronizes gear and shaft speeds *(center)*. A firmer contact with small teeth on the gear's side then locks the gear *(bottom)*.

The drive-train system serves two functions: it transmits power from the engine to the drive wheels, and it varies the amount of turning force —or torque. The latter function is necessary because the engine alone does not produce enough torque at low speeds to put the car in motion from a stop. An assist is provided by two sets of gears in the drive train—the transmission and differential.

Both manual and automatic transmissions commonly use three forward gears to blend speed and torque. First gear delivers maximum torque and minimum speed for starting. Second gear offers medium torque and speed for acceleration and hill-climbing. Third gear allows maximum speed with minimum torque for highway travel. A reverse gear permits backward movement.

The transmission sends power along a drive shaft to the differential gears in the rear axle. There, the torque is boosted and transmitted to the rear wheels, which drive the car.

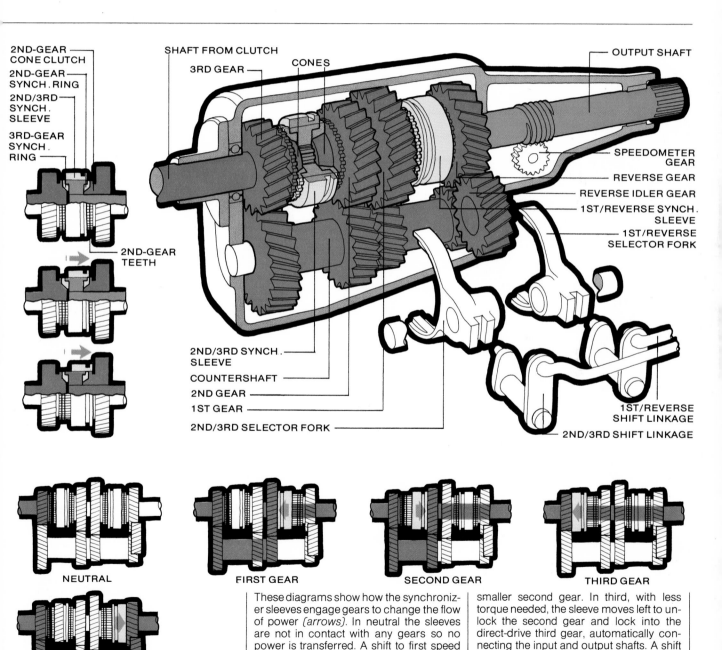

These diagrams show how the synchronizer sleeves engage gears to change the flow of power *(arrows)*. In neutral the sleeves are not in contact with any gears so no power is transferred. A shift to first speed locks a sleeve into the largest and most powerful gear. A shift to second neutralizes the first sleeve and locks the other into the smaller second gear. In third, with less torque needed, the sleeve moves left to unlock the second gear and lock into the direct-drive third gear, automatically connecting the input and output shafts. A shift to reverse locks in a three-gear combination. The output shaft is then driven by the reverse gear in the opposite direction.

THE DRIVE-TRAIN SYSTEM: Automatic transmission

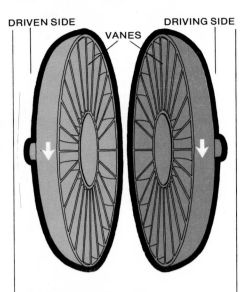

DRIVEN SIDE   DRIVING SIDE

VANES

FLUID COUPLING

A fluid coupling such as the one shown above in simplified form is the heart of the torque converter *(below)* that transmits power from the engine to the gears in the automatic transmission. The coupling consists of two unconnected halves of a doughnut-shaped unit. The driving side is powered by the engine, while the driven side is linked to the transmission shaft.

When the halves are placed together in an oil-filled enclosure, the driving side sets up a rapid rotary movement of oil that strikes the vanes of the driven side, forcing it to rotate in the same direction at virtually the same speed when the car is cruising.

AUTOMATIC TRANSMISSION ▶

Only a relatively small part of an automatic transmission *(right)* is occupied by the gears. Most of the space is filled by the versatile torque converter *(below, left)* and a system of clutches and brake bands that activate the proper gear ratios to provide power to the output shaft.

When the transmission selector is set in the drive position, pressurized oil courses through a complex series of valves in the valve body. The valves, which open and close automatically according to the engine's speed and load, tighten or loosen both the brake bands and the clutches in the transmission to provide the various gear ratios required for driving.

DRIVING SIDE

DRIVEN SIDE

ENGINE SHAFT

OUTPUT SHAFT

STATOR

TORQUE CONVERTER

While fulfilling the function of a fluid coupling *(above, left)*, the torque converter also acts like a gear by boosting the engine's driving force. It does this through a complex arrangement of vaned sections, called stators, in the center of the coupling.

In this cutaway view, the driving side churns the oil that rotates the driven side at the left. The stator vanes are angled to intercept oil thrown off by the driven side vanes and to direct it at high velocity back against the driving side vanes. This speeds up the driving side, which in turn speeds up the driven side, causing the output shaft to turn faster. As a result of this torque multiplication, the torque converter's output shaft receives more thrust than the input shaft originally received from the engine.

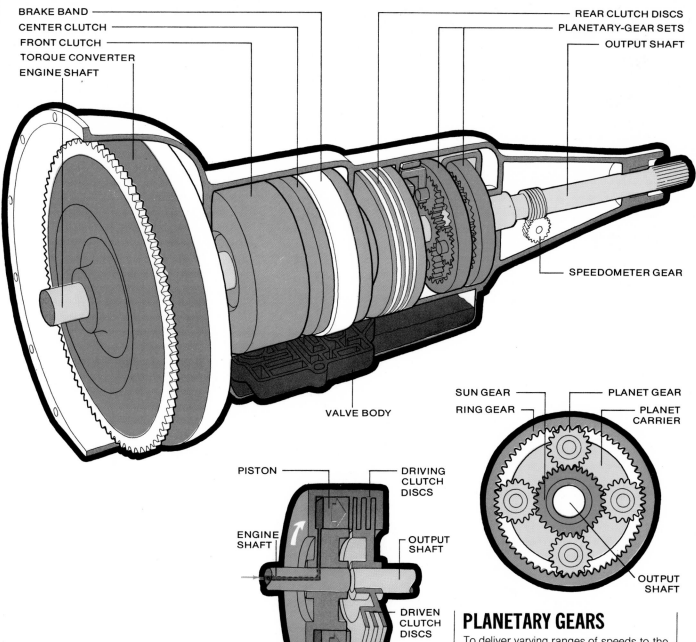

BRAKE BAND
CENTER CLUTCH
FRONT CLUTCH
TORQUE CONVERTER
ENGINE SHAFT

REAR CLUTCH DISCS
PLANETARY-GEAR SETS
OUTPUT SHAFT

SPEEDOMETER GEAR

VALVE BODY

PISTON

DRIVING CLUTCH DISCS

ENGINE SHAFT

OUTPUT SHAFT

DRIVEN CLUTCH DISCS

SUN GEAR
RING GEAR

PLANET GEAR
PLANET CARRIER

OUTPUT SHAFT

FLUID CLUTCH

The fluid clutch is activated by hydraulic pressure. Oil, forced into the clutch housing through a boring in the engine shaft, presses against the piston. This pressure squeezes together a series of clutch discs that are connected alternately to the rotating driving side of the clutch and the stationary driven side. When the discs lock, the driven side turns with the driving side. Power is then delivered to the output shaft and the gears that are attached to it.

PLANETARY GEARS

To deliver varying ranges of speeds to the driving wheels, the automatic transmission employs a pair of two identical planetary-gear sets. Each of these sets, one of which is shown above, consists of four small planet gears that are mounted on a planet carrier. They rotate around a sun gear that is attached to the output shaft of the torque converter and also around the inside edge of a still-larger ring gear.

The two sets operate in unison. Reacting to the speed of the engine, the transmission automatically engages or disengages the gears in various combinations to provide low, medium or high gear. Another combination, activated by the gear selector on the steering wheel, puts the car in reverse.

45

THE DRIVE-TRAIN SYSTEM: Final drive

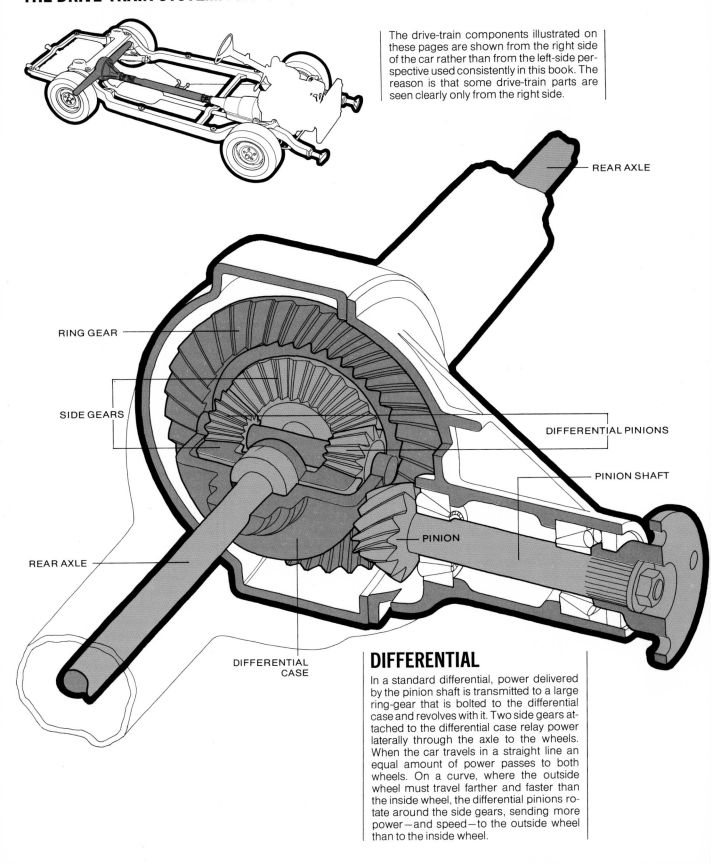

The drive-train components illustrated on these pages are shown from the right side of the car rather than from the left-side perspective used consistently in this book. The reason is that some drive-train parts are seen clearly only from the right side.

REAR AXLE

RING GEAR

SIDE GEARS

DIFFERENTIAL PINIONS

PINION SHAFT

PINION

REAR AXLE

DIFFERENTIAL CASE

DIFFERENTIAL

In a standard differential, power delivered by the pinion shaft is transmitted to a large ring-gear that is bolted to the differential case and revolves with it. Two side gears attached to the differential case relay power laterally through the axle to the wheels. When the car travels in a straight line an equal amount of power passes to both wheels. On a curve, where the outside wheel must travel farther and faster than the inside wheel, the differential pinions rotate around the side gears, sending more power—and speed—to the outside wheel than to the inside wheel.

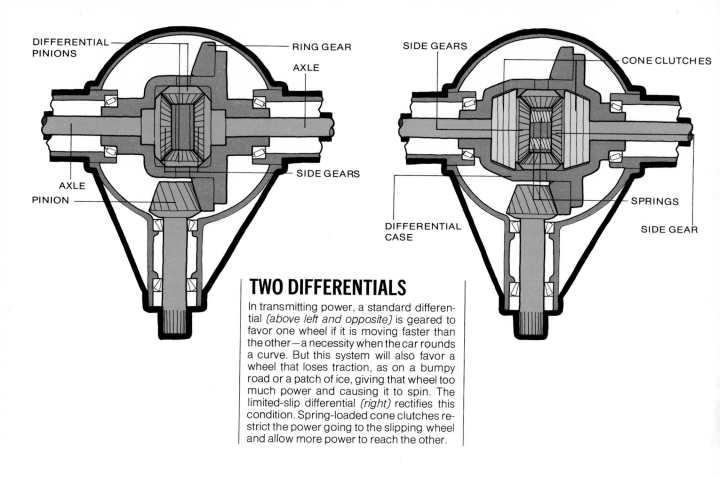

DIFFERENTIAL PINIONS

RING GEAR

AXLE

SIDE GEARS

AXLE

PINION

SIDE GEARS

CONE CLUTCHES

SPRINGS

SIDE GEAR

DIFFERENTIAL CASE

TWO DIFFERENTIALS

In transmitting power, a standard differential *(above left and opposite)* is geared to favor one wheel if it is moving faster than the other—a necessity when the car rounds a curve. But this system will also favor a wheel that loses traction, as on a bumpy road or a patch of ice, giving that wheel too much power and causing it to spin. The limited-slip differential *(right)* rectifies this condition. Spring-loaded cone clutches restrict the power going to the slipping wheel and allow more power to reach the other.

UNIVERSAL JOINTS

If the drive shaft were a single rod extending from the transmission to the rear axle, the bends and flexes caused by the moving car would snap it. Universal joints are used to absorb this stress. The flexible joints, formed by joining the shaft yokes with a cross-shaped unit called a spider, rotate freely to transfer power when angled up, down or sideways. A double-link yoke often is used for still greater flexibility.

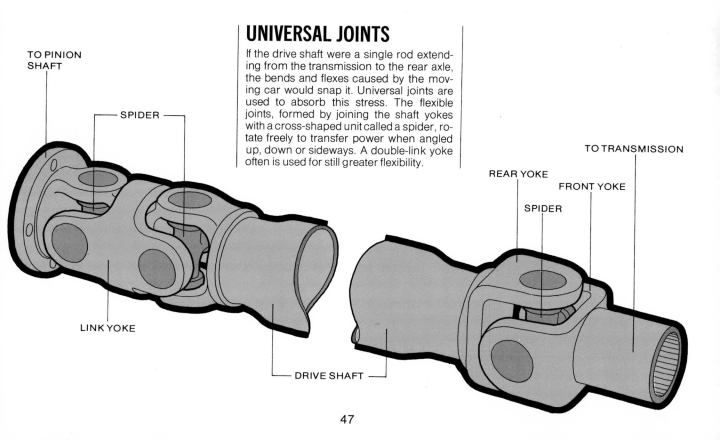

TO PINION SHAFT

SPIDER

LINK YOKE

DRIVE SHAFT

REAR YOKE

SPIDER

FRONT YOKE

TO TRANSMISSION

THE STEERING SYSTEM

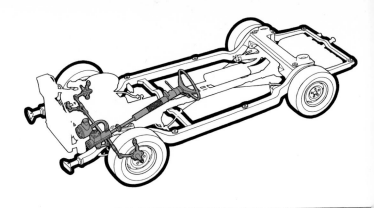

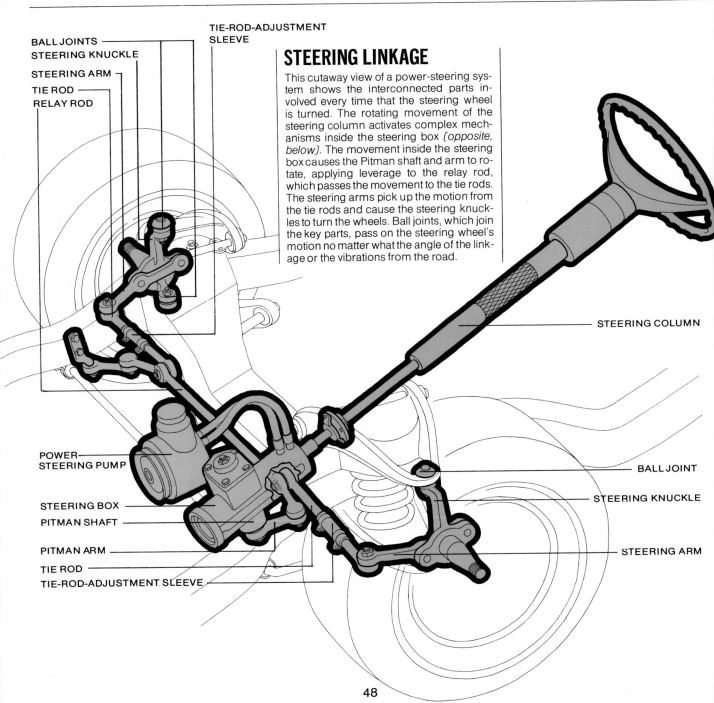

BALL JOINTS
STEERING KNUCKLE

STEERING ARM

TIE ROD
RELAY ROD

TIE-ROD-ADJUSTMENT
SLEEVE

STEERING LINKAGE

This cutaway view of a power-steering system shows the interconnected parts involved every time that the steering wheel is turned. The rotating movement of the steering column activates complex mechanisms inside the steering box *(opposite, below)*. The movement inside the steering box causes the Pitman shaft and arm to rotate, applying leverage to the relay rod, which passes the movement to the tie rods. The steering arms pick up the motion from the tie rods and cause the steering knuckles to turn the wheels. Ball joints, which join the key parts, pass on the steering wheel's motion no matter what the angle of the linkage or the vibrations from the road.

STEERING COLUMN

BALL JOINT

STEERING KNUCKLE

STEERING ARM

POWER-
STEERING PUMP

STEERING BOX
PITMAN SHAFT

PITMAN ARM

TIE ROD
TIE-ROD-ADJUSTMENT SLEEVE

Back in the earliest days of the horseless carriage when most of an automobile's weight—including the engine—was on the rear axle, steering was a simple matter of turning a tiller that pivoted the entire front axle. But when the engine was moved to the front of the car, more complex steering systems had to evolve.

Two of the most common steering mechanisms are shown here: rack and pinion and the standard, or recirculating-ball, system that can be either manual or power-assisted.

Designed for sports cars, rack and pinion requires too much driver muscle at low speeds to be serviceable in larger, heavier cars. For big automobiles, power steering is practically mandatory equipment. It makes a two-ton car respond easily to the steering wheel, whether at highway speeds or inching into a narrow parking place.

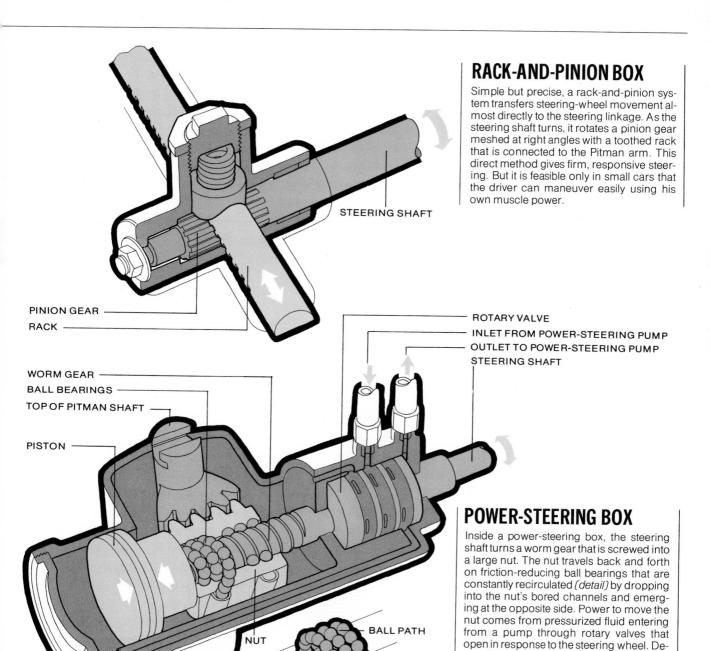

RACK-AND-PINION BOX

Simple but precise, a rack-and-pinion system transfers steering-wheel movement almost directly to the steering linkage. As the steering shaft turns, it rotates a pinion gear meshed at right angles with a toothed rack that is connected to the Pitman arm. This direct method gives firm, responsive steering. But it is feasible only in small cars that the driver can maneuver easily using his own muscle power.

STEERING SHAFT

PINION GEAR
RACK

WORM GEAR
BALL BEARINGS
TOP OF PITMAN SHAFT
PISTON

ROTARY VALVE
INLET FROM POWER-STEERING PUMP
OUTLET TO POWER-STEERING PUMP
STEERING SHAFT

POWER-STEERING BOX

Inside a power-steering box, the steering shaft turns a worm gear that is screwed into a large nut. The nut travels back and forth on friction-reducing ball bearings that are constantly recirculated (detail) by dropping into the nut's bored channels and emerging at the opposite side. Power to move the nut comes from pressurized fluid entering from a pump through rotary valves that open in response to the steering wheel. Depending on the turn direction, the fluid moves a piston forward or backward. This action moves the nut, which turns the Pitman shaft and steering linkage.

NUT
BALL PATH
PITMAN SHAFT

THE SUSPENSION SYSTEM

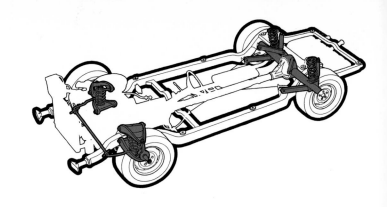

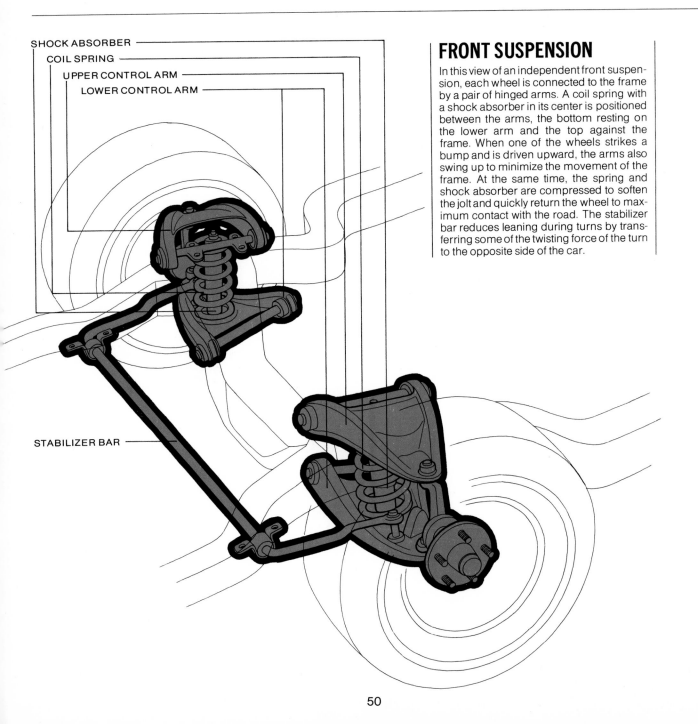

SHOCK ABSORBER

COIL SPRING

UPPER CONTROL ARM

LOWER CONTROL ARM

STABILIZER BAR

FRONT SUSPENSION

In this view of an independent front suspension, each wheel is connected to the frame by a pair of hinged arms. A coil spring with a shock absorber in its center is positioned between the arms, the bottom resting on the lower arm and the top against the frame. When one of the wheels strikes a bump and is driven upward, the arms also swing up to minimize the movement of the frame. At the same time, the spring and shock absorber are compressed to soften the jolt and quickly return the wheel to maximum contact with the road. The stabilizer bar reduces leaning during turns by transferring some of the twisting force of the turn to the opposite side of the car.

Each wheel of today's car has its own suspension system consisting of a steel spring or, in some cars, a torsion bar *(overleaf)* and a shock absorber to soak up the impact caused by uneven road surfaces. In addition, there are mechanical linkages to guide the movement of the wheels. As a whole, the system has two basic functions: to keep the car's wheels in firm contact with the road and to provide a comfortable ride for the passengers.

Much of the suspension's work is done by the springs. Under normal road conditions they support the body on an even keel by compressing and rebounding with every up-and-down wheel movement. But if the car were suspended only by springs, it would bounce and sway uncomfortably after each bump. These undesirable effects are reduced by the four shock absorbers that dampen much of the up-and-down motion.

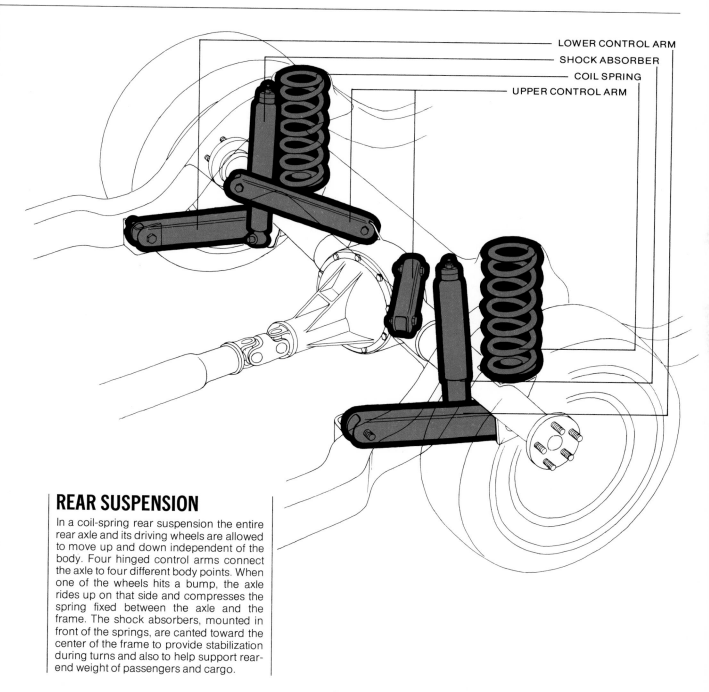

LOWER CONTROL ARM
SHOCK ABSORBER
COIL SPRING
UPPER CONTROL ARM

REAR SUSPENSION

In a coil-spring rear suspension the entire rear axle and its driving wheels are allowed to move up and down independent of the body. Four hinged control arms connect the axle to four different body points. When one of the wheels hits a bump, the axle rides up on that side and compresses the spring fixed between the axle and the frame. The shock absorbers, mounted in front of the springs, are canted toward the center of the frame to provide stabilization during turns and also to help support rear-end weight of passengers and cargo.

THE SUSPENSION SYSTEM: Torsion bars, leaf springs, shock absorbers

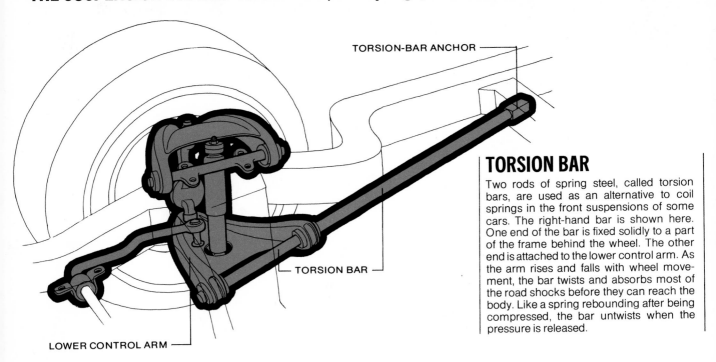

TORSION-BAR ANCHOR

TORSION BAR

LOWER CONTROL ARM

TORSION BAR

Two rods of spring steel, called torsion bars, are used as an alternative to coil springs in the front suspensions of some cars. The right-hand bar is shown here. One end of the bar is fixed solidly to a part of the frame behind the wheel. The other end is attached to the lower control arm. As the arm rises and falls with wheel movement, the bar twists and absorbs most of the road shocks before they can reach the body. Like a spring rebounding after being compressed, the bar untwists when the pressure is released.

LEAF SPRING

A holdover from horse-and-buggy days, leaf springs often are used in heavy-duty rear suspensions. Several layers of spring steel, clipped together to form a single unit, support great axle weight. A hinged shackle at one end permits the springs to flex with axle movement while a shock absorber dampens the oscillations between the center of the spring and the frame.

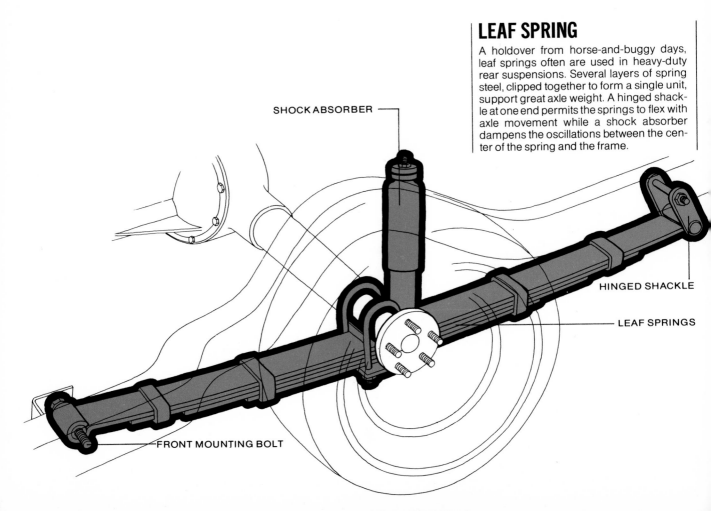

SHOCK ABSORBER

HINGED SHACKLE

LEAF SPRINGS

FRONT MOUNTING BOLT

SHOCK ABSORBER

Designed to dampen the force of any sudden impacts, the double-action hydraulic shock absorber works equally well whether being squeezed together or pulled apart. When the wheel travels over a bump, the lower cylinder moves with the wheel and is telescoped *(left, large arrow)* into the upper cylinder, which is bolted to the frame of the car. A piston attached to the upper cylinder eases this telescoping action by plunging into thick fluid at the bottom of the pressure tube. The pressure slows the piston's motion and forces some fluid to flow upward through the compression valve *(small arrow)* and downward through the reservoir valve into the reservoir tubes.

As the shock absorber rebounds after the impact *(right)*, the lower cylinder is pulled downward *(large arrow)*. The piston then works in reverse, easing the rebound impact by pressing the fluid in the top of the pressure tube. The rebound valve allows pressurized fluid to enter the lower part of the tube *(small arrow)* at the same time that the tube is being refilled from the supply of fluid in the reservoir tubes.

RESERVOIR TUBE

PISTON

COMPRESSION VALVE

PRESSURE TUBE

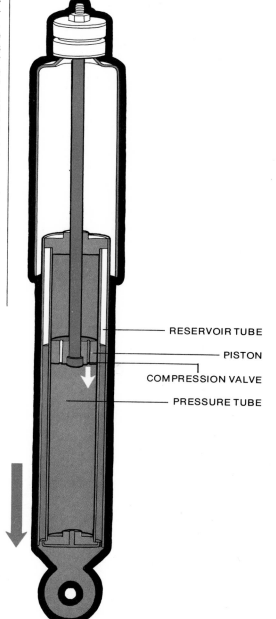

RESERVOIR TUBE

PISTON

COMPRESSION VALVE

PRESSURE TUBE

THE BRAKING SYSTEM

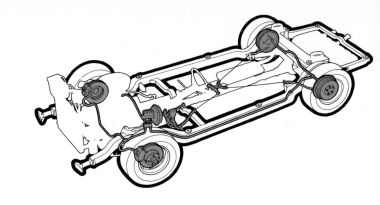

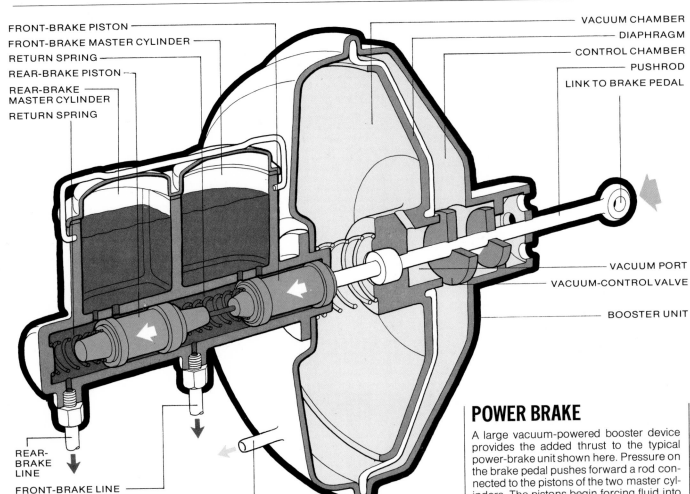

FRONT-BRAKE PISTON
FRONT-BRAKE MASTER CYLINDER
RETURN SPRING
REAR-BRAKE PISTON
REAR-BRAKE MASTER CYLINDER
RETURN SPRING

VACUUM CHAMBER
DIAPHRAGM
CONTROL CHAMBER
PUSHROD
LINK TO BRAKE PEDAL

VACUUM PORT
VACUUM-CONTROL VALVE

BOOSTER UNIT

REAR-BRAKE LINE
FRONT-BRAKE LINE
ENGINE VACUUM LINE

POWER BRAKE

A large vacuum-powered booster device provides the added thrust to the typical power-brake unit shown here. Pressure on the brake pedal pushes forward a rod connected to the pistons of the two master cylinders. The pistons begin forcing fluid into the front and rear brake lines.

At the same time, the brake-pedal pushrod positions the vacuum-control valve so that it closes the vacuum port and seals off the forward half of the booster unit. The engine vacuum line then draws off the air, creating a low-pressure vacuum chamber. Atmospheric pressure in the control chamber reacts by pushing against the diaphragm dividing the two chambers. The pressure on the diaphragm, which is locked to the pushrod, forces it forward, supplying additional pressure on the pistons.

WARNING SWITCH

This special brake warning switch *(right)*, standard equipment since 1970, is connected to the front and rear brake lines. It alerts the driver if either set of brakes is not working properly. When pressure in one of the lines is sharply reduced, pressure from the other side forces a piston to move *(arrow)*. A plunger pin then drops into a groove in the piston, activating a switch that turns on a dashboard warning light.

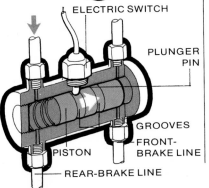

ELECTRIC SWITCH
PLUNGER PIN
GROOVES
FRONT-BRAKE LINE
PISTON
REAR-BRAKE LINE

When you step on the brake pedal you command a stopping force 10 times as powerful as the force that puts the car in motion. In an all-out emergency stop, the wheels of a heavy, speeding automobile can be locked to a standstill almost instantaneously—in scarcely one second. The braking system can exert as much as 1,000 pounds of hydraulic pressure on each of the four brakes. In modern systems a power-assisted master cylinder

(below, left) separately activates the front and rear brakes. Should one set fail, the other can provide adequate, though reduced, temporary braking power. High-performance disc brakes (below), originally developed for racing, often are used on the front wheels. On most American cars when the front brakes are of the disc type the ones in the rear are of the traditional drum type (overleaf). The parking brake works only on the rear wheels.

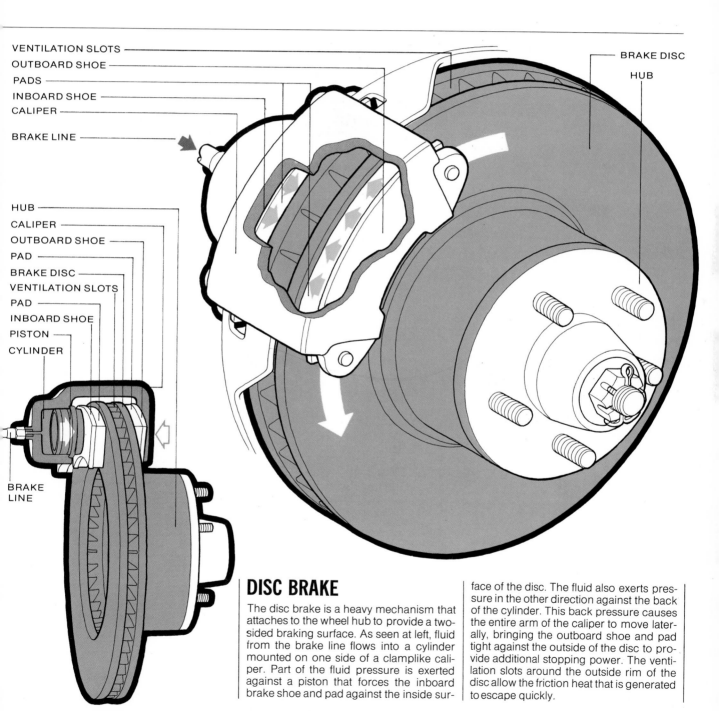

DISC BRAKE

The disc brake is a heavy mechanism that attaches to the wheel hub to provide a two-sided braking surface. As seen at left, fluid from the brake line flows into a cylinder mounted on one side of a clamplike caliper. Part of the fluid pressure is exerted against a piston that forces the inboard brake shoe and pad against the inside surface of the disc. The fluid also exerts pressure in the other direction against the back of the cylinder. This back pressure causes the entire arm of the caliper to move laterally, bringing the outboard shoe and pad tight against the outside of the disc to provide additional stopping power. The ventilation slots around the outside rim of the disc allow the friction heat that is generated to escape quickly.

THE BRAKING SYSTEM: Drum brakes

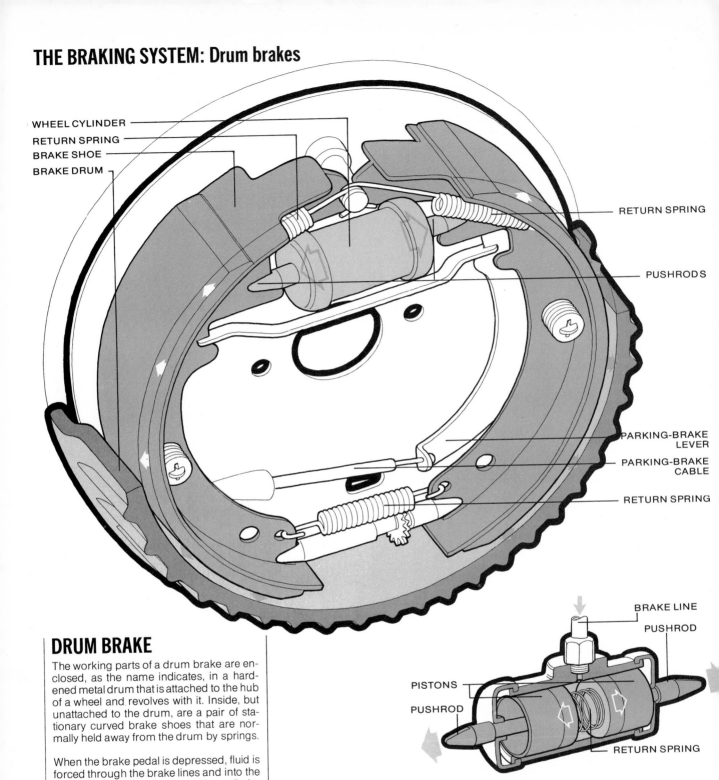

WHEEL CYLINDER
RETURN SPRING
BRAKE SHOE
BRAKE DRUM

RETURN SPRING

PUSHRODS

PARKING-BRAKE LEVER

PARKING-BRAKE CABLE

RETURN SPRING

BRAKE LINE

PUSHROD

PISTONS

PUSHROD

RETURN SPRING

DRUM BRAKE

The working parts of a drum brake are enclosed, as the name indicates, in a hardened metal drum that is attached to the hub of a wheel and revolves with it. Inside, but unattached to the drum, are a pair of stationary curved brake shoes that are normally held away from the drum by springs.

When the brake pedal is depressed, fluid is forced through the brake lines and into the wheel cylinder. Pushrods in the cylinder *(right)* then apply pressure to both shoes, overcoming the spring tension and pressing the shoes against the drum. Because of the intense friction caused by braking, the brake shoes must be lined with a heat-resistant asbestos compound. Hydraulic drum brakes also can be activated mechanically as parking brakes by means of cables attached to a lever *(opposite)*.

WHEEL CYLINDER

Two-way pressure is applied when the wheel cylinder is activated. Brake fluid enters the center of the cylinder, forcing the pistons apart *(arrows)*. Pushrods at the piston ends then apply equal pressure to the brake shoes. A return spring pulls the pistons together when pressure is released.

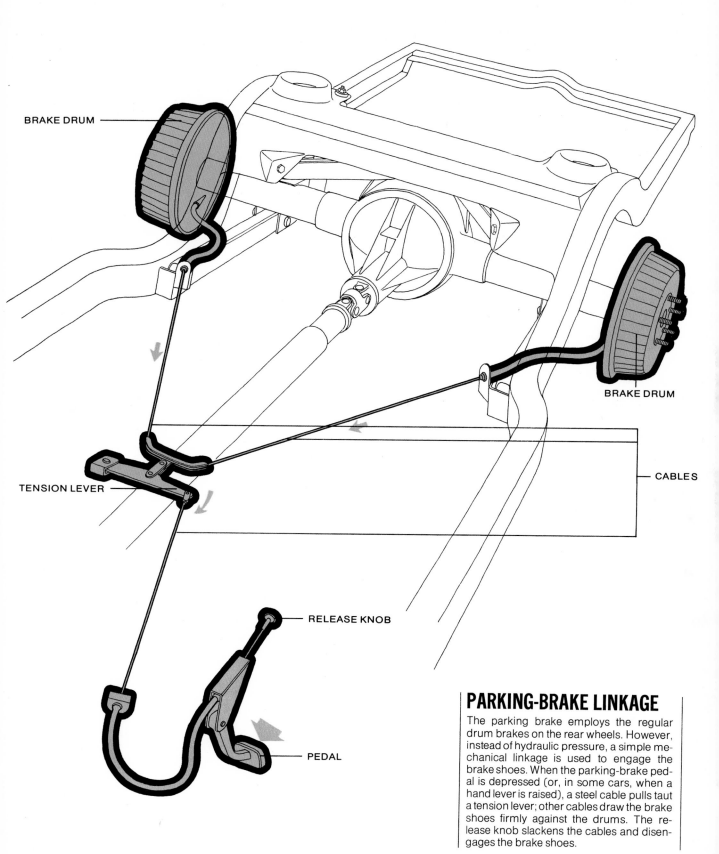

BRAKE DRUM

BRAKE DRUM

CABLES

TENSION LEVER

RELEASE KNOB

PEDAL

PARKING-BRAKE LINKAGE

The parking brake employs the regular drum brakes on the rear wheels. However, instead of hydraulic pressure, a simple mechanical linkage is used to engage the brake shoes. When the parking-brake pedal is depressed (or, in some cars, when a hand lever is raised), a steel cable pulls taut a tension lever; other cables draw the brake shoes firmly against the drums. The release knob slackens the cables and disengages the brake shoes.

NEW CARS

GETTING THE ONE YOU WANT AT THE BEST PRICE

2

Too many Americans do too little planning before buying a new car. Except for a house, automobiles are the biggest investments most families make—and both ventures, if they are handled intelligently, demand attention to a long list of considerations. In buying a car, decisions must be made about size, power, body type, added options and accessories, the availability and quality of service, and, of course, the price. American automobile manufacturers build more than 400 different models, and when these are coupled with all the possible lists of buyer-specified extras, the number of combinations runs into the millions. In addition to all this, American dealers offer an ever-increasing assortment of foreign models.

The prime prerequisite for picking a car is to decide how it is to be used (box, page 65). Form follows function: the way a family lives and where and how far it travels should be the main factors in the choice. A student or a city couple with no children probably would opt for compactness over big-car spaciousness; vice versa for parents who chauffeur five kids and their friends around a suburb. Most families, of course, find themselves in different situations, with different requirements, at different times—in town and country, alone or with passengers, on short hops or on cross-country vacation jaunts. There is no easy way out of the size dilemma. But it makes sense to have a car that is right most of the time and too large or too small only occasionally.

Let's examine the decision-making experience of one family that is, according to recent statistics from the government and the automobile industry, typical of American car buyers in age and situation (though perhaps atypical

59

in wisdom). Bill, a 30-year-old engineer for a Midwestern electronics firm, uses his four-year-old compact to drive to work daily; it is still in good shape. Wife Ann's six-year-old Behemoth Eight, however, is gasping its last breath. It gets heavy use: it goes to the supermarket two or three times a week, it delivers son Mike to football practice and daughter Kathy to dancing classes, and on Sunday afternoons the whole family often piles in for a drive in the country. They took the Behemoth on a vacation tour of New England last summer, but both Ann and Bill are convinced it would not survive the Rocky Mountains trip they plan for next summer.

During the months in which they thought about replacing the Behemoth, they had visited many dealers and talked to many salesmen. They had looked at floor models and built up a large library of brochures that listed the specifications and options available for each line. One night they got out all the brochures and sat down to talk about a new car.

Practically the only occasions when the whole family rode in the Behemoth, they agreed, were on their Sunday excursions and on summer vacations. In a typical week most of Ann's trips were for distances of less than five miles. Usually she was driving alone or with only one of the children; she could get along splendidly with a car smaller than the Behemoth. But what about those Sundays, what about those vacations? The classic dilemma.

Choosing the size best for you

Not so many years ago, Ann and Bill would not have had a choice; all cars were pretty much the same length, width and height. Now, however, there is a wide range of sizes to choose from (chart, page 66). American manufacturers offer cars in four basic sizes. (Imports generally fall into the first two categories.)

■ SUBCOMPACTS, the smallest cars made, are shorter than 172 inches overall and their suggested retail price, without any options, is below $2,500.

Ann and Bill knew that subcompacts are the least expensive cars to buy and operate. Small and light, they achieve the best gasoline mileage, and are easiest to maneuver. On the other hand, a subcompact offers the least interior space, and generally the least engine power. It promises to seat a maximum of four adults, but those in the rear seat very likely will feel uncomfortable if they ride for any distance. Bill and Ann decided a subcompact was simply too small for the family.

■ COMPACTS are between 173 and 204 inches in length. Detroit's models cost from $2,200 to $2,900, without options; foreign makes start at $2,200 and climb to more than $4,300 with factory equipment.

Bill had found that his compact was economical to run, easy to handle and a dream to squeeze into his plant's parking lot. It could easily seat two adults in front, but legroom in the rear was minimal and the kids, when they were along, had little room to move. "What we really need," Bill told Ann, "are a couple of compacts that expand like accordions for trips with the kids."

■ INTERMEDIATES do not shrink or stretch, but they do fill the gap between the compacts and today's full-sized models—the big standards like Ann's old Behemoth. Intermediate models measure from 207 to 215 inches, and in price range from about $2,700 to over $3,000, factory equipped. For many years, until the late 1950s, this length was the automobile industry's top of the line. In fact, during the first decade after World War II nearly all American-built cars were about this size. Most curbside parking spaces, garages and parking lots were designed for them. In the mid-'50s, however,

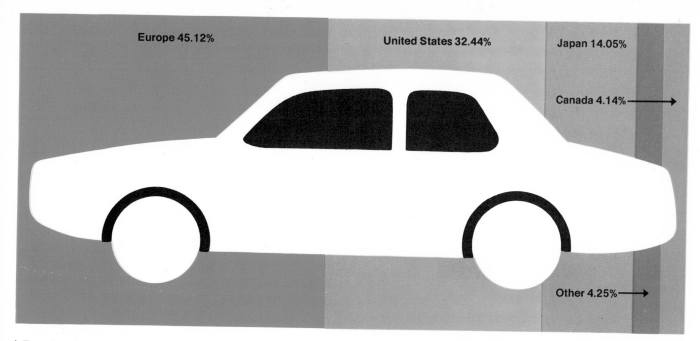

Europe 45.12% United States 32.44% Japan 14.05%

Canada 4.14%→

Other 4.25%→

Two decades ago three of every four passenger cars were built in the United States. But European and Japanese production has expanded vastly. Today, though American production stands at an all-time high, the United States produces slightly less than one of every three passenger vehicles.

cars began to sprout soaring tail fins and elaborate chromed bumpers, and in the process they grew a foot or so in length. Homeowners who continued to buy the same make of car found their garages strangely smaller. At the point when large numbers of people began switching to smaller imported cars, the major auto manufacturers expanded their production lines and cranked up to add compact and intermediate models in volume. Buyers thus found themselves with a choice of sizes they had never had before.

Because so many U.S. driving situations —roads, garages, parking spaces—were designed for cars of their dimensions, today's intermediates increasingly represent a popular compromise. For shorter trips, they can seat three in front and three in back in relative comfort. They offer a wide choice of engines and accessories, and provide a respectable amount of luggage space.

Poring over the brochures, Ann and Bill came to feel that their use pattern indicated the wisdom of choosing an intermediate. "It would carry my whole bridge club, or Kathy's dancing-school friends, or several of Mike's friends in their football gear," Ann mused. "It would be easier to park than the Behemoth and we'd still have room in the garage to store the bicycles." Bill, who secretly hoped one day to take the family on a camping trip, was willing to accept an intermediate, because he had learned that it is the smallest size capable of safely towing a camper or trailer. But he was reluctant to give up the feeling of power, solidity and luxury that is built into a big car. He remembered the pleasure of driving the Behemoth when it was new. It was, after all, a standard. And a standard is a standard, isn't it? Well, yes and no.

■ STANDARDS, by the early 1970s, accounted for only about 40 per cent of the cars sold in the United States (against about 35 per cent for compacts and subcompacts combined), and that percentage is still diminishing. The standard, or full-sized, model is no longer the average American's everyday car; it's a big and often richly appointed vehicle. Standards include the largest, most expensive cars you can buy. They measure in length from 213 to 235 inches (nearly 20 feet) and range in price from $3,600 to more than $11,000.

Typically each nameplate comes in three lines, differing widely in price and power and comfort features. There are the economy models, with a bare minimum of standard factory-installed equipment; the middle line, with more deluxe trim and equipment; and the high-priced luxury versions. With few exceptions any one of these three lines offers greater stability and riding comfort than smaller cars. Most standard models will seat three adults comfortably in both front and back, and they offer many advantages for a driver or a family that takes frequent high-speed, long-distance trips. But a full-sized car can be cumbersome in city traffic and difficult to park.

Bill liked the looks of the Belchfire Brougham, a top-of-the-line full-sized sedan. But he was also mindful that Ann was cool to driving another car with the proportions of the Behemoth. She complained that it was "like driving a Sherman tank down Main Street." Bill countered by saying he would not be averse to an intermediate-sized wagon—the body style that year after year accounts for one of every nine automobile sales in America.

Nearly every model line offers station wagons, so they are available in all sizes from subcompacts to standards. Usually they are a few inches longer than the comparable sedan and they command a price premium over the sedan version. Subcompact wagons usually have two side doors and a rear door hinged at the top. The bigger models usually have four side doors, but a variety of arrangements is used to provide access to the cargo compartment in the rear: a door that lifts upward; or a door that opens to one side; or a door that opens downward (to provide additional load surface); a door that can be opened either downward or to the side, or a door that opens like a clamshell —the top half slides up under the roof and the bottom half slides downward under the floor. With this variety the station wagon lends itself to many use patterns, from the transporting of Little Leaguers to the hauling of snow blowers and plywood panels.

"I still think the Belchfire can carry or pull everything we'll want it to, and it's smooth-handling, with power everything. It's no Sherman tank," Bill said. "Yes, but a big car costs more in every way," said Ann. "What about all that gasoline they burn?"

The average car is driven about 12,000 miles a year. A large car that got 10 miles to the gallon, she estimated, would burn up at least 500 gallons of gasoline more than a smaller car that got 18 miles per gallon; and even if they used the same grade of fuel, the cost of that difference was dizzying.

Another important consideration, Ann reminded Bill, is how quickly a particular model will depreciate in value and what it will be worth when the time comes to resell it. Depreciation is the largest cost of owning a car. But since the money isn't paid out in cash, most people tend to underestimate the amount. During its first year, a new car typically loses one quarter to one third of the manufacturer's suggested retail price—the price listed on the sticker that is pasted, by law, on one of its windows. Each year thereafter the car continues to depreciate, although more slowly, until it is junked. Few people want to keep a car until it is ready for the junkyard, however, and the average family trades in its old car for a new one about every three and a half years.

By choosing a car that appears likely to have a high resale value, you can significantly reduce the cost of owning it. Unhappily, there is no easy or sure way to tell which cars will depreciate less than others. The popularity of different cars varies by model, by region and even by season. Spring usually contributes to the re-

With changing life styles—including an exodus of the affluent from city to suburb (where a high degree of mobility is needed) —nearly 80 per cent of American families have acquired at least one automobile. Furthermore, the number of multicar households has been climbing steadily: 30.2 per cent of all families own two automobiles and 5.6 per cent own three or more cars.

lease of budget inhibitions; a large station wagon, for example, can be worth $300 more in April than it was worth the previous December, because many families want a large car for their summer vacation trip. In early fall every existing car automatically declines in value because that is when the next year's models are introduced and put on sale.

Bill promised to stop the next day to ask one or two used-car dealers which models would be likely to depreciate least in their area. Certainly, depreciation would not determine what car they would buy, but it was an important consideration. He took the Behemoth, freshly washed, on this errand so that the used-car dealers could give him a ball-park appraisal; knowing its approximate value would help later in bargaining with the new-car dealer over its trade-in price.

Bill found out that, because smaller cars have been becoming more popular and standard-sized models less so, the trend is for smaller cars to depreciate less than larger ones. "The dealer said that kids and retired people like the economy and handling of the little jobs," Bill told Ann, "and since they buy a lot of the cars that are traded in, the smaller ones keep their value better."

Imports do, too. The sales of imported cars soared for several years in the late 1960s because many models were less expensive than any American-made car. But with the introduction of the American subcompacts in 1970 and subsequent devaluation of the dollar, that price advantage virtually disappeared. Domestic subcompacts and compacts are now competitive in price with comparable imports.

Most imported cars, even luxury models, are more compact than their American equivalents. Few imports provide as much interior space as an American-made standard car or a station wagon.

But many imports do offer attractive alternatives to American small or intermediate cars. Several achieve better gasoline mileage than most U.S. cars do. A number have won reputations for excellent quality and have built up creditable service networks. Some are more comfortable to drive than American small cars, and some offer mechanical features unavailable on Detroit's models. On the other hand, if you are driving an imported car in an area where there is no dealer service for that make, you may run into difficulty having it repaired. And replacement parts for imported cars may be expensive and hard to get if they, too, have to be shipped substantial distances.

Some styling considerations

After looking over their brochures, recalling the features of models they had seen or ridden in, and asking judicious questions of neighbors and friends who recently had bought new cars, Ann and Bill concluded that, after size and price, the most significant difference among cars was in styling. "I like the looks of the imports," said Ann. "They're cute and, well, I think they're exotic."

"Not me," said Bill. "Sure, I want a car that looks sleek and streamlined, but it also has to be roomy, comfortable and solid."

"What you want," said Ann, "is your TV chair stuffed into the cockpit of a space rocket with wheels on it." In the end, of course, they compromised. For their particular needs at that particular time, they decided, an intermediate was the thing. It would be within their budget, even after adding options; it was small enough for Ann's local driving, and it was still large enough for the family's summer trip. Then they zeroed in on the make they both thought had the nicest appearance—sleek enough for Bill, but with a hint of continental lines pleasing to Ann. They chose an alternate, too, in case they couldn't find a satisfactory dealer or a good price for their first pick.

They still had to decide on the body type (chart, page 68). Their car was available as a sedan or hardtop, and with two or four doors. For several years the hardtop was the most popular body style by far. Unlike a sedan, which has roof-supporting pillars behind the front doors, a hardtop has completely open sides when the windows are down. It has a feeling of spaciousness that a sedan lacks, and automobile designers are pleased by its uncluttered look. But the hardtop is more prone than a sedan to rattles, leaks and wind noise. Because it has no center pillar to support the roof, a hardtop is less safe in an accident, hence the steady trend to sedans.

A sedan is the most solidly built type of car. The side pillars help to keep the body rigid, and a two-door sedan is especially likely to be free from rattles and vibration. But it is sometimes hard to tell just what is a sedan and what is a hardtop. Some models are called "colonnade hardtops" or "pillared hardtops" and some are even called "hardtop sedans." You can end the confusion easily: it's a sedan if it has a pillar behind the front doors.

Time was when a sedan was simply a sedan, and a car had either two or four doors. Now some two-door models, called hatchbacks, have fold-down rear seats and a third door, or liftgate, in place of a trunk. The hatchback door is handy for loading bags of groceries or other cargo, but such models have no cargo space that is out of sight, as it is in the ordinary car's trunk.

The decision to buy a two-door or a four-door car should also depend on how you weigh personal considerations. The Behemoth had only two doors because Ann and Bill, six years before, had been concerned that their small children might accidentally open a rear door. Now the kids were bigger. "It would be easier to load things with four doors," Ann said, "and the bridge club ladies grumble some when I make them climb into the back seat." Bill agreed that for them four doors would be worth the slightly higher price.

Picking out the options

At this point the car Ann and Bill decided on was somewhat like a prefabricated house that can be bought as a "shell." They now had to decide how to furnish and landscape it.

There are dozens of options and accessories available, and it is possible, as Ann and Bill learned, that by adding enough options the price of a car can be almost doubled. In this situation an aggressive salesman may try to "load you up." If the buyer has decided firmly in advance which options he really wants, he will be able to resist such a salesman's blandishments more successfully. Some options (e.g., an automatic transmission or a heavy-duty suspension) must be built into the car when it is made; they cannot be added later. And some options that might otherwise be easily dismissed will add considerably to the resale value of the car. Dealers say it is difficult to sell a standard or intermediate-sized used car unless it is equipped with automatic transmission, power steering, power brakes, a radio and, in most regions of the United States, air conditioning as well.

THE CAR'S VARIED JOBS

For most Americans the car is an indispensable member of the family rather than a luxury. The chart below shows how the average family uses its car.

Purpose of trip	Percentage of trips
EARNING A LIVING	
Travel to and from work	32.3%
Travel related to business	4.4%
	36.7%
FAMILY DUTIES	
Shopping	15.4%
Visits to doctor and dentist	1.7%
Rides to school, church, etc.	9.4%
Other	14.2%
	40.7%
RECREATION	
Vacations	0.1%
Visits to friends and relatives	9.1%
Pleasure rides	1.4%
Other (dining out, social events, etc.)	12.0%
	22.6%
Total	100%

Some functional options, such as a higher axle ratio to increase pulling power, usually add surprisingly little to the basic cost of a car. Others, such as automatic transmission, are fairly expensive. And some options may require still other options: air conditioning, for instance, usually demands a more powerful engine, a heavy-duty radiator and alternator, and a stronger battery.

That more powerful engine is the first option to consider. The base price of every car includes a standard engine. In general this is the most economical, lowest powered engine that the manufacturer thinks will adequately propel the car. But for every model there is at least one—and sometimes four or five—more powerful engine. Which to choose depends, again, on how the car is to be used. In some subcompacts, for example, the standard four-cylinder engine teamed with an automatic transmission provides barely enough power to accelerate the car safely onto a high-speed turnpike. As a rule, if a buyer plans to use the car mostly for local driving in flat country, with relatively little driving in hilly country or on superhighways, the standard engine should be sufficient. But if many power-draining options are to be added, especially an air conditioner, the next-more-powerful engine almost certainly will be more satisfactory. If towing a trailer is planned, a still stronger engine is indicated.

With a pencil and pad, Bill began listing the options he and Ann wanted. He started by replacing the car's standard 250-cubic-inch, six-cylinder engine with the smallest available V8. Ann wasn't very certain she now needed a 140-horsepower, 300-cubic-inch engine, but Bill just said, "Wait and see." Then he asked Ann how she felt about an automatic transmission. "I wouldn't drive a car without it," she said. Bill smiled and added it to his list. Then Bill elected a heavy-duty axle ratio.

He knew that this slightly higher ratio of drive shaft to wheel speed cuts down a bit on a car's maximum-speed performance—but it provides additional power to the rear wheels, a valuable assist if you plan to pull a trailer's weight. (Still another kind of axle is the economy option, which has a slightly lower ratio than the regular axle. It provides a little less power to the wheels, but lets the engine work less hard and saves gasoline.)

Power steering? On large cars, of course, it's pretty much standard, since the power boost is almost essential for parking and for maneu-

SIZING UP NEW CARS

The first step in buying a new car is to select a size that best meets your needs in terms of function, performance, comfort and economy. Each of today's four size categories includes a complete assortment of body styles *(page 68)*.

The data and comments below do not apply to sports or specialty cars or exotic imports. The prices listed are for factory-equipped cars, i.e., only those with features and accessories that are strictly standard equipment.

SIZE	MAJOR ADVANTAGES	MAJOR DISADVANTAGES
**Subcompact** Length: 154" to 172" Passengers: four Price: $2,000 to $2,500	Best maneuverability Lowest initial cost Best fuel mileage Low insurance rates Low upkeep costs Low depreciation	Vulnerable in accident Poorest highway performance Harsh ride Lack of power for towing Noisy Close quarters, especially in rear Limited trunk space Fewest available options

**Compact**
Length: 173" to 204"
Passengers: five
Price: $2,200 to $2,900
(some imports $4,000 and up)
	Good maneuverability and
	  adequate highway performance
	Less noise than smaller cars
	Low initial cost and depreciation
	Good fuel mileage
	Low insurance rates
	Moderate upkeep costs
	Good choice of options
		Vulnerable in accident
		Harsher ride than larger cars
		Lack of power for heavy-duty
		  towing
		Close quarters for rear-seat
		  passengers

**Intermediate**
Length: 207" to 215"
Passengers: six
Price: $2,700 to $3,000
	Good blend of maneuverability,
	  highway performance and
	  operating economy
	Less noise than smaller cars
	Enough room for small families
	Good trunk space
	Generous choice of options
		Higher initial cost than smaller
		  cars
		Mediocre fuel mileage, especially
		  if large engine is needed
		  for power options and heavy
		  towing
		High upkeep costs

**Standard (Full sized)**
Length: 213" to 235"
Passengers: six
Price: $3,600 to $12,000
	Most protection in collision
	  with another car
	Best highway performance
	Powerful enough for heavy
	  towing
	Roomiest interior
	Large trunk space
	Largest choice of options
		Least maneuverability, even
		  with power steering
		Highest initial cost
		Poorest fuel mileage
		Highest insurance rates
		Highest upkeep costs
		Highest depreciation

vering in heavy traffic. Power steering makes it easier to drive any car, and the option will repay much of its original cost by increasing the car's resale value. (Most subcompacts, with small, four-cylinder engines, are so light and maneuverable that power steering isn't really necessary.)

Power brakes are similarly useful on large cars. They greatly reduce the strain of constant braking in traffic. Disc brakes—whose friction comes from the contact of flat pads on metal discs rather than that of rounded linings on metal drums—are less subject to fading, or losing effectiveness, because of heat that is produced by continuous braking. They also are less affected by moisture than drum brakes. Bill opted for power steering and power disc brakes. Then he and Ann discussed air conditioning, an expensive extra that is rapidly increasing in popularity.

Installed in about 60 per cent of all the cars built in the United States today, "air" was initially introduced as a luxury item for cars sold in the South and in the Western desert states. But it made driving so much more pleasant —providing not only cooling comfort in summer but interior quiet year-round (because the windows stay closed)—that it's now equally attractive to drivers in Northern states. Bill wasn't certain whether they really needed air conditioning. It is one of the most expensive options, typically increasing the price of a car by 10 per cent. It also increases gasoline consumption because of the additional power it requires. But when Ann reminded him of the pressure cooker their local highways became in summer, and of their planned summer trip across the plains, they decided to include air conditioning—particularly since Bill was well aware that they would recoup roughly half the original cost of this option when it came time to trade the car in.

They considered several other options that would make driving the car more pleasant—an electrically adjustable driver's seat, a stereo tape player; and some that were purely cosmetic—a vinyl roof, a deluxe exterior-trim package. (A check list of options will be found on pages 70 to 72.) However, in the end all they added to their list was an outside left-hand rear-view mirror that was adjustable from inside; intermittent windshield wipers that could be set to sweep only every two to 10 seconds—slowly enough so the blade doesn't smudge against dry glass in drizzle or light snow—and an AM-FM radio.

Perhaps the most obvious option was the color. They had pretty much settled on what the manufacturer called winter green for the outside and black for the interior, but they put off making the final choice until they could see actual colors on a car or sample swatches in the showroom.

The dealer and the test drive

One Saturday soon after, Bill and Ann took their list of options and visited a nearby dealer. They planned to accomplish three vital steps on this trip. They would pin down the total list price of the car they had chosen, equipped with their list of options. They would test-drive the model they wanted. And they would inspect the dealership and appraise its service facilities. These are the three steps most people do not fully pursue when they buy a car. Most discontent with a car arises because the buyer isn't confident that he paid a reasonable price, didn't test-drive the car or didn't buy from a dealer who would provide reliable service.

"Can I help you folks today?" a salesman asked, rather indifferently, as they walked in. The salesmen had been watching them through the plate-glass window and had decid-

HOW THE BODY STYLES SHAPE UP

After you pick a new car of suitable size *(page 66)*, your next choice is a body style. This requires juggling considerations of safety, comfort, looks and cost. The permutations are many, but whatever size/style combination you want, one or more auto makers offer it. In the comments below, sedans are defined as cars with central side pillars. The comments about station wagons also apply to the hybrid hatchbacks, which have a tailgate-like third door.

STYLE	MAJOR ADVANTAGES	MAJOR DISADVANTAGES
 **Four-door sedan**	Rear seat is more accessible than in two-door cars Initial cost is lower than for four-door hardtop Pillar adds rollover support Design cuts drafts and noises	Depreciation is higher than for hardtop Rear doors can be opened accidentally by children
 **Two-door sedan**	Initial cost is lower than for hardtop No rear doors for children to open accidentally Pillar adds rollover support Design cuts drafts and noises	Depreciation is higher than for hardtop Rear seat is less accessible than in four-door models
 **Four-door hardtop**	Depreciation is lower than for sedan Rear seat is more accessible than in two-door models Side vision is unobstructed Styling is more streamlined than sedan's	Initial cost is higher than for sedan Rear doors can be opened accidentally by children Absence of pillars means less support in case of rollover Pillarless windows admit more noise and weather
 **Two-door hardtop**	Depreciation is lower than for sedan No rear doors for children to open accidentally Side vision is unobstructed Styling is more streamlined than sedan's	Cost is higher than for sedan Headroom and kneeroom in rear are less than in sedan Absence of pillars means less support in case of rollover Pillarless windows admit more noise and weather
 **Convertible**	Open-air feeling with top down is unmatched even by sunroofed car Depreciation is lower than for roofed cars	No rollover protection Fabric top is noisier, less weathertight and more vulnerable to vandalism—and replacements are costly Sun-heated leather or vinyl seats can scorch flesh
 **Station wagon**	Passenger space equals or exceeds that of most sedans Cargo space exceeds capacity of sedan trunk Depreciation is lower than for sedan	Most cargo space is exposed Tailgate and folding seat generate rattles Cargo area amplifies noises Interior is harder to heat and cool Cost is higher than for sedan

ed they were not buyers but merely lookers —or, in the jargon of the new-car salesman, tire kickers *(box, page 74)*.

The test drive

Ann and Bill spent more time examining closely a floor model approximating what they were interested in. When Bill began asking about prices, the salesman brightened up, invited them into his cubicle and pulled out a contract. There are salesmen who won't discuss prices until a customer is seated in an office, where it is harder to avoid a sales pitch. "We don't plan on buying quite so soon," said Bill, "but we'd like to get your prices on that sedan we've been looking at, and ask about a few options, and then we'd like to take a test drive."

"You folks look like you already know what you want," said the salesman. "You have your options all written out. All you have to do is sign on the dotted line and you can drive home in a new car tomorrow." But when Bill still insisted that he was not ready to buy, the salesman gave him the list prices.

The list price of the car and most options are on the car's window sticker, of course, and current prices are also listed in paperback books available at many newsstands. But if the dealer has a discount policy, it may show up at this early stage of negotiation.

After the salesman gave Ann and Bill the list, all three climbed into a demonstrator car and went off for a test drive that took the best part of an hour. The salesman wasn't exactly ecstatic about being away from the sales floor that long, but Bill was determined to test the car until all his questions about it were answered.

Even dealers agree that the biggest mistake most customers make is failing to test-drive the model they buy. Only by actually sitting in one and maneuvering it on the road can a driver be sure the car that looks so good also handles well and rides comfortably. If the dealer has a demonstrator to lend for a weekend, that's even better. Or renting the particular model for a day or two can be a wise investment.

They began with Ann riding in the back, to check on legroom and rear-seat comfort. As Bill drove, the salesman described the car's features. Bill tried parking the car along the curb, drove rapidly over an unpaved road nearby, and finally took the car along a superhighway at maximum legal speed. After a half hour he stopped and changed places with Ann, who retraced his route. By this time both had driven the car over several different kinds of roads, and they had been in it long enough to decide whether it was comfortable and as well designed as it looked.

But the car they had driven had not been equipped with some of the options they wanted, and when they returned to the dealership they checked these out more briefly on other demonstrators. After thanking the salesman and taking his card, Ann and Bill looked around the dealership. The salesman had been helpful, and the business seemed cleanly kept and well managed. Before leaving, they walked into the back end, or service department, to look it over. The write-up man (assistant manager) on duty told them that the shop managed to complete most repairs in one day and that a special effort was made to handle minor repairs quickly, while the customer waited. He also said the service department would provide a "loaner" for a customer to drive if his car was in the shop for more than a day. To Bill this was a clear signal that service was good.

One evening the following week, Ann and Bill visited a dealer who sold the make that was their second choice and went through the entire three-step routine again. Both Ann and Bill liked the car, but decided it really didn't excite them. They made up their minds to return only

OPTIONS FOR EVERY NEED OR WHIM

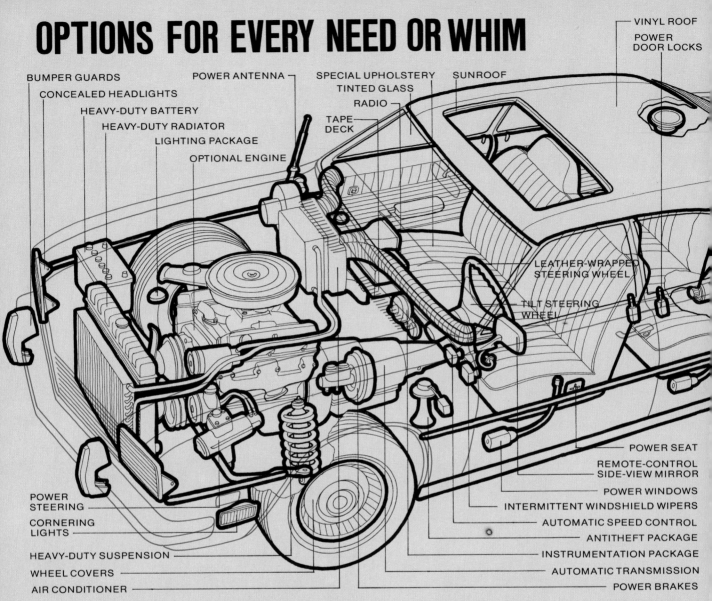

BUMPER GUARDS
CONCEALED HEADLIGHTS
HEAVY-DUTY BATTERY
HEAVY-DUTY RADIATOR
LIGHTING PACKAGE
OPTIONAL ENGINE
POWER ANTENNA
TAPE DECK
SPECIAL UPHOLSTERY
TINTED GLASS
RADIO
SUNROOF
VINYL ROOF
POWER DOOR LOCKS
LEATHER-WRAPPED STEERING WHEEL
TILT STEERING WHEEL
POWER SEAT
REMOTE-CONTROL SIDE-VIEW MIRROR
POWER WINDOWS
INTERMITTENT WINDSHIELD WIPERS
AUTOMATIC SPEED CONTROL
ANTITHEFT PACKAGE
INSTRUMENTATION PACKAGE
AUTOMATIC TRANSMISSION
POWER BRAKES
POWER STEERING
CORNERING LIGHTS
HEAVY-DUTY SUSPENSION
WHEEL COVERS
AIR CONDITIONER

Options can transform an assembly-line product into a vehicle that is virtually custom-built to the buyer's specifications.

The most common factory-installed options are discussed here under their generic names; nomenclature varies from one manufacturer to another. Those for which costs generally can be largely recovered at trade-in, or whose absence in larger or luxury models decreases resale value, are marked with an asterisk (*).

There are no hard-and-fast buying rules for options: one man's imperative is another man's frivolity. It is possible, of course, to buy a stripped car —one without a single option. But hardly anyone does: for instance, more than 90 per cent of all new cars are ordered with a radio. On the other hand, if a spendthrift buyer tacked all of the options dis-cussed here onto a $3,800 standard-sized car —which is physically possible—he would double the car's price.

Buyers who want a number of related options, such as a cluster of dashboard gauges to replace the usual "idiot lights," often can take advantage of bargain packages put together by the manufactur-er. This is not mere merchandising gimmickry. By selling the options as a group the manufacturer cuts assembly-line costs and passes on significant savings to the customer. Such packages should be evaluated carefully. Each option within a pack-age usually can be purchased separately, but if you want most of the add-ons that have been pack-aged in a group, you often can order all of them for little more —and sometimes even less—money than you were already prepared to pay.

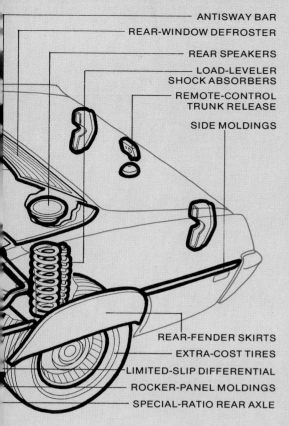

ANTISWAY BAR
REAR-WINDOW DEFROSTER
REAR SPEAKERS
LOAD-LEVELER
SHOCK ABSORBERS
REMOTE-CONTROL
TRUNK RELEASE
SIDE MOLDINGS

REAR-FENDER SKIRTS
EXTRA-COST TIRES
LIMITED-SLIP DIFFERENTIAL
ROCKER-PANEL MOLDINGS
SPECIAL-RATIO REAR AXLE

A

Air conditioner*—Factory installation is preferable to after-purchase addition because the unit is built into the car, out of sight and out of the way. Furthermore, an air conditioner usually requires a larger engine and heavy-duty support from the cooling system, battery, alternator and suspension, and these should be factory-installed with it. A more sophisticated version, with automatic temperature control, can be set to maintain a preselected year-round temperature by mixing heated air and cooled air. More expensive than a manual model, it tends to produce warm and cool air drafts as it cycles on and off.

Antisway bar—This option will improve handling by preventing excessive leaning when the car is turned.

Antitheft package—The basic items include a lockable inside hood release, decals and a spare tire lock. Some versions provide an automatic alarm.

Automatic speed control—Offered on larger cars, this accessory allows the driver to set a desired speed and take his foot from the accelerator. The control is disengaged by a tap on the brake pedal. Critics say this option, though useful on long trips over uncrowded highways, invites driver inattention.

Automatic transmission*—A clear convenience, especially for motorists who do much stop-and-go driving; but it cuts

gas mileage, and on small-engine subcompacts can sap engine power.

B

Body stripes—This styling touch, usually in the form of decals, is often part of an exterior-trim package.

Bumper guards—These vertical bars protect the grille and rear deck by intercepting very-low-speed impacts. They also forestall interlocking with cars that have lower or higher bumpers.

C

Concealed headlights—These are offered only on some larger cars and sporty compacts. This option features power-operated lids that drop or rotate to cover the lights when not in use. More cosmetic than functional, if the mechanism fails, the car may be without lights.

Cornering lights—Offered only on larger cars, these lights are located in the front side fenders. Activated by the turn indicator, they give side illumination when the car is rounding a corner.

D

Disc brakes—In comparison with most drums, disc brakes generally stop a car with less swerve, and operate more effectively when hot or wet.

H

Heavy-duty battery—Often included in a power accessory package such as air conditioning, this option can also assist starting in cold weather.

Heavy-duty radiator—Typically this option, which affords a larger coolant capacity, is part of a package such as air conditioning or towing.

Heavy-duty suspension—Often part of an air-conditioning or towing package also, this option is a substantial plus for cars frequently driven on rough or unpaved roads, for cars used to carry heavy cargos and for drivers who prefer a firmer ride.

I

Instrumentation package—This option usually includes a cluster of gauges (replacing dashboard warning lights) that precisely register water temperature, oil temperature and battery condition. Some packages add a trip odometer, an electric clock and/or a tachometer.

Intermittent windshield wipers—This is a variation that permits wipers to be operated at preset intervals of two to 10 seconds—a benefit in light precipitation.

L

Leather-wrapped steering wheel—Often part of an interior trim package, this racy touch is also promoted as a convenience in sticky weather.

Lighting package—In addition to the most common interior lights, this group adds, in various combinations, spots of

illumination over the ashtray, inside the glove compartment and trunk, and under the dash for map reading. There may also be a light at the ignition switch (which turns on when the driver's door opens and goes out after a set interval) and one in the engine compartment.

Limited-slip differential—This mechanism, designed to improve traction on slippery surfaces, prevents one wheel from turning faster than the other. If a rear wheel begins to slip in snow, ice or mud, this device transfers more engine power to the drive wheel that has the better grip. Should both wheels begin to slip, it attempts to balance the power it transmits to prevent one wheel from spinning freely. Such differentials, for which different manufacturers have different proprietary names, vary in efficiency from make to make. Some may be relatively noisy and some of them can—by repeated, rapid overcompensation—cause fishtailing on slick roads.

Load-leveler shock absorbers—Sold often as part of a towing package, the shocks replace the standard rear units. By adding or bleeding compressed air, the driver can vary the level of his car according to the weight of the load being carried or pulled.

O

Optional engine—A new car's standard engine is designed by the manufacturer to provide power adequate for normal use. But if the vehicle is laden with power accessories such as air conditioning, or if a towing package is ordered, or if the car is to be used in hilly country or in other demanding circumstances, consider a larger engine.

P

Power antenna—This feature is a convenience on long trips. It raises the radio antenna to its optimum extension in fringe-reception areas and permits the driver to retract the antenna fully upon parking—out of the reach of vandals.

Power brakes*—Teamed with either disc or drum brakes, this power assist lessens the pressure needed on the brake pedal, a particularly valuable feature on heavier cars.

Power door-locks—This option can be a safety feature for car owners with small children, and it also can be a back saver for drivers who often travel alone or who must otherwise reach across wide seats to lock doors.

Power seat*—Convenient in a car driven by people of various sizes, each of whom prefers a different driving position for comfort and better control or visibility. Two-way seats go front and back; four-way seats add an up-and-down motion; six-way seats add a tilting motion. If the power mechanism fails, the seats cannot be adjusted manually —and repairs can be expensive.

Power steering* — Standard on larger cars, this option improves maneuverability, especially in parking. In some cars it may significantly decrease the driver's feel of the road. Still, it should be considered for virtually every car with an engine of six cylinders or more.

Power windows* — A convenience for drivers going through toll booths and for easy ventilation control, this option also is a possible hazard to small children, who can be injured if a careless adult in the front seat raises a window without looking back. Also, if the mechanism fails, it is stuck in one position until costly repairs can be made.

Premium paint — One popular way to make a car stand out is to pay extra for a nonstandard paint job. But certain hot and metallic colors require more careful maintenance and the paint may be difficult to match should body work and touch-ups be needed.

R

Radio* — Automobile radios come in a variety of forms: AM or FM or both, AM-FM stereo, with or without tape decks (below). The prime consideration is where the car will be driven most of the time. An FM radio provides reception that is cleaner and of higher fidelity than AM, but its range is limited — to perhaps 50 miles of a broadcast source. AM stations can be tuned in at much greater distances.

Rear-axle gear ratio — Heavy-duty ratios provide more wheel-turning force to haul heavy loads and climb hills, but in doing so they trade off some pickup. Economy ratios provide less wheel-turning force but give better gas mileage under light loads.

Rear-fender skirts — A stylistic accessory on larger cars, skirts cover the rear wheel wells. They can make checking pressure or changing tires awkward.

Rear speakers — For use with radio or tape deck, additional speakers provide better sound quality. In addition, when equipped with a switch or knob they permit the driver to direct programs to music or sports fans in the rear while conversing up front — and vice versa.

Rear-window defroster — Often called a defogger or demister, this accessory comes in two forms. One type consists of electric heat-carrying wires sandwiched within the glass; it is better at melting outside ice and snow. The other type consists of a blower, much like the front-window defroster; it is better at dissipating interior condensation.

Remote-control side-view mirror — This mechanism allows a driver to adjust the outside mirror from within the car. It is handy for families with several drivers or for use in bad weather.

Remote-control trunk release — Handy for shopping and other errands that require repeated use of the trunk. The driver can stay in the car, and does not have to fumble with keys while someone else loads bundles or other cargo into the trunk.

Rocker-panel moldings — Attached to the bottom edges of the car's exterior, these moldings protect vulnerable areas against corrosion.

S

Seats — Basically, there are two types: buckets and split-bench. Well-designed bucket seats give more support but limit the number of side-by-side passengers to two. On some models, swivel bucket seats are available in front; they turn to allow easier — and more modest — entries and exits. Split-bench seats are, like buckets, individually adjustable, but their backs meet flush in the middle so that three people can sit side by side — though not comfortably for long distances. On some larger cars, foldaway armrests are standard or optional with bench or split-bench seats.

Side moldings — Placed along the sides of the car at their widest and most vulnerable points, these moldings protect paint from being chipped when doors of other cars are thrown open against the body. Moldings inset with strips of resilient vinyl give the most protection.

Sunroof* — Manual sunroofs usually are offered on subcompact and compact cars; a more expensive, powered version is offered on standard-sized cars and sporty intermediates. This option is fast becoming an alternative to the convertible, a body style that is being phased out by American auto makers. Powered sunroofs can be expensive to repair should the motor fail.

T

Tape deck* — For music lovers, this accessory can be a desirable alternative to the radio — even FM or AM-FM stereo — since control of programming is complete and the sound does not deteriorate when signals are weak or fade out completely in tunnels and underpasses. For decks that play eight-track cartridges, cassette adapters are available.

Tilt steering wheel — This option, which permits the steering wheel to be raised or lowered to several different positions, and locked there, is a convenience in a car used by several drivers. It also allows a driver to vary his own position during long-distance trips. The wheel swings all the way up for easier driver exit and entry.

Tinted glass — Usually ordered as part of an air-conditioning package, tinted glass cuts out some of the sun's hot rays and helps keep the vehicle's interior cooler. The more lightly hued the glass, the less it reduces nighttime vision.

Tires (extra cost) — Tires are a complicated subject. You can, of course, order a better grade of tire than is standard for the new car of your choice. A full discussion of tire design is on pages 132–133.

U

Undercoating — A thick, waterproofing, tarlike compound, this material is applied to a car's underside to fight corrosion. It also cuts down on rattles and squeaks. Undercoating may come with a sound-dampening underhood blanket as part of an insulation package.

Upholstery — Vinyl, which comes in solid or woven form, is the easiest surface to keep clean, but unless the plastic is woven it is hot in summer and cold in winter. Cloth, being porous, is more comfortable but harder to keep clean. In combination cloth/vinyl upholstery, the seats are cloth and the edges, which suffer most from friction, are in vinyl. Leather is expensive and luxurious, but it stains easily and may crack with age. In leather/vinyl upholstery, the plastic is used on the heavy-wear edges.

V

Vinyl roof* — The value of this option is primarily in its styling appeal. Dark vinyl tops are heat-absorbing and put an added load on an air conditioner.

W

Wheel covers — They are larger and dressier than standard hubcaps.

Station-wagon options

Most of the options for passenger cars can be ordered on station wagons. The following are solely for wagons:

Deflector vane — This roof accessory comes either alone or as part of a luggage rack. Mounted at the rear of the roof, it deflects the slipstream away from the tailgate window as it flows along the roofline and prevents exhaust fumes, dust and dirt from being sucked into the window, if open. It also wards off any accumulations of mud and salt. Some deflectors are built into the roof.

Luggage rack — Bolted to the roof, a rack greatly adds to the cargo-carrying capacity. It also is useful as a lashing post for over-sized cargo. But security from theft is minimal; on trips, luggage should be unloaded every night.

Power tailgate-window — With this option the driver can operate the tailgate window from the front seat or with a key at the door itself. But a careless operator or one whose vision is obstructed by cargo could hurt an unwary passenger, particularly a small child.

Tailgate defroster — The two types are similar to passenger-car rear-window options. Tailgate defrosters are not available on all models.

Tailgate window-washer — This option cleans the tailgate window by remote control. Not available on all models.

---

* Options that usually increase resale value and whose absence usually decreases the resale value of larger or luxury models.

if a satisfactory deal could not be swung for their first choice.

Meanwhile, they asked friends about the reputation of each dealer. On his way to work one morning, Bill stopped at the service departments of both dealers and talked with a few of the customers to learn if they were satisfied.

Since a purchaser usually depends on his dealer to provide service, it is always worthwhile before buying to find out how well he runs his service department. Perhaps the best way is to take in the old car for a tune-up or repair. Does the shop seem efficient? Are customers courteously greeted? Is the car's problem carefully noted by the write-up man? Is the car ready when promised, and is the problem remedied? Does the bill seem reasonable for the service performed? It's a good idea, also, to check on the dealer's reputation. The Better Business Bureau will have records of customers who have complained about sales techniques or service. Bill and Ann were lucky —both dealers seemed to be reputable businessmen who dealt honestly with their customers and provided good service. There are dealers, however, who are neither so honest nor so helpful and they have had a bad effect on the reputations of dealers everywhere. An opinion poll within the last decade indicated that automobile dealers were the most distrusted businessmen in America. The public's generally poor view of both the quality of their service and the prices they charge conceivably would improve if more people understood how an automobile dealership operates. Most people think that dealers make much bigger profits than they really do.

How the dealership works

An automobile dealer runs four complicated businesses: selling new cars, buying and selling used cars, and selling parts and service. The most profitable of these is selling new cars —which is why some dealers concentrate on sales and neglect service.

But even their profits on new cars are much less than many people think. Most new-car buyers get a better deal than they realize. A dealer's income comes from two sources: his salary, which he pays himself and which is included in his costs of operation, and the dealership's profit. In one recent year, the average new car was sold for $3,693 and the average dealership profit was 1 to 2 per cent, or $37 to $74 on each car sold. The profits on used cars were even less.

Most dealers lose money on their service departments. Many provide service only because their franchise agreement with a manufacturer requires them to. The costs of running a service department can be enormous. The dealer must buy expensive tools, must constantly retrain his mechanics to repair new models and often must provide free loaner cars to his customers. It's not surprising that a dealer wants to make as large a profit as he can on a new car. When the figures from all the dealer's businesses are totaled, including service and used-car sales, the average dealership earns a profit of only about 1 per cent on the total amount of its sales.

Since the purchaser will be depending heavily on the dealer during the period of the new-car warranty, it's worth the effort to find a good one—even if this means driving to the other side of town or choosing a different make of car. A poor dealer can cost far more in inflated service charges and in exasperation than a buyer might be able to save on a slightly lower initial price.

With their list of prices from the salesman, Ann and Bill set out to unravel the mystery of car prices, that befuddling, arcane system of fig-

WHAT THE SALESMAN'S JARGON MEANS

Some words and phrases used by automobile salesmen constitute a code for communicating with colleagues over the customer's head. Others are merely conversational shorthand. An awareness of the jargon may help a customer negotiate. A condensed glossary follows.

Back end: The dealership's service department.

Budget buggies: Used cars selling for $95 to $295.

Bushing: Inducing the customer to buy unwanted options.

Comebacks: Cars brought in two or more times for the same mechanical repair.

Cream puff: A low-mileage used car in excellent condition.

Decked out: Loaded with optional equipment.

Demonstrator: A car maintained by the dealer for test drives, sold at reduced prices after a year or less of use.

Handshaker: A car with a standard manual gearshift.

Has ice: The car is air conditioned.

Highball: The practice of citing an impossibly high trade-in allowance to a customer who is known to be comparison shopping. When the customer finds that other dealers cannot match the trade-in allowance, he will return to the original dealer, only to be told that the inflated figure was a mistake. Many customers will then accept a new, lower allowance because they are tired of shopping.

Holdback: A 2 per cent markup that the dealer pays the manufacturer on each new car that is added to his stock. This amount is rebated to the dealer after the car is sold.

Junker: A used car in the $25-to-$75 price bracket. Other synonyms are: pieces of iron, skillets, rats, dogs and sleds.

Loaner: A car lent by the dealer to a customer while the customer's car is under repair.

Lowball: The practice of quoting an impossibly low price for a new car in order to lure a customer back to the salesroom after he has sampled prices elsewhere. As with the highball, the customer is then told that the original price was wrong. The term also may refer to the practice of offering so low an allowance on an unwanted trade-in that the customer will try to sell his car elsewhere.

Pipe smoker: A hard-to-sell prospect.

Putting a customer to sleep: Giving a purchaser a price that is no bargain and having him accept it.

Straight car: A first-rate traded-in car.

Tire kicker: An individual who is just looking.

T.O. man: The take-over man steps into negotiations after a salesman has obtained a signed purchase agreement and a deposit from a customer. The T.O. man's function is to raise the bargain price quoted by the salesman and agreed to by the customer. The T.O. man looks at the signed agreement, shakes his head and says, "Oh, no, no. I couldn't sell the car for that—it's less than the car cost me."

---

ures, percentages and jargon that sometimes finds one buyer paying $500 less than another for the same model identically equipped.

Unlike most kinds of merchandise, a car does not have a fixed price that everyone pays. To begin with, the options a buyer chooses alter its price. Furthermore, when he trades in a used car he is selling to the dealer as well as buying from him; the price he gets for his used car will affect the price he pays for a new one.

Because the cars being bought and sold each time are paired in a unique transaction, the price is subject to negotiation between salesman and customer. But if the customer knows as much as the dealer does about the true cost of a new car, it's not all that difficult to bargain for a reasonable price.

Federal law requires every new car to have pasted on one of its windows a sticker *(page 76)* giving the manufacturer's suggested retail price for the car without options, plus a list of the options built into the car and their prices. The total of all these prices is the "sticker price" of the car.

Unlike the tags in a supermarket, however, the sticker price does not dictate the exact amount that every buyer must pay. It is, rather, a maximum price that is established as a protection for the gullible and to limit somewhat the opportunity to extract an unreasonably high price from a naïve buyer.

How much can one expect to shave from the sticker price? If the buyer knows how to decode a sticker, he can tell within a few dollars how much the dealer himself paid for the car, and that can be his bargaining guide.

The first price on the sticker shows the maximum retail price of the basic car, with its standard engine and without any options. The dealer buys the car at a discount from that price; the size of his discount depends upon the size of the car. He also gets a discount on the options, and an additional rebate of 2 per cent (called the holdback), which is paid to him by the manufacturer after the car is sold. By adding together the base price of the car, the charges for options and the holdback, you can determine approximately what the dealer paid for the car *(page 77)*.

But some additional costs must be included in the price. The freight, or destination, charge shown on the sticker is the cost of transporting the car from the assembly plant to the dealer. It varies by car model and location (it can even be different for two dealers of the same make in the same city). The dealer receives no discount on this freight charge; he simply passes it on to the buyer. Another charge shown on the sticker is for "preparation," or "predelivery service." It covers the dealer's cost of repairing or adjusting minor defects in the car as delivered to him by the manufacturer, cleaning it and generally getting it shipshape for the buyer to take delivery.

The total of the dealer's discounted cost plus the freight and service charge is the dealer's actual cost for the car. To this amount he must then add his cost of doing business. He must include the salesman's commission, his own rent, his bills for utilities and insurance, the wages he pays (including his own salary, etc.). These items usually add roughly $200 to $300 to the dealer's total cost of selling a car.

All of these items totaled together represent the lowest price at which he can sell a car without a loss. But this price is still substantially less than the sticker price, though it does not include any profit for the dealership. A government survey covering sales during recent years indicated that more than half of all intermediates were actually sold for 10 to 15 per cent below their sticker prices, and that half the full-sized models were sold for 15 to 20 per cent below the sticker price. The dealership does earn a reasonable profit per car, even with discounts at these levels. Dealers give smaller discounts on compacts and subcompacts because their own discount is smaller on those cars and because the dealer's cost of operation is a larger proportion of the total price.

Since the sticker price is so far above the price for which most cars are actually sold, many consumer groups—and dealers—think it should be reduced to reflect more closely the real price. The wide gap permits dishonest dealers to use shady sales methods. Some dealers, for example, advertise cars at "$100 over dealer's cost." To the uninitiated this might seem like a very low markup, but in actual fact the figure already has the dealership profit built right into it.

Car-buying services

There are other ways to purchase a car for somewhat less than a price fair to a dealer. There are, for example, the buying services that operate in a number of large cities. Buying services offer to sell cars at prices ranging from $100 to $200 above the invoice price. Their leverage is volume and they usually operate through unions, fraternal lodges and social clubs. Members often can purchase a car through a buying service for significantly less than a dealer would charge an individual.

But such services have at least one big disadvantage: the buyer usually is not able to choose the dealer who actually delivers the car. If the dealer who has contracted to supply cars to the buying service is more interested in high-volume sales than in service (as he is likely to be), the buyer may end up the prey of an unreliable and expensive service operation. Other busy dealers in the same name plate, whose locations may be more convenient to the purchaser, often are reluctant to work on a car they themselves did not sell.

Every new car must, by federal law, carry a manufacturer's sticker on one of its windows. Affixed at the factory, it cannot be altered or removed until the car is delivered to its buyer. The sticker legally identifies the car it is on, lists all features and equipment installed at the factory and sets the ceiling price for that package as a whole.

A The identification number on the sticker should match the one on the engine block.

B The suggested retail price is exclusive of options, taxes, shipping, etc.

C The destination charge (i.e., shipping cost from factory to dealer) is fixed: the dealer makes no profit on it.

D Factory-installed options are spelled out along with their prices.

E Standard features on cars of this model, including required safety items, are listed. There should be no additional charge.

F The dealer preparation charge covers any shipping-damage repair, plus cleaning the car and making final adjustments to mechanical and safety-related parts.

G The subtotal figure combines the prices of options and the preparation charge.

H The total price does not include state or local sales taxes. This bottom-line figure is the maximum any buyer should pay: by bargaining over the suggested retail price and the options prices, the total price may be decreased substantially, depending on the size of the car *(box, opposite)*.

Dealer: ROCK FALLS MOTORS
ROCK FALLS, CONN.

COLUMBIA MOTORS CORP.

Make: JEFFERSON

A Vehicle Identification Number   15GR27442R6

B Manufacturer's Suggested Retail Price of This Vehicle: $ 3845.80

Model 89320   V8 GAZELLE 4-DR SEDAN   45.00

C Destination Charge

This vehicle was manufactured in compliance with all applicable Federal motor vehicle safety and emission-control standards.   subtotal   3890.80

Manufacturer's suggested retail delivered prices for options and accessories installed on this vehicle by manufacturer:

D H22 DELUXE SEAT BELTS   12.00
B37 EZ-EYE TINTED GLASS   41.00
L79 ALL-CLIMATE AIR CONDITIONING   385.00
645 195 HP TWIN-DYMO 400 V-8 ENGINE   54.00
GK5 FULL WHEEL COVERS   26.00
BV2 AM PUSHBUTTON RADIO   62.00
9G5 BLUE VINYL INTERIOR   19.00
8WQ G-4 MERMAID GREEN   no extra charge   ------

E THIS CAR INCLUDES ALL THESE FEATURES--DYMO AUTO-TRANSMATIC, POWER STEERING, POWER DISC/DRUM BRAKES, CONCEALED WIPERS, POWER VENTAIR, WOOD-GRAIN INTERIOR TRIM, BELT BUZZER, FRONT SEAT BACK LATCHES, FRONT SHOULDER BELTS, CARPETING, GLOVE COMPARTMENT LIGHT, LIGHTER, LUGGAGE COMPARTMENT LIGHT AND MAT.

F DEALER PREPARATION   50.00

Factory installed options and accessories   (does not include dealer installed options, or accessories, state or local taxes or license fees)   **G** subtotal   649.00

H Total Amount $ 4539.80

There also are companies that use computers to produce, for prospective purchasers, a comparison of the dealer cost with the sticker price of desired models. These companies also offer to sell a car at a smaller markup than most dealers will charge, but the dealers through whom they sell the cars offer the same disadvantage—service that may be unreliable.

Bill and Ann had one remaining decision: what to do with the Behemoth. Several used-car dealers had appraised it, but Bill thought their estimates low. Classified newspaper advertisements for similar models carried prices $300 to $400 higher. What Bill failed to consider was that dealers buy used cars at wholesale prices, while the ads list the retail prices, which include the costs of cleaning and reconditioning the cars. He could have found the average wholesale and retail prices for used cars of all models by checking in the National Automobile Dealers Association's *Official Used Car Guide (page 88).*

Bill and Ann considered selling the Behemoth on their own. By doing so, they probably would receive more than from a dealer. But they would be kept busy showing the car and going along on test drives. Depending on when their car was sold, they might have to do without a second vehicle for several days—or even a month or two.

They decided that, for them, the possible gain from selling privately wasn't worth the inconveniences. But Bill was convinced that if he cleaned up the Behemoth before getting it appraised, the dealer would place a higher value on it. The dealer, after all, judges a car basically in the same way a potential used-car customer does—by how it looks. Before Bill drove back to the showroom to close the deal for the new car, he spent a morning carefully cleaning the Behemoth, inside and out. He got some paint and covered several nicks and rust spots. He polished the chrome and even waxed the body. He replaced a broken light bulb. He made the old car look as attractive as possible.

Then Bill drove back to the dealer, ready to buy a new car. The same salesman greeted him, obviously aware that this time Bill was not a tire-kicker but a customer ready to buy. They went into the salesman's office again, and this time, as Bill read off his list of options, the salesman wrote them on a contract.

When Bill had finished, the salesman said, "You're in luck. We happen to have a car just like that in stock, except that it's cerulean blue instead of winter green and it has a power sunroof. If you'll take that car, I can let you drive it home tomorrow and I'll let you have the sunroof at $100 off list."

There were two reasons for the salesman's proposal. First, by selling Bill a car already on the dealer's lot he could reduce the finance charges that the dealer was already paying on the car. Second, he was trying to "bush" Bill: sell him an option that upped the price of the car—and his own commission. Bill would get a car without having to wait six weeks or more, but he would have a car in the wrong color and with an expensive option he didn't want. The list price of the sunroof was about $375 and it cost the dealer about $300. By selling it at $100 under list price, the dealership would lose $25 —a sum that the salesman could easily recover by reducing the discount he'd offer Bill on the entire car.

COMPUTING THE DEALER'S TRUE COST

The list price of a new car *(bottom line of sticker, left)* is the maximum the dealer can charge. An informed buyer should be able to shave a respectable amount off this price. To gain a bargaining position, use the information on the sticker to gauge the dealer's true cost. First take the top figure, the suggested retail price, and multiply it by the following amount, based on the size of the car:

Subcompacts, Compacts	0.85
Intermediates	0.81
Standards	0.77

Now total the suggested retail prices of all your options and multiply that figure by 0.80. To the sum of these figures, add the listed transportation and preparation charges, which are fixed fees on which the dealer makes no profit. This total is within a few dollars of the actual price the dealer paid for the car. The difference between this sum and the list price is the bargaining range; how much a dealer is willing to come down depends in large part on his overhead, annual volume, the time of year and whether you are trading in your old car.

Since Bill had compiled his option list carefully, he declined. Then the salesman said: "We'd like to help finance your car, and I'd also suggest that you get some creditor life insurance." By earning sales commissions on financing and insurance, a dealer can double his profits on a new car. (For a full explanation of these important and complicated subjects, see Chapters 4 and 5.)

"Do you have a trade-in?" asked the salesman. "Yes, I have a six-year-old Behemoth," Bill said, "but I'd like to settle on the price for the new car first." That avoided any possibility that the salesman might juggle the prices of the two cars. Once in a while a salesman will ask at the outset of negotiations for the keys of a car to be taken in trade. He explains that to save time the used-car manager will appraise it while he's recording the specifications for the new car. He shouldn't get the keys; nor should he be allowed to appraise the old car until the price of the new one has been settled. It isn't a bad idea for the purchaser to park a block or two away so the salesman cannot see the make or model of his car.

After some bargaining over the prices of the options, Bill agreed on a total figure for the new car. Then he went with the salesman to have the Behemoth appraised. The appraiser looked over the car carefully, checked the mileage and asked Bill for the keys so he could start the engine. Bill was right there to reclaim the keys when the brief process was over.

An unscrupulous salesman may use possession of an owner's keys as a lever to force him to change his mind about buying a car already in the showroom. And, more rarely, he may spring a $5 or $10 "appraisal fee"—after the fact—on prospects who decide not to buy. A reputable dealer will never levy any such fee.

The trade-in offer came to about what Bill had expected, and he agreed to it. The salesman then deducted the trade-in price from the new-car price and gave the contract to Bill to sign. Bill read it carefully, front and back, to see that it described both deals correctly.

In most states there is a standard printed purchase contract used by all dealers. But in any case, before a buyer signs he should be certain that his contract does not, in print or by written-in amendment, permit the dealer to impose any hidden or delayed charges. He should be sure that it allows for an increase in the agreed-upon price for the new car only in the event that the manufacturer increases his sales price to the dealer—and if he can get the dealer to agree to absorb any price increase, he should by all means do so.

Further, the contract should not permit any later reappraisal of the traded car, unless it is seriously damaged before it is turned over to the dealer. The used-car manager's appraisal allows for normal depreciation until then. In addition, the purchaser should try to have the dealer add to the contract a clause specifying that, upon delivery, the dealer will provide written assurance that all predelivery work has been done (it will help in any later dispute about warranty charges).

Most dealers don't permit their salesmen to sign on behalf of the dealership; and if one does, the commitment may not be valid. The contract should be signed by the sales manager or another officer of the dealership (and he should also initial any changes in the form).

When the salesman came back with the signed contract, Bill took a copy. They shook hands, and the salesman gave Bill a tentative delivery date for his car—about six weeks away. When that happy day arrived, and Ann and Bill saw their car, buffed and gleaming to the hubcaps, they were delighted.

Inspecting a new car

Many buyers are similarly smitten when they take delivery on a new car. But when this moment arrives, the few obvious blemishes and defects should not be blotted out by euphoria. Enthusiasm is better restrained for a time. Go over the car carefully. Check for dents or nicks in the body. Look for misassembled parts. The auto is, after all, an immensely complicated and mass-produced item, and on a busy assembly line small parts, and occasionally one not so small, may be attached improperly or not at all. See that the spare tire and jack are there. Look under the hood for any obvious omissions. Be sure all the options you've ordered are installed. Test the engine, the lights, the radio, the windshield washers, all the mechanisms. Look under the car to see if anything appears amiss. Despite all the inspections the car has been given by both the manufacturer and the dealer, some defect may have slipped by. The more thoroughly the car is examined before the deal is finally sealed, the less chance that there will be an unpleasant surprise for the new owner.

Bill made a complete inspection and noticed only two flaws: the interior rear-view mirror was so loosely affixed to its bracket that it couldn't be made to hold its proper angle, and the armrest on the driver's door was off kilter. In a couple of minutes a mechanic had tightened the mirror and secured the armrest, whose trouble proved to be a missing screw.

Bill then asked the salesman to introduce him to the service manager. He was careful to get the written statement, provided for in his contract, that all predelivery servicing had been done. Only then did Bill turn over his keys and his title to the old Behemoth.

Once again the salesman explained to Bill and Ann the control layout for their model and urged them to read the owner's manual carefully when they got home. He explained the new car's warranty. The warranty coverage on cars varies, but most guarantees provide for free repair or replacement of any defective part for the first year or the first 12,000 miles. Some components are guaranteed by their manufacturer, not by the automobile firm. The salesman handed Bill all the appropriate papers *(box, right),* including a booklet that described all the provisions of the warranty and told him what to do if a part failed.

"You drive it, honey," said Bill, gallantry overcoming his own pride. And on the blissful ride home, amid the FM music and the new-car smell, he told her for the first time why he had ordered the bigger engine: he was buying a new trailer for their camping trip to the Rockies. For her, of course.

DETAILS THAT MAKE A CAR LEGAL

The purchaser of any car, either new or used, must obtain various certificates, plates and stickers that attest to his compliance with his state's motor-vehicle regulations. These essentials of automobile legality, not all of which are required in all states, are:

Certificate of title: This documents the buyer's ownership of the car. Its possession is mandatory in almost all states. The certificate gives the owner's name and address, describes the car by make, model and identification numbers, and records whether a lien exists against the car. Should the car be stolen, the certificate would support the owner's claim for insurance. If the owner wants to sell the car, the certificate will prove his right to do so. Since the certificate of title is never needed on the road, it should not be kept in the car or on the driver's person; it should be stored in a safe place.

Certificate of registration: All motor vehicles operated on public highways must be registered with the state's department of motor vehicles. Most states require that the certificate of registration be kept in the car or on the driver's person for display on demand by a policeman or the other party to any accident in which the driver is involved. Registration fees are determined by the car's weight or, in some states, by its horsepower rating. In states where automobile liability insurance is mandatory, applications for registration must be accompanied by proof of insurance.

Plates and stickers: License plates are issued when a car is registered. At the same time, a registration sticker is provided; it gives the registration's expiration date and must be affixed to the license plate or to the inside of the windshield.

Inspection sticker: In many states safety-related equipment must be inspected regularly—once or twice a year and whenever the car's ownership changes. When a car is approved, the inspector issues a windshield sticker. If a car is driven without a valid sticker, the driver faces a fine.

Insurance card: In some states liability insurance is required on all automobiles. In a number of such states, proof of insurance—a punch card or a certificate issued by the insuring company—must be kept in the car.

Driver's license: All states require the licensing of drivers, and a driver's license is proof that a driver is competent and knows the motor-vehicle laws. The license must be on the driver's person or in his car whenever he is at the wheel.

USED CARS

HOW TO AVOID PICKING A LEMON

DECIPHERING ADVERTISEMENTS
WHAT IS THE BOOK PRICE?
AN ON-THE-LOT CHECK LIST
HOW TO SPOT THE TROUBLE CAR
CONDITION VERSUS MILEAGE
A PROPER ROAD TEST
CLOSING THE DEAL

3

Florence is a teacher who needs a car to get to school. But her eight-year-old workhorse has logged more than 80,000 miles, and even her mechanic is saying it's time to get rid of it. Florence was hoping that the old car would last until she had saved enough money to buy a new one. Now it's going to cost $230 for a rebuilt transmission. She has spent $600 on repairs and maintenance during the past year, and her savings account is down to $920.

Harry is an accountant who has just paid the last installment on the loan he took when he bought his compact sedan three years ago. Now he's ready to begin all over again by trading for another compact. But Harry has been having some second thoughts after driving his father-in-law's expensive full-sized sedan. He likes the comfort, luxury and performance of a big car. He's busily jotting down figures, try-

ing to see if he can fit a larger monthly auto payment into his tight family budget.

Lester is a prosperous businessman who recently bought a home in a fashionable suburban community. He commutes to work in the city by train, which has created a problem for his wife Louise. She has to get up at 6:30 to drive Lester to the station, and then return each evening to pick him up. "We need two cars," she says. "Three," says their 16-year-old son, Lester Jr., who has just completed his high-school driver-education course. Lester has most of his available cash tied up in the new house and is wondering if he will have to dig into his savings or postpone that vacation trip he had his heart set on.

Florence, Harry and Lester are typical of the millions of Americans who buy used cars every year. Florence will buy a used car because she has no other choice. Harry will trade his compact for a two-year-old full-sized sedan in top condition, and his monthly payments will be about the same as if he had bought a new compact. Lester will solve his problem by buying two used cars for the price of a single new one: a six-year-old sedan to use as a station car and a four-year-old subcompact for Lester Jr.

There was a time when buying a used car carried something of a stigma. You bought a used car because you couldn't afford a new one. But today there are millions of people who aren't self-conscious about buying and driving used cars; in fact, about three people buy them for every two who buy new cars. The average purchaser spends about $1,300 for a used car, an amount equivalent to the down payment on a $4,000 new car. And if he pays cash, as more than half of all used-car buyers do, there is an additional saving in loan interest.

Buying a late-model, full-sized used car instead of a smaller new car has come to be a very tempting proposition. In fact, it so attracts buyers who have budgeted $2,000 to $3,000 that some manufacturers have found it necessary to increase the advertising budgets for their new compacts and subcompacts to meet the growing competition of used cars.

An even more tempting alternative to buying a new car is to buy two used cars, as Lester did. One of the greatest boons to the used-car business has been the increase in two-car families. Nearly a third of all American families own two or more cars. In families with incomes of more than $15,000 almost half own at least two cars and 15 per cent own three or more. In many cases, those second and third cars were bought to meet the needs of a specific family driver. Dad might want a sturdy old sedan to take him back and forth to work or to the station. Mom might need a station wagon for shopping and the inevitable suburban car pools. If there's a teenager at home you may find a jalopy or a subcompact in the driveway. Sometimes the second car isn't a car at all, but a light truck or recreational vehicle (Chapter 12).

Facts of life about used cars

But before you dash off to your nearest used-car dealer, there are three universal truths about used cars that you should keep in mind:

■ ALL USED CARS ARE WORN MACHINERY. No matter how well maintained by a previous owner or reconditioned by a dealer, a used car has a greater chance of a breakdown than a new car. There are many variations on the familiar story of the used car that conks out on the way home from the lot. Dealers stoutly maintain that such stories are grossly exaggerated; nevertheless, they seldom will guarantee a used car for more than 30 days.

■ MILEAGE DOESN'T TELL ALL. For years American drivers have been living with the myth that every car has a certain number of relatively trouble-free miles built into it—usually from 35,000 to 50,000. The remaining life expectancy of a used car was determined by deducting the mileage recorded on the odometer from the "built-in" total, usually considered to be 100,000 miles. Such people have been doubly misled. Not only is mileage an unreliable measure of wear, but many dealers have routinely "spun" the odometers of their cars to show lower mileage. Before odometer tampering became a federal offense in 1973, a Massachusetts survey indicated that 25 per cent of all used cars sold in the state had altered odometer readings.

While the new law has doubtless reduced odometer tampering, there is no guarantee that the practice has been eliminated. When you consider that a two-year-old luxury car with 24,000 miles on its odometer will bring about $600 more than the identical car with 50,000 miles, the motive for tampering is obvious. Actually, the car with 50,000 "good" miles—well maintained and used mostly on highways, where most American cars are designed to deliver maximum performance—may be in better condition than one with 24,000 "tough" miles, carelessly maintained and used mostly in stop-and-go city traffic.

■ DON'T LOOK FOR BARGAINS. Competition being what it is, the price nearly always indicates the condition a car is in. In fact, you should be prepared to pay a fair price and budget an additional $200 to $300 for a complete tune-up and minor repairs after purchase. But when the list price is significantly lower than the car seems to warrant—for example, $999 for a two-year-old full-sized sedan—beware of what dealers call the trouble car. It may be a repainted taxi or police car, a skillfully repaired victim of a major accident, or a car that was once windshield-deep in floodwater and is loaded with hidden rust.

If, having weighed the pros and cons, you decide that a used car is just what you need, the next question is: where is the best place to buy one? There are three principal sources of used cars: the used-car lots of new-car dealers, independent used-car dealers and private sellers (these and other sources are compared on the chart on page 84).

■ THE NEW-CAR DEALER. On his used-car lot —which may be a considerable distance from his new-car showroom—he sells the best cars obtained as trade-ins. Since there are many people who routinely buy new cars every two or three years, the new-car dealer is the best source for late-model cars. They are generally tuned up and given minor repairs, in addition to a thorough cleaning, before being placed on the lot. The prices are usually high because each car is expected not only to provide a prof-

KING OF THE USED-CAR DEALERS

If there were a hall of fame for used-car dealers, Earl "Madman" Muntz would rate a prominent pedestal. During and shortly after World War II, when cars were scarce, he pioneered volume buying and selling techniques that justified his claim to being "the largest used-car dealer the world has ever known." At the peak of his career he was selling more than 750 used cars each month from just two locations in Glendale and Los Angeles, California.

Muntz's "nom de gimmick" was the premise of a massive advertising campaign that made him a household word. Billboards by the hundreds carried his outrageous slogans ("You too can be a wealthy pedestrian—sell your car to Muntz"), skywriters filled the air with his name and radio stations blared his jingles ("Oh get the most, the top at once/ And sell your car to Muntz").

Although Muntz posed as an eccentric who paid ridiculously high prices for his used cars and then sold them at ridiculously low prices, he was in fact a shrewd and highly successful businessman. By 1948, however, profits had begun to drop as other dealers adopted his techniques, and Muntz quit the used-car business. But he left behind a personal and not altogether mythical creation: the archetypal image of the fast-talking, fast-dealing used-car salesman.

A BUYER'S GUIDE TO THE USED-CAR MARKET

There are no exclusive dealer franchises for used cars. Just as a person buying used furniture can take his business to an antiques dealer, a garage sale or a thrift shop, a used-car buyer has a wide choice of marketplaces, ranging from his neighborhood gas station (listed below as a consignment seller) to auctions. The list below summarizes the advantages and disadvantages of the principal used-car sources discussed in this chapter.

SOURCE	MAJOR ADVANTAGES	MAJOR DISADVANTAGES
New-car dealer	More late-model cars Service facilities Best guarantees Dealer's reputation verifiable	Higher prices Reluctance to accept trade-in on another used car
Independent dealer	Competitive prices due to low overhead Greater willingness to accept trades	Prevalence of older models Minimal guarantees Probable inadequacy of service facilities
Private seller	Low prices	Absence of guarantees Unavailability of trades Possible difficulty of establishing ownership Scattered locations Choice usually of only one car
Consignment seller	Low prices Convenient neighborhood locations	Absence of guarantees Unavailability of trades Possible difficulty of establishing ownership
Commercial auction	Low prices	Infrequency of sales Time-consuming procedure No guarantees or trades Little or no opportunity to check condition of cars
Government auction	Low prices Honest evaluations	Infrequency of sales Poor condition of many cars Need to bid against dealers for best cars No guarantees or trades
Liquidation auction	Low prices	Infrequency of sales Poor condition of many cars Absence of guarantees Unavailability of trades
Rental/lease agency	Late-model cars Availability of some guarantees	Abused condition of many cars Unavailability of trades

it on the original trade-in deal and any reconditioning cost, but also to meet a share of the dealership's total overhead, which can be considerably more than you might expect.

Many new-car dealers assign to each used car an amount (the "nut") to be added to the wholesale book price. The total is the minimum at which the car will be sold. On some late models, the nut may be as much as $500.

Partially offsetting the new-car dealer's high prices is a guarantee of some sort. This may range from the minimum guarantee of 30 days or 1,000 miles, whichever comes first, to a guarantee of a year or 12,000 miles. But the buyer should be aware that used-car guarantees usually limit the responsibility of the dealer to half the cost of the repairs, and sometimes to as little as 15 per cent. Since the dealer also establishes the cost of the repairs under the guarantee terms, he rarely loses money under the arrangement.

Most new-car dealers prefer to keep a high percentage of late-model used cars—less than five years old—on their lots because they sell more quickly and at higher prices than older cars. Such dealers are often reluctant to take your old car in trade for a newer used car. A favorite technique for discouraging such trades is to offer deliberately such a low price that you're tempted to cry out, "Why, I can get twice as much as that selling it myself." That's just what the dealer wants you to do.

■ THE INDEPENDENT DEALER. His stereotype, dating from the late 1940s, is the guy with the flashy clothes, big smile and outstretched hand, a master at peddling repainted wrecks as low-mileage cream puffs driven by grandmothers. Today, he may turn out to be an ordinary-looking businessman who will answer your questions matter-of-factly and may have to excuse himself occasionally to answer the telephone in his little office.

The old days of the high-volume, hard-sell independent dealers have vanished along with fabled operators like California's Earl "Madman" Muntz (box, page 83).

Strong competition from new-car dealers, as well as stronger government regulations, has greatly reduced the number of independent dealers since their heyday in the years immediately following World War II. Their lots can be found tucked in among new-car dealers in the familiar "automobile row" of every major city. In small towns the independent dealer may double as the local auto repairman.

Whatever his location, the cars he has to sell are often the new-car dealer's leftovers. The independent dealer buys these cars directly from the new-car dealer or at auction sales, and bases his retail price on his cost. Because his overhead is usually low (he may be the only employee), the independent dealer can offer competitive prices. Generally, his cars are somewhat older and less expensive than those of the new-car dealer.

Guarantees, where they exist at all, are minimal. However, some independent dealers, who depend on neighborhood patronage and repeat sales, will provide repairs on an informal basis even when not required to do so. An independent dealer to avoid is the "cheapie" specialist, often found in low-income neighborhoods. His cars are the culls of the auction market, often bought for as little as $50 each. If the dealer can put these derelicts in some kind of working order, he can get double or triple what he paid for them. Most of his customers can't afford anything better, and the down payment required for the advertised "instant credit" is often more than the car's wholesale cost.

■ PRIVATE SELLERS. It may be your neighbor or your brother-in-law. Maybe it's the fellow who drives around town with a For Sale sign in his window. It could be the person who pinned the handwritten advertisement on the bulletin board at the office or the supermarket, or had it published in the classified columns of the local newspaper or shopping guide. There are always people trying to sell their own cars.

Often the prices are tempting. Private sellers usually want cash and want it quickly, and will sometimes sell their cars for less than a dealer's wholesale cost. This is because owners tend to think of the money they receive as a profit. While a dealer must add his overhead onto the cost of his cars, the private seller has no overhead and often feels that an old car has "paid for itself," especially if he has just gotten a good cash discount on a new car because he had no trade-in.

If you want to take the time to shop through a list of private sellers—who seldom have more than one car to sell—you can expect to pay somewhere between the dealer's wholesale and retail price. On late-model cars, you might be able to save several hundred dollars. But you will be buying the car with no guarantees and with no legal recourse if you should later discover that you purchased a damaged or defective car. Because private sales are usually handled by cash or certified check, they may also require a larger amount of money than the down payment to a dealer on a financed purchase.

A nagging problem with private sales is the matter of obtaining a clear legal title from the previous owner. Clear title is important in avoiding stolen or encumbered cars, such as those pledged as security for unpaid loans. In either case, the car can be repossessed from an unwary buyer without repayment—and sometimes without notice. When dealing with a private seller, always insist on proof of ownership. Don't settle for the car's current registration. Ask for the certificate of title, which not only names the owner but lists all liens

THE HARD-TO-SELL BARGAINS

Used-car dealers try to stock the kinds of cars that will sell easily. But sometimes they find themselves saddled with unpopular cars that are hard to sell even though they may be in excellent condition. If you can find one of these cars on a lot or among the listings of private sellers you may be able to buy it at a bargain price—if you can overlook the reason it was a hard-to-sell car in the first place. Most of the unpopular cars fall into one of these four categories:

1. The rare birds. These are cars, mostly imported, that were sold new in relatively small numbers. Used-car buyers find them unfamiliar and may be concerned about the limited number of service facilities.

2. The orphans. When a manufacturer discontinues the production of a particular make, the used cars of that make tend to drop in value. Buyers are concerned about availability of spare parts—even though the major manufacturers often stock parts that are interchangeable among several makes.

3. The losers. For every hot new car that sets sales records in its class, there are a couple of competitive makes or models that are showroom disappointments. They lack one of the winner's essential features—price, performance or styling. The losers are usually well-built and mechanically dependable cars, but nobody likes a loser and the stigma often carries over to the used-car lot.

4. The oddballs. They're perfectly good cars that fail to sell because of their appearance. They would include the boxy sedan that looks dowdy in an age of racy fastbacks, or the garishly designed station wagon whose styling clashes with the less flamboyant lines of newer models. Even the color of a car can make it an oddball. A black sports car, for example, could be expected to have about the same appeal for a teenager that a hot-pink family sedan would have for his father.

against the car. Be cautious in dealing for a car whose owner has recently died. The car may be part of an estate, legally salable only by the estate's administrator.

In addition to the three principal sources of used cars already listed, there are several others that occasionally can provide the kind of car you may be looking for.

■ THE CONSIGNMENT SELLER is usually a gasoline-station manager or the owner of a repair garage who sells used cars as a sideline. Unlike the dealer, he does not own the cars. He sells them for their private owners and takes part of the sale price as his commission. Consignment sellers generally are not licensed used-car dealers, offer no guarantees and cannot be held legally responsible for any damage or defects. The chief advantage, and often the only advantage, that they have to offer is a convenient display place for private sellers and prospective buyers.

If you like a little excitement, and don't mind killing a few hours, you might consider buying a used car at an auction sale. While most auto auctions are restricted to dealers, there are three types of auctions where you can take part in the bidding:

■ COMMERCIAL AUCTIONS are little more than dealer gimmicks. Instead of posting a price on his cars and allowing himself to be bargained down to his real selling price, the auction dealer starts with a temptingly low figure and lets the bidding lift the selling price. Chances are you will wind up paying about the same. But it's more fun to bid than to haggle, even though your choice is confined to what the auction dealer has available. While most own the cars they auction, some work on consignment by selling the car for the owner.

■ GOVERNMENT AUCTIONS permit you to bid on just about anything from a de-sirened

police car or a sleek black limousine to a station wagon. Many city, state and federal agencies are required by law to dispose of their surplus cars at public auction, and the bidding is often temptingly low.

The best organized of the government auctions are those conducted every few weeks at various locations throughout the country by the Property Management and Disposal Service of the General Services Administration, the federal government's housekeeping agency. You might find yourself bidding on a plain gray sedan once driven by a Navy recruiting officer, or a flashy sports car used by an undercover agent. Most of these cars have been regularly maintained, and the government is usually candid in describing any known defects. The cars are available for inspection several days before the auction, at which time their motors may be started for on-site testing.

The government also conducts auctions by mail for surplus cars in relatively isolated locations. But a mail bidder should think long and hard about what he's buying and how he is going to take delivery. Information on both types of auctions can be obtained from the General Services Administration's Business Service Center in the nearest major city.

■ LIQUIDATION AUCTIONS in most cases are court-ordered dispositions of business and personal property, designed to raise cash to pay off debts. They include sheriff's auctions where property, including cars, is sold by court order in cases of bankruptcy, nonpayment of taxes and lawsuits. Banks and other lending institutions often are legally empowered to take cars for nonpayment of debt and to sell them at repossession auctions.

Estate auctions are a common way of raising cash to pay the debts of an estate. You can safely buy a stolen car at auctions conducted by some insurance companies, which own re-

HOW BOOK PRICES OF USED CARS ARE DETERMINED

The bible of the used-car industry is the monthly *Official Used Car Guide* published under the auspices of the National Automobile Dealers Association (NADA). Other guides, some derived from this one, are discussed in the text *(page 90)*.

The sample page at right, reproduced actual size, shows the type of information provided for all makes and models of used cars up to six years old. The important figures, shown in color, are the latest "book" prices. They are compiled monthly by taking the averages of more than 100,000 sales and finance transactions throughout the United States. The average trade-in, or wholesale, price is at the left. At the right is the average retail price and the average loan price, which is the amount that can be financed. The prices in the column titled Fact. A.D.P. (factory advertised delivery price) represent each car's original sticker price.

Additions for certain optional equipment—or deductions for the lack of it—are also included, along with a frequently repeated bottom-of-the-page reminder to the dealer to "deduct for high mileage."

Av'g. Trade-In	Ins. Sym.	BODY TYPE	Model	Fact. A.D.P.	Ship. Wgt.	Av'g. Loan	Av'g. Retail
							DODGE

VEHICLE IDENTIFICATION NUMBER: See explanation on page 67.

1971 DODGE—DART—continued

Av'g. Trade-In		BODY TYPE		Fact. A.D.P.		Av'g. Loan	Av'g. Retail
50		Add Power Steering		$ 95		50	75
175		Add Factory Air Conditioning		363		175	225
100		Add V8 318 CID Eng.		124		100	125
150		Deduct Manual Trans.				150	150

1971 DODGE—CHALLENGER   Start Sept. 1970
EQUIPPED AT and PS

W.B. 110". Length 192". Width 77". Tires 7.35x14, RT F70x14. ENGINES: 6 Cyl.; Std. Models "JH". Opt. "JL" 225 CID. B&S 3.4x4.12. Tax HP 27.7. BHP 145. "JL" 198 CID. B&S 3.4x3.64. Tax HP 27.7. BHP 125. V8: 318 CID. B&S 3.91x3.31. Tax HP 48.9. BHP 230. Std. "RT". Opt. other Models. 383 CID, B&S 4.25x3.38. Tax HP 57.8. BHP 300. Opt. 275. Opt: 340 CID. Tax HP 52.2. BHP 275. 426 CID. Tax HP 57.8. BHP 425. 440 CID. Tax HP 59.7. BHP 385.

Av'g. Trade-In	Ins. Sym.	BODY TYPE	Model	Fact. A.D.P.	Ship. Wgt.	Av'g. Loan	Av'g. Retail
CHALLENGER-6		Veh. Ident.: (Model)( )1( )100001 Up.					
1650	4	Coupe 2D	JL23	$2727	3020	1500	2075
1750	4	Hardtop 2D	JH23	2848	3065	1575	2175
1675	4	Convertible 2D	JH27	3105	3150	1525	2100
CHALLENGER-V8		Veh. Ident.: (Model)( )1( )100001 Up.					
1750	4	Coupe 2D	JL23	$2853	3080	1575	2175
1850	4	Hardtop 2D	JH23	2950	3120	1675	2300
1775	4	Convertible	JH27	3207	3210	1600	2200
CHALLENGER R/T-V8		Veh. Ident.: (Model)( )1( )100001 Up.					
1950	i	Hardtop 2D	JS23	$3273	3495	1775	2400
75		Add Vinyl Top		$ 82		75	100
225		Add Factory Air Conditioning		375		225	300
200		Deduct 3 Spd. Trans.				200	200
175		Deduct 4 Spd. Trans.				175	175
125		Deduct Conventional Steering				125	125

1971 DODGE—CORONET   Start Sept. 1970
EQUIPPED AT and PS

W.B. 118". Length 207", S/W 214". Width 78", S/W 79". Tires E78x14, S/W H78x14, Broug & Crest. F78x14. ENGINES: 6 Cyl.; 225 CID. B&S 3.4x4.12. Tax HP 27.7. BHP 145. V8: 318 CID. B&S 3.91x3.31. Tax HP 48.9. BHP 230. Opt. 383 CID. Tax HP 57.8. BHP 275/300.

Av'g. Trade-In	Ins. Sym.	BODY TYPE	Model	Fact. A.D.P.	Ship. Wgt.	Av'g. Loan	Av'g. Retail
CORONET-6		Veh. Ident.: (Model)( )1( )100001 Up.					
1325	4	Sedan 4D	WL41	$2777	3245	1200	1750
1500	4	Station Wagon 4D 2S	WL45	3101	3745	1350	1925
CORONET CUSTOM-6		Veh. Ident.: (Model)( )1( )100001 Up.					
1425	4	Sedan 4D	WH41	$2951	3250	1300	1850
1625	4	Station Wagon 4D 2D	WH45	3278	3750	1475	2050
CORONET-V8		Veh. Ident.: (Model)( )1( )100001 Up.					
1450	4	Sedan 4D	WL41	$2872	3360	1325	1875
1625	4	Station Wagon 4D 2S	WL45	3196	3810	1475	2050
CORONET CUSTOM-V8		Veh. Ident.: (Model)( )1( )100001 Up.					
1550	4	Sedan 4D	WH41	$3046	3365	1400	1975

DEDUCT FOR HIGH MILEAGE

---

covered stolen cars under the terms of their theft insurance, and at auctions conducted by police departments, which have the right to sell stolen or abandoned cars if the owners cannot be found within a reasonable time.

In liquidation auctions, the cars vary greatly in condition. But the low prices can be enticing, even though the bidding of dealers —and sometimes of former owners—will probably prevent you from getting superbargains.

There is one more source of used cars to be aware of: rental and leasing firms. While many of these companies prefer to sell directly to dealers or to put their cars on the block at dealers' auctions, there are some significant exceptions. One of the nation's largest car-rental firms not only sells cars through its local offices but also maintains regional showrooms where the best cars are displayed and sold.

Rental cars usually are sold when about one year old or when they have racked up 20,000 miles. They are popular models and most are fully equipped. But the low mileage can be deceptive because it was logged by scores of drivers, whose different driving habits can inflict an incredible amount of abuse in a short time. A less risky purchase may be the leased car. It usually has been driven for months or years by one person, who is more apt to take care of a car than a series of renters. Rental and leased cars are usually sold for cash "as is," but the larger agencies may offer some sort of guarantee and financing arrangement. Ask local agency managers for full information.

How the dealers deal

Unless a good friend or relative comes along with a used-car offer that's too good to refuse, it pays to do some homework before venturing into the marketplace. No Arab bazaar ever offered a greater variety of merchandise, prices and deceptive claims than what used-car dealers call "the last of the great horse-trading businesses in America." Just as there are no two used cars quite alike, neither are there two dealers who operate quite the same way.

Smiling Sam is waiting to greet you effusively the moment you set foot on his lot. He follows you around as you examine his cars, every one of which is a beauty, a gem, a cream puff. Interested? He'll make you a deal that's a positive steal, a giveaway, a once-in-a-lifetime bargain. Smiling Sam is a hustler with disarming charm, a type that thrives in a bazaar.

Greasy George is likely to be wearing mechanic's overalls and wiping his hands as he ambles over. "Just finished tuning that station wagon," he will say. "We don't put 'em on the line until they're in tip-top shape." Actually, he has been salvaging some parts from a junk car, but there's something reassuring about a man who at least seems to be a mechanic. When he says that clunk in the engine doesn't mean anything, you're tempted to believe him.

Homespun Hank believes in low-key selling. He wears sweaters and lumberjack shirts, and will chat about the rotten weather and the rising price of groceries. He's studiously modest about his wares and may even amble off while you examine a car. But Homespun Hank sells a lot of cars because he seems such a nice guy.

Regardless of the dealer's approach, he won't stay in business long if he can't provide cars that appeal to his customers. But it's up to you to determine what sort of car you need; one of the worst mistakes you can make is to let a dealer decide for you. Don't just drive over to a lot on the spur of the moment. An astute dealer can spot you before you can say "Just looking, thanks," and you'll find yourself slamming doors, tooting horns and listening to glowing spiels until you lay out a deposit on a car that's probably bigger, flashier and more expensive than the one you really need.

Much of the information provided for new-car buyers in Chapter 2 also applies to used cars. But after you have weighed the merits of a subcompact station wagon against an intermediate sedan, there are some other things that you should keep in mind:

■ USED IMPORTS COST LESS. Many imported cars depreciate faster than their domestic equivalents and cost less as used cars. But this should be weighed against the availability of parts and service in your neighborhood.

■ LOOK FOR LATE MODELS. Where the price and make are the same, a late bottom-of-the-line model usually is more trouble-free and a better buy than an older luxury model.

■ DON'T BE SOLD BY OPTIONS. Be cautious about cars loaded with accessories. The rule in selecting a used car is: the simpler, the better. Extra equipment is likely to require more maintenance and repair.

■ LOSERS CAN BE BARGAINS. If you don't plan to resell the car later, and can overlook depreciation, consider the merits of a late model that failed to sell well when new (box, page 86). A classic example is Ford's Edsel of 1958 —a big, overstyled car that hit the market just as tastes were shifting to smaller, less expensive models; the Edsel was therefore discontinued shortly after its introduction.

The best place to get straight information about used cars is from the people who own them—your friends, relatives and neighbors. If you're thinking about a compact sedan like the one in your neighbor's driveway, ask him about it. But be prepared to ask specific questions about such things as riding comfort, gasoline mileage and recent repairs. If you simply ask, "How do you like the car?" you may get almost any kind of answer. Your neighbor's wife, who doesn't keep track of maintenance costs and uses the car for shopping and driving the kids around town, may praise it lavishly: it rides beautifully, has never given her a bit of trouble. But ask her husband, who has just paid for a tune-up, muffler, brake linings and a new fender, and you may hear the same car damned as the worst car ever made. The truth, of course, lies somewhere in between.

Your local library can provide a great deal of information about used cars. Ask to see the back copies of various automotive and consumer publications that give detailed specifications and road test data on various cars. Many libraries also subscribe to the *Official Used Car Guide* of the National Automobile Dealers Association *(box, page 88)*. It provides specifications and current prices, wholesale and retail, for used cars up to six years old. If your library hasn't the latest edition, you probably can see one at your bank's loan department.

There are a number of other used-car price guides published by various organizations, including the Kelly Blue Book, widely used in California. While most such guides are sold only to subscribers, particularly dealers and auto loan specialists, a few can be found on newsstands. But remember that guide prices are only averages based on recent sales and that actual prices differ substantially from guide to guide, dealer to dealer, city to city, and even from month to month.

USED-CAR SHORTHAND

Used-car sellers often use a kind of shorthand to describe their wares in newspaper advertisements. Although it helps them cram the maximum amount of information into a minimum amount of space, the result can be confusing to the would-be buyer. While variations are numerous, this guide to commonly used abbreviations should help to decipher most used-car advertisements:

a/c (or AC) - air conditioner
ACC - accessories
all discs - disc brakes on all four wheels
AM - AM radio
auto (or AT) - automatic transmission
conv - convertible
cpe - coupe
cyl - cylinders (usually preceded by the number 4, 6 or 8)
discs - disc brakes on front wheels only
dlr - dealer
dr - door (usually preceded by 2 or 4)
fac - factory installed (as in fac a/c)
FM - FM radio
h - heater
lo (or lo mi) - low mileage
man - manual transmission
pb - power brakes
ps - power steering
p disc - power-disc brakes, front wheels only
pw - power windows
r - radio (often joined with heater as rh or r & h)
rad ti - radial tires
reblt - rebuilt
sed - sedan
ss - stick shift (manual transmission)
st - stereo
tape - tape player
tr - transmission
V8 - V-shaped eight-cylinder engine
warr (or wty) - warranty
wgn - station wagon
ww - white sidewall tires

Should you confront a dealer with a book price, don't be surprised if he pulls out a different guide and shows you a higher book price. The typical used-car dealer subscribes to several different guides, and can usually find one with a price to suit his purpose. But if he can't meet your book price, he can always fall back on a standard line: "Sorry. You'd better buy your car from the publisher."

Another good place to get information about used cars is in the newspaper advertisements of local dealers and private sellers. In reading them, you will find that most are printed in automobilese *(list, left)*, a kind of shorthand evolved by used-car dealers to cram the maximum amount of information into the minimum amount of space. For example:

'72 Chev Imp Cust HT cpe, V8, AT, A/C, PS, PB, W/W, r&h.

What's being offered is a 1972 Chevrolet Impala custom hardtop coupe (two doors), with an eight-cylinder engine, automatic transmission, air conditioning, power steering, power brakes, white sidewall tires, radio and heater.

The advertisements of private sellers may be as succinct, but they sometimes go on to tell more about a car than the owner intended to reveal. Ads that mention rebuilt transmissions, new paint and new tires on a late-model car ought to give any would-be buyer pause. So should lines like "needs work," "good transportation" and "best offer." They are sure tipoffs that the car leaves a lot to be desired.

Once you have a pretty good idea of what kind of car you want, and how much you can expect to pay for it, you're ready to begin shopping. A good way to begin is to check out the used-car dealers nearest to your home. Though their prices may not be any better than those of dealers in the next town, a local dealer is easier to return to if you have a problem with your car —and a lot more likely to do something about it, if only to maintain his reputation in the neighborhood. In the used-car business a dealer's reputation is more crucial to the buyer than the number of cars he has for sale, so it pays to find out just what kind of reputation he

has. Ask your neighbors for the names of people who have bought cars from him. Call your local Better Business Bureau or Chamber of Commerce to find out if any complaints have been filed against him.

If all this snooping seems excessive, remember that buying from a reputable dealer is the best insurance you can get. It gives you a fair shot at getting a sound car at a fair price, and with a guarantee that will be honestly met.

"I don't ask to see the guarantee if one of my customers comes back a few weeks or a few months later for some little thing," says one such dealer. "If it's a loose wire or a burned-out bulb, I'll fix it and won't charge anything. Once, for a good customer, I even replaced a starter in a car I'd sold three months before."

Knowing what to buy and where to buy, as important as that information is, counts for little if you don't know how to buy. To get the best possible used car at the best possible price requires more than door-slamming, tire-kicking and haggling. It requires careful checking from the moment you set foot on a dealer's lot.

In fact, even that moment should be well planned. The best time of year to go used-car shopping is in a slack period, when demand is not at a peak. Winter, for example, is a time when most dealers are well stocked with cars traded in on new models introduced in the fall. The supply of good late-model cars dwindles quickly during the spring and summer buying seasons. The best time of all to buy: immediately following a siege of bad winter weather, such as a heavy snowstorm. Dealers are generally anxious to make up for lost sales and are likely to offer unusually good deals.

But whether you do your buying in winter or summer, always do it during the daytime. The reflections from the bright lights illuminating some lots make even a repainted wreck look like a factory-fresh beauty. It's also a good idea to stay away when it's raining or drizzling. The dullest paint looks shiny and new when wet.

The strategy of smart shopping

And so, let us assume you are ready to go shopping on a sunny winter day. But whatever the time of year, there are some practical hints for dealing with dealers.

First of all, take your time. You may need the car desperately, but if you grab the first car offered, you may be more desperate later. Allow an entire day to visit used-car lots in your vicinity and promise yourself that you won't buy unless you find the car you want at the price you want to pay. At each lot, limit yourself to consideration of no more than two or three cars. If you feel there are no cars that meet your specifications, don't waste the salesman's time and your own by looking over cars that *almost* meet your needs. There will always be time to consider alternatives after you have visited other lots.

At this point, it is a good idea to be aware of the role of the used-car salesman. Actually he has two roles. Sometimes he can even become two different people. When he first introduces himself he is Mr. Agreeable, the friendly persuader whose job is to find a car that meets the buyer's requirements.

"You're planning to take some trips? Here's a beauty. Look at all that trunk space. Or maybe you'd like to look at a small wagon?"

The buyer is encouraged to examine and test some cars. Finally he finds one he wants. That is when Mr. Agreeable is subtly but unmistakably transformed into Mr. Business. Or he may go right on being Mr. Agreeable while he turns the buyer over to a "takeover man," whose job is to close the deal. Whoever he is, he must handle the second role carefully. The give-and-take might go like this:

Buyer: "I like the car but not the price. Will you take $1,500 for it?"

Seller: "You can't be serious. This car is $2,200. That's a fair price, but if you're ready to buy right now I'll sell it to you for $2,000."

Buyer: "Gee, that's a lot of money. Can't you do any better? After all, the tires are kind of worn and there's that dent in the fender."

Seller: "How about if I have the dent fixed and throw in a new set of tires?"

Buyer: "I'd rather take it as it is but I'd also like a better price."

Seller: "Look, I don't like to argue. Would another $100 make a difference?"

Buyer: "Well . . ."

Seller: "That's really about the best I can do and still make a profit. Here, look at the book price. See? That car sells for $1,850. I'm making only $50 on the deal!"

The salesman has neglected to point out that the book price is for a car in excellent condition, or that the car cost him only $1,450 at a dealer's auction the week before. The buyer feels he's getting a bargain on the best car he's tested by cutting $300 from the original price. The salesman knows he can make a handsome $450 profit. Both are pleased with the prospective agreement, the buyer smiling with the knowledge that he was prepared to spend $2,000 and the seller smiling with the knowledge that he was prepared to drop to $1,700.

In most cases it pays to be frank with the salesman at the outset. By telling him what sort of car you're looking for, and perhaps by giving him some idea of what you plan to pay, you can save yourself the trouble of personally examining all of his cars to find the two or three most suitable ones. If he believes you have done your homework and know what you want, he will quickly indicate the cars he feels will meet your needs. He probably will steer you to models a bit newer and more expensive than

VERBAL TRAPS IN USED-CAR ADS

The used-car advertisement at right, a composite derived from actual newspaper ads, is loaded with booby traps for the unwary buyer. Although deceptive come-ons are less prevalent than they once were, the technique is not dead. Knowing how to translate the seemingly straightforward promises can save any buyer time, money and not a little grief.

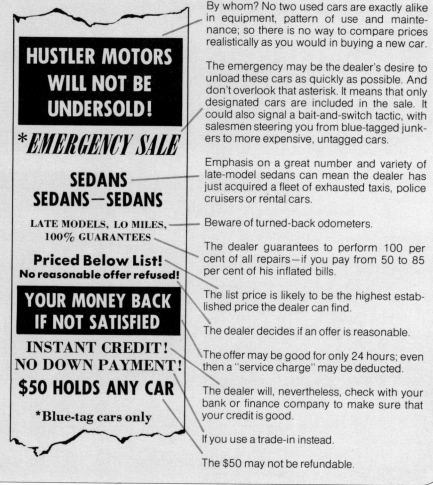

HUSTLER MOTORS WILL NOT BE UNDERSOLD!

***EMERGENCY SALE**

SEDANS SEDANS—SEDANS

LATE MODELS, LO MILES, 100% GUARANTEES

Priced Below List!
No reasonable offer refused!

YOUR MONEY BACK IF NOT SATISFIED

INSTANT CREDIT! NO DOWN PAYMENT!

$50 HOLDS ANY CAR

*Blue-tag cars only

By whom? No two used cars are exactly alike in equipment, pattern of use and maintenance; so there is no way to compare prices realistically as you would in buying a new car.

The emergency may be the dealer's desire to unload these cars as quickly as possible. And don't overlook that asterisk. It means that only designated cars are included in the sale. It could also signal a bait-and-switch tactic, with salesmen steering you from blue-tagged junkers to more expensive, untagged cars.

Emphasis on a great number and variety of late-model sedans can mean the dealer has just acquired a fleet of exhausted taxis, police cruisers or rental cars.

Beware of turned-back odometers.

The dealer guarantees to perform 100 per cent of all repairs—if you pay from 50 to 85 per cent of his inflated bills.

The list price is likely to be the highest established price the dealer can find.

The dealer decides if an offer is reasonable.

The offer may be good for only 24 hours; even then a "service charge" may be deducted.

The dealer will, nevertheless, check with your bank or finance company to make sure that your credit is good.

If you use a trade-in instead.

The $50 may not be refundable.

---

you had in mind, but within your bargaining range. It is a poor salesman who shows a $2,000 car to a buyer who has made it plain that he plans to spend no more than $1,000.

Once you have found the kind of car you want, at a price that seems about right, the most important part of used-car buying begins: determining the condition of the car. It is probably the least understood and most poorly performed ritual confronting the average car buyer. Yet, with a few guidelines—and a lot of common sense—it is fairly simple to determine what shape a used car is in. It is essentially the same technique used-car dealers employ when appraising cars they themselves plan to buy.

You begin with a couple of basic rules. The first is to pay little or no attention to the odometer reading. You need not, as one expert advises, deliberately avoid looking at the reading until your examination is completed. But if you do peek at the numbers, remember that even if they reflect the true mileage, they do not necessarily reflect the true condition of the car. The average used-car dealer assumes a car has been driven about 12,000 miles per year, regardless of the odometer reading, and uses that figure as a basis for deciding what condition the car should be in. So, with a three-year-old car, he expects to find the sort of wear that goes with 36,000 miles of use. If he finds less wear, he happily proclaims the existence of a cream puff. If he finds more wear, even though the odometer may read a delightful 20,000

SOME OLD CARS WITH VERY NEW PRICES

Most cars depreciate in value every year until eventually they are worthless. But some old cars, after being lovingly restored to pristine power and beauty, can be worth many times their original prices. The most valuable are classics such as the 1929 Cadillac and the 1930 Packard below: cars that were outstanding in styling, engineering and high-quality craftsmanship. Other cars, especially an-

1932 AUBURN $5,500

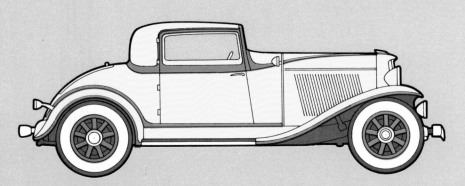

In the depths of the 1930s Depression this two-tone Auburn coupe cost $805 —including a rumble seat that was handy for a double date, a mother-in-law or the children. It also had a two-speed axle, an early form of overdrive that permitted the car to run at top speed on a straightaway without increasing revolutions of the engine.

1924 MODEL-T FORD $1,900

From 1909 to 1927 Henry Ford produced 15 million Model-T Fords—his most famous design. The more cars he made, the lower he managed to bring prices. The 1909 model cost $850, but this 1924 version could be bought for $290 (an electric starter sold for $60 more). Despite their popularity among collectors, Model Ts even today are relatively inexpensive to buy because the hardy little cars are still easy to find.

1929 CADILLAC FLEETWOOD ROADSTER $25,000

Sleek roadsters like this $3,450 Cadillac were a symbol of the high-living affluence of the Roaring Twenties. Cadillac introduced the first synchromesh transmission, chromium plating and safety glass in 1929. At last count only six of this rare model were left in the world.

tiques such as the 1924 Model T and the 1912 Hudson, draw their value mainly from the nostalgia of old-car buffs who enjoy tinkering with the engines, restoring worn or missing parts, polishing every bit of metal to a dazzling brilliance and then chugging down back roads to wave proudly at curious folk who point and smile.

Collecting old cars for profit, however, is not a hobby for casual backyard mechanics. The demand for the classics in recent years has driven their cost well beyond the reach of the average collector. Even cars with less than aristocratic pedigrees often can be bought only at highly inflated prices. Furthermore, the cost of restoring them can run into many thousands of dollars—and only then are they worth the top prices indicated below.

$50,000

Packard produced a limited series of this sports model—called a boattail because of its pointed rear end—in 1930 for a price tag of $5,200. It featured a four-speed transmission and a powerful eight-cylinder engine. Buffs claim that only seven of the original 150 boattails still exist today.

1930 PACKARD "734" SPEEDSTER

$4,000

The refreshingly clean lines of the Thunderbird—a radical advance in styling—have made this car a much-sought-after collector's item despite its relatively recent vintage. Ford produced this two-seater "personal car" for only four years before expanding it into a less sporty five-passenger sedan. You could have bought the original model for $2,900.

1955 FORD THUNDERBIRD

$4,000

New, this pre-World War I touring car with a special six-cylinder engine listed for $2,450. Although the cars weighed more than 3,000 pounds, even the standard four-cylinder engines could get them rolling at 50 miles per hour—more than fast enough for the primitive roads of the day. In 1916 a similar Hudson made the first round-trip transcontinental drive between New York and San Francisco.

1912 HUDSON PHAETON

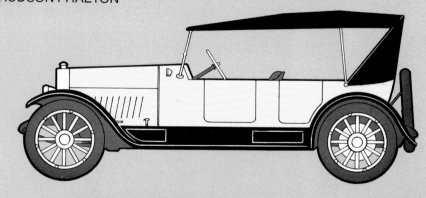

miles, the car is dubbed a dog, a sled—or an unprintable equivalent.

The second rule in determining the condition of a used car is to concentrate on the car's basic structure and mechanical systems. Don't be concerned with minor flaws that can be inexpensively corrected, such as a scratched fender or a broken taillight. They can be repaired or replaced quickly and at nominal cost.

With those two rules in mind, you're ready to examine a used car the way the dealer does. The first step is to size up the exterior. Have you ever watched a used-car appraiser casually circle a car from a few feet away, glancing here and there but never seeming to look at anything in particular? The technique is called a walkaround, and the dealer is evaluating a number of things that help him place the car in one of four categories before he ever touches it. The categories, as standardized by the National Automobile Dealers Association, are:

■ SHARP. The car is "like new"; it has been unusually well maintained, with shiny paint and chrome, good tires and no visible signs of rust or body damage. This is the rare cream puff, which commands the top price for its model and year.

■ CLEAN. The car is neat and attractive with acceptable signs of wear. It's the kind of car that dealers love to have in their front lines because it requires relatively little preparation and is easy to sell at a reasonable price.

■ FAIR. Signs of wear and neglect are clearly visible, although some effort has been made to keep the car in shape. The body and chrome are dull or have been repainted. There may be dents and scrapes caused by minor collisions, but no major damage. Some dealers fix up these cars and sell them as "clean"; others prefer to keep them in the back of the lot as inexpensive "transportation specials."

■ ROUGH. It may run reasonably well, but it

WATCH OUT FOR THE USED-CAR RECALL

When you buy a used car the burden is on you to discover whether the car has an uncorrected safety defect. It is unrealistic to expect a dealer to bring up the issue of defects, much less point one out on a car in which you may be interested.

More than 42 million cars have been recalled since the National Traffic and Motor Vehicle Safety Act became law in 1966. When a defect is discovered the law requires the manufacturer to notify the purchaser, describe the defect and instruct him to have it repaired.

Unfortunately for the used-car buyer, the owner of a defective vehicle cannot always be located by the manufacturer. Worse yet, some owners receive the warnings but ignore them.

The quickest and surest way to find out whether the used car you have chosen has ever been recalled is to telephone the customer-service representative at the manufacturer's nearest divisional zone office. You can find this information listed in the owner's manual.

Be sure to state the exact year and model, and include the vehicle identification number. If you find that the car has indeed been recalled, ask for a complete description of the defect and the manufacturer's corrective action. Then take the car to a mechanic to determine whether or not the work has been done. If it has not, the manufacturer's new-car dealer will very likely make the repair without charge for either parts or labor.

looks awful—two or three different shades of paint, mismatched fenders and doors, missing chrome and rust-riddled rocker panels. As far as the dealer is concerned it is a dog, and will cost more to fix up than it is worth—and that's the way you should look at it, too.

Casing a car from the outside

Assuming you have eliminated the obviously rough cars—which many dealers won't permit on their lots—how do you go about determining the condition of a car that *looks* good?

Kicking the tires and listening to the doors thud will tell you next to nothing. What you need is a systematic plan for inspecting a car that will reveal most hidden faults—including those the dealer himself may not be aware of. The plan should begin with a brief but careful on-the-lot inspection (check list, page 98). Only if the car passes this first test should you get behind the wheel for the longer and more critical road test (page 100).

So let's begin outside the car, as the dealer does. Your first chore: look for new paint. The acrylic paint sprayed on new cars at the factory is capable of surviving almost any sort of weather conditions for at least three years. So if you find new paint on a late-model used car, it's a pretty safe bet that it's covering a repaired body—and, even more serious, perhaps concealing the evidence of a major accident. In any event, new paint is something to arouse your suspicions and should be a signal for you to inspect the rest of the car very carefully.

Some body shops apply new paint so skillfully as to defy detection. But there is usually a clue or two, even if the car has been entirely repainted. Look for a different color on the inside edges of the door frame, under the hood and on the fire wall separating the engine from the passenger compartment. No paint shop can remove and replace all the wires, locks and latches, so they either paint lightly around these parts or skip such areas entirely.

More difficult to detect is new paint that matches and blends with the old. A favorite dealer's trick is to look for tiny paint spots that inevitably spatter the adjoining portion of chrome trim. At the factory such chrome is added after the body is painted, and therefore it is spotless. In repainting, the chrome is masked with tape or paper. But no matter how well the masking is done it is almost impossible to keep a few spots from hitting the chrome.

Look for telltale ripples by sighting along the sides of the body from the front or rear. Look also for rough spots or a bubbling effect along the lower part of the body. They usually indicate painted-over rust that has not been properly scraped and primed.

Look for rust also along the lower edges of the body, at the bottom of door frames and the floor of the trunk. If the rust is superficial, it can be arrested after proper conditioning and repainting. But if it's deep and extensive, your best bet is to start looking at another car.

While you're examining the car for rust, keep an eye open for salt corrosion. Salt can devastate a car by dulling its paint, pitting its chrome and rotting away its underside. Salt-corrosion damage is most common in cars driven during the winter in places where chemical compounds are used to help melt snow and ice. But it is also a hazard for cars whose previous owners have lived near the ocean.

Just as new paint on a late-model car should be a danger signal, so should new or refinished chrome parts: bumpers, grilles and trim strips. They may have been put there by a meticulous owner, since these parts do get nicked and dented easily. If this is the case, fine. But the odds are also good that extra-shiny parts disguise deeper damage to the body, chassis or mechanical parts of the car. So take a close look around the area the new chrome covers.

You might think that a nice set of new tires would be a big plus for a used car. More probably, it's a minus. Except in the rarest of cases, no owner trades in or sells a car with four brand-new tires on it. What you may be admiring is a set of inexpensive tires, or even retreads, installed by the dealer. Retreads, with a little paint artfully applied, can pass for new tires on casual inspection. Look closely; worn lettering on the sidewall is a sure giveaway.

ON-THE-LOT CHECK LIST

In your initial examination of a used car, check the list below. Each of the items is discussed more fully in the text of this chapter.

Exterior. The following clues indicate a poorly maintained car (items 1 to 4 could be the result of an accident):

1. New paint on late model
2. Ripples in the body metal
3. New or refinished chrome
4. Misaligned doors, hood, trunk lid
5. Black smudges inside tailpipe *(right)*.
6. Worn shock absorbers
7. Retreaded or unevenly worn tires

Interior. The following items also indicate poor maintenance (items 1 to 8 can adversely affect safety):

1. Excessive steering-wheel play
2. Sticking accelerator pedal
3. Brake pedal with little resistance
4. Inoperative parking brake
5. Inoperative door locks
6. Inoperative windshield wipers or washer
7. Inoperable dashboard gauges or warning lights
8. Worn or loose safety belts
9. Worn upholstery or sagging front seats
10. Seat that will not adjust
11. Faulty windows
12. Inoperable heater/defroster
13. Inoperable options, e.g., radio and air conditioning
14. Faulty courtesy lights
15. No spare tire or tools

Lights. With a helper, check the operation of outside lights:

1. Headlights (including dimmer switch)
2. Brake lights
3. Turn signals
4. Emergency flasher
5. Parking lights
6. Back-up lights
7. Rear license-plate light

Idling engine. Be suspicious of any of these symptoms:

1. Sluggish starting, requiring long cranking
2. Rapid, noisy idle that may hide other noises
3. Slow engine response to accelerator-pedal pressure
4. Unusual engine noises —chatter, knocks, ticks

Take a look at how the doors, hood and trunk lid fit onto the car body. Poor alignment could mean a poorly assembled car—or one knocked out of shape in an accident. Open the doors —all of them—and make sure they close easily and tightly without slamming.

Examine the tailpipe opening. Its coating of exhaust residue can reveal some interesting information about how the car was cared for by the previous owner. The residue inside the tailpipe of a pre-1972 car should be an evenly distributed, dark-gray color. A very light, pearl-gray color in a pre-1972 model signifies a hot-running engine that may be due to improper ignition timing, and the car probably is a gas-gulper. The pearl-gray color is normal, however, in late-model cars, whose emissions-control equipment requires hotter combustion temperatures. The presence of black, gummy deposits in the tailpipe of any car indicates an oil-burning engine, most likely the result of worn piston rings.

You should also check the shock absorbers with a simple test. At each corner of the car, press down as hard as you can on the fender —or jump on and off the bumper. When the pressure is suddenly released, the body should bounce upward one time, then settle at a level position and stay there. If it bounces more than once, the shock absorbers need replacing. This is not, however, an unreasonable expense.

Casing a car from the inside

With your stroll around the car completed, now is the time to take a look inside that handsome piece of iron. Slide behind the wheel and take a look around you. What sort of shape is the upholstery in? If the seats are concealed beneath brand-new covers, it is a fair bet the upholstery is in bad shape and that the car has seen hard use. If the upholstery is exposed, look for signs of abnormal wear. A sagging driv-

While good-quality retreads can be perfectly serviceable (they are used on trucks and airplanes), those installed by a used-car dealer are apt to be inexpensive and risky.

Look instead for four matching tires—or, at least, two matching pairs—with uniformly worn treads; they suggest that the owner was a careful driver who knew how to maintain a car properly. Be sure the car has a usable spare tire and tire-changing tools.

What else can the outside of the car tell you?

er's seat and worn armrest indicate the car may have had longer and heavier use than you thought. You should expect the front seats to show more wear than those in back. Don't worry about dirt and scuff marks. Usually they can be removed fairly easily, especially from vinyl upholstery. Cuts and cracks, depending on their extent, may be another matter.

One of the most popular places to look for wear is the pedals—accelerator, brake and clutch. The trouble is that dealers know that people always look there, so they routinely replace pedals that show a lot of wear. But more important than wear is how well the pedals work. Try them with the engine off. The accelerator should feel firm and should not wobble when depressed; it should spring back promptly when pressure is released.

Now try the brake. It should not sink more than an inch or two, no matter how hard it is pressed; and you should not feel as if you were stepping on a wet sponge: a spongy pedal spells trouble in the braking system.

If the car has a clutch pedal, you can check it for firmness, but the real test of the clutch must wait until you get the car on the road.

Now check out the rest of the driver's controls. You probably will have to turn the ignition key to unlock the steering wheel and activate the dashboard warning lights, buzzers and gauges. It's important to know what they all mean, but it's more important to look for signals that aren't working when they should be. The problem may be nothing more than a loose wire, but it is essential that everything on the dashboard works correctly.

Turn the steering wheel left until you feel pressure, and then right until you feel pressure again. Most steering wheels have a bit of free play built into them. But more than two inches of free play is unsafe and could indicate a serious problem with the steering mechanism. If the car has power steering, this test must be done after the engine is started.

Now, with the engine running, pause and listen. It should start quickly and quietly. With your foot off the accelerator, the engine should idle smoothly. A too-slow idle, which can lead to stalling, usually can be adjusted easily. But a fast idle that sounds as if the car is ready to take off may be a deliberate attempt to conceal sounds of a worn-out or damaged engine. Ask the salesman to slow the idling speed. If he can't or won't, consider passing up the car.

Your first hard look at the engine should come now, while it is idling but before it has had time to warm up fully. However, when you lift the hood of the purring power plant, remember that what you hear is usually more important than what you see. Listen to the sound of what's happening inside the engine—a symphony of explosions, squishes and hums.

Listen for unusual noises like pings, scrapes, knocks, grinds and squeals. It is difficult for the untrained ear to pick out normal from abnormal sounds in an engine, but you should be suspicious of any noise loud enough to be heard above the relatively quiet engine sound. If you do hear an objectionable or frightening noise, it's best to assume the worst and reject the car. Don't dismiss the noise because it disappears after the engine warms up. Cold engines are more revealing than hot ones.

Casing the car on the road

If you're satisfied with the idling engine, you're ready for a road test. Since this is the ultimate performance test, don't simply settle for a spin around the block. Tell the salesman you want to take the car out for a half hour—or longer. He may not be happy about the idea, so be prepared for a variety of negative responses.

"Sorry, we don't have plates for that car." Don't believe it. All dealers have special

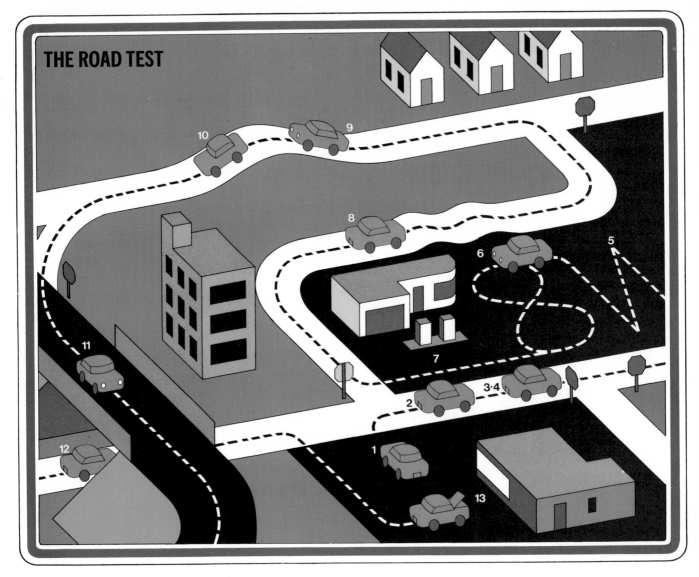

THE ROAD TEST

No car—especially a used one—should be bought without a thorough road test. This 13-item check list, keyed to the illustration above, can be completed in 30 minutes.

Dealer's lot: (1) With the car in neutral, race the engine and check the exhaust. White smoke is normal, blue smoke means an untuned carburetor, black smoke hints at a worn engine. Engage the parking brake, shift into gear and depress the gas pedal slowly. If the car will not overcome the brake, the clutch or transmission may be faulty. (The problem may be with the brake, of course, but that test comes later.)

Starting out: (2) Accelerate smoothly to 30 mph. If a manual shift's gearbox sticks or grinds and the clutch offers little resistance, or if an automatic hesitates noticeably between shifts, the car's transmission is questionable. **(3)** Slow from 30 mph by gently pumping the brake pedal. If the pedal is not firm, suspect leaky brake cylinders. **(4)** Now brake hard from 5 mph. Squealing or swerving indicates worn brake linings.

Empty parking lot: (5) Brake to a halt, then rapidly shift from drive to reverse to drive, braking to a halt each time and accelerating to no more than 10 mph each way. Chattering or stalling suggests a worn automatic transmission. **(6)** Drive a tight figure 8 at a moderate speed. Slow steering response may mean worn steering linkage. **(7)** Accelerate to 25 mph and take your hands from the wheel. Veering means improper wheel balance or alignment.

Bumpy road: (8) Drive over an uneven road at a moderate speed. Bouncing or swaying indicates a bad suspension.

Hill: (9) Pick a hill steep enough to be troublesome if it were covered with snow. Stop on the upslope. Accelerate to 30 mph. Sluggishness points to engine or transmission trouble. **(10)** Brake on the downslope. If the car stops slowly or noisily, suspect worn brake linings. Park on the downslope and set the parking brake; it should hold.

Highway: (11) From a full stop accelerate quickly to 60 mph. If it takes more than 20 seconds, the engine may need tuning.

In town: (12) Pick a street with an underpass, or lined with buildings or parked cars, which amplify noises. With the driver's window down, brake and accelerate several times and listen for unusual engine, transmission or exhaust sounds. Make note of them for later discussion with a mechanic.

Dealer's lot: (13) Park, but leave the engine idling. After a few minutes, move the car and check the pavement for leaks. Turn off the ignition, lift the hood and look for fresh leaks in the engine compartment.

plates that they can use on any of their cars.

"Sorry, we're not insured." Dealers carry blanket policies that cover all their cars.

"Won't you take my word for it? The car's a jewel!" If it's really a jewel, he should be proud to have you appraise it.

"You don't have to take a test ride. Our guarantee covers everything." Let it cover problems that turn up *after* the test ride.

"You'll have to sign this paper. It just guarantees that you'll be responsible for any damage." Careful! It might also guarantee that you will buy the car.

"We don't permit test drives." Find yourself another dealer.

Often the salesman's reluctance to permit a test drive is based not so much on any apprehension about the car's performance as on personal inconvenience. Many dealers make the salesman go along on test drives and the longer he is off the lot, the fewer cars he can sell.

The ideal solution is to schedule the test drive at a mutually convenient time. But even if that is not possible, insist on the test drive as a condition of the sale. You wouldn't buy a used house without checking out the heat, electricity, water pressure and sewerage. So you are equally justified in checking out the various systems—such as engine, drive train, steering and brakes—of a used car. The check list and map on page 100 provide an assortment of suitable tests for this purpose.

But what if you want that car so badly that you're willing to put your money down after a quick run around the block—or simply around the dealer's lot? Consider the experience of Vinnie, who fell in love with a sporty red hardtop on the front line at Rockbottom Used Cars. The car was an absolute doll. Brand-new tires, spotless engine, gleaming paint—and only 22,000 miles on the odometer. A steal at $999, the salesman said as he accompanied Vinnie

for a short ride. Notice how fast the engine started? Get a load of that pickup. Listen to that engine. That's power. Vinnie could hardly get his money out of the bank fast enough.

Behind the wheel of his new used car, Vinnie shrugged off the fact that the engine now seemed to grind for quite a while before starting up. He didn't even mind too much when he drove over a pothole and the car lurched heavily to one side. He was only mildly annoyed when he went out that night and found that one of his headlights wasn't working. The muttering began when it started to rain and Vinnie discovered that his windshield wipers didn't work. As each day went by, he found other disconcerting things. He began to hear odd noises—thumps, rattles, pings and chatters. A smelly blue cloud seemed to follow him everywhere. At high speeds Vinnie had to hang on to the steering wheel to keep from veering. To make matters worse, after only a few weeks the shiny red paint looked dull and vaguely purple.

The people at Rockbottom Used Cars fixed the headlight and the windshield wipers, but assured Vinnie there was nothing else wrong with the car—or at least nothing he hadn't had a chance to find out before he bought it. The salesman who had been so helpful shrugged as Vinnie recited all the things that had gone wrong with the car. "It's a used car," he said. "You have to expect these things."

The day of reckoning came when the car simply quit while Vinnie was trying to drive to work one morning. At the garage where it had to be towed, a mechanic examined the car and shook his head sadly.

"So far, you've got a burned-out transmission, a cracked block and a welded axle. This car has had a lot of hard miles and it's been in a wreck. It'll cost more to fix than it's worth."

Vinnie had learned—the hard way—that a cheap coat of paint, a set of retreads, and a steam-cleaned engine can make a dog look like a cream puff. And he had also learned that a little artful doctoring—charging up an old battery, adjusting the carburetor to a high idle, heavily greasing worn gears and bearings—can make a worn-out car seem full of pep for a little while.

Getting a fair price and a guarantee

If Vinnie had subjected the car to a thorough road test, he probably wouldn't have bought it. And if he had taken it to a garage for a checkup, he would have rejected it—and Rockbottom Used Cars—immediately. Such a checkup is an excellent way to find out things about a car's condition that no amount of testing by the buyer can reveal. For a flat fee, many garages will run your car through a battery of tests that provide accurate information ranging from cylinder compression to front-end alignment (*check list, opposite*). You can also get your car checked at one of the diagnostic centers that have sprung up across the nation in recent years. These centers provide a standard series of tests. The findings are recorded on a printed form. A careful reading of the form, combined with your own observations on the lot and behind the wheel, should tell you all you would want to know about a used car.

Which brings us to the final step in the process of buying a used car. Now that you have found a car you like and have checked it thoroughly enough to satisfy yourself of its condition, you're ready to buy. Or, to use the terminology of the car business, you are ready to close the deal. It might be well to review here just what goes into a used-car deal.

■ DEALER'S PRICE. This is the price you were given when you first saw the car. It is merely a base for bargaining. The final price should be lower—and never higher.

■ YOUR PRICE. It should be based as closely as possible on current competitive prices and not on hearsay. Your own brother-in-law, who bought a used car a couple of years ago and who is sure you can buy your car for half of the dealer's price, usually is not the best authority. Be prepared to revise your price upward or downward to reflect the condition of the car and the estimated cost of repairs.

■ DEALER'S REPAIRS. Dealers will sometimes agree to make repairs as a precondition of sale. This is a good bargaining point for the dealer. But do not assume that he will use top-quality parts; he may use rebuilt ones or some from junk cars.

■ BUYER REPAIRS. You might prefer to make a list of repairs you will have to pay for after purchase, and use it to get the dealer to lower his price. But don't expect him to deduct the full amount of your estimate. Repairs that may cost you $300 will cost him about half that, and his cost is the best offer you can expect.

■ TRADE-IN. Many used-car dealers don't like to take older used cars in trade and will tell you so. But if your old car is clean and has been well maintained, the dealer should offer you at least the minimum wholesale value, a price he can recover at the next dealer's auction. Should you decide to sell your old car privately, or keep it around for a second or third car, make sure the dealer knows about it. By relieving him of the chore of selling your old car, you should be able to bring down the price.

■ GUARANTEE. The type of guarantee provided by the dealer can greatly affect the selling price. Obviously, a deal with no guarantees means that the buyer is trading the risk of future repairs for an attractive purchase price.

Most used-car dealers offer a standard guarantee that covers the car's basic systems, such as the engine and drive train, for 30 days or 1,000 miles. But even within the limited period

A CHECK LIST FOR YOUR MECHANIC

The final, and most important, examination of a used car should be made by an experienced and reliable mechanic. The check list below covers most of the places where trouble is likely to occur —or already has. The potential buyer should go over the check list with the mechanic before and after commissioning the work: before, in order to make clear the extent of the examination and to fix the charge for the service; afterward, to pin down needed repairs and probable trouble spots.

Under the hood

1. Loose or worn belts
2. Worn or leaking hoses
3. Radiator leaks
4. Engine cracks or leaks
5. Ignition timing
6. Spark-plug examination
7. Cylinder compression
8. Carburetor examination
9. Crankcase ventilation valve
10. Exhaust-system damage
11. Clutch-pedal free play
12. Oil level and condition
13. Battery voltage and electrolyte level
14. Brake-cylinder fluid level
15. Alternator efficiency
16. Brake-pedal travel and free play
17. Air-conditioning system

On the lift

1. Axle damage or leaks
2. Drive-shaft lubricant leaks
3. Transmission-oil leaks
4. Exhaust-system damage
5. Shock-absorber damage or leaks
6. Ball-joint play
7. Steering play
8. Brake-fluid leaks
9. Brake-lining wear
10. Gas-tank damage and leaks
11. Underbody corrosion

Wheels and tires

1. Wheel alignment and balance
2. Tire condition

covered by the guarantee, repairs are made on no better than a 50-50 basis; you pay at least half the cost. It is not uncommon for dealers to farm out guarantee work to private shops. These shops may be told to double the bill and then charge the customer half the amount. In any case a 50-50 guarantee should have little if any impact on the car's price.

Be wary of the dealer's offer of the unused portion of a new-car warranty. Few used cars are sold with new-car warranties still in effect. When they are, the warranties can be transferred only if the manufacturer approves. Even then, there may be a charge.

Some dealers offer various types of extended guarantees that may be worth something. Be careful, however, because used-car guarantees are never models of generosity. A typical arrangement might call for extending the period covered by the 50-50 repairs to six months or even a year. Such extensions, however, usually cost the buyer an extra fee.

Once the various parts of the deal have been determined and evaluated, and the cash payment agreed upon, you can proceed with the final steps that will put you in the driver's seat. Financing (Chapter 4) a used car is much the same as financing a new car. But if you plan to take out a car loan, you should be aware that most banks and lending institutions require larger down payments and charge higher interest rates for used cars than for new ones.

Once the deal has been made, it is customary to leave a deposit until the car has been registered at the local office of the state motor vehicle department—or the registration of your old car has been officially transferred. In some states this may require an inspection of brakes, suspension system, tires, lights, windshield wipers, horn, steering, exhaust system and seat belts. In New York State, for example, it is the responsibility of the dealer to make sure that any car he sells meets state requirements. (It can, however, be sold as "junk" and restored by the buyer to meet inspection.)

With ownership documents in hand, license plates in place and key in ignition, you are now the owner of a used car. Or, if you prefer the tonier euphemism, a previously owned car. It may be a year-old Cadillac or a 12-year-old Plymouth, but if you bought well you have the car you want, in good condition, at a price you can afford. And remember, it's the only one exactly like it in the whole world.

FINANCING

HOLDING DOWN THE COSTS OF OWNERSHIP

SHOPPING FOR THE BEST LOAN
SHOULD YOU PAY CASH?
SOME CAUTIONS BEFORE YOU SIGN
IMPORTANCE OF THE APR
A HARD LOOK AT OPERATING EXPENSES
KNOWING WHEN TO TRADE
LEASE OR BUY?

4

"Oddly enough," says a recent study done by the U.S. Department of Transportation, "many owners do not seem to be aware of many of their automobile costs." Only when a motorist is faced with a major outlay—for new tires or for major repairs, for example—does he show some concern. "Otherwise," continues the government report, "he drives his vehicle and seems to conclude that his trips are costing very little." In fact, the very opposite is true. For many American families, annual automobile expenditures exceed what they have to spend on food or clothing or even on shelter.

Apart from considering any financing charges (which add several hundred dollars to the cost of the majority of cars bought in the United States), the study examined a fairly typical situation and offered the following analysis of costs for a $4,379 standard-sized sedan owned by a suburban family and driven an average of 12,000 miles per year over a four-year period:

Depreciation	$3,301.00
Repairs and maintenance	$735.95
Tire replacement	$102.07
Accessories	$12.08
Gasoline	$969.21
Oil	$46.50
Insurance	$623.00
Garaging, parking, tolls, etc.	$778.60
State taxes and fees	$549.36
Federal taxes	$152.90

The grand total works out to $7,270.67—or an average of $1,817.67 per year.

A head-on look at the costs involved in owning a car can be a dismaying experience, but it also should be a challenge—because there almost always is room for improvement. Any car owner can hope to beat the averages by driving carefully and maintaining his car properly, thus minimizing his repair bills and operating expenses. And in the matter of insurance, the cost of which varies a good deal, there are a number of ways to save money (Chapter 5).

Still another road to economy lies in knowing when to trade your car for a new one. This decision hinges on the relationship between depreciation and the costs of maintenance, including tire replacement (graph, page 108). Depreciation (the car's loss of value as it grows older) is not constant; rather, it occurs at a decreasing rate through the years. A car will depreciate a great deal the first year after it is purchased, less the next year, still less the third year, and so on. Maintenance follows an opposite trend, starting low and rising. As the car grows older it will require replacement of its tires and other equipment, and suffer more frequent mechanical troubles, all of which often can more than offset the money saved by the decreased depreciation.

According to a consensus of experts in the field, the most economical course is to trade a car that is driven about 12,000 miles a year during the fourth year of ownership. However, this recommendation is based on statistical averages and may not apply to you. If, for instance, you have a trouble-prone car, you may be better off getting rid of it early. On the other hand, if you have a particularly trouble-free car or one that depreciates slowly, and if you take good care of the vehicle, you may be wise to keep it for an additional year or two past the indicated trade-in point.

Clearly, there are numerous variables. And, in fact, your own decision about when to trade may well be based on something quite unrelated to cost. For instance, you simply may have a preference for recent models. But you should at least be aware that substantial sums of money are at stake.

The cost of borrowing money

There is another major expense over which car owners have considerable control, although they don't always realize it. This item is the cost of the money you use to purchase the car. If you pay cash, the real cost is more than the sum you actually hand over to the dealer, since, if you had left the cash in a savings account or invested it, the money at least would have earned interest or dividends. On the other hand, if you borrow the money, your cost is the interest on the loan. In short, money costs money—sometimes a little, sometimes a lot.

About four of every five buyers take out an installment loan when they buy a car, paying off the debt in fixed monthly sums. In most cases the collateral for the loan is the car itself. If the borrower defaults on his payments, the car can be repossessed—in effect, forcibly seized—and sold to someone else. If the resale price does not cover the balance of the note (and it almost never does) the borrower may be sued for the difference, plus repossession charges, court costs and attorney's fees.

Auto financing can be obtained from a variety of sources: a commercial bank, a savings bank in one of the 12 states where such institutions are permitted to make consumer loans, a credit union, a finance company or the automobile dealer himself. The costs of auto loans vary widely and you should shop for financing just as carefully as you would for the car. Before 1969, comparison shopping for loans often was difficult and very frustrating because lenders described their loans in a variety of ways—in terms of monthly payments, for instance, or various methods of charging interest. But in 1969 the Truth in Lending Law

AUTOMOBILE OPERATING COSTS

The costs of operating a standard V8 sedan (with automatic transmission, power steering, power brakes and air conditioning) and those of a six-cylinder compact have been compiled by the Department of Transportation on the basis of a survey in a suburban Baltimore neighborhood. Some costs, such as insurance premiums, vary greatly from area to area but most of those given below are typical for most parts of the country.

The assumption of declining mileage over a four-year period is based on studies of drivers' experience. An owner who annually drives his car fewer miles than the norms given in the table does not, however, lower his costs per mile. He saves on gasoline, oil, tires and repairs, but insurance, garage rent and depreciation are the same as for a car with higher mileage, so the average cost per mile may be even greater.

	First year (14,500 miles)		Second year (13,000 miles)		Third year (11,500 miles)		Fourth year (10,000 miles)	
	Standard	Compact	Standard	Compact	Standard	Compact	Standard	Compact
Depreciation	$1,226.00	$674.00	$900.00	$519.00	$675.00	$394.00	$500.00	$305.00
cents per mile	8.46¢	4.65¢	6.92¢	3.99¢	5.87¢	3.42¢	5.0¢	3.05¢
Repairs, parts, maintenance, tires and accessories	$102.95	$97.92	$134.50	$123.93	$269.33	$185.70	$343.32	$256.00
cents per mile	.7¢	.68¢	1.03¢	.96¢	2.34¢	1.62¢	3.43¢	2.56¢
Gas and oil (excluding taxes)	$298.00	$254.75	$268.41	$229.47	$239.58	$204.93	$209.72	$179.64
cents per mile	2.06¢	1.75¢	2.07¢	1.77¢	2.08¢	1.79¢	2.1¢	1.79¢
Insurance	$164.00	$155.00	$156.00	$147.00	$156.00	$147.00	$147.00	$140.00
cents per mile	1.13¢	1.07¢	1.20¢	1.13¢	1.36¢	1.28¢	1.47¢	1.40¢
Garaging, parking and tolls	$208.36	$208.36	$199.22	$199.22	$190.08	$190.08	$180.94	$180.94
cents per mile	1.44¢	1.44¢	1.53¢	1.53¢	1.65¢	1.65¢	1.81¢	1.81¢
Federal and state taxes and fees	$326.01	$231.12	$136.62	$110.80	$125.12	$100.34	$114.51	$91.69
cents per mile	2.25¢	1.59¢	1.06¢	.85¢	1.09¢	.87¢	1.14¢	.92¢
TOTAL COSTS	$2,325.32	$1,621.15	$1,794.75	$1,329.42	$1,655.11	$1,222.05	$1,495.49	$1,153.27
cents per mile	16.04¢	11.18¢	13.81¢	10.23¢	14.39¢	10.63¢	14.95¢	11.53¢

ECONOMICS OF THE AGING CAR

Ever since the first automobile took to the road, car owners have pondered and debated the questions: "How long should I keep my car? When does it become more expensive to hold on to it than to trade it in?" There are no pat answers—if there were, the debates would have ended long ago.

The chart *(below)*, based on a study by the U.S. Department of Transportation, shows *(blue line)* the rate over a 10-year span at which the average car's value depreciates, as a percentage of its original cost. The chart also shows *(red line)* the average cost of repairs and maintenance, including tire replacement, as a percentage of the car's value in each of the 10 years.

In the car's seventh year, maintenance costs are greater than the vehicle itself is worth, as the crossing of the blue and red lines indicates.

But some experts point out that the optimum time for trading actually comes substantially earlier: at the end of a new car's fourth year of ownership. From then on the gap between the car's value and the cost to keep it going begins to narrow sharply, making ownership uneconomical.

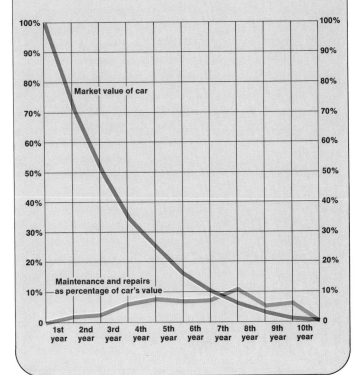

became effective. It compels all lenders to speak to their customers in the same easy-to-understand language.

The Truth in Lending Law requires a lender to reveal a number of essential facts about a loan. For shopping purposes, two of these facts are particularly important:

■ THE TRUE ANNUAL PERCENTAGE RATE (APR). This figure represents in percentage form the effective annual interest rate, and it also reflects all other compulsory finance charges, such as credit-report fees.

■ THE TOTAL FINANCE CHARGE. This figure represents the dollar sum of all interest charges plus additional fees.

At this point there is one caution. Insurance is included in the APR and in the total finance charge only if the insurance is compulsory and is so specified in the contract of purchase. Some lenders get around that provision by having the borrower sign a separate entry on the contract. That device makes the car insurance technically an option and therefore exempt from inclusion in the APR and finance charges. Lenders almost always require that you have insurance covering the car for the life of the loan. But remember—you do not have to buy the insurance from the lender.

Despite the Truth in Lending Law, when you ask a lender about the cost of a loan he might begin, even today, by talking in terms of the monthly payments you can elect to pay, or you may find yourself trying to cope with such words in the financing lexicon as add-on or discount *(box, page 110)*. Insist that he tell you the true annual percentage rate as well as the total finance charge. He cannot legally refuse to give them to you.

Either of these numbers will give you a basis for comparing the offers of different lenders. Many experts advise shopping for the lowest APR and then arranging terms to fit your ability to meet payments. The APR, they insist, is the better yardstick. On the other hand, some people still find dollar figures easier to comprehend than percentages; they prefer to consider first the total finance charge. Unlike the APR, the finance charge will reflect the important effect time has on the cost of a loan. For example, a 36-month loan (available to anyone with a good credit rating) will cost half again as much as a 24-month loan bearing the same true annual percentage rate, since interest would be paid over three years instead of two. Of course, there is another side to this particular borrowed coin: the monthly payments for the shorter term will be higher, since the loan must be paid off sooner.

So, in choosing a repayment period for a loan, your optimum course should be obvious: take the loan for as short a time and for as high a monthly payment as you can manage—realistically, without endangering your ability to meet all your other monthly obligations and unforeseen emergency expenses. That way, if you have obtained the lowest APR available, you'll be money ahead.

Which lender should you choose?

■ AUTOMOBILE DEALERS. Approximately 50 per cent of all buyers who finance the purchase of a new car get their loan through the dealer. This course is convenient, but it is not necessarily the most economical. Dealers do not ordinarily finance customers out of their own funds. Instead, to avoid tying up their capital, they "sell the paper" at a discount to a lending institution—a bank, or a sales-finance company. The latter is a lending institution that does not normally deal directly with consumers. The category includes independent companies, as well as subsidiaries of auto manufacturers, whose primary function is to provide credit financing to dealers and buyers.

EXAMINE THE FINE PRINT

Before you sign up for an automobile loan, read —and make sure you understand—every word of the contract. Since the enactment of the Truth in Lending Law in 1969, certain facts about the agreement must be clearly specified; of these, the first two listed below are of basic importance:

☐ The loan's true annual percentage rate, to the nearest quarter of 1 per cent.

☐ The total finance charge in dollars and cents —i.e., interest plus any other compulsory fees conditional to the granting of credit. An example of such a fee would be a charge for a credit report.

☐ The total amount being financed.

☐ The number, amounts and dates of payments.

☐ The penalty for default or late payment, and a definition of what the lender considers lateness.

☐ The opportunity for a rebate. The contract must stipulate the amount of money, if any, to be returned if you pay off the loan ahead of schedule.

☐ The insurance premiums for which you are being asked to sign up. Collision and comprehensive insurance policies executed in the name of the lender usually are required to protect him should the car be stolen, damaged or destroyed. Insurance on the borrower's life for the duration of the loan also may be demanded. But the premiums on policies for which the lender personally makes arrangements may be substantially greater than those available from other sources, and the claim service of the designated company inferior. If you provide the required insurance, you may buy it wherever and as inexpensively as you wish.

☐ The extras that may have been slipped in. If the contract includes compulsory credit, accident and health insurance, the cost of such coverage must be clearly disclosed in the finance charge. On the other hand, if the coverage is elective, you are under no obligation to buy it.

A MUST QUESTION FOR BORROWERS

The 1969 federal Truth in Lending Law requires that all lenders disclose the cost of credit, including all finance charges and the true annual percentage rate (APR) of interest on each loan. The APR takes into account not only the fact that any stated simple-interest charge does not reflect the month-to-month decline of the balance owed, but also the fact that many lenders use either the add-on or the discount method in calculating their charges. In shopping for the best possible deal, it will help if you understand the particulars of how add-on and discount loans work:

■ THE ADD-ON. With this kind of loan, the entire amount of interest to be paid is added at the outset to the amount the borrower requests. The APR is then calculated on this total figure.

Assume, for example, that you need a two-year $3,300 loan and the lender says your annual simple-interest charge will be only $5 per $100, or $165 per year; on a two-year loan the total comes to $330. That $330 added to the $3,300 will make your total debt $3,630—which will be payable in 24 monthly installments of $151.25. On that basis the APR is 9.3 per cent—not 5 per cent—because for all but the first of the 24 months, your steadily declining debt will be less than $3,630. (On a three-year loan at the same rate, the added finance charge will be $495—i.e., three times $165—and your monthly payments $105.42. The APR will still be 9.3 per cent.)

■ THE DISCOUNT. With this kind of loan, the interest charge is deducted in full at the start. So, to obtain all of the $3,300 you require in cash, the amount of your loan actually would have to be $3,667. Your monthly payments would come to $152.79 and the true APR would be 10.3 per cent. (To get $3,300 in cash on a *three*-year loan, you would have to borrow $3,882—the $3,300 plus $582 in interest—and your 36 monthly payments would be $107.83 each. The APR would increase to 10.9 per cent.)

So, whenever you must borrow money—for a car or anything else—be sure you ask the one indispensable question of every potential lender: What is the true annual percentage rate? The answer could help save you a lot of money.

The rate of interest the dealer offers depends pretty much on current market conditions in your area. If a competitor is offering a relatively low rate, your dealer may find it wise to match that rate. Your own credit rating also is a factor. If your income is substantial and your financial reputation is good, you may get a better deal than the next buyer.

If, however, the dealer can induce a customer to accept an APR several percentage points above the rate charged by his own credit source, he can pocket some of the difference. There are large-volume dealers who actually make more money financing loans than they do by selling cars.

Dealers occasionally use the sales pitch that their loan rates are somehow "official." But there is no such thing as an official rate. Any lender, including a car dealer, can charge anything up to the limit set by the state's installment sales act (an APR of 15 per cent is about the maximum for new cars in most states). Do not accept at face value any claims that the dealer's rates are the best available, although sometimes they may be. Always check elsewhere to be sure.

One other caveat needs mentioning. Some car buyers choose to finance their purchase through the dealer because they think they can get better service by threatening to stop payment on the loan. This may only lead to trouble, because installment payments do not go to the dealer but to the bank or finance company that holds the loan contract. Stopping payment may well cost you your car. (There are other safeguards if you do have trouble with the car. When you buy, you sign two contracts—one with the dealer, for the purchase, and the other for your loan. The contract with the dealer should provide a warranty against defects in the automobile.)

■ BANKS. As a rule, banks offer the general

public the best terms available anywhere —about 2 per cent below the average APR charged by dealers. Although many banks still require a car buyer to make a down payment of about 25 per cent of a new car's retail price, some are relaxing this requirement and will finance the entire purchase.

Large banks will charge most of their customers a uniform rate, but if you are an especially good customer, you may be able to get favorable treatment. Bargaining is more likely to work at small banks. In any case, it is worth your while to check with more than one bank. Banks, too, are competing with one another for business, and a bank that is especially aggressive in the auto-loan field may offer terms at a given time that are substantially better than those of its competitors. Some banks occasionally even hold "loan sales," dropping their rates to lure customers.

■ CREDIT UNIONS. A credit union is a voluntary association of people who share some bond, such as employment by the same company or membership in the same church. Some 23,000 such associations exist in the United States, and millions of people belong. Chartered either by the federal government or the state, credit unions are empowered to pay interest on deposit accounts and to make loans. Because they are nonprofit organizations and often are subsidized by employers, they usually are able to offer rates as low as or lower than those of a bank. A standard APR among credit unions is 9 per cent, and this figure includes life insurance to cover the amount of the loan. Also, credit unions often are more forgiving than banks when loan payments are occasionally late.

Usually, members can borrow up to $2,500 from a credit union on their signatures alone. If a car is used as collateral, there is hardly ever a limit, although a down payment equal to 25 per cent of the car's price is a standard requirement. A larger down payment is likely to gain an interest rate below the norm.

■ CONSUMER FINANCE COMPANIES. People who do not belong to a credit union and who cannot get a loan from a bank because they are considered poor risks usually can arrange credit financing through one of these small-loan firms. But, because they are high-risk lenders, finance companies by and large charge the highest rates around. Furthermore, in some states the amount of the loan is restricted by law, although there is a trend away from such limitations.

Before going to a finance company, you certainly ought to investigate other sources of credit; in the trade, finance companies are sometimes referred to as lenders of last resort.

Take advantage of your savings

Paying cash is usually the cheapest way to buy a car, although anybody who is fortunate enough to be earning 12 per cent or better annually on invested money doesn't have to be told that taking out a loan would be more economical than wiping out the investment. Yet even when a cash payment makes the most sense and the money is available, many people nonetheless opt to take out a loan, for reasons that are more psychological than economic. They feel that it's worth paying a little extra in order to keep their savings account intact and to have the discipline of paying off a loan, rather than relying on their will power to replenish the account. But they still can gain some advantage from their savings by using the money as collateral for a passbook loan. Such loans are obtainable from commercial banks, savings banks and savings-and-loan associations.

The passbook loan is a way of borrowing money from yourself. Since the loan is thoroughly secured by cash, it will have a lower cost than a conventional auto loan; the lender is taking no risk. In fact, the compound interest that your savings account continues to earn will be greater than the finance charges you pay for the loan (box, opposite).

Savings-and-loan associations customarily make passbook loans for 1 1/2 per cent more than the rate of interest they pay on your account. The rate differential is more than overcome by the compound interest earned. With savings banks the usual rate is 2 per cent more. And commercial banks, which pay lower interest on savings accounts, usually exact 4 per cent or more. The interest you pay on a passbook loan is, like other interest charges, deductible in computing your income tax. On passbook loans, you generally are allowed to borrow against 95 per cent of your savings.

Buy it or lease it?

Companies that need cars for business purposes sometimes discover that leasing is more economical than buying. Company cars typically suffer much more abuse than vehicles that are privately owned, and with leased cars the company doesn't have the problem of disposing of these vehicles. Individuals, too (especially doctors, lawyers and small-business owners), sometimes lease cars because they can afford the convenience and can charge off a large portion of what becomes a demonstrable nonpersonal expense as a business cost. But for the average individual, leasing is substantially more expensive than buying.

If, for example, you sign a 24-month lease for a car that carries a manufacturer's list price of $4,400, the leasing charge would be about $125 per month, or $3,000 over two years. What if you purchased this car instead of leasing it? Assuming you can negotiate a typical discount of 15 per cent from the car's $4,400 sticker price, you will buy the car for $3,740. Let's also

assume that you finance the entire purchase with a 24-month loan that has an APR of 10 per cent. Your monthly loan payments would be $172.59—or $47.59 per month more than for the leasing arrangement. Over a two-year period, that difference will add up to $1,142.16.

However, at the end of the two-year period you will own the automobile, which (assuming good condition) would have a book value of just about half its original sticker price, or $2,200. Subtracting the $1,142.16 in additional payments, you still would be $1,057.84 ahead by buying rather than leasing.

If you do decide to lease a car, you will be offered a choice of two different types of contract: open end and closed end. The former is open because at the end of the lease period it is an open question as to whether—and how much—you still owe the leasing company. Sometimes the car's estimated wholesale value at the end of the period will be stipulated in the open-end contract as the buy-back price. When the lease expires, you can purchase the car yourself for the same figure. You also have the option of selling the car. Or you can turn it back to the lessor to be sold for the best price. If the best price the leasing company can get is less than the buy-back price agreed on originally, you have to make up the difference.

A person who chooses an open-end contract might find himself owing a considerable sum of money he hadn't anticipated if the car cannot be resold for the buy-back price. On the other hand, if he has taken exceptionally good care of the automobile, it might be worth more than the buy-back price and he could pocket the difference.

On a closed-end lease, you turn in the car at the termination of the lease, and that's the end of it. Obviously such an arrangement is more conducive to peace of mind since your costs are more predictable. But they are not quite so

THE BENEFITS OF A PASSBOOK LOAN

If you have money in a savings account, you can use it as collateral for a low-cost passbook loan. The bank or savings-and-loan association that offers this type of loan is taking no risk. It can, therefore, offer you money at a rate of interest slightly higher than the interest your savings earn.

Let's say you want to borrow $3,300 in order to buy a new car. The chart below lists the important figures for a passbook loan in that amount when repaid in one-, two- or three-year periods.

For example, suppose you have $3,300 earning interest at a rate of 5 per cent compounded quarterly. You obtain a passbook loan and pay 6 1/2 per cent interest on the loan. However, that interest will be charged on a loan balance that declines with each monthly payment, making your total interest charge for two years $228.03. During these same two years, however, your savings account will earn $352.12, a difference of $124.09.

On the other hand, if you have lots of will power, you can do even better than that. If you draw the whole $3,300 from your account, and then discipline yourself to make monthly deposits equal to the payments of principal and interest on a passbook loan—$147.01 on $3,300 at 6 1/2 per cent—you would have $3,702.59 in two years.

	One-year loan	Two-year loan	Three-year loan
Interest earned in savings account	$171.60	$352.12	$542.03
Interest charge on loan	117.48	228.03	341.22
Net earnings on account after paying off loan	54.12	124.09	200.81
Bank balance at end of loan	$3,471.60	$3,652.12	$3,842.03
Balance after self-motivated monthly payments	$3,496.94	$3,702.59	$3,919.87

predictable as you might think. Most closed-end contracts have a clause that permits the lessor to charge you extra money at the end of the period if there is excessive wear and tear on the car. Furthermore, if you drive more than a stated number of miles, you can be charged up to three cents per extra mile.

What about the numerous other expenses involved in operating a leased car? The way these charges are handled depends on another pair of contract options. Under one kind of lease you are responsible for the costs of gasoline, oil, maintenance, tires, registration and insurance. Alternatively, some leasing companies offer a full-maintenance lease under which the leasing company will pay for everything except gas and oil, and will even provide another car while repairs are being made on the original one.

The virtue of the full-maintenance lease is that it offers maximum convenience and protects your budget against sudden disruptions. But it will add substantially to your monthly charge and it may not be a very good bargain. Chances are that you would be able to get insurance at a considerably lower rate than that procured by the leasing company. And while the maintenance provision will cost you $20 to $30 per month, the actual cost of maintenance usually is below that range during the first 24 months of a car's life.

For the average individual, leasing is a luxury no matter how the contract is written. The decision should be approached cautiously, with eyes wide open to the costs—both immediate and latent—that are involved in the convenience of using a car that isn't your own.

Similar advice applies, of course, to anyone who buys a car. Too many Americans spend more than they realize on cars, and certainly more than they have to.

INSURANCE

HOW MUCH YOU NEED AND WHERE TO GET IT

WHAT KIND OF COVERAGE?
COMPARISON SHOPPING FOR POLICIES
HOW TO RATE INSURERS
HOW TO CUT YOUR COSTS
NO-FAULT: WHAT IT IS AND ISN'T
WHAT DETERMINES YOUR PREMIUM
IF NO COMPANY WILL INSURE YOU

5

If you still wonder why car owners must pay so much for insurance coverage, accident statistics provide an incontrovertible answer. The harrowing odds are that virtually every person who drives a car for 10 years will be involved in at least one accident during that time. Expert insurance actuaries have calculated that 24 per cent of all drivers will be tapped by the statistical finger of fate during the first year they operate a car. After three years, the toll rises to 56 per cent. Three fourths of all drivers will have had an accident within five years and after 10 years the probability is just about 100 per cent. That's the reason underwriters sell more than $17 billion worth of automobile insurance each year.

The purpose of auto insurance is, of course, to guard your assets or those of a victim in the event that these statistics catch up with you.

Since insurance serves to pool the financial risks of a large number of clients, the cost of a particular accident is, in effect, spread around. If this were not so, the cost to the individual of protection against sudden financial disaster would be prohibitive. Nevertheless, insurance premiums represent one of the major costs of owning and operating a car.

While there's no escaping the fact that insurance is a major expense, the cost frequently can be cut down. Too many people assume that there is little difference between one company's rates and another's. This is a costly misconception. To prove how shopping around can repay the effort, the Illinois Insurance Department conducted an extensive comparison of premiums charged by different companies. In one extreme case, premiums quoted to the

THE TOLL OF THE AUTOMOBILE

The percentages of change since 1940 in three vital motor-vehicle statistics are traced in the graph below. By 1970 the number of miles traveled in motor vehicles by Americans *(green line)* went up 271 per cent following a slight decline during the years of World War II. The number of accidents of all kinds *(red line)* rose in the 1940-1970 period by about 162 per cent. But the number of traffic fatalities *(black line)* went up by a relatively small 59 per cent.

Experts cite a broad range of factors behind this heartening trend, including improvement of roads, safer cars, more effective laws and better drivers.

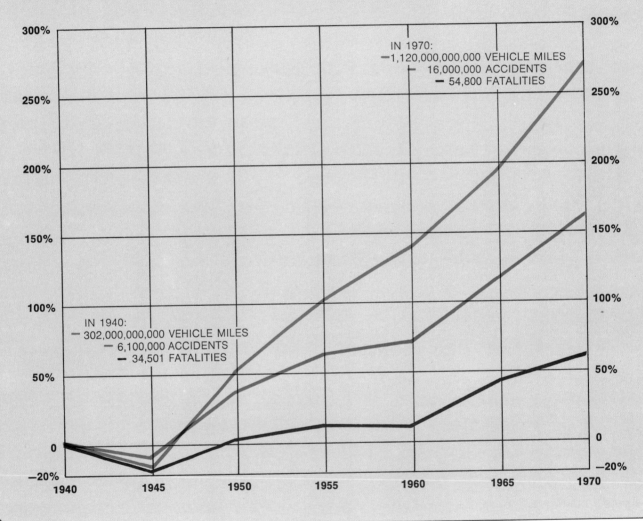

IN 1970:
— 1,120,000,000,000 VEHICLE MILES
— 16,000,000 ACCIDENTS
— 54,800 FATALITIES

IN 1940:
— 302,000,000,000 VEHICLE MILES
— 6,100,000 ACCIDENTS
— 34,501 FATALITIES

same driver for the same car, for virtually identical policies, ranged from a low of $257 to a high of $992 a year.

Before you can shop sensibly for insurance you must decide exactly what kinds of coverage you want and how much coverage of each kind. In approaching these questions you will quickly discover that automobile insurance is a rather complicated and subtle commodity. The typical policy is in reality an assemblage of a number of different financial protection components.

Most of the components in the policy pay for damage to the policyholder's car or for medical bills incurred by the policyholder and his passengers in an accident. If your car is stolen, if it burns, or if you collide with a telephone pole or with another car—to name just a few contingencies—your own losses are covered by parts of the policy called *comprehensive* and *collision*. Bodily injuries to you or to your passengers are covered by a part of the policy called *medical payments*. A coverage called *uninsured motorist* pays for bodily injury—and, in a few states, for physical damages, too—if you are in an accident caused by a hit-and-run driver or a driver who carries no insurance. All of these coverages are optional, with the occasional exception of *uninsured motorist*, which is compulsory in some states.

In addition to the coverages that compensate the policyholder and his passengers, there is another type that also pays for the property damage and bodily injuries sustained by the victims of an accident caused by the policyholder. This is *liability* coverage. You buy it for the benefit of others, not yourself, and you will never collect on it. Nevertheless, it may well be the most important part of your policy, and in a number of states it is compulsory to have liability coverage.

So far, we have been talking about the typical auto-insurance policy—but it may not be typical for long. In the near future every motorist may be required to carry a simpler straightforward kind of policy that is widely described as *no-fault*. As its label suggests, no-fault insurance is not concerned with who is to blame for an accident: it directly reimburses a motorist for his medical bills, lost wages or, if the worst should happen, burial expenses. (Property losses, however, are generally

THE LIABILITY SYSTEM: TWO VIEWS

Liability, in the context of automobile insurance, is a fancy word for fault. Traditionally motorists and insurers alike have believed that the person who causes an accident should be held accountable and he, or his insurance company, should pay all the costs. The traditionalists still believe so.

In recent years this view has been challenged by those who contend that nobody in his right mind would willfully cause an accident and so no liability—no fault—can be properly assigned. Under this concept, each party in an accident would be reimbursed by his own insurer for specific financial losses.

The biggest point of contention between opponents and advocates of no-fault is how to compensate victims for such intangibles as pain and suffering. No solution yet proposed satisfies everybody. But both sides agree the present system has major flaws:

Blame may be difficult to prove. In most states, a motorist who seeks to recover his losses in court (rather than settle out of court) must prove that responsibility for an accident lay entirely with the other driver. But it often is difficult to establish precisely what happened in the split second of collision. If the defendant's lawyer can show that the plaintiff bears even a small fraction of the blame, there will be no reimbursement at all. Fully 45 per cent of all persons seriously injured in auto accidents never recover anything from liability insurance.

The system is expensive. Of every premium dollar paid by policyholders, 56 cents is consumed by legal fees and overhead, leaving only 44 cents for accident victims.

Reparation is slow. Because of congestion in the courts and the necessity to investigate facts carefully in order to establish fault, an average of 16 months elapses between the time of an accident and the time when payment is made. In big-city courts the delay can stretch to four or five years.

The system is inequitable. To avoid legal expenses, insurance companies tend to settle smaller claims out of court—often overpaying—whereas they fight hard over large claims. Victims whose loss is less than $500 receive, on the average, four and a half times the amount the accident cost them. But victims with actual losses of more than $25,000 who manage to collect are reimbursed, on the average, for only one third.

117

not covered, and a motorist would have to carry *collision* to collect on damages to his car in an accident.) Under the ideal no-fault plan there would not be a need for the medical-payments, liability and uninsured-motorist coverages, since each driver would be entirely reimbursed by his own insurer, regardless of how an accident occurred or who was responsible. But the ideal does not yet exist.

Although a number of states already have adopted plans labeled no-fault (Massachusetts was the first, in 1970), all such plans are partial measures that leave the question of blame very much alive, thereby continuing to expose motorists to legal action for liability claims. For instance, one state's no-fault plan lets another driver sue you for any claim larger than $200 if he alleges that you were at fault. Certain other so-called no-fault plans don't have that limit but expose a driver to liability claims of any amount; such plans completely vitiate the intentions of the no-fault concept.

A thoroughgoing no-fault system would eliminate a great deal of the financial inefficiency and injustice that occurs regularly under the usual system *(box, page 117)*. Even the partial no-fault plans have brought some encouraging improvements. But if you live in a state whose insurance goes by the name of no-fault, do not take the description literally. You will still need some of the old-style coverages.

What coverage do you need —and how much?

■ LIABILITY. Whether your state makes this coverage obligatory or not, you need it—and don't skimp. More than any other kind of coverage, liability stands between you and utter ruin. You might find it financially inconvenient or even painful to smash your car against a telephone pole. But this expense is likely to be minuscule compared to the cost of injuring another person in an accident that is your

WHY HIGH LIABILITY COVERAGE IS A BARGAIN

Liability coverage pays for damage claims made against you when you are to blame for an accident. Naturally, as the amount of coverage goes up so does the premium—but nowhere near as fast. Modest rises in premiums bring disproportionately large boosts in coverage because big claims are less common.

Assuming, as a yardstick, that 10/20/5 coverage *(box, right)* carries a premium of $100, then:

    25/50/10 will cost about $118

    50/100/10 will cost about $127

    100/300/25 will cost about $136

    250/500/50 will cost about $145

Thus, in this representative example, 2,400 per cent more bodily injury coverage will cost only 45 per cent more than the premium for the lowest coverage.

fault. Juries tend to be generous to the victims of auto accidents. Some jury awards have exceeded one million dollars.

In the shorthand used by insurance salesmen, liability coverage usually is indicated by three numbers separated by slash marks: for instance, 10/20/5. The first two numbers are the limits on bodily injury coverage in thousands of dollars; if you carry 10/20/5, the 10 indicates that your insurance company will pay up to $10,000 for injuries to any single victim. The 20 indicates a maximum payout of $20,000 if more than one person is injured. (Bodily injury coverage includes claims for lost wages, burial expenses and "pain and suffering," as well as for medical bills.) The final figure, 5, refers to property damage; it indicates that if you are to blame for an accident, your insurance company will pay no more than $5,000 for damages to another car or a house or to other valuable property. The usual combinations in which liability coverage is sold are 10/20/5, 25/50/10, 50/100/10 and 100/300/25. Some insurance companies offer a "special package auto policy," which sets a single liability limit instead of multiple limits *(box, right)*.

If you are wise, you will choose a large amount of liability coverage. Many motorists are content to buy liability insurance to cover their personal assets—a strategy that makes sense only if you are willing to face bankruptcy in the event an injured party sues you for double that amount, thus taking your insurance plus all your assets.

It is far more sensible to carry high liability coverage—especially because the high combinations are a bargain. The box at left shows that, in buying liability insurance, protection increases dramatically with only modest increases in the premium price.

More affluent individuals who feel uneasy about the frequency with which enormous financial awards are being granted in accident cases might well consider buying a separate liability "umbrella." This feature typically raises your liability coverage to one million dollars for an extra yearly premium of about $60. It pays off claims for any kind of damage or injury you have caused, whether at home or away, in your automobile or out of it. Usually a liability umbrella is sold only to individuals who already have 100/300/25 auto liability and $50,000 worth of homeowner's liability. Many people who do not have a great deal of cash but who have nevertheless accumulated substantial physical assets through the years find the peace of mind worth the additional price.

■ COMPREHENSIVE. Apart from accidents, a great many unpleasant things can threaten your investment in a car. Comprehensive covers practically anything that can happen to a

A GOOD DEAL FOR GOOD DRIVERS

Some insurance companies make what is known as a special-package policy available to motorists whom they measure as good risks. It automatically includes liability, medical-payments and uninsured-motorist coverages, and is about 15 per cent cheaper than equivalent coverage under a standard policy. The reduction is possible partly because only good-risk drivers qualify, and partly because the medical-payments coverage does not pay for bills already fully covered by other medical insurance such as Blue Cross or any major-medical or surgical policies. On the other hand, standard automobile-insurance policies do provide such expensive duplicate compensation.

In addition to a lower premium, the special-package policy has an advantageous liability feature. Instead of stipulating three separate limits of liability, it has a single limit. Thus, where a 10/20/5 standard policy would pay $10,000 for bodily injuries to one person, $20,000 for all injuries and $5,000 for property damage, an equivalent amount of liability coverage would pay $25,000 for any combination of claims of whatever kind. Higher limits than those given in this example are available.

car when it is standing still and it covers a couple of kinds of collision as well. In the standard policy, comprehensive will pay you for physical damage or loss through fire, theft, flood, falling objects (including airplanes), explosion, earthquake, windstorm, lightning, hail, water, vandalism, riot and collision with a bird or animal. Comprehensive may also include an allowance for car rental if your vehicle is stolen, and some companies include coverage for theft of personal effects.

As a rule, comprehensive is well worth having, since it represents one of the lesser costs in your total insurance package. However, many car owners choose to put a lower limit, known as a deductible, on their coverage. The usual deductibles are $50 or $100. A deductible simply means that you will personally pay for your losses up to that limit and the insurance company covers the rest.

The deductible clause frees insurance companies from overhead costs for processing all small claims in addition to relieving a portion of their financial responsibility. And logically enough, the cost of your premium always goes down as your deductible goes up. In a typical policy, a $50 deductible may result in a 35 per cent decrease in the premium for comprehensive; a $100 deductible might reduce the premium by 56 per cent.

■ COLLISION . This coverage reimburses you for damage done to your car when you strike an object or when your car turns over. Collision coverage applies regardless of who is to blame for an accident.

As with comprehensive, collision claims are almost always limited by actual cash value, or ACV—the fair market value of the car or any of its parts. The insurance company's claims department determines the ACV by looking up your car in a pricing guide that is published primarily for used-car dealers (page 88). However, "stated amount" coverage can be obtained for antique cars, cherished older cars in superb condition or others for which regular used-car values are inappropriate. Naturally, stated amount coverage is more expensive than ACV and it will generally require an inspection by the insurance company's appraiser before the policy is issued.

Practically all collision insurance is written with a deductible provision, ranging from $50 all the way up to $1,000. As with comprehensive coverage, the more of the risk you personally assume—that is, the higher the deductible—the lower your premium (box, above).

THE TRADE-OFF IN COLLISION DEDUCTIBLES

Because the frequency of minor damage to automobiles would swamp insurance companies with claims, virtually all collision coverage is written with a deductible clause. This arrangement requires you personally to pay for damages up to the specified deductible amount; the insurance company pays the rest. The more risk you assume through your deductible, the less the coverage will cost.

Thus, if $50-deductible coverage costs $100 annually:

$100 deductible will cost about $85

$150 deductible will cost about $68

$250 deductible will cost about $51

$500 deductible will cost about $38

$1,000 deductible will cost about $21

Even with high deductibles, collision insurance is quite expensive. You are not compelled to carry it unless you are buying a car on time (understandably, lenders usually require collision insurance to protect their investment). But remember, you don't have to buy the policy from the lender; you may get a better rate elsewhere by making a few calls.

Many car owners feel that collision insurance is a waste of money on a car more than two years old. They think that it is more sensible to act as their own insurer, paying for damages out of their own savings rather than buying protection from an insurance company. They may well be right. For one thing, about 35 per cent of their premium dollar goes to pay insurance-company overhead; obviously, if you put money in a savings account as an emergency fund for accident repairs, you will save on overhead. For another thing, collision damages are tax deductible. Thus, a motorist in a 30 per cent tax bracket might reason this way when he analyzes the need for collision coverage on his four-year-old Skyblaze Special: "With $100-deductible collision, I'm paying for all damage up to that amount anyway. If the car is really wrecked, the ACV would be around $800, so after the deductible I'd collect $700. Without insurance, I could take the casualty loss on my income-tax return—minus $100, as required by the law. This would cut my net loss to around $590—so I'm actually paying $80 a year for collision coverage to insure against a loss of $590. It doesn't seem worth it."

There is no easy answer. Perhaps the best rule of thumb is this: If you can afford to replace your car without borrowing money, you will probably save by doing without collision coverage. You may regret the decision if you have a bad accident shortly after dropping the coverage, but if you enjoy a few accident-free years, the money saved on premiums may put you ahead of the game.

■ MEDICAL PAYMENTS. Regardless of who was at fault in an accident, this coverage reimburses you for medical or burial expenses incurred within one year of an accident, and it also takes care of medical expenses if you are hit by a car while bicycling or walking. If you are driving your own car, it covers any guest passengers. If you are driving someone else's car it will cover members of your immediate family, but no other passengers. (In such a situation, nonfamily passengers are covered by the car owner's medical payments or by the driver's liability if he is grossly negligent.)

Usually the coverage pays for medical bills whether you carry health insurance or not. Such duplicate coverage actually enables you to profit from an accident, although few people would care to earn a profit this way. Many motorists feel that they don't need medical-payments coverage if they now have health in-surance. In fact, they should have it because of the possibility that they might be carrying passengers when an accident occurs.

Policies generally are available in amounts ranging from $500 to $10,000. If you can, choose a high limit; it will be a bargain, since the premium for the highest coverage will be only a few dollars more than for the lowest amount (box, page 122).

■ UNINSURED MOTORIST. Accident statistics should rightly make any motorist blanch at the thought of getting behind a wheel without insurance. Yet an estimated 15 per cent of all drivers carry none. Even in states that require proof of insurance before a car can be registered, some owners buy installment insurance, get their registration and then let the policy lapse. In states where insurance is not mandatory, an uninsured driver who has caused an accident must post cash or a bond up to a certain amount determined by the local financial responsibility law—usually a liability limit of 10/20/5; if he cannot prove financial responsibility after the accident, his car will be impounded and his driving privileges revoked. But that doesn't help you.

Uninsured-motorist coverage is designed to protect against drivers who lack liability coverage and against hit-and-run drivers. The policyholder and all members of his immediate family are covered, whether in a car, walking or bicycling. Nonfamily passengers in the policyholder's car are protected too.

In all but eight states, uninsured-motorist coverage is for bodily injury only, and the maximum payout is limited by the financial responsibility law of the state. If the bodily injury limits of that law are 10/20, any one person can recover up to $10,000, and $20,000 is available to cover all injuries.

Why would you want uninsured-motorist coverage if you already have a policy providing *medical payments*? The reason, basically, is that an *uninsured-motorist* policy offers a higher maximum payout, and it will also compensate you for lost wages, which a *medical-payments* policy does not cover. This added protection will cost you only four to eight dollars per year. Considering the number of uninsured motorists—and the terrible accidents they can cause—it is a bargain.

■ TOWING. This coverage, sometimes called emergency road service, is really a frill. Usually it costs two or three dollars a year and pays up to $25 per tow. For most car owners, it isn't a very good deal. However, some insurers set no claim limit; if you can get such unlimited coverage, it may well be worth the money, especially if you travel in sparsely populated areas where the cost of towing a disabled car to a far-off garage may be very steep.

Why does it cost what it costs?

The premium you pay for your auto insurance is determined by the amount of financial responsibility that the insurer assumes and by the statistical likelihood that the insurer will ever have to pay off. These basic considerations depend, in turn, on a whole array of factors applying to individual car owners:

■ THE DRIVER'S SAFETY RECORD. A history of accidents or serious moving violations will burden a driver with a high premium, and new accidents or violations may result in another premium increase.

■ THE RATING TERRITORY. In the eyes of insurance companies, the United States is divided up into numerous areas where accidents occur at statistically different rates. The rating territory can be a part of a large city, an entire smaller city, a suburb or group of suburbs, or a fairly large expanse of nonmetropolitan or rural areas. If the accident rate in the territory is high, then liability, collision and medical-

payments premiums are high. Comprehensive will be high where theft and vandalism are prevalent or in areas subject to frequent fierce wind- and hailstorms.

■ WHO DRIVES THE CAR. Young drivers in the family, particularly males, mean a drastically higher premium, since insurance companies know that young people are involved in a disproportionate share of accidents.

■ CAR USE. How far your car is driven yearly and under what conditions obviously affects its exposure to potential accidents.

■ THE NATURE OF THE CAR. The premium is affected by a car's age, value, horsepower, size and safety features. As an example, a high-performance "muscle car" rates a significantly higher premium than a standard car for equivalent coverage because of the greater frequency and greater severity of accidents involving such vehicles.

Many of these factors are beyond your control. After all, you are who you are: you live in a certain place, have a certain family make-up, travel a certain distance each year and so on. Nevertheless, you can exploit some of the premium determinants to your advantage—by maintaining a good driving record, for example, or perhaps by buying a low-horsepower car rather than a rubber-burning flash.

Money also can be saved through discounts. Many insurance companies offer discounts if young drivers have taken accredited driver-training courses in high school; there are also "good-student discounts," since insurers have discovered that high grades go hand in hand with safer driving. (Incidentally, you should be sure to notify your insurance company if a young driver in your family gets married or goes away to college; your premium may be reduced). And if you buy a second or third car, insure it with your present company; you may be eligible for a multiple-car discount.

Be a comparison shopper

The cost of identical coverage may vary greatly among different insurance firms since companies rate the accident probability in a given territory differently or because their overhead and operating costs are unequal or because they have varying degrees of interest in selling insurance in a particular area. Because of such disparities *(box, page 124)* you should shop around and compare price tags.

After you have decided on the kinds and amounts of coverage you want, you are ready to enter the marketplace. There is no way you can cover the entire field, of course, since auto insurance is sold in the United States by more than 900 companies. Ask friends or neighbors to suggest insurance companies so that you can narrow the choice to workable limits—five or six companies, say. Check also with your employer or union to see if you are eligible for low-cost group insurance.

Other car owners' advice can be helpful. Most have opinions about their insurer, and they can probably tell you whether the company pays claims quickly, is satisfactory to deal with and sticks with the policyholder after he

has been in an accident. This last point is particularly important; in a recent survey 14 per cent of all motorists queried said that their insurer failed to renew their policy after they had been involved in an accident.

Insurance companies are closely regulated by state governments. But if you are in any doubt about an insurer's solvency, ask an independent insurance broker to look up the company's financial rating in Best's Insurance Reports. Don't buy from any company whose rating isn't a healthy A-plus.

You can buy auto insurance through several different channels. About 57 per cent of the industry's dollar volume is sold through the mail or through agents or salaried employees who represent one company only. The rest is sold through independent agents or brokers. Independent agents have contracts with several companies; brokers can place insurance business with almost any company.

You might get the lowest premium on a policy bought from any one of these sellers since they are all competing directly for the consumer's dollar. But, aside from prices, the broker or independent agent does have a certain marketing advantage in terms of convenience. Not only can he offer you a wide choice of policies and companies, but he can also fill your other insurance needs since he usually handles a broad line of property and casualty insurance—and often health and life insurance as well. If you are a valued client whose auto insurance, homeowner's policy, health insurance and other policies have long been handled by your broker or agent, you should be able to expect personal attention to your problems.

But a broker or agent may not be the best source of insurance for you. If you find that you can get a substantially better price from a reputable company that sells through the mail or

THE CASE FOR COMPARISON SHOPPING

Ample proof that it pays to shop around is provided by a buyer's work sheet *(below)* that shows the premiums charged by six different companies for identical coverage. This buyer was a married man who lived in Cleveland, anticipated that he would drive his new sedan about 10,000 miles a year, had no youthful drivers in his family and boasted an unblemished driving record. The least-expensive company charged $113.60 less than the most expensive.

Type of coverage	Limits of coverage	Annual premiums					
		Company A	Company B	Company C	Company D	Company E	Company F
Liability:							
Bodily injury	$100,000 per person	(sold as package)	(sold as package)	$100.40	$125.00	$99.00	$109.00
	$300,000 per accident						
Property damage	$10,000 per accident	$125.28	$151.00	41.30	46.00	49.00	50.00
Physical damage to insured vehicle:							
Comprehensive	Actual cash value	60.48	68.00	83.00	78.00	98.00	110.00
Collision	$100 Deductible per accident	78.24	79.00	118.10	106.00	118.00	112.00
Medical payments	$2,000 per person	12.00	15.00	11.00	14.00	10.00	11.00
Uninsured motorist	$12,500 per person	6.40	6.00	4.20	6.00	7.00	4.00
	$25,000 per accident						
		$282.40	$319.00	$358.00	$375.00	$381.00	$396.00

its own agents, and if you have established that this company treats its customers well, take your business there.

Ideally, careful shopping should link you up with an insurance company that provides prompt and fair service at a good price. If for some reason your insurer fails to meet that expectation, you can switch to another company before your present policy expires and obtain a refund of the unused portion of your premium. But be sure you get a firm commitment in the form of a written binder from the new company before you cancel your present policy. A salesman's assurance that your application will be accepted is not enough, because companies sometimes change their minds.

An alarming number of people, however, lose their insurance through no act of their own. Nearly everyone seems to know a story about some friend who suddenly and inexplicably got a letter from his insurance company saying that his policy would not be renewed (outright cancellation is illegal, unless a driver loses his license or doesn't pay his premiums). The company's refusal to renew the policy usually was for reasons involving either geography or its driver-classification system. A company may simply decide not to write any more policies in a certain territory—almost always an urban area where damage claims have been high. Or you may, for any of several reasons such as age and occupation, fall into a driver classification with a high claims rate. The company declines to insure anybody in that class —good drivers or bad.

You can in such cases sound out other companies, with a reasonably good chance of finding one that hasn't decided to eliminate the territory you live in or doesn't put you in one of its "unwanted" classifications. A broker or agent often can influence his company's decision on accepting a car owner who has been turned down elsewhere. Your chances will be greatly enhanced if you make it clear to him that, if you become an auto-insurance customer, he will also get other business from you —your homeowner's policy, for instance, or any other casualty insurance you carry for yourself or other members of your family.

You may, of course, be unable to renew the policy because you have compiled such a poor driving record or been involved in so many accidents that the insurance company regards you as too much of a risk to keep on its books.

If this is the case, other companies are not likely to look kindly on you either.

Assuming that ordinary insurance companies reject all your applications, you have several options. You can seek out a standard insurance company that has a subsidiary offering high-risk (or "substandard") policies. You can turn to a private company whose sole business is writing such policies. Or you can apply for coverage under the assigned-risk plan that exists in every state; this plan requires insurance companies to accept quotas of drivers who have been denied standard insurance.

No matter where you turn, your insurance costs are going to increase—in some cases, hugely. Furthermore, your coverage probably is going to be restricted. Under an assigned-risk plan, the liability coverage that you can buy generally is limited to the minimum specified by the state's financial responsibility law; other kinds of coverage, such as comprehensive, collision and medical payments, often are not available. Still another drawback is that a number of states require advance payment of the full year's premium, frequently a matter of several hundred dollars.

The companies that specialize in high-risk insurance may give you a way around some of these restrictions. They will permit installment payments, will sell you excess-liability coverage and will make the various other coverages available. But they usually charge hefty premiums. Another sobering fact about such companies is their high rate of bankruptcy. When they go out of business, they sometimes fail to notify their customers, who lose their premiums as well as their insurance.

The moral is plain: don't let reckless driving place you in the position of requiring high-risk insurance. And if you do find yourself in that situation, be sure to do intensive comparison shopping for both price and quality.

UPKEEP

PROLONGING THE LIFE AND LOOKS OF YOUR CAR

THE CRUCIAL BREAK-IN PERIOD
SECRETS OF OCTANE RATINGS
ADDITIVES—GOOD OR BAD?
DOING ROUTINE CHECKS PROPERLY
BUYING AND CARING FOR TIRES
CLEANING INSIDE AND OUT
GARAGING AND STORING

6

Howard has bought a new full-sized sedan. He was disappointed, however, that the trade-in value of his old compact was much less than he had expected. Three different dealers explained to him that the condition of the compact could not justify any higher allowance.

Howard admitted to himself that he had been careless with the old car from the beginning. It always had burned oil; perhaps he should have followed more conscientiously the break-in suggestions in his owner's manual. And those summers by the ocean had taken their toll of the car's finish; he had made a mistake in believing that a car's exterior doesn't require as much attention these days as it once did. So, to guarantee a better price when the time comes to trade in his new car, he has promised himself that he will follow from the outset the instructions in his owner's manual.

After reading the manual, though, he still has questions about the how and why of breaking in a new car and preserving it in optimum condition. Also, to keep operating expenses as low as possible, he wants to know what maintenance services he can do for himself.

In fact, a great many new-car owners find they have similar questions that the manual doesn't cover. This chapter will answer those questions by explaining the correct break-in procedure. It will also detail the routine maintenance services that extend the life and looks of a car and help to prevent mechanical problems from developing.

Breaking in a new car

You may have heard that cars are "broken in at the factory." Don't believe it. Although some manufacturers test engines by operating them briefly before they are installed, a new car isn't driven far enough or its engine run long enough after leaving the assembly line to even start the break-in process.

The first 200 to 500 miles of driving your car are critical. During this period, while you're familiarizing yourself with the car, its major mechanical components—the engine, the transmission, the differential and, if you have one, the clutch—are undergoing the first strains of sustained operation. If you handle a new car judiciously, this break-in period will set up the engine for a long, trouble-free life. If, however, you are careless and ignore the guidelines discussed here, you may be setting the stage for premature mechanical failure and inviting costly repair bills.

Get the piston rings seated properly

When the engine is new, its parts fit together so tightly that the pistons need extra lubrication to move freely up and down. For this reason the walls of the piston cylinders—far from being perfectly smooth—are lined with finely machined microgrooves that, like minute canals, distribute oil between the piston rings and the cylinder walls.

During the first 200 to 500 miles of driving, the engine should not be allowed to operate at a steady, unvarying speed—either high or low. Nor should there be any prolonged idling of the engine. Vary the speeds by a few miles per hour so that the piston rings will wear off the microgrooves and ensure a close, oil-tight fit within the cylinder (drawing, right). The rings will then be properly seated. The driver who treats a new car as though it were a museum piece may not get the pistons moving fast enough to smooth the cylinder walls properly. If the rings on the pistons are not perfectly seated during the break-in period, the engine will continue to use oil unnecessarily.

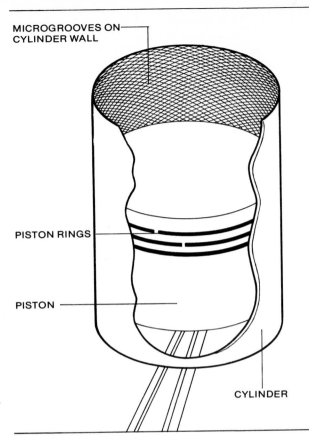

MICROGROOVES ON CYLINDER WALL

PISTON RINGS

PISTON

CYLINDER

Crisscrossing microgrooves on the inner walls of a new car's cylinders serve as channels to carry lubricating oil. As the piston is broken in, its rings wear down the ridges of the microgrooves. When the cylinder wall is smooth, the rings are said to be seated. Thereafter, oil flows evenly along the wall and the rings form a seal, closing off the combustion chamber above the piston and preventing the entrance of excess oil from the crankcase below.

Most experts agree that an additional step toward avoiding later cylinder trouble is to accelerate the car occasionally. You should do this in short spurts, no longer than a couple of miles each time, during the break-in period. Take your new car onto a secondary highway —not a turnpike, where sustained high-speed driving is the rule—and bring it up to the speed recommended in your owner's manual. When the road is clear, slow the car to 30 or 35 mph to slack off the strain on the engine. Then put your foot down hard on the accelerator and quickly bring the car back up to the recommended limit. By increasing the power suddenly, you also increase the pressure in the combustion chamber and force the piston rings to push harder against the cylinder walls. Keep repeating the procedure, slowing down and speeding up. This is hardly normal driving behavior, and unless you display a "breaking in" sign, you'll have to endure the baleful looks of other drivers who may not understand what you are up to. But don't let them deter you; stick to this unusual procedure. Breaking in a new car is serious business.

New engines no longer need break-in oil —the very-light-weight oil formerly used to prevent strain on new parts. The multiviscosity oil currently put into new cars is the same product that you will continue to use; it needs to be changed only after the normal driving interval specified in the owner's manual.

You can, however, expect to use some extra oil during the break-in period. Until the rings are seated, oil will flow into the combustion chamber and burn. For example, you may have to replace a quart of oil after the first 500 miles of driving, but not need the next quart until another 1,200 miles have gone by. After the break-in period is over and you have faithfully followed instructions, if you still have to add oil substantially before each complete change, take the car back to the dealer. The rings may have failed to seat properly or perhaps there is a leak; these conditions should be corrected under the terms of your warranty.

Go easy on the gears

Starting and accelerating with care during the break-in period will help the gears to mesh smoothly, polishing off any microscopic irregularities. Jack-rabbit starts and screeching acceleration, on the other hand, will slam the gears together and their teeth may chip or even break off. The result can be early transmission or differential failure.

If your new car has a manual transmission, your clutch may need special attention during this period. The clutch is the link between the engine and the transmission driveline, and it must be adjusted to engage and release fully; otherwise, the engine will race faster than the turning force it delivers and this strain can wear out the engine. Since a new clutch will loosen with use, you may want to have it checked for adjustment at the first maintenance servicing.

The cardinal rule for driving with a manual transmission: never ride the clutch pedal. Driving with the pedal partly depressed and thus the clutch partly in operation wears out the clutch rapidly. When you stop for a traffic light on an ascending hill, don't ride the clutch to hold the car from sliding back; this is a sure way to ruin the clutch. Instead, depress the pedal completely so that the clutch is disengaged, and hold the car with the brake.

Some additional tips

The breaking in of a new car consists mainly —but not entirely—of driving with care and tending to the engine. But there are other considerations to keep in mind during the first few weeks or months of ownership:

■ USE YOUR WARRANTY. New cars are complicated, mass-produced machines. A certain number of defects are inevitable. Keep a note pad and pencil beside you during the break-in period, and jot down a description of any trouble you have. Before returning the car for its first servicing of any kind, make up a written list (in triplicate, if possible, as described on page 265) of all the items you want to call to the dealer's attention.

■ WATCH YOUR TIRES. New tires need about 50 miles at the start of the break-in period for their different components—belts, plies, tread —to settle into proper conformity with each other. Treat them carefully and be on the lookout for any defects.

■ PROTECT THE EXTERIOR. Today's acrylic paints, chrome and vinyl tops on new cars are tough, but dirt, grime and corrosion can damage them in a matter of weeks. As a precaution, wash the car frequently, and apply a vinyl sealer to the top as soon as possible. Wax the paint and chrome at the first opportunity recommended in your service manual.

■ PROTECT THE INTERIOR. To keep the carpet looking new, install rubber floor mats throughout, fitting them carefully around the pedals on the floor in the front of the car.

■ POSTPONE TOWING. Do not pull a trailer until you have driven a new car 500 to 1,000 miles—and never unless the car is properly equipped for towing *(Chapter 12)*. The heavy strain of a trailer load can cause damage to the tight new parts of the engine, transmission and differential.

■ DON'T STAY IN THE CITY. Slow city driving puts more strain on your engine than any other kind of travel. While you're turtling around town, moisture that builds up inside the engine may mix with the crankcase oil and form sludge and carbon—two archenemies of moving parts. A bit of fast driving every week or two during the break-in period—and afterward as well—will permit the engine to run hot enough and fast enough to burn up or expel the contaminants. If you simply can't get out of town, it is wise to have the oil and the oil filter changed at more frequent intervals as recommended for these special conditions in your owner's manual.

Choosing gasoline

The labels on the pumps in service stations often are so confusing, and so different from brand to brand, that buying gas may seem more complicated than it really is.

Basically all gasolines are blends of various refined petroleum products combined with such chemical additives as detergents, rust- and gum-preventives, and anti-icers. Blends vary from company to company, region to region and season to season, but all are designed to produce dependable fuel. Grade designations (such as premium, intermediate, regular and economy, or subregular) indicate the knock, or detonation, resistance of a gasoline and usually are measured in terms of octane numbers. Other designations such as low lead and unleaded indicate the lead content of the gasoline as well as its octane rating. The higher the octane number, the greater that fuel's ability to resist detonation. In recent years the average octane number of regular gasoline sold in the United States has been about 93 to 94, the average octane number of premium gasoline about 98 to 100.

Because cars are less prone to knock in higher altitudes, octane levels in mountainous regions generally are lower than elsewhere. For example, in the southern mountain states, according to the latest nationwide survey, regular gasoline had an average octane number of 92.4; to achieve equivalent performance in New England, a similar grade gasoline there had an octane number of about 94.9. Within a given region, however, brands of gasoline of the same grade seldom vary by more than one or two octane points.

The octane number of a gasoline is determined in a laboratory by comparing its ability to withstand detonation with that of a blend of two fuels used as laboratory standards: isooctane and n-heptane (the n stands for normal). Since isooctane has maximum resistance to detonation it has an arbitrary octane rating of 100. N-heptane has minimum resistance and an octane rating of 0. So if a given fuel is rated 96, it has the same resistance to detonation as

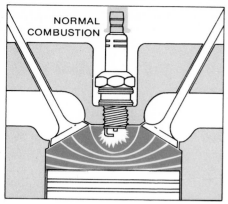

NORMAL COMBUSTION

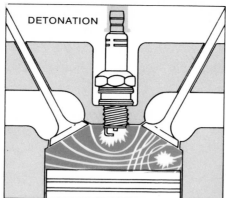

DETONATION

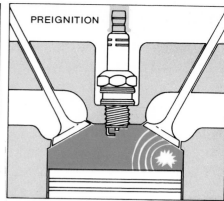

PREIGNITION

When an engine is running normally the fuel-air mixture in each cylinder burns evenly *(above)*. Under abnormal conditions, however, two types of aberrant combustion can take place.

Gasoline with a low octane rating can cause detonation *(center)*. Here the spark plug ignites only part of the fuel and the rest explodes spontaneously a moment later.

Where the problem is preignition *(right)*, impurities inside a hot cylinder—usually carbon deposits—can ignite the fuel before the spark plug fires.

a mixture of 96 per cent isooctane and 4 per cent n-heptane.

Since 1923, octane ratings of gasoline have been improved with a lead additive, most commonly tetraethyl lead. The more lead added —up to a certain point—the higher the octane rating becomes. Adding lead can even raise the octane rating of a gasoline above the laboratory standard of 100.

Unleaded gasoline

In recent years widespread concern about air pollution has led to a demand for gasolines that do not expel lead fumes into the atmosphere. The development of a new device to control exhaust pollutants, called a catalytic converter (page 319), has intensified this demand because leaded gasoline reduces the efficiency of the device. If used to treat exhaust containing lead, metals in the converter become ineffective and the converter has to be replaced.

In response to growing concerns about the environment and in anticipation of the catalytic converter, some oil companies early in this decade began producing gasolines containing no lead. These fuels achieve a good detonation

resistance without lead additives by employing complex and expensive refining methods. Because of the time and investment needed to change techniques and products on a huge scale, many companies have compromised, at least temporarily, by producing a low-lead gasoline that combines somewhat more highly refined gasolines with a minimum of lead. Where conventional gasolines may contain lead compounds up to 4.2 grams per gallon, the low-lead types contain only .5 gram or less per gallon.

Beware of detonation

With or without lead, knock-free gasoline is an essential for any car. Knock, or detonation, is a spontaneous second explosion of the fuel-air mixture inside the cylinder after the spark plug has fired. The ignited fuel does not explode: it burns smoothly and progressively, in expanding circles out from the spark plug *(drawings, above)*. The pressure of the gases released by this combustion reaches its maximum force at about the time all the fuel is burned and the piston in the cylinder is just at the top of its upstroke. This combustion design delivers the greatest possible power to the downstroke of the piston.

However, when detonation occurs, the fuel does not burn evenly. A split second after the spark plug fires, the rest of the fuel in the farthest reaches of the combustion chamber explodes. The piston, which has not quite started its downstroke, is left without the powerful push of normal combustion since the fuel has completed its burning prematurely. With this downward push of the pistons reduced, the en-

TIRES: THE OVERLOOKED UNDERPINNINGS

Four sections of tread—each smaller than one of these pages—are, at any given instant, the only contact between a car and the road. The tires must support loads of 2,500 to 6,000 pounds or more at speeds approaching 80 mph, revolving and flexing for up to 40,000 miles. No other parts of a car are more crucial to its performance or deserve more faithful maintenance and careful selection.

Size, shape, materials and type of construction, all are factors that govern a tire's longevity and your ride. The first rule in choosing tires is to follow the recommendations in your owner's manual. Then checking out the information embossed on the sidewall *(below)* can help you choose a set of tires that will suit both your car and your own personal driving requirements.

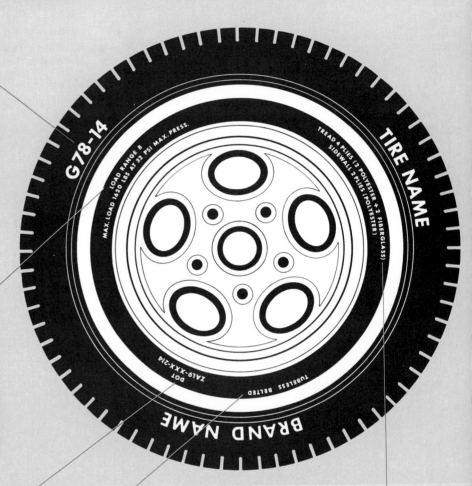

SIZE DESIGNATIONS

This combination of one letter and four numbers on the sidewall is a three-part code. The letter denotes the sidewall-to-sidewall width of the tire; the two numbers grouped with the letter refer to the tire's height-to-width ratio *(profiles, opposite)*; the numbers following the dash indicate in inches the diameter of the wheel rim the tire will fit. Should you want to replace a set of tires, you will find the sizes that will fit your car specified in your owner's manual.

LOAD AND PRESSURE

The weight, or load, a tire can support is designated by a letter. Car makers usually suggest the B tire shown; the C is rare and the stronger D tire generally is recommended only for heavy-duty hauling or for station wagons. Under one of these letters, the specific load-carrying and tire-pressure capacities are spelled out. This tire, at its maximum safe air pressure of 32 pounds per square inch, can carry up to 1,620 pounds. The total weight of a fully loaded car should not exceed four times the limit of each tire—in this case 6,480 pounds.

CERTIFICATION AND CODES

DOT certifies that the tire meets the minimal performance standards of the U.S. Department of Transportation. The encoded letters and numbers beneath DOT are a tire's serial number. This code provides the name of the manufacturer (a brand name on the sidewall may represent only the distributor), the tire's size, materials and date of manufacture. The last three digits, 214 in this instance, would mean the tire was made in the 21st week of 1974.

TIRE TYPE

Government regulations require that every passenger tire be stamped either "tubeless" or "tube-type"; actually, more than 90 per cent of them are tubeless. "Belted" indicates that a tire has extra strength in its construction *(opposite)*. In addition, if the tire shown here were a radial, it would be designated as such—a necessary precaution because radials should not be mixed with other tire types except when the radials are used as the pair on the rear axle.

CARCASS CORDS

The foundation of a tire is a strong but resilient fabric carcass made up of paired plies (or layers) of rubberized fibers called cords. Whatever material the fibers are—nylon, polyester, rayon, fiberglass or steel strands—they must be identified. Polyester does not "flat spot" after standing, as nylon does, causing temporarily bumpy rides; nor does it deteriorate when wet, as rayon can. Fiberglass, while not as durable as steel, affords a smooth and quiet ride.

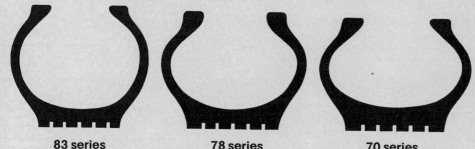

TIRE PROFILES

The percentage ratio of a tire's tread-to-wheel-rim height in relation to its sidewall-to-sidewall width establishes its profile size and series number. Greater tread width gives better traction and stability, so today's trend is away from conventional 83-series tires *(far left)* toward 78s or 70s for family cars, to 60s and 50s for sports models.

83 series   **78 series**   **70 series**

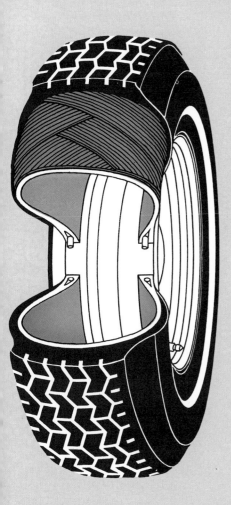

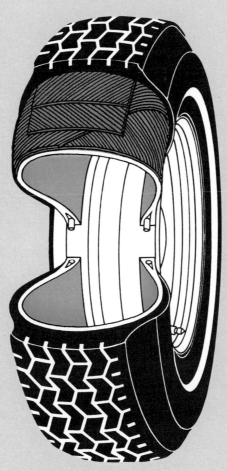

BIAS PLY

The standard—and least expensive—tire is a bias ply. Its cord strips are arranged diagonally (that is, at a bias) to the center line of the tread and alternate plies are reversed to cross at a 30° or 40° angle. The result is a uniformly firm body, satisfactory at moderate speeds—with sidewalls that can stand curb bruises. In fast driving or hard turning, however, the tread elements squirm together then spring apart, producing heat that weakens the tires.

BELTED BIAS

The body plies of belted-bias tires criss-cross diagonally, like those of bias-ply tires, to ensure strong sidewalls. The added belts are two or more cord strips that are cut on the bias and alternated, in herringbone fashion, around the perimeter of the tire between the body plies and the tread. Belts not only strengthen the tire against impact and puncture damage, but also serve to stiffen the tread so that it has less tendency to squirm on the road.

RADIAL

The body cords of radial tires run at right angles (radially) to the center line of the treads; the belt cords are arranged in a herringbone pattern. The radial body cords allow sidewalls to flex so that the tread maintains maximum surface contact with the road during turns, whereas the stiff sidewalls of bias-type tires would lift the edges of the tread. Radials are well suited to high-speed driving—but some may produce noise or roughness at low speeds.

133

gine suffers power loss. Another consequence is that shock waves meet those resulting from normal combustion within the cylinder to cause a knocking sound in the engine.

Detonation generally is brought on by low-octane gasoline that cannot withstand the extreme compression and high temperatures in the combustion chamber—and thus explodes when it should not.

To avoid detonation, you should use a gasoline that has just enough resistance to the pressure and heat your engine produces to ensure that it does not knock. As a guide, most cars now being built are designed to use unleaded or low-lead gasoline with an octane rating of about 91.

A new engine's octane appetite usually increases somewhat during the first 5,000 to 10,000 miles. If you ever hear your engine knocking, experiment with other brands of gasoline of the same grade in the hope that their octane rating may be slightly higher, or you can try the next higher grade of gasoline. (Some drivers let their tank get only about half empty between gas stops and fill the tank alternately with regular grade and premium to get a blend of the two.) If knocking persists, check your car's cooling system, ignition timing and carburetor. A malfunction of any of the three can lead to detonation.

In no event can you afford to ignore the problem. Operating a new car under conditions of continuous detonation is considered misuse of the engine and may invalidate the warranty on the parts affected.

Listen for preignition

Another form of faulty combustion, called preignition, is sometimes mistaken for detonation, although the two problems are quite different. Preignition occurs when the fuel in a cylinder burns before it should—even before

the plug sparks to set it off. You can recognize preignition by its pinging or knocking sound.

The cylinders in an engine (whether there are four, six or eight) are set to fire in a specific order. The firing order of a six-cylinder engine might be 1-5-3-6-2-4. If the fuel in cylinder three should ignite before the fuel in number five, that's preignition—a malady of older cars and those used for long periods on short hauls, both situations in which carbon deposits build up. These carbon deposits can get so hot that they ignite the fuel in a cylinder ahead of its proper firing order.

Preignition ruins engines. If the piston in the contaminated cylinder is on its upward stroke when fuel ignites prematurely, the counterforce knocks the piston back down, much like running full tilt into an oncoming punch. Preignition knocks holes in piston heads and bends connecting rods. If you ever hear heavy pinging or knocking coming from your engine—particularly if the car has more than 30,000 miles on it—don't wait for the noise to go away. Take the car to a mechanic at once.

Purchasing gasoline

For your well-being, and that of the engine, remember these cautions when buying fuel:

■ BE WARY OF VAPORS. Gasoline vapors are highly explosive. When gas is pumped into your tank, be sure that the engine is turned off and that no one smokes outside the car. Do not restart the engine until the gas-tank cap has been replaced and secured.

■ BE WARY OF ADDITIVES. Major gasoline producers supply fuels that contain all necessary additives. The use of special additives is not only unnecessary and wastefully expensive, but may risk your warranty coverage—with one exception. To remove the water that invariably collects in your gas tank, you may wish to put in a can of commercial gasoline dry-

bald spots	**wear at shoulders**	**wear at center**	**wear on one side**	**feathered edge**

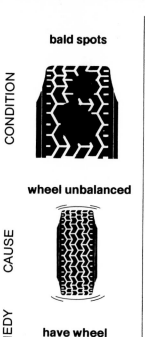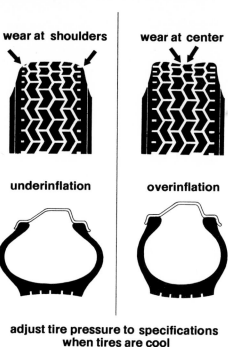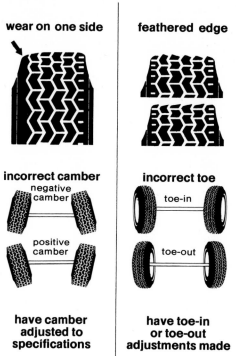

CONDITION

CAUSE

wheel unbalanced	**underinflation**	**overinflation**	**incorrect camber**	**incorrect toe**
			negative camber / positive camber	toe-in / toe-out

REMEDY

have wheel balanced	**adjust tire pressure to specifications when tires are cool**		**have camber adjusted to specifications**	**have toe-in or toe-out adjustments made**

ing agent every month or so. Also known as gasoline antifreeze, it is available at most service stations, discount stores and auto-supply stores. This additive, which consists mainly of alcohol, will combine with the water to form a mixture that will burn readily in the engine.

■ BE WARY OF FOREIGN BRANDS. Before you operate a car outside the United States or Canada, find out if the octane rating of the gasolines sold in the countries you'll be visiting is high enough to prevent excessive detonation. Write to the customer-service department of the manufacturer of your car (the address is in the owner's manual), giving a description of your car and the names of the countries to be visited. The company will furnish the necessary information.

Judging tires

Tires are so critical to your safety and comfort that you should never buy them on a whim or leave responsibility for their care entirely to a service-station attendant.

Cars are designed to give best performance with certain sizes and types of tires, so the wise practice in choosing tires is to follow your

The tire diagrams above depict *(top row)* various erratic wear patterns, and in each instance, directly underneath, the cause of the problem as well as the corrective adjustment required. The tire flaw may be something as simple to fix as underinflation or overinflation of the tire, in which case the owner himself can attend to it. If the trouble is caused by improper balancing—or, on the front wheels, by misalignment—the car should be taken as soon as possible to a shop that specializes in doing this kind of work. A program of personal inspections and prompt corrections of any flaws will ensure longer tire life.

Tread-wear indicators *(above)* are smooth horizontal bands about half an inch wide that become visible when only 1/16 of an inch remains of the original tread. When the bands appear across two or more adjacent grooves, replace the tire.

CHOOSING YOUR OWN PATTERN FOR TIRE ROTATION

The 12 tire-rotation procedures diagramed below are not as formidable as they seem. At any given time, only one of them will apply to your car. First, read across the top line to locate the number and type of tires you will be rotating. Then read down the column at left. The top entry is for regular rotation without snow tires, usually done every 6,000 miles. See the second and third rows when snow tires *(in color)* are part of the rotation. Remember, you must use radial snow tires if you have radials up front. When you put tires in storage, record on the inner face of each one, using chalk or tape, its position. This will help when remounting the tires.

	four tires (nonradial)	five tires (nonradial)	four tires (radial)	five tires (radial)
routine rotation				
putting on snow tires in fall	 to storage	 to storage	 to storage	 to storage
removing snow tires in spring	 to storage	 to storage	 to storage	 to storage

136

owner's manual to the letter. The drawings on pages 132-133 illustrate and explain the different types and profiles of tires, and interpret the information that appears on the sidewalls.

Your chief consideration should be to get tires—either when ordering a new car or buying replacements—that will be appropriate for your car, your driving needs and your budget. For use around town, for example, inexpensive bias-ply tires may be the best buy. But if you expect to use the tires mainly on long, high-speed trips, you should spend additional money for the extra strength and durability of belted-bias or radial tires.

Whenever you are replacing tires, remember that both tires on the same axle should be identical or at least a closely matched pair. Tires with different construction, size, profile or radically different tread patterns are likely to have different traction, steering and braking characteristics.

And, if you value your life, remember that radial tires—which are constructed very differently from either bias-ply or belted-bias types —should never be mixed with other tires, except when they are bought and used as the pair on the rear wheels of the car.

Selecting tire pressure

The pressure a tire can safely hold—usually referred to as the tire's maximum pressure —depends not only on its size but also on the strength and resilience of its fabric carcass. Check the sidewall to find the tire's maximum safe pressure: the manufacturer stamps the figure and the initials PSI (for pounds per square inch) on every tire. Maximum safe pressure means exactly that: it is the highest level to which the tire can be safely inflated. But to avoid confusion, remember, maximum PSI and the proper pressure for a given car are not necessarily the same.

In use on a specific car model, a tire may perform best at a pressure less than the maximum figure on the sidewall. For that reason, when the car manufacturer specifies what tires you should use, he also recommends the PSI at which you should maintain them for riding comfort and driving ease and for the longest tire wear. These recommendations are listed in the owner's manual and pasted either inside the door frame on the driver's side or inside the glove compartment.

Running tires at the proper PSI gives extended and even tread wear, maximum traction on curves, and resistance to damage from rocks and potholes. Tires run at too-low air pressure will flex and squirm more than they are designed to, resulting in faster wear on the outside edges of the tread. Underinflated tires can also generate excessive heat that may lead to premature tire failure. Too much air pressure will lead to rapid wear in the center of the tread (drawings, page 135). Rarely is it advisable to inflate the tire to maximum pressure. Some possible exceptions: handling very heavy loads or driving at very high speeds.

The recommended inflation pressures are sometimes different for the front and the back tires. For example, some station wagons require higher pressure in the rear tires than in the front. But remember, tires on the same axle —whether front, or rear—always should be inflated to identical pressures no matter what the driving conditions. This assures even tread wear, steering control and braking.

Even if you faithfully follow the manufacturer's recommendations for routine driving, you should increase the tire pressure by four pounds before going on any lengthy trip. (If doing so would exceed the figure stamped on the sidewall, add pressure only to the limit stated on the tire.) This higher PSI will help the tire to withstand the heat generated at turnpike speeds and give better mileage. After you return—but only after the tires cool down—reduce the pressure to the normal figure.

Checking the PSI

Although many experts recommend that tire pressure be checked once a month, you should do it weekly. Every 10° change in temperature will affect the PSI by about one pound. If the thermometer falls from 70° to 40°, for example, your tires will lose three PSI.

The pressure gauges on service-station air pumps often are inaccurate. Don't rely on them. Instead, buy a reliable pocket gauge of the type shown at right and keep it in your glove compartment so that you can periodically check tire pressure yourself.

Take your readings only when the tires are cold—that is, when they have been idle for three or more hours, or have been driven less than a mile after being idle for three or more hours. When you are driving, tire pressure can increase as much as six PSI. Allowance for this normal increase is built into the recommended pressures for cold tires. Never bleed what may seem to be excess pressure from hot tires; they will be underinflated when they cool off.

Frequent inspection of the treads will help you to keep wheels correctly balanced and aligned —crucial factors in safe driving (drawings, page 135). Check the treads for damaging bits of glass, nails and stones. All tire valves should have caps to keep out dirt and moisture. Finally, rotating the tires at recommended intervals will distribute wear more evenly and extend their tread life (drawings, page 136).

Scheduling routine checks

Inspection of the oil level in the crankcase or the tension on the fan belt is the kind of chore most car owners leave to gasoline-station at-

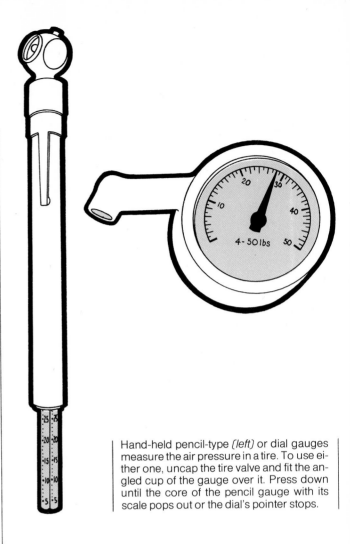

Hand-held pencil-type *(left)* or dial gauges measure the air pressure in a tire. To use either one, uncap the tire valve and fit the angled cup of the gauge over it. Press down until the core of the pencil gauge with its scale pops out or the dial's pointer stops.

tendants. This policy is fine as long as the service at the gasoline station is competent and careful, but too often it is neither. So, make the simple fluid-level and drive-belt checks yourself and know that the jobs are done right (pages 139-140).

Keep the battery full

Before your battery is charged for operation, its cells are filled with solution called electrolyte, which is 1 part sulfuric acid and 2 parts water. This mixture is the battery's lifeblood. The lead plates in the cells must be constantly immersed in electrolyte in order to generate the electricity you need to start the car and to operate the various accessories when the engine is not running.

To be sure that the plates are covered with electrolyte at all times, check the battery once a month in cold weather. In hot weather, when the water content of the electrolyte evaporates faster, check the battery once a week. Short of spillage the volume of the sulfuric acid will never change: while the battery is giving off electricity, the lead in the plates reacts with the acid to form lead sulfate among other compounds. But the chemical reaction reverses when the battery is receiving electricity from the engine generator or alternator, and lead sulfate becomes sulfuric acid again. When you check the level of the electrolyte, uncap all six cells in the battery and inspect them one by one (page 140). Do not assume that simply because one cell is full, the others are too. Each cell is a separate compartment and functions independently; all of the cells must operate together to provide the power you need. If the liquid level in any cell is below the ring indicator, you should add a few ounces of clean tap water (or distilled water).

Handle the battery cautiously and never strike a match or smoke under the hood of the car. A battery constantly gives off highly explosive hydrogen gas; even when the battery is cold, the gas may be present at the vents in the cell caps. Resting a wrench or other metal tool on top of the battery is just as perilous; if metal touches both battery posts—the protruding knobs to which the power cables are attached—it will cause a short circuit and the resulting sparks may ignite the hydrogen gas.

Never overfill a battery with water. The electrolyte will bubble up through the cell-cap vents. It is highly corrosive, and in time may corrode the cable clamps; if you see white deposits of acid around the terminals, clean them off as described on pages 148-149 and 196. Worse, electrolyte may splash on your clothes and skin, in which case it should be washed

Check the tension of the fan belt by pushing it down, midway between the pulleys, with your thumb. The fan belt should flex enough to depress about half an inch. If it stretches beyond that, it needs to be tightened or replaced (page 175).

off immediately with a weak solution of baking soda and water, which neutralizes the acid. If electrolyte ever gets into your eyes, flush immediately with copious amounts of water and see a doctor at once.

In cold weather, add water to the battery only just before driving, so that it will mix into the acid before it has a chance to freeze. If your battery needs water every month (or every week in summer), your electrical system may be overcharging. Have a serviceman check it.

When your car is slow to start, the energy stored in the battery may be nearly used up. In most cases, this is not a serious problem: storage batteries are readily rechargeable. You can check the charge level yourself with a battery hydrometer (page 142) or have it done at a

CHECKING FLUID LEVELS

The fluids that keep your battery, radiator, brakes, power steering, engine and automatic transmission functioning smoothly need to be checked and replenished periodically. When you do these simple jobs park your car on level ground and follow the prescribed procedures.

Battery electrolyte should be checked monthly in winter and weekly in summer when its water content evaporates faster. Uncap and inspect each of the six cells separately. The electrolyte must cover the lead plates in each cell. If the level is below the ring in the neck of the filler well, add tap water or distilled water.

Radiator coolant needs checking every one to two months. Remove the radiator cap when the engine is cold if convenient. If it has been running, however, the coolant will be under pressure. Holding a protective rag, turn the radiator cap counterclockwise to its first stop; allow the pressure to escape, then turn the cap further to remove it. The coolant should cover the vertical pipes inside the radiator. Pour in a mixture of half coolant, half water.

Brake fluid should be checked at regular intervals as recommended in your owner's manual. With a screwdriver, pry off the retaining wire clip that holds the cover on the master cylinder and lift off the cover. Pour in enough brake fluid to keep both master-cylinder compartments filled to within 1/4 inch of the top.

Power-steering fluid should be checked periodically as recommended in your owner's manual. The dipstick, attached to the cap on the filler neck, must be wiped clean, then reinserted and the cap tightened. Loosen the cap and withdraw the dipstick. Pour in power-steering fluid only if the liquid level on the stick is on or below the add mark. To avoid overfilling, add the fluid gradually, then test its level again.

Engine oil should be checked each time the gas tank is filled. Pull out the dipstick, wipe it clean, then reinsert it to its full depth. Make sure it has seated fully, then pull it up again to read the oil level. Add a quart of oil only if the level is on or below the add mark. If the level is between the full and add lines, do not add oil.

Automatic-transmission fluid should be checked regularly as specified in your owner's manual. Warm up the engine for at least 10 minutes. With the engine running at idle, engage the parking brake and put your foot on the brake pedal. Shift the selector lever to low and then to reverse. Put it in park and leave the engine running.

Pull out the automatic-transmission dipstick, wipe it clean and reinsert it. Be sure the stick seats. Add fluid only if the level is on or below the add mark. Pour in the fluid gradually and check the dipstick repeatedly to avoid overfilling.

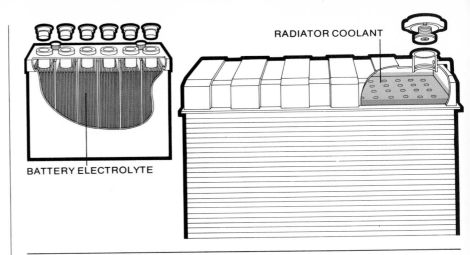

BATTERY ELECTROLYTE

RADIATOR COOLANT

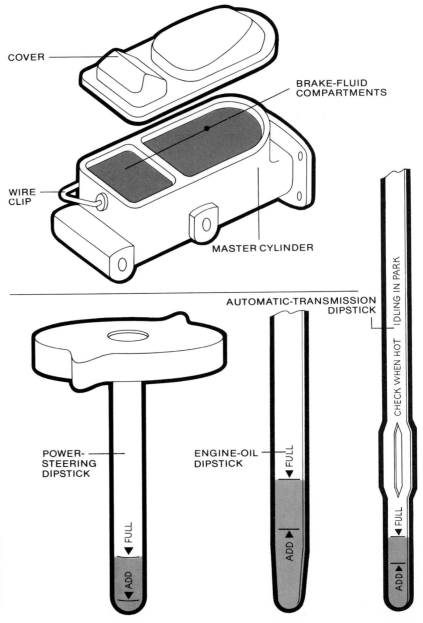

COVER

BRAKE-FLUID COMPARTMENTS

WIRE CLIP

MASTER CYLINDER

AUTOMATIC-TRANSMISSION DIPSTICK

POWER-STEERING DIPSTICK

FULL

ADD

ENGINE-OIL DIPSTICK

FULL

ADD

IDLING IN PARK

CHECK WHEN HOT

FULL

ADD

service station. Only if the readings among the cells differ widely does the battery actually need to be replaced.

Replenish oil regularly

Engine oil not only lubricates metal parts but also helps to keep them working clean. Check the oil level every time you need gasoline (page 140). You can let the service-station attendant do the checking and filling. Or you can do both jobs yourself, and save money by buying oil in five-quart cans.

Use only the class and viscosity of oil recommended in your owner's manual. The viscosity, or flowability, of oils is indicated by the initials SAE (Society of Automotive Engineers) and a classification number, plus the letter W (for winter), signifying oils that are suitable for cold weather. Today most oils are multiviscosity types that flow well in winter and also resist thinning out in summer. Generally, car manufacturers recommend SAE 10W-30 or SAE 10W-40 for use all year round, except in climates where winter temperatures remain below zero for extended periods. In these frigid regions either SAE 5W-20 or SAE 5W-30 is recommended.

The best time to check the oil level is when the engine has been cold so that the oil has had time to drain back down into the crankcase. When you are on a trip, have the gas tank filled and other chores attended to before checking the oil. This will allow most of the oil to drain downward into the crankcase and make possible a correct reading.

Because the engine oil gradually becomes clogged with combustion by-products, it must be changed—that is, drained and replaced—at the intervals prescribed in your owner's manual. The oil filter needs changing every time you change the oil. By changing the oil and filter yourself (pages 162–163), you can save con-

siderable time and money, and avoid the inconvenience of making an appointment at a service station.

Keep the radiator full

The liquid level of the antifreeze and water mixture—called the coolant—in your radiator should be checked every month or two. This mixture must be maintained at the proper strength so that it will keep the engine cool in summer and prevent it from freezing in winter.

It is best to make routine checks of the coolant when the engine is cold. You can also check the coolant after the engine has been running—but be very careful. Most radiators have a pressure cap. If the cap is released while the engine is hot, the coolant may boil over and spout up dangerously.

Using a rag to protect your hand, remove the cap by turning it slowly to the first notch; wait briefly for the pressure inside to escape before unscrewing the cap completely. Then establish that the coolant is at the level recommended in the owner's manual—usually one and a half to three inches below the bottom of the filler neck. Many owners and service stations add plain water when the coolant level gets low, but it is a better practice to add a half-and-half mixture of coolant and water that will keep the fluid in the radiator from becoming diluted. This mixture can be made up in advance and kept for months in an old antifreeze container whose cap still can be tightly closed.

Although ethylene glycol, the antifreeze agent in the coolant, does not evaporate, it loses its effectiveness in time, particularly if it is diluted repeatedly with water. You can check the percentage of ethylene glycol in the coolant by using a radiator antifreeze hydrometer as shown on page 142.

Any time your hood is up is a good time to look over the drive belts. All cars have one: the

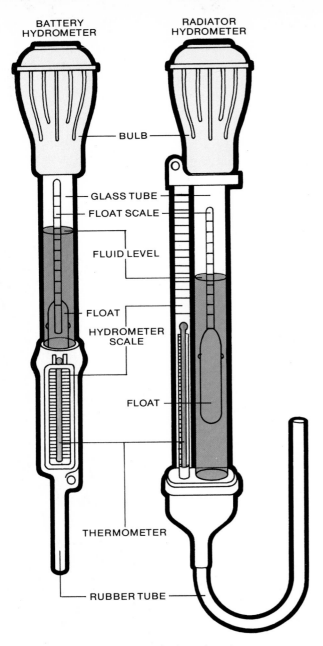

BATTERY HYDROMETER

RADIATOR HYDROMETER

BULB

GLASS TUBE
FLOAT SCALE

FLUID LEVEL

FLOAT

HYDROMETER SCALE

FLOAT

THERMOMETER

RUBBER TUBE

Both of the highly accurate hydrometers shown above—one for testing the charge in a battery, the other for checking the effectiveness of antifreeze in a radiator—are used in the same basic manner.

First, hold the hydrometer vertically and squeeze the bulb repeatedly to draw fluid into the glass tube until the float bobs freely. Then look at the scale on the float stem and read off the number, or letter, of the line at the fluid level. Next, check the thermometer reading. Finally, consult the scale on the hydrometer. The scale will correlate the two readings you have taken: for a battery it will tell you if recharging is needed; for antifreeze, it will indicate the lowest temperature at which the coolant protects.

belt that turns the radiator fan, alternator and water pump. And many cars have an additional belt—or belts—to operate a power-steering pump, an air-injection pump and/or a compressor for an air conditioner.

Any belt will, in time, wear or stretch, and in most cases it announces its trouble by squealing. Keep an ear tuned, especially when you make a sharp turn or switch on the air conditioning. Whether you hear squeals or not, check the belts periodically. Test their tension as shown in the drawing on page 139, and inspect their appearance as well. The cracking that usually appears first along the bottom edges and sides indicates that a belt is wearing out; a slick glaze on the surface means the belt has begun to slip. Replacing belts is another job you can do for yourself; the steps are described on page 175.

Perform periodic checks

As long as the car behaves properly and handles easily, you can schedule inspection of the fluid levels of the brake cylinder, automatic-transmission reservoir, and the power-steering fluid at intervals recommended in your owner's manual. To get accurate readings of all these fluid levels, be sure the car itself is level and parked on a flat spot.

■ BRAKE FLUID. The fluid in the brake system evaporates gradually. Pry off the retaining wire on the brake-cylinder cover as described on page 140 to check the level of the fluid inside. Supplement the fluid, if necessary, with whatever product your owner's manual recommends. Handle the fluid and the cylinder cover with care: if fluid drips on the car's exterior, its chemicals will eat into the finish.

■ AUTOMATIC-TRANSMISSION FLUID. The level of fluid in the automatic transmission, unlike the others, must be checked with the engine warmed up and running at idle. Follow exactly the directions on page 140. If the level is low, add only the kind of transmission fluid specified in your owner's manual and only enough to bring the level to a point between add and full. Do not overfill the transmission; the fluid needs space for expansion and without it it will boil from its reservoir.

■ POWER-STEERING FLUID. The fluid in the power-steering reservoir is similar to that which is used in the automatic transmission. It should be checked as described on page 140. If necessary, add a few ounces at a time, rechecking the level with the dipstick until the fluid reaches the full mark.

Maintaining your car's appearance

Service stations and auto-supply stores are well stocked with products to keep your car looking like new: polishes, waxes and cleaners for body and chrome, glass cleaners, vinyl cleaners, tire cleaners and paints, stain removers for upholstery, engine degreasers, and many others. If you buy products other than those specifically recommended by the car manufacturer, be sure they are suited to the job at hand. For example, if the owner's manual tells you to use a nonabrasive cleaner, make certain the product you buy states on the label that it is nonabrasive.

Clean windows inside and out

Check the cleanliness of all of your car's windows every time you start out—as a safety measure, if not for appearance' sake. Plain dirt is easy enough to remove with water or a household glass cleaner. For more stubborn spots, including bug splatters, you can buy a commercial automobile-window cleaner or try the detergent-alcohol recipe in the chart on pages 146-147. Applied with vigorous rubbing, this homemade mixture usually does the trick. On a long trip, it is wise to take along a con-

tainer of the fluid, plus clean rags, paper towels or tissues for on-the-road cleaning.

Vinyl upholstery materials contain some substances that vaporize and form a stubborn film on interior glass surfaces. Also, tobacco smoke leaves a similar film. Water or commercial cleaners merely smear the film. To remove it, use plain white vinegar diluted 1 to 1 with water. The film will disappear immediately and the odor of vinegar will go quickly if the car is well ventilated.

Keep the exterior shining

The finishes on today's cars are tougher than they used to be, but they are by no means immune to corrosion by chemicals spread on highways in winter, by salt air near the ocean, and by industrial haze—not to mention ordinary rust. Washing the car as often as convenient is the best way to prevent road film and airborne chemical deposits from damaging the paint and rust from taking hold.

If you care about the appearance of your car, you probably ask yourself at least once a week if the car needs washing. There are various options to consider. You can take the car to the local wash where a quick job may cost 98 cents at the beginning of the week. But then, if it rains at midweek, the car will not look its best for the weekend. Would it be better to wait till Saturday, even though the cost will go up to $1.45? Or should you get out the pails, rags and hose and do it yourself at home? Could the teenager who lives next door be persuaded to do a decent job?

If, finally, you decide to wash the car yourself, the suggestions offered in the box on page 144 will help you to get the job done well.

When it's time to polish or wax your car, common sense should tell you so. If the finish looks cloudy and gray, it needs protection. If raindrops bead up—that is, hold their round

WASHING, POLISHING AND WAXING

Circumstance and time will dictate whether your car needs only a wash to remove surface dirt, a waxing to protect its shine or a polish to restore the color's glow. All three chores should be done when the metal feels cool and the car is parked in the shade; heat and sun streak the finish.

The cleanest wash
Spray strong jets of water from the garden hose on the under parts most susceptible to salt and rust—wheel wells, fenders, bumpers.

Squirt jets of water along the edge of metal trim moldings to flush out any dirt trapped there.

If your car is covered with a light film of dust, use only cold water to wash it. If dust and dirt form a heavier coating, mix some mild nondetergent liquid soap with cold water in a gallon bucket. Check the label on the soap container for the proper amount to use. If the dirt requires stronger treatment, mix some commercial car-wash solution with cold water, following the label directions. Never use heavy-duty soaps or detergents, which may bleach your paint.

Wash one panel or section of the car at a time, starting with the roof and upper areas. Swab on the soap with a clean, soft cloth, a car-wash mitt, a sponge or, handiest of all, a string-mop refill.

To prevent streaks, use the hose to rinse off the sudsy residue immediately.

To remove bits of hardened tar or bug and bird marks, hold a cloth saturated with cooking oil over the spot until the blemish lifts off easily.

Repeat soaping and rinsing until the entire car has been washed. Rinse one final time with the hose. Dry at once with another soft cloth or, best of all, a chamois.

The brightest polish
After the car is washed and dried, pour some car polish or cleaner-polish on a clean cloth.

Using a circular and overlapping motion, coat one panel or section of the car at a time. Press down vigorously on the cloth to remove the film of oxidized paint from the surface.

Let the polish dry completely. When it looks hazy, rub it off with another cloth. Turn the cloth regularly so that its surface is always clean.

The shiniest wax
Wash and dry the car (and polish if necessary).

If you are using liquid car wax or a combination of cleaner and wax, pour a generous amount onto a clean, soft cloth. If you are using paste-type wax, soak the cloth in water and wring it dry before applying a light coat of wax.

Rub on the wax vigorously, employing a circular, overlapping motion and concentrating on a small section of the car at a time.

Let the wax dry to a haze, then wipe the haze away and buff with a clean cloth or chamois.

Change the cloth whenever it is caked with wax.

shapes—when they land on the car, there still is enough wax to protect the car's finish. But if the drops spread out, little or no wax is left.

The difference between polish (sometimes called cleaner or prewaxer) and wax is this: polish removes oxidized particles of pigment from the surface and exposes the paint beneath while leaving a film on top to make the paint shine. Wax applies a protective coat over the finish to maintain its brilliance and guard it from deterioration. There is also a wide variety of combination, or one-step, polishes and waxes—liquids, pastes, gels (or presoftened pastes) and spray foams. But for the longest-lasting job, traditionalists still swear by a body polish followed by a coat of hard paste wax. Some hints on how to get the best results are given in the box at left.

To keep vinyl tops looking their best, clean them using a soft-bristled brush while washing the car. Never use a wire brush; the vinyl is a thin sheet that will tear. If the top loses its luster, there are liquid vinyl-top restorers that require buffing as well as dressings that shine without buffing. Both these restorers are available at auto-supply stores in colors to match your top or in a neutral shade.

To restore the appearance of white sidewall tires, use a cleaner made for the purpose. Gasoline, kerosene or other petroleum-based products will eat into the rubber.

Preserve the interior

If you use a vacuum cleaner and a whisk broom regularly before dirt has a chance to get embedded—once every week or so—you may be able to put off washing the seats and floor coverings for a long time.

Sooner or later, though, the upholstery will begin to look dull and grimy. In most cases the answer is to pick out a few clean terry-cloth face towels you are ready to discard (or make several oversized cheesecloth pads) and mix up a bucket of warm, sudsy water *(pages 146-147)*. Apply the suds sparingly and rub gently without letting them soak through the upholstery. Rinse by wiping with clear water, and then open the car's doors and windows to let things dry out.

An alternate method is to buy an upholstery cleaner—but be sure to get the kind that is intended for synthetics: vinyl, nylon, rayon, viscose and orlon. Cleaners that are intended for natural fabrics—rarely used in cars today—form a soapy foam that may leave a dull film on the synthetics.

Do not use chrome polish on the bright trim pieces inside the car unless you are certain they are metal. Usually, though they may look like chrome, these shiny bits are plastic, made to resemble metal. Wipe them with a damp sponge and buff with a soft, dry cloth. Whatever the trim is actually made of, avoid abrasive cleaners when cleaning it.

The ideal time to remove a stain from the seats or carpets is immediately after it appears, before it has a chance to set. When that is not possible, wipe or blot up the spot as thoroughly as you can and resolve to work on the stain at your first opportunity. The chart on pages 146-147 shows how to remove most kinds of stains. Never use carbon tetrachloride: its fumes can result in serious injury or even death. Be careful even with commercial cleaning compounds; some are flammable or toxic. Read the labels carefully.

Keeping the engine clean

The oily grime that collects on the outside of your engine should be removed before the engine becomes thickly coated. Dirt on electrical connections can actually result in the cross-jumping of the current and result in faulty starting. Dirt on the gas-pedal linkages can in-

TIPS ON STORING YOUR CAR

There are certain steps you should take if your car is not going to be used for more than two weeks. If you are storing your car for more than a month, there are additional measures to be taken.

Storage from two weeks to a month
Wash the car *(box, opposite)* to remove excessive dirt and grime that might cause paint and chrome to deteriorate.

If the weather is cold, be sure to check the level of the radiator coolant as well as the protective capacity of the antifreeze *(pages 140, 142)*.

Put the automatic transmission selector in park or a manual transmission in first gear. Do not apply the parking brake; if left engaged, the brake may freeze in that position.

Disconnect the positive battery-cable to avoid fire as a consequence of possible faulty wiring.

Close the windows and lock the car.

If the car is not to be stored in a garage or carport, protect it with a securely tied plastic cover. Park it on high, firm ground that will not be transformed into a sea of mud after a rain or thaw.

Storage for longer than a month
Wash and wax the car *(opposite)*.

If the weather is cold, be sure to check the level of the radiator coolant as well as the protective capacity of the antifreeze *(pages 140, 142)*.

If the car is to be stored in warm weather or a warm place, simply disconnect the positive battery-cable. But if the car will be idle in freezing temperatures, remove the battery, first being sure that the positive and negative terminals are clearly marked. Do not leave the battery where vagrant sparks may ignite the hydrogen given off by the electrolyte. To keep spilled electrolyte from damaging an adjacent surface, place the battery in a heavy plastic or stainless-steel pan in your basement, heated garage or any other convenient, warm place where it will not freeze.

Remove the windshield-wiper blades; to interrupt the process of normal deterioration, wrap them in rags and store them flat.

Put the automatic-transmission selector in park or a manual transmission in first gear. If the car is to be stored for more than 90 days, put the car on jack stands so the tires are raised off the ground. Reduce tire pressure to 25 per cent of normal. Both these steps take pressure off the tires—continued pressure over an extended period leads to deterioration of the rubber.

To return the car to operating condition
Reverse all the steps taken in preparing the car for storage. Before driving, check the tire pressures—reinflate if necessary, using a tire pump or a can of compressed air—and check all fluid levels. After reconnecting the battery and before turning on the ignition, check the charge *(page 142);* recharge if necessary.

CLEANING UP—INSIDE AND OUT

These days cleaning your car is a lot less troublesome than was the case just a few years ago; both the exterior *(page 144)* and the interior are finished in materials designed to make them easier to maintain. However, the materials used vary widely by manufacturer and as a result there is no single, universal procedure. Before undertaking to restore your own car's finish, upholstery and trim, consult your owner's manual for the manufacturer's specific recommendations and follow them explicitly. Steps that supplement those recommendations are listed below.

GLASS

Wash exterior glass with a household window cleaner or a clean lint-free cloth dampened with lukewarm water. Dry with paper towels. For stubborn glass areas, use a mixture of 1 part mild household detergent, 4 parts rubbing alcohol and 5 parts lukewarm water. Be sure to rinse with clear water and dry with paper towels. To remove hardened bug spots and bird droppings, rub gently with a plastic pot-scrubbing pad.

Tobacco smoke and the vaporization of chemicals in vinyl upholstery and trim often leave a stubborn film on interior glass. This film can be removed with a clean cloth dampened in a mixture of 1 part white vinegar to 1 part lukewarm water.

HARD INTERIOR SURFACES

To clean chrome, metalized plastic trim and the dashboard, wash with a soft cloth dipped in a sudsy mixture of warm water and mild household detergent. Rinse with a clean cloth dampened in lukewarm water. Buff with a soft cloth or chamois. Dirty chrome—but not metalized plastic—can be cleaned with a commercial chrome polish.

RUBBER

Wash floor pads and tires with a soft-bristled brush dipped in a mixture of warm water and mild household detergent. Rinse with lukewarm water. Wash whitewall tires with a special cleaning solution manufactured for that purpose and sold at any auto-supply store. Never wipe rubber with gasoline, benzene or other petroleum-based cleaners; they will attack the rubber.

LEATHER

To clean leather upholstery use only the suds of a mixture of mild soap and lukewarm water. Rub the suds gently into the leather with cheesecloth or any soft cloth. Do not let the soap saturate or soak through the leather. Remove suds with a clean cloth dampened in lukewarm water, and buff dry with cheesecloth or a soft cloth. To restore faded luster, dust the leather lightly with baby powder and buff with a soft cloth.

VINYL UPHOLSTERY

Wash vinyl upholstery with a mixture of mild household detergent and warm water. Rinse off with a cloth dampened with lukewarm water.

VINYL ROOF

Never use a metal or other stiff-bristled brush to scrub your vinyl roof. Though the vinyl is rugged, it still is only a relatively thin sheet stretched over the steel top of the car. Use a soft brush dipped in mild soapsuds. Rinse with clear water to remove all soap. For stubborn stains or streaks use a commercial vinyl-roof cleaner. For discolorations, use a vinyl restorer (available from your dealer or an auto-supply store) the same color as your roof.

REMOVING STAINS FROM NYLON AND RAYON

The finishes that make vinyl or leather upholstery almost impervious to spills unfortunately cannot be used for nylon or rayon upholstery and carpeting. As a result, these synthetic fabrics remain susceptible to stains of many kinds. To keep the fabrics spotless, deal with accidents as soon as they occur: scrape off spilled food or blot away grease immediately to prevent stains from setting. Then follow the steps described below, which spell out the first measures to take and, in addition, the ways to deal with stubborn blemishes.

Never resort to gasoline, naphtha, acetone or other solvents, laundry detergents or bleaches; all these will weaken or discolor rayon and nylon. If the remedies detailed here do not work, even when you repeat them, seek advice from specialists at a commercial dry-cleaning company.

Blood: Wipe as soon as possible with a clean cloth dipped in cold water; do not use soap or hot water, or the stain will set. Then pour two or three drops of household ammonia over the stain. Let the ammonia soak in for a few moments, then wash it off with a cloth dampened with cold water.

Butter, crayon, grease, oil: Scrape off the surface accumulation with a dull knife, then moisten a clean cloth (preferably cheesecloth) with a cleaning fluid labeled safe for use on synthetic fabric and rub at the stain from its rim toward the center. Use a clean absorbent towel to soak up excess cleaning fluid and the loosened stain particles.

Candy: For chocolate, wipe with a clean cloth dipped in lukewarm water. For nonchocolate candy, wipe with a clean cloth dipped in warm water. Then, if necessary, apply cleaning fluid as you would for butter or grease *(above)*.

Catsup: Wipe with a clean cloth dipped in cold water. Then, if necessary, apply a small amount of a commercial detergent-foam upholstery cleaner with a clean sponge or soft-bristled brush and rub the stain lightly. Wipe clean with a damp cloth. Dry with an absorbent towel or cloth.

Chewing gum: Rub an ice cube over the gum to harden it; then scrape it off with a dull knife. Ap-

ply cleaning fluid as described for catsup stains.

Coffee, fruit, ice cream, milk, soft drinks: Wipe with a clean cloth dipped in plain cold water; do not use soap or hot water. If necessary, use cleaning fluid as described for catsup stains.

Enamel, lacquer, oil-base paint: Wipe with a clean cloth dipped in turpentine. If the stain remains, wipe with a clean cloth soaked in a mixture of 1 part denatured alcohol to 1 part benzene. Finally, wash with another cloth dipped in mild soapsuds; then rinse with cold water.

Lipstick: Scrape off the surface accumulation with a dull knife. Then apply cleaning fluid as described for catsup stains.

Mustard: Wipe with a clean cloth dipped in plain warm water. Moisten a cloth with foam detergent and rub at the spot from the rim toward the center. Rinse with another cloth dampened in cold water.

Shoe polish (paste or wax): Scrape off the surface accumulation with a dull knife and apply cleaning fluid as described for catsup stains.

Tar: Scrape off the surface accumulation with a dull knife and apply cleaning fluid as described for catsup stains. Scrape again until all solid tar is off, then rub lightly with additional cleaner.

Urine: Wipe with a clean cloth dipped in a lukewarm solution of mild soap and rinse with a cloth dipped in cold water. Then saturate a clean cloth with a mixture of 1 part household ammonia to 5 parts cold water. Set the cloth on the spot, let it stand for a minute, then remove; rinse the spot with a clean cloth dipped in clear cold water.

Vomit: Blot up with paper towels and wipe the spot with a cloth dipped in cold water. Wash with a clean cloth dipped in a lukewarm solution of mild soapsuds and rinse with a cloth dipped in cold water. If odor persists, dip a rag in a solution of one-half cup baking soda dissolved in one quart of lukewarm water, wipe it over the stain and rinse with a clean water-soaked rag.

terfere with the proper operation of the carburetor. The complete degreasing procedure is detailed in the box at right.

Housing and storing your car

While washing and waxing go a long way toward saving a car's finish, garaging is added insurance that the paint will stay bright. A car that frequently stands out in the hot sun or in ice and snow will turn dull or pale and develop rust spots long before one that is kept under cover. If you don't have a garage or even a carport, consider investing in a plastic car cover, especially if you live near the ocean or in an area of heavy industrial fallout. Since these waterproof, greaseproof and fireproof coverings slip on or off quickly and fold into a compact bundle for storage, they can be used to cover your car when it must be left exposed.

Whenever your car will be out of service for a month or longer, you should take special protective measures to keep it in first-class condition. The fundamentals of car storage are listed in the box on page 145.

Finally, remember that part of the adventure of buying a car, new or used, is that no two cars are exactly alike. Every automobile will perform and handle slightly differently—and will respond somewhat differently, too—to the standard break-in and upkeep techniques. Furthermore, no two drivers are exactly alike. If you fancy high-speed driving, you cannot expect the same fuel economy you might get at lower speeds. The brake linings stand up longer in a car that travels mostly on turnpikes than in one that spends its life on city streets. Like so many rules, therefore, those set up for car maintenance are no more than general guidelines that you may have to adapt to suit your own car, your own driving needs and your personal preferences.

DEGREASING A DIRTY ENGINE

Before you undertake to clean the grime off an engine, buy a spray can of commercial degreaser, which costs about two dollars. A word of caution: follow the warnings on the label.

The numbers on the illustrations refer to the appropriate text paragraphs.

Tools and materials: scrub brush, soft-bristle brush, old tooth- or nailbrush, pail, masking tape or toothpicks; garden hose, baking soda, kerosene or parts-washing solvent, engine degreaser.

1 Warm up the engine for about 10 minutes, then turn off the ignition.

2 Seal off the holes in the battery caps with tape or rounded toothpicks. Dissolve three tablespoons of baking soda in a quart of water. Wash the battery with an old scrub brush or tooth- or nailbrush dipped in this solution. Rinse with clean water.

3 (Picture) Loosen the carburetor air-cleaner by unscrewing its wing nut. Disconnect hoses attached to the air cleaner. If a hose cannot be freed at the cleaner, trace it to its other end and release it there.

4 (Picture) Lift off the air cleaner and put it in a clean place.

5 Using either kerosene or a commercial parts-washing solvent, clean the outside of the carburetor and linkages with a tooth- or nailbrush.

6 (Pictures) Cover the distributor, coil, carburetor and the openings of any hoses with cling-type plastic wrap and secure with rubber bands, twist-ties or string.

7 Using a soft bristle-brush, clean the thin metal fins of the radiator.

8 From the engine itself remove as much caked grime as you can, using a putty knife. Spray the degreaser over the entire engine and all dirty areas under the hood.

9 Allow 15 minutes for the degreaser to work. Then spray the engine with the garden hose.

10 Turn off hose, remove plastic wraps and replace the air cleaner and hoses.

11 Start the car immediately and let it idle 10 minutes to dry out the engine.

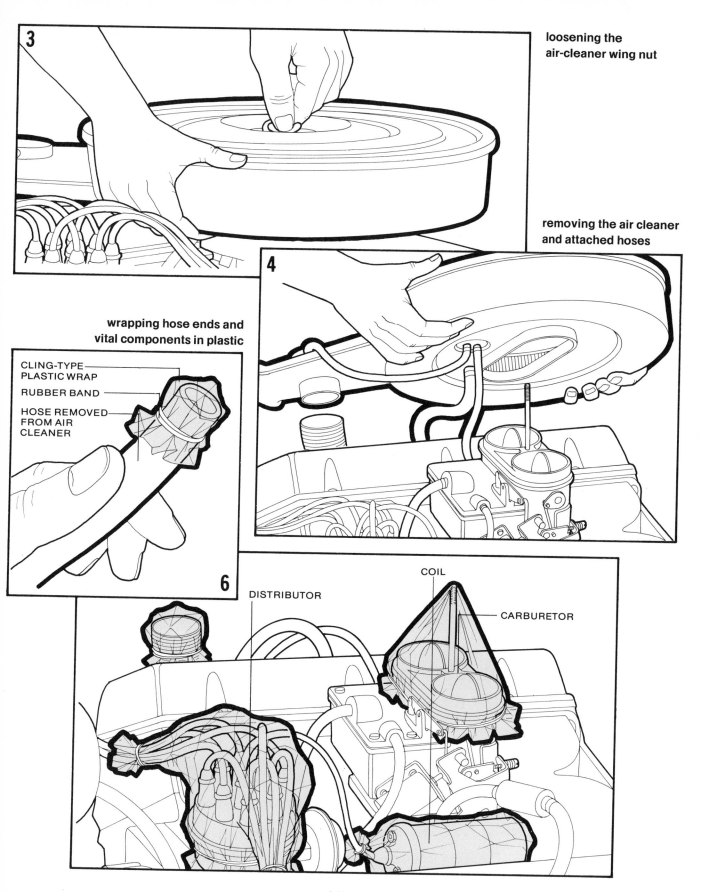

3

loosening the
air-cleaner wing nut

removing the air cleaner
and attached hoses

4

wrapping hose ends and
vital components in plastic

CLING-TYPE
PLASTIC WRAP

RUBBER BAND

HOSE REMOVED
FROM AIR
CLEANER

6

DISTRIBUTOR

COIL

CARBURETOR

MAINTENANCE AND REPAIRS

JOBS YOU CAN DO TO SAVE TIME AND MONEY

7

The modern automobile is designed to have a useful road life of at least 100,000 miles—almost a decade of driving for the average motorist—if its various systems and components are kept in good repair.

Best left to specialists are a number of maintenance and repair tasks, including all major overhauls; work involving such crucial systems as brakes and steering; and relatively infrequent jobs that may require expensive special equipment, such as wheel alignment and exhaust-system replacement.

There are a lot of jobs, however, that you can perform safely and efficiently, even if you have never tried them before. To do them, you must have all the right tools, most of which are inexpensive and pay for themselves quickly (pages 154-155). And you must be willing to get your hands and old clothes dirty as you work.

There are many advantages to doing the labor yourself. First, you will save money. In today's economy, doing a job that takes a mechanic just an hour can mean a saving of $6 to $18, depending on the wage scale in your region. By shopping for your own parts at discount stores you can buy them, in most cases, for less money than a dealer or repair shop would charge you. With products that you will use regularly, such as crankcase oil, transmission fluid and engine coolants, you can save by buying larger containers.

Besides saving money, you will gain something else just as important: peace of mind. By doing the work yourself—following all instructions carefully and conscientiously, and using the best-quality materials—you will have the satisfaction of accomplishment and know for certain that the job is done right.

And finally, it can be more convenient: no appointments to make long in advance, no doing without the car for a day, or more.

Each of the maintenance, troubleshooting and repair procedures in this chapter has been organized as a self-contained unit. The text that explains each job has been written in numbered steps for easy comprehension. Steps that benefit by pictorial explication are accompanied by specially prepared drawings. Each drawing is marked with the same number as the step it illustrates in the text.

Don't be alarmed if a particular part in your car looks slightly different from the one in the drawing. The part may not be the same in exact detail, but its function will be the same and the method of dealing with it will be similar.

The specific preventive-maintenance schedules necessary for trouble-free performance are listed in your owner's manual. That booklet will also provide specifications for replacement parts and lubricants necessary to do the jobs dealt with in this chapter. The manual will also help you to identify and locate parts that have failed or are deteriorating noticeably, so that you can replace them promptly.

For most of the tasks described in this chapter, you will need only your owner's manual. A detailed service manual (box, opposite), although not essential, may be of substantial help. Inexpensive and available from your dealer, this thick book lists every specification down to bolt torques for your particular car, information that will increase your understanding of the car and make every job easier. If you are planning to do your own tune-ups (Chapter 8), a service manual is required.

Before you start any job, read the appropriate section here, in its entirety, several times. When you fully understand the task at hand,

purchase all the replacement materials you are likely to need. You can determine the correct size and type of parts either by consulting the service manual for your car or by identifying the vehicle's make, model, year and engine size at the parts store. Always buy nationally known brands of replacement materials; check with your dealer about the acceptability of specific brands for your car.

All the jobs discussed here demand the same basic procedures and precautions:

■ BE METHODICAL. Assemble all tools and materials and put them in a convenient place in the order in which you will need them. Jot down for easy reference the applicable specifications for the task you will be performing.

■ BE NEAT. When working around dirty or greasy areas, be sure to keep the area and the components on which you are working clean. You can do this by using water, or a solvent-soaked cloth or paper towel.

■ BE PATIENT. The first time you perform a task, proceed slowly. Be sure you understand exactly what it is you must do before starting each step. When unsure, reread the section.

■ BE SAFE. When you must raise part of the car, always follow safe jacking procedures (pages 156-157). Before you begin any repair work, move the car onto a flat, even surface. To prevent your car from rolling accidentally, the parking brake must be engaged; also place automatic transmissions in park and manual transmissions in first gear, except where otherwise noted.

Never get under the car when it is held up only by the bumper jack—it could slip and cause a serious accident. Always use jack stands or wheel ramps before sliding underneath. Never get beneath a vehicle when the engine is running, and when you do get under the car, wear a cap to keep grease out of your hair.

TWO MANUALS MADE FOR YOUR CAR

Two important publications—the owner's manual and the service manual—are put out to help you understand the methods of operation and the maintenance and repair procedures that apply specifically to your car. The two manuals should not be confused, since each has been written to fill certain needs:

Owner's manual: Tucked in the glove compartment of every new car, this booklet supplies all the necessary routine information about operating and servicing your car. Among other things, it explains the proper way to start the engine and change a flat tire; how to operate the heater, air conditioner and radio; and when to lubricate and change the engine oil. The manual also provides guides for minor troubleshooting, and lists such vital statistics as the capacity of the gas tank, recommended tire pressures and the types of fuses required for the electrical system. This manual is must reading for every car owner. If you have lost yours, get another from your dealer. It will cost about a dollar.

Service manual: The size and thickness of a major metropolitan telephone book, the service manual for your car is packed with technical information that will fascinate anyone with a mechanical flair. It lists every conceivable detail of maintenance and repair, from the smallest engine part to the exact torque needed to tighten every nut and bolt. It describes the parts and the operation of all the vital components and explains complex procedures. One key word of caution, however: the service manual is written for the professional mechanic. It is not light, or even easy, reading. You will have to spend the time and exert the patience needed to understand the technical language. Nevertheless, the service manual is an indispensable supplement to this book if you are planning to do extensive work on your own car.

The service manual costs about seven dollars. It can be ordered with a postcard that is included in your owner's manual.

Particularly watch your head while working under the vehicle in the engine compartment or, as a matter of fact, anywhere else near a car. A nut or rust and dirt dropped into your eyes or a faceful of engine oil or transmission fluid is painful and can be dangerous.

■ AVOID SHOCKS. Never use a trouble light if the ground or car is wet—as it would be, for example, while flushing the cooling system. Water can transmit deadly electricity. To be safe, use a flashlight if illumination is required in wet or damp areas.

On many of the jobs, your biggest problem will be deciding how much force you can safely use to remove or replace parts and how best to dispose of old parts and fluids. Generally, you can free even the most stubbornly rusted fastener if you first squirt on penetrating oil and give it sufficient time to do its work. Still, you might have to apply considerable muscle to disassemble a component; just make sure that you use the correct tool. Never try to gain leverage by striking one tool with another and never hammer or jimmy any fastener. If the fastener should break, you will be stuck with a difficult —and probably expensive—repair problem.

When you reassemble parts, you should not have to use much force, since the components should fit together smoothly. If they do not, double check to see that you are placing the correct part in the correct slot. In this phase of the job, do not use more force in tightening a fastener than you would in firmly securing the lid of a jar, unless the service manual calls for the application of a specific amount of force with a torque wrench (page 154).

Old parts such as burned-out bulbs and cracked hoses can be chucked into the trash can. Crankcase oil and transmission fluid, however, can be taken to your local gas station; they will dispose of it for you.

TOOLS FOR JOBS YOU CAN DO

This basic set of tools, shown grouped with the paragraph numbers in the text, will enable you to perform the jobs described in this chapter.

Don't sacrifice quality to save money: cheap tools wear out faster and may damage car parts. The price ranges given represent the spread between adequate quality and professional quality tools. If you bought every item shown, your total expenditure should be less than $150.

The tools you will need—plus the parts and materials—are listed in the introduction to each job.

1 Screwdrivers: for slotted screws, one with a 6-inch blade and 1/4-inch tip and one with a 4-inch blade and 1/8-inch tip; for Phillips-head screws, one with a 3-inch blade and one with a 6-inch blade. Total price: $6 to $11.

2 Pliers: locking-grip type that can be used as pliers, as an adjustable wrench or as a vise; needle-nose type for use in cramped spaces and electrical work; standard type for routine gripping jobs. Total price: $6 to $15.

3 Wrenches: a combination of open- and box-end wrenches in graduated sizes from 3/8 inch to 7/8 inch. Total price: $17 to $25. Adjustable-jaw wrench, for bolts up to 7/8 inch. Price: $2 to $5.

4 Socket-wrench set with 3/8-inch drive: includes extension shafts 3 inches and 6 inches long; sockets come in graduated sizes from 3/8 inch to 7/8 inch (or, for metric bolts, from 7 mm to 19 mm); forward-and-reverse ratchet handle 8 inches long; universal joint for working around corners; socket for shock-absorber removal. Total price: $30 to $60.

5 Tools for specific jobs: torque wrench for tightening bolts to exact specifications ($15 to $40); test light for checking electrical connections (about $2); grease gun with adapters for chassis lubrication (about $8); jack stand (two recommended, $10 to $35 per pair); work light (about $4); funnel for adding engine oil (about $.50); flexible-spout funnel for adding transmission fluid (about $1.50); fuse puller for the safe removal of burned-out fuses (about $1); rubber mallet for replacing wheel covers and hubcaps and for pounding out body dents (about $2); oil-filter wrench for removing slippery oil filters (about $2).

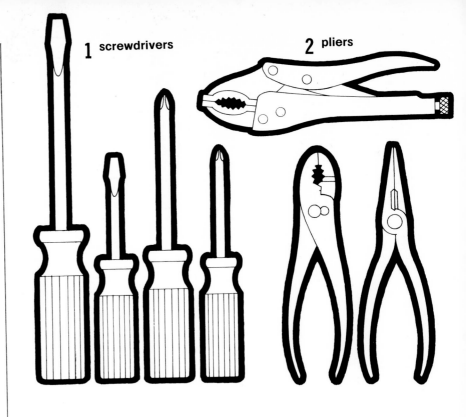

1 screwdrivers

2 pliers

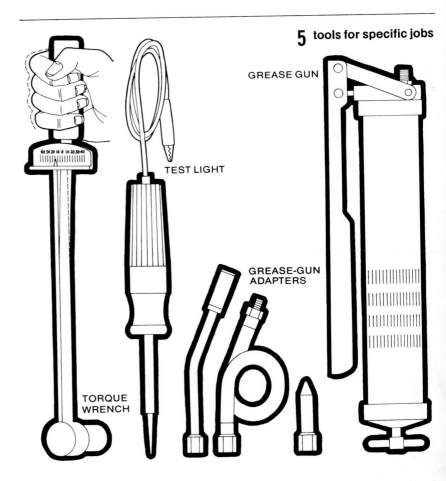

5 tools for specific jobs

GREASE GUN

TEST LIGHT

GREASE-GUN ADAPTERS

TORQUE WRENCH

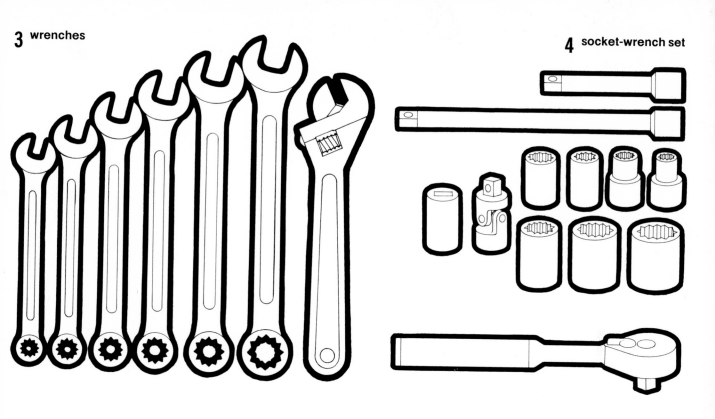

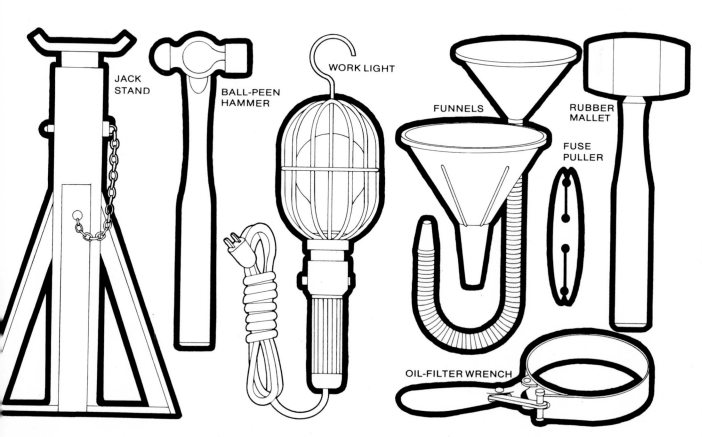

JACK
STAND

BALL-PEEN
HAMMER

WORK LIGHT

FUNNELS

RUBBER
MALLET

FUSE
PULLER

OIL-FILTER WRENCH

RAISING THE CAR

Every automobile comes from the factory equipped with a jack to be used in changing flats. However, if you plan to work beneath the car, you must support it more solidly with jack stands *(steps 5 and 6)* or wheel ramps *(step 7)*.

Never get under the car unless it is on these special supports. Also, always use them in pairs at either the front or rear ends of the car.

1 Before jacking a car always be sure the ignition is off, the parking brakes are engaged and the automatic-transmission lever is in park. If your car has a manual transmission, make sure that you effectively lock the transmission by shifting into first gear. This helps brake the rear wheels.

If you're going to be working on the front of the car, be sure to place wooden or metal chocks in front of and behind the rear wheel diagonally opposite the front wheel being raised, as illustrated below. If you're going to work on a rear wheel, you should chock both of the front wheels.

2 (Picture) Most American cars come equipped with upright jacks that raise the wheel by hooking under the bumper; cars of recent vintage frequently have special slots in the bumper to engage the jack hook. Many subcompact cars have jacking brackets, mounted along the rocker panels, that are designed for special scissor jacks. (If your car does not have a bumper jack, consult your owner's manual or look for a sticker in the trunk that will explain how to use the jack.)

The base of a bumper jack must be positioned so that, at first, the jack is angled slightly under the car. As the car is raised, the jack should become absolutely vertical.

3 To raise the car, set the small metal ratchet-control tab on the jack hook to its horizontal-up position. Using the tire iron as a jack handle, pump up and down.

4 To lower the car, flip the ratchet-control tab to its vertical-down position and pump until the jack hook is disengaged.

5 (Picture) To position jack stands before working under a car whose front wheels must be removed, chock the rear wheels. Then jack up one side until the lower suspension arm that connects the wheel and chassis is lifted higher than the top of the jack stand. Place one of the stands under the outside end of the arm, directly be-

neath the coil spring. Lower the car onto the stand. Repeat the procedure on the opposite side to position the second stand.

6 (Picture) To position jack stands at the rear end of a car first chock the front wheels. Then jack up one side until the rear axle is higher than the top of the stand. Place the stand under the axle within six inches of the springs. Lower the car onto the stand. Repeat the process on the opposite side of the axle. This forces the rear wheels high into their wheel wells. If you want to remove the wheels, place the stands under the chassis beams forward, but within 12 inches, of the rear axle.

7 (Picture) Wheel ramps may be used if you do not need to remove the wheels or leave them free to spin, as when checking brakes or bearings. Position the ramps directly in line with the wheels that are to be raised. With someone to guide you, drive very slowly—forward or back depending upon which end of the car is to be raised —onto the ramps.

Be extremely careful not to overdrive the edges of the ramps or to let the wheels slide off the sides. When the car is positioned on the ramps, turn off the engine and engage the parking brake. Place a manual transmission in first gear and an automatic transmission in park. Chock the wheels that are still on the ground.

2

**raising front end
with bumper jack**

WHEEL CHOCKS ——————— ROCKER PANELS

5

**using jack stands
to hold up front end**

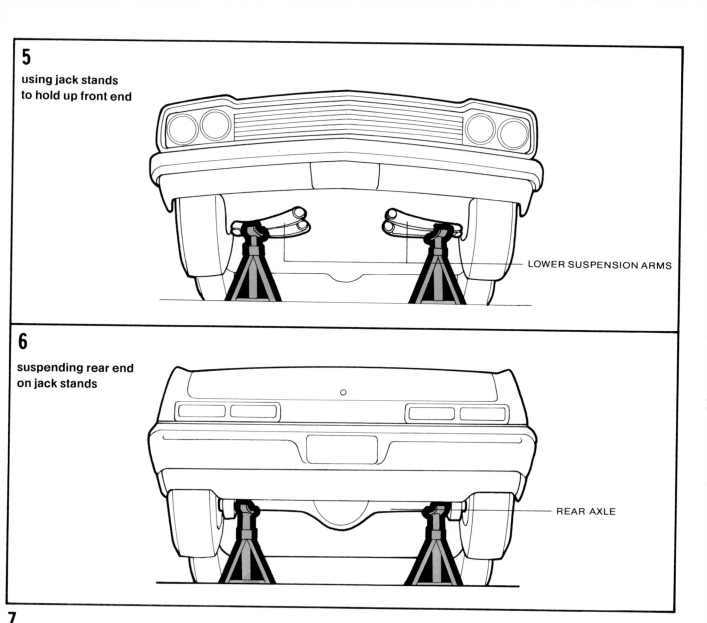

LOWER SUSPENSION ARMS

6

**suspending rear end
on jack stands**

REAR AXLE

7

**perching front wheels
on wheel ramps**

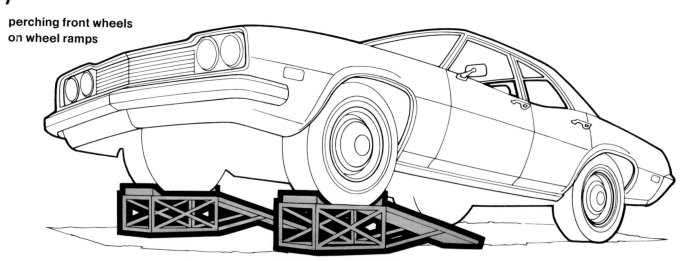

CHANGING A FLAT TIRE

Flat tires occur less frequently than they used to, but every motorist eventually gets stuck with one. Removing the flat and putting on the spare is simple when an orderly series of steps is followed. To make the changing both easier and safer, carry two wooden chocks, a rubber mallet, a small can of light oil, and warning flares or reflectors *(page 291)*.

CAUTION: Be sure the car is on level ground before you change a tire.

1 To change a front tire, place a manual transmission in gear, an automatic transmission in park. Engage the parking brake. Chock the front and back of the rear wheel that is diagonally opposite the one you are changing. To change a rear tire, chock both front wheels.

2 Remove the tire iron, jack and spare tire from the trunk.

3 (Picture) Using the tapered end of the tire iron, pry off the wheel cover.

4 (Picture) With the lug-wrench end of the tire iron, loosen each lug nut two turns. The lugs may be tight; hold the tire iron as shown for greater leverage.

5 Set up the jack and raise the car *(page 156)* until the wheel you are replacing is two to three inches off the ground.

6 (Picture) Remove the lug nuts and put them in the upturned wheel cover.

7 (Picture) Pull off the wheel and squirt several drops of light oil onto the studs to prevent rusting.

8 Mount the spare tire on the studs and screw in the lug nuts by hand. Tighten with the tire iron until the wheel turns.

9 Using the jack, lower the car until the tire touches the ground.

10 (Picture) Finish the tightening of the lug nuts in the crisscross sequence shown. Turn them as tight as you can.

11 (Picture) Slip the wheel cover into position and tap around its rim with a rubber mallet until it is firmly seated.

12 Disengage the jack and pull out the chocks. Place all the equipment and the flat tire in the trunk before you leave.

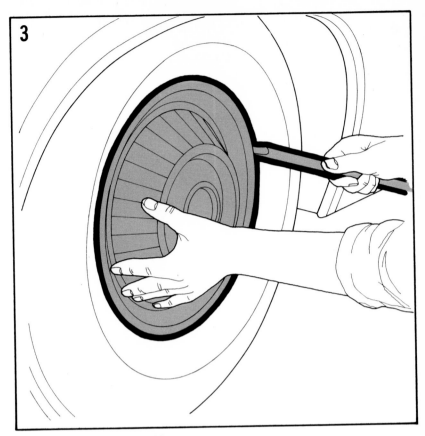

removing wheel cover with tapered end of the tire iron

applying light oil to studs of the hub

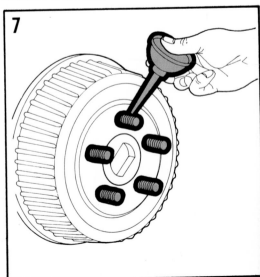

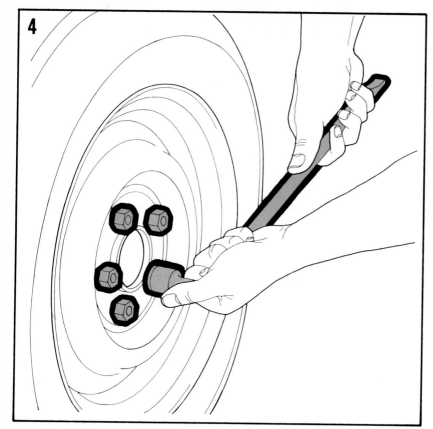

**grasping tire iron
for best leverage**

**safeguarding lug nuts
against loss**

**using rubber mallet to
secure wheel cover**

**proper sequence
in tightening lug nuts**

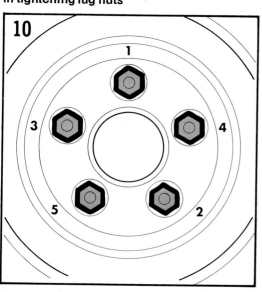

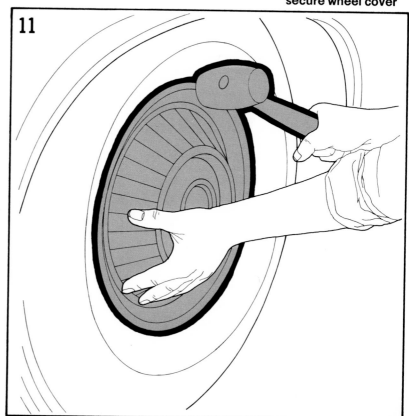

SILENCING RATTLES AND SQUEAKS

As it accumulates mileage, every car develops unwanted body noises. Unless a noise is symptomatic of a deep-seated problem *(Chapter 9)*, it usually can be easily quieted.

Tools and materials: socket wrench; silicone-spray lubricant; stainless silicone-stick lubricant.

1 If a door, hood or trunk lid squeaks when you open and shut it, apply a stick of stainless silicone lubricant to all hinges.

2 (Picture) If the noise persists, hold a piece of stiff material—a credit card, for example—across the gap where the door, hood or trunk lid meets the body. Determine if the surfaces are flush and in line *(top drawing)*. An examination of the chrome molding also may indicate improper alignment *(bottom drawing)*. If the parts are out of line, refer to your service manual before adjusting the hinges. Or have a garage or body shop do the job.

3 To find the source of a noise heard only on the road, remove all loose objects from the glove compartment, passenger compartment and trunk. Make sure the jack, tire iron and spare tire are secured. Drive at a moderate speed over a bumpy road and listen. If the noise comes from the body, see step 4; if it comes from under the car, consult step 5.

4 (Picture) Noises from the bumpers, fenders and grille usually are the result of loose bolts. By opening the hood and doors, these body bolts are easily accessible. With a socket wrench, tighten every accessible loose bolt. Also tighten all bolts or screws on the door, trunk and hood hinges, as well as those that fasten the lock and latch components. Some door hinges are mounted with large screws that can be tightened only with special tools; in this case the job must be done by a professional. Then rub stainless silicone lubricant on the lock latch. If the hood noise continues, see if the two rubber bumpers on top of the grille are in firm contact with the closed hood. If they are not, raise them by turning slightly counterclockwise.

For unaccountable noise in a door, partially open and close it with a quick, swinging motion; something may have fallen into the recess between the metal and the interior trim. To reach the object, you must have a body man remove the trim panel.

To cure squeaking in either the door or trunk lid, spray silicone lubricant on the rubber weather stripping.

5 (Picture) Noises emanating from the undercarriage near a wheel usually mean some part of the suspension assembly is loose or binding. Tighten all loose control-arm mounting bolts and spray all rubber bushings around the bolts. If the bushings are badly deteriorated, the silicone may be of little help and the bushings will have to be replaced. If your car is equipped with leaf springs in the rear, spray them with the silicone lubricant—do not use lubricating oil, which will cause the rubber fittings to deteriorate.

For noise coming from the center of the undercarriage, tighten the fasteners on all exhaust-system clamps. Now try to wiggle the muffler and exhaust pipes. If they still are so loose that they bang against the chassis, they must be replaced.

4

locating body bolts, hinges, latches and locks

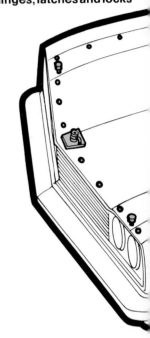

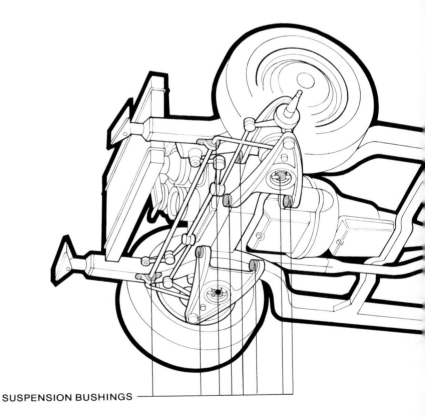

SUSPENSION BUSHINGS

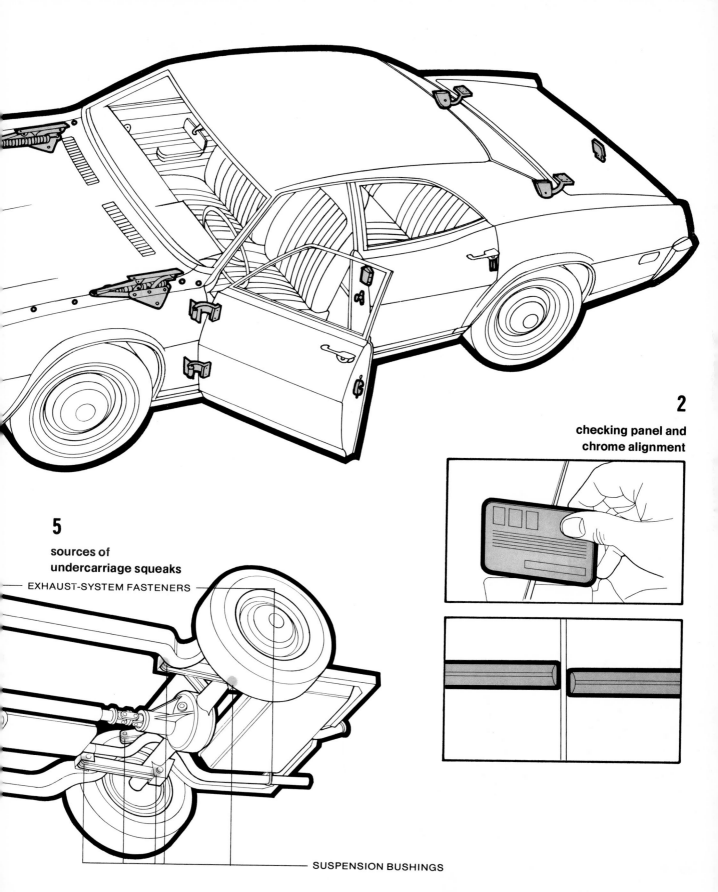

2

**checking panel and
chrome alignment**

5

**sources of
undercarriage squeaks**

EXHAUST-SYSTEM FASTENERS

SUSPENSION BUSHINGS

161

CHANGING ENGINE OIL

The engine's crankcase oil should be changed at specified intervals. The oil filter usually is replaced with every second oil change. Use only the specified grade of replacement oil.

Tools and materials: open-end wrench, oil-filter wrench, funnel, drain pan; oil, oil filter (if being replaced).

1 Idle the engine for five minutes so that the oil will flow easily; then turn it off. Find the crankcase drain plug in the sump under the engine and place a pan under it.

2 (Picture) Loosen the drain plug with a wrench, then unscrew it slowly by hand. Be ready to pull it away quickly to avoid the gush of warm oil.

3 When the oil has drained, wipe the plug and its recess. Replace the plug and tighten it. (If you're not changing the filter, proceed to step 7.)

4 (Picture) Move the drain pan beneath the oil filter. Clamp the oil-filter wrench around the unit and loosen it. Finish unscrewing the filter by hand. Empty the filter into the drain pan, then discard it. Also discard the oil-filter gasket.

5 Wipe the filter recess with a clean cloth to remove any dirt, grime or old oil.

6 (Picture) Lightly coat the gasket of the new filter with several drops of fresh engine oil. Screw it in by hand until you meet resistance, then give it three quarters of a turn. Do not use the oil-filter wrench.

7 (Picture) Remove the oil-filler cap located atop the rocker-arm cover. Recheck your manual for the crankcase capacity; include an extra quart if you changed the filter. Pour in fresh oil; replace the cap.

8 Start the engine and let it idle for a minute. Turn off the engine.

9 See if there is any seepage around the drain plug or filter. If there is, wipe them clean and tighten a bit further. Start the engine, let it idle for a minute and check again. If there still is seepage, either the plug or the filter gasket is defective.

10 If there is no leakage, check the oil level with the engine's dipstick. If the level is below, or even with, the bottom line, add another half quart.

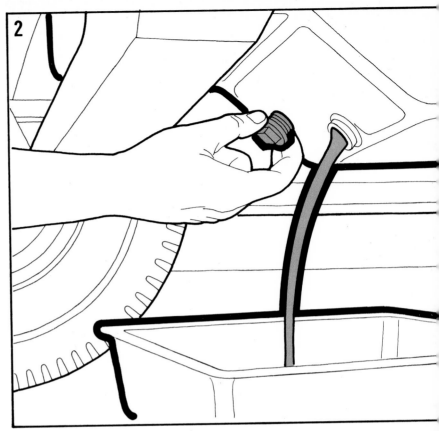

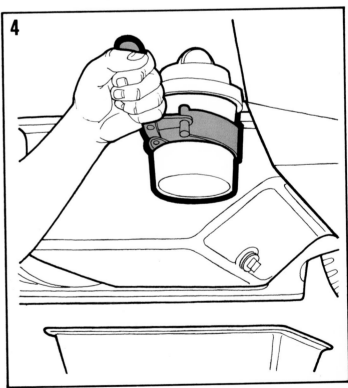

loosening old filter with an oil-filter wrench

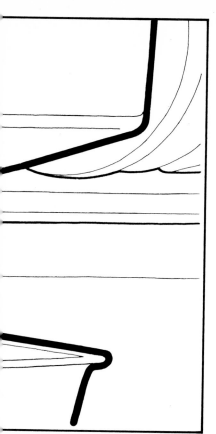

removing drain plug
from the oil sump

applying engine oil to
gasket of new filter

6

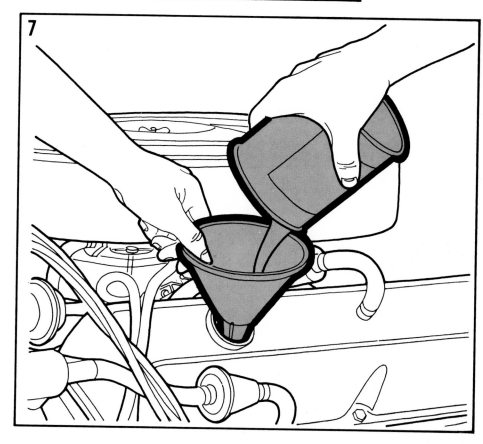

7

adding fresh oil through
filler atop engine

163

LUBRICATING THE CHASSIS

Certain bearings and close-fitting joints must be lubricated according to schedules in your owner's manual. Once you have located the grease fittings of these joints, lubricating requires only a hand-operated grease gun. Use the grease specified in your owner's manual. Also check the lubricant level in the rear axle.

Tools and materials: grease gun with appropriate fittings; chassis lubricant.

NOTE: If outside temperatures are below freezing, park the car for 30 minutes in a heated garage so the grease flows easily.

1 (Picture) With the aid of the drawing *(below, right)*, find the joints to be greased. Some fittings may be positioned differently in your car; check your service manual.

2 Raise the car's front end onto jack stands *(pages 156–157)*.

3 (Picture) Check the type of grease fittings on your car and place the appropriate attachment on the grease gun.

The nipple fitting at left in drawing 3 calls for a recessed attachment. When you·lubricate, apply grease until it begins to ooze out through the middle of the joint.

The sealed fitting at right in drawing 3 has a threaded metal access plug that must be removed with a wrench. For this particular fitting you will use a rubber-tipped attachment on the grease gun.

CAUTION: With the sealed fitting, apply grease only until the middle rubber boot begins to swell; do not force in lubricant after this reaction or the boot will rupture.

4 (Picture) Fill the grease gun and wipe each fitting with a cloth before lubricating with the gun.

Replace and tighten the access plugs as you finish with each sealed fitting.

5 Lower the car from the jack stands and set them to one side.

6 (Picture) Use a wrench to loosen the lubricating plug located on the rear-axle housing. If lubricant begins to seep out, the level is acceptable; tighten the plug. If you can remove the plug and nothing comes out, you may need to add lubricant. Let your gasoline station do it.

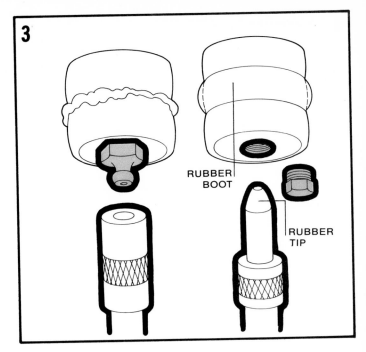

two types of fittings and grease-gun attachments

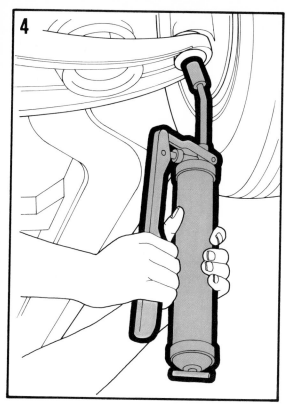

4

forcing lubricant into a
fitting with a hand grease gun

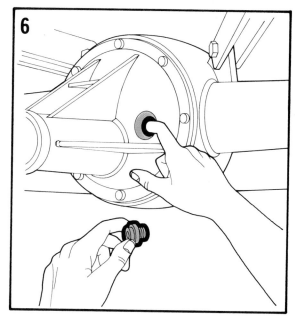

checking lubricant level
with rear-axle plug out

6

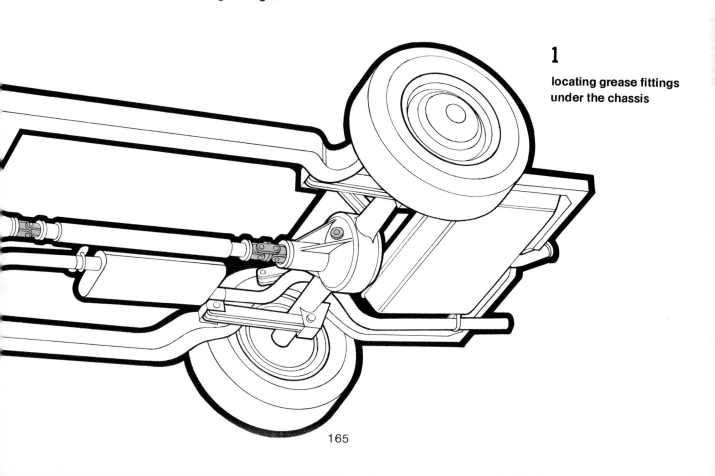

1

locating grease fittings
under the chassis

REPACKING FRONT-WHEEL BEARINGS

The bearings on the front wheels must be cleaned and packed with grease at about 30,000-mile intervals. To repack the bearings you will require the information in your service manual.

Tools and materials: tire tools and jack stands, socket wrench, pliers, screwdriver, torque wrench, hammer, wood block, steel punch; wheel-bearing grease, two new grease seals, two new cotter pins, a rubber mallet, kerosene, a length of heavy-gauge wire looped at the ends, a piece of cardboard 1/4 inch thick, polyethylene gloves, small paintbrush, clean cloth or paper toweling.

1 Pry off the hubcap or wheel cover of the front wheel you are working on. If your car has disc brakes, loosen the lug nuts, raise the front end of the car on jack stands *(page 157)* and remove the lug nuts and wheel. If your car has drum brakes, leave the front wheel on and the lug nuts tight.

NOTE: You will be cleaning various nuts, washers and bearings by soaking them in kerosene. The inner and outer bearings on each wheel must be kept separate and replaced in their original positions. An easy way to avoid mistakes is to use two carefully labeled plastic containers of kerosene: one for the inner bearing of the wheel and another one for the outer bearing. As you work, place each bearing and its associated parts into the appropriate container.

2 (Picture) Brush dirt from the spindle and pry off the spindle cap with a screwdriver. Use pliers to unbend the cotter-pin arms, which will be wrapped around the lock nut; discard the pin. Pull off the lock nut, unscrew the adjusting nut, pull off the metal washer and drop all these parts into the same outer-bearing container.

Grasp either the disc brake—or the still-attached wheel if the car has drum brakes—and draw it slightly toward you. Then push the disc or wheel back to its original position. This movement will bring the outer bearing outward along the wheel spindle so that you can pull the bearing off.

CAUTION: Do not remove either of the bearing cups from the hub. (They are shown removed in the exploded drawing for clarity only.)

Slide the outer bearing from the spindle and put it in the outer-bearing container.

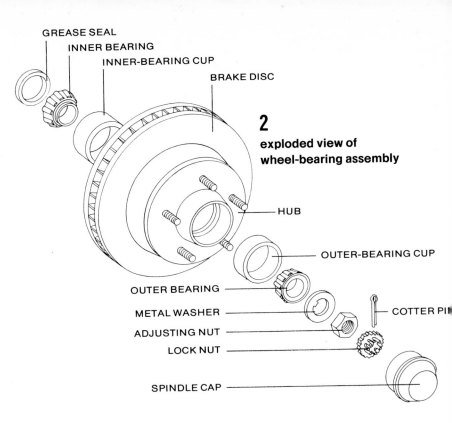

GREASE SEAL
INNER BEARING
INNER-BEARING CUP
BRAKE DISC

2

**exploded view of
wheel-bearing assembly**

HUB

OUTER-BEARING CUP

OUTER BEARING

METAL WASHER

ADJUSTING NUT

LOCK NUT

COTTER PIN

SPINDLE CAP

**unbolting the caliper
of a disc brake**

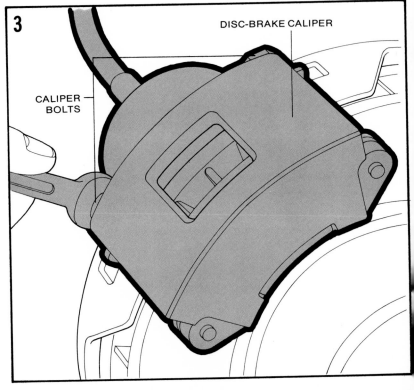

3

DISC-BRAKE CALIPER

CALIPER
BOLTS

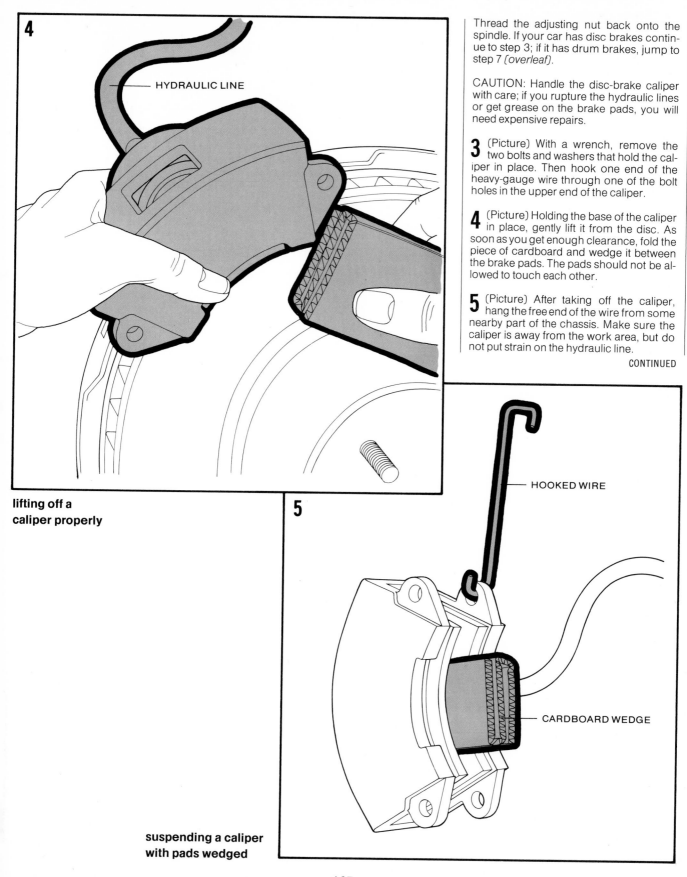

4

HYDRAULIC LINE

**lifting off a
caliper properly**

Thread the adjusting nut back onto the spindle. If your car has disc brakes continue to step 3; if it has drum brakes, jump to step 7 *[overleaf]*.

CAUTION: Handle the disc-brake caliper with care; if you rupture the hydraulic lines or get grease on the brake pads, you will need expensive repairs.

3 (Picture) With a wrench, remove the two bolts and washers that hold the caliper in place. Then hook one end of the heavy-gauge wire through one of the bolt holes in the upper end of the caliper.

4 (Picture) Holding the base of the caliper in place, gently lift it from the disc. As soon as you get enough clearance, fold the piece of cardboard and wedge it between the brake pads. The pads should not be allowed to touch each other.

5 (Picture) After taking off the caliper, hang the free end of the wire from some nearby part of the chassis. Make sure the caliper is away from the work area, but do not put strain on the hydraulic line.

CONTINUED

5

HOOKED WIRE

CARDBOARD WEDGE

**suspending a caliper
with pads wedged**

REPACKING BEARINGS

CONTINUED

6 After removing the caliper, grasp the disc and pull; it should come off easily. The inner bearing and grease seal should be held on the spindle by the adjusting nut. If the adjusting nut does not hold the bearing and seal on the spindle, place the disc face down on a clean cloth and use a hammer and punch to tap the bearing and grease seal free.

7 (Picture) If you are working on a wheel with drum brakes, grasp the wheel itself and pull it off. The inner bearing and grease seal should be held by the adjusting nut.

8 Remove the adjusting nut, inner bearing and grease seal from the spindle. Place the adjusting nut in the first container and the bearing in the second container; discard the seal.

9 Now clean the spindle thoroughly with a kerosene-soaked cloth. If you are working on a car with drum brakes, cover the spindle with a clean cloth and use a dry paintbrush to flick away dirt from the surrounding brake assembly. Leave the protective cloth in place.

10 With a kerosene-soaked cloth, clean the inside of the hub and the inner- and outer-bearing cups that were left inside the hub of the disc or drum.

NOTE: Inspect the cups for scratches, pitting or signs of excessive wear. Should a cup be scratched or pitted, finish the repacking job. But when the wheels are back on, drive to a service station at your first opportunity and have the cups replaced.

11 (Picture) Use a screwdriver blade to spread fresh grease evenly around the interior of the hub and its grease cups.

12 Use clean cloth to dry the two bearings and examine them for cracks, nicks or worn spots. Should a bearing be damaged, both it and its bearing cup must be replaced by a professional.

13 (Picture) Put on disposable polyethylene gloves. Scoop a glob of grease into the palm of your hand and knead the inner bearing into it; the grease must get between the rollers. Insert the inner bearing, narrow end first, into its cup. Then pack the outer bearing with grease and set it on a clean piece of cardboard.

14 (Picture) Smear a light film of grease on both sides of a new grease seal. Carefully place the seal over the inner bearing. Position a block of wood over the seal. Tap the wood gently with a hammer, rotating it with each tap. When the seal is level with the hub lip, it is seated.

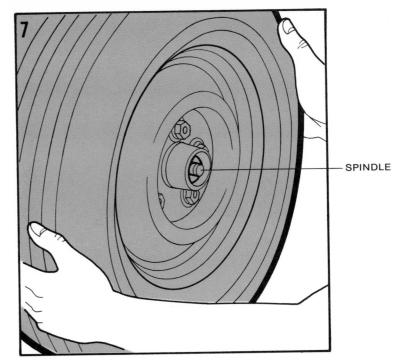

SPINDLE

**pulling off the
wheel and drum**

**applying grease to
the hub with screwdriver**

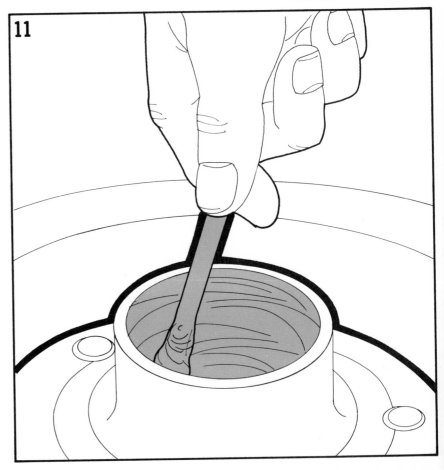

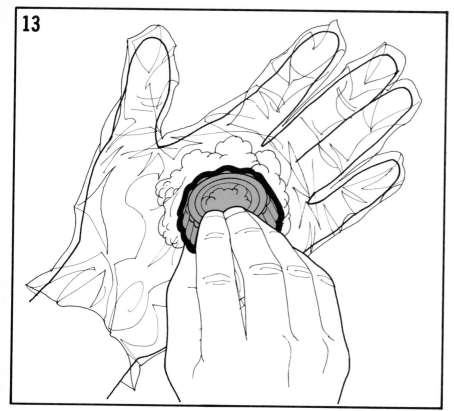

13

**packing the
bearing with grease**

**tapping the inner seal and
bearing into position**

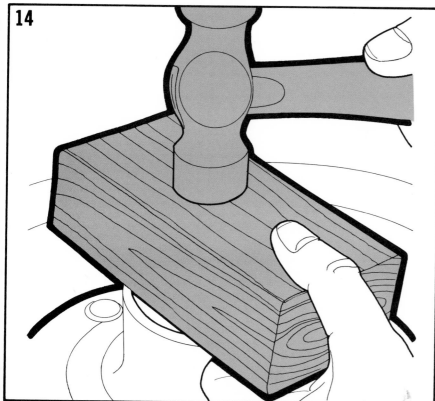

14

CAUTION: Inspect the seal for cracks. If this fragile part sustained any damage during installation, you must remove it and put in another one.

15 Remount the disc—or the entire wheel and drum if you have drum brakes—over the wheel spindle. The spindle must be held steady while you move the disc or wheel in place.

16 Slide the outer bearing over the spindle. The narrow end of the outer bearing must face inward.

Put on the washer and adjusting nut, then finger-tighten the nut. If your car has disc brakes continue to step 17; if it has drum brakes, jump to step 18.

17 With a clean cloth, wipe both the inner and outer surfaces of the disc. Carefully remove the caliper from its hanger wire. Position the base of the caliper, remove the piece of cardboard and tilt the top into place. Using a torque wrench, tighten the caliper bolts and washers to the torque specified in your service manual. Then place the wheel over the lugs and finger-tighten the lug nuts.

18 Consult your service manual for the torque—in foot-pounds—required to seat the bearings. Set your torque wrench at that number and tighten the adjusting nut. Then use a socket wrench to loosen the adjusting nut half a turn. Consult your service manual for the second torque setting and retighten the adjusting nut to that specification.

19 Slip the lock nut over the spindle. Position the nut so that its slots line up with the cotter-pin hole in the spindle.

20 Insert a new cotter pin through a slot in the lock nut and spindle. Bend its two halves around the lock nut.

21 Rotate the wheel in both directions. It should move smoothly and silently. If it does not, retrace all previous steps—or seek professional help.

22 Gently tap the spindle cap into place with a rubber mallet.

23 Lower the car from the jack stands. If you have been working on a car with disc brakes, you must use a tire iron to finish tightening the lug nuts of each wheel, following the proper sequence *(page 159)*.

24 Before you start to drive, pump the brake pedal several times to make sure that the brakes operate properly. If you have disc brakes, the pedal may go to the floor the first time you press down; however, it will return to its normal position after you pump the pedal two or three times.

CHANGING FLUID IN AN AUTOMATIC TRANSMISSION

The fluid in the automatic transmission should be changed regularly, usually at 24,000-mile intervals.

Tools and materials: screwdriver, socket wrench, flexible-necked funnel; transmission filter replacement kit, new transmission fluid, gasket sealant.

1 Warm the transmission fluid by driving for at least 10 miles making frequent stops and starts. Position the car on a level work area and turn off the engine. Raise the front end on jack stands *(pages 156-157)*.

2 Place a pan under the shallow pan-shaped sump under the transmission.

3 (Picture) If there is a drain plug, unbolt it with a wrench, let the fluid run out and replace the plug. If there is no plug, remove the sump and unfasten three bolts on each side of the transmission sump. Some of the fluid will drain into the pan. When the draining stops, remove the sump and empty the rest of the fluid. Wipe the sump clean.

4 (Picture) Unfasten the filter attached to the valve body. Make sure that the O-ring gasket between the filter and the valve body above also comes off. If the filter is a reusable type, clean it by soaking it in kerosene; otherwise, discard it.

5 With a kerosene-soaked cloth, wipe the surface areas where the sump is bolted to the transmission.

6 With a new O-ring gasket in place, put the new filter in position and secure it.

7 (Picture) Brush the rim of the sump with sealant and put the new transmission gasket in place.

8 (Picture) Replace the sump and tighten evenly, securing the bolts in the numbered sequence shown.

9 (Picture) Place a funnel with a long flexible tube into the filler neck, and pour in the new transmission fluid.

10 Drive the car for about 10 miles. With the engine still idling, check the fluid level. If the fluid is below the low mark, add fluid in half-pint increments until you reach the full mark. Be very careful not to overfill.

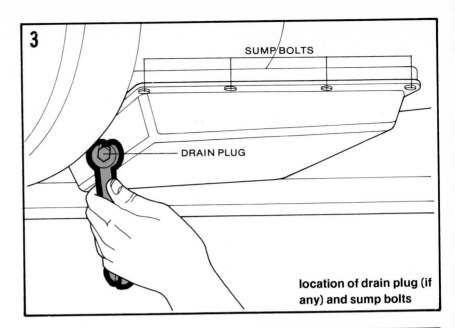

3

SUMP BOLTS

DRAIN PLUG

location of drain plug (if any) and sump bolts

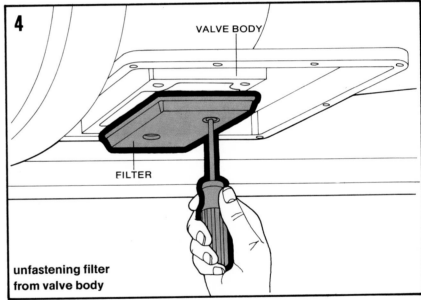

4

VALVE BODY

FILTER

unfastening filter from valve body

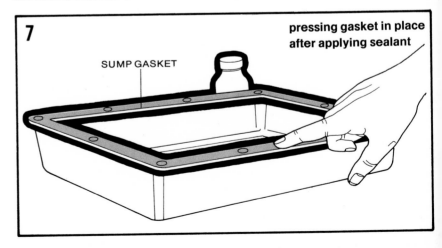

7

pressing gasket in place after applying sealant

SUMP GASKET

sequence for tightening sump bolts

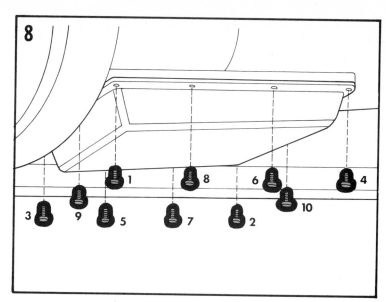

adding fresh fluid through filler neck

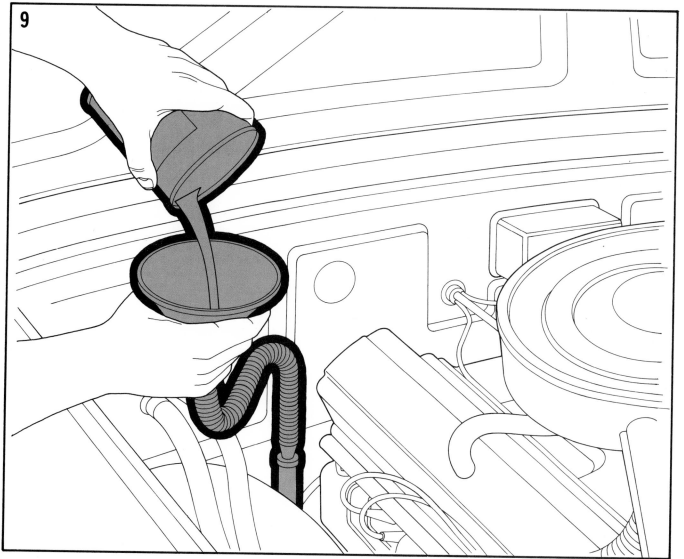

FLUSHING THE COOLING SYSTEM

The cooling system should be drained and cleaned according to the schedule recommended in your service manual However, if you notice a film of sludge on the inside of the filler neck when you make your monthly coolant check *(page 140)*, flush the system as soon as possible. Always start cooling-system service when the engine is cold.

Tools and materials: wrench, pliers; radiator flush, new coolant.

1 With the ignition off and when the engine is cool, remove the radiator cap.

2 (Picture) With a pair of pliers, open the petcock at the bottom of the radiator.

3 (Picture) With a wrench, remove the engine-block drain plugs. In-line engines have one plug; V8s have two, one on each side of the block.

4 When the engine block is empty, tighten the petcock and secure drain plugs.

5 (Picture) Fill the radiator almost to the top with water. Add a can of fast-flush solvent. Run the engine for about 15 minutes at fast idle with radiator cap off.

6 Turn off the engine and drain the system again as in steps 2 and 3. Leave the petcock open and the plugs out.

7 (Picture) Place the garden hose in the radiator's filler neck and flush with water under pressure.

8 With water from the hose still running, start the engine and let it run at fast idle for at least five minutes before turning it off.

9 Tighten the radiator petcock and replace and tighten the drain plugs.

10 Consult your owner's manual for the correct proportions of antifreeze and water. Pour the mixture into the radiator.

11 Replace the radiator cap, start the engine and let it idle for two minutes. Turn off the engine, remove the radiator cap and check to see that the level of the coolant is correct.

12 Replace the radiator cap and secure it tightly. Check for leaks from the drain plugs and petcock.

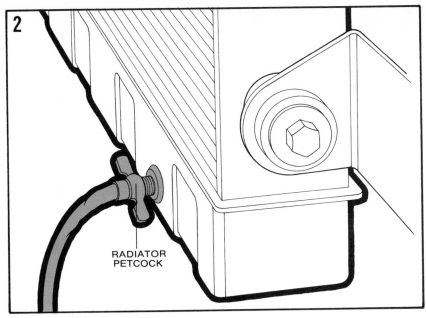

2

RADIATOR PETCOCK

opening petcock at bottom of radiator

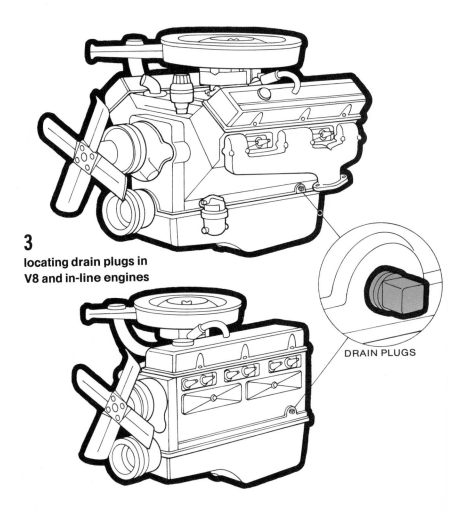

3

locating drain plugs in V8 and in-line engines

DRAIN PLUGS

172

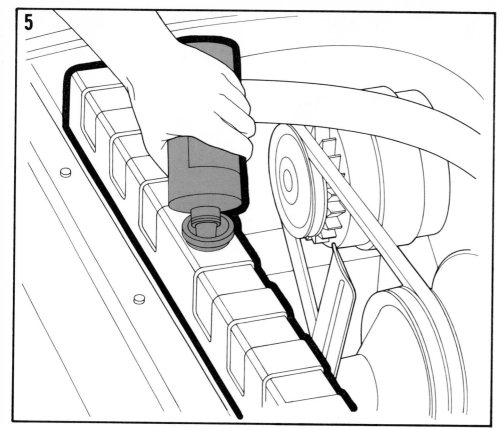

**adding fast-flush
solvent from can**

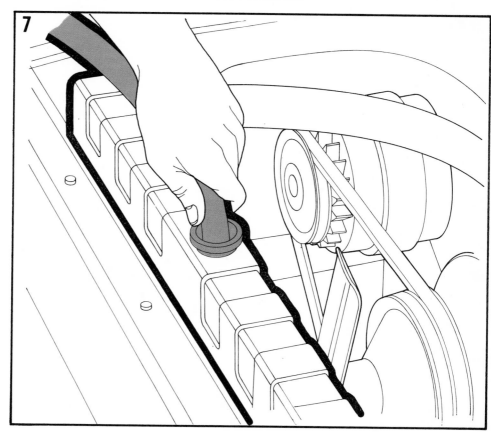

**running water through a
garden hose into radiator**

REPLACING HOSES

All the rubber hoses in the engine compartment should be checked periodically for signs of deterioration beyond the hairline cracks that are the natural consequence of age. If the hose is swollen or feels mushy, replace it before it bursts while you are on the road. The instructions here deal with the more trouble-prone radiator hoses, but also apply to heater hoses.

Tools and materials: a screwdriver, new hoses, new clamps, water-resistant adhesive, new coolant (if needed).

CAUTION: Change hoses only when the engine is cold.

1 If you are replacing only the upper hose, remove the radiator cap and open the petcock at the bottom of the radiator. Drain two quarts of coolant into a container. Tighten the petcock.
  To replace the lower hose, you must fully drain the radiator *(preceding pages)* and partially drain the engine block. But instead of removing the engine-block drain plugs, unfasten the lower-hose connection at the radiator, as in steps 2 and 3, permitting the coolant to flow into a container.

2 (Picture) Locate the connecting joints of the hose you wish to replace. Using a screwdriver, loosen the screws that hold the clamps at each end. If a clamp is badly corroded, snip it off and replace it.

3 Twist the hose free of the metal connecting joints.

CAUTION: If the hose is stuck, do not force it; you might break the connecting joint. Slit the end, then pry it off with a screwdriver.

4 Position the clamps on the new hose, about a quarter inch in from each end.

5 Clean the metal connecting joints at both ends. If bits of the old hose have stuck to the surface, scrape them off with a putty knife. Coat the connecting joints with a light film of water-resistant adhesive.

6 Twist the new hose over each connecting joint. Be sure the clamp slides past the joint's ridge. Tighten the clamp screws.

7 Make sure the radiator petcock is securely tightened. Replace the coolant.

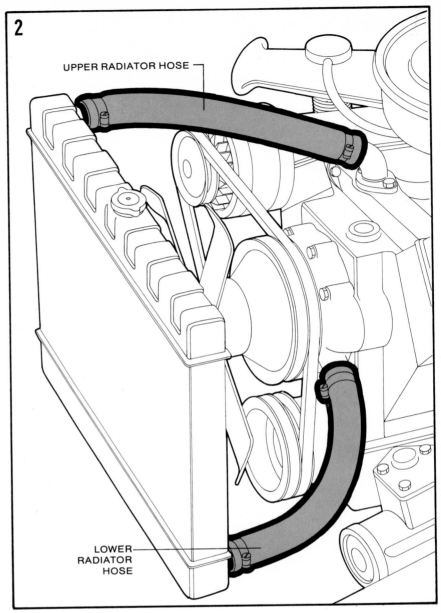

locations of upper and lower radiator hoses

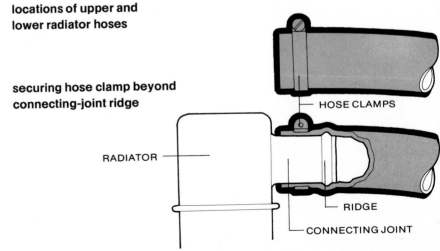

securing hose clamp beyond connecting-joint ridge

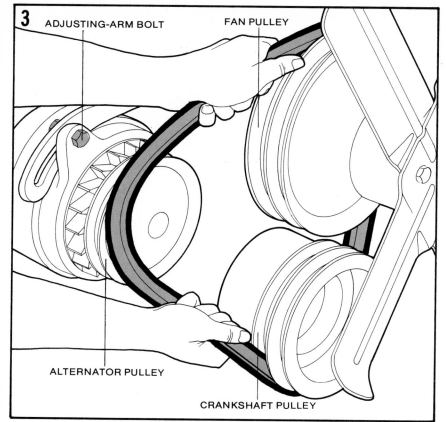

3 ADJUSTING-ARM BOLT　　　FAN PULLEY

ALTERNATOR PULLEY

CRANKSHAFT PULLEY

**with alternator loose,
placing belt on pulleys**

**applying pressure with tire
iron while tightening bolt**

5

ALTERNATOR
HOUSING

REPLACING BELTS

The various belts in the engine compartment should be checked periodically for tension *(page 139)* and for signs of deterioration. If a belt is glazed or cracked, replace it before it begins to emit unpleasant squeals or, worse, snaps while in use. The instructions here deal with the drive belt attached to the alternator. But they also apply to the belts from the crankshaft pulleys that operate such options as the air conditioner, power steering and air-injection pump.

1 To loosen the alternator, use a wrench to turn the adjusting-arm bolt two full counterclockwise revolutions.

2 Use a tire iron as a pry bar. Put it against the alternator housing, and force the alternator toward the fan pulley until the belt slackens enough for you to slip it off.

CAUTION: When using a tire iron or any pry bar, always lever against the part to which the movable pulley is attached, never against the pulley itself.

3 (Picture) Loop the new belt over the fan and crankshaft pulleys, then stretch it over the alternator pulley.

4 Using the tire iron as a lever, force the alternator away from the fan pulley until the belt is taut.

5 (Picture) With the tire iron, hold the alternator in the taut position. With your free hand, check the tension with a tension tool or by the method described on page 139. When the tension is correct, tighten the alternator's adjusting-arm bolt.

6 After the bolt has been fastened, recheck the tension; the alternator may have moved slightly as you tightened. If so, loosen the bolt, and repeat steps 4 and 5.

COOLING-SYSTEM MAINTENANCE

To check the cooling system, regularly inspect the radiator cap *(step 1)* and clean the fins *(step 2)*. If the system behaves erratically, test the thermostat *(steps 3-9)*.

Tools and materials (to check thermostat): wrench; high-temperature thermometer; new gasket for thermostat, gasket cement, and new thermostat (if being replaced).

1 (Picture) Remove the radiator cap; the rubber gasket should be uncracked and pliable. The spring should feel firm. If any part has deteriorated, buy a new cap.

2 (Picture) Clean the radiator fins, both front and back, using full pressure from a garden hose and a soft brush.

3 If you are going to drain and flush the cooling system, proceed to step 4. If not, remove the radiator cap, open the petcock at the bottom of the radiator and drain two quarts of coolant into a container for reuse. Tighten the petcock.

4 (Picture) With a wrench, unfasten the two bolts that secure the metal thermostat housing where the upper radiator hose meets the engine block. Lift out the exposed thermostat and discard the gasket.

5 Jot down the number stamped on the thermostat. It indicates the temperature at which the valve on the thermostat opens.

6 (Picture) Place the thermostat and a reliable thermometer into a pan of undiluted antifreeze.

7 (Picture) Heat the liquid. When it gets to within 15° of the opening temperature, jiggle the thermostat with a spoon. When the liquid reaches 20° above the opening temperature, the valve should be open at least one quarter of an inch. Turn off the heat. When the temperature has dropped to 10° below the opening temperature, the valve should be closed. If the valve has not operated properly, replace the thermostat.

8 Wipe clean all the exposed surfaces of the housing and place the thermostat —valve end up, spring end down—into it. Coat the housing flange with gasket cement and put on a new gasket. Slip the housing into place carefully—if it's misaligned, it may crack—and tighten the bolts.

9 Fill up the radiator with coolant and secure the radiator cap.

testing radiator cap's
rubber gasket

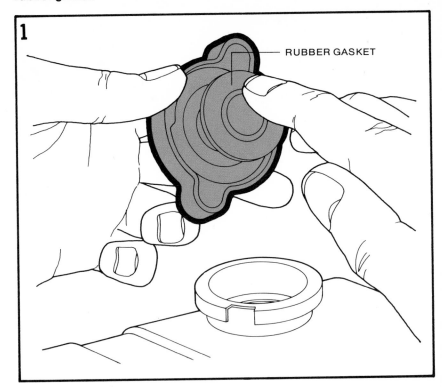

RUBBER GASKET

insects and debris
clogging radiator fins

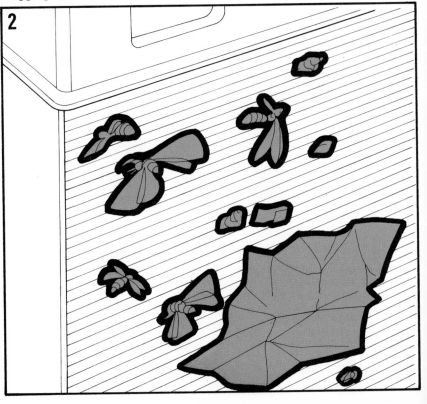

thermostat resting under its housing

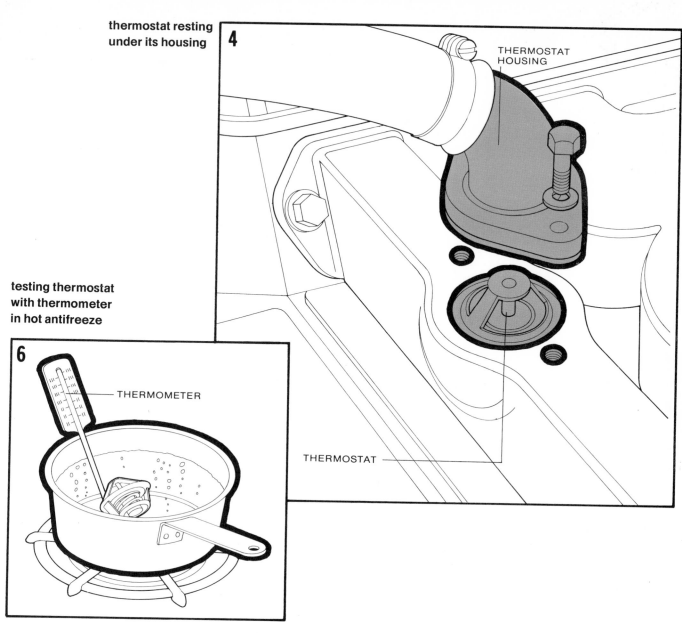

THERMOSTAT HOUSING

THERMOSTAT

testing thermostat with thermometer in hot antifreeze

THERMOMETER

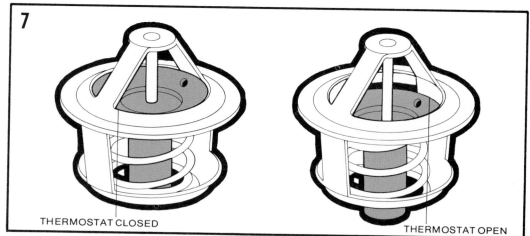

inspecting valve's responses to temperature changes

THERMOSTAT CLOSED

THERMOSTAT OPEN

ELECTRICAL PROBLEMS

Though an automobile's electrical system is complex, many common problems are not difficult to remedy, as is shown here.

CAUTION: Turn off the ignition before replacing fuses.

Tools and materials: test light, screwdriver, wrench; new fuses, bulbs, electrical tape, solder or crimp connectors.

1 (Picture) Using a flashlight, examine the fuse panel (located under the dashboard, and usually mounted on the fire wall) for burned-out fuses. If all the fuses are good, proceed to step 3.

2 (Picture) Pry free a burned-out fuse with a fuse puller or a nonmetallic object, such as an ice-cream stick. Never use a screwdriver—its metal shaft could short-circuit the wiring even with the ignition off. The fuse's capacity will be stamped on one of its metal ends. Snap a replacement of the same capacity into the panel.

CAUTION: Before working on the instrument lights *(below)*, disconnect the negative cable on the battery. Limit your work here to bulb replacement.

3 (Picture) To reach the instrument panel lights, unfasten the screws that hold the dashboard panel in place. Gently pull this panel toward you and prop it on the steering column. On most cars, you now have access to all the dashboard bulbs. On some larger cars, though, you will have to remove the panel completely; consult your service manual. Replace the defective bulb and screw back the dash panel. Finally, remember to reattach the negative cable on the battery.

4 (Picture) Some exterior lights come out as a unit. Using a screwdriver or wrench, reach behind the fender and unfasten the retaining screws or bolts. Then pull the entire light unit out of its recess. The lens and gasket will now disengage. Examine the bulb and replace if necessary.

5 (Picture) Other exterior lights, such as many taillights, are mounted permanently into the body. To gain access to the bulb, unfasten the screws that hold the lens and gasket. To remove the bulb, press the bulb inward, turn slightly counterclockwise, then pull it from the socket. Taillight bulbs on some cars can be reached by merely opening the trunk.

CONTINUED

1

METAL FILAMENT

distinguishing a good fuse *(top)* **from a burned-out fuse** *(bottom)*

removing a burned-out fuse with a fuse puller

2

unscrewing the dashboard panel

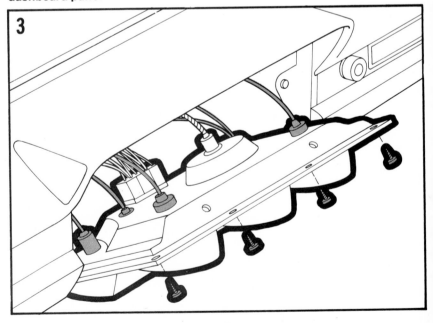

3

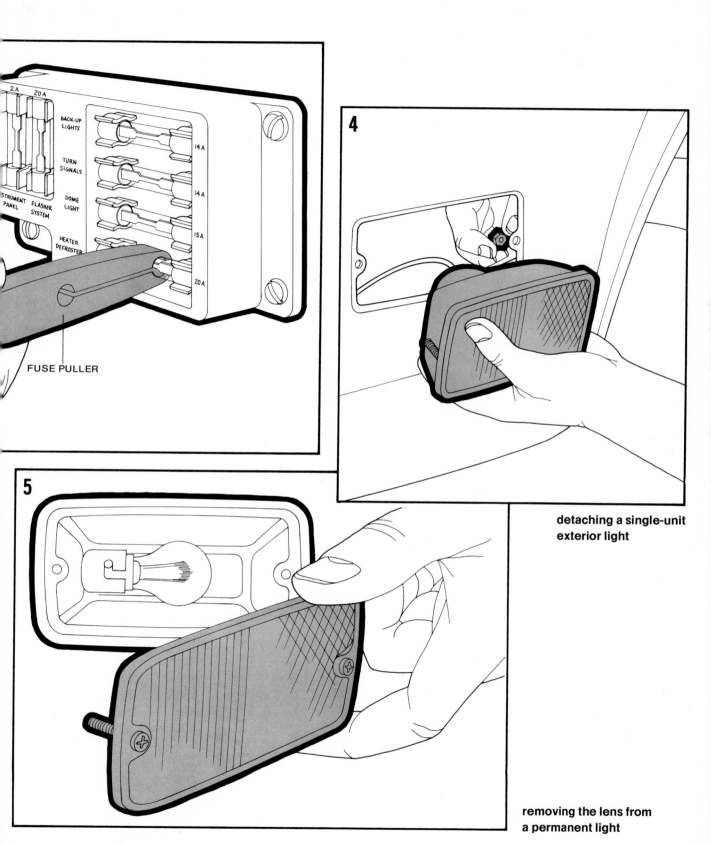

2 A 20 A

INSTRUMENT PANEL FLASHER SYSTEM

BACK-UP LIGHTS

TURN SIGNALS

DOME LIGHT

HEATER DEFROSTER

14 A

14 A

15 A

20 A

FUSE PULLER

4

detaching a single-unit
exterior light

5

removing the lens from
a permanent light

ELECTRICAL PROBLEMS
CONTINUED

6 (Picture) If a light is out, but its fuse and bulb are good, remove the bulb and use fine sandpaper to remove any corrosion in or around the socket and the bulb contacts. Replace the bulb. If the light still does not go on, remove the bulb and, with the circuit still on, fasten the alligator ground-clip lead of a test light to a clean metal part of the socket. Insert the pointed probe of the test light into the socket. If the test light does not glow, there is either a loose connection or a broken wire.

7 You can gain access to all light connections by opening the hood or trunk lid, reaching into wheel wells or removing an entire socket assembly to get at its wires. Tighten all screws around the suspect socket assembly and check the connections of all wires leading to it.

8 (Picture) Trace the wires that lead to the socket. Use electrical tape to cover any frayed insulation. Repair breaks in the wire by one of the following two methods.

Soldering. Follow the steps illustrated *(top, far right)*, from top to bottom: Strip about an inch of insulation from the ends of the broken wire. Scrape or sandpaper the wire to bare metal. Braid the bare wires together. Heat the new connection with a soldering iron, then touch the solder to the wires until the solder runs freely over the connection. Let the solder cool a few seconds. Wrap the connection with electrical tape.

Crimping. Prepare the ends of the broken wires as in soldering, but do not braid them together. Slip the bare wires into a crimp connector. Squeeze each end of the connector with pliers. Tug lightly on both wires; the connection should feel tight.

9 (Picture) If all the brake lights fail, locate the switch on the brake-pedal arm. Pull the connector from the brake-light switch. Test to see if the switch is faulty: insert the bare ends of a short length of insulated wire into the connector openings to complete the circuit. If the brake lights now work, the switch is broken. The old unit can be removed by unscrewing it from its mounting bracket. Screw in a new switch. Reattach the connector after taking out the test wire. Tap the brake pedal to make sure the brake lights go on instantly. If they do not, screw the switch further into its bracket.

10 (Picture) Should the turn signals fail, inspect the flasher unit mounted under the dashboard either on the fuse block or near it. Unplug the connector and insert an insulated wire to test it, as in step 9. To replace a broken unit, pull it from its clamp or from its mounting in the fuse block. Install a new unit and attach the connector.

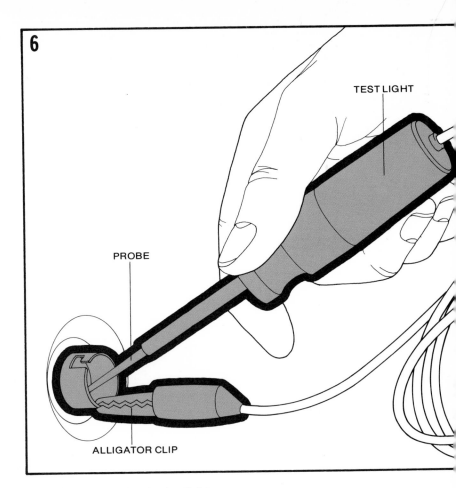

6

TEST LIGHT

PROBE

ALLIGATOR CLIP

testing brake-light switch on pedal arm

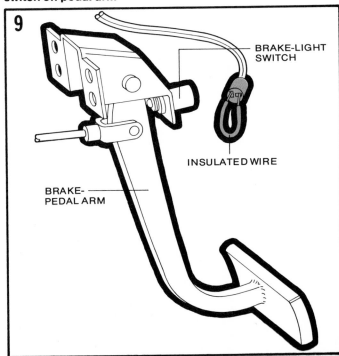

9

BRAKE-LIGHT SWITCH

INSULATED WIRE

BRAKE-PEDAL ARM

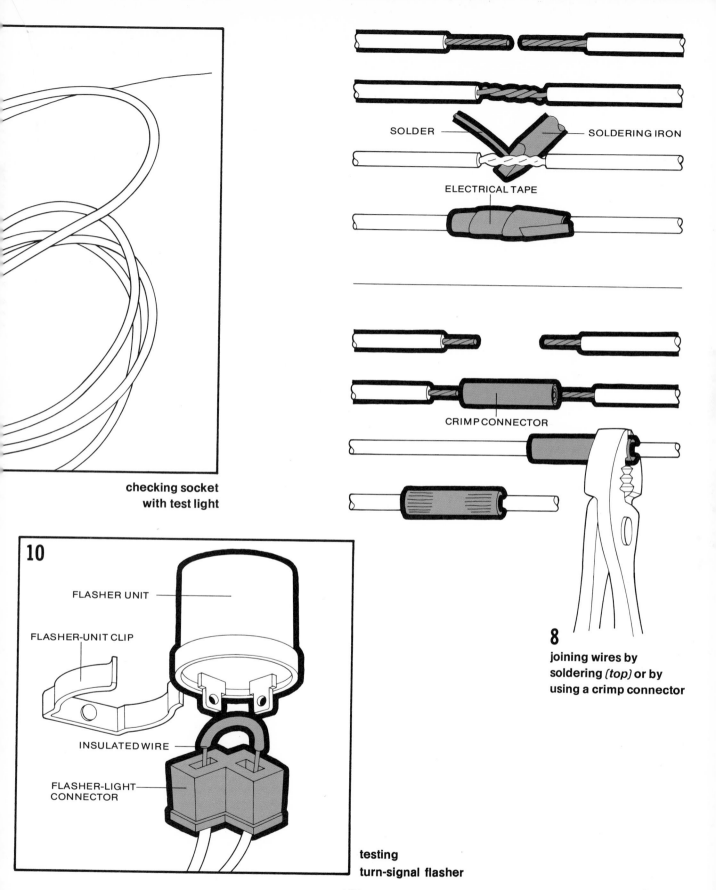

checking socket
with test light

SOLDER — SOLDERING IRON

ELECTRICAL TAPE

CRIMP CONNECTOR

8
joining wires by
soldering *(top)* or by
using a crimp connector

10

FLASHER UNIT

FLASHER-UNIT CLIP

INSULATED WIRE

FLASHER-LIGHT
CONNECTOR

testing
turn-signal flasher

181

REPLACING AND ALIGNING HEADLIGHTS

Before you replace a headlight, examine its lens. A number will be embossed on the glass; be sure the replacement bulb has the same number or it will not fit.

Alignment should be checked at least once a year or each time a headlight is replaced. Save the alignment screen you must make *(opposite)* and, if possible, paint marks on your driveway fixing the precise spot where the car should be parked. That way you will be able to align your headlights quickly at any time.

Tools and materials: screwdriver, pliers, tape measure, 25-foot string, T square, chalk or paint, aiming-screen materials.

1 (Picture) Remove the screws that hold the headlight trim ring.

2 If there is a spring from the retaining ring to the headlight socket disengage it.

3 Loosen the screws that hold the retaining ring in position and then rotate the ring until it is disengaged from the screws. On some cars it may be necessary to remove the screws. Do *not* touch the larger adjustment screws.

4 (Picture) Pull the sealed-beam bulb forward and disconnect the plug.

5 Plug in the new bulb. Orient the bulb so that it fits into the indentations in the adjusting ring or headlight socket.

6 Replace the spring that connects the retaining ring and the headlight socket. Slip the retaining ring back on and tighten or replace the three screws that hold it. If you are going to align the headlights, now is the time; if not, replace the trim ring.

ALIGNING HEADLIGHTS

Before you align the headlights, consult your service manual to see that the tires are properly inflated and how much gasoline should be in the tank.

1 (Picture) Your first requirement is an alignment screen. Any flat surface—a garage door, a large sheet of paper or cardboard larger than the front of your car—will do. But the screen must be perpendicular to level ground with 25 feet between the screen and the front of the car.

2 Using a T square or any right-angled object, draw a straight, vertical line through the center of the screen to represent the center line of the car.

3 With a tape measure, measure the distance between the ground and the center of the car's headlights. Make two small marks on the screen, each at the same height as the distance between the ground

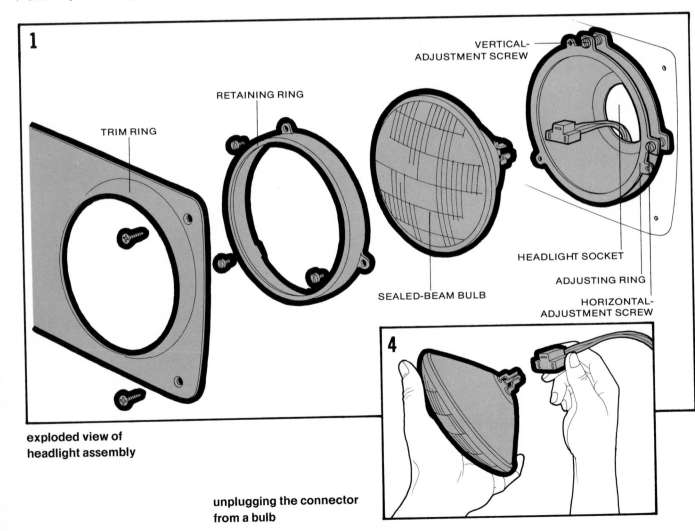

1

VERTICAL-ADJUSTMENT SCREW

RETAINING RING

TRIM RING

HEADLIGHT SOCKET

ADJUSTING RING

HORIZONTAL-ADJUSTMENT SCREW

SEALED-BEAM BULB

4

exploded view of headlight assembly

unplugging the connector from a bulb

and the headlights. Now draw a horizontal line connecting the marks.

NOTE: If your car has stacked headlights —one bulb set above the other—you will need to draw two horizontal lines.

4 Use the tape measure to find the distance from the center of each headlight to the center of the car. Then go to the screen. From the intersection of the vertical and horizontal lines, measure on each side of the horizontal line the distance between the car's center line and the headlights; put marks on the line at both points. Next, draw vertical lines through the marks from the top to the bottom of the screen. You now have a screen showing the height and position of your car's headlights.

NOTE: If your car has four horizontal (side-by-side) headlights, follow the above procedure to draw four vertical lines.

5 To align the headlights, the car's front must be centered exactly 25 feet from the screen and precisely parallel to it. The center of the grille must point directly at the center line on the screen.

To position the car, use a piece of string 25 feet long. Stretch it on the ground from the vertical center line of the screen down the driveway, using a T square to make sure it is perpendicular to the screen. Put a mark on the driveway at the end of the string.

Make two more marks on the driveway, following the same procedure, but starting from points a few feet to the left and right of the screen's center line. Then draw a straight line connecting the three marks on the driveway. Accentuate the center mark.

6 Wait until dusk or after dark when headlight beams are clearly defined. Have someone guide you in positioning the car. Its front must be directly over and parallel to the positioning line on the pavement, and the center of its grille must be directly over the center mark. Any error will make the alignment incorrect.

7 (Picture) Unscrew the headlight trim rings and expose the adjustment screws. The top screw moves the light vertically, the side screw moves it horizontally.

8 Turn on the high beam. Work on one light at a time, covering the others with dropcloths or newspapers.

9 Adjust the lights until their hot spots —the bright center areas—are two inches below the intersection of the horizontal and vertical center lines on the screen.

Set the lights on low beam. The outer perimeter of the low-beam hot spots should be two inches to the right of the vertical headlight center lines and just touching the horizontal line with its upper edge. If your car has only two headlights, the low-beam pattern should be correct if the high-beam alignment was done properly. If it is not, the light is defective and should be replaced.

10 Now reinstall the headlight trim rings back on their housings.

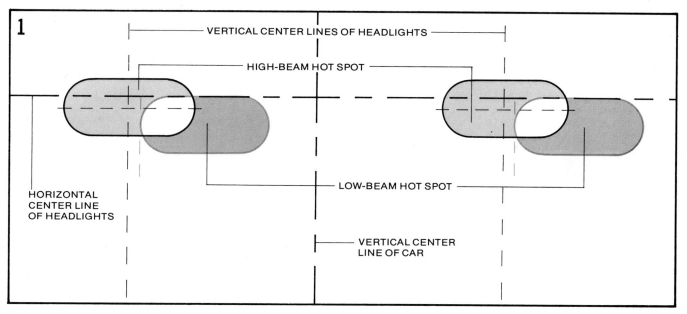

aligning screen with reference lines

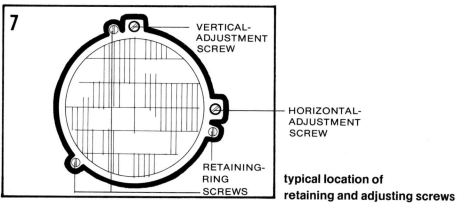

typical location of retaining and adjusting screws

REPLACING SHOCK ABSORBERS

Worn shock abosrbers not only make for an uncomfortable ride, they can dangerously affect a car's road-holding capability. Give the shocks a periodic rebound test *(page 98)*, and if they fail, replace them promptly. Whenever you buy new shocks, specify the heavy-duty or double-action type. Install a complete set of shocks; if you replace just one pair, you may experience fore-and-aft swaying. If your shocks have shaft-type mounts, you will have to buy a special shock-absorber socket for your wrench *(page 154)*.

1 The evening before you install the new shock absorbers, get underneath the car and liberally squirt penetrating oil onto the upper and lower mounts of the old shocks. This special oil will make the job of loosening rusted and frozen nuts easier and faster the next day.

2 (Picture) Shock absorbers are held in place by one of three types of mounts: shaft, one bolt and two bolt. The shaft type, often used on the upper front-end mounts, is fastened by a series of rubber bushings, metal washers and a locking nut. Use the special socket to hold the shaft itself firm as you manipulate the nut with the use of an open-end wrench.

The one- and two-bolt types, used interchangeably on upper and lower mounts both front and rear, are unfastened with a socket wrench.

All the shock-absorber fasteners loosen counterclockwise. Expect to use muscle, but do not hammer on the wrench or the fastener; doing so could strip the nut. Instead, squirt more penetrating oil on any fastener that refuses to budge, and wait.

When you remove a mount, note carefully the relative positions and sequences for all washers and rubber bushings. Typical arrangements are illustrated at far right. Do not immediately discard these parts; many replacement shock kits contain various sizes of washers and bushings. But to be sure you have the right ones for your car, you may have to match some of them with the original parts.

3 (Picture) Lift the hood and see if you have access to the upper mounts of the front shocks. If you do, remove the fasteners; if not, see step 5.

4 Raise the front end of the car onto jack stands *(page 157)*.

5 (Picture) If you have not already unfastened the upper mounts, do so from the underside of the car. Then unfasten both lower mounts and pull out each old shock through the coil spring. On some cars you also may have to unbolt a lower mounting plate, attached to the lower control arm, to obtain the clearance you will need to remove the shock.

CAUTION: Never grasp the shaft of a new shock with any tool other than the proper socket; otherwise you may cause the hydraulic fluid in the shock to leak later.

6 Push up the new shock through the coil spring. Fasten, but do not tighten, the upper mount, making sure that you have installed all washers and bushings in the

**top shaft mount
of front shock**

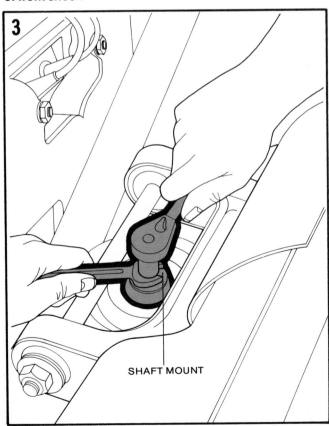

SHAFT MOUNT

**bottom two-bolt mount
of front shock**

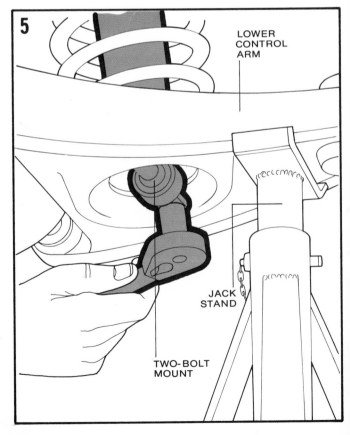

LOWER CONTROL ARM

JACK STAND

TWO-BOLT MOUNT

proper sequence. Repeat this procedure with the other shock.

7 Fasten the bottom mounts of both shocks but don't tighten them yet.

8 With a torque wrench set to the specifications in your service manual, tighten each mount. If you loosened the upper mounts from the engine compartment, tighten them from above. Generally, the torque for the upper mounts is different from that for the lower mounts. If you do not have a torque wrench, tighten each type of mount until the flattened bushing is pressed out no farther than the diameter of the largest washer.

Tug from side to side on each fully installed shock to be doubly sure that it will not rub or bump against any underbody part or hydraulic line.

9 Lower the front end of the car. Then, jack up the back end of the car and place it on the jack stands.

10 (Pictures) Repeat steps 5 through 9 on each of the rear shocks. Replacing rear shocks is quicker since they are not installed within coil springs.

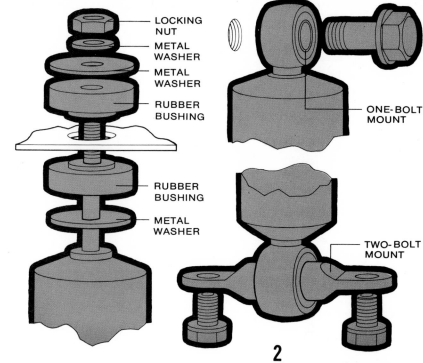

LOCKING NUT

METAL WASHER

METAL WASHER

RUBBER BUSHING

RUBBER BUSHING

METAL WASHER

ONE-BOLT MOUNT

TWO-BOLT MOUNT

2 three mountings: shaft *(left)*, one bolt and two bolt

bottom one-bolt mount of rear shock

top shaft mount of rear shock

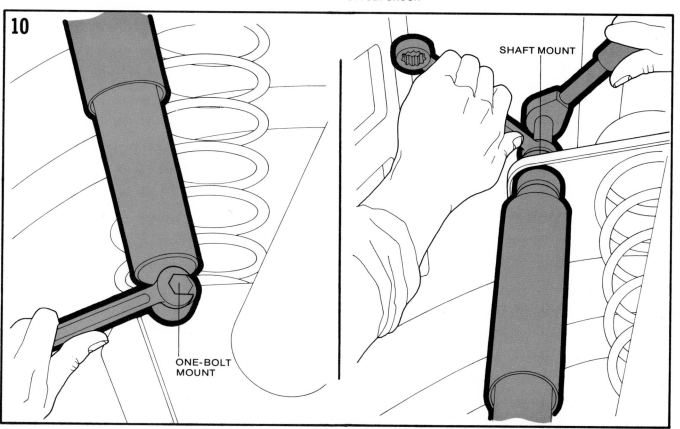

ONE-BOLT MOUNT

SHAFT MOUNT

FILLING BODY DENTS

The small dents, nicks and scratches that accumulate on a car's body are expensive to have fixed professionally. However, you can repair these minor blemishes without undue difficulty.

If you come upon corrosion that has not eaten through the metal, sand all rust away. But if it has eroded a hole larger than a dime, see a professional body-man to have it fixed.

1 If the deepest part of the dent or crease to be repaired is depressed not more than half an inch below the body surface, proceed to step 5. If the dent is deeper, you must first make it shallower, or the putty may pop out or crack later.

2 On any area that you can reach behind, such as hoods and truck lids, place a wooden block on the outer surface and pound out the dent from the inner surface, using a rubber mallet.

3 (Picture) If you cannot reach behind the dent, as in a door, use an electric drill to pierce the surface at two-inch intervals.

CAUTION: Do not let the bit plunge in; you may damage wires or mechanisms.

4 (Picture) Thread a self-tapping sheet-metal screw halfway into each drilled hole. Grip the screw with vise-grip pliers and tug until the dent is slightly concave — within a half inch of the surface.

5 (Picture) Use coarse sandpaper to remove the paint. Sand to bare metal within the dent and roughen a one-inch border around its contours.

6 Wipe the freshly sanded area with a damp cloth, and allow the area to dry.

7 (Picture) Plastic body-putty generally comes with an applicator; use it to press the putty into the cavity. Fill the dent higher than the surrounding surfaces, since the putty will shrink slightly as it dries. Allow the putty to cure for the length of time specified on the can label — as much as 48 hours.

8 (Picture) With a flat file, stroke the hardened putty until it is level with, and contoured to, the surrounding surfaces. File away lumps or edges in the putty.

9 Wrap fine sandpaper around a block and buff the putty until it is smooth. You are now ready to paint [overleaf].

CONTINUED

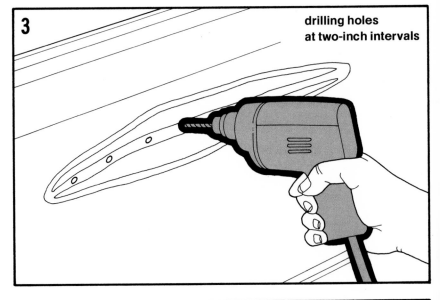

3   **drilling holes at two-inch intervals**

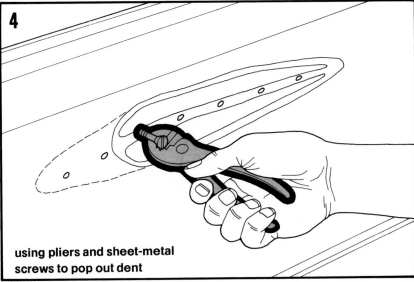

4

using pliers and sheet-metal screws to pop out dent

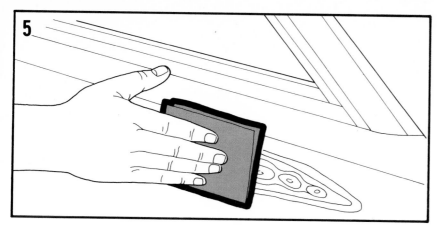

**sanding to bare metal
with coarse sandpaper**

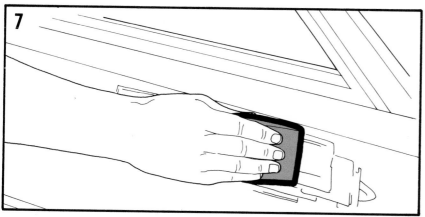

**smoothing putty
with applicator**

**contouring putty
with flat file**

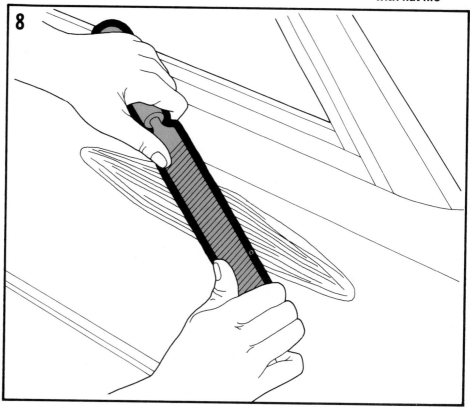

REPAINTING SHEET METAL

Small nicks in a car's finish are best repaired with an inexpensive touch-up kit available from your dealer. With a little more effort, you can repaint cracked or scratched areas or putty-filled dents *(preceding pages)*. But if the area to be repainted is quite large, let a professional body-man do the work.

1 If you are painting a putty-filled dent, proceed to step 2. If you are painting an unputtied blemish, use coarse sandpaper to remove the damaged paint. Sand to bare metal in the marred area; roughen a one-inch border of the good paint around the contours of the damaged finish.

2 With an alcohol-soaked cloth, wipe the sanded area clean of dust, abrasive particles and paint flecks.

3 (Picture) Carefully mask all glass and metal trim around the area to be painted. Tape newspapers over the glass; cover chrome moldings with masking tape.

4 Use a sharp knife to make a template by cutting a hole in the center of a piece of lightweight cardboard. The hole's perimeter should match the area to be painted.

5 (Picture) Hold the template in position about eight inches above the area to be painted and mist on a thin coat of primer. Allow the primer to dry for the length of time specified on the label.

6 (Picture) Dip fine sandpaper of the wet-and-dry type in water and sand the dried primer just enough to roughen its surface. When you work with this abrasive, keep it wet. After sanding, wipe the area with an alcohol-soaked cloth.

7 (Picture) Again using the template, mist on the first coat of paint. Allow the paint to dry for the time specified on the label.

8 Wet-sand the dried paint as in step 6, clean the surface and spray on the second coat of paint.

9 (Picture) When the final coat of paint is fully dry, remove all tape and masking papers. Apply rubbing compound over and slightly beyond the entire painted area. Work in the compound with a damp cloth, then buff it with a soft, clean cloth.

10 Finish by waxing the entire body panel on which you worked.

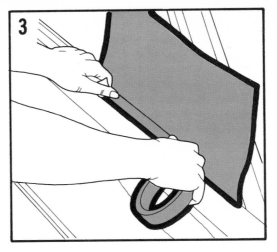

masking adjacent areas to protect them

using template to protect adjacent areas from primer

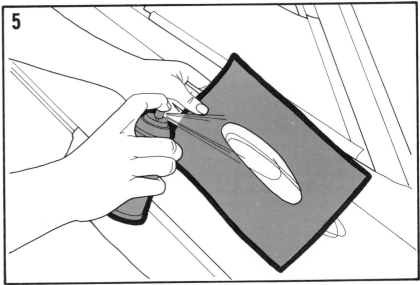

applying wet-and-dry sandpaper to roughen dry primer surface

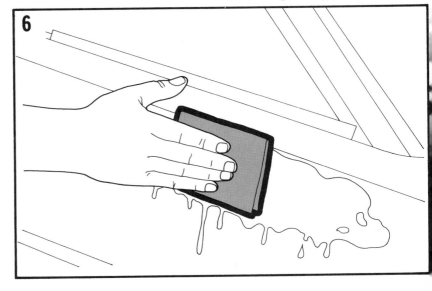

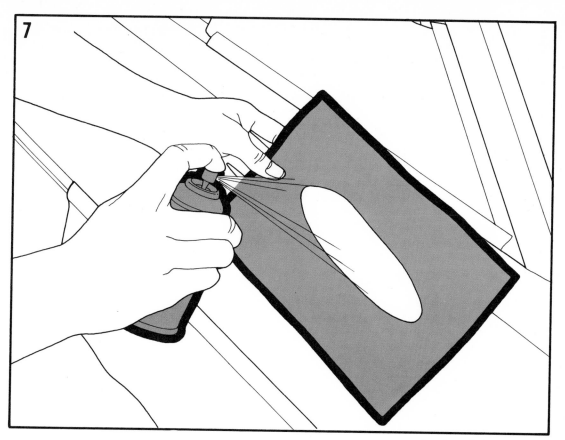

**using template to protect
adjacent areas from paint**

**bringing out paint's gloss
with rubbing compound**

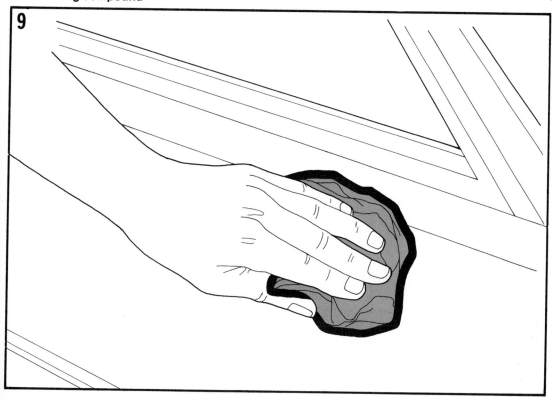

TUNING AN ENGINE

A SYSTEMATIC APPROACH TO A PRECISION TASK

SELECTION OF ELECTRONIC AIDS
WHEN TO REPLACE THE PLUGS
INSIDE THE DISTRIBUTOR
SETTING THE POINTS
USING A DWELL TACHOMETER
TIMING, A CRITICAL PROCEDURE
ADJUSTING THE CARBURETOR

8

For an automobile engine to give peak performance, operation of the carburetor and of the ignition system must be precisely coordinated —or tuned—so that the correct fuel-air mixture is supplied to the cylinders and ignited at the correct moment. Since parts wear out and even the best-adjusted automobile engine will be thrown slightly out of kilter by the stresses of normal driving, all engines must periodically receive a good tune-up.

The process is at once restorative and preventative. That is, regular adjustment restores the engine to its optimum operating efficiency. At the same time, replacement of deteriorating parts helps prevent later problems.

Manufacturers normally recommend a tune-up after every 12 months or 12,000 miles. But if you subject your car's engine to continual stop-and-go driving or make short trips, which do not permit the engine to warm up sufficiently, you may have to tune it more frequently. A tune-up also is in order any time you notice a decline in your car's performance, such as increased fuel consumption, lack of pep, rough idling or hard starting.

The tune-up job is performed primarily on the carburetor, which provides the fuel mixture to the engine, and on the ignition system, which creates the spark for firing the fuel.

When the time comes for a tune-up, you should consider performing this meticulous work yourself, especially if you have sharpened your mechanical skills on some of the other regular maintenance tasks (Chapter 7).

Armed with several moderately priced test instruments and tools (which will pay for themselves by the third tune-up), and also with the specifications listed in the service manual for

drive car until engine warms up
park on level spot
set out tools
check fluid levels

clean battery
replace PCV valve
service air cleaner

your car *(page 153)*, you can tune even the most intimidatingly large engine.

There are three good reasons for performing the job yourself. One is the security of knowing that the necessary adjustments have been done completely and correctly. Even the most expert and otherwise conscientious mechanic may take short cuts if he faces a backlog of jobs. Though these short cuts are unlikely to cause any damage in themselves, the fact remains that every step in a tune-up is important; if one is skipped, the engine will not perform up to its potential.

A second reason is economy. The largest part of any tune-up bill is the charge for labor —most flat-rate manuals *(box, page 261)* suggest two to three hours for thoroughly adjusting most V8 engines, and today most garages demand from $6 to $18 per hour for their mechanics' time. In addition, garages charge the full retail price for replacement parts. You can save money by purchasing such components as spark plugs, breaker points and filters from a reputable discount or auto-supply store.

Finally, by doing the tuning yourself, you will become familiar with the ignition and fuel systems. This knowledge may well come in handy later, for these systems are the cause of most on-the-road problems *(Chapter 9)*.

Despite the addition of complex emission controls to today's engines, tuning remains a straightforward job. There is little difference in the basic technique whether you're working on the old commuting jalopy or the new family car. But regardless of the car you're working on, always use replacement parts that meet the specifications of your service manual.

The tune-up described in this chapter applies to all automobile engines except rotaries and diesels and those having fuel-injection or electronic-ignition systems. The individual tasks that constitute a thorough tune-up are arranged in the sequence that most good mechanics follow: first, the spark plugs and breaker points are refurbished or replaced, and then adjusted; next, the spark timing is set; finally, the carburetor is adjusted.

The drawings in the chapter show the recommended way to perform the more complicated tasks on various components. The components on which you work may differ slightly from those illustrated. However, the way they work and the techniques for servicing them are the same as for the models shown.

One decision you will need to make is whether to replace spark plugs, breaker points and filters as a matter of course or whether to reuse them. If these parts have deteriorated beyond salvage (how to determine their condition is described in this chapter) you must, of course, replace them. However, though some parts can safely be reused, you should carefully consider replacing them if you follow the schedule specified in your owner's manual and perform a tune-up only once a year. By cleaning and refurbishing these parts, you do not restore them to their original condition; you merely slow their rates of deterioration. Thus, you might well have to go under the hood again to replace them before the interval for another tune-up has elapsed.

Before you start your initial tune-up, read through this chapter to get an overview of all

```
┌─────────────────────┐     ┌──────────────────────────┐     ┌──────────────────────┐
│ remove spark plugs  │     │ remove and examine       │     │ check automatic choke│
│ test engine compres-│ ──▶ │   distributor cap        │ ──▶ │ replace fuel filter  │
│ sion                │     │ remove and examine rotor │     │ adjust engine idle   │
│ clean, gap and      │     │ check spark advances     │     │                      │
│ install spark plugs │     │ install breaker points   │     │                      │
│                     │     │ set breaker-point gap    │     │                      │
└─────────────────────┘     │ adjust breaker points    │     └──────────────────────┘
                            │   using dwell meter      │
                            │ check ignition timing    │
                            └──────────────────────────┘
```

the steps involved and the sequence in which they are performed. Then, determine the various specifications you must meet: cylinder compression, ignition timing, breaker-point gap, dwell angle, spark-plug gap and idle speed. On post-1960 cars these specifications are on a decal inside the engine compartment; for older models, the specifications are listed in your service manual and it will be helpful to jot them down on a piece of paper for quick reference when you need them.

Allow a full day for your first tune-up, so you will have time to become fully familiar with each step. Subsequent tune-ups should require only a few hours. Make sure that you are dressed safely: wear short- or tight-sleeved shirts, remove wrist watches, rings and other jewelry, tie long hair behind your head or tuck it under a cap.

Prepare the car by first driving several miles until the engine reaches its optimum operating temperature. Then, park in a level spot where you will be able to work undisturbed. If you work inside a garage, be especially sure to have adequate cross-ventilation because your engine must be run at idle speed during some procedures of the tune-up.

A car with an automatic transmission should be left in the park position, a manual transmission in neutral. On any car, always engage the parking brake and place chocks on both sides of the drive wheels. For additional illumination, use a work light. If the car or pavement is wet, however, avoid shocks by using a flashlight or a battery-powered lantern.

Assemble your tools, test instruments and replacement parts (overleaf) on a nearby table or on a dropcloth draped over the fender nearest the distributor.

Finally, check the fluid levels in the battery, radiator and the crankcase. If all is well, you are now ready to begin the tune-up procedures that start on page 196.

As you work, proceed slowly. Pay attention to the cautionary notes in the chapter, remembering always to stay well clear of any moving fan blades or belts.

The parts you will be removing during the tune-up should come loose fairly easily. If you have trouble with a rusted fastener, squirt on a few drops of penetrating oil. Use only the prescribed tool; and never hammer, pound or jimmy any engine component. As you take a component apart, arrange the various parts, including washers and nuts, in the same order as you removed them; that will help you to reassemble the component properly.

Be especially patient when adjusting a precise tolerance or specification; even an experienced mechanic may need several tries to set a breaker-point gap correctly.

Finally, after you have finished the tune-up, double check the engine compartment before closing the hood to make certain that you have removed all instruments, tools and materials.

After completing a tune-up, if you still are not satisfied with the engine's performance, there probably is a deeper problem. Go to a professional mechanic for help. However, the odds are very good that if you carefully follow the instructions in this chapter, when you finish your own tune-up the engine will perform at a level that could not be improved upon even by the most skilled professional.

TOOLS FOR
THE TUNE-UP

The special tools and the test instruments (*drawings*) you will need to perform a thorough tune-up should cost no more than $100. It's an investment well worth making when you consider that a major tune-up by a mechanic costs between $40 and $80, depending on the engine and the area of the country. By doing the job yourself, you can recoup more than the cost of your equipment—which can be used again and again—by the time that you have completed your third tune-up.

If you have been performing other maintenance jobs, you already will own such basic tools as the pliers, screwdrivers and wrenches (*pages 154-155*) that you will need to do a tune-up.

Two of the four test instruments required are described in detail in this chapter (*dwell tachometer, page 213; timing light, page 216*). Before purchasing a remote starter switch, make sure you can attach it easily to the starter solenoid of your car; some solenoids, especially on large V8 engines, are so inaccessible that it may be simpler to have a helper start and stop the engine at your command, using the car's ignition key. Before you purchase a compression gauge, select the type that screws rather than plugs into the spark-plug openings; it is usually more accurate.

A useful rule when buying tools and test instruments is to stick to well-known products. Many manufacturers offer several price lines. Don't feel that you must buy the most expensive equipment. But by the same token, don't buy the least expensive. Tuning an engine requires precise fits and measurements, which are more difficult to make with cheap tools.

Purchase all of the replacement parts you may need—they are listed at right—before you begin the tune-up; few situations are as irksome as finding yourself lacking a small but indispensable part in the middle of the job—especially if the stores are closed. Anything you decide not to use can always be saved for the next tune-up.

To make sure the parts you buy are the correct ones, you will need to know, in addition to the make and model of your car, the year it was built and which engine it has. This information will help the clerk at the store to find the specified parts. It also will enable you to use special charts prepared by independent manufacturers that show which of their replacement parts meet your engine's specifications.

Tune-up tools

1 battery-cable puller
2 battery cleaning brush
3 hose-clamp pliers
4 spark-plug socket
5 remote starter switch
6 compression gauge
7 ignition file
8 spark-plug tool
9 thickness gauges
10 Allen wrenches
11 dwell tachometer
12 timing light
13 distributor wrench

Other tools

electric work-light
wrenches (socket and open end)
pliers
screwdrivers
torque wrench

Miscellaneous

service manual
wheel chocks
baking soda
petroleum jelly
paper towels or clean rags
kerosene
engine oil
masking tape
soda straw
toothpicks
distributor-cam lubricant
lighter fluid
clothespin
chalk
carburetor solvent
small mirror

Replacement parts

spark plugs
PCV valve
air-cleaner filter
PCV filter
breaker-point assembly
condenser
spare screws for distributor parts
fuel filter

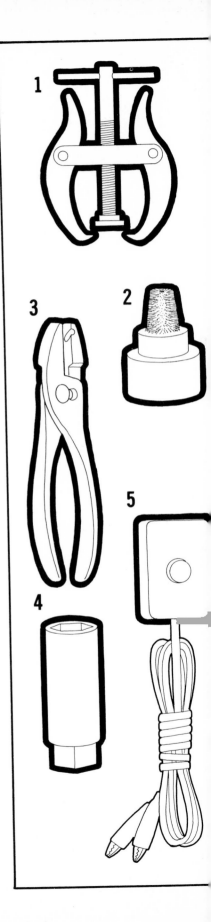

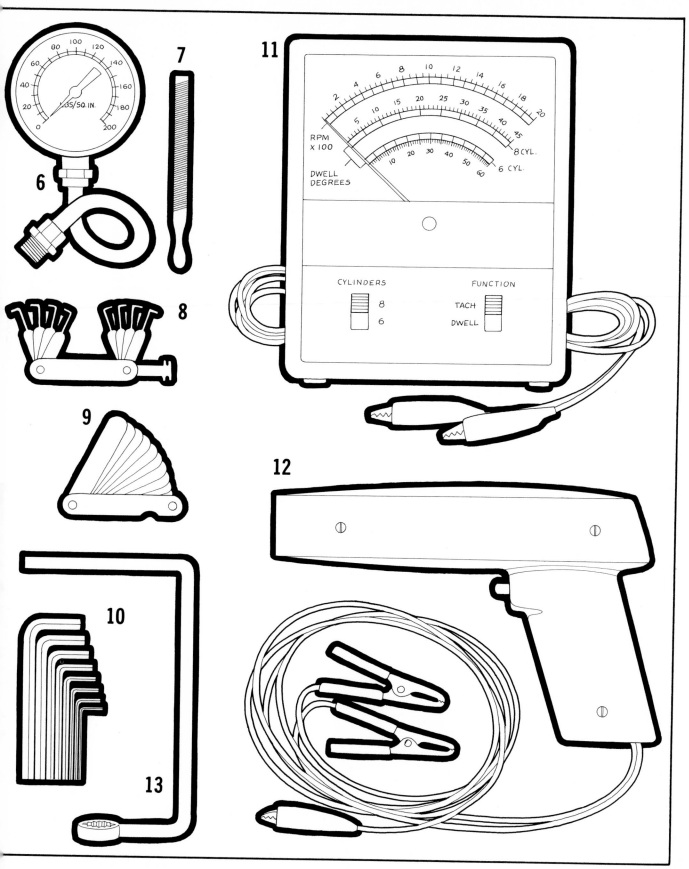

PRELIMINARY STEPS

The tools that will be needed for the tune-up should be laid out in an orderly manner. Then several preliminary operations should be carried out.

1 Because much of the tune-up involves electrical circuits, it is essential that the battery be in good condition and the connections clean and tight. If the battery case is corroded, rinse it with a baking-soda solution *(page 148)*.

2 (Pictures) Remove the battery cables, negative cable first. On some batteries loosen the bolt at each post; on others squeeze a spring clamp with pliers to release it. If the clamp cannot be lifted off easily, remove it with a battery-cable puller.

3 (Pictures) Brighten each post and terminal with a battery cleaning brush to improve the contact.

4 Replace the terminals on the posts, negative cable last. Make sure they are tight. Spread petroleum jelly over terminals and posts to reduce corrosion.

5 (Picture) Remove the PCV valve from the hose that leads to one of the rocker-arm covers. Some valves are clamped and some pull loose. If the time interval for replacement has elapsed (see your service manual), install a new valve. Otherwise shake the valve; if it rattles, it is working properly and can be reused. If it makes no sound, install a new valve with the larger end toward the rocker-arm cover.

6 (Pictures) Remove the air-cleaner lid *(pages 148-149)*. Remove the filter. If it has been in use longer than your service manual specifies, discard it. If not, clean it by knocking it against a flat surface. If you see holes or dirt clogs, discard the filter.

7 (Picture) Remove the rest of the air-filter container *(pages 148-149)*. Insert a screwdriver into the air-cleaner snorkel and gently move the flapper valve. If it binds, lubricate it with several drops of engine oil. Inspect the small mesh filter attached to the inside edge of the air cleaner. If it is made of a permanent material such as is used in air conditioners, rinse it in kerosene. If not, replace the mesh filter.

8 Wipe any dirt or grease from all parts of the air-cleaner container. Drop in the filter and put the whole assembly aside.

CONTINUED

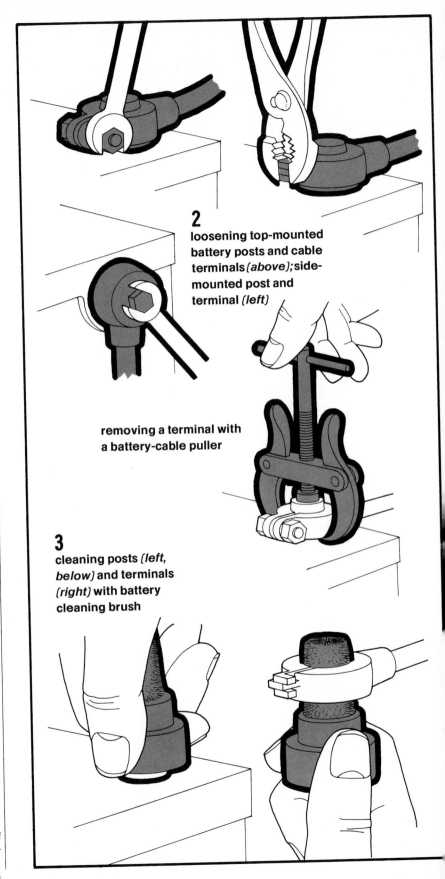

2 loosening top-mounted battery posts and cable terminals *(above);* side-mounted post and terminal *(left)*

removing a terminal with a battery-cable puller

3 cleaning posts *(left, below)* and terminals *(right)* with battery cleaning brush

5

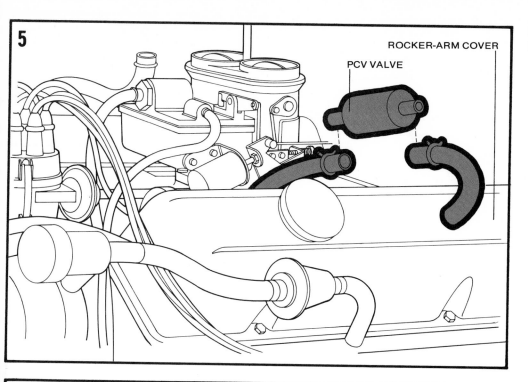

locating the PCV valve

PCV VALVE

ROCKER-ARM COVER

cleaning and inspecting the filter element

6

FILTER ELEMENT

7

AIR-CLEANER SNORKEL

PCV FILTER

SCREWDRIVER

FLAPPER VALVE

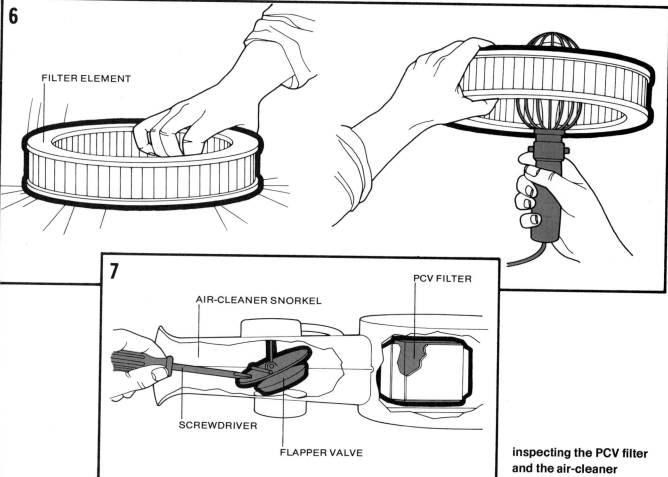

inspecting the PCV filter and the air-cleaner flapper valve

PRELIMINARY STEPS CONTINUED

CAUTION: In the following steps you will be reaching into the engine compartment, parts of which may still be hot.

9 (Picture) Use short strips of masking tape to label each spark-plug cable before removal; they must be replaced later in the same sequence. On in-line engines, simply number each cable from front to rear. On V8 engines, mark the plugs on the driver's side D-1 through D-4 and those on the passenger's side P-1 through P-4.

10 (Picture) Grasp each cable by its protective boot and wiggle it off. Never tug on the cable itself; the electrical conductor inside the cable might break.

11 When the cables are free, wipe them with kerosene to remove any dirt, grease or road salt that might cause the rubber to deteriorate.

12 (Picture) Bend each cable slightly to check for cracked insulation. If any cable is brittle or cracked, replace all of them (the cables are sold as complete sets).

13 (Picture) Clean around each spark-plug recess by blowing through a soda straw. It is vital that you clear away debris, because dirt dropped into the cylinder after the spark plugs are removed could cause costly internal damage.

CAUTION: You will next be removing and handling the spark plugs. They and the engine may be hot. When removing spark plugs near the battery, keep the wrench from touching the live (positive) post of the battery. Be careful when handling the plugs; if you drop them and their porcelain insulators crack, you cannot reuse them.

14 (Picture) Attach a spark-plug socket to a socket wrench and, turning counterclockwise, remove each plug. On some cars, especially those with power accessories, the plugs may be hard to reach. If so, extensions and universal-joint attachments that fit between the socket and the wrench will make the job easier. If the spark plugs have metal gaskets, be sure not to lose them; they will be needed if you decide to reuse the same plugs [overleaf].

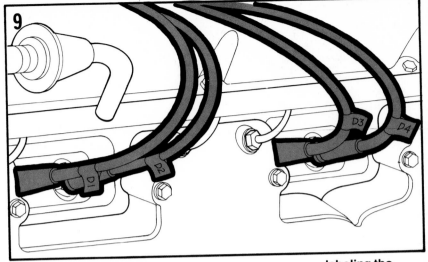

labeling the spark-plug cables

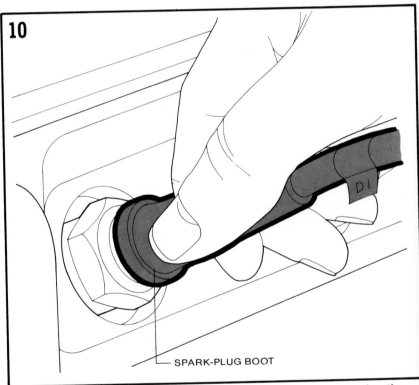

SPARK-PLUG BOOT

removing the spark-plug cable

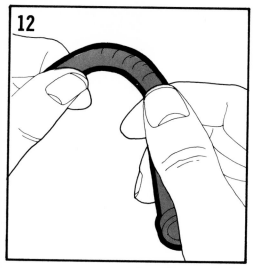

checking spark-plug
cables for cracks

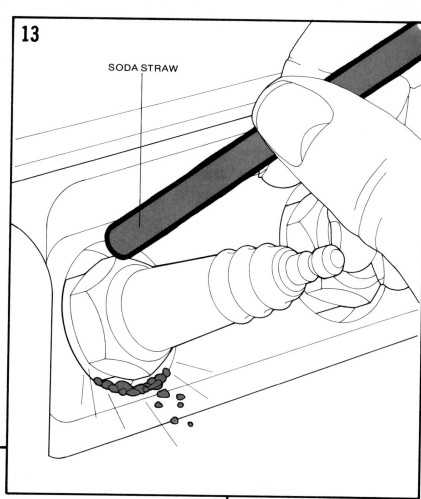

SODA STRAW

blowing debris from the
spark-plug recess

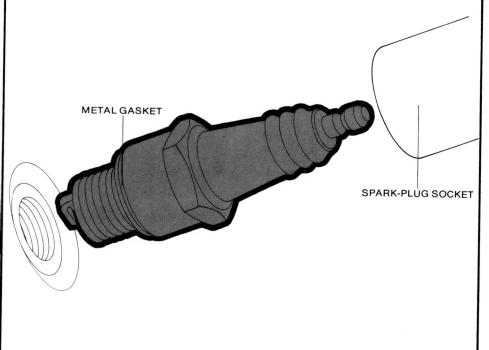

METAL GASKET

SPARK-PLUG SOCKET

removing the plug with
a spark-plug socket

TESTING COMPRESSION

A key factor in good engine performance is compression: the pressure exerted on the fuel-air mixture in the cylinders before ignition. Therefore, the first step in any tune-up is to test compression. If it is abnormal, even in one cylinder, your car may need a ring or valve job.

1 (Picture) Locate the choke's butterfly-valve atop the carburetor and push it open, that is, into a vertical position. Carefully insert a screwdriver into the carburetor barrel to hold the choke open. Then find the throttle lever and move it to open the throttle at the bottom of the barrel. Position the screwdriver to prop open both choke and throttle. (This same step also will open the linked chokes and throttles of a multibarreled carburetor like the one shown here.)

2 (Picture) Locate the coil and disconnect the side terminal wire linking the coil to the distributor. Secure or tape the wire away from moving engine parts.

CAUTION: In the next step, beware of hot metal nearby.

3 (Picture) If you plan to use a remote starter switch instead of the car's ignition switch to crank the engine, now is the time to connect it. Locate the starter solenoid, mounted on top of the starter motor or against the fire wall. Attach one of the leads of the remote starter switch to the solenoid terminal, marked S; attach the other lead to the battery's positive (+) terminal.

CAUTION: Turn on the ignition. In some models failure to do so may destroy a ground contact in the ignition switch.

4 (Picture) Screw in the compression gauge to any spark-plug opening and crank the engine until the needle stops rising—about five seconds. Jot down the reading, then press the gauge's release button. Repeat the process at each spark-plug opening. Turn off the ignition.

5 Check to be sure that all readings are in the normal range, as listed in your service manual. If the compression meets this test, continue with the tune-up. If not, replace the plugs and go to a mechanic.

BEFORE PROCEEDING: Lift the screwdriver out of the carburetor, leaving the coil's side terminal wire disconnected and the remote starter in place.

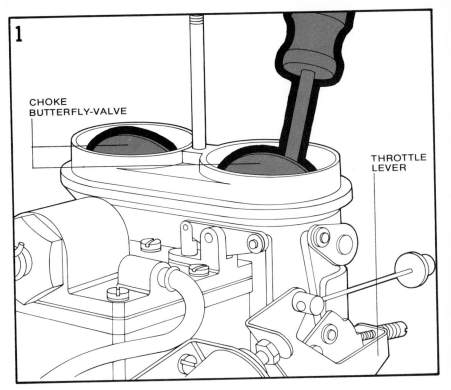

CHOKE BUTTERFLY-VALVE

THROTTLE LEVER

blocking the choke and throttle with a screwdriver

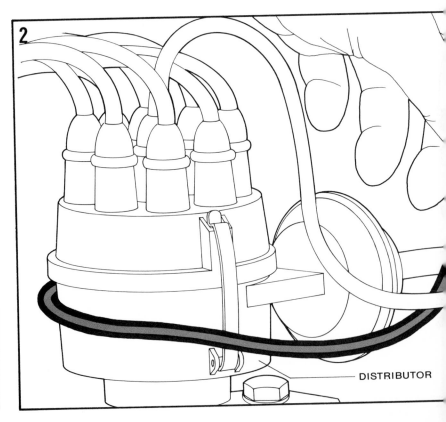

DISTRIBUTOR

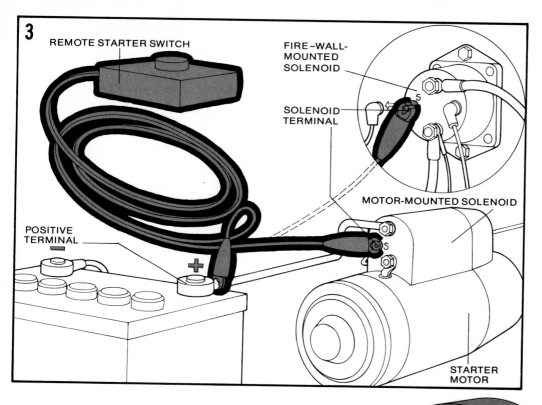

3

REMOTE STARTER SWITCH

FIRE–WALL–MOUNTED SOLENOID

SOLENOID TERMINAL

S

MOTOR-MOUNTED SOLENOID

POSITIVE TERMINAL

+

S

STARTER MOTOR

reading the compression gauge

removing the coil's side terminal wire

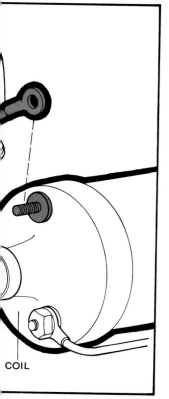

COIL

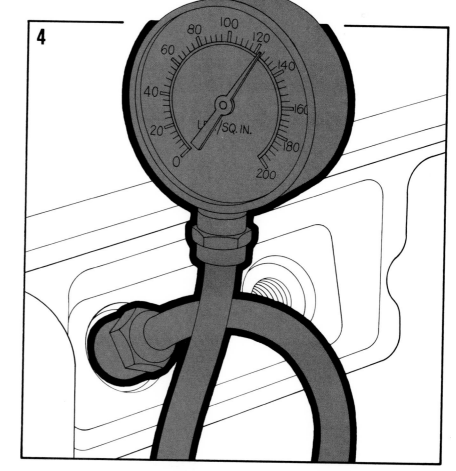

4

80 100 120
60 140
40 160
20 180
0 200
LBS./SQ. IN.

SERVICING THE SPARK PLUGS

The spark plugs ignite the fuel mixture in the cylinders by means of bursts of high-voltage electricity carried from the distributor. Each burst travels to the bottom, or firing end, of the plug where it creates a powerful spark by jumping across a tiny gap between two electrodes. The ability of the spark to ignite the fuel is adversely affected if the plugs are damaged or the spark gaps are abnormal. That's why it is vital to examine used plugs closely and to clean them periodically, and also why gaps of old and new plugs should be checked before installation.

1 (Picture) Examine each spark plug and compare it with the examples in this chart. A plug can be safely reused if the electrodes are coated with a gray or tan deposit but show no burn marks—evidence of excessive heat in a cylinder. The white porcelain insulator can be slightly stained, but must not be cracked or chipped. Visible damage to the electrodes or insulator calls for immediate replacement of the plug. It's a good idea to save badly damaged plugs and show them to a mechanic, who may be able to diagnose and correct the cause of the damage.

Plugs also can be damaged by overheating and by various kinds of fouling that coat the electrodes and change the size of the spark gap—or even close the gap completely so that no ignition occurs. While it is best to replace fouled plugs, they sometimes can be salvaged if the coating has not formed a solid crust. In the examples illustrated, the plugs fouled by oil, carbon and gasoline additives can be salvaged; the others cannot be salvaged and must be replaced.

CAUTION: To avoid having to replace plugs one at a time as they wear out, always replace the entire set of plugs if even one is bad. Don't reuse plugs that have been in the engine for most of their useful life—typically about 12,000 miles.

2 If plugs are to be reused, soak them in kerosene and then clean their threads with a wire brush. Use a toothpick to scrape softened deposits off the electrodes and the bottom part of the insulator.

3 (Picture) With an ignition file, flatten the center electrode until it is smooth. Rinse the firing end in kerosene to remove any metal filings. Then wipe each plug clean with a paper towel and set it aside to dry.

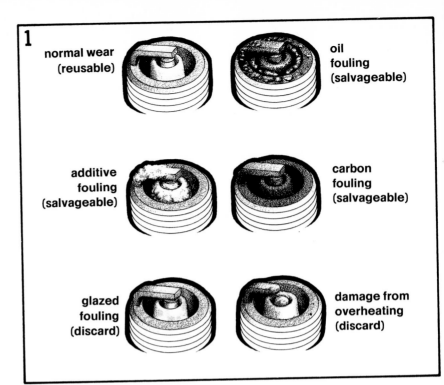

normal wear (reusable)

oil fouling (salvageable)

additive fouling (salvageable)

carbon fouling (salvageable)

glazed fouling (discard)

damage from overheating (discard)

filing the center electrode

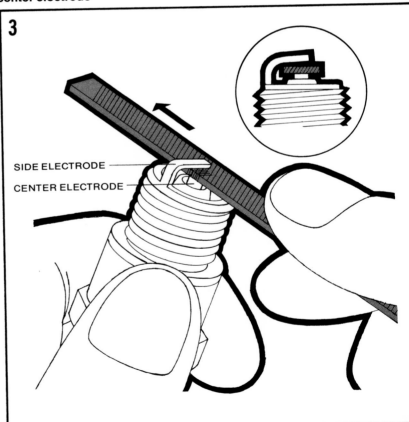

SIDE ELECTRODE

CENTER ELECTRODE

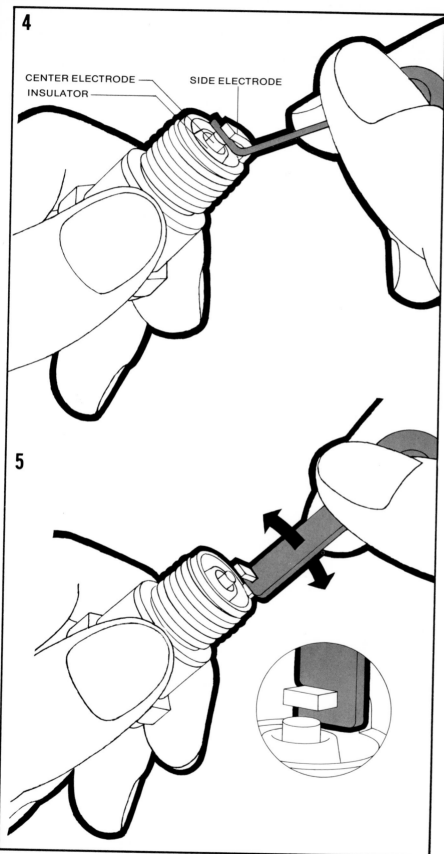

4

CENTER ELECTRODE
INSULATOR
SIDE ELECTRODE

5

4 (Picture) All spark plugs—old or new —must have their gaps adjusted before being installed. Use a round wire feeler-gauge of the thickness specified by your service manual. Pull the gauge through the gap between the two electrodes. If the gap is correct, the gauge will pass through it smoothly with only a slight amount of friction detectable.

5 (Picture) If the gap is incorrect, fit the notched bending bar of a spark plug tool over the side electrode and gently bend the metal to narrow or widen the gap. Use the feeler-gauge to check the gap. Do not be discouraged if it takes you several tries to set the gap correctly; few professionals get it precisely right on their first—or their second—effort.

6 When all the plugs have been correctly gapped, dab several drops of engine oil onto their threads to ease installation. If the engine of your car has an aluminum cylinder-head, you may need to treat the threads with an antiseizing compound in the event the engine is still hot.

CAUTION: As you install the spark plugs, you will again be reaching into engine areas that might still be hot.

7 Screw the plugs into their openings by hand until you no longer can tighten them with your fingers. Should one of the plugs bind, take it out and begin again; if you apply too much force, you risk stripping the threads. For holes that are difficult to reach, use the spark-plug socket on a wrench extension.

Finish tightening the plugs by using a torque wrench according to the specifications in your service manual. Plugs with gaskets may be tightened with a half-turn of a socket wrench.

8 Using the coded masking tape as your guide *(page 198)*, reconnect the spark-plug cables to the plugs. Make sure that the cable boot fits fully over the exposed portion of the plug.

BEFORE PROCEEDING: Pull the masking tape off of the cables.

**bending the electrode to
adjust the gap**

SERVICING THE DISTRIBUTOR

The distributor is the heart of the ignition system which controls cylinder firing. It consists of a number of components that relay the battery's low-voltage electricity to the coil and distribute high-voltage electricity from the coil to the individual spark plugs. Each one of these distributor components—cap, rotor, advance assemblies, breaker points and condenser—has to be kept in suitable condition and properly adjusted so they will deliver the correct amount of electricity to the correct plug at the correct moment.

Since the distributor is the most complicated part that you will be dealing with, its disassembly and servicing will occupy a considerable part of your tune-up time. But if you follow the directions that begin here and continue through page 209, you will be handling the components in a logical sequence and this should make the work proceed smoothly.

If your car has an electronic-ignition system, it does not have a distributor like the one shown here. But it does have some of the components, including a rotor and cap. Check your service manual to see what maintenance may be necessary before proceeding to the task of adjusting the timing (pages 216–221).

1 Before tackling the distributor, locate the nearby coil; clean dirt and oil from its outer casing with a dry paper towel. (The coil is a virtually trouble-free component that needs replacing only rarely—for example, when cracks appear in the casing. Replacement involves first a simple transfer of the coil's wires—some have three, some four—to the new unit and then the transfer of the coil itself, which is fastened in position by a clamp.)

2 (Pictures) Begin the distributor disassembly by removing the cap. If the cap is secured by a pair of clips, insert the tip of a screwdriver behind each clip and then twist until the clip is unsnapped. Where the cap is secured by L-shaped latches, insert a screwdriver into the slotted heads and press down slightly before turning each head a half turn. This will release the latches underneath.

3 (Picture) Lift the cap off the distributor housing and clean it of dirt and oil, inside and out, with a dry paper towel. Inspect the plastic material closely for cracks, chips

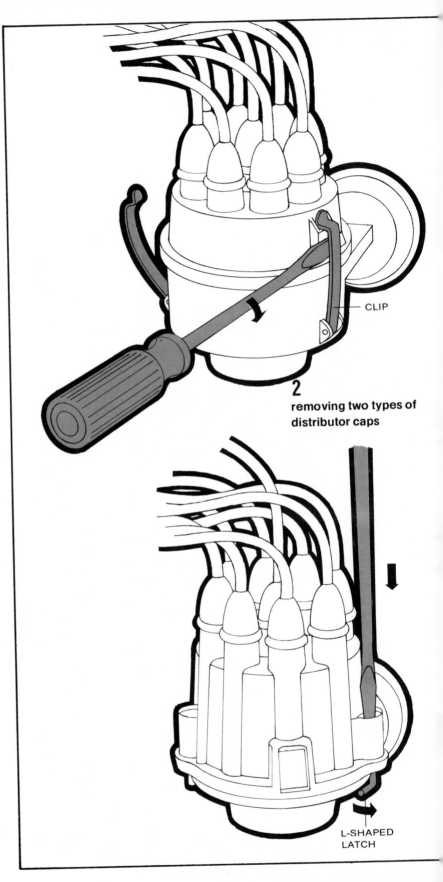

removing two types of distributor caps

CLIP

L-SHAPED LATCH

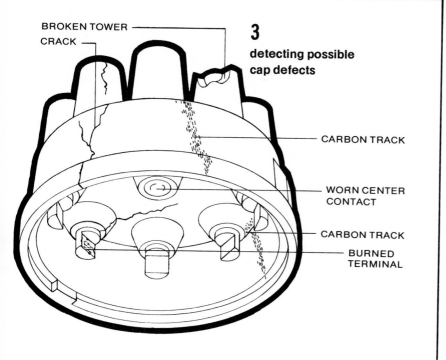

BROKEN TOWER
CRACK

3

**detecting possible
cap defects**

CARBON TRACK

WORN CENTER
CONTACT

CARBON TRACK

BURNED
TERMINAL

and for carbon tracks, which are etched into the sides of the cap by leaking electricity conducted along paths provided by spattered oil.

Look at the ring of metal terminals inside the cap to see if any are missing or show signs of burning or corrosion. Holding the cap in one hand, remove and replace each cable, one at a time, to see if any of the towers are damaged or corroded inside.
If any of these conditions are present, replace the cap. If the terminals are only slightly blackened or corroded, the cap can be reused after the deposits have been scraped off with fine sandpaper.

4 (Picture) If you do replace the cap with a new one, be sure to reattach the cables in the correct firing sequence. The best way to do this is to align the two caps side by side, with their markings and distinctive features in the same position. Then transfer the cables, one at a time, from the old cap to the new one. Push down on each cable until it snaps into place.

5 Push the cap to one side so that it will not interfere with your work on the other distributor components.

CONTINUED

4

**replacing
a defective cap**

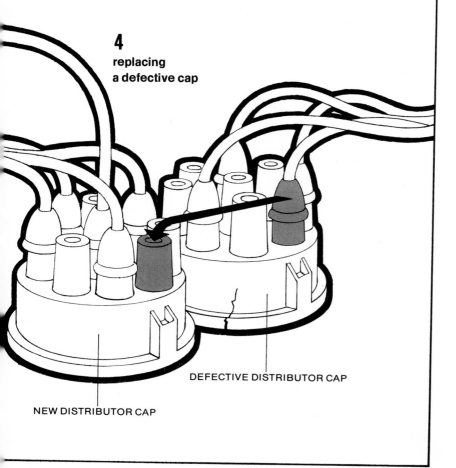

DEFECTIVE DISTRIBUTOR CAP

NEW DISTRIBUTOR CAP

DISTRIBUTOR CONTINUED

6 (Pictures) Remove the rotor from atop the distributor shaft. It usually can be lifted off, but on some distributors you may have to remove two screws and washers.

7 (Picture) If the distributor contains a radio frequency interference (RFI) shield, remove the two retaining screws and lift off the two halves of the shield. They require no servicing; set them aside.

8 (Picture) After wiping the rotor clean with a dry paper towel, examine it carefully for cracks and corrosion. If you find either of these flaws, replace the rotor. If the rotor is reusable, set it aside and proceed with the disassembly.

9 (Picture) Make sure that the centrifugal-advance mechanism is working freely. With your fingers, turn the distributor shaft approximately 5° in the same direction that it normally rotates. You can determine the direction by cranking the engine briefly. If the centrifugal-advance mechanism is inaccessible beneath the breaker points, as in the distributor shown in this step, check it by turning the top of the distributor shaft. Release the shaft, which should return immediately to its original position. If the centrifugal-advance mechanism is accessible, as in the type of distributor shown in step 7 *(lower left)*, check it by turning the mechanism until its crescent-shaped arms open. Then release it; the arms should pop back to their original position.

10 (Picture) To examine the vacuum-advance mechanism, find the breaker points and press against them in the direction opposite to that of the normal shaft rotation. This will cause the base plate to move. When you release the points, the base plate should swivel quickly and smoothly back to its original position.

CAUTION: If either the centrifugal or the vacuum-advance mechanism seems to be balky, retest it several times in rapid succession. If it continues to bind, reassemble the distributor and have a mechanic make whatever repair is needed.

CONTINUED

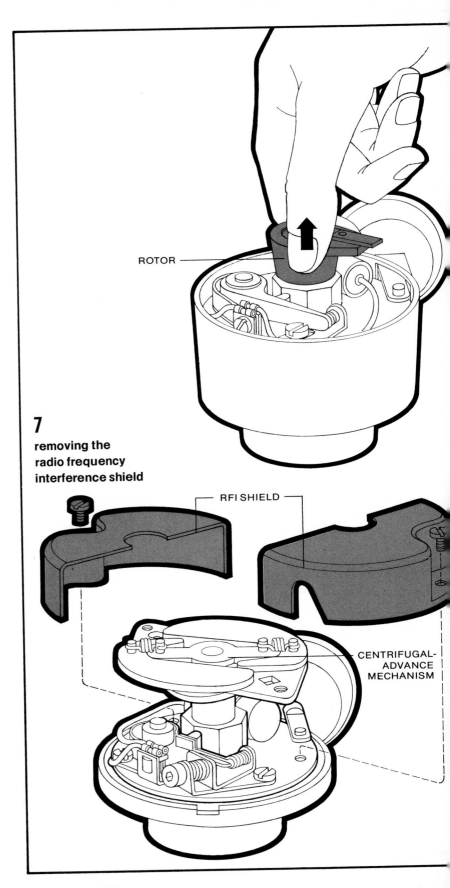

ROTOR

7
removing the radio frequency interference shield

RFI SHIELD

CENTRIFUGAL-ADVANCE MECHANISM

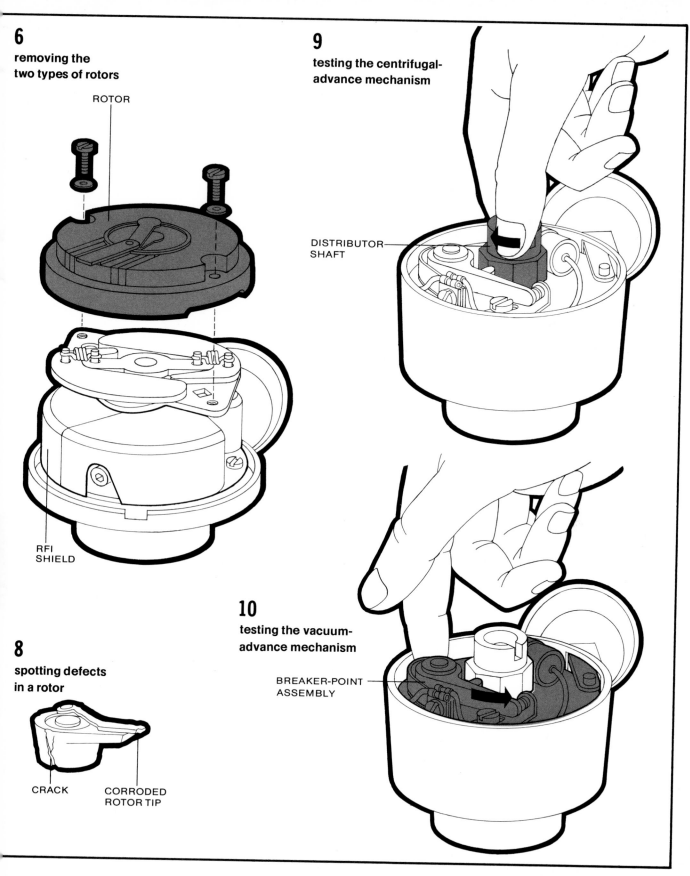

6

removing the
two types of rotors

ROTOR

RFI
SHIELD

8

spotting defects
in a rotor

CRACK

CORRODED
ROTOR TIP

9

testing the centrifugal-
advance mechanism

DISTRIBUTOR
SHAFT

10

testing the vacuum-
advance mechanism

BREAKER-POINT
ASSEMBLY

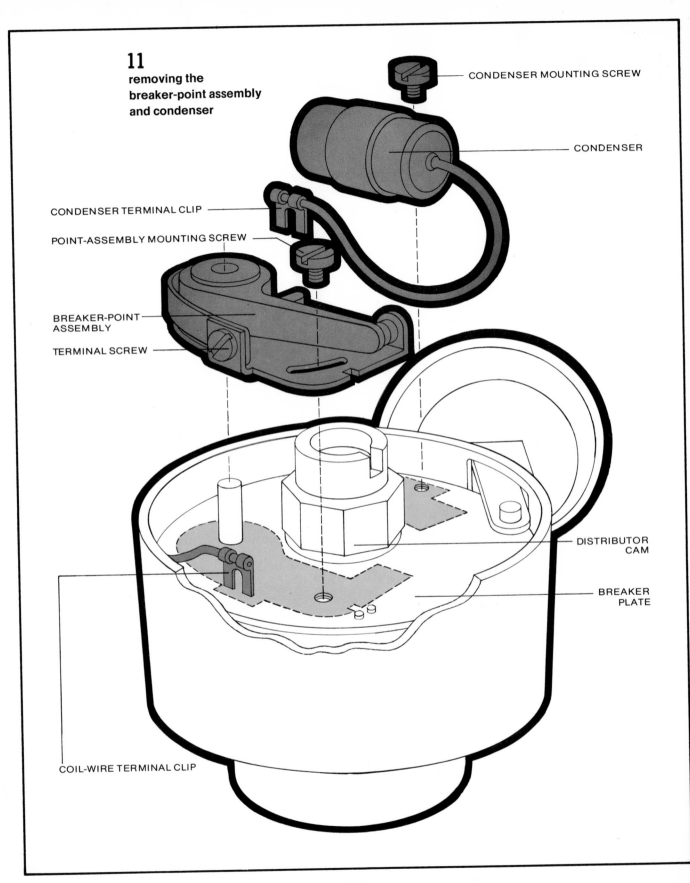

11
removing the breaker-point assembly and condenser

CONDENSER MOUNTING SCREW

CONDENSER

CONDENSER TERMINAL CLIP

POINT-ASSEMBLY MOUNTING SCREW

BREAKER-POINT ASSEMBLY

TERMINAL SCREW

DISTRIBUTOR CAM

BREAKER PLATE

COIL-WIRE TERMINAL CLIP

DISTRIBUTOR CONTINUED

CAUTION: In the steps that follow, be careful not to drop a screw into the bottom of the distributor; it could be difficult to remove. Whenever you handle the point assembly, keep your fingers away from the two circular contact areas.

11 (Picture) If the two advance mechanisms are functioning correctly, proceed to the removal of the breaker-point assembly. Loosen the terminal screw that holds the terminal clips of the wires linking the points to the coil and condenser. Lift the two wires out of the way, noting their position so that later they can be correctly replaced. Unfasten the point-assembly mounting screw (or screws) holding the breaker-point assembly. Lift the unit free.

12 (Picture) Examine the points carefully. While many mechanics routinely install new points with every tune-up, it often is possible to reuse them. If the points are coated with light gray deposits but are not burned or pitted *(top right)*, they can be safely reused after light buffing with an ignition file. Do not attempt to clean them down to bare metal; you may destroy the points' alignment.

If, however, the points appear severely burned or pitted *(center and bottom right)* — or if they have completed their specified useful life — you must replace them.

One of the causes of burned points is leaking oil. If the points are burned, check the breaker plate for an oil streak that indicates a leak somewhere in the distributor. If you find oil, continue the tune-up but take your car to a mechanic as soon as possible to have the leak traced and stopped.

13 If you replace damaged points, you should also replace the condenser. Remove the condenser mounting screw that holds the condenser in place *(picture 11)* and screw in the replacement tightly.

14 Clean dirt and grease from the breaker plate with a dry paper towel.

15 Use your finger to dab a light coat of distributor-cam lubricant on the cam.

16 Install the new or refurbished breaker-point assembly, making sure that it is correctly positioned before screwing it to the breaker plate *(picture 11)*.

17 Reconnect the two terminal clips and tighten the terminal screw. Be sure the clips do not touch the breaker plate. Tuck the wires back into their original positions, out of the way of moving parts. You are now ready to adjust the breaker-point gap.

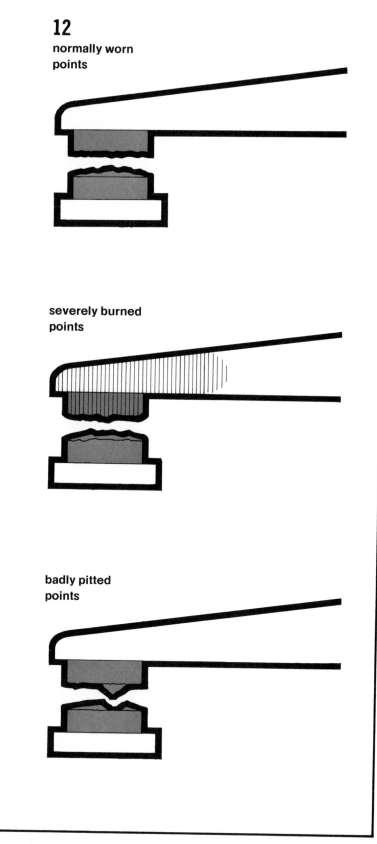

12
normally worn points

severely burned points

badly pitted points

GAPPING THE POINTS

Once the breaker points have been installed, the gap between the points must be set to the proper opening. The engine will not start if the spacing of the points is substantially off and will not run properly unless the spacing is exact. There are two methods of adjusting the breaker-point gap, depending on the type of distributor that is used in your car. Both types are discussed and illustrated here.

1 In all distributors, before the points can be adjusted, the rubbing block of the breaker-point assembly must rest on one of the lobes, or raised portions, of the distributor cam. It is often necessary to turn the cam to get it into the proper position, and this is achieved by turning the engine slightly. With the ignition turned on, use a remote starter switch (or have a helper turn the ignition key) to "bump" the engine in very short spurts until the rubbing block is centered on one of the lobes.

2 (Picture) Select a gauge the same thickness as the point gap specified in your service manual or on the tune-up decal that is located in the engine compartment of newer cars.

In distributors whose point gaps are held in place by the mounting screw, begin by loosening the screw slightly. Then insert a screwdriver into the notches or slots next to the mounting screw. Twist the tip of the screwdriver until the points open slightly wider than the thickness gauge. The same opening is achieved in other distributors simply by turning an adjustment screw with an Allen wrench.

Now, with either kind of distributor, insert the thickness gauge between the points. Make sure that you hold the gauge so that its sides are parallel to the surfaces of the points; if you twist the gauge, it will spread the points too far apart and the resulting gap will be too wide.

Using either the screwdriver or the Allen wrench, close the points until you can first sense a slight friction on the gauge as you slide it back and forth between the points.

3 When the gap is set, remove the gauge and tighten the mounting screw or withdraw the Allen wrench. Then reinsert the gauge and double check the gap width. If the points have shifted even slightly, repeat this adjustment until the gap is correct.

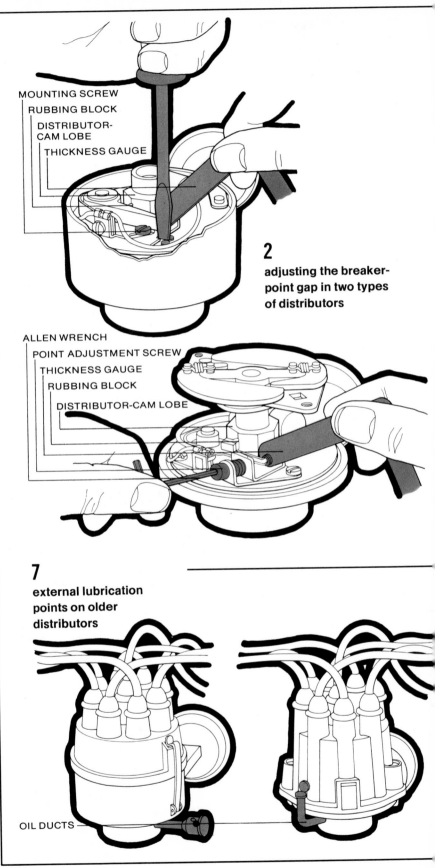

MOUNTING SCREW
RUBBING BLOCK
DISTRIBUTOR-CAM LOBE
THICKNESS GAUGE

2
adjusting the breaker-point gap in two types of distributors

ALLEN WRENCH
POINT ADJUSTMENT SCREW
THICKNESS GAUGE
RUBBING BLOCK
DISTRIBUTOR-CAM LOBE

7
external lubrication points on older distributors

OIL DUCTS

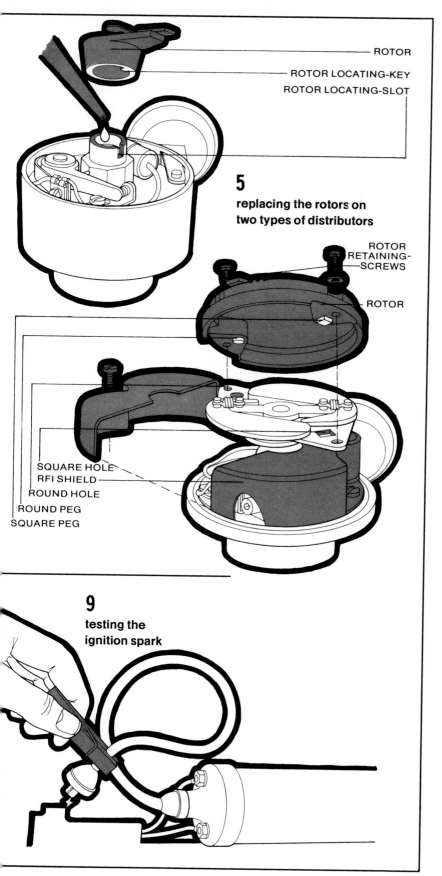

ROTOR

ROTOR LOCATING-KEY

ROTOR LOCATING-SLOT

5

**replacing the rotors on
two types of distributors**

ROTOR
RETAINING-
SCREWS

ROTOR

SQUARE HOLE
RFI SHIELD
ROUND HOLE
ROUND PEG
SQUARE PEG

9

**testing the
ignition spark**

4 Squirt lighter fluid into a clean paper towel. Gently draw it through the narrow breaker-point gap to remove any oil or fingerprints from the points.

5 (Picture) If the distributor has a small rotor that fits into a key slot in its shaft, lubricate the wick inside the shaft with three drops of engine oil. Be careful not to spill any oil outside the shaft. Then slip the rotor onto the shaft, making sure that the locating key fits into the corresponding slot in the shaft. Push the rotor all the way down.

If the distributor has a large pancake-shaped rotor, you may have removed an RFI shield (page 206). Now is the time to replace the shield. First position the half that covers the points; then position the other half and replace the retaining screws. Do not let any parts inside the distributor touch the shield. Now replace the rotor itself so that the square peg fits into the square hole and the round peg into the round hole. Finally, secure the rotor with its two screws.

6 Replace the distributor cap and fasten its latches. Press firmly on each of the spark-plug cable boots to seat them firmly in the distributor cap.

7 (Picture) On some older cars, the distributor has an oil duct at its base for lubricating an internal bearing. (On newer cars, this bearing is permanently oiled.) Put three drops of engine oil in the duct.

8 Reconnect the wire that you removed from the coil before you made the compression test (page 200).

9 (Picture) Remove the cable from the center tower of the distributor cap by gently pulling on its boot. To avoid getting a shock during the test that follows, grasp the cable with a wooden clothespin or any insulating material. Hold the end of the cable about one quarter of an inch from a clean, bare area of metal. With the ignition turned on, use a remote starter switch (or have a helper turn the ignition key) to crank the engine briefly. If the distributor and coil are operating correctly, a thick blue spark will jump from the cable to the metal.

If, however, the spark is thin and yellow in color, go back and check the point gap and wiring connections in the distributor. If the spark still is weak, proceed with the tune-up since this will not affect the rest of the job. However, the weak spark does indicate some other defect in the ignition system; have it corrected by a mechanic.

10 Switch off the ignition. Remove the clothespin and reinsert the cable into its socket in the center of the distributor cap. Push it down until it snaps into place.

CAUTION: Before proceeding to the steps on the following pages, remove all hand tools from the engine compartment, but leave the remote starter switch attached.

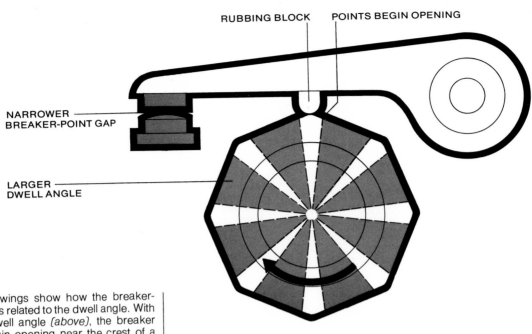

RUBBING BLOCK   POINTS BEGIN OPENING

NARROWER
BREAKER-POINT GAP

LARGER
DWELL ANGLE

These drawings show how the breaker-point gap is related to the dwell angle. With a large dwell angle *(above)*, the breaker points begin opening near the crest of a distributor-cam lobe; therefore, they open only a small distance. With a smaller dwell angle *(below)*, the breaker points begin opening farther from the crest, so they open wider. When you adjust the breaker-point gap with a thickness gauge, you indirectly set the dwell angle, since the gap determines how far from the crest the breaker points must begin opening.

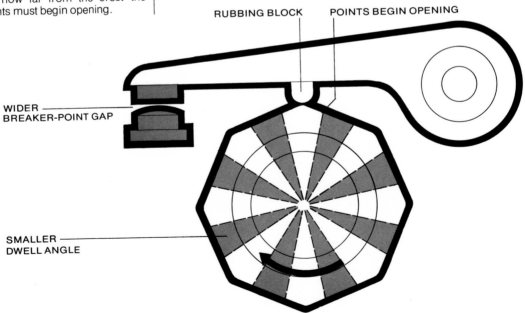

RUBBING BLOCK   POINTS BEGIN OPENING

WIDER
BREAKER-POINT GAP

SMALLER
DWELL ANGLE

MEASURING THE DWELL ANGLE

Setting the breaker-point gap using a thickness gauge *(page 210)* determines how long the points, as they repeatedly open and close, will be in contact—or, in automotive parlance, how long they will dwell together—thus allowing electricity to flow through the primary windings of the coil. However, a more accurate method of setting breaker-point dwell is to use a special meter *(below)* to measure the dwell angle. This angle is the distance, in degrees, that the distributor cam rotates while the points are closed. If the points stay closed for too long or too short an interval, insufficient electricity is transmitted to the spark plugs and the engine will perform poorly.

The instrument used to measure the dwell angle is called, naturally enough, a dwell meter. It is simply a voltmeter calibrated to tell the average amount of voltage that passes through the ignition system's primary circuit as the points open and close. If the points remain closed for a long interval, the average voltage is high and the meter shows a large dwell angle. The opposite is true if the points remain closed for a short interval.

Most instrument makers combine a dwell meter with a tachometer—which measures an engine's speed in revolutions per minute—into a single testing device called a dwell tachometer. The combination is convenient because you will also need a tachometer to check the engine's idling speed *(overleaf)* before you can set the dwell angle precisely. A dwell tachometer that will give adequate service costs about $25. One of professional quality costs about four times that amount.

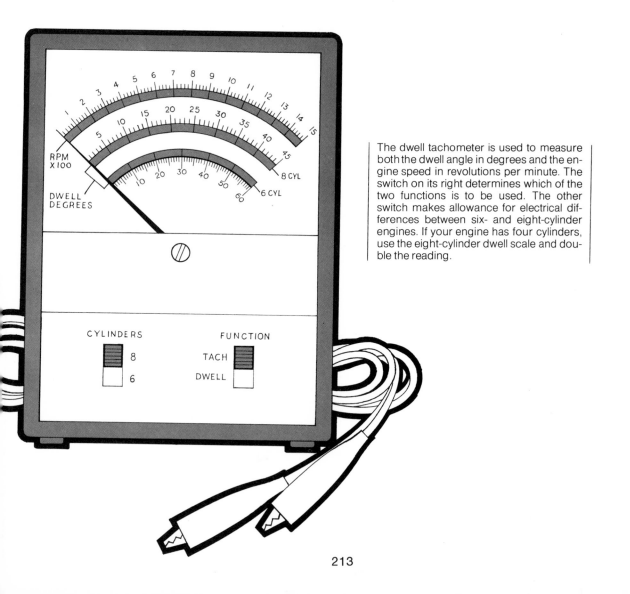

The dwell tachometer is used to measure both the dwell angle in degrees and the engine speed in revolutions per minute. The switch on its right determines which of the two functions is to be used. The other switch makes allowance for electrical differences between six- and eight-cylinder engines. If your engine has four cylinders, use the eight-cylinder dwell scale and double the reading.

SETTING THE DWELL ANGLE

Because the dwell tachometer makes its measurements while the engine is running and works as well with old points as with new ones, the device permits a precise final adjustment of the point gap.

1 (Picture) Attach the dwell tachometer's lead wires according to the instructions that come with it. Usually, the red-colored lead goes to a side terminal of the coil; attach it on top of the wire leading to the distributor points. Attach the other lead, which serves as a ground wire, to any clean metal part of the engine.

2 Move the function switch to "tachometer." Then move the other switch to correspond with the number of cylinders in your car's engine.

CAUTION: You will be using the dwell tachometer while the engine is running. Be sure to keep yourself, your clothing, the instrument and its lead wires clear of moving fans and belts.

3 (Picture) Consult your service manual (or refer to the decal in the engine compartment) for the speed at which the engine must idle while you check the dwell angle. If you are using a remote starter, turn on the ignition. With the gearshift in neutral or park, start the engine and let it run. Read the tachometer scale. If the idle is within the prescribed specifications, proceed to step 4.
   If it is not, you will first have to adjust the idle. With the aid of your service manual, locate the screw or solenoid that controls low-speed idling. Turn the screw or solenoid clockwise to increase idle speed or counterclockwise to reduce idle speed, until the reading on the tachometer scale is within specifications.

4 (Picture) Let the engine idle and move the function switch to "dwell." Consult your service manual for the correct dwell angle. If the reading on the dwell scale is within the specified range, turn off the engine and proceed with timing the ignition *(overleaf)*. If it is not, you will have to change the dwell angle.

To change the dwell angle on an externally adjusted distributor, such as the one shown, let the engine run. Lift the sliding door in the distributor cap to uncover the point-adjustment screw and insert an Allen wrench into the screw. Turn it slowly while you watch the dwell scale. Turning the screw clockwise reduces the dwell angle, turning it counterclockwise increases the angle. When the pointer indicates the correct dwell angle, remove the wrench and close the sliding door.

For points that are adjusted by loosening the mounting screw, turn off the engine. Remove the distributor cap and rotor, and then reset the gap according to the instructions on pages 210 and 211. If the dwell angle is too small, move the points closer together; if the angle is too great, move the points farther apart. Put the rotor and cap back on the distributor, restart the engine and check the new dwell-angle setting with the dwell tachometer. You may have to repeat this procedure several times to set the correct dwell.

connecting the dwell tachometer

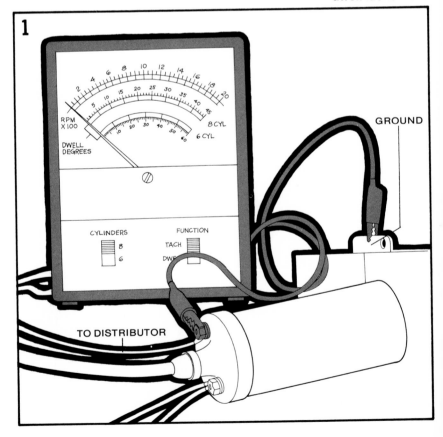

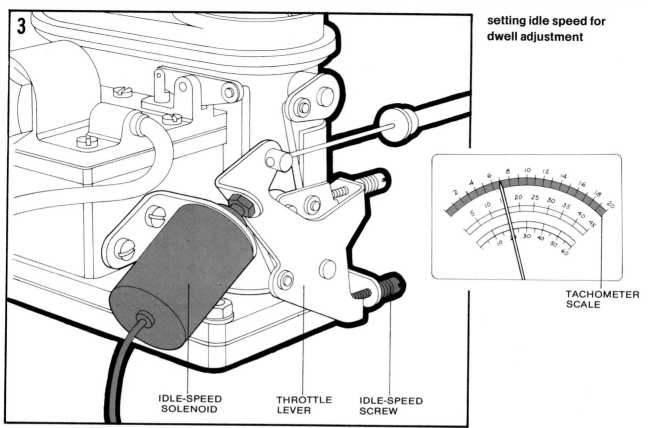

setting idle speed for dwell adjustment

TACHOMETER SCALE

IDLE-SPEED SOLENOID   THROTTLE LEVER   IDLE-SPEED SCREW

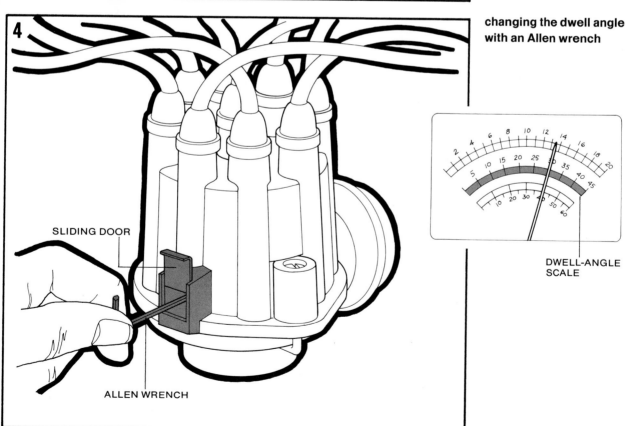

changing the dwell angle with an Allen wrench

DWELL-ANGLE SCALE

SLIDING DOOR

ALLEN WRENCH

PRINCIPLES OF IGNITION TIMING

Even though the breaker points are perfectly gapped to deliver electricity to the spark plugs at the precise intervals required, there remains the task of coordinating—or timing—the sparks with the position of the pistons inside the cylinders. This adjustment is one of the most critical procedures in the tune-up—and one of the easiest.

As the engine runs, each piston goes through a compression stroke that starts at the bottom of the cylinder and ends near its top at a point called top dead center (TDC). In most engines, the spark plug fires just before the piston reaches TDC.

Timing specifications, which vary from engine to engine, are expressed in degrees. For example, if an engine's timing is 5° before TDC, the spark should fire when the crankshaft still has 5° to turn before the piston reaches TDC. Timing marks engraved or raised on the crankshaft pulley, engine block or flywheel indicate where the No. 1 piston is in relation to its TDC; one mark is a groove or pointer and the other is a scale marked in degrees *(overleaf)*. One is fixed and the other rotates.

Timing is checked with a timing light. When properly connected to the engine, a timing light will flash brightly each time the spark plug in the No. 1 cylinder fires. Because of the light's stroboscopic effect, the rotating timing mark seems stationary and, aligned with the fixed mark, it shows how many degrees from TDC the spark plug fires.

Simply turning the distributor changes the timing by changing the position of the breaker points' rubbing block *(opposite)*. Timing the No. 1 cylinder automatically times all the others.

A good-quality timing light, like the one shown here, usually is a pistol-shaped device equipped with leads that connect to both battery terminals and to the No. 1 spark plug *(overleaf)*. Most timing lights of this kind draw their power from the car battery, although some can be connected to electrical outlets.

The cost of a good timing light varies widely, from as little as $20 to as much as $65, depending on its construction. Less expensive lights use dim neon bulbs that are effective only when triggered close to the ignition timing marks—which can be both difficult and dangerous. Better lights use brilliant flash tubes that have blue-tinted beams visible even in bright sunshine.

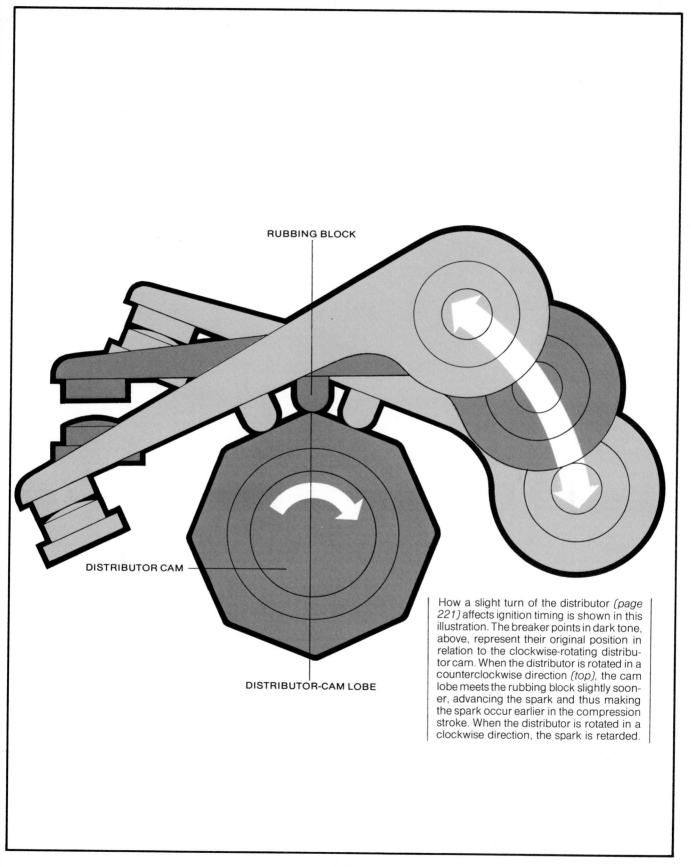

RUBBING BLOCK

DISTRIBUTOR CAM

DISTRIBUTOR-CAM LOBE

How a slight turn of the distributor *(page 221)* affects ignition timing is shown in this illustration. The breaker points in dark tone, above, represent their original position in relation to the clockwise-rotating distributor cam. When the distributor is rotated in a counterclockwise direction *(top),* the cam lobe meets the rubbing block slightly sooner, advancing the spark and thus making the spark occur earlier in the compression stroke. When the distributor is rotated in a clockwise direction, the spark is retarded.

ADJUSTING IGNITION TIMING

The final task in ignition tuning is to adjust the timing so that the spark plugs fire at the correct instant.

CAUTION: In the first and later ignition-timing steps, you will be working near engine areas that may be hot.

1 (Picture) Attach the timing light according to the manufacturer's instructions. Connect the more heavily insulated of the three leads to the No. 1 spark plug (see your service manual) after removing the plug's cable. The light has an adapter that can be inserted between the spark-plug terminal and its cable to provide a connection for the lead. The other two leads are clamped to the battery terminals, with the red lead going to the positive terminal and the black to the negative terminal.

2 (Picture) Use your service manual to locate the timing marks on your car's engine. Usually the marks are located at the front of the engine, as illustrated. On some cars, however, the marks are located on the flywheel at the rear of the engine and can be observed through a peephole in the flywheel housing. The timing marks show the position of the No. 1 piston in relation to top dead center (marked TDC, or 0) either after top dead center (ATDC) or before top dead center (BTDC).

Clean the scale and pointer, if they are accessible, using a paper towel dampened with kerosene. Then consult your service manual to see which timing mark should align with the pointer; accentuate that line with paint or chalk.

3 (Picture) Pull off the tube connected to the vacuum-advance mechanism. Plug the tube with a pencil, then secure the tube out of the way of moving parts.

CAUTION: You will be working with the engine running. Stay clear of moving parts.

4 (Picture) Start the engine and leave the transmission in neutral or park. Recheck the idle speed and adjust the idle-speed screw or solenoid until the idle is satisfactory [pages 214-215].

CONTINUED

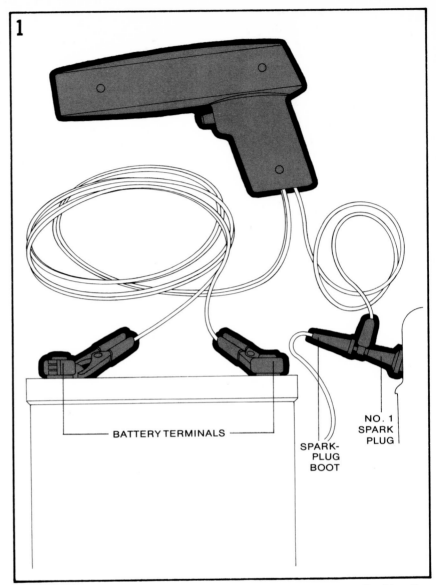

1

BATTERY TERMINALS

SPARK-PLUG BOOT

NO. 1 SPARK PLUG

attaching the timing light

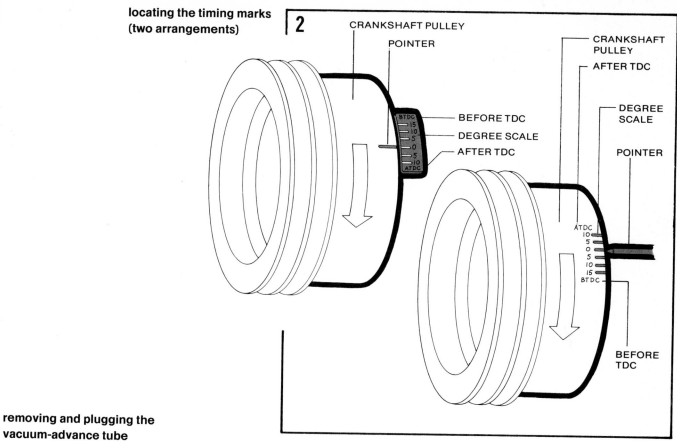

2

CRANKSHAFT PULLEY
POINTER
BEFORE TDC
DEGREE SCALE
AFTER TDC

CRANKSHAFT PULLEY
AFTER TDC
DEGREE SCALE
POINTER
BEFORE TDC

**removing and plugging the
vacuum-advance tube**

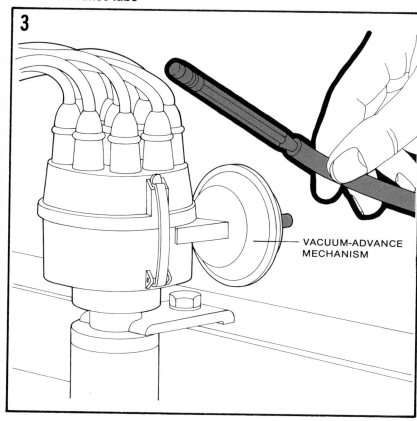

3

VACUUM-ADVANCE
MECHANISM

**typical tachometer reading
after idle adjustment**

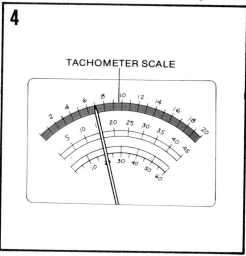

4

TACHOMETER SCALE

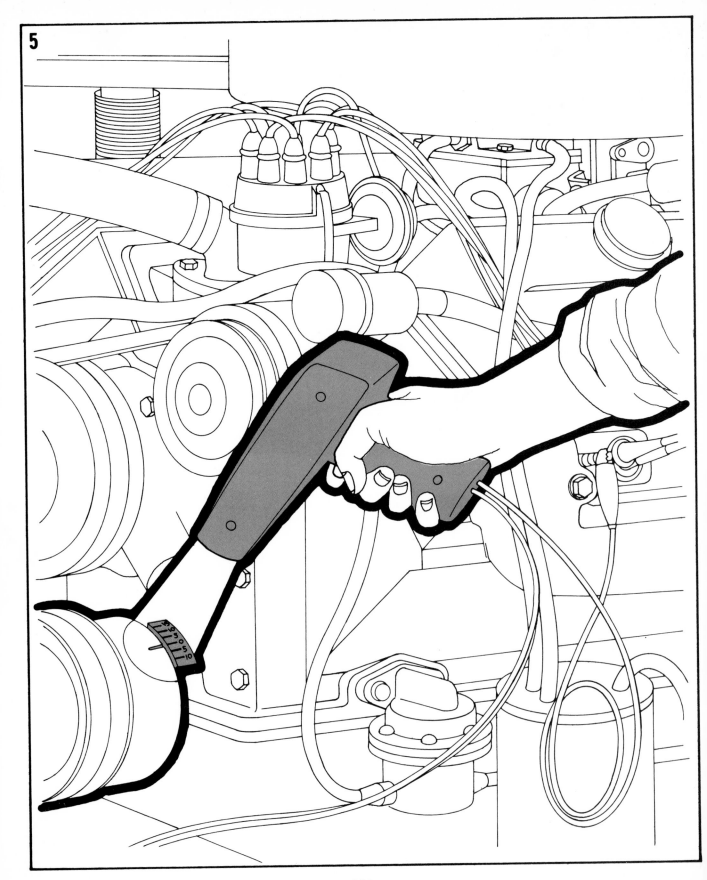

ADJUSTING TIMING CONTINUED

5 (Picture) With the engine idling, aim the timing light at the timing marks and pull its trigger switch. The stroboscopic light will make the rotating mark appear to be stationary. See if the pointer aligns with the accentuated mark on the scale. If it does not, the ignition timing is incorrectly set.

6 (Picture) If the timing is off, turn off the engine and loosen the distributor hold-down bolt. If this bolt is difficult to reach, you will require a distributor wrench *(pages 194-195)*. Loosen the bolt until you can rotate the distributor with one hand.

7 (Picture) Turn on the engine. With the timing light in one hand, grasp the vacuum advance with the other hand. Keep the light aimed at the timing marks while you use the vacuum advance to rotate the distributor slowly. If the pointer moves farther away from the correct timing mark, rotate the distributor in the other direction. When the pointer and correct mark align, turn off the timing light and the engine.

8 Tighten the hold-down bolt at the base of the distributor, being careful not to disturb the position of the distributor.

9 Restart the engine and use the timing light to recheck the timing. If the timing marks are not now correctly aligned, the distributor probably moved when you tightened the hold-down bolt. In this event, repeat steps 6 and 7.

10 Check the centrifugal-advance mechanism with the engine running. Aim the timing light at the timing marks and open the throttle with the throttle lever *(page 215)* until the engine reaches 1,500 rpm. The timing mark should advance as the engine speeds up, then return to its original position when the engine resumes idling. If it doesn't, consult a mechanic after you finish the tune-up.

11 Stop the engine, unplug the vacuum-advance tube and reattach it. Check the vacuum advance by aiming the timing light at the timing marks while the engine runs at 1,500 rpm. The timing mark should show the spark advanced farther than in step 10. If it does not, continue the tune-up but have a mechanic check the vacuum advance later.

BEFORE PROCEEDING: Turn off the engine. Detach and remove the timing light. Make sure all hand tools and the pencil used to plug the hose are out of the engine compartment. Leave the dwell tachometer and the remote starter switch connected.

using the timing light

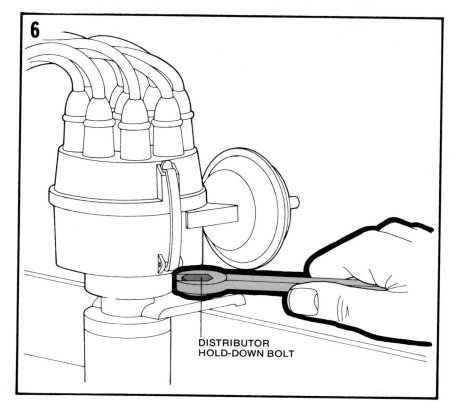

**loosening the distributor
hold-down bolt**

DISTRIBUTOR
HOLD-DOWN BOLT

**rotating the
distributor**

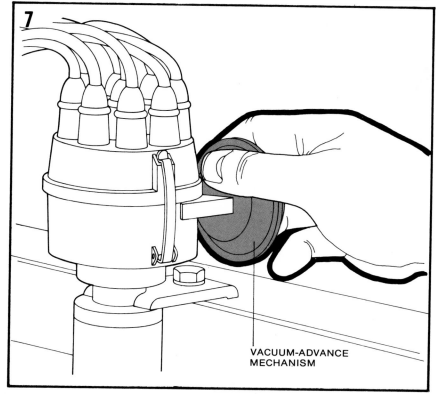
VACUUM-ADVANCE
MECHANISM

ADJUSTING THE IDLE

Your final tune-up tasks involve the fuel system. You must be sure that properly filtered gasoline is reaching the carburetor and that the correct fuel mixture is being produced and fed into the cylinders in the correct amounts. After the preliminaries of checking the automatic choke and fuel filter, this procedure will involve the adjustment of three idle settings.

CAUTION: Some engine parts may still be hot, so take care not to touch them.

1 (Picture) Use one finger to gently move the choke butterfly at the top of the carburetor. The butterfly should swivel freely. If it doesn't, clean the pivots with carburetor solvent before proceeding.

2 (Picture) Consult your service manual for the location of the fuel filter and then remove the filter. If the filter is recessed into the carburetor, disconnect the fuel line and unscrew the retaining plug. If it is an in-line filter—that is, inserted in the fuel line between the fuel pump and the carburetor —release the clamps and pull out the filter. If the filter is attached to the fuel pump, detach the fuel line and unscrew the filter.

Install a new filter and reconnect the fittings. Be sure to replace—in the same order—any washers, gaskets and springs that were removed with the old filter.

3 Hold the choke butterfly-valve open and look directly down the carburetor barrel. (You may need a small mirror to help you.) Rotate the throttle lever quickly and see if tiny squirts of fuel enter the barrel. Repeat the procedure for the other primary barrel of a multibarreled carburetor. If a squirt fails to appear in either barrel, continue the tune-up but see a mechanic later to have the problem corrected.

4 Start the engine and let it warm up by idling in neutral for 20 minutes.

5 While the engine is idling, consult your service manual to determine what gear the car should be in while adjusting the idle, and also to see whether other setting-up procedures (such as turning on the headlights) are necessary. If the manual requires the transmission to be in drive, be sure to set the parking brake, block the drive wheels and have an assistant sit in the driver's seat, foot firmly positioned on the brake pedal as a safety precaution.

CONTINUED

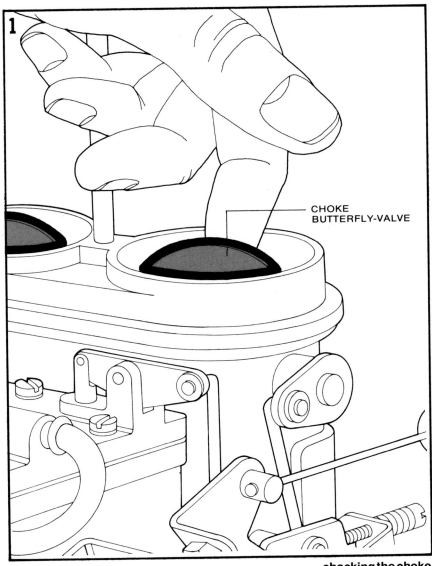

CHOKE
BUTTERFLY-VALVE

**checking the choke
butterfly-valve**

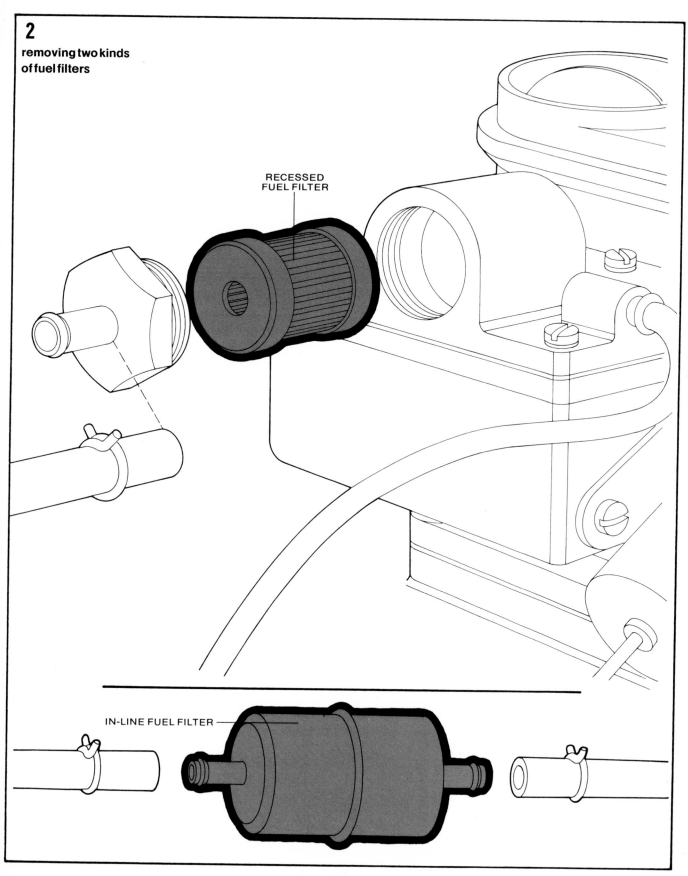

2
removing two kinds of fuel filters

RECESSED FUEL FILTER

IN-LINE FUEL FILTER

223

ADJUSTING IDLE CONTINUED

CAUTION: You will be setting three basic idle adjustments while the engine is running—curb idle, idle fuel mixture and fast idle. Keep yourself, your clothing and test-instrument leads clear of all moving engine parts during this time.

6 (Picture) Use your service manual to locate the idle-adjustment devices of the carburetor: curb-idle solenoid; idle-speed screw; idle-mixture screws; and fast-idle screw. Don't confuse a cylindrical throttle solenoid and a disc-shaped antistall dashpot. The manual will also tell you what your engine's idle speeds should be, and what accessories should be turned on, turned off or disconnected while you make the various idle adjustments.

7 Using the tachometer, set the curb-idle speed, typically about 700 rpm, by turning the idle-speed screw or the curb-idle solenoid. If your carburetor has both screw and solenoid, adjust the curb-idle speed with the solenoid. Then disconnect the plug in the solenoid's single wire before using the screw to obtain a lower idle speed as specified in your service manual. Reconnect the solenoid before proceeding.

8 To set the correct mixture of gasoline and air at curb idle, use a screwdriver to turn the idle-mixture screw located near the bottom of the carburetor barrel *(picture 6)*. If there are two such screws, as is the case with two- and four-barrel carburetors, adjust one of them completely before repeating the process with the other. Turn the screw only an eighth of a turn at a time—and wait about 30 seconds for the engine to react before giving the screw another eighth of a turn.

If the idle-mixture screw has a plastic head with tabs to limit how far it can be moved, simply turn the screw until the engine idles at its smoothest. Should the engine idle roughly even after you have turned the screw—or screws—as far as possible, do not tamper with the tabs; take the car to a mechanic for the proper adjustment.

If there are no tabs, turn the idle-mixture screw clockwise until the engine begins to slow. Then turn the screw slowly in the opposite direction. When you reach the point where the engine stops speeding up, the setting is correct.

On recent cars equipped with emission controls, it may be necessary to perform an additional clockwise adjustment of the same idle-mixture screw to make the fuel mixture leaner. Check your service manual or tune-up decal, found under the hood, for instructions on how far to rotate the screw, or how much of a decrease in rpm's should be registered by the tachometer.

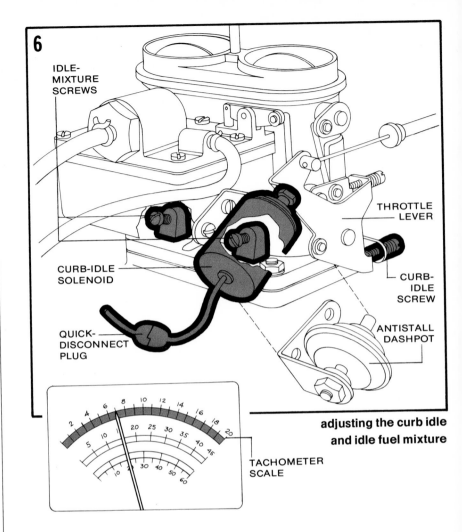

adjusting the curb idle and idle fuel mixture

9 Check your tachometer to make sure that the curb-idle setting is still correct. If it is not, repeat step 7.

10 (Picture) Locate the fast-idle screw, which is usually attached to the throttle lever and rests against a stepped cam. Rotate the cam *(top arrow)* until the screw rests on the highest or second-highest step, whichever your manual specifies. Turn the screw until the tachometer shows you have obtained the specified fast-idle speed, which must be about twice the curb-idle speed. Then open the throttle slightly *(bottom arrow)* and release the lever to slow the engine to curb-idle speed.

11 (Picture) If your carburetor is fitted with an external antistall dashpot, adjust it now. Open the throttle by turning the throttle lever; release it suddenly.

If the engine stalls or nearly stalls, use a wrench to loosen the dashpot lock nut.

Then turn the dashpot by hand until its plunger allows the throttle lever to close gently to curb-idle speed without stalling. Check the tachometer to be sure that the throttle closes all the way to curb idle. If it does not, slowly screw the dashpot away from the throttle lever until the tachometer registers curb-idle speed. Tighten the lock nut. Turn off the engine.

12 Reconnect any components that had to be disconnected before the idle adjustments were made. Replace the air cleaner if you have not already done so. Make sure that you reattach all hoses leading to the cleaner.

13 Disconnect the dwell tachometer, and if you used one, the remote starter switch. Make sure that all tools, lights and other equipment used during the tune-up are out of the engine compartment. Put your transmission into the park position before you unchock the wheels.

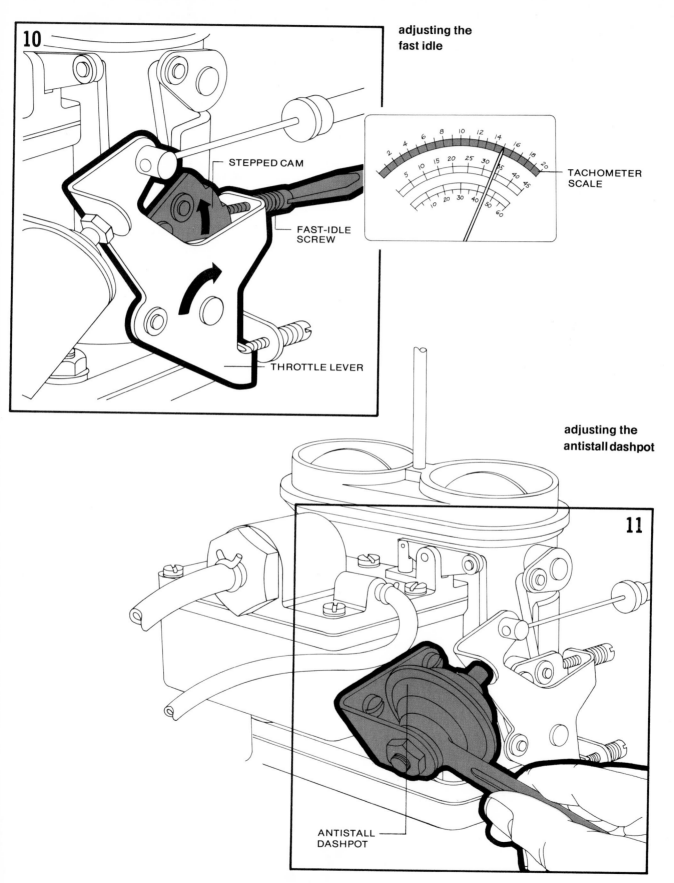

adjusting the fast idle

STEPPED CAM

FAST-IDLE SCREW

THROTTLE LEVER

TACHOMETER SCALE

10

adjusting the antistall dashpot

ANTISTALL DASHPOT

11

TROUBLESHOOTING

WHAT TO DO WHEN THE CAR MISBEHAVES

9

Even if a car has been most carefully driven and maintained, there comes a time when —Something's Wrong. The problem may announce itself dramatically, with a backfire like a shotgun blast, for instance. It may signal itself without a sound, by means of one of the dashboard warning lights *(overleaf)*. Or maybe some morning the car simply won't start when you turn the ignition key.

Of course it's always irritating. Something wrong with the family car is one of the major threats to domestic tranquillity, right up there with the overdrawn bank balance and "you should never have asked for that third cocktail." It is not, however, a cause for panic. Even if you are innocent of any mechanical bent, you can—with the aid of the troubleshooting guide that follows—diagnose most of the troubles that are likely to afflict your automobile

—that bang, that whimper, that silence—and even fix a good many of them without limping to a garage or calling a tow truck.

Each of the major categories of problems the motorist is likely to encounter is stated in large headline type. After the headline and a brief commentary, the particular circumstances under which the problem occurs are singled out so that you may identify your own situation. Each circumstance is numbered and printed in boldface type. Following each numbered entry is an alphabetical list of the possible causes and probable cures. The same background color separates each problem and the suggested solutions from the next grouping.

The recommended procedures are listed alphabetically in the order enabling you to try the easiest and most obvious solution first. The sequence is not always the one a skilled me-

THE CAR'S BUILT-IN WARNING SYSTEM

Standard dashboard instruments have shrunk in number and function over the years. Replacing them, in some instances, are "idiot lights"—so called because, instead of measuring the performance of the car's systems, they merely announce the fact that the system is performing poorly—or that it has already failed.

Three of the lights warn of difficulties with the alternator, the oil pressure or the engine temperature. When any of these lights come on and stay on while you are driving, pull off the road immediately and stop the engine until you can determine something about the cause of the trouble.

A fourth light, found in most of the recent models, warns of trouble in the braking system. It functions a bit differently *(last item, opposite)*.

ALTERNATOR LIGHT

The problem. When this light goes on, the alternator is not recharging the battery. Sooner or later —sooner, if the headlights are burning—the engine will stall because the supply of electricity stored in the battery will be exhausted. This cuts power to the spark coil, shutting down the ignition system.

What causes it. There are three possibilities: the alternator may not be rotating fast enough to produce the required voltage, a deficiency in the circuit may be preventing electrical current from reaching the battery or there may be a malfunction in the alternator itself.

What to do about it. Pull off the road and stop the engine to conserve the remaining electricity.

Check for a loose, glazed or broken drive belt *(page 175)*. If the belt is loose, tighten it, restart the engine and see if the light goes out. If the belt is glazed or broken and you carry a spare, install it.

Otherwise, head for the nearest service station to get it replaced. You can drive without a belt for a short distance, utilizing the remaining power stored in your battery.

If the belt is apparently functioning properly, check the tightness of the wiring connections at the alternator and also at the voltage regulator if the two are separated. Inspect the wires for breaks or worn insulation. Tape or splice as necessary for an emergency repair *(pages 180-181)*.

Loose, corroded connections between battery cables and posts can make the light come on by damaging the alternator or voltage regulator. Cleaning the connections now won't help.

If you find poor battery-cable connections or if you can't trace the defect, turn off all electrical accessories and drive to a mechanic. A fully charged battery is capable of running an engine for two to four hours with headlights and other accessories off, 30 to 60 minutes with headlights on.

OIL-PRESSURE LIGHT

The problem. This light warns that oil pressure in the engine is low. Running an engine whose oil pressure is inadequate can destroy it in minutes.

What causes it. Oil may be leaking out of the engine. If there are no leaks, a mechanical defect, possibly of the oil pump, has caused a reduction in the pressure required to keep the lubricating oil flowing through the engine.

What to do about it. Pull off the road immediately —coasting in neutral, if possible. Turn off the engine the moment you come to a full stop.

Check the oil level in the crankcase *(page 140)*.

If oil is visible on the dipstick, even though below the recommended minimum, and the light came on only intermittently when cornering or accelerating, drive slowly to the nearest gas station to add oil. If the light glowed steadily, even if the oil level is adequate—indicating a problem in the engine more complex than a simple leak—don't attempt to drive any farther. Have the car towed.

Have the mechanic check for massive leaks. Small leaks—even some that lose enough oil to affect pressure in a relatively short time—can be hard to find. If the leak is small, you may be able to continue driving after adding oil. Make frequent checks of the oil level until the leak is fixed.

TEMPERATURE LIGHT

The problem. This light means that the engine's coolant is overheating.

What to do about it. If you are stuck in traffic on a hot day, the cooling system is probably overworked. Turn on the heater and turn off the air conditioner. Place the transmission in neutral and run the engine at moderately high speed. If the warning light doesn't go out in a few minutes, pull off the road and stop the engine in order to keep it from overheating further.

Look for bugs or leaves blocking the radiator, then check for a broken, loose or glazed fan belt. Tighten or replace it if necessary (page 175). If you can't fix the belt, drive to a mechanic. But stop each time the warning light goes on. Wait until the light goes out, then continue.

If the fan belt is all right, wait until the warning light goes out, then check the radiator (or the overflow tank, if there is one) for coolant loss — removing the radiator cap with great care since the coolant is very hot and under pressure. Avert your face, protect your hand with a rag and turn the cap counterclockwise to its first stop. Let pressure escape before turning farther, then remove the cap.

If the coolant level is correct (page 140), there is a mechanical defect or blockage in the cooling system and you must drive slowly to a mechanic. Stop each time the engine overheats.

If the coolant level is low, look for leaks from the radiator or its hoses (page 174). Tighten loose hose connections. Add water to the radiator while the engine is running. Suddenly introducing cold water to a hot engine can cause it to crack. Keep the engine running and replace the radiator cap, tightening it only halfway. Doing so reduces pressure against the leak and slows the flow of coolant. A loose radiator cap reduces the efficiency of the cooling system, but may let you drive farther before the engine overheats again than a fast leak would. If a hose has burst, do not attempt to drive the car; have it towed to a garage.

If you find no leaks, look for water in the exhaust pipe, especially if overheating was preceded by roughness and power loss in the engine. Water in the exhaust pipe would indicate a failure of the cylinder head, engine block or cylinder-head gasket, the seal that confines combustion to the individual cylinders and restricts the coolant to the engine's water jacket. Any of these failures permits water to enter the cylinders. There it contaminates the fuel mixture and affects combustion before being expelled through the car's exhaust system and winding up in the tailpipe.

Check the engine-oil dipstick (page 140). If the oil has risen to an abnormally high level, water probably has leaked into the crankcase.

If you find water either in the exhaust pipe or in the crankcase, don't attempt to drive any farther. Have the car towed to a garage for repairs.

BRAKE-SYSTEM WARNING LIGHT

The problem. This light, found in cars of recent vintage, flashes on when either of the car's separate hydraulic braking systems fails. Unlike the other warning lights, it does not automatically signal a malfunction. Instead, a switch closes as you hit the brake pedal, as explained on page 54.

What causes it. The hydraulic pressure in one of the two braking systems has been reduced to a point where it can no longer activate the brakes for two of the wheels. The fluid may have leaked out of the master cylinder, the wheel cylinder or at any point between them. A sharp object in the road can cut a brake line and knock out one system.

What to do about it. Even though the warning light remains on, you probably still have braking power in two wheels. It is not necessary to stop, but you should slow down and test your brakes to see how much braking effort is required. Widen the distance between your car and the one in front of you, to allow more time for braking. Try to anticipate stops and begin braking earlier than you customarily would. If you find that pushing on the brake pedal doesn't slow the car at all, you can stop your car by shifting to a lower gear and carefully engaging the parking brake. But you shouldn't attempt to drive any farther. Have the car towed to a garage for repairs.

chanic, using sophisticated test instruments, would follow, but it is the sequence a mechanic might use if he were caught away from the shop and wearing a sports jacket.

The solutions do become more complicated as the list continues, and if the problem has not been solved after all practical alternatives have been exhausted or if your troubleshooting points to a difficulty with which you should not try to cope personally, this guide will advise you that professional help is indeed in order.

Prevention is always best

Proper maintenance, including well-spaced tune-ups, will make a lot of troubleshooting unnecessary by heading off malfunctions before they reach the critical stage. And there are some factors, quite apart from the power plant, that may make the engine seem to be malfunctioning when it isn't. Tire pressures that are too low, for instance, besides being harmful to the tires themselves, can result in decreased performance: the engine must work harder to drive the car. Dragging brakes, including the hand brake, can have the same effect; and so can faulty wheel alignment. Kinks or obstructions in the exhaust system force the engine to work harder during the exhaust strokes, thus robbing the wheels of power.

Major repairs themselves can sometimes impair performance temporarily. New parts fit together more tightly than old ones, resulting in more friction for the engine to overcome until the replacements have been broken in.

Learn to start your car correctly

Engines often get blamed for not starting up fast enough, although the fault may be the driver's. Older-model cars and many imports and sports cars have manually controlled chokes. But most current American cars have automatic chokes and require strict adherence to start-ing procedures, which many drivers blithely ignore. Check your owner's manual. Does it tell you to depress the gas pedal to the floor before turning on the ignition if the engine is cold? Many do. What about starting the car in the winter or when the engine is hot? Most owner's manuals outline different starting procedures for each of these conditions. You can save yourself unnecessary annoyance by always starting the car exactly as your owner's manual recommends.

Cold weather poses other problems that do not necessarily mean something is malfunctioning. Low temperatures stiffen lubricants in the engine, making it harder to turn over. The starter motor therefore needs more electrical power. But the battery cannot produce electricity as easily in cold weather as in warm because the chemical reactions in its electrolyte (page 321) slow down when the temperature drops. At freezing, a new, fully charged battery can produce only 65 per cent of the power it delivers at 80° F.; and at zero, the power output drops to 40 per cent. Thus, in cold weather the engine's greater demand for electricity is coupled with a smaller supply of it. Furthermore, because the cold inhibits vaporization of gasoline, the engine may have to be cranked longer by the starter before it receives a fuel mixture rich enough in gasoline to be ignited.

How to use the guide that follows

To use the troubleshooting guide, find the symptom first. For example, if one of your dashboard warning lights is aglow, turn to the chart on the preceding page. If the symptom is a suspicious new noise, find it on the check list on pages 249 to 251. Otherwise, seek out the particular symptom most appropriate to your situation and follow the procedures in the following pages that apply.

WHEN THE CAR WON'T START

This perhaps most disconcerting of all problems associated with automobile ownership may stem from a bewildering variety of causes. Starting a car's engine involves four major elements: the starter motor, the ignition system, the fuel system—and the person at the wheel. Here, as in any troubleshooting situation, begin by seeking the simplest possible cause, however obvious. Proceed methodically, as necessary, in the following order.

1 If there's no response from the starter motor

A In a car equipped with an automatic transmission, be sure the gearshift lever is firmly set in the park position. If the starter doesn't work in park, try neutral. If it still doesn't work, jiggle the gearshift lever to both sides of the neutral position. A safety switch connected to the lever may have become misaligned so that it cuts the starting circuit even when the indicator on the transmission quadrant appears to be correctly positioned. If the car now starts, have that safety switch checked anyway.

B Test the battery's charge by turning on the headlights and then trying to start the car. If the lights burn brightly, the problem is not likely to be in the battery itself, but in some other part of the starting system. Double check the battery's condition with a hydrometer, if you have one *(page 142)*. If the hydrometer shows an adequate charge—or if you believe the battery is good because of the bright headlights—skip to step 1E. If, however, the headlights dim dramatically when you try to start the car, so much that they turn yellow or orange, the battery is probably discharged. Proceed to the following step.

C In cold weather, warming the battery by placing a light bulb beneath it may achieve a start. Low temperatures weaken batteries by slowing down the chemical reaction that produces electricity.

D Jump-start the engine with another vehicle's battery. This operation is common enough—and safe, provided proper precautions are taken.

First turn off your ignition to avoid draining any power that may be left in the battery. Park a vehicle that has a fully charged battery of the same voltage near the disabled car so that the two cars do not touch. The jumper cables to be used should not have to reach across either engine, where they might drop accidentally into the fans. Using old gloves or a rag, remove all the cell caps from both batteries. Cover the holes with clean rags to contain any splashing acid. Another reason for doing this is that one of the chemical reactions inside a battery produces hydrogen gas. Removing the caps allows the gas to escape.

CAUTION: In extremely cold weather, look into the cells to be sure the battery fluid is not frozen. If it is, pockets of hydrogen gas may have formed and the gas could explode when the jumper cable is attached. Thaw the battery before using the jumper.

First, attach the ends of one jumper cable to the positive posts of both batteries *(drawing, overleaf)*.

Next, attach one end of the second cable to the other post of the charged battery. Ground the other end by clipping it to a clean, unpainted part of the disabled car's engine. Be sure all four cable clips are so positioned that they cannot accidentally contact each other or drop onto moving parts once the engine turns over and begins to run.

CAUTION: Be sure to attach the second cable (i.e., the ground cable) as directed, not to the ground post of the discharged battery. This is because a few sparks occur when this final connection is broken after the car starts. If the connection is made on the battery itself, the sparks could ignite any hydrogen gas that has accumulated near it.

With the assisting vehicle's engine running and all the accessories in both cars turned off, start the engine.

Remove the second cable from the problem car's engine and then from the post on the booster battery. Disconnect the first cable from the positive posts of the two batteries.

Remove the rags from the vent caps on both batteries and dispose of them. Replace the vent caps.

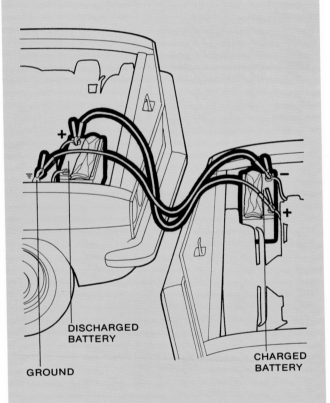

DISCHARGED BATTERY

CHARGED BATTERY

GROUND

E If the test in step 1B indicated that the battery is adequately charged, the problem may be loose or corroded connections at the battery posts. If you're in a hurry, force the tip of an insulated screwdriver between each battery-cable terminal and its post *(drawing, right);* that way you may improve the connections enough to start the engine. Clean the connections thoroughly at the earliest opportunity.

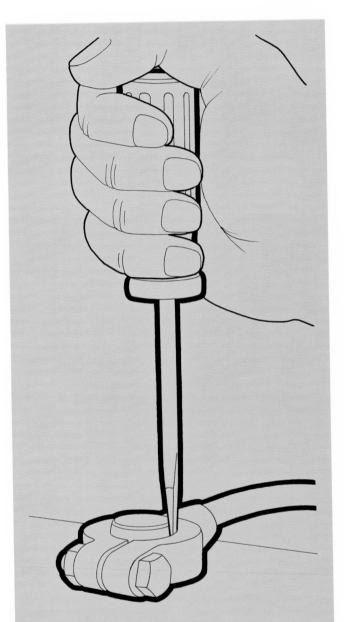

F Follow the heavy cable from the battery's positive terminal to the solenoid and make sure the connection is tight. If your car has a fire-wall-mounted solenoid, you will find a second cable leading from the solenoid to the starter. Make sure that this cable's connections to the solenoid and the starter are tight also. Defective insulation on the cables—if you find any—will not keep the engine from starting, but you should replace a deteriorated cable.

G Follow the cable from the negative side of the battery. Check its connection to the engine and tighten the connection if it is loose.

H The problem may be in the ignition switch or in one of the wires that connect it to the starter. To by-pass the wiring between battery and starter, attach one end of a jumper cable to the positive post and the other end either to the starter motor, if the car has a fire-wall-mounted solenoid *(drawing, right)*, or to the solenoid, if the solenoid is mounted on the starter *(drawing, below)*. Don't let the cable's clip touch the car frame; it will spark dangerously. Be sure your clothes and hands are clear of moving engine parts; since you have by-passed the ignition switch, the engine may turn as soon as the second connection is made. If it does, work the throttle from under the hood to keep it going. Disconnect the jumper, first from the relay or solenoid and then from the battery, then take the car to a mechanic.

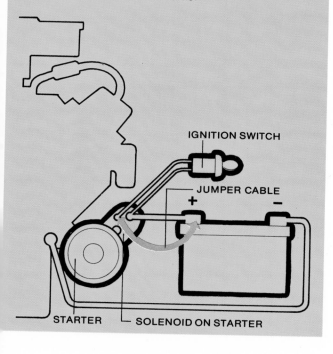

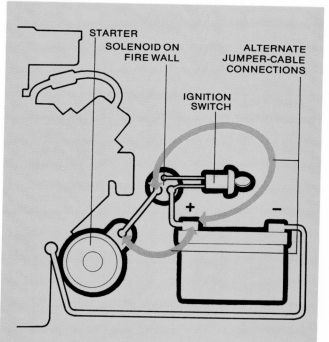

I Sometimes the starter drive-gear jams in the engine flywheel-gear. In a car with an automatic transmission, the repair job required should be left to a mechanic. In a car with a manual transmission, set the shift in high gear and rock the car gently, forward and back, to release the jam.

J If none of the steps so far has worked, and you have a manual transmission, try starting the car by getting a push from another vehicle. Cars with automatic transmissions cannot be started, and may even be damaged, by pushing.

If the transmission is manual, be sure the bumper of the pushing car meets yours. Move the shift into high, turn on the ignition and depress the clutch pedal. Have the pusher accelerate slowly and, at 5 mph, let in the clutch gradually. If the engine offers resistance or makes extraordinary noises, depress the clutch immediately and stop. You will have to call a mechanic. If the engine turns freely with the clutch engaged, signal the pusher to accelerate gradually to 20 to 25 mph. If the engine doesn't catch in the space of two blocks, get a mechanic.

2 If the engine cranks normally but does not start

A Does the gas gauge read empty? Even if not, the gauge could be faulty. Bounce the car's rear up and down while listening for the slosh of fuel in the tank.

B The smell of gasoline inside the car indicates a flooded carburetor. Protracted cranking with the choke closed or pumping the accelerator to start a reluctant engine draws so much gasoline through the carburetor that the fuel mixture reaching the cylinders is too rich for the engine. Percolation, caused by gasoline vaporizing in the carburetor on hot days, also can cause flooding.

Remove the top of the air cleaner *(pages 148-149)* and block open the choke's butterfly valve with a pencil or screwdriver, as in the illustration on page 200. Get in the car and push the gas pedal to the floor; keep it there without pumping. Crank the engine with the starter to pull air through the carburetor and dispel the excess fuel.

If the engine does not start in 20 to 30 seconds of cranking, stop and let the starter cool for two minutes before trying again. Do not release the gas pedal between tries: each time the pedal is depressed, more gasoline is pumped through the carburetor.

An alternative to blocking open the choke is to wait at least 15 minutes for the excess fuel to evaporate.

C If the engine is cold but not flooded, make sure the choke butterfly is fully closed. Remove the air cleaner's cover *(pages 148-149)* and see if the butterfly is open. If it is, push the gas pedal to the floor to close it. If that does not close the butterfly, hold it closed with a long stick while someone starts the engine. Hold it closed until the engine runs on its own.

Carburetor solvent should be applied as soon as possible to free sticky butterfly pivots. If the butterfly seems free but still stays open, have a mechanic adjust or repair the choke.

D Check the fuel filter and the fuel lines that extend from both sides of the fuel pump *(drawing, below)*. Remove the fuel filter *(pages 222-223)* if it is obviously dirty, discard it and connect the fuel line directly to the carburetor; the filter's absence for a short time will do no harm. Be sure the connections at both ends of each fuel line are tight and that there are no cracks or holes. Most fuel lines under the hood are made of rubber; and if the lines are long enough, loose or split ends can be fixed simply by cutting them off and reconnecting them. Leaks not at the ends may be patched temporarily with tape, but a damaged line should be replaced promptly.

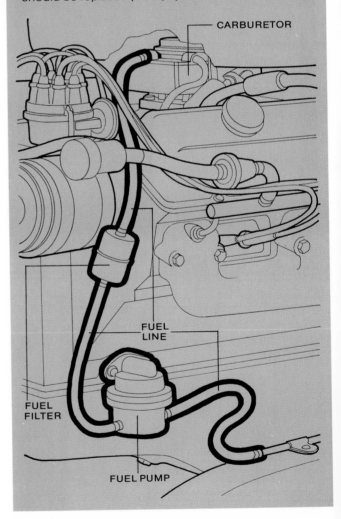

CARBURETOR

FUEL LINE

FUEL FILTER

FUEL PUMP

E Moisture or greasy dirt on the ignition system can provide an alternate path for the electricity intended for the spark plugs. Wipe clean and dry the distributor cap, spark-plug cables, spark coil and engine areas around the plugs. In very wet conditions, dry off all ignition parts, removing the distributor cap *(page 204)* to dry the inside and also the cable from each spark plug *(page 198)* to dry its insulator.

F See that the wires to the spark coil's two side terminals are securely connected. Push in the thick cable at the center of the coil as far as possible. Wrap tape around any breaks or worn spots in the insulation of the wire that connects the distributor to the coil's side terminal. Breaks in the wire itself sometimes can be spliced *(pages 180-181)*. Also remove the distributor cap and see that the two wires inside are tightly connected to the points *(pages 208-209)*.

Check for breaks or worn insulation in the wires attached to the coil's other side post. See that all spark-plug cables are firmly seated in their towers in the distributor cap and pushed tightly onto each plug.

G Test the primary circuit for spark delivery. Pull the heavy cable from the center tower of the distributor cap and hold it a quarter inch from a clean area of the engine while a helper turns the ignition key *(page 211)*. If a strong blue spark jumps the gap, reinsert the cable in its tower and proceed to the next step. If there is no spark, or a weak yellow one, remove the distributor cap. Crank the engine and see if the points open, as they must for the coil to produce a spark. If they do not, file them lightly *(page 209)* and set the gap *(page 210)* 3/1,000 of an inch narrower than the service manual recommends for new points. Check the gap with a dwell meter, if possible.

See if the breaker points are burned or pitted so deeply that they do not allow the coil to produce a spark. If so, they should be replaced, but they may be rejuvenated temporarily by filing them down to bare metal with an ignition file, then resetting the gap.

Inspect the condenser connections. The lead should be attached securely to the points. Remove the screw that holds the condenser in place and wipe clean both condenser and breaker plate *(pages 208-209)*. Reattach the condenser to the breaker plate. If there is no spark, see a mechanic.

H Test the secondary circuit for spark delivery by removing the spark-plug cables one by one and holding them near a clean area of the engine while it is cranked. A strong blue spark should jump a 1/4-inch gap. If only half the cables provide strong sparks, that should be enough to start the engine. If more than half produce weak sparks, remove the distributor cap and check both cap and rotor for defects such as cracks and corrosion *(pages 204-207)*.

Clean the rotor's spring contact if it is dirty. If the contact is poor between the rotor and the carbon button in the center of the cap, both parts must be replaced, although bending the spring away from the rotor may improve the connection temporarily.

I If cap and rotor are clean and dry, and free of defects, the trouble probably is in the spark-plug cables. Look for defective insulation *(pages 198-199)* on those that give weak sparks. If you find any poorly insulated cables, replace the whole set.

J See if the fuel system delivers gasoline to the carburetor. First remove the air cleaner from the top of the carburetor *(pages 148-149)*. Then, if there is a drain plug at the bottom of the bowl, remove it. If the carburetor has no drain plug, rotate the throttle lever while looking into the carburetor barrel. Fuel squirting into the barrel—or flowing from the bowl when you removed the plug—shows that the fuel supply to the carburetor is adequate.

K If there was no gasoline in the carburetor bowl, remove the two fuel lines under the hood and blow through them. Clean out clogged lines with a thin stick or a coat-hanger wire. If the fuel lines are open, the trouble lies elsewhere: in the fuel pump, the carburetor, the fuel lines beneath the car, or the gas-tank filter screen. You need a mechanic.

L Remove one or two spark plugs *(pages 198-199)* and see if they are dry and clean. Plugs wet with oil, gasoline or water will not fire. Dry them by heating them with a match or on the stove. Clean and adjust their gaps *(pages 202-203)* before reinstallation.

If the engine still won't start, the timing may be incorrectly set or there may be internal defects in the spark-plug cables. You need a mechanic.

3 If the engine cranks too slowly to catch

A Repairing a faulty starter is a job for a mechanic. When there is no defect, slow cranking usually means that the starter is not getting enough electricity, or that the engine for one reason or another is putting up more resistance than usual to the battery's kick—or the problem is a combination of both. In cold weather, stiffening of summer-weight oil can reduce cranking speeds; changing to a winter grade may solve the problem. Hot weather also can impede cranking; when the engine is shut off after a long stretch of high-speed driving—say, for a turnpike lunch-stop—the engine's temperature, with no air to lower it, rises, with the result that engine parts expand, fit together more tightly and are therefore harder to move. The only solution here is to wait for the engine to cool.

If the problem is not the result of a hot engine, first refer to step 1 and try procedures B through H. If these do not work, try the following procedures:

B Follow every other spark-plug cable in the distributor cap to its plug *(drawing)*. Loosen the four plugs several turns to reduce compression and thus the drain on the battery. If the engine starts, working against the compression of only half the cylinders, let

it run a few moments to warm up, then turn it off and tighten the loosened plugs.

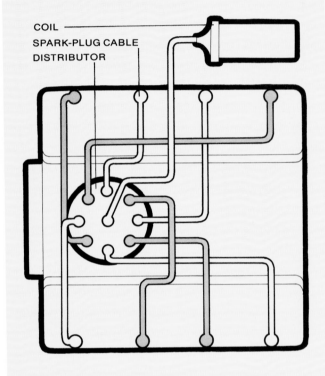

COIL
SPARK-PLUG CABLE
DISTRIBUTOR

C If the engine does not start, reinstall the plugs. If your car has a manual transmission, get a push *(step 1J)*; if it doesn't, call a mechanic.

4 If the starter motor whines but does not turn the engine over

A In cold weather, splash-water from the road may have frozen on the starter motor's drive gear, preventing it from engaging the flywheel gear of the engine. Or lubricants in the starter may have congealed, similarly keeping it from engaging with the engine. Try warming the starter by running it in one-minute bursts at one-minute intervals or by simply pouring hot water over it. This may let you start the engine.

B The starter's drive gear may not be engaging the engine's flywheel gear because of wear or damage. With an automatic transmission, there is nothing you can do but call a mechanic. With a manual transmission, shift to high gear, hold down the clutch and have the car pushed about five feet. Release the clutch when the car is in motion. This will turn the engine and reposition the engine's flywheel gear against the starting motor's drive gear. Even if the engine starts, you still must get the gears adjusted or repaired.

C The trouble may be some other malfunction of the starter or its gear system. Start the car by pushing it *(step 1J)*—again, only if it has a manual transmission.

5 If the engine backfires and does not start

A Clean the ignition-system components of dirt, grease and moisture *(step 2E)*.

B Make sure spark-plug cables are securely attached to the right plugs. Find the engine's spark-plug-cable arrangement plan in your service manual. Compare your engine's cables with the diagram and correct any differences you find.

C Look for spark-plug cables with faulty insulation *(pages 198-199)* and inspect the distributor cap for carbon tracks *(pages 204-205)*. Both faulty insulation and carbon tracks—between terminals inside the distributor cap—provide routes for the coil's charge to pass to the wrong plugs—cross-firing. If you find any poorly insulated cables, replace the whole set. Replace a distributor cap with carbon tracks.

D If you have just performed a tune-up, be sure the

distributor rotor is the right one for your engine and has been correctly installed on the distributor shaft *(pages 210-211)*. If the new rotor seems wrong for your engine and you still have the old one, use it temporarily. If none of the foregoing helps, the engine's timing may require adjustment.

6 If the car starts, dies and will not restart

A In freezing weather, remove the top of the air cleaner *(pages 148-149)* and look into the carburetor barrel while opening the throttle. If there is no stream of gasoline from the accelerator pump *(page 222)*, water in the gas may have frozen and blocked the fuel line (the engine having run initially on gas already in the carburetor). Melt the ice by pouring hot water over the fuel pump and the lower sections of the fuel lines. Ice in less accessible parts of the fuel system must await warmer weather—or a push into a heated garage—before the ice will melt.

After the ice is melted, pour a commercial gasoline additive or alcohol into the gas tank to absorb water that may have condensed there. The engine will burn the water-alcohol mixture. (To reduce the possibility of such winter condensation, it is a good idea to keep the gas tank as full as possible.)

B Remove a spark plug *(pages 198-199)* and see if the electrodes are wet. If they are, remove the rest of the plugs and dry them off by heating them with a match or on the stove.

Water vapor is a by-product of the fuel mixture's combustion. When the air is damp and the engine cold, condensation can wet the spark plugs' firing ends. If wet plugs are a chronic problem, however, water may be leaking into the cylinders from the engine's cooling system, a serious problem that calls for a mechanic. If the plugs are dry and the car still won't start, try the procedures in step 2 (when the engine cranks normally but won't start).

WHEN THE ENGINE RUNS POORLY OR STOPS RUNNING

Engine misbehavior, no matter how unsettling, rarely indicates imminent disaster. At least the car is still running and will get you to your destination or to the next service station. Moreover, most engine malfunctions begin as small problems, so you generally have time to study the symptoms, isolate the problem and have it corrected before it can do any major damage.

7 If the engine backfires and runs unevenly

Rough running accompanied by backfiring often is caused by a too-lean fuel mixture, by cross-firing *(step 5C)* or by a faulty cylinder-head gasket *(page 229)* that allows flame from one cylinder to ignite the fuel mixture in an adjoining one. Backfiring occurs when the fuel mixture is ignited while a valve is still open; the hot gases escape into the carburetor or the exhaust system with a loud report.

A Tapping the carburetor bowl lightly with the handle of a hammer or a screwdriver will dislodge a fuel-metering valve that has stuck closed. If that solves the problem, add carburetor cleaner to the gas in the fuel tank to remove gums that may be making the valves sticky. If the problem persists, have a mechanic disassemble and clean the carburetor.

B If the engine is cold, make sure the choke is fully closed. Push it closed if necessary.

C Use a work light to check the air-cleaner element for dirt *(pages 196-197)* and replace if clogged.

D Clean ignition-system components of dirt, grease and moisture *(step 2E)*.

E Make sure spark-plug cables are securely attached to the correct plugs, and look for spark-plug cables with faulty insulation *(pages 198–199)*.

F Remove the distributor cap and check both cap and rotor for defects such as cracks and corrosion *(pages 204–207)*. Replace if necessary.

G Check the operation of the spark-advance mechanisms *(pages 206–207, 221)*. If either one is not working, have a mechanic repair it.

H Remove the fuel filter *(pages 222-223)* and replace it if it is obviously dirty. You can reconnect the fuel lines of some cars without the filter, but you must replace it as soon as possible.

I Check the idle-mixture adjustment *(page 224)*.

J Test the engine's compression *(pages 198-201)*. Poor compression accompanied by backfiring may indicate a faulty head gasket or sluggish valves. Either job requires a mechanic.

8 If the engine idles poorly

A When the engine is up to operating temperature —the true character of an engine's idle can be judged only at operating temperature—make sure the choke is completely open; otherwise the engine will continually stall or threaten to stall. If the choke does not open all the way, having it adjusted or repaired by a mechanic will improve your engine's idle.

B Check the PCV valve *(pages 196-197)* and inspect hoses in the PCV and air-injection (emission-control) systems *(pages 34-35)* for cracks.

C Test the primary and secondary ignition circuits for spark delivery *(steps 2G, 2H, 2I)*.

D See that the idle speed and idle mixture are adjusted *(pages 224-225)* to the specifications in the service manual or on the tune-up label under the hood.

E Make sure the ignition timing is set to specifications *(pages 218-221)*.

F Test the engine's compression *(pages 198-201)*. Correcting compression is a job for a mechanic.

G After the compression test, clean and regap the spark plugs *(pages 202-203)* before reinstalling them. If any one of the plugs cannot be thoroughly cleaned, replace all of them.

H If the idle remains rough and all cylinders have adequate compression, the carburetor might be clogged—a problem for a mechanic.

9 If the engine loses power

A Make sure that both the throttle and choke are completely open when the engine is at operating temperature. When the engine has warmed up, remove the air-cleaner cover *(pages 148-149)*. With the accelerator pressed to the floor, see if the choke but-

terfly is open all the way. If it is not, go to a mechanic and have him adjust it. Meanwhile, through the opening—if necessary, hold it open with a finger—gently try to open the throttle farther with a screwdriver. If it moves, have a mechanic adjust the throttle linkage.

B Examine the carburetor barrel for ice. In high humidity at temperatures near freezing, air can be chilled enough in passing through the carburetor barrel to freeze the water vapor in it, blocking passages and cutting power. Wait for engine heat to melt the ice or pour hot water over the carburetor's sides.

C Check the air-cleaner element for dirt *(pages 196-197)*, and replace it if it is clogged.

D Check the fuel filter and the fuel lines that extend from both sides of the fuel pump *(step 2D)*.

E Test the primary and secondary ignition circuits for spark delivery *(steps 2G, 2H, 2I)*.

F Make sure the ignition timing is set *(pages 218-221)* to the specifications in the service manual or on the label under the hood. A distributor that is loosely attached, even slightly, can rotate and retard timing *(pages 216-217)*.

G Check the operation of the spark-advance mechanisms *(pages 206-207, 221)*. If either one is not working, have a mechanic repair it.

H Test the engine's compression *(pages 198-201)*. Correcting compression is a job for a mechanic.

I After the compression test, clean and regap the spark plugs *(pages 202-203)* before reinstalling them. If any of the plugs cannot be thoroughly cleaned, replace all of them.

10 If the engine misfires

Misfiring occurs when one or more spark plugs fail to ignite the cylinder's fuel charge. Mechanics call this a "missing" cylinder or cylinders. The most obvious clue: part of the engine's smooth roar is absent, as if there were a hole in the sound.

Misfiring at idling speeds causes rough idling *(step 8)*. It also tends to occur under two other conditions: at high engine speeds without a heavy load, as when nipping along a level highway (a situation that calls for checks A through H, below); and under a heavy load, as in hard acceleration or a tough pull up a hill *(steps I through M)*. In both cases, misfiring will mean loss of power, and the trouble usually will be in the ignition system.

A Look for defective insulation on the spark-plug cables *(pages 198-199)*. If you find any poorly insulated cables, replace the whole set.

B Remove the distributor cap and check both the cap and rotor for defects such as cracks and corrosion. Replace if necessary *(pages 204-207)*.

C Check the alignment of the breaker points *(drawing)*. Install a new set *(pages 208-209)* if the point surfaces have become misaligned.

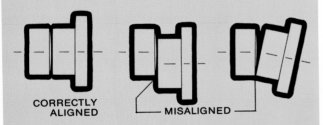

CORRECTLY ALIGNED MISALIGNED

D Inspect the condenser connections *(step 2G)*.

E See that the point dwell is adjusted to specifica-

tions *(pages 214-215)*. If you do not have a dwell meter, a thickness gauge 3/1,000 of an inch thinner than your service manual recommends for new points will approximate the proper gap if the points are not excessively pitted.

F Test the engine's compression *(pages 198-201)*. Correcting compression is a job for a mechanic.

G After the compression test, clean and regap the spark plugs *(pages 202-203)* before reinstalling them. If any one of the plugs cannot be thoroughly cleaned, replace all of them.

H Replace the breaker points and the condenser *(pages 208-209)*. If the tension of the breaker-point spring is too low, the points might bounce at high engine speeds, causing misfiring. A faulty condenser also can cause misfiring even if the points appear to be in good condition. If these steps have not solved the problem, it may be caused by trouble in the spark coil or fuel system. You need a mechanic.

I If the misfiring occurs under a heavy load, look for defective insulation on the spark-plug cables *(pages 198-199)*. If you find any poorly insulated cables, replace the whole set.

J Test the primary and secondary ignition circuits for spark delivery *(steps 2G, 2H, 2I)*.

K Check the accelerator pump. Remove the air-cleaner cover *(pages 148-149)*, look into the barrel of the carburetor and open the throttle by moving the throttle lever. Gasoline should squirt into the carburetor's primary barrels. If it does not, have a mechanic fix the accelerator pump.

L Test the engine's compression *(pages 198-201)*. Correcting compression is a job for a mechanic.

M After the compression test, clean and regap the spark plugs *(pages 202-203)*. If any one of the plugs cannot be thoroughly cleaned, replace all of them.

Any problems not uncovered by the foregoing tests probably are fuel-system defects and require the services of a mechanic.

11 If the car gets poor gas mileage

To establish that your mileage actually has decreased or that it is significantly below your model's average, begin keeping a record as soon as you suspect a decrease. The procedure is simple: fill the tank to the brim and record the odometer reading. Each time you buy gas thereafter, fill the tank to the brim and record both the precise number of gallons purchased—fraction included—and the odometer reading. Dividing the exact number of miles traveled between fill-ups by the gallons purchased yields the miles per gallon you are getting.

Remember, though, that stop-and-go driving in city traffic gives the worst mileage; long highway trips at moderate speeds, the best. You should characterize the kind of driving done between fill-ups and record that information as well. If you are convinced that your mileage is seriously off:

A Evaluate your driving habits and the conditions under which you drive. Poor gas mileage may not be the car's fault. Is your highway driving done at top speeds? Do you race away from stops—"leave rubber?" Both practices exact a heavy premium in gas. Do you make many short trips during which the engine does not warm up to best efficiency? Is the car subject to frequent idling in heavy traffic?

B Check your tire pressures *(page 138)*. Underinflated tires waste a lot of gas, since the engine has to work against the added friction.

C Check for fuel leaks. Look for traces of gas on the ground under the gas tank and check fuel lines that extend from both sides of the fuel pump *(step 2D)*.

D Faulty wheel alignment also can waste power by creating added running friction. See a mechanic.

E See that the car's exhaust system is clear of possible obstructions.

F Make sure that brakes are not dragging for any reason. Have them adjusted or repaired if necessary.

G Check the air-cleaner element for dirt *(pages 196-197)*. Clean it or replace it.

H Test the primary and secondary ignition circuit for spark delivery *(steps 2G, 2H, 2I)*.

I Make sure the ignition timing is set to specifications *(pages 218-221)*.

J Check the operation of the spark-advance mechanisms *(pages 206-207, 221)*. If either one is not working, have a mechanic repair it.

K Clean and regap the spark plugs *(pages 198-199, 202-203)*. If any one of the plugs cannot be thoroughly cleaned, replace all of them.

12 If the engine overheats

An engine overheats when its cooling system cannot disperse heat as fast as it is produced. This may come about when unusual driving conditions cause the engine to produce more heat than usual, when there is a defect in the cooling system or when the very air itself—on which both air- and water-cooled engines ultimately depend for cooling—is hot and therefore less efficient at cooling. Under heavy loads, engines produce more heat because they burn more fuel to maintain a given speed. Pulling a trailer in torrid weather can overtax an otherwise adequate cooling system.

A The obvious first step is to check the coolant level in the radiator—assuming the car is water cooled. If the coolant is low, replenish it *(page 140)*. If the level drops again within a couple of weeks, the hoses may be leaking *(step 12E)* or coolant may be leaking into the engine. See a mechanic.

B Clean the front of the radiator: remove all bugs, leaves or other obstructions. In the case of an air-cooled engine, clear grease and dirt from the spaces between the cooling fins on the cylinder block and head. Any obstruction reduces the surface area of the fins and, therefore, their capacity to radiate and dissipate heat.

C If your car has a fan shroud, a kind of wind tunnel between the radiator and fan, make sure it is intact.

D Adjust the fan-belt tension if the belt is loose; replace the belt if it is worn or glazed *(page 175)*.

E Look for leak stains on the radiator's side and on the hoses. Tighten leaking hose connections *(page 174)*. Replace hoses that have deteriorated.

F See that the car's exhaust system is clear of possible obstructions.

G Have the radiator cap tested at a gas station to see if it holds its rated pressure. If it fails to hold the pres-

sure, parts of it may have weakened. Replace the cap.

H Make sure the ignition timing is set to specifications *(pages 218-221)*.

I Check the cooling system's thermostat and replace it if the valve fails to open or close at specified temperatures *(pages 176-177)*.

J Flush the cooling system *(pages 172-173)*.

13 If the engine stops running without warning

Of the engine's four essential systems only two —the fuel system and the ignition system—can cut out without some warning from your dashboard instruments, rough operation or suspicious noises.

A Make sure the ground strap of your battery has not come loose *(step 1G)*. Tighten it if necessary. If the cable is broken, replace it temporarily with a jumper. Route the cable to stay clear of the engine, and wire or tape it in place.

B Test the primary and secondary ignition circuits for spark delivery *(steps 2G, 2H, 2I)*.

C Check the fuel filter and the fuel lines that extend from both sides of the fuel pump *(step 2D)*. Particularly during a hot day in the spring, suspect vapor lock in the fuel system. Heat can make gasoline vaporize in the fuel lines under the hood or in the fuel pump. Bubbles of gas vapor rather than liquid fuel are then pumped to the carburetor, causing the engine to lose power and even stall. Cooling is the only answer: pour water over the fuel pump and lines or wait for the engine to cool.

WHEN THE CAR IS HARD TO CONTROL

Relatively simple things can make the car difficult to control, but they are never unimportant. Since any handling problem can be dangerous, especially in high-speed driving, you should have such problems—or even symptoms of impending problems—attended to at once. Repair or adjustment of the brake system and the front-end suspension is a delicate matter and should be left to a specialist.

14 If the front wheels shimmy

Besides being annoying and tiring, this wobbling motion, transmitted to the driver through the steering wheel, can cause accidents. A severe shimmy can, for instance, loosen wheel lugs enough for a wheel to come off.

A Check for a bent tire rim. The bent rim throws the wheel out of balance and causes it to shimmy. Have a mechanic put your tire on a new rim and then balance the tire and rim.

B Make sure the front-wheel lugs are adequately tight (pages 158–159).

C Be sure the front shock absorbers are securely attached to the car; replace them if they are worn out (pages 184-185).

D See that the front-wheel bearings are correctly tightened (page 169). They seldom loosen in normal use but if they were removed recently they may have been reinstalled improperly.

E Other causes of shimmy—out-of-balance front wheels, loose parts in the front suspension or in the steering mechanism, incorrectly aligned wheels— are best handled by a mechanic.

15 If the car is hard to steer

A Check for bent tire rims on the front wheels.

B Check the fluid level in the power-steering unit (page 140). Add fluid if the level is low.

C Check your tire pressures (page 138). Low pressure in front tires makes steering more difficult.

D Make sure the front-wheel lugs are adequately tight (pages 158-159).

E Inspect the drive belt from the engine to the power-steering pump. A loose or glazed belt may turn too slowly to provide adequate pressure, and steering becomes more difficult. Tighten it if it is loose; replace it if it is glazed (page 175).

F Lubricate the front suspension (pages 164-165).

G Other causes of stiff steering are problems for a skilled mechanic. They include faulty front-wheel alignment, a worn steering mechanism, binding of the steering linkage because of wear or misalignment, and looseness of the bolts that hold the steering gear to the chassis.

16 If wheels don't straighten out after a turn

A Check the fluid level in the power-steering unit *(page 140)*. Add fluid if the level is low.

B In cold weather, lubricants in the steering box and front suspension may have congealed. You must use the steering wheel to return the wheels to their original position. When engine heat raises the temperature under the hood, the lubricants will thin out and steering then becomes normal.

C Lubricate the front suspension *(pages 164-165)*.

D Faulty front-wheel alignment can also cause poor steering-return. See a mechanic.

17 If the car tends to drift or wander

External conditions—roads with high crowns, side winds, road-surface irregularities, as well as mechanical defects—can cause a car to veer even though the steering wheel is held steady.

A Find a smooth, flat, straight stretch of road, at least a half mile long. Drive in both directions on a windless day (or with wind blowing along rather than across the road). If there is no trace of drift, blame the car's previous misbehavior on conditions at the time. If there still is a tendency to wander, look for the mechanical causes listed in B through E.

B Check for incorrect tire pressures *(page 138)*.

C Make sure the brakes are not dragging for any reason. Have them adjusted or repaired if necessary.

D See that the front-wheel bearings are correctly tightened *(page 169)*. They seldom loosen or tighten in normal use, but if they were removed recently they may have been reinstalled improperly.

E Loose front-suspension parts and faulty wheel alignment also can cause drifting. See a mechanic.

18 If the car pulls to one side during braking

A Check for unequal tire pressures *(page 138)*.

B Wet brakes—or, worse yet, a wet brake on one side—can cause a car to veer dangerously. Disc brakes are less susceptible than drums to this trouble because the pads constantly dry the discs as the wheels turn. Apply light pressure on the brake pedal as you drive to generate heat from the friction; this will dry the brakes.

C Make sure the tires on both front wheels are identical in construction, closely similar in tread design and have undergone approximately equal wear. Pairing a bias-ply with a radial-ply tire on the same axle is, of course, extremely dangerous because of their different handling characteristics; but even when the plies are the same, mismatched tires can differ in traction and running characteristics.

D See that the front-wheel bearings are correctly tightened *(page 169)*. They seldom loosen or tighten in normal use, but if they were removed recently they may have been reinstalled improperly.

E Other causes of brake pull, requiring the services of a mechanic, include: improperly adjusted brakes, loose calipers on front disc brakes, sticking wheel cylinders and blocked hydraulic-brake lines, a loose steering assembly, incorrect wheel alignment, worn or scored drums or discs, mismatched brake linings, and brake fluid or grease on linings. Not only must contaminated linings be replaced but the source of the contaminant must also be traced and repairs made. See a mechanic.

19 If one wheel locks during braking

A Compare the tread depths of both tires on an axle, front and rear. The more worn the tire, the more likely the wheel will be to lock and skid.

B Inspect the brake linings. If they are gummy from leaking hydraulic fluid, have a mechanic replace them—and fix the leak.

20 If both rear wheels lock during hard braking

As a car pitches forward during hard stops, weight is shifted from the rear wheels. Because they then support less weight than the front wheels, they tend to lock. A proportioning valve near the master cylinders counters this tendency by partially redistributing hydraulic pressure from the rear brakes to the front brakes. Bald rear tires may, however, defeat this valve.

A See whether the tread on the rear tires is badly worn. The more worn the tires, the more likely the wheels will be to lock and skid.

B Have the proportioning valve replaced. Replacing this valve requires bleeding the brake lines to remove air from them, a critical procedure you should leave to a skilled mechanic.

WHEN LITTLE THINGS GO WRONG

Little things can be dangerous as well as annoying. A nonfunctioning windshield wiper in a downpour, for example, can effectively disable a car. It makes sense to study your service manual and familiarize yourself with how the little things work. Then you won't sit by helplessly when—nightmare of the mechanically illiterate —the horns start blowing and refuse to stop.

21 If an electric motor fails

Electric motors power a variety of accessories, from windshield wipers to power seats and windows. The motors vary in size and shape but all work basically the same way.

An electric-motor circuit consists of the motor, a switch, a fuse, a ground and a wire that runs from battery to switch to motor. The fuse usually is inserted between the switch and the battery. The ground is a short wire that runs from the motor to a near point on the car frame (unless the motor is attached to the frame, which itself serves as a ground) to complete the circuit. A burned-out electric motor must be replaced. But electrical failure frequently is traceable to faulty wiring, switch or fuse.

Two recommendations: First, when tracing a wire for breaks and worn insulation, follow it only until it disappears among a group of wires taped together; bundled wire is well protected against breaks and wear, and unwrapping it is a mechanic's job. Use a test light to check the continuity of wires and connections *(pages 180-181)*. Second, when you have found the trouble and are ready to make repairs more complicated than replacing a light bulb or a fuse, disconnect the ground terminal from the battery to avoid accidental short circuits.

A When an electrc motor stops working, look for a blown fuse in the fuse block. Replace the fuse with an identical one *(pages 178-179)*. If the fuse continues to fail, refer to your service manual and be sure you're using a fuse of the correct size. If you are, there is probably a short circuit somewhere, either in the wiring, in the switch or in the motor.

B Use a jumper wire to connect the positive side of the battery to the motor terminal at the point where its wire from the battery is connected *(drawing, below)*, thus by-passing the motor's fuse, switch and wiring. Clamp the cable first to the battery, then to the motor terminal with the other end of the wire. If the motor runs, the problem is in the switch or wiring.

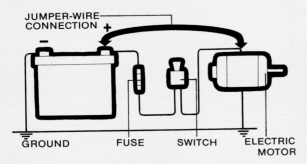

JUMPER-WIRE CONNECTION +

GROUND   FUSE   SWITCH   ELECTRIC MOTOR

C Trace the wiring from the electric motor to the switch and battery, seeking breaks, worn insulation and loose connections. Splice, tape *(pages 180-181)* or tighten as necessary. If the motor has only one wire leading to it, make sure the motor itself is attached tightly to the car. If corrosion where the motor and car frame meet is impeding electrical contact, remove the motor and clean the area with sandpaper.

22 One horn doesn't sound

The horn circuit consists of the horns, a relay (that reroutes the powerful current the horns require so that it doesn't pass through the steering column), a switch in the steering wheel, the battery and the wiring that connects them all. In many recent models there is an additional switch operated by the ignition key to silence the horns when the ignition is off. The horns blow when the driver pushes the horn ring, closing a switch to complete a circuit.

A Follow the wire leading to the malfunctioning horn. Splice breaks and tape any worn insulation you find *(pages 180-181)*.

B Look for a loose connection at the silent horn. If the base of the horn appears corroded, remove the horn by loosening its mounting bolt and sandpaper the area of contact between the horn and the car.

C If neither remedy works, get a new horn.

23 If neither horn sounds

A Look for a blown fuse in the fuse block under the dashboard. Replace it with an identical one if it is burned out *(pages 178-179)*.

B Tighten any loose connections in the horn circuit. See if any wires are broken or rubbing against the car frame. Splice breaks and tape any worn insulation you find *(pages 180-181)*.

24 If the horn sounds intermittently

A A "nervous horn," which sounds only part of the time when the ring is pushed, and sometimes when it is not, usually results from the looseness of parts in the horn switch inside the steering wheel. Fixing it is a job for a mechanic.

25 If the horns won't stop blowing

When the horn won't turn off, it usually is because either the relay or the horn-ring switch has remained closed. However, horn systems do vary in detail among car manufacturers; consult your service manual to establish how the system works in your car, where the relay (if there is one) is located and what to do if a horn suddenly starts blaring.

A Turn off the ignition.

B If you can't remember immediately where to disconnect the horns, remove the ground cable from the battery. This will stop the racket and give you time to collect your thoughts.

C Disconnecting the wires at the horns *(drawing, below)* will always silence them, though horns can be difficult to reach.

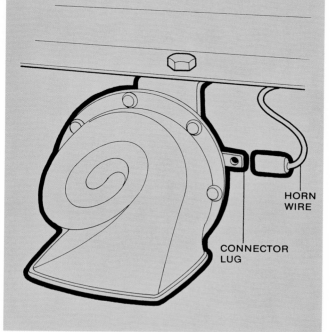

HORN WIRE

CONNECTOR LUG

D After disconnecting the horns, reattach the ground cable to the battery. Have a mechanic check out your car's horn system.

26 If turn signals don't light

A When none of the lights work, look for a blown fuse in the fuse block under the dashboard *(pages 178-179)*. If a fuse is burned out, replace it with one of the same capacity.

B When some bulbs work and others do not, check the unlit bulbs. Replace any that are burned out. Clean any sockets that are corroded *(pages 180-181)*. If all unlit bulbs are on the same side of the car, the turn-signal switch in the steering column may be defective. See a mechanic.

27 If a turn-signal lights up but doesn't flash

A Replace the flasher unit *(pages 180-181)*. Flasher units cannot be repaired, but are inexpensive. Plugging in a new one takes only a few minutes.

28 If turn-signals flash too fast or too slowly

A Check for burned-out bulbs. Dead bulbs change the amount of resistance in a circuit, a factor that can affect the flash rate even if the flasher unit is good. Replace with bulbs of the same size, since a change in bulb size also can affect the flash rate.

B Replace the flasher unit *(pages 180-181)*.

29 If a turn-signal switch won't stay on or fails to cancel after a turn

This fault usually lies in the switch itself. Fixing it is a job for a mechanic.

30 If the windshield-wiper arms collide or cover the wrong area

A A wiper errant in position or timing usually is set incorrectly on its drive shaft. With one hand, lift the wiper arm as far away from the windshield as possible. Using a screwdriver, with the other hand gently pry the wiper arm from its shaft *(drawing, below)*. Reposition it so that it does not collide with the other wiper and push it back onto the shaft. If necessary, reposition both arms on their shafts so that they do not collide with each other.

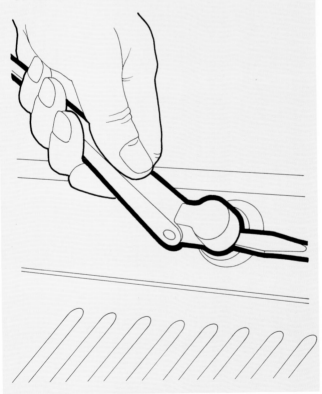

B Excessive wear where wiper arms and drive shafts meet also can cause blades to wobble and hit each other. A mechanic must handle this problem.

31 If wiper motors won't turn on

A Refer to step 21 for what to do.

32 If the wipers otherwise malfunction

There are other ways in which wipers can misbehave: the motor runs but they don't budge; they won't turn off; they stop instantly when the switch is turned off instead of continuing to their parked position; they work at only one speed; they work at the wrong speed; the washer spray goes on when you turn on the wiper alone. Let a mechanic handle all these jobs for you.

33 If the radio cuts in and out or stops working

A When the radio seems dead and its dial light is out, check the fuse *(pages 178-179)*.

B Loose connections or wires accidentally grounded can cause the radio to work intermittently or not at all. Check the radio's ground connection and connections to the battery, remote speakers (if any) and antenna. Tighten loose connections and splice or replace broken wires.

C See a mechanic about interference from the ignition system and poor reception.

NOISES AND WHAT TO DO ABOUT THEM

To be intelligently analytical of unusual noises, you first must know the normal sound of your car. Or, rather, sounds, because car noises —normal or abnormal—change according to the weather, the environment, the road surface and whether the windows are open or closed. When your car is running normally, listen to its engine at idle—from the driver's seat and from the outside, with the hood closed and with the hood open. Take a run down the street and a spin on the highway, paying close attention to the sounds of the car in motion.

The perception of suspicious noises is, of course, subjective: one man's ping is another man's knock. The car's construction—a steel box attached to a steel frame—adds to the confusion by transmitting sounds so that a noise from the front of the car can sound as though it were in the rear, and vice versa. For this reason it is not surprising that pinpointing noises and deciding what causes them are difficult tasks.

One rule of thumb: the loudest noises are the most serious. If a loud noise develops suddenly —in any part of the car—stop immediately and investigate. If you can't locate the source of the noise or if the noise is a metallic hammering apparently centered in the engine, continued driving may severely damage your car. Get a tow.

Fortunately, most noises are neither loud, sudden or dangerous. When you hear a new one, take your time. Note the pattern of its occurrence, and decide whether you'd call it a snap, a crackle or a pop. Look for it on the partial list below. If you don't find it described as a snap, try pop—before concluding that your particular problem has not been included. The terms listed are the commonest descriptions mechanics hear from complaining car owners. After each listing, the nature of the sound is described in italic type, together with a pattern of occurrence—that is, when and under what conditions the sound most often manifests itself. The likeliest cause of the sound and the corrective action required are printed in regular type.

BANG *Backfire—explosive sound from the rear.*
Check the ignition timing *(pages 218-221)*. If the timing is correct, the fuel mixture may be too lean *(pages 224-225)*—or rocker arms or valve springs may be defective (see a mechanic).

BUMP *Heavy, muffled sounds from the rear, especially when negotiating bumps or corners.*
First check for loose items in the trunk—the spare tire and jack for example. If the rear shock absorbers are loose, tighten them *(pages 184-185)*. Spring clips may be loose (see a mechanic).

BUZZ *Vibrations from the front at highway speeds.*
Air passing through vents can cause thin pieces of the heating and ventilating systems to oscillate.

CHATTER *Clattering from the rear end of a car with a limited-slip differential—more evident during turns than on the straightaway.*
The differential may have been refilled with the wrong lubricant. Have it drained and refilled.

CHIRP *An intermittent high-pitched noise when front wheels are turned as far as they will go. Most noticeable when the engine is idling.*
The belt to the power-steering pump is loose. Tighten it *(page 175)*.

CLICK *A rapid, rhythmic sound, soft or loud, that speeds up and slows down with the engine.*
A fan blade may be striking a part of the car because it is bent or loose (see a mechanic).

Regular clicking that diminishes, or even ceases, as the engine warms up.

The pistons are tipping back and forth, striking the cylinder walls—a phenomenon known as piston slap. More annoying than dangerous, it cannot do much damage (but see a mechanic).

CLUNK *Rhythmic noise under the rear at low speed.*

Universal joints or parts of the differential may be out of adjustment (see a mechanic).

GRIND *An abrasive noise in cars with manual transmission, occurring when the clutch is depressed, accompanied by a rubbing sensation transmitted to the foot through the pedal.*

The throwout bearing in the clutch needs lubrication or replacement (see a mechanic).

GROAN *A protesting noise from the power-steering mechanism when the wheels are turned, whether the car is stationary or moving.*

The steering system needs fluid *(page 140).*

Groaning from brakes as the car is gradually braked to a stop or is gradually released from one.

This is normal. Use more pedal pressure in stopping or release the brake pedal more decisively.

GROWL *A low, guttural sound from the front wheels that diminishes with light application of the brakes while maintaining speed.*

The front-wheel bearings may be worn. Raise the front of the car and spin the front wheels. If they make a noise, replace the bearings *(pages 166-169).*

Growling from the rear during turns, more audible in left than in right turns.

Some parts in the differential probably are worn (see a mechanic).

An intermittent growl from the rear during acceleration or deceleration.

Differential bearings may be sliding back and forth in what is called bearing endplay (see a mechanic).

A steady growl from the rear when coasting.

Rear-wheel bearings may be worn or damaged.

Jack up the car and spin the rear wheels by hand. If they make a noise, see a mechanic.

HISS *A sibilant sound in the forward part of the car.*

Hisses come from leaks wherever a gas is under pressure, as in (most obviously) tires or the air conditioner or the engine itself, from which air can leak past a loose spark plug. Check for leaks in power brakes or any vacuum-operated accessory. Some hiss is normal in many power-steering systems.

Hissing in the rear during acceleration.

This noise may indicate a restriction in the exhaust pipe (see a mechanic).

HUM *A continuous monotone outside the car when it is in motion.*

Most snow tires and some radials deliver a hum at high speeds. If you are not using snows, increase tire pressure to 50 pounds for a short test run on asphalt. If the hum doesn't change, reduce the air pressure and have a mechanic check the rear axle.

KNOCK *A rapidly occurring noise (also known in the trade as a ping) during acceleration. It also may sound like a light rattle.*

Try using a fuel with a higher octane rating. If this does not quiet the knock, it may be the result of incorrect timing. Reset the timing *(pages 218-221).* A third cause could be a malfunction in the distributor-advance mechanisms. Check them *(page 221).*

A sharp double knock at idle.

Piston pins probably are loose (see a mechanic).

PING See *knock*

POP *A nonrhythmic noise from the front end while turning the front wheels during cold weather.*

The tie rods or ball joints in the front suspension are worn (see a mechanic).

RAP *A regular, light metallic sound most noticeable when the engine is "floating"—neither accelerating nor decelerating—at about 30 mph.*

The connecting-rod bearings probably are worn (see a mechanic).

RASP *A grating noise, continuous or intermittent, from the dashboard, which speeds and slows as the car does and may be accompanied by erratic speedometer readings.*

The speedometer cable needs lubrication or replacement (see a mechanic).

RATTLE *A sound suggesting looseness emanating from disc brakes at low speeds on rough roads.*

This noise may indicate the absence of a spring designed specifically to keep brakes from rattling; or the brakes may need new pads.

A rattle from the front suspension that does not cease upon light application of the brakes.

The front-wheel bearings may be loose or defective. Raise the front of the car and spin the front wheels by hand. If they make a noise, replace the bearings *(pages 166-169)*. The sound also can be caused by loose or worn shock absorbers. Replace them *(pages 184-185)*.

SCRAPE *A sharp rubbing sound from the brakes.*

The brake pads or linings may be worn out, requiring replacement. The wheel bearings may need tightening *(page 169)* or an excessively long mounting bolt scraping on the disc may be causing such a noise (see a mechanic).

SCREECH *A high-pitched noise when the engine is raced in neutral and during fast acceleration.*

One of the drive belts under the hood probably is loose. Tighten it *(pages 174-175)*.

SNAP *A sharp, snapping sound as the car begins to move, either forward or backward.*

Bolts may be loose in the rear suspension (see a mechanic).

SQUEAK *A high-pitched sound during braking.*

In drum brakes, this noise indicates a problem with brake linings, perhaps dirt (see a mechanic). Disc brakes sometimes squeal, but the noise does not always indicate a malfunction.

Squeaks as the car takes dips and bumps in the road.

Rubber bushings in the suspension may be deteriorated. Silicone lubricants made for rubber will quiet the noises temporarily, but the bushings should be replaced (see a mechanic).

SQUEAL *A high-pitched noise underneath cars with manual transmission that disappears as soon as the clutch pedal is depressed slightly.*

The throwout bearing in the clutch needs lubrication or replacement (see a mechanic).

A squeal from the front of the car at idle that is independent of the steering.

The water pump may need lubrication. Add water-pump lubricant to the coolant. The fan or alternator also could be responsible (see a mechanic).

TAP *A light, hammering sound—rhythmic but intermittent—heard when the engine is cold but that may cease when the engine warms up.*

This sound may be caused by too little oil in the crankcase. Check the dipstick. The noise also may be caused by sticking valves or faulty hydraulic valve-lifters (see a mechanic).

THUD *A heavy, low noise from the engine, particularly when it is under heavy load.*

The engine's main bearings may be loose or worn, or the flywheel may be loose (see a mechanic).

THUMP *Nonrhythmic, rapid pounding under the hood during acceleration.*

The engine mounts may be worn or loose (have a mechanic replace or tighten them).

Rhythmic thumping from the tires.

The sound means a swelling or a depression in a tire, which can indicate a serious defect. But some tires, particularly those containing nylon, may form temporary flat spots when the car is parked for a long period, or even overnight during cold weather. If a thump does not cease after a few miles' driving, check for swelling or damaged tread.

WHIR *A continuous sound under the car at highway speeds, sometimes accompanied by vibration.*

This noise can be caused by worn universal joints or an unbalanced driveshaft (see a mechanic).

GARAGES AND MECHANICS

HOW TO FIND GOOD ONES AT FAIR PRICES

THE WIDE CHOICE OF SERVICES
GETTING THE MOST FROM YOUR WARRANTY
AFTER THE WARRANTY HAS EXPIRED
DEALING WITH THE REPAIRMAN
UNDERSTANDING A WORK ORDER
TWO WAYS TO FIGURE REPAIR CHARGES
AVOIDING THE GYPS

10

"What is there about peppermint ice cream that keeps my car from starting?" Thelma asked the service manager of the garage. "The car starts fine when I buy vanilla ice cream. But when I buy peppermint . . ."

The service manager assured Thelma that peppermint ice cream had nothing to do with a car's ignition problems. As an elderly widow who knew little about automobiles, she was used to being humored at the garage, but this time she was positive that she was right. Since Thelma was a longtime customer, the service manager agreed to take a test ride with her to the ice-cream store.

She went inside and bought a pint of vanilla. When she came out, the car started immediately. Then she drove around the block a few times, returned to the store and bought peppermint. Now when she tried to start the car,

the engine refused to catch; and she almost ran down the battery.

"You see," she said with some satisfaction, "the peppermint flavor does it every time."

"Hold the gas pedal to the floor," the service manager suggested. Thelma followed his instruction, and the engine immediately came to life. The man now had his clue. He examined the vanilla ice-cream container, then the peppermint. The peppermint, he noted, was not prepackaged, and Thelma had had to wait an extra few minutes for it to be hand packed. During this time the fuel in the car's hot carburetor percolated from its bowl into the engine, flooding it.

This did not happen when she bought vanilla, because she came out of the store before the problem had time to develop. "Lots of engines behave this way when they're hot," the service manager told her. "Press the accelerator to the floor, hold it there as you turn the ignition key and the engine should start. Even if that doesn't work, the problem will solve itself. Wait a few minutes and the excess fuel will evaporate, and the engine will catch. But you were right in a way: the peppermint ice cream *did* cause the trouble."

In another part of town, the family car's behavior prompted a tiff between a husband and wife. Evelyn told George that the car was bucking and stalling. Yet when he took it for a test drive, it performed beautifully. The next day, she complained about the car; George took another test drive, and again detected no trouble.

To settle the spat over who was right, George took the car to a shop where he explained the problem.

A mechanic checked the engine and then took a test drive himself. But he could find nothing wrong either. He told George to have Evelyn bring the car by the next time it ran roughly. The following day there she was.

Searching for clues, the mechanic took another test drive and found that the car did indeed misfire when driven over rough roads. He checked out the connections in the ignition circuit but they were all clean and tight.

Then he noticed that the trouble only occurred when Evelyn's key chain, which had a dozen other keys on it, was in the ignition. When he detached the ignition key from the chain and drove the car over a rough road, it ran perfectly. Now he was closer to the problem. Obviously there was a looseness in the ignition switch. On a rough road the weight of the keys on the chain made the ignition key vibrate, causing the contacts in the switch to separate and intermittently stop the flow of electricity through the ignition system. This interrupted the firing of the spark plugs. Without the weight of the key ring, the ignition key

did not vibrate, the switch was not disturbed and the car performed normally. A new ignition switch solved the problem—and ended the family argument.

Both these stories ended well because the people involved were among the lucky car owners who have perceptive and conscientious mechanics to turn to in time of need.

The phrase "time of need" is a relative one, of course. Many motorists possess some mechanical expertise—and practically anyone can reduce his or her increasing dependence on auto-repair shops by learning how to maintain a car properly, and by personally taking on some of the minor repair jobs *(Chapters 6 through 8)*. But modern automobiles are exceedingly complicated pieces of machinery, and eventually a time will come when the services of an expert mechanic will be necessary.

The crucial role played by the automobile mechanic in today's world can be measured in dollar terms. Americans spend about $30 billion each year on car repairs and maintenance, which includes about $20 billion for accident repairs. Yet their experience with repairs may be expressed more meaningfully by some other figures that show how the increase in the number of mechanics has lagged behind the increase in the number of cars on the road. In 1950 there were approximately 670,000 mechanics to service about 36 million vehicles—a ratio of about one mechanic for every 54 cars. Since then, the number of automobiles has swelled to more than 86 million but there are now only 800,000 mechanics to service them —roughly one for every 108 cars. The consequences are unfortunate but undeniable: the average person has a harder time getting his car repaired and he pays more for the work.

There are several reasons for this situation. Converting men with mechanical aptitudes into mechanics is not an easy process. A me-

Diagnostic Center Inc.

417 CENTRAL STREET
WAYNESBORO, WASHINGTON

TELEPHONE 555-2104

3554

REPORTED PROBLEM AREA
ENGINE
BRAKES
STEERING
OTHER

NAME

ADDRESS

CITY   STATE

YEAR   MAKE   MODEL   DATE

BUSINESS PHONE   LICENSE NO.

RESIDENCE PHONE   MILEAGE

UNDER CAR INSPECTION				ENGINE & TRAN. PERFORMANCE				GENERAL INSPECTION					
TIRE CONDITION - GENERAL				TRANSMISSION MOUNTS				ROTOR GAP			HEATER HOSES		
BALL JOINTS - UPPER				UNDERCOATING				MAXIMUM COIL OUTPUT			WATER PUMP		
BALL JOINTS - LOWER				**WHEEL ALIGNMENT**				INITIAL TIMING			COOLANT CONDITION		
TIE ROD ENDS				TOE - IN				TIMING ADVANCE			RADIATOR PRESSURE TEST.		
IDLER ARM				CASTER				CENTRIFICAL WEIGHT OPERATION			ENGINE OIL		
PITMAN ARM				CAMBER				CRANKING - VOLTAGE			TRANSMISSION OIL		
STEERING RELAY ROD				STEERING FREE PLAY				CHARGING - VOLTAGE			POWER STEERING OIL		
FRONT SHOCK ABSORBERS				STEERING CENTRALIZATION				IGNITION WIRES			MASTER CYLINDER FLUID		
POWER STEERING LEAKS				TURNING RADIUS				DISTRIBUTOR CAP			AIR CONDITIONER HOSES		
MUFFLERS				WHEEL BALANCE				DYNAMIC COMPRESSION			VACUUM HOSES		
RESONATORS				**ENGINE & TRAN. PERFORMANCE**				HEAD GASKET CONDITION			AIR FILTER ELEMENT		
EXHAUST PIPES				FUEL PUMP PRESSURE				**GENERAL INSPECTION**			BELTS - STRG/GEN/A.C.		
TAIL PIPES				FUEL PUMP VOLUME				HEADLIGHTS - HIGH ☐ LOW ☐			OIL FILLER CAP		
HANGERS & CLAMPS				COMBUSTION	IDLE			PARKING LIGHTS			CRANKCASE VENTILATION SYSTEM		
UNIVERSAL JOINTS				EFFICIENCY	CRUISE			RADIO ANTENNA			BATTERY CABLES		
DRIVESHAFT CENTER SUPPORT					FULL THROTTLE			WINDSHIELD - FRONT ☐ REAR ☐			BATTERY HOLDER		
PINION SEAL				ENGINE IDLE SPEED				SIDE WINDOWS			BATTERY CONDITION - VISUAL		
DIFFERENTIAL GASKET (LEAKS)				CARB. LINKAGE & MOUNTING				STOP LIGHTS			BATTERY CONDITION - % OF CHARGE		
GAS TANK & LINES				MAXIMUM AVAILABLE TORQUE				SIGNAL LIGHTS			BATTERY CONDITION - LOAD TEST		
TRANSMISSION SEALS				TRANS. SHIFTPOINTS				BACK - UP LIGHTS			HEAT RISER VALVE		
TRANS. VAC. MOD. & HOSE				PASSING GEAR				LICENSE PLATE LIGHTS			FUEL SYSTEM - VISUAL		
OIL FILTER & PAN (LEAKS)				SPEEDOMETER	30 H L			EMERGENCY - FLASHER LIGHTS			VALVE COVER GASKETS		
REAR GREASE SEALS				ACCURACY	50 H L			SIDE VIEW MIRROR			FAN & PULLEYS		
REAR SHOCK-ABSORBERS				CLUTCH SLIPPAGE				REAR VIEW MIRROR			HORNS		
SPRINGS				STARTER - DRAW - AMPS				WINDSHIELD WIPER ARMS & BLADES			**HEADLIGHTS**		
BRAKE LININGS % REMAINING				CAM ANGLE				WINDSHIELD WASHERS			LOW BEAM FOCUS		
WHEEL CYLINDERS				CAM ANGLE VARIATION				DASHBOARD GUAGES			HIGH BEAM FOCUS		
BRAKE DRUMS				CONDENSER OSCILLATION				HEATER & DEFROSTER BLOWER			LOW BEAM INTENSITY		
FRONT GREASE SEALS				DIST. POINT ARCING				AIR CONDITIONER			HIGH BEAM INTENSITY		
FRONT WHEEL BEARINGS				IGNITION POLARITY				EMERGENCY BRAKE RESERVE					
BRAKE SHOE HOLD DOWN SPRINGS				SPARK PLUGS - VISUAL									
BRAKE LINE & HOSES				SPARK PLUGS VARIATION				**GENERAL UNDERHOOD INSPECTION**					
BRAKE PEDAL RESERVE				PRIMARY CURRENT IRREGULARITIES				HOOD LATCH & SAFETY					
BRAKE STATIC HYDRAULIC TEST				SECONDARY CURRENT IRREGULARITIES				RADIATOR CAP					
MOTOR MOUNTS				SPARK VOLTAGE				RADIATOR HOSES					

Column scale (right margin): UNSATISFACTORY · MARGINAL · SATISFACTORY

I hereby authorize the above repair work to be done along with the necessary material, and hereby grant you and/or your employees permission to operate the car or truck herein described on streets, highways or elsewhere for the purpose of testing and/or inspection. An express mechanic's lien is hereby acknowledged on above car or truck to secure the amount of repairs thereto. Not responsible for car or contents in case of fire or theft. STORAGE WILL BE CHARGED 24 HOURS AFTER REPAIRS OR ESTIMATES ARE COMPLETED.   **TERMS—STRICTLY CASH**

X

---

chanic's work is physical, sometimes tedious and usually dirty. It is often highly complex as well, since a first-rate mechanic is expected to have a working knowledge of virtually all aspects of the automobile. While he is not disappearing, his services are in greater demand today than ever before (box, page 257).

To find a good mechanic—or, more precisely, the place where he works—is the abiding goal of every American motorist. As you search for him, keep these three basic principles in mind: the mechanic must be competent, skilled at diagnosing your car's problem and able to make the necessary repair. To meet these standards he must have good equipment and the knowledge of how to use it correctly; he, and

This sample check list used by an automobile diagnostic center reflects the scores of possible trouble areas in a car, ranging from simple devices such as hood latches and mirrors to intricate components such as the transmission and differential.

For more than a decade these centers have offered customers a thorough technological assessment of their car's mechanical functions. Using sophisticated monitoring equipment—such as oscilloscopes as well as dynamometers that simulate road conditions—the centers attempt to reduce the amount of guesswork in automotive troubleshooting. Many of their customers are owners whose new-car warranty is about to expire or used-car buyers who want to check a car they are considering.

The cost of an examination usually runs from $10 to $20. Today many dealerships and other repair shops also are equipped with the testing devices, and in turn most diagnostic centers offer—but do not insist on doing—the indicated repairs.

ROSEBUD AUTO REPAIRS INC.
WHEEL ALIGNMENT · BRAKES · IGNITION
8 MAIN STREET, ROSEBUD, NEBRASKA   PHONE 555-7543

REPAIR ORDER N⁰ 16139

MATERIAL USED

QUAN	DESCRIPTION	PRICE	
5	qts oil	5	00
1	oil filter	5	50
1	qt trans oil	1	00
1	set spark plugs	10	80
1	set ignition points	4	00
1	condenser	1	20
1	gas filter	2	00
1	air filter	4	00
1	radiator hose, upper	2	50

NAME Bob McKee
ADDRESS Cowles Street
Rosebud, Nebraska

DATE 5/9/73
PHONE 555-4858
PROMISED

LICENSE NO. AND STATE	MOTOR NO.	MAKE AND MODEL	MILEAGE
YR 5108 Neb.	1075Y452	1970 Madison	19,730

TUNE ENGINE: retime ignition, adjust dist. dwell, adj. carb, clean or replace PCV valve, replace carb air cleaner, Clean and tighten battery terminals, refill master cyl, check antifreeze, adjust belts.   24 00

Lubricate chassis   2 00

Check pull to left

Check rattle, left rear   ⟩ Call cust. if repairs needed

THIS COMPANY ASSUMES NO RESPONSIBILITY FOR LOSS OR DAMAGE BY FIRE OR THEFT TO VEHICLES OR PERSONAL EFFECTS PLACED WITH US FOR STORAGE, SALE OR REPAIR. REPAIRS ARE GUARANTEED FOR 90 DAYS OR 4,000 MILES, WHICHEVER OCCURS FIRST. NOTE: NO ADJUSTMENTS FOR ERRORS IN ARITHMETIC WILL BE MADE UNLESS CLAIMED WITHIN 10 DAYS AFTER THE COMPLETION OF THIS ORDER AND ON PRESENTATION OF THIS COPY.

TOTAL

TOTAL FOR LABOR	
TOTAL FOR PARTS	
GAS, OIL AND GREASE	
ACCESSORIES	
TOTAL AMOUNT	

I HEREBY AUTHORIZE THE ABOVE REPAIR WORK, INCLUDING THE REPLACEMENT OF PARTS AS NECESSARY.

SIGNED Robert McKee

Many garages use a combination work order and billing form similar to the sample above. Make sure the service manager fills in all identifying information—especially the mileage—at the top of the form. You will need this record should you have any complaints in the future.

Have each repair or maintenance job listed individually. Before committing yourself, obtain a reasonably accurate estimate of the costs. The exact labor charges—and all the materials used for the repairs—will, of course, have to be put on the bill when the work is completed.

If a problem needs precise diagnosis before the work can be done, the work order should carry a notation that the shop must call you with the results of that diagnosis and an estimate of the repair cost.

You have to sign the work authorization when you leave the car. Before doing so, check the form for a statement of the shop's guarantee (center, bottom).

---

the shop where he is employed, must have integrity—an interest in doing the job right.

Determining a mechanic's competency is the most difficult task. The industry has taken its first steps toward certifying mechanics in an effort to give the public—and the mechanics —standards of workmanship (box, opposite).

Judging the adequacy of a shop's equipment is an easier job; so is judging its integrity. Some hints of how to locate a well-equipped, honest shop are discussed in the following paragraphs. The mechanic who is honest, reliable and talented will carry a good reputation in any community. One who consistently does good

THE NEED FOR BETTER CRAFTSMEN — AND TWO PROMISING PROGRAMS

For most automobile owners, a bill for car repairs represents one of the more frustrating mysteries of daily life. Typically such a bill reads: "Parts—$29.75. Labor—$69.80," though the job may have taken only part of one mechanic's morning. Sadly reaching for his overdrawn checkbook, the motorist envisions the mechanic climbing out of the grease pit at day's end, washing up and driving off in a Silver Ghost.

It isn't necessarily so. A mechanic—even a skilled one—generally earns less than a master plumber or electrician. From a mechanic's wages he often must pay for the cost of his personal tools: an initial investment of $1,500 may rise further each year because tools get lost, stolen, broken or wear out.

The labor charge in the bill does not make the mechanic rich—he gets about half of it. The remainder goes to his boss—the garage owner —who uses it to cover business expenditures including rent, insurance, taxes, phone and electric bills, equipment costs and all the other components of overhead, plus, of course, a profit. While an owner also makes a profit on the sale of parts, the margin is not enough to keep his garage in the black. Additional profit thus must come from the labor charge.

The relatively low wages alone may suffice to explain why there is a serious shortage of qualified mechanics. But the reasons are social and economic as well:

American society tends to look down on manual labor. Parents with mechanically gifted sons steer them to colleges or technical schools that will prepare them for professional or white-collar careers.

It takes more than a mechanical bent and a love for tinkering to make a good mechanic. Many skillful young men who have been considered whizzes at fixing the family car have gone off to manufacturers' training schools only to fail at mastering the complex repair manuals and lessons directed at the modern automobile's 15,000 parts.

A relatively few unscrupulous shops have given the business a bad name, discouraging young men from entering it. Two states—California and Connecticut—have established licensing bureaus for repair shops, and garages that cheat in those states can be closed down. But until licensing becomes much more widespread, thus adding prestige to the total trade, parents presumably will continue to discourage sons who would like to become professional automobile mechanics.

In an effort to raise the status of mechanics, members of the service industry, manufacturers and dealers in 1972 founded the National Institute for Automotive Service Excellence. Under the institute program, which is voluntary, a mechanic pays a small fee to take any, or all, of five tests on different systems of the car. (The tests are administered and graded by a wholly independent testing organization.) If a mechanic passes any one test, he is entitled to wear an orange, white and blue shoulder patch. If he passes all five tests, he qualifies as a certified general automobile mechanic—a master craftsman. This does not guarantee more money, though that may come eventually. It does provide recognition of skill and experience.

A related way of offering incentives to mechanics has been encouraged by the National Automobile Dealers Association. In cooperating facilities, each repair job is rated according to the amount of skill a mechanic needs to complete it. Then the mechanic and the job are matched—the most skilled man is assigned the most complex job.

The mechanic is then paid according to the rating of the job. A man doing complex work, such as repairing an automatic transmission, would earn more than another, less experienced mechanic would make for, say, doing an engine tune-up—even though both jobs might take the same amount of time.

When the craftsman with the finest skill earns the highest pay, experienced mechanics should find little reason to leave the profession, and mechanics with lower skills would have a real incentive to increase their capabilities.

WHERE TO GO FOR REPAIRS

Deciding where to take your car for maintenance or repairs often is half the job. Guidance of the kind offered here can only be general because so many variables affect each task. Your choice should depend upon the competency of the mechanic, the adequacy of equipment, the integrity of the shop and the rates. Mass merchandisers offer repairs, but the kind of work they do often depends on the size of the shop.

In the chart below, stars indicate the places that usually can do a given job properly and at the best price. Dots denote places that can also do the job but may be less convenient or more expensive, or both. Blanks indicate that the service required is not normally provided. And remember: it may be faster, cheaper—and in the long run easier—to do some of the jobs *(right column)* yourself.

Job	Dealer	Independent garage	Specialty shop	Gasoline station	Do it yourself
Tune-up	●	★		●	★
Replace drum-brake linings	●	★	★	●	
Replace disc-brake pads	★	★	★	●	
Replace muffler	●	★	★	●	
Replace shock absorbers	●	★	★	●	★
Automatic transmission	★	●	★		
Air conditioning	★	●	★		
Wheel alignment	●	★	★	●	
Wheel balancing	●	★	★	●	
Rebuild starter	●	★	★		
Rebuild alternator	●	★	★		
Lubricate chassis	●	●		★	★
Replace ball joints	★	★	●		
Change oil, oil filter	●	●		★	★
Repair upholstery	★		★		
Body work	★		★		
Overhaul engine	●	★	★		
Electrical accessories	★	★	●		
Replace wiper blades	●	●	●	★	★
Replace headlamps	●	●	●	★	★
Tire repair	●	★	★	★	

work for you will quickly establish his integrity and earn your esteem.

These are general guidelines to keep in mind. But your quest for the right mechanic will undoubtedly take you to several different types of automotive establishments.

When your car develops troubles, you can seek help from any one of a number of sources: the service department of a new-car dealership, an independent garage, a specialty shop that concerns itself primarily with one aspect of the car (the automatic transmission, for instance), a mass merchandiser who mainly sells and installs parts but also does some repair work or a gasoline service station. You also may want to visit a diagnostic center for periodic checkups or prior determination of a problem. Such establishments do not always perform repairs themselves, but they can be a useful auxiliary service (box, page 255).

With all these factors in mind, then, where should you go for service?

The dealer's service department

As long as the warranty on your car is in effect, a dealer must be your automatic choice. The reason is obvious: his service department will correct any flaw in workmanship or replace any defective part without charge. You should not be reluctant about asking for warranty repairs, since the dealer is being reimbursed by the manufacturer. And, in any case, you have already paid for the warranty work indirectly, because the projected costs of the work over a specified period were calculated by the manufacturer in determining the list price of the new car.

To know what to expect when problems develop during the warranty period, you must, first of all, be aware of how responsibility for the car's various elements are portioned out among the dealer, manufacturers other than

the car maker, and yourself. These are some of the key points:

■ THE DEALER'S OBLIGATIONS. The warranty is limited by time and mileage. Usually it is in effect for 12 months or 12,000 miles, whichever comes first. However, some manufacturers give longer warranties, one offering it at an extra, but reasonable, fee.

■ YOUR OBLIGATIONS. Under most warranties, the owner is responsible for seeing that scheduled maintenance is done at specified intervals. This includes such things as regularly changing the oil and oil filter and checking the fluid levels of the automatic transmission, brake master cylinder and power steering. Those items replaced during routine maintenance—spark plugs, fuel, air or oil filters—must be paid for by the owner. The exception is the part that fails prematurely, indicating it was defective originally. If the premature failure can be traced to owner abuse, however, the warranty does not cover it.

To keep the warranty valid, the car must be maintained according to the schedule in your owner's manual. But you do not have to get the maintenance work done at an authorized dealer's service department. Any gasoline station or independent garage can do such jobs as oil and filter changes, as long as the products meet the specifications set in the owner's manual. Keep your receipts as proof that the maintenance was done.

■ OTHER WARRANTIES. Batteries and tires have special warranties. Tires normally are covered by their manufacturer for the life of the tread. Generally, if there is a premature failure due to a defect in the tire before 20 per cent of the tread is used, you will get a new tire free. After 20 per cent of the tread has been worn, the manufacturer will give you a prorata allowance toward a new tire, based on the amount of tread remaining. If half the tread re-

BEWARE OF THE MECHANIC'S LIEN

If you ever have your car repaired and fail to pay the bill, you may unhappily become acquainted with the term "mechanic's lien." A lien is a legally recorded claim against property. A mechanic is anyone who has performed work—whether it be car repairing or plumbing or landscaping. The purpose of the lien is to permit the creditor to seize the property—be it a car, a house or a piece of land —and have it sold to obtain money that is due him both for his labor and any materials used.

The procedure requires that the claimant first notify the debtor of his intention to obtain a lien if the bill is not paid within a specified time. If the bill remains unpaid, the claimant applies to the courts for a lien. As a legal technicality the authorities advertise the claim in small-type newspaper notices. If the debtor fails to respond, the lien is issued and the property is seized and sold at auction by the court; the mechanic is then paid from the proceeds. If the proceeds are greater than the bill the difference is turned over to the owner.

The use of the mechanic's lien in the automobile repair business is, fortunately, rarely necessary. Usually a lien is invoked only when an owner brings in a car that requires extensive repairs, agrees on an estimate, and then, after the work is done, decides that the repair bill is disproportionate to the car's value. So the owner simply abandons the car. The shop is not only stuck with the repair costs but also loses valuable space, an especially important consideration in smaller shops. The only recourse is to get the car off the premises and recover all or part of the repair costs.

In cases involving disagreement over size of a bill or the quality of workmanship, the best recourse for the car owner is to pay the bill, then make a formal complaint to the proper authorities (box, page 269) or, as a last resort, to sue the shop.

mains, you should get a new tire of the same make for half price.

The car battery, too, is backed by its manufacturers. The warranty normally provides for free replacement if the battery fails due to a manufacturing defect within a 12-month or 12,000-mile period. After that there is generally additional coverage for 24 months. If a battery fails when it is two years old, 12 months remain of the warranty. You should get a one-third discount on a new battery.

■ WHERE TO GET WARRANTY REPAIRS. Warranty work normally should be performed at an authorized dealership, though not necessarily the one you bought the car from. However, you probably will want to go there, since your original dealer is likely to be more attentive to your problems. If an emergency repair is needed and an authorized dealer is closed or not in the area, you will have to get the work done at an independent garage. Be sure to get receipts for these jobs and keep any part that has been replaced. Later, when you apply for reimbursement at the dealership or regional office of the car manufacturer, you will have to document your case.

Even if your car is out of warranty, you may be able to get it fixed without charge or be partially reimbursed—not because of any legal right but because the dealer or manufacturer may want to keep your good will. If something major goes wrong and you're just past the warranty period, ask the dealer to seek the reimbursement for you. Or you can call the manufacturer's nearest regional office and ask for an appointment with a service representative to discuss the problem.

If you're on good terms with the service writer, he may set up your appointment with the regional office. Discuss the problem calmly with the service representative, but make your

HOW SHOPS COMPUTE LABOR CHARGES

In preparing a bill for service or repairs on your car, the service manager calculates the charge for labor on the basis of time spent on the job. But rather than clock the work, most managers consult a flat-rate manual, sometimes known as a labor guide *(page 266)*. The book specifies, in hours and tenths of hours, how long a job should take. In arriving at the charge to you, the manager then multiplies the hourly charge for labor by the amount of time the book suggests. The following list offers examples of times given in a manufacturer's flat-rate manual as compared with those published by an independent publisher.

For the most part, the manufacturer allots less time to a given job. One reason for the difference in times is that manufacturers assume their mechanics will have access to special tools while other shops' mechanics may not; also, their manuals are used largely in warranty work that is done on newer and, therefore, cleaner cars. For one thing, that means fewer fasteners locked by corrosion, and so less time needed to do a job.

JOB	DEALER'S MANUAL	TRADE MANUAL
alternator, replace	.4 (24 min.)	.8 (48 min.)
brake hoses, replace both front	.5	.7
brake shoes, reline all	.8	.8
carburetor, adjust	.3	.4
distributor, replace	.4	.8
distributor cap, replace	.3	.4
door handle (outside), replace	.5	.6
front wheels, balance	.4	.9
fuel pump, replace	.4	.5
hood lock, replace	.3	.4
ignition coil, replace	.4	.5
parking brake, adjust	.2	.4
piston rings, replace	10.1	14.1
rear springs, replace both	.4	.9
shock absorbers, replace two, front or rear	.6	.8
water pump, replace	1.3	2.0
windshield glass, replace	1.2	2.4

points clearly. If they are cogent, the service representative can authorize an adjustment.

Recently, for example, one motorist discovered that the ball joints on her car were heavily worn after only 33,000 miles. Before she had the dealer replace them, she reread the company's maintenance schedule for the car. She then went to the service representative and pointed out that the ball joints were supposed to be lubricated every 36,000 miles. "This means that there is no maintenance that I've failed to perform," she told him, "since I still have 3,000 miles to go before the first lubrication is due." She won her case. The new ball joints were installed free.

After your warranty expires, you may want to continue taking your car to the dealer for repairs, on the logical grounds that his mechanics are particularly familiar with your type of automobile. However, now you will be charged for all work that is done; and as a general rule, dealers' service departments are the most expensive of all repair shops.

Several factors account for the dealer's higher prices. He usually has a large showroom and service department, plus a payroll of executives, salesmen, trained mechanics and office personnel. He also must purchase an expensive array of new-vehicle tools and equipment to perform all conceivable repairs on the many models he sells. And he may spend heavily on advertising. Inevitably, all these built-in expenses will be reflected in your repair bill.

The independent garage

A powerful argument for going to an independent garage after the warranty period is over is the fact that it is likely to have lower overhead than a dealer has. In seeking out a good independent garage, recall the basic criteria for finding a good mechanic discussed above.

Also, there are things you can observe that will help you find the right place:

■ REPUTATION COUNTS. If you're new to the area, ask your neighbors about their repair shop. If several patronize the same shop and are satisfied, that's a good sign.

■ NEATNESS COUNTS. Look for cleanliness and order when inspecting a shop. Cleanliness reflects attitude; mechanics in an excessively dirty facility with tools scattered around cannot work efficiently.

■ MODERN TOOLS COUNT. Make sure that the shop has good equipment. For example, any competent garage should have modern electronic meters for setting the distributor dwell and measuring engine revolutions when tuning an engine. Current editions of general-repair manuals and manufacturers' literature on new cars should be at hand in the manager's office or work area.

The specialty shop

After the expiration of the new-car warranty, many of your subsequent problems can be diagnosed and solved at specialty shops, which come in all shapes and sizes. Independent specialty shops, dealing with specific jobs, such as wheel alignment, have been around for decades. And today there are now major chains of franchised shops that heavily advertise their expertise in such specifics as mufflers, transmissions or brakes. Tire dealers, too, have joined the parade by expanding their line to include work on brakes, front-end suspension and cooling systems.

Any of these specialty shops—franchised chain outlets and independent alike—can offer good bargains. But the astute motorist will be aware that some owners or managers of large franchise shops know little about repairs. More often they are businessmen whose profits come from turning over a large volume of goods and services. Be sure to get a second opinion before allowing them to do any extensive, expensive work.

The mass merchandisers

With the rise of suburban shopping centers in recent years, many big department stores have plunged into or expanded their auto-repair business, bringing all their polished marketing skills with them. Their service outlets concentrate on installing rapid-turnover items, including batteries, tires, shock absorbers, mufflers, and various accessories. Sometimes the shops also perform fast and relatively easy repairs—tune-ups, replacing shock absorbers, wheel alignment and the like.

Because they deal in high volume, the mass merchandisers often can sell parts at a lower price than is available elsewhere. Another advantage is their location in large shopping complexes: you can leave the car and do your shopping while repairs are being made. However, these outlets may not be the best place to go if the car has serious trouble. The men who work there are usually not highly trained mechanics who can diagnose difficult repair problems. But they can install such parts as shock absorbers, mufflers and batteries.

The gasoline station

Even in this day of complicated engines, America's first choice for maintenance and light repair work remains the gasoline station. As they have for decades, motorists continue to take the car to the gasoline station for oil changes, lubrication and tire patching. Some stations these days are equipped to do somewhat more complex jobs, such as engine tune-ups.

A gasoline station's advantages are well known: convenient neighborhood locations, long hours of daily operation and comparatively low prices. An attendant who pumps gas

THE LIFE EXPECTANCY OF PARTS

How long should any given part of a car last? There can, of course, be no precise answer—no specific number of days, or years, or miles. A part's life span depends a great deal on how well the car has been treated: how regularly it has had checkups and tune-ups, how it has been driven, and what kind of road and weather conditions it has encountered. But an owner has a right to expect that a part, with normal use, will endure for at least the minimum mileage given on the chart below. The figures are worth remembering or consulting from time to time: if your automatic transmission, say, has logged 75,000 miles, it would be wise to check it before undertaking a trip from Boston to Chicago. If, on the other hand, a mechanic whom you do not know well tells you your shock absorbers are shot after only 5,000 miles, you would do well to seek confirmation of his diagnosis at another shop before having them replaced.

PART	MINIMUM MILES	SPECIAL NOTES
Automatic transmission	50,000 to 75,000	
Radiator	75,000	
Pistons	100,000	The estimate assumes the oil and oil filter are changed regularly.
Connecting rods	100,000	
Piston rings	100,000	The estimate assumes oil of the grade and weight recommended in the owner's manual is used.
Brake drums, front and rear	100,000	Barring accidents, drums require replacement only in the unlikely event that they have been damaged by extended use without adequate linings.
Brake-drum linings	20,000 to 25,000	
Wheel cylinders, on each brake	40,000	Wheel cylinders are prone to corrosion and should be checked when brake linings are being replaced.
Valves	100,000	
Shock absorbers	20,000	
Wheel bearings	100,000	Wheel bearings should be washed in a solvent and packed in wheel-bearing grease about every 30,000 miles.
Muffler	20,000 to 25,000	This mileage is applicable only if the car is used regularly and under optimum conditions. If it is driven only occasionally, condensed moisture will rust the part, as will winter driving on salted roads and, to a lesser extent, leaving it ungaraged.
Exhaust pipe	20,000 to 25,000	See note on muffler.
Tailpipe	20,000 to 25,000	See note on muffler.
Carburetor	50,000 to 70,000	
Fuel pump	50,000 to 75,000	

PITFALLS FOR PASSING MOTORISTS

The great majority of gasoline-station attendants are honest. But there are, unfortunately, in this trade as in all others, devoted gyps—particularly at "last chance" stations—who attempt to earn a quick profit from transient customers, at times even resorting to downright dishonest tricks. The best protection is vigilance: never allow an unknown attendant to check or service your car unless you are watching. If you slip, the advice below may help to soften the blow.

ADVISED REPAIR	POSSIBLE TRICK	WHAT TO DO
new tire	An unscrupulous attendant while ostensibly checking air pressure will actually puncture a tire with a pointed screwdriver or slash it with a blade set in a finger ring or embedded in the toe of his boot.	Put on your spare and take the damaged tire to another service station or garage to be repaired or replaced.
new fan belt	A fan belt is easy to cut so that it hangs by a thread, if the car owner is not carefully watching the attendant.	Always carry an extra fan belt. Ask the attendant to put it on for you and thus at least deprive him of the profit on a new belt.
new alternator	An attendant can pull off the wires to the alternator and thus activate the warning light on your dashboard. He also can create misleading smoke by secretly dropping a pinch of titanium tetrachloride (a chemical used by the military to make smoke screens) or even a pinch of barbecue sauce on the hot alternator.	If the alternator light was off when you drove in, suggest that some wires must have come loose accidentally and ask the attendant to tighten them. Do not panic if a cloud of smoke suddenly rises from underneath the hood. Wait for it to dissipate, then check the wires going to the alternator. If they show no sign of burning, drive on.
new gas cap	There is an old trick of forgetting to replace gas caps and then recycling them; yours will be sold to the next victim. Before leaving the gas station, always check to see that the cap has been replaced.	Unless you are sure that this attendant, at this station, took your cap (and you are bigger than he is), it's best not to argue. Pay him a dollar or two for a replacement.
new ball joints	If your car is up on a lift for something as minor as a routine lubrication, the mechanic can shake a free-hanging front wheel and point out a "dangerous" wobble.	Front wheels are supposed to have a bit of free play—it only looks like a wobble. If you have any doubts, however, have them double checked at another shop.
new radiator hose	A quick jab with a sharp screwdriver is all it takes to puncture this hose.	There's nothing to do but buy a new one and have it installed right there.
new shock absorbers	An attendant can squirt crankcase oil on your shocks and say their seals are broken.	Be suspicious of this claim if your car has been riding smoothly. Look at the shocks. A real leak would start from the seal-cover area, not from the middle of the shock. Also press down on the car's bumper and let go. If the car does not bounce more than once or twice, the shocks are all right.
more engine oil	Another subterfuge is short-sticking: pushing the oil dipstick only partway down when checking the oil level.	If you suspect you have enough oil, tell the attendant the dipstick is tricky and have him check it again as you watch.

may handle simple repair and replacement jobs, and since he need not be highly trained for such tasks, his wages are comparatively low—a factor that hopefully will be reflected in your bill. Some stations may also have a qualified mechanic, either renting a service bay or in the employ of the owner.

Dealing with the repair shop

As with a doctor-patient relationship, dealings between car owners and the various kinds of repair shops often are considerably less efficient and comfortable than they should be. Just remember that you, the owner, can do a lot to build a satisfying business relationship. Whether discussing with a dealer a repair covered under the new-car warranty or arranging for a job at an independent shop, there is a definite procedure you can follow that will help establish a mutually beneficial rapport.

Except in an emergency—if you have a breakdown while on a trip, for instance—always call ahead of time for an appointment. The motorist who breezes into a shop demanding immediate service is starting out with two strikes against him; the shop may not have either the time or the incentive to do a good job. By preparing the way with a phone call, the shop will be able to assign the best-qualified mechanic to the job, to allow the proper amount of time and possibly to have the needed parts on hand. By the same token, if you cannot keep the appointment, call and cancel. The shop will appreciate your awareness of its workload—almost always heavy these days.

Before you take the car to the shop, draw up as precise a list as you can of what is wrong with the car—and make two carbons if it is warranty work. You will leave the original with the service manager and keep the carbons. If there is trouble over what the shop will or won't repair under the warranty, you'll have a copy to send or take to the manufacturer's regional office and still have a copy of your own.

Do not try to pinpoint the precise trouble unless you're quite sure of its origin. But give the service manager all the clues you can, in clear, unambiguous language. By doing so you will save his time and your money.

Here are some examples of the kinds of reporting you can do that may be valuable in helping the mechanic make his diagnosis:

■ STARTING TROUBLE. Does the problem occur only when the engine is cold, only when hot, only when the weather is humid or wet? When the key is turned, does the engine crank normally, slowly or intermittently?

■ BRAKE TROUBLE. Do the brakes squeal? Does the pedal go to the floor? Is there a pulsating feeling in the pedal when you apply pressure to it? Do the brakes fade badly after several hard stops from high speeds?

■ ENGINE TROUBLE. If the engine stalls or misfires, does it happen only when the engine is cold, or during hot or humid weather? Does it happen only on acceleration or on braking?

■ TRANSMISSION TROUBLE. Does the engine seem to be running very much faster than normal during acceleration? Is the shifting harsh? Does the transmission shift at proper speeds? Does it shift at all? Is it noisy? Does it work normally at low speed, but seem to be holding back at high speed? Or is the problem just the reverse? Does the car fail to move forward when you first put it into drive? Does the problem occur only when you first start out, or only for the first few miles, or all the time?

■ HANDLING TROUBLE. Is the problem excessive vibration, or a bouncing up and down on a washboard road or railroad crossing? Does the problem only occur when you're accelerating, or coasting, or at all times? Is it most noticeable only at certain road speeds? Does it occur only on braking?

At the shop you probably won't deal directly with the mechanic who will work on your car. Instead you will explain your problem to the service manager (in larger shops, he is known as a service writer or write-up man) and he will tell the mechanics what work to perform on the car. Present him with the list of your car's ailments. If the problem is poor riding or poor handling, ask him to take a test drive with you so that he'll understand the exact nature of the trouble (this kind of problem is particularly difficult to describe accurately). Tell him that he can have all the time necessary to do the job correctly. If you do not demand the car by 5 o'clock that night, chances are he will reciprocate by seeing to it that the work is done as quickly as possible.

The service manager will enter the items to be fixed on a form called a work order (page 256). You will then be asked to sign it. Be careful! A signed work order is a promise to pay for the job. Read the work order carefully and make sure you understand each entry. Auto repairmen often use a kind of shorthand to describe their service operations, such as "R&R" (which means "remove and replace"). If you can't make sense out of the work order, ask the man to clarify any obscure notations.

Not knowing what you are signing can be extremely expensive. If you approve a work order that says, "Check engine noise and correct," you might be agreeing to finance a complete engine overhaul. To prevent this, request that a "call you" notation be marked on the order whenever the problem does not have a specific solution or the service manager is not sure how much work will be necessary.

When the shop does call to get your go-ahead, never say, "Do whatever you think is necessary"; you might as well hand over a blank check. Ask what measures are being taken and what they will cost.

When you pick up the repaired car scrutinize the bill closely. Check to see that all labor costs have been listed separately; never pay a lump sum for labor without knowing the price of each specific job. Be certain that you understand all the charges and that no unauthorized repairs have been made. Keep on the lookout for such unrequested items as gas line antifreeze in winter or an additive in the oil. Their cost is slight but will add up to a tidy sum if a repair shop tacks such unwanted products onto your bill every time you take your car there. With a car still under warranty, additives should never be put in the oil without your permission. Their inclusion may violate the conditions of the warranty; you might be unable to collect should there be engine damage.

Before you pay the bill, ask the service manager to take a test drive with you; attune your senses to the car's performance; and if you discern even a hint of remaining trouble, lodge an immediate protest.

Disputes that arise between car owners and repair shops cannot always be settled by discussion—but one tactic that you should not resort to is refusing to pay the bill. In any financial dispute, the shop holds the trump card: it can put a claim on your car under a statute known as a mechanic's lien (box, page 260). Since you certainly don't want this to happen, pay up—then sue later to recover your money.

The makings of a repair bill

A repair bill consists of two main ingredients —parts and labor—and if you have any doubts about the fairness of either, you may have a way to double check.

Dealers set the price for a part by looking it up in a list provided by the manufacturer. Other repair shops will utilize a number of price lists from the manufacturers of parts or from independent publishing organizations serving

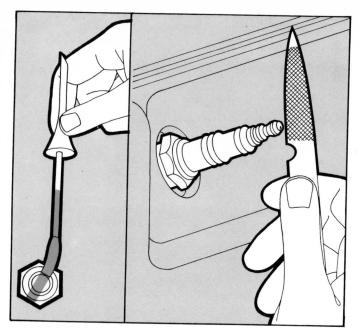

When you must take your car to an unfamiliar shop, you can take precautions to ensure that a job actually has been carried out by marking parts on which work will need to be done or parts that are to be replaced. If, for instance, the spark plugs are to be changed, nick the top of an old plug with a small file.

If a part is to be removed and later put back again—for example, a wheel that must be pulled off to check the brake linings—put a dab of paint on one of the lug nuts. The paint will be rubbed off if the mechanic does indeed remove the bolt.

the trade. In any case, you have every right to ask to see the price list to make sure you have not been overcharged. The figures will be list prices and the shop will be making a profit on the parts by getting them at a discount—perhaps 30 per cent or more. But you should not be charged more than the list price.

The shop will calculate labor charges either by what they call a clock hour or by a flat-rate hour. Under the clock-hour method, you are charged for the actual time the mechanic takes to do the job. If the shop's rate is $12 an hour and the work takes exactly an hour to complete, the labor charge will be $12. If it takes an hour and 20 minutes, the labor charge will be $16. Regrettably, you have no way of checking on the time a mechanic spent on the job.

If, however, your shop uses the flat-rate system—and the great majority of shops do—you can check to see that the charge is correct. Under the flat-rate system, labor charges are determined by how long a job should take on a specific make of car rather than how long it actually did take. The theoretical time that will be spent on any given repair task is listed in a flat-rate manual compiled and issued by either the car manufacturer or an independent trade publisher. If the manual assigns to a particular job a flat rate of, say, 0.7, this means that it should take a good mechanic seven tenths of an hour. The flat rate of 0.7 will be multiplied by the hourly labor rate—$12, for instance—giving a labor charge of $8.40. This is what you will pay, whether the job in fact took only a few minutes or more than an hour.

Flat-rate figures are based on studies of mechanics working under normal shop conditions. It may seem strange that flat rates drawn up by many manufacturers for their dealers' warranty work almost always are lower than those in the manuals published by independent organizations, but there are logical reasons for the discrepancy. A mechanic at a dealership will be working on a car that is relatively clean and rust free. And he also will have special tools designed for work on the make of car that the dealer sells. These factors speed up repair work—hence the flat-rate times are lower.

When the warranty period is over, the dealer may continue to apply the manufacturer's flat rates, but some dealers switch to the higher flat rates of the independent manuals.

Understandably, the flat-rate system has come in for a good deal of criticism. No one wants to pay for more time than was actually spent on a job—a situation that sometimes does occur. Furthermore, the flat-rate system denies you an opportunity to save money by finding the mechanic who works fastest. However, the system does have some advantages. It allows a repair shop to give you an exact price or at least a close estimate on a job even before the work begins. And it gives you a way of checking against possible overcharges for labor. If the cost of labor on your bill seems exorbitant, you can ask the service manager to show you the figure in the manual that tells how long the job was supposed to take. If you do spot an overcharge and no extensive complications are mentioned on the bill, don't let the service manager get away with an explanation that the mechanic spent longer on the job than the manual stated. This may be true, but unless there were complications and they were reported to you, the shop should only charge you by the stipulated flat-rate figure.

It may be that you can save money by finding a shop that has efficient mechanics and figures its charges fairly by the clock hour—but you will have to trust the shop's word about the time spent on the job. With the flat-rate system, you at least will be dealing with a time factor that you can check on, even if it is only an average that may have been improved upon.

The shop's guarantee

Every repair shop should guarantee its repair work. The guarantee should either be printed on the bill or given to you in writing. When you pay for repair work, your guarantee ought to specify the length of time or the amount of mileage during which it remains in effect. The usual guarantee is for 90 days or 4,000 miles, whichever comes first. Read over the agreement carefully so that you will know whether both parts and labor are covered, or only parts. Be wary of such sweeping phrases as "Good for the life of your car." This could mean that the guarantee lasts only as long as you personally keep the car; it may not include labor charges,

IF THE JOB ISN'T DONE RIGHT

Car owners often take a death-and-taxes attitude when they feel a repair job has not been done properly: they throw up their hands and assume they have to accept the inevitable. They should not.

First, try to reason calmly with the garage owner or the customer-service representative; shouting, threatening and fist pounding rarely bring the desired results. If you're still dissatisfied, you can make a written complaint to one or more of the agencies listed below. Explain the situation, giving all important details: your name and address, the name and address of the shop, the nature of your complaint, and the make, model and year of your car plus its identification number and its present mileage.

Council of Better Business Bureaus, Inc., 1150 17th Street, N.W., Washington, D.C. 20036 (or your local Better Business Bureau)

Independent Garage Owners of America, 624 South Michigan Avenue, Chicago, Illinois 60605

Federal Trade Commission, Bureau of Consumer Protection, Pennsylvania Avenue at 6th Street, N.W., Washington, D.C. 20580 (or its regional offices)

National Automobile Dealers Association, 2000 K Street, N.W., Washington, D.C. 20006

White House Office of Consumer Affairs, New Executive Office Building, Washington, D.C. 20506

The State Attorney General, in your state capital

U.S. Department of Transportation, 400 7th Street, S.W., Washington, D.C. 20590

and while the main part will be replaced free if it fails, you may have to pay for various necessary auxiliary parts.

The auto-repair business has its share of unscrupulous operators who prey on the fears or ignorance of motorists. Many car owners who have been once burned by a dishonest shop thereafter regard all shops with distrust or outright hostility. Obviously this is not a very constructive attitude, since a hostile approach quite often engenders a hostile reaction. Your best protection against dishonest operators is to be aware of them by learning their favorite tricks *(box, page 264)*.

Travelers are the easiest targets for cheats. Beware of those "last chance" gas stations located at the beginning of a long stretch of highway traversing an unpopulated area; be wary of the glib mechanic there who tries to sell you a major repair job on the spot, allegedly to save you from imminent disaster. If your car isn't obviously misbehaving, don't undertake a big repair job without getting a second opinion from another shop.

You don't have to be on a trip to be taken advantage of. Another common gyp occurs at the disreputable specialty shop that has advertised a $20.95 brake job or a free transmission checkup. Once in the shop you may become a candidate for whatever they can sell you. The $20.95 brake job, for example, might only cover adjustments on two wheels; since all four should be adjusted at once, the bill may be doubled—and you might be charged further unexpected amounts for resurfacing the brake drums and rebuilding the wheel cylinders.

At a transmission shop, don't let the mechanic take apart the transmission "to discover the trouble." Almost all transmission problems can be diagnosed by a road test alone. If you allow the shop mechanic to remove the transmission, he may charge you a large fee to reinstall it whether he finds anything wrong or not.

To be certain that repair shops actually install the parts you pay for, mark your old ones in the manner suggested on page 267. When you pick up the car, look for your mark on the part the mechanic says he removed. (Even if you find your mark on a component that has supposedly been replaced, question the mechanic before you accuse him. If he says that the part was rebuilt and the original casing still used, check your bill. A rebuilt part costs less than a replacement.)

Even dealers working under the new-car warranty stipulations are not always aboveboard. The profit that a dealer's service department makes on warranty work may be low compared to what it could make on repairs made after the warranty if it switched to an independent flat-rate manual. A good dealer accepts this situation and relies on volume—and pleased customers who return later with non-warranty repair work—to maintain profits. But occasional unscrupulous dealers will disdain warranty-repair work by giving the car what they call a wall job or sunbath. After it is left by the customer, the car is parked in a back lot (against a wall or in the sun). It remains there without being touched by a mechanic. You pick it up assuming that the fault has been corrected, only to find that nothing was done.

If you're the victim of such a practice, inform the service writer at the dealership that you plan either to call the regional office of the manufacturer or use the hot line that some manufacturers have set up for direct complaints to Detroit. This warning may elicit an instant change of tune since the dealer could be stripped of his franchise. If you experience any kind of shoddy treatment at any type of repair shop, you can write to one of the agencies that deal with consumer complaints *(opposite)*. But no one wants to have to cope with cheaters after the fact. The surest path to getting your money's worth is to know the potential pitfalls, be aware of your rights, and make every effort to establish a firm but friendly continuing relationship with the supervisory personnel and mechanics at a repair shop.

ON THE ROAD

DRIVING WITH LESS STRAIN ON YOU AND YOUR CAR

THE ART OF BEING DEFENSIVE
TECHNIQUES FOR CITY DRIVING
HIGHWAY MANEUVERING
A MANUAL OF NEW ROAD SIGNS
OVERCOMING BAD WEATHER
ITEMS FOR A TRAVEL KIT
IF YOU HAVE AN ACCIDENT

11

As a famous race driver once observed, few men will admit that they are not simply marvelous drivers. Nor, he might well have added, will many women or teenagers. Each year, however, the National Safety Council reports that more than 55,000 people are killed in motor vehicle accidents and two million more suffer disabling injuries. Despite these awful statistics, the slaughter on our highways goes on. Why? No one knows.

Perhaps the main problem is the difficulty in translating dry figures, however devastating, into gushing blood and broken bones. Safety slogans—"If you drink don't drive, if you drive don't drink," "Buckle up for safety," "Speed kills"—are now so familiar they have lost much of their original impact. Accidents, after all, happen only to the other guy.

This chapter is designed to help you avoid becoming the other guy. It assumes you are legally licensed, obey traffic regulations and possess common sense. It is mainly about defensive driving, a familiar and well-worn safety term but still the one that best describes a way of thinking and behaving behind the wheel that marks the difference between a good driver and someone who simply has a license to drive.

The National Safety Council defines defensive driving as "minimizing risks by anticipating the actions and errors of others." And so, you ask, what's new? If you are a driver of long experience, there will be only a few surprises awaiting you in what follows. Even those few, however, should be valuable additions to your existing body of knowledge and skills. And if there is a relatively inexperienced driver in the family—perhaps a teenager just learning to

271

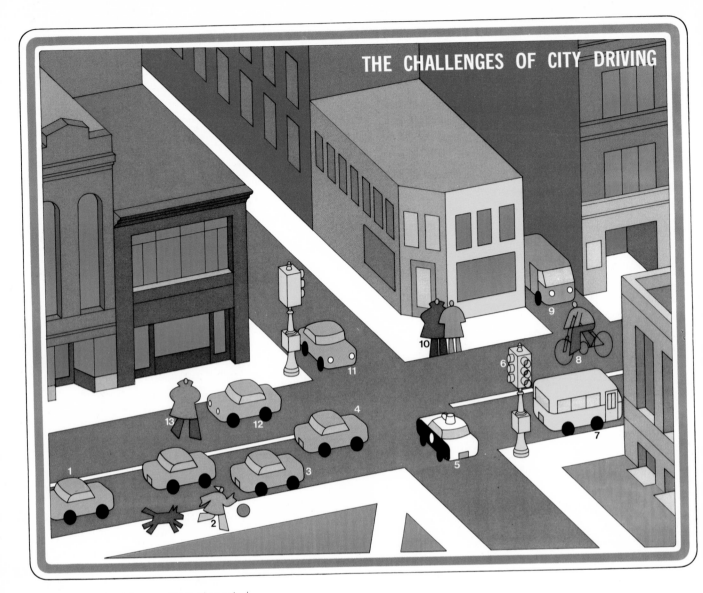

City driving, at best, is something of an adventure; the possibilities for misadventure are ever-present. Just in from the country, the careful driver of the orange car *(second from left)* must in the space of seconds take into account (1) the car close behind him, (2) the child and the dog that may dart into the street, (3) the parked car on his right, (4) the car ahead, which may have to stop abruptly, (5) the police emergency car that is crossing the intersection against the traffic light, (6) the light itself, (7) the school bus that is about to disgorge children, (8) the bicyclist who may swerve suddenly, (9) the truck emerging from an alley, (10) the pedestrians who may carelessly become jaywalkers, (11) the car waiting to dash across the intersection, (12) the immediate response of the car headed in the opposite direction, (13) the pedestrian who already is risking his life by jaywalking.

drive—this chapter should expand his understanding far beyond the scope of the typical learning process. A good driver will have mastered all the information to the point where his behavior behind the wheel is instinctive. On that basis, consider the following.

Do you always make your turns and park correctly? Do you prepare properly for the long trips you take? Are you as careful as you should be on an open-access highway? On an expressway? Do you do all the right things when the weather is inclement—or while driving at night? If a mechanical failure or other emergency occurred while you were traveling at substantial speed, would you know how to handle the situation?

This chapter deals with all of these matters —and much more.

Defensive driving also means knowing everything there is to know about how you can ensure a safe and comfortable drive—from maintaining your car in tip-top shape to reading maps accurately. It even offers advice on how to think about routine daily trips before you start out: defensive driving really begins in your own driveway.

Before you turn on the ignition

Seat belts and shoulder harnesses have been mandatory equipment on all new cars since 1968. And though the value of using both restraints together cannot be overemphasized, the percentage of people who have worn them has been pitifully small. This has been true despite the rasping buzzer, first used on most 1972 models, that does not stop until the seat belt is hooked up. In the 1974 models, however, an ignition interlock system was introduced. This system is intended to force a motorist to use both of his restraints by preventing the engine from being started until the restraints are fastened.

Accident researchers have found that seat belts alone reduce deaths and serious injuries by 32 per cent in front-end crashes. Indeed, several surveys suggest fatalities can be eliminated entirely at speeds up to 60 mph if the driver is restrained by both his seat belt and shoulder harness. The reason is simple. If you have an accident and are not wearing the proper restraints, your body will keep moving until it, too, hits something.

If this so-called second collision is with a steering column, a dashboard or a windshield, the chance of injury or death is quite high; but if the second collision is absorbed by the restraints, you could escape with just minor bruises. Another important reason for using seat and shoulder restraints is that, in the event of a collision, a skid or other violent movement, the restraints hold the driver firmly in place and may enable him to regain control of his vehicle.

So, as the first rule of defensive driving, the seat belt should be fastened; it should be positioned comfortably but firmly across your hip bones (not your middle). The shoulder harness should restrain your upper body so that it is just free enough for you to put your fist between the harness and your chest. Fastening both should be your first priority every time you enter an automobile, whether you're heading out cross-country or just driving to the corner grocery store. Safety experts maintain that one fourth of all auto accidents happen within 25 miles of home.

To reduce the possibility of whiplash—a severe injury to neck muscles and tissue caused when a car is struck from the rear—you should also be sure, if your car has headrests, that they are adjusted to the proper height for driver and passenger. And lock all doors: even in the worst accidents it is better to stay in the car than to be thrown into oncoming traffic.

Finally, adjust your rearview and sideview mirrors to minimize your blind spots. The inside mirror should be aimed to pick up as much traffic as possible directly behind you. The outside mirror should be set to disclose any vehicle passing on your left until it is almost even with your left shoulder. As soon as you get on the road, let a car or two pass by so that you can check the mirrors' positions.

Driving defensively in the city

Call him David Cameron. He is the consummate defensive driver and his vigilance has paid off: in 20 years he has never so much as

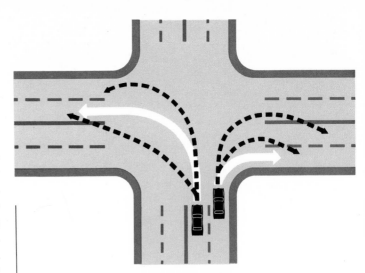

What could be more simple than turning a corner? Unfortunately, many drivers pay so little attention to this frequent maneuver that they repeatedly execute it not only poorly but dangerously. The dashed arrows above trace the most common errors: turning too soon or too late. The solid arrows chart the correct paths.

put a dent in his fender. He knows that even on a short business trip to the city he's likely to encounter every conceivable traffic situation from the serenity of a quiet residential neighborhood to the madness of a downtown traffic jam. He knows that the keys to sane city driving and all other driving are patience, courtesy, and the assumption that something unusual can always happen and probably will.

He also knows that driving defensively must be honed by intelligence and practice until it is largely instinctive. He has worked at it a long time; and so, en route to his downtown office, his mind is alert. If it were a computer, the conscious and subconscious inputs would read something like this:

"Watch the car ahead. Remember, rear-end collisions are the most common kind of accident. Correct following distance is one car-length for each 10 mph up to 30 mph; above that speed, make it two car-lengths for each 10 mph. Avoid race-and-brake driving, which is annoying to other drivers and cuts gas mileage.

"It's the rush hour; crosswalks are crowded. People are hurrying and tend to move impulsively, to ignore traffic signals and stop signs.

"Check the mirrors constantly—about once every five seconds; traffic patterns change abruptly and without warning.

"Don't ride the brakes. It's confusing to other drivers, and wears brakes out faster. Overheated brakes can fade at a crucial moment.

"Parked cars, narrow street—always a problem. Some impatient driver might pull out abruptly or open his car door without looking.

"Intersections. I must remember to slow down at every one and be ready to stop even when the right of way is mine.

"Traffic light. Assume another car will run a red light or a stop sign.

"That car's directional signal is blinking for a turn—but maybe the driver doesn't realize

it is on. Wait until the car begins to turn.

"If I stop here, I won't block the pedestrian walkway or the crossflow of traffic. And when I can start up again, I won't move at all until I'm sure I won't be blocking other cars.

"A lot of bicycles these days and motorcycles, too. Although they're subject to the rules of the road, they can be unpredictable.

"Children en route to school and pets being walked. They're also unpredictable."

Obviously, in the time it took to share this small part of Dave Cameron's experience, he would be far down the street. But that is just the point. Defensive driving is an acquired skill and must be worked at until it becomes second nature. Every now and then check yourself, as Dave Cameron frequently does, to see just how aware you really are of potentially dangerous situations everywhere you drive.

How to turn

Next time you are standing at an intersection, note how many drivers make their turns safely and correctly. The low percentage probably will surprise you. The diagram above illus-

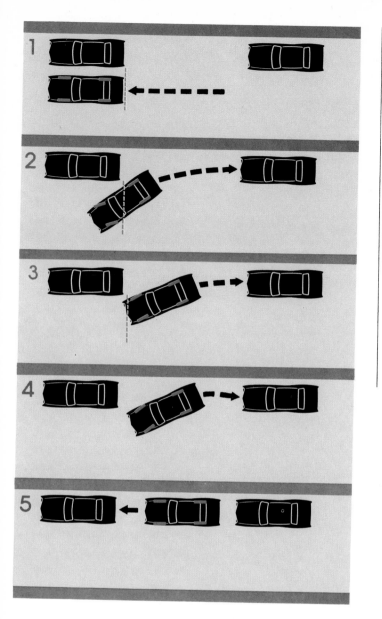

Parallel parking ranks high among the challenges of driving. But with practice and adherence to a five-point procedure, no one should have to circle the block endlessly looking for a better spot. (1) Find a space at least five feet longer than your car —this will give you a two-and-a-half-foot buffer zone front and rear once you are parked. Signal a stop. Pull up beside the car ahead—exactly parallel to it and two feet away—and align the rear bumpers. Check; the position is important. (2) Shift to reverse. Inch backward, turning the steering wheel sharp right until your car is at about a 45°angle to the curb and your steering wheel is opposite the other fellow's rear bumper. Stop and check. (3) Resume inching back, meanwhile beginning to straighten your front wheels. Keep on backing until the right tip of your front bumper is opposite the left tip of the other car's rear bumper. Stop and check; your right rear wheel should be about 18 inches from the curb. (4) Creep backward again, now turning your steering wheel sharply to the left as far as it will go. (5) Shift to forward and move slowly ahead, straightening the wheels. When you are equidistant from the car ahead and the car behind, and parallel to the curb, you've done it.

trates some turning errors and also indicates how to make correct left- and right-hand turns. To review the essential rules:

■ SLOW DOWN EARLY. Move into the proper turning lane and begin braking well before you reach the corner, especially if traffic is heavy or fast-moving.

■ SIGNAL EARLY. Flip on your turn indicator at least 100 feet before the corner.

■ BE ALERT AT THE INTERSECTION. Make sure the road is clear in all directions and be especially wary of pedestrians. When the light

is in their favor, they have the right of way.

■ TURN AT A RIGHT ANGLE. Make sure your turn is neither too wide nor too short. (Before making a U-turn, be sure it's legal to do so. In many congested areas U-turns are prohibited.)

How to park

The diagram above illustrates the correct way to parallel park.

For angle parking—the kind most often required at places such as shopping centers —the procedure is even simpler. Approach the

WHAT TO KEEP IN YOUR CAR

A wise car owner will carry equipment adequate to cope with the variety of situations that occur on the road. The check lists below contain some suggested items to have in your car for three different types of driving.

While some larger articles will have to be carried in the trunk, the items that you will need most frequently — or in case of an emergency — should be kept within easy reach. If your glove compartment is not big enough, a shallow container kept under a seat or a flight bag set on the floor will provide safe and organized additional carrying space.

Everyday driving

It's a good idea to keep the following items in your car at all times:

accident-report form	litter bag
adjustable wrench	owner's manual
collapsible umbrella	paper toweling
drive belts (extras)	pencil and paper
facial tissues	pliers
fire extinguisher	screwdriver
first-aid kit	spare tire, jack
flares or warning lights	street maps (local)
flashlight	sunglasses
ice-snow scraper	tire-pressure gauge
insurance-policy data	work gloves

On a trip

Whenever you're going a considerable distance and expect to be in your car for extended periods, these additional articles can be very handy to have:

blankets	keys (extra set)
cleaning tissues	maps
coins (for phone)	whisk broom
flashlight batteries (spares)	window-cleaner spray

Into the wilds

If you are traveling to remote areas where service stations are scarce, these additional items — which obviously presume some mechanical ability — may save you much time and trouble:

air pump	gasoline (extra can)
engine oil (extra quart)	insulated bottle (with
fuel filter (spare)	beverage)
fuse puller	tire-repair kit
fuses (spare)	wiper blades (spare)

empty space slowly with your turn indicator on and keep about five feet out from the line of parked cars into which you plan to move. As your leading fender draws even with the space, turn hard. Creep forward. Be mindful of the rear quarter of your car on the side you're cutting. If it seems uncomfortably close to the parked car on that side, stop; turn your wheels sharply in the opposite direction, back up slowly, turn your wheels into the parking space and move forward again. Gradually straighten your wheels so your car will be centered within the allotted space and parallel with the other parked cars.

When you leave an angle-parking space, reverse the procedure. But this time be mindful of traffic behind you, and go extra slowly.

Planning a trip

Driving defensively becomes a more acute, magnified responsibility when a long business or pleasure trip will take you into territory that is less familiar or even totally new. Planning for it can be time consuming. But a responsible driver will always follow a seven-point check list. Minimally, the list promises to save many lost hours and avoid frayed tempers:

■ KNOW WHERE YOU'RE GOING. Highways in strange metropolitan areas can be identified by road signs in a bewildering variety of ways. To avoid getting lost, or having to make split-second decisions at high speed, plan your route in advance and know the roads by both their names and numbers. Automobile clubs and some gasoline companies provide free prerouted maps to members or customers. But if you prefer to do your own planning, comprehensive road atlases can be purchased for a few dollars, and service stations usually have up-to-date maps of their areas.

■ BE SURE YOUR CAR IS TUNED. Have the job done before any long trip, and in the hour or so before departure personally recheck such things as tire pressure (including the spare), as well as gas, oil and battery-fluid levels.

■ PACK YOUR CAR SAFELY. Distribute the total weight, including that of the passengers, as evenly as possible over the entire car. If too much weight is in the rear, you could overload the rear shock absorbers and make your car difficult to control. Consider a luggage rack, carefully installed on the center of the roof, as a way to achieve better weight distribution; and if you habitually travel under heavy loads, consider using heavy-duty shock absorbers.

■ PREPARE A TRAVEL KIT. Use the check list opposite as a guide for personal-comfort items as well as safety items. Consider what equipment to carry if you expect to encounter unusual driving conditions. Store at least three or four flares and a first-aid kit inside the passenger compartment (even a slight rear-end collision could jam the trunk lock).

■ SECURE LOOSE OBJECTS. If you stop quickly, loose items inside the passenger compartment could fly about and cause serious injury.

■ BE EXTRA CAREFUL WITH CHILDREN. Babies and other small fry can get hurt more easily than adults since their lightweight bodies are more likely to be hurled about in a collision. An example of a safe, well-designed baby carrier is shown above. Explain to children the importance of not bothering the driver. Car games and frequent rest stops along the way will help keep them quiet.

■ KNOW YOUR TOW. If you're driving an oversized vehicle such as a camper or a van, familiarize yourself with its safety requirements before you start out (Chapter 12).

Road signs and what they mean

A good defensive driver knows that next in importance to the rules of the road are the signs along the highway. These road signs perform

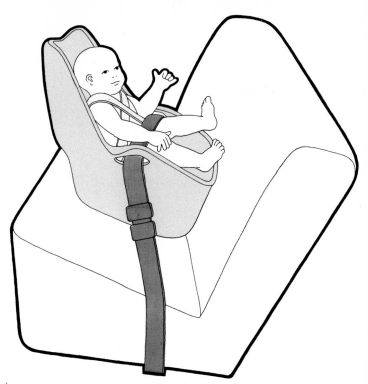

Baby seats come in many shapes—and not all of them are safe. The design shown here is particularly effective because it faces the rear and employs a double diagonal harness to confine the infant. The carrier itself is also anchored by the car's seat belt.

three basic functions: they control traffic, warn of possible hazards and give information. The three categories of signs have different shapes depending on what their function is: warning signs, for example, are typically diamond shaped; stop signs are octagonal; no-passing-zone signs are pennant shaped.

Whatever their purpose, most signs traditionally have used words to convey their instructions. Recently, however, worded signs began giving way to signs that rely mainly on easily recognizable symbols. The most important of these are shown on pages 278-279. Memorize the shapes and symbols so that their meanings will be instantly clear when you encounter them from a distance or at high speed.

Roads with open access

Outside the city, roadways are of two general types: controlled access and open access. Both have their peculiar hazards, but the latter kind —whether it is a meandering two-lane coun-

CHANGES IN SIGNS: MORE VISIBLE, LESS VERBAL

Traffic signs along American streets and highways are being redesigned because traffic experts have discovered that drivers react much more quickly to symbols than to words. The two signs at right mean the same thing, but the new one *(bottom)* is emphatically wordless: a red slash through the black arrow cancels permission for a right-hand turn. The new signs are similar to the international signs that multilingual areas like Europe have successfully employed for years.

Some new signs still use words *(below)*, but even these rely heavily on standardized shapes and especially on colors for ready recognition. Red indicates a stop or prohibition; yellow, a warning; blue, motorist services; brown, recreational and scenic areas. Most of the yellow diamond-shaped warning signs *(right)*, which are the most varied kind of sign, eventually will become completely wordless; but until the motoring public gets accustomed to them, many will also carry a word equivalent, or subtitle, on a separate sign beneath the symbol.

round: railroad ahead

pennant: no passing ahead

blue rectangle: motorist services

inverted triangle: yield right-of-way

circle in square: traffic regulation

pentagon: school area

octagon: complete stop

trapezoid: recreational area

divided highway ahead	merge	divided highway ends	right lane ends
two-way traffic	road jogs ahead	right turn	right curve
winding road	crossroad	branch road	T-intersection
Y-intersection	signal ahead	hill ahead	farm-machinery traffic
bicycle crossing	pedestrian crossing	cattle crossing	deer crossing

279

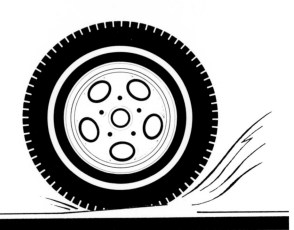

This drawing demonstrates what happens during hydroplaning — a dangerous driving phenomenon that can develop during a heavy rainfall. If a car is traveling too fast for the grooves in the tire tread to displace the water on the road, the tire will ride up on the wedge of water that it pushes ahead. Front tires usually will hydroplane first; but if the rear tires are more worn, they can lose road contact before those up front.

try roadway or a heavily traveled multilane highway—is without question the more dangerous on which to drive. The less familiar you are with driving on such open-access roads the more hazardous they are.

Trust nothing—not even your eyes. Hidden drives, traffic-control devices and intersections are everywhere. You may encounter anything from late-model sports cars to huge trailer trucks to ancient farm vehicles. Traffic lights often are difficult to spot, especially if they are set against the gaudy neon signs of a shopping center.

Stop signs may be obscured by summer foliage; on country roads they may have been knocked down and never replaced. Lane markers often are misleading or worn away. So, always be alert—doubly alert. Here are some tips to help you along:

■ EASE BACK IN TROUBLE SPOTS. As you approach an intersection, the crest of a hill or even a gentle curve, let up on the gas momentarily. This won't slow you much, but it will considerably reduce the time necessary to hit the brakes if you have to stop unexpectedly.

■ BE ALERT TO SIGNS. However battered or faded the signs may be, believe all warnings of curves, hidden drives, narrow bridges and the like. If a sign says SLOW! SHARP CURVE AHEAD you can believe it. Never trust your sense of speed if you think you have to brake suddenly. Let your speedometer, not the seat of your pants, tell you how fast you're going.

Be aware of reduced-speed signs close to towns, congested areas and schools. Now and then the limits they impose are unreasonably low, but it is better to crawl along for a while than to be an unwilling contributor to the local treasury—or to hit a child.

■ MIND YOUR LANES. Stay in the right lane except when passing. On two-lane roads, of course, there isn't any choice. But even on multilane highways without a median strip, it is always better to keep as far away as possible from oncoming cars. Besides, if you stay in the left lane, you could hinder other drivers who might want to pass.

Proper passing procedure

If you follow the rules of courtesy and common sense, passing on a two-lane road does not have to be the white-knuckle experience it is generally made out to be.

First, the don'ts. Never pass as you approach a curve, the crest of a hill, a railroad crossing, an intersection, a bridge or an underpass. In all cases, your vision will be partially obstructed. Never pass if there is a solid stripe dividing the road, and never pass just because the driver ahead signals you by. Despite his good intentions, an error of judgment by him may lead you into a fatal trap. Finally, never pass more than one car at a time. If you're in a line of cars, grin and bear it and wait your turn.

Now, a rundown of the correct—and crucial —rules for passing:

■ BEGIN FROM A SAFE DISTANCE. Start your pass well back—at the correct following dis-

When driving through fog, even in daytime, you should always use your headlights—but only the low beams. Fog is nothing more than a low-lying cloud made up of tiny water particles that not only restrict visibility—sometimes drastically—but also bounce back the light from your high beams. Low beams, however, which shine downward toward the road, will not cause a blinding reflection. Your low beams will not only help you to see better on a foggy road, but they will also allow other drivers to see your car more readily.

tance for your speed. You need to see as much of the road ahead as possible; and if you're tailgating, there is simply no way you can see around the car ahead of you. If you happen to be following a truck too closely, the huge blind spot directly behind it won't allow the truck driver to see you either. Check the road ahead to make sure it is clear of traffic and will remain clear until you finish your pass. If you're going 65 mph it will take almost a quarter of a mile to pass safely a car going 55 mph.

■ SIGNAL EARLY. Flip on your left-turn indicator well before you cut your wheels to turn into the passing lane.

■ CHECK BOTH MIRRORS. Make sure no other vehicle is about to pass you.

■ CHANGE LANES QUICKLY. Your passing speed should not be more than 10 mph faster than the speed of the other car. If you have to go faster, you're passing unsafely. As you overtake the car ahead, gently tap your horn or flash your lights if you have any doubt at all that the driver knows you are there. If he's not watching and you surprise him, a slight swerve could send you both careering off the road.

■ SIGNAL YOUR RETURN. When you are well past the other car, use your right-turn indicator and glance over your right shoulder to make sure you can move back in front of the other car without cutting him off.

■ AVOID LEAPFROGGING. Once back in line, maintain a steady speed at least equal to that of the car you just passed. There are few highway maneuvers more annoying than a me-first driver who slows down after passing and immediately forces the trailing driver to hit his brakes or do a leapfrog of his own.

Three-lane, two-way roads are particularly hazardous. If such a road is otherwise unmarked, the first car into the center lane from either direction has the right of way. Use the center lane only for passing, and spend as little time in it as possible.

Expressways: entrances and exits

Controlled-access highways—usually called expressways but sometimes known as interstates, freeways, tollways, turnpikes, thruways and parkways—first appeared in the late 1930s and by the 1950s had begun to multiply. Designed to move a large number of vehicles (nearly 250,000 per day on some expressways) from one place to another in the shortest possible time, they are basically safer than old-fashioned roads but require an additional set of driving skills.

Getting on and off them is an art in itself. The proper procedure:

■ SIGNAL YOUR ENTRANCE. When you pull into the acceleration lane—a merging one-way road designed to help you join the traffic flow without hindering it—flip on your left-turn indicator and make sure there are no cars just in front of you. If there are, slow down, keep alert and be prepared to come to a complete stop in case a car ahead suddenly halts.

■ WATCH ALL LANES. When it is safe to proceed, begin to accelerate. At the same time, carefully check the traffic in all the lanes moving in your direction, not just the traffic in the lane with which you'll be merging.

As you pace yourself for a safe gap in the traffic, also keep a sharp lookout behind and well ahead of you. An exit is often just down

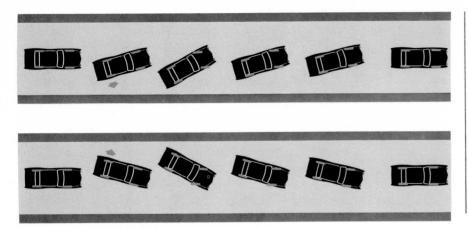

Skids occur when traction is lost by a car's front wheels, rear wheels or all four wheels. The three most frequent causes are maladjusted brakes, panic braking or overacceleration. The car can skid to the right *(top)* or to the left *(bottom)*. In either instance, the corrective action is exactly the same: suppress the instinct to brake, but stop feeding gas. Then, in the language of driving experts, steer into the skid. This cryptic advice may confuse a layman caught in a split-second emergency. But to end confusion once and for all, the phrase simply means: steer in the direction you were going and want to go. (Note the wheel positions in the drawings.) If done in time, the car will straighten itself out.

the road from an entrance and a car preparing to exit could easily cut into your lane right in front of you without warning. If you do have to slow suddenly, you'll want to know the traffic situation behind you.

■ BE SURE YOUR SPEED IS UP. The gap you choose should be big enough so that your entrance does not appreciably slow the traffic flow, and whenever possible your entrance speed should not be less than 10 mph under the lower limit for expressway traffic.

When your entrance is completed, accelerate gradually, but as quickly as possible get your speed up to that of the cars around you.

Before considering the proper procedure for exiting an expressway, remember again that knowing the roads to be traveled is indispensable to safe driving. You should have studied carefully the road maps of any unfamiliar area before you started out. Or minimally, you should have asked for explicit directions, and mastered them. Local signs are notoriously inadequate or misleading to a stranger.

When you're ready to exit a high-speed, multilane roadway:

■ PLAN YOUR EXIT. Think about it well in advance. Begin to move into the exit lane—usually the right-hand lane—at least one mile before the actual exit, and keep your right-turn signal flashing until you leave the expressway.

■ WATCH THE SPEEDOMETER. When you reach the deceleration lane, begin gentle braking almost immediately. Many exit ramps have tight curves, and you should not have to brake

abruptly when you reach them. Again, don't depend on feel to tell you if you have slowed down sufficiently.

While on expressways

Although expressways are by far the safest kind of road on which to drive (the death rate on interstates of 2.5 persons per 100 million vehicle-miles is about half the average for all roads), traffic engineers and safety experts have realized for years that they present other unique driving problems. What applies to a casual Sunday drive on a quiet country lane simply doesn't hold for the specially engineered roads where top speeds in some Western states are 80 mph. Some tips on basic defensive driving for the open road:

■ LOOK AHEAD. At 60 mph you need 360 feet in which to stop; at 80 mph, 650 feet. Be able to anticipate trouble far beyond that distance. Watch not only the car directly in front of you, but the cars beyond it as well. Often a car far ahead of you will tip off the first signs of trouble. Something as innocuous as a flash of brake lights or a puff of dust could mean the start of a devastating high-speed crash. If you react to that warning, and if the cars between you and the trouble have been maintaining a safe driving distance, you have greatly improved your ability to cope with an emergency.

■ USE YOUR MIRRORS CONSTANTLY. If you are traveling at a speed of 50 mph, a car moving at 70 mph will be able to overtake you in a matter of seconds.

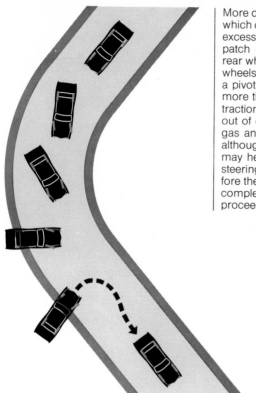

More dangerous than a skid is a spin-out, which occurs mainly on curves because of excessive speed, or when the car hits a patch of gravel, water or ice. First, the rear wheels lose all traction while the front wheels, still in contact with the road, act as a pivot. Then, when the car has swerved more than 25° off course, all wheels lose traction and the car slides completely out of control. As in a skid, stop feeding gas and avoid jamming on the brakes—although short, intermittent stab-braking may help. Try to regain some control by steering in the direction you were going before the spin-out, but let the car come to a complete stop. Then, hopefully, you can proceed on your way.

■ MAINTAIN YOUR SPEED. Keep it equal to that of the cars around you. Your speed will vary with conditions, but it should never be more than the posted maximum and never under the posted minimum—if there is one. Remember that traveling too slowly often is as dangerous as moving too fast. Any time a car is passing you, the chances of an accident are increased enormously by the fallibility of human judgment—and by impatience.

■ WATCH YOUR SPEEDOMETER. Check it frequently to make sure you're moving at the speed you have set for yourself. A clear stretch of road invites a heavy foot on the accelerator and plays tricks with your speed perception. A slight downhill grade, for example, can add speed that you will hardly notice.

■ BE A LONER. Keep to yourself as much as possible. Don't drive beside other cars and especially don't hold a position in another car's blind spot. At high speeds, a slight gust of wind can cause a car to swerve two feet or more.

Avoid wolfpacks—several cars driving together at high speeds. A swerve or a panic stop by any one of them could quickly turn into a multicar holocaust. If you see a wolfpack ahead, stay behind until it breaks up. If one approaches you from behind, slow down so it can get by you quickly.

■ STAY TO THE RIGHT. This applies on all expressways—with two exceptions. If your road is multilane, you may use all but the far left lane for normal driving; but no matter how many lanes there are, the left lane should always be used only for passing. As you approach an expressway entrance, check the traffic in front and behind and move one lane to the left if conditions permit, to help those drivers trying to merge.

■ DON'T CHANGE LANES ABRUPTLY. Signal your lane-change well in advance, and once you've made sure the lane is clear (and that nobody else wants to occupy it), ease in.

While passing another car, boost your speed by about 10 mph—no more, but no less either. The shorter time you spend next to another car, the better off you are.

■ TAKE CURVES PROPERLY. On a multilane road, stay in the center of your lane throughout the turn. When traveling at a fair clip on a two-lane road where you may not be able to see as far around a curve as you'd like, flatten your turning arc. That is, for a curve to the left, begin taking the turn toward the right-hand side of your lane and then cross slightly toward the apex of the curve within your lane. When you are through the corner, slide right back into the center of your lane. For a curve bearing right,

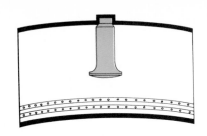

The grooves of conventional tires *(far left)* grip dry roads and shed water on wet ones. For winter driving in soft snow, the deeper grooves of snow tires *(center, left)* give better traction. But never use snow tires for high-speed nonwinter driving; they heat up quickly and are more prone to blowouts.

For ice and packed snow, you may want to mount studded tires *(left)*—snow tires equipped with studs *(above)*—in states that permit their use. Beware: studs damage dry roads and are of no help in soft snow.

begin toward the left side of your lane and drive toward the apex. This cornering technique allows you to see oncoming traffic a little bit farther down the road, but clearly it should not be used if there is an oncoming car in the adjoining lane.

You should never have to brake after you start to turn the steering wheel. If you have to brake violently, you've entered the turn too quickly; if you have to brake while in the middle of a turn, you run the risk of going into a deadly spin. These rules apply whether your cornering speed is 65 mph or 25 mph.

■ BE ALERT FOR ACCIDENTS. If you approach a group of slow-moving cars, assume that something has happened or is about to happen and slow down long before you reach the congested area. Tap your brakes lightly three or four times as a warning to cars behind you. Should you have to slow to a crawl, turn on your flashers and reinforce the warning, if possible, by using the left-hand stop signal —your arm extended out the window, bent downward at the elbow with the palm of your hand facing the rear.

Check your mirrors to make sure the fast-moving cars behind you are slowing down, too. If you stop completely, leave a substantial gap between you and the car ahead. If the worst happens and you are unavoidably going to be

rear-ended, the extra cushion will leave you room to lurch ahead without additional damage. If you can see a rear-end collision coming and the shoulder is clear, pull over out of the way as quickly as you can.

■ STAY ALERT, KEEP COMFORTABLE. In Michigan, a driver slams on his brakes to avoid a nonexistent deer. In Georgia, another driver rolls his car down an embankment to avoid hitting a stalled car—also nonexistent. Both were victims of highway hypnosis, that is, the mental lapse caused by miles of unobstructed driving, the gentle curves of an expressway and the steady hum of tires at high speeds.

To help avoid all these hazards of fatigue and boredom, wear loose-fitting, comfortable clothes on long trips, and make sure your car is well ventilated. Don't eat heavily, especially at night. Play the radio. Change your driving posture fairly often and the position of your hands on the steering wheel. If you do become drowsy, pull off the road and sleep; often a 10-minute catnap is a sufficient refresher.

If there is another driver along, make it a rule to change off every two hours by the clock —tired or not, inconvenient or not. That way, even long, forced stretches of travel are covered without fatigue, with maximum alertness.

■ WATCH YOUR GAS GAUGE. Expressway exits often are spaced rather far apart, and late at night the distance between open service stations, especially in the sparsely populated Western states, might be well over 100 miles. Also, fuel consumption increases with speed. If you have been getting 300 miles to the tank while driving at 50 mph you might get only 240 miles to the tank at 70 mph.

Night driving

There are more than 110 million licensed drivers in the United States and, theoretically at least, every one is a potential hazard. This consideration, plus the vagaries of weather and geography, means you will rarely drive under ideal conditions.

Night driving is the most common of all difficult driving situations. It is three times as dangerous as daytime driving. Why? To start with, obviously you can't see as well at night. Furthermore, one driver in five has a vision defect, ranging from impaired depth perception (which darkness aggravates) to nyctalopia —night blindness. Moreover, drivers generally are more tired at night, and drunks abound. A recent five-state survey found that between 7 p.m. and 4 a.m. one of every 25 drivers was drunk, by legal definition of the word.

To reduce at least some of the hazards of driving at night:

■ CLEAN UP FOR GOOD VISIBILITY. Before starting out, make sure your headlights are working, clean and aimed properly. Wash your windshield and rear window. Grimy glass not only reduces your ability to see out, but also spreads the glare of oncoming and trailing lights. On long night trips, have paper towels and window cleaner at hand.

■ USE HEADLIGHTS PROPERLY. Turn them on before they are strictly necessary. Among other things, they help other drivers to see you. And remember, driving at dusk is almost as dangerous as driving in total darkness.

IF YOU ARE STRANDED

Every year many motorists are stranded —and some perish—on deserts or in blizzards because their cars have broken down. You can avoid becoming another digit in the statistics by following a few simple rules.

In a desert

☐ If you must cross a desert in summer, do it before 11 a.m. or after 4 p.m. Midday temperatures often exceed 120°F. and cause overheating of engines and tires—the most common causes of desert misadventures.

☐ If you plan an excursion on a little-traveled road, tell a local postmaster, storekeeper or any responsible person where you are going. Ask him to notify the police if you have not returned or telephoned by a given time.

☐ Before you depart, stock up on extra water, not only for drinking but also for the radiator. Take plenty of canned fruit juice: in an emergency it will nourish you as well as quench your thirst.

☐ If your car breaks down, use distress signals (page 287). Stay in the car and be patient. If you start walking, you may be felled by the extreme heat or lose your bearings and become lost in a sandstorm.

☐ Stay out of the direct sun—and remember, even inside the car, the back seat is especially exposed. Keep snacks out of the sun, too: if they spoil, and you eat them, they will sicken you. Use the air conditioning in the car for only a few minutes at a time: otherwise the engine will overheat and suffer damage.

In a blizzard

☐ Before starting on any trip where a substantial snowfall is a possibility, listen to weather reports.

☐ Take along an insulated bottle of hot soup or beverage; high-energy foods such as raisins, candy and cookies; and blankets and extra clothing.

☐ If the car breaks down in a blizzard, use distress signals and wait patiently in the car, unless you are certain that help is nearby and that you can reach it.

☐ Keep warm with blankets and extra clothes, and add insulating layers of newspapers, floor mats—anything.

☐ If the engine is working, use the heater. But first run the engine at a speed equivalent to about 30 mph—not at idling speed—to warm it up quickly and keep the battery charged. After the engine has run a few minutes, turn on the heater to maximum and keep it there five or six minutes. Then shut off the engine to save gas. Restart it only when the cold becomes unbearable.

☐ Warning: Use your heater only if you know the muffler and the rest of the exhaust system are in good condition: carbon monoxide in the exhaust fumes can seep into the passenger compartment and kill quickly.

☐ Check the tailpipe periodically—it may have become blocked with drifting snow.

☐ Open a window slightly as a further precaution against the danger of carbon monoxide.

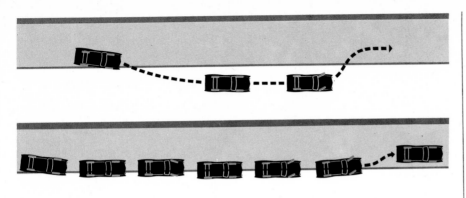

Most drivers have felt the jolt of a front wheel slipping off onto the shoulder. The instinct is to steer right back onto the road. Don't. That maneuver can throw the car out of control. If the shoulder is hard and unobstructed *(top)*, slow down and move over gradually until all four wheels are on the shoulder. Then, when the road is clear, turn sharply back onto it.

If the shoulder is soft *(bottom)* or is obstructed, slow down, ease over until both the front and rear wheels on that side straddle the pavement's edge, and only then turn sharply back onto the road. Be ready instantly to straighten your wheels, so that you don't veer into the oncoming lane.

Use your high beams only when the road ahead of you is absolutely clear of traffic in both directions. If an oncoming driver does not dim his brights, flick your own on and off very quickly as a reminder, but if he still keeps on his brights don't retaliate.

Don't overdrive your lights. That is, make sure you can stop safely within the length of road illuminated by your headlights.

When you approach the crest of a hill or a blind curve, flick your lights as a warning signal to oncoming drivers.

■ INCREASE YOUR INTERVAL. Follow other cars at a greater distance; darkness severely reduces depth perception.

■ SIGNAL BEFORE PASSING. Flick your lights to warn the driver in front of you.

Driving in the rain

Any time it begins to rain, immediately slow down and increase your normal following distance. There are no exceptions to these rules. Rain will increase your stopping distance by about two thirds in all speed ranges and sharply reduce your visibility. Furthermore, there are two conditions when the road actually is more hazardous than it looks:

In the first 30 minutes of even a light shower, water mixes with the dust and oil on the pavement and sometimes makes the road almost as slippery as ice.

In heavy rain—any time the road is dimpled by the falling droplets—a car's tires actually can begin to ride up on a thin but tough layer of water in the same way that a motorboat rides the waves. This phenomenon, called hydroplaning, begins at around 35 mph; at 55 mph your tires may have lost their traction entirely *(drawing, page 280)*. Further, there is no safe way to find out whether or not your car is hydroplaning; the best rule is to assume that it is and act accordingly.

So, if you were driving at 60 mph, a speed of 55 mph might be perfectly safe for the first half hour of a light rain. But in moderate rain slow down to at least 40 or 45 mph. And in heavy rain consider any speed over 35 mph extremely dangerous. If it's raining so hard that your wipers cannot keep your windshield clear, pull off the road and wait for the deluge to end.

Some other hints:

■ WAIT TO START YOUR WIPERS. Your windshield should be wet enough to clean itself with the first swipe or two of the blades. If you switch on the wipers too soon your windshield will streak or smudge.

■ DRIVE SLOWLY THROUGH PUDDLES. Hitting still water at high speeds is like hitting a brick on the road and the impact could jerk the steering wheel out of your hands. If you must drive through deep water, do it slowly and afterward pump your brakes frequently to help dry the brake linings.

Fog and smog

Fog—or smog—can descend gradually or can envelop you suddenly. Either way, when it arrives you're in a driving crisis of the worst sort.

let it pass, then follow it. The big vehicle's lights are more powerful and sit higher off the road than yours, and its driver probably will be able to see farther ahead.

■ KNOW WHEN TO STOP. If the fog is impenetrable, pull off the road and immediately turn on your flashers. Then set out flares according to the instructions on page 291.

Skids and spins

A skid or a spin can be caused by a number of things—slamming on the brakes, a patch of ice, excessive speed in a turn—and the end result often is calamitous. Either your rear wheels break loose from the pavement and your car starts to swap ends or your front wheels break loose and you can't steer.

There are, as well, various combinations of the two. In any event, a skid can be terrifying and it always is extremely dangerous; by definition, your car is out of control. For detailed instructions on how to cope with such situations, see the illustrations on pages 282 and 283. Meanwhile, don't forget that the best defense against a skid is never to get into one. Skids contribute to one fourth of all serious accidents and they are almost always the result of driver error.

Winter driving

Even if there is no snow, cold-weather driving is both difficult and hazardous. Ice can form anywhere, even on a road you think is salted or well sanded; and at night ice that has melted and refrozen often is indistinguishable from dry pavement. If the temperature is anywhere near freezing, assume the road ahead (especially on bridges) is icy and reduce your speed significantly. Remember:

■ REGULAR TIRES ARE INADEQUATE. When the snow season approaches, put on your snow tires. The illustration on page 284 shows the

Occasionally you'll be forewarned. If you see ground fog in a field or a nearby hollow beside the road, chances are you will soon run into a patch on the road itself. Slow down and be ready to turn on your lights. Even if they don't help you to see, your taillights will help the driver behind keep track of your position.

When you find yourself in fog or smog:

■ NEVER USE HIGH BEAMS. The droplets of water will reflect the light and bounce it back into your eyes, severely reducing your vision *(drawings, page 281)*.

■ USE YOUR WIPERS. Fog will often reduce visibility by depositing a fine mist or spray on the windshield.

■ DON'T OVERDRIVE YOUR HEADLIGHTS. Again, this means slowing to a speed at which you can stop safely within the stretch of road illuminated by your lights. And always be ready to stop suddenly.

■ FOLLOW A LEADER. Try to pick up a pair of taillights attached to a car ahead that is traveling at a cautious speed, and let those lights help guide you through the crisis. Better yet, if a bus or a truck is crowding you from behind,

IF YOU HAVE AN ACCIDENT

Even the best of drivers may become involved in an accident: statistically, mishaps occur to roughly one of every four licensed drivers each year—reason enough to be prepared for trouble at all times. Minimal emergency supplies that should be kept in the car include warning flares, a powerful flashlight, a first-aid kit, a first-aid manual and blankets. Keep three of your flares within easy reach in case your trunk should be jammed in a rear-end collision. Always keep the required legal documents in your car. Then, if you do have an accident:

Do these things immediately:

1. Turn off the ignition.

2. Turn on your car's flashers and place lighted flares at appropriate intervals *(drawing, page 291)*.

3. Determine whether anyone has been injured.

4. Summon the police, and medical aid if necessary. Do so by flagging down drivers of passing cars and asking them to carry your message. Do not rely on one such driver; make your request to two—going in opposite directions if possible. If there have been injuries, cover the victims with blankets but administer first aid only if you are sure you know what you are doing. Do not try to lift a car under which someone is pinned unless there is enough manpower on the scene to keep the car from falling on the injured person.

5. If your car is movable and if you have police permission, pull off the road out of the way of traffic.

Do these things next:

1. If another automobile has been involved, jot down the names, addresses and phone numbers of the other driver and of all occupants of the other car. Note the seating position of each occupant of the other car, the car's license plate number and its registration number, and the number of the other driver's license.

2. Take the names, addresses and phone numbers of all witnesses on the scene and record their pertinent remarks, such as "He was swerving all over the road," carefully noting the identification and address of the speaker.

3. Record the shield number, name and headquarters address of the policeman in charge.

4. Sketch the scene, and if possible photograph it, indicating the point of contact between the cars, the directions in which they were going and their positions after the accident. Jot down notes about road conditions: the time of day or night, the weather, the visibility, the amount of traffic, the presence of oil slicks and the posted speed limit.

What NOT to do:

1. Do not offer any information to the police or the other driver beyond what is legally required: your name and address, your driver's license number, your automobile's registration number, the name of your insurance company and the obvious facts concerning the accident.

2. Do not admit to any degree of culpability, no matter how minor; the factors contributing to the accident may be more complex than you can know at the time. Even an expression of compassion to an injured passenger ("Gee, I'm sorry") may sound different in a court of law.

3. Do not sign any authorization for towing without reading the tow-truck agreement carefully: it may authorize excessively costly repairs before an insurance adjuster has inspected and appraised the damage to your car.

In the aftermath, and as soon as possible:

1. Notify your insurance agent in all circumstances, even if the other driver has said "My insurance company will take care of it."

2. Fill out and file reports of the accident with the proper local and state authorities and with your own insurance company.

3. Go to your doctor for a complete checkup, even if you were examined by a physician at the scene of the accident. Some physical effects do not become immediately apparent.

differences in the treads of regular tires, and those of snow tires (including studded snow tires whose treads are embedded with blunt-tipped pieces of metal or plastic). Studded tires are best in glare-ice conditions or hard-packed snow; the rest of the time they may be of dubious value; they also are illegal the year round in five states and part of the year in many of the others. A full set of chains may serve you better for the really desperate conditions of glare ice and heavy, wet snow.

■ TAKE EXTRA PRECAUTIONS. Adding more weight over the drive wheels (luggage, for example, or sandbags) often is a good way to improve traction. In addition, keep the maximum possible distance between you and the car ahead, proceeding at a slow, steady speed; and within the bounds of safety don't come to a complete stop unless it's absolutely necessary. Your car's weight and momentum will help propel you through all but the deepest accumulations. And always be prepared with a small snow shovel.

If you do get stuck:

■ DON'T SPIN YOUR TIRES. This only succeeds in deepening the rut.

■ STRAIGHTEN YOUR FRONT WHEELS. Often this simple move will allow you to drive right out of a snowbank. If not:

■ ROCK YOUR CAR GENTLY. Shift to reverse and back up until just before the wheels spin, then quickly shift to low and drive forward —again, until just before the wheels spin. And repeat. Do not race your engine; the wheels will only dig in deeper. Often the rocking motion itself will be enough to free your car.

Warning: With an automatic transmission rocking your car recklessly may damage the gears. However, you may get out by leaving your car in gear and stepping gently on the gas until just before the wheels spin, then taking your foot off the gas and letting your car roll in the opposite direction under its own momentum as far as it can. And repeat.

If you're still stuck and must shovel out:

■ CLEAR A BROAD AREA. Shovel away the snow behind and in front of all four wheels, and any packed snow from beneath the car.

■ YOU CAN MAKE YOUR OWN TRACTION. Use any gritty substance you can find—pebbles, dirt that has collected inside the fender well, even an old blanket. Put whatever you can find behind and in front of the rear wheels. (If you've been foresighted enough to weigh down your rear end with a sack of sand in the trunk, a few handfuls from that ready supply can now serve another useful purpose.) Often a movement of just a foot or so may be enough for your tires to gain traction again.

Mechanical failures

If your car is properly maintained, you will rarely, if ever, experience a dangerous mechanical failure at high speed. But the suddenness with which such a failure can take place will frighten even the most alert and defensive-minded driver. Prepare your responses to the following emergencies:

■ TIRE FAILURE. If your car starts to weave suddenly, a blowout could be imminent. If you hear a *thwak, thwak, thwak* sound from the vicinity of a wheel, your tire could be chunking —that is, throwing its tread. In either case, grab the steering wheel firmly and take your foot off the gas. Steer in a straight line and don't brake until your car has slowed down enough to pull it off the road safely.

Find a safe pull-off area. Don't stop on a bridge or on a road with a narrow shoulder, even if you have to drive a couple of hundred extra yards. Keeping your car in or near the flow of traffic invites disaster. After you stop, set out flares. See page 158 for the correct way to change a tire.

■ LOSS OF BRAKES. If your brakes fail, first pump them hard. Often you can build up enough pressure this way to get back at least partial braking. Shift to a lower gear, permitting the engine to help slow the car. Look for a safe place to guide your car. Even a brake loss on a downhill grade doesn't have to be serious. For example, if there is little traffic and if you can steer to the bottom of the hill, the force of gravity on the uphill side will then bring you to a safe stop. You can use your parking brake if it is the lever type that is set by hand. Even then, be careful. Apply it rhythmically—on again, off again. The parking brake works the rear wheels only and its sudden full application could send your car into a skid. If all else fails, look for a soft place to hit—a snow bank or a dirt embankment—or even a guard rail if the choice is between it and another car.

■ LOSS OF STEERING. If you lose your steering, there just isn't a lot you can do except slow down and brake intermittently until your car stops. Use your flashers and honk loudly to warn other cars.

■ A STUCK ACCELERATOR. In Detroit, a woman found her gas pedal jammed against the floorboard. Her car gained speed and at 70 mph she opened the door and jumped out. Incredibly, she wasn't killed, but her panic was hardly necessary. She simply should have turned off her ignition and braked to a halt. Have a balky accelerator fixed immediately. If it sticks once, it will stick again.

■ LOSS OF LIGHTS. If your lights fail, brake hard in a series of quick stabs and try, blind as you are, to steer in a straight line—unless you are positive there's a curve ahead. When the car stops, pull it over as far as possible onto the shoulder of the road, if there is one. Quickly light flares or turn on a flashlight.

■ FIRE. First be sure that what you think is a car fire is not just a boiling radiator. Most fires are relatively minor and involve the electrical system. These can easily be put out with a fire extinguisher or a blanket—or, in extreme circumstances, smothered with dirt. If a fire appears to be out of control, move at least 100 feet away; your gas tank could explode.

Fast-moving emergencies

Occasionally, even a good driver finds himself in emergency situations that require quick thinking and heavy braking:

■ HUNG UP WHILE PASSING. On a two-lane road you have just drawn even with the car you're trying to pass when you realize that another car in the oncoming lane is traveling much faster than was originally apparent. It's a classic emergency. You don't know whether to gun the accelerator and try to complete the pass or to fall back docilely into line. There is only one correct response, however, and that is to brake firmly and pull back into line.

If you began your move with enough distance between you and the car you planned to pass, there should be no hazard about slipping back into line. If you press on, you depend on the good judgment of the other two drivers to help you out. And remember, the primary rule of defensive driving is not to rely on anybody's good sense except your own.

■ ONCOMING CAR IN YOUR LANE. Again, on a two-lane road a car suddenly veers to its left and heads right for you. The other driver could be guilty of atrocious passing judgment. He could be a drunk or he may have fallen asleep. But whatever the reason, this is possibly as desperate an emergency as you will ever face.

Your instinctive response is to hit the brakes hard. Wrong. If your brakes lock, you'll lose steering control. Instead, you should stab-brake—hitting and releasing in a rapid sequence—and look for an escape route. With steering control you may be able to drive

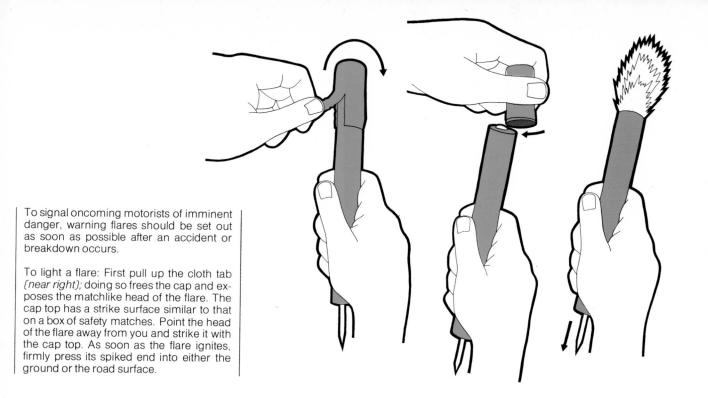

To signal oncoming motorists of imminent danger, warning flares should be set out as soon as possible after an accident or breakdown occurs.

To light a flare: First pull up the cloth tab *(near right);* doing so frees the cap and exposes the matchlike head of the flare. The cap top has a strike surface similar to that on a box of safety matches. Point the head of the flare away from you and strike it with the cap top. As soon as the flare ignites, firmly press its spiked end into either the ground or the road surface.

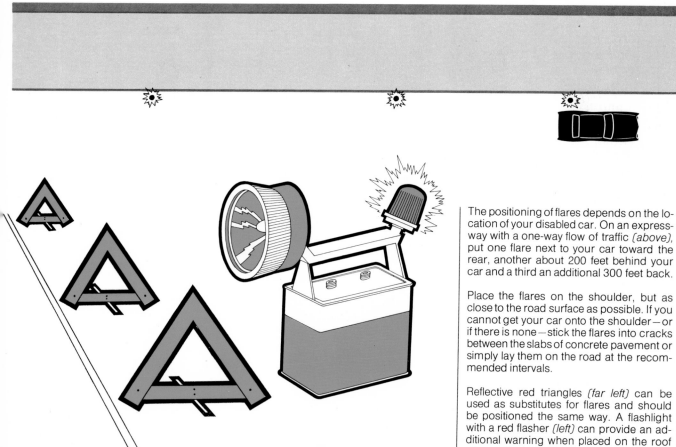

The positioning of flares depends on the location of your disabled car. On an expressway with a one-way flow of traffic *(above),* put one flare next to your car toward the rear, another about 200 feet behind your car and a third an additional 300 feet back.

Place the flares on the shoulder, but as close to the road surface as possible. If you cannot get your car onto the shoulder—or if there is none—stick the flares into cracks between the slabs of concrete pavement or simply lay them on the road at the recommended intervals.

Reflective red triangles *(far left)* can be used as substitutes for flares and should be positioned the same way. A flashlight with a red flasher *(left)* can provide an additional warning when placed on the roof of your disabled vehicle.

TIME OF ACCIDENT	MONTH DAY YEAR June 2 1973	DAY OF WEEK Saturday	HOUR OF DAY 7.30	AM (PM)

LIGHT CONDITION	☐ 1. DAYLIGHT	☐ 2. DAWN	✓ 3. DUSK	☐ 4. DARK ROAD LIGHTED	☐ 5. DARK ROAD UNLIGHTED

LOCATION	COUNTY Green	CITY OR TOWN Leeds

ROUTE NO. OR STREET NAME Route 142

☐ AT INTERSECTION WITH   Triste Street

☐ NOT AT INTERSECTION: ☐ MILES OR FEET   ☐ N ☐ E ☐ S ☐ W   (NEAREST CROSSROAD, INTERSECTION, OR LANDMARK)

VEHICLE NO. 1

DRIVER'S FIRST NAME Pamela	MIDDLE INITIAL	LAST NAME Walker	DRIVER'S IDENTIFICATION NO. TL163775480 037977-44

NUMBER AND STREET 41 Ellis Street	CITY Emery	STATE Colorado	ZIP CODE	STATE OF LICENSE Colorado

OWNER'S FIRST NAME Pamela	MIDDLE INITIAL	LAST NAME Walker

NUMBER AND STREET 41 Ellis Street, Emery	CITY	STATE Colorado	ZIP CODE

PLATE NUMBER 54131	VEHICLE MAKE AND YEAR Tyler 1972	VEH. IDENT. NUMBER 1N69R351	STATE OF REGISTRATION Colorado	EXPIRATION MONTH YEAR Oct. 1974

VEHICLE NO. 2

DRIVER'S FIRST NAME David	MIDDLE INITIAL	LAST NAME Harrison	DRIVER'S IDENTIFICATION NO. TL4755 39374 152012-48

NUMBER AND STREET 3 Laufer Street	CITY Treeview	STATE Colorado	ZIP CODE	STATE OF LICENSE Colorado

OWNER'S FIRST NAME David	MIDDLE INITIAL	LAST NAME Harrison

NUMBER AND STREET 3 Laufer Street	CITY Treeview	STATE Colorado

PLATE NUMBER 70038	VEHICLE MAKE AND YEAR Polk 1970	VEH. IDENT. NUMBER 4F34T854	STATE OF REGISTRATION Colorado	EXPIRATION MONTH YEAR Aug. 1973

INJURED IN ACCIDENT	NAME Janet Hubbard		25	SEX F	INJURIES whiplash
STREET ADDRESS 12 Vine Street		CITY AND STATE Emery, Colorado			
NAME		CITY			
STREET ADDRESS		CITY AND STATE			
NAME					
STREET ADDRESS		CITY AND STATE			

DESCRIPTION AND APPARENT CAUSE OF ACCIDENT

As I was just about to complete a right turn onto Rt. 142 from Triste Street, the car going west on Rt. 142, rather than slowing down at the flashing yellow light, continued at a high speed and collided into the rear of my car. My car ended up hitting a guard rail and car #2 bounced off my car twice and ended up right behind me.

DIAGRAM OF ACCIDENT NUMBER EACH VEHICLE AS ON FRONT OF REPORT. SHOW DIRECTION BY ARROW. USE SOLID LINE TO SHOW PATH OF VEHICLE OR PEDESTRIAN BEFORE ACCIDENT. DOTTED LINE AFTER ACCIDENT TO. SHOW PEDESTRIAN BY O. SHOW RAILROAD BY ++++++

INDICATE NORTH BY ARROW

If you are a driver involved in an accident resulting in an injury, a death or property damage, you must file a report with the proper authorities as soon as possible.

The accident form at right is a composite of those required by various states, since no nationwide standardized form yet exists. The facts on this form represent the minimal information you should record at any accident scene. Obtain a copy of the form required in your own state and keep it in your car. Police departments, insurance companies or motor clubs can supply the form and also specific information about the state's reporting requirements.

around the other car. If necessary, go off the road and into a ditch. Anything is better than a head-on collision. Never swerve to your left. If you do, you're taking away the most obvious escape route of the car racing toward you. Furthermore, if the car heading your way was trying to pass, you're creating the same emergency for the driver of the car being passed.

■ SOLID OBJECT IN THE ROAD. A boulder falls off a dump truck 200 feet ahead and at 65 mph you know you cannot stop in time. So don't try. Stab-brake rapidly and heartily—this is no time to be timid—as long as you can. You'll scrub off enough speed either to minimize injuries or to drive around the obstacle.

Animals are something else. Try the same stab-and-steer technique just described, but don't risk a skid or a collision with a guard rail or another car if the animal is reasonably small. The options aren't pleasant, but often the lesser evil is to hit a small animal rather than seriously injure yourself and others.

■ A WHEEL OFF THE ROAD. This is among the most common driving emergencies—and greatly underrated. Your attention strays for just a moment and suddenly your right front wheel drops onto a soft shoulder. In this case, avoid braking and don't try to bring the car back onto the road with a quick twist of your steering wheel. If the shoulder is an inch or so below the level of the road, your right front wheel will catch on the edge and the overcorrection could send your car skidding into an oncoming lane. For the correct response, see the illustration on page 286.

The accident is going to happen

It's an emergency. Following the rules of defensive driving, you take all the proper steps, but they haven't worked. You are about to become a statistic—the other guy.

Even if a crash is imminent, the rules of de- fensive driving apply right up to and beyond the moment of impact. Don't give up. There is always something you can do:

■ GRIP THE WHEEL TIGHTLY. You might bruise or even break your arms in a high-speed crash, but it is better to stay put by holding onto the steering wheel than to be thrown forward into the steering column or the windshield. If you're wearing your seat and shoulder restraints as you should be, there is little or no danger of being thrown from your seat.

■ STAB-BRAKE HARD. And keep doing it right up to and beyond the first impact. If you career onward after initial contact, braking will reduce the effects of the next impact.

■ SEIZE ON ALTERNATIVES. Aim for relatively soft and flexible objects, and always try to hit a glancing blow rather than head-on. For example, if the choice is between a big tree and a shallow ditch, choose the ditch. If it's between a stalled car and a guard rail, pick the guard rail. Swerve into another lane as a last resort.

The accident has happened

If you have an accident there are many things you must know and several things you should do immediately. For detailed guidance see the boxes on pages 288, 291 and opposite.

Well now, that's a lot to know when all you were trying to do was get from *here* to *there*. But that is just the point: knowing your destination and steering *there* is not enough. Driving is a very great responsibility, and every moment you are behind the wheel your life is at stake. So are the lives of others. To be a really good driver you must not only know everything you've just read, but practice it, always. Only when you can confidently say that you do will you fully realize the potentials for comfort and convenience, pleasure and safety that the miracle of the automobile provides.

RECREATIONAL VEHICLES

HOW TO CHOOSE AN RV TO FIT YOUR FAMILY'S NEEDS

12

Perhaps the most revolutionary phenomenon in modern motor travel is the recreational vehicle—a rolling shelter that blends creature comforts and heady independence. Recreational vehicles, or RVs, come in a multitude of shapes and sizes. But for practical discussion, they can be divided into four categories.

■ THE CAMPING TRAILER: a compact low-profile box on two wheels that can be towed by almost any kind of vehicle. At a campsite its collapsible sides open up to produce a tentlike dwelling. Camping trailers, when open, range in length from 11 to 22 feet.

■ THE TRAVEL TRAILER: another towed shelter, with either two or four wheels. It differs from a camping trailer in that it is a live-in unit, which is the reason it often is referred to as a house trailer. It has rigid sides and top and measures from 10 to 35 feet long, including the hitch that attaches it to the towing vehicle. Larger, and generally more elaborate and expensive than camping trailers, travel trailers account for more than half of all RV sales.

■ THE SLIDE-IN TRUCK CAMPER: a housing unit that slips onto the bed of a pickup truck. From eight to 11 1/2 feet long, this RV usually features a sleeping area over the truck's cab. A related version is the pickup cover or shell —an inexpensive enclosure that fits over the back of a pickup truck but does not provide the conveniences found in truck campers.

■ THE MOTOR HOME: a self-powered efficiency apartment on wheels. In this category are several subspecies. The conventional motor home is built onto a truck-sized chassis and engine, and it ranges in length from 16 to 35 feet. Another type, the chassis-mounted camper, is somewhat smaller and has the living

quarters permanently mounted on the back of a regular truck chassis where the truck bed would otherwise sit; but, unlike the walk-through motor home, a chassis-mount camper retains the truck cab except for a crawl-through space to the living area. Two other types of motor home employ the chassis and engine of a delivery-type van; the van may be modified by either raising its roof to provide more headroom or by substituting a camper body that replaces the van behind, and over, the cab portion.

Within this spectrum of recreational vehicles a buyer can find a rig that will fit practically any budget and meet almost any taste in comfort and convenience. For $300 or so, you can get a pickup-camper shell that provides little more than a roof over your head. For prices ranging from $3,000 to upwards of $30,000, you can have a motor home or travel trailer with a fully equipped kitchen, a hot-water heater, flush toilet, shower or bathtub, air conditioning, central heating and sleeping accommodations for eight. Options include a built-in color television set, a multispeaker radio and tape system, a microwave oven, a bar, and a long list of other luxury features.

The majority of buyers want their RVs to be self-contained—a term that simply means the recreational vehicle can be used, if necessary, without access to outside electricity or plumbing. An on-board supply of liquid-petroleum gas (butane or propane) runs a furnace, stove, water heater and refrigerator. A self-contained RV carries its own water supply and also has a holding tank for sewage. Interior lights usually have both 12-volt and 110-volt circuits, so that they will function either on outside power or on the RV's own 12-volt battery. Some RVs even have a special generator for lights and other electrical accessories and appliances.

The only regular stops a self-contained RV need make are for gasoline and to empty waste from the holding tank (dumping facilities are provided by most big campgrounds and at many service stations on well-traveled routes). The RV owner who has already invested in this kind of rig is in a position to enjoy a weekend trip, an extended vacation or full-fledged retirement living at remarkably low cost. Recently an Iowa family of five traveled 4,800 miles in their motor home, vacationing in Yellowstone Park and visiting the West Coast. They spent only $250 on gas, oil, road tolls and parking fees. And since they shopped in local stores, fixed all their own meals, and slept in their RV, their daily living costs were virtually the same as if they had remained at home in Iowa.

Small wonder, then, that millions of Americans have decided to take advantage of the opportunities offered by RVs. Since the 1960s the market has enjoyed explosive growth. There are now more than 800 companies making RVs, including automobile manufacturers who have entered the field. The number of dealers tops the 10,000 mark. Private campgrounds, operated individually or in conjunction with nationally franchised chains, are springing up everywhere, and RV owners have a choice of some 20,000 public and private campgrounds in the United States, Canada and Mexico. If present trends continue, some eight million recreational vehicles will be rolling along America's highways by the year 1980—an astonishing projection, considering that large-scale production of RVs did not get underway until the 1960s.

Because the RV field is so new and offers such a variety of models, many would-be owners hardly know where to begin. Certainly, any

buyer should start out carefully. Says one dealer, "This is a nonnecessity business. You don't need to buy on the spur of the moment, so you should take a lot of time and care to pick out exactly what you want."

The first consideration, of course, is your budget. One tempting factor in the RV market is the advantageous financing available: five- and seven-year payment plans can be had in many cases. Another appealing feature of the market is that RVs depreciate less rapidly than passenger cars—according to most dealers, anyway. But these considerations are just the beginning of the cost analysis you should make to figure out if you can afford an RV.

Storage may present an additional cost. Some communities ban overnight parking of RVs on the street—and sometimes even on a homeowner's private property. But this need not be an insuperable obstacle to RV ownership—many dealers offer parking facilities, and RV storage lots are appearing in densely populated areas. (There is a storage charge, averaging about one dollar per foot per month.)

Another concern is insurance. It must be purchased separately, since most automobile policies do not include the family RV (even a camper that is clamped onto the back of a pickup truck is not covered by the truck's insurance). Operating costs also are a primary consideration. Gasoline will be the main expense. The larger and heavier the RV, the higher its gas consumption—or that of the vehicle used to tow it. For motor homes, the range is anywhere from four to 12 miles per gallon, depending on the size of the rig, how fast it is driven and whether it is used on level or hilly roads.

Even when you are sure that you can afford an RV, hold your buying impulse in check until you have rented one or, better yet, several. The more experience you have with RVs through renting, the easier it will be to decide whether you want to invest, and if so, in what kind of vehicle. Rental operators are not hard to find and most dealers are happy to rent as well as sell, since they know that about half of all rental customers will eventually become buyers.

Rental prices vary from place to place and season to season, but the averages are not too dismaying. A 14-foot camping trailer can be rented for about $65 a week, a 16-foot travel trailer for about $110 a week, a truck camper, including the pickup truck, for about $100 a week plus 10 or 12 cents a mile, and a motor home for about $225 a week and 10 or 12 cents a mile. Generally a deposit of $50 to several hundred dollars is required when renting, depending on the size of the RV.

When out camping in your rented RV, talk to other owners. They can give you scores of tips, including who the best dealers are. One of the most successful dealers recently confided to a prospective buyer: "Out at the camping ground, owners love to gossip. What they say out there can make or break a dealer."

As might be expected in a business that has grown as fast as the RV industry, the caliber of dealers is uneven, particularly in their ability or their willingness to service their products. There are dealers who offer poor service—especially those who do a small volume of business or sell RVs as a sideline.

But the size of a dealership does not necessarily indicate how easily a buyer will be able to get his rig repaired. A big part of the service problem is that the various parts of an RV may be guaranteed by their individual manufacturers rather than by the dealer who sold the RV or the manufacturer who assembled it. Thus, if an RV owner finds that his stove is faulty, he might have to return it to the stove manufacturer. For engine problems, he might have to take his RV to an auto dealer who represents the manufacturer of the engine. The dealer from whom he bought his RV may be responsible only for what goes wrong with the RV living module—the shell of the rig.

This system has led to misunderstandings between buyers and RV dealers, and to infighting between the RV manufacturers and the suppliers of the various parts. Fortunately, more and more RV dealers are standing behind their sales with a single warranty, and the entrance of the auto giants into the field is accelerating this trend. Nevertheless, don't let a dealer talk you into buying a rig without an ironclad service agreement. Quiz him extensively and in precise detail to see just how much of the vehicle he backs and how much may be covered by other warranties. You should also take a close look at the dealer's service facilities to make sure that promises about repairs can be kept. One leading figure in the industry says frankly: "A buyer ought to shop for a good dealer at least as carefully as he shops for his RV." This is good advice, and all the rules for choosing a car dealer (*Chapters 2 and 3*) apply equally well to the RV field.

An RV for every taste

There is no such thing as a perfect all-purpose RV. But for every buyer a certain kind of RV will come closest to meeting the requirements posed by his budget, the size of his family, the kinds of trips he will be taking.

What follows is a series of stories—based on a survey of market trends—that indicate some typical match-ups between buyers and RVs.

Sam and Jane, a young married couple, had wanted an RV ever since they went on a weekend trip with friends who owned a camping

BEFORE YOU BUY—THINK

Falling in love at first sight with a recreational vehicle can be as risky as with the opposite sex. But many a motorist, encountering an RV beauty on a dealer's lot, is moved to marry the thing immediately. The union may last, but it really should not be attempted without a good deal of thought:

Cost
Motor homes and big trailers require a sizable initial investment. Will the vehicle be used often enough to justify the expenditure?

Upkeep
A motor home or a big trailer is a second house, with all the problems of houses. Roofs leak on occasion; sinks and toilets stop up; wiring becomes defective. Windows have to be washed and carpets cleaned; and before winter storage, tanks and pipes must be drained, as with a summer bungalow. On top of all the household chores add the mechanical malfunctions that beset gasoline-powered vehicles from time to time.

Operating expenses
The engine in a big RV burns gasoline faster than your furnace burns oil. In addition you will need another fuel, such as bottled gas, for heating and cooking.

Long-term storage
When an RV is not on the road, it has to be stored. Most are too big—and too vulnerable to theft and vandalism—to be parked on the street, even if that were legal, which it usually is not. Unless you own a home with plenty of parking space, rent fees for storage must be fitted into your monthly budget.

Mobility
Not all RVs can go everywhere you would like to go. Motor homes and trailers with bottled-gas tanks often are banned from tunnels unless the tanks are emptied before entering. This is because of potential danger from explosion and because changes in air pressure can cause leaks in the gas systems. They are banned on some limited-access roads such as scenic parkways because they are too big or too heavy for the roads. Occasionally they are banned on bridges and mountain roads because high winds or steep grades may make them difficult to handle. Finally, you cannot always pause on a road and camp at the spot of your choice; often you must find a commercial campsite and pay a fee.

Maneuverability
Even a well-designed RV is more difficult to maneuver than a car: harder to steer, park, brake and accelerate.

None of these considerations is a compelling reason not to buy an RV. But be sure you know what you are taking on.

trailer. But they were hesitant for several reasons. They owned only one car, an imported subcompact that wasn't powerful or heavy enough to pull a trailer. And storage was a problem: they lived in an apartment building and hence had no space of their own where a trailer could be conveniently stored. When they explained the situation to a local RV dealer, he said, "You could buy a larger car for towing, of course, and you could always store a trailer here for a few dollars a month. But it seems to me that the best solution would be to trade in your present car for a converted van. It would serve double duty as a family car and an RV, and you could park it on the street."

Jane protested that a van would be too cramped for comfortable camping—until she saw what the dealer had in mind. He showed them a van with a roof that could be raised to provide more headroom when parked. Although it was hardly bigger than an average station wagon, it contained foldaway bunks, a galley, a portable toilet and air conditioning to boot. After renting a similar model for a weekend, they concluded that it was just the thing for them. For less than $6,000 they purchased an RV that presents no storage difficulties, can be used around town, and gives them about 10 to 12 miles per gallon. The couple contends that, for all-around usefulness, they have the best value on the market.

Jim and Billy were brothers, but they had entirely different tastes, as could be judged in their choice of trailers. Before their wives demanded that they put a stop to it, they livened many a family gathering with discussions of the merits of their vehicles—and their vacation styles. It is an argument familiar among RV owners, a good-natured feud between those who like to camp out literally, and those who want to take the comforts of home with them.

The older brother, Jim, believed in economic, unostentatious camping. At vacationtime he and his wife and their four preteenagers piled into the family sedan, hitched on a camping trailer and set off for the wilds. When traveling, the camping trailer was a four-foot-high box on wheels that offered little wind resistance and was so light—less than 1,200 pounds—that it towed without strain on the car. Once at their destination, Jim and his family unhitched the camping trailer, leveled it with its own stabilizing jacks and opened it up into a surprisingly commodious vinyl dwelling that could sleep six people comfortably. For little more than a thousand dollars Jim had an easy-to-haul trailer with its own galley, tap water and portable toilet.

There were drawbacks, of course. Because of the collapsible design of the unit, the family had to break camp every time they moved, although folding the dwelling back into its base was not a lengthy project. And on longer trips, Jim wished for more storage space than his compact rig offered. But all things considered, he felt that the camping trailer was tailor-made for his budget and life style.

Jim's brother Billy placed a premium on comfort. When he drove off with his wife and their teen-age twins he hauled a luxury travel trailer that compared favorably with any motel suite they could afford.

Billy's trailer was 23 feet long and weighed 3,940 pounds. To handle this load he had traded in his compact car for a new standard-sized sedan with a special "towing package"; it came with heavy-duty cooling components, power-disc brakes and a heavy-duty suspension and frame. The carefully engineered towing package on this new car virtually guaranteed trips that were free from engine overheating, faulty braking and the strain on the suspension and

soft-sided camping trailer

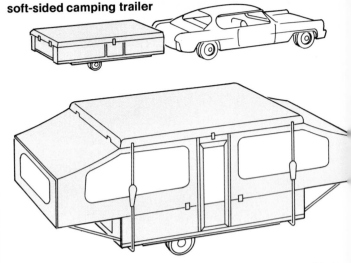

drive-train that might have occurred if he had retained his old car.

Unlike a light camping trailer, a travel trailer requires a special hitch that distributes the weight through the chassis of the towing vehicle and keeps the rig on an even keel. Since there are various kinds of hitches for different trailers *(box, page 310)*, the hitches are not included in the factory-installed towing package. So, for $200 Billy had the RV dealer install the appropriate hitch for his trailer.

His total outlay on the car and trailer was $8,200, but he considered it money well spent. Wherever he went, he had all the amenities he desired. At large campgrounds he could plug the RV into electrical outlets provided there. Elsewhere he could use the trailer's own 4,000-watt generator, whose sounds were muted by wall-to-wall carpeting and an acoustical-tile ceiling. He and his wife prepared their meals in a glistening, highly efficient galley complete with modern appliances. After an evening of watching his color TV, he could step into his full bathroom for a steamy shower. Emerging in his dressing gown, he could flick on the galley lights and rummage through the refrigerator for a midnight snack.

Billy readily admitted—even to his brother —that he was not interested in traditional camping. He saw no reason to leave the comforts of home behind just because he was spending a few weeks in the country.

When John decided to invest in an RV, a slide-in truck camper seemed to be the obvious choice since he already owned a pickup truck for everyday hauling jobs on his farm. But he didn't take the plunge immediately. He rented a travel trailer and a truck camper on successive weekends, then asked his family which they preferred. His two children cast a strong vote for the slide-in camper. With a trailer they

Dimensions: From 7 to 12 feet long and 6 to 6 1/2 feet wide, folded; 14 to 24 feet long. Road height in towing position from 3 to 4 1/2 feet. Headroom when erected, from 6 to 6 1/2 feet.
Weight without optional equipment: From 490 to 2,000 pounds.
Accommodations: Sleeps four to eight.
Hitch: Any of the three types on page 310.
Advantages: Low initial cost; light weight makes for easy, economical driving.
Disadvantages: Because both hard- and soft-sided camping trailers fold down on themselves while on the road, there is little or no room inside them for carrying gear.
Suitability: Good for small, young families willing to rough it.

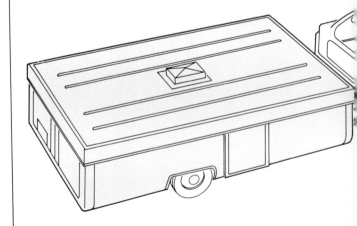

CAMPING TRAILERS

The least expensive recreational vehicles to operate, and in their simplest form the lowest priced, are the camping trailers, which can be towed by even the smallest of family cars. They cost from $350 for a model that merely provides sleeping quarters to $3,000 for a unit equipped with a stove, sink, refrigerator and dining space *(below, right).* These camping trailers are not self-contained; they depend on campground facilities for electricity and plumbing.

Camping trailers come in two basic versions: soft sided, with canvas or other fabric walls; and hard sided, with plastic, aluminum or fiberglass walls. Both versions fold compactly and their light weight and low profile on the road reduce wind resistance and gasoline consumption. When camping trailers are erected, they can stand alone, leaving the car free for shopping, sightseeing or going to the movies. Camping trailers rank third in popularity among recreational vehicles.

Dimensions: From 10 to 12 feet long and 7 1/2 feet wide, folded; 18 to 20 feet long. Road height (folded) about 4 1/2 feet. Headroom (erected) from 6 to 6 1/2 feet.
Accommodations: Sleeps four to eight.
Weight without optional equipment: 500 to 2,500 pounds.
Hitch: Same as for soft-sided camper.
Advantages: Solid construction provides more comfort and security. When folded, its low profile does not obstruct rear vision.
Disadvantages: Higher initial cost than soft-sided camper and greater weight. Takes longer to set up.
Suitability: Good for young families with several children and a need for more than a bare minimum of conveniences.

hard-sided camping trailer

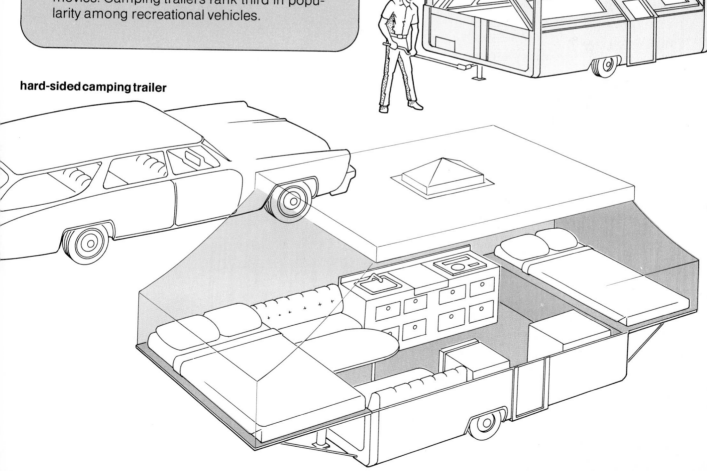

had to squeeze into the truck cab when on the road, since the laws of most states do not allow passengers to ride in a trailer under tow. But it was perfectly legal to ride in the back of a truck camper; and they particularly liked to climb up into the bunk that juts out over the truck's cab. From there they could lie down and look out the little front window that served as their own private windshield.

When John's wife first saw the slide-in camper she had her doubts, thinking that it would be difficult to remove from the pickup once it was in place. She soon found that the special jacks attached to the unit made the job easy (drawings, pages 304–305). Placed on the ground at campsites, the unit made an excellent stationary home, complete with galley and plumbing. Meanwhile, the truck, which had a high ground clearance, was freed to strike off into wild country. It was capable of making trips that would have defied low-slung passenger cars as well as such self-powered RVs as vans or the larger motor homes.

For John, the clincher was the rig's driving characteristics. The piggyback arrangement of the housing unit atop the truck resulted in more compactness and maneuverability than a trailer-plus-towing-vehicle combination. True, the high profile of the rig made him well aware of crosswinds on turnpikes, but the ease of parking and turning more than made up for that deficiency. There was no doubt about it, he thought: the slide-in camper was the ideal RV for his family.

standard travel trailer

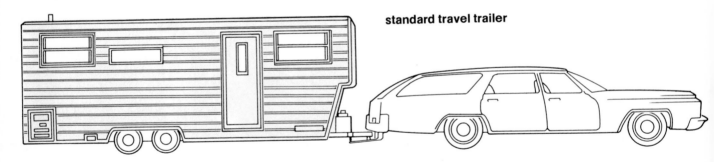

TRAVEL TRAILERS

Like camping trailers, travel trailers are towed, but they are much more elaborate and thus more expensive, ranging in price from $900 to more than $18,000. They come with many —and sometimes all—of the comforts of home, as shown in the cutaway view (opposite).

There are two basic versions, similar in most respects except in the hitch that is used and in the kind of towing vehicle required. The standard travel trailer (above), which has been around since the 1930s, can be hauled by a full-sized family sedan. The ultramodern variety (opposite), known as a fifth-wheel trailer, must be towed by a specially fitted pickup truck. (The fifth wheel is a turntable mounted on the truck, into which a kingpin slides easily.) Both varieties can be unhitched, freeing the towing vehicle for other duties. With 250,000 units sold annually in recent years, these models are the most popular of all RV types.

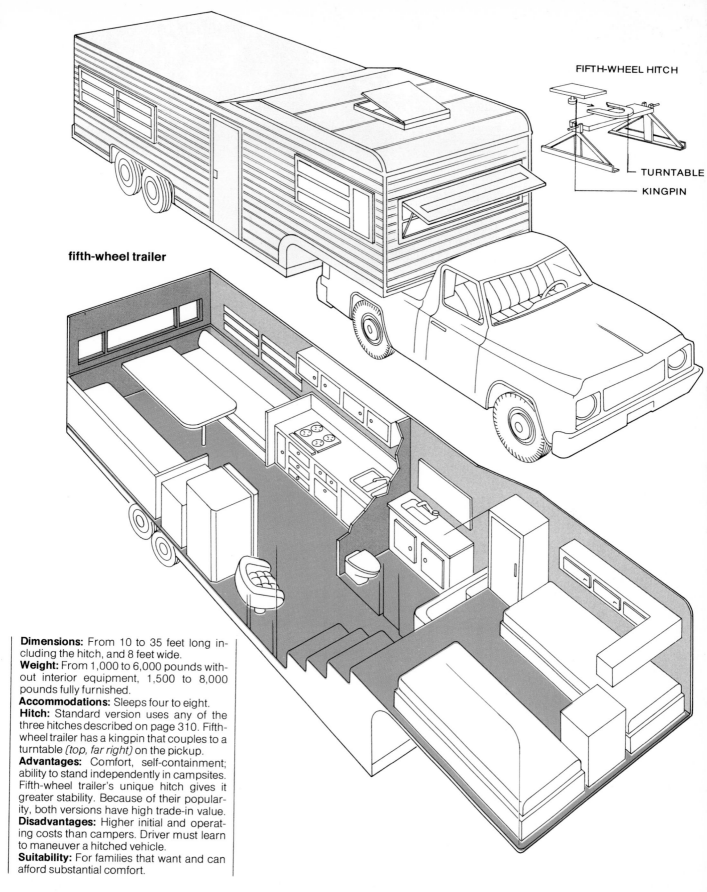

FIFTH-WHEEL HITCH

TURNTABLE

KINGPIN

fifth-wheel trailer

Dimensions: From 10 to 35 feet long including the hitch, and 8 feet wide.
Weight: From 1,000 to 6,000 pounds without interior equipment, 1,500 to 8,000 pounds fully furnished.
Accommodations: Sleeps four to eight.
Hitch: Standard version uses any of the three hitches described on page 310. Fifth-wheel trailer has a kingpin that couples to a turntable *(top, far right)* on the pickup.
Advantages: Comfort, self-containment; ability to stand independently in campsites. Fifth-wheel trailer's unique hitch gives it greater stability. Because of their popularity, both versions have high trade-in value.
Disadvantages: Higher initial and operating costs than campers. Driver must learn to maneuver a hitched vehicle.
Suitability: For families that want and can afford substantial comfort.

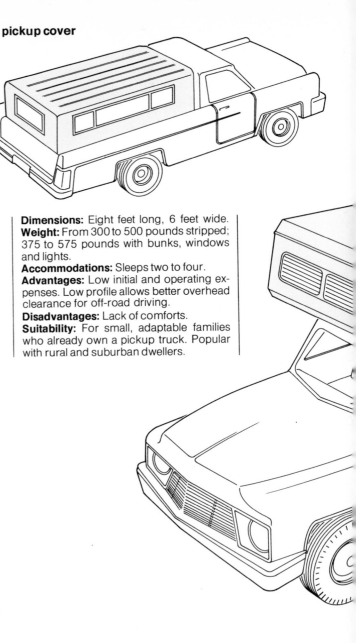

Arnold and Elizabeth, an elderly couple, had decided upon their ideal RV—a conventional motor home. They visited a local dealer regularly, asking questions that indicated they had done their homework. Eventually they decided to rent for a few days one of the cheaper motor homes—a 19-foot model that sold for $8,000. Later they rented a larger $18,000 model for a weekend. After that the dealer didn't see them for a month or so and he thought they had bought somewhere else. Then one morning they returned to tell him that they wanted to buy the luxury model. They had been renting other motor homes from local dealers, comparing floor plans, appliances and driving characteristics. Having surveyed the market scrupulously, they were sure they were ready to make a choice that was right for them.

"How would you like to pay for it?" the dealer asked his customers.

"Cash," Arnold replied. "We've just sold the house. The kids are grown and married. Real-estate taxes are eating up my pension check. We're going to climb into this motor home and drive away. We'll come back and see the kids and grandchildren, but we're cutting the old ties. We're off to see the country."

The model they had selected was well outfitted for this new way of life. It was fully self-contained, with all of the conveniences they could possibly require. They particularly liked the idea of having the entire unit under the same roof so that they could park and move from the oversized bucket passenger seats to a dinette table and then, if they wished, to built-in beds for a nap. What made the large outlay of $18,000 sensible for them was the degree of use they would get out of their home on wheels. Retirees who own RVs use them an average of 92 days a year (as opposed to 51 days a year as an average for younger families), and Arnold and Elizabeth planned to exceed the av-

Dimensions: Eight feet long, 6 feet wide.
Weight: From 300 to 500 pounds stripped; 375 to 575 pounds with bunks, windows and lights.
Accommodations: Sleeps two to four.
Advantages: Low initial and operating expenses. Low profile allows better overhead clearance for off-road driving.
Disadvantages: Lack of comforts.
Suitability: For small, adaptable families who already own a pickup truck. Popular with rural and suburban dwellers.

Dimensions: From 8 to 11 1/2 feet long and 7 to 8 feet wide.
Weight: From 1,000 to 4,000 pounds fully equipped.
Accommodations: Sleeping capacity for eight, with some bunks extending over the cab. Kitchen area, dinette and shower.
Advantages: Ease of driving a single vehicle; much of the comfort of a motor home *(following pages)* at lower initial cost and good ground clearance and traction. Can be detached to free truck for other duty.
Disadvantages: Tendency to sway unless the truck and camper unit are carefully matched for size and weight distribution.
Suitability: For large families with moderate financial resources who already own a truck that can be spared from business uses for vacation trips.

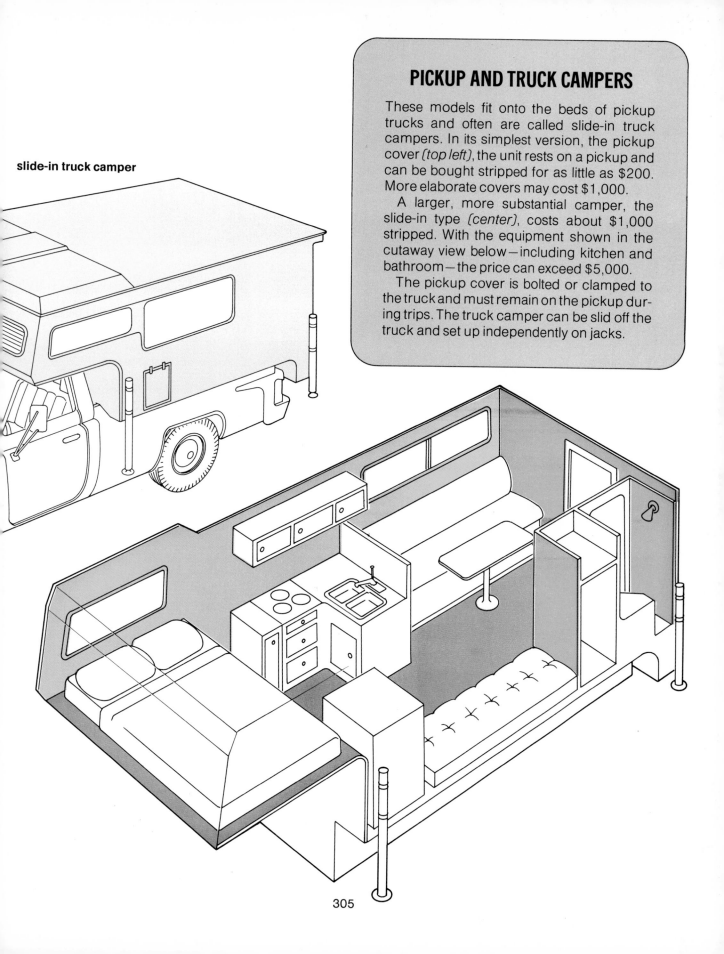

slide-in truck camper

PICKUP AND TRUCK CAMPERS

These models fit onto the beds of pickup trucks and often are called slide-in truck campers. In its simplest version, the pickup cover *(top left)*, the unit rests on a pickup and can be bought stripped for as little as $200. More elaborate covers may cost $1,000.

A larger, more substantial camper, the slide-in type *(center)*, costs about $1,000 stripped. With the equipment shown in the cutaway view below—including kitchen and bathroom—the price can exceed $5,000.

The pickup cover is bolted or clamped to the truck and must remain on the pickup during trips. The truck camper can be slid off the truck and set up independently on jacks.

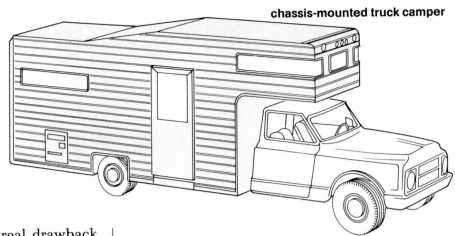

erages considerably. The only real drawback was that the motor home was rather bulky for local shopping trips, but they figured that its great storage space would allow them to stockpile whatever they needed.

Buying a used RV

Steve and Sylvia knew what they wanted—a travel trailer—but they didn't see how they could possibly afford one on their budget. Then a friend, Joel, suggested that a used trailer might be the answer. At first the idea made them uneasy since they felt that they lacked the expertise to judge the condition of a used RV. But Joel, an experienced trailerist himself, offered to serve as their consultant. "Don't be afraid of a used RV," he told them. "More than a quarter of the RVs sold every year are used. Almost all dealers have them, and you'll see For Sale signs on RVs at many campgrounds. It's not hard to tell how well an RV has been treated." Reassured, the couple spent several weekends looking at used trailers. Finally they spotted one that, for their purposes, looked perfect. They called their friend and asked him to meet them at the dealer's lot.

The salesman had assured Steve and Sylvia that he would welcome a close inspection of the vehicle but he knew he didn't have an easy sale when he saw Joel appear in overalls, carrying a bag of tools and a seven-foot ladder. Joel's first act was to have the dealer roll the trailer onto level ground. Then, with his pocket gauge, he checked the pressure of the tires and, as Steve and Sylvia watched in admiration, removed all supporting jacks under the trailer except the jack that held up the tongue.

Dimensions: From 20 to 28 feet long, 8 feet wide, 9 feet high.
Weight: From 7,000 to 12,000 pounds, equipped.
Accommodations: Sleeping space for four to eight: kitchen, dinette, toilet and optional amenities, including TV and stereo.
Advantages: Roominess. Ease of driving a single vehicle and elimination of hitching and unhitching chores.
Disadvantages: High initial cost. High cost of operation.
Suitability: For large, well-off families who make long trips.

Dimensions: From 18 to 24 feet long, to 8 feet wide, 8 to 9 1/2 feet high.
Weight: From 6,000 to 9,000 pounds, equipped.
Accommodations: Sleeping space for six, plus cooking, eating and sanitary facilities, and optional amenities.
Advantages: Lower initial cost. Lower operating cost than chassis-mounted truck camper. Free access to interior.
Disadvantages: Driving compartment is not as roomy as in a motor home.
Suitability: For smaller, well-off families who make frequent, extended trips.

MINI MOTOR HOMES

The three mini motor homes illustrated here are self-propelled mobile dwellings that have been built onto or into existing trucks or vans. (In the truck version the driver sits behind the engine in a cab with only a small crawl-through space to the camper; in the van versions the driver sits beside the engine and has free access to the van behind him.)

The chassis-mounted truck camper at left costs from about $5,000 to $15,000 or more. The "chopped van" *(below, left)* costs from $5,500 to $12,000. Van conversions *(right)*, whose original van bodies are adapted for living quarters, sell for from $4,500 to $10,000 or more. All three versions provide living essentials and even some comforts — as shown in the cutaway view, below — for extended trips. But when the occupants want to go sightseeing, shopping or to a movie, the whole house has to go along.

Dimensions: From 16 to 26 feet long, 7 to 8 feet wide, 6 to 8 feet high.
Weight: From 4,000 to 7,000 pounds, equipped as below.
Accommodations: Sleeping space for two to four, plus all facilities for comfort.
Advantages: Shorter models will fit into most garages due to lower height of vans. Easy handling.
Disadvantages: Limited living accommodations compared to both standard motor homes and the other mini motor homes.
Suitability: For small families who travel far and frequently, but prefer to avoid expense of a chassis-mounted truck camper.

van conversion

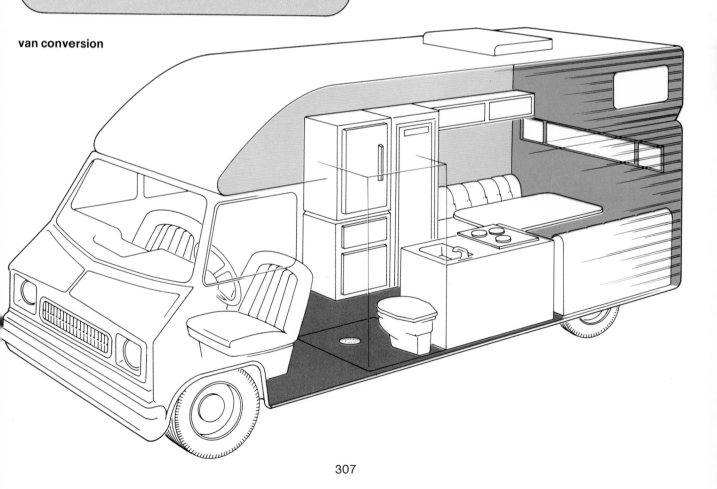

STANDARD MOTOR HOMES

Unlike the mini motor homes on the two preceding pages, standard motor homes such as the one shown here are originally designed and built as integral mobile dwellings. They are the aristocrats of recreational vehicles—a distinction they have enjoyed since they went into mass production in the mid-1960s. And they are priced accordingly, starting at $6,000 for the smallest, least elaborate models and rising to above $25,000.

Because a motor home does not have to be adapted to an existing chassis, its floor plans can efficiently use every square inch of space. A deluxe motor home thus may incorporate, as the cutaway view *(right)* shows, a tub, a shower, a wash basin with a shaving mirror, a toilet with a sewage-disposal unit, a combined dining area and sitting room that quickly converts to a bedroom, plus stove, refrigerator and sink. Optional equipment includes a 110-volt generator for lighting, a water purifier, air conditioning, television, and a water heater that operates from a unit that burns liquid propane gas.

They are indeed "dream rigs," but not everyone should try to realize the dream: they are costly to buy and costly to operate. Nevertheless, deluxe motor homes represent the fastest-growing segment of the RV business.

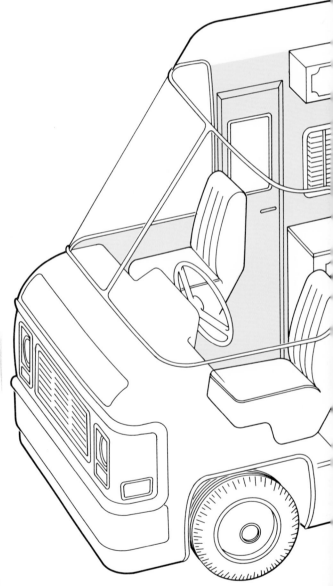

Dimensions: From 16 to 35 feet long, 8 feet wide, and up to 9 feet high.
Weight: From 6,000 to 20,000 pounds, equipped.
Accommodations: Sleeping space and all essentials and comforts for a party of four to eight during weeks of travel. (But measure the beds before you buy. They may prove to be too short or too narrow.)
Advantages: Complete mobility and independence from campsites or motels. Largest load capacity of all RVs.
Disadvantages: High initial cost. High op-

erating cost: the smallest model consumes gasoline at the rate of 10 to 12 miles per gallon, the largest model at the rate of four to six miles per gallon.
Suitability: For prosperous retired couples who spend most of the year traveling, and for large, well-off families who tour in the summer, fish in the spring, hunt in the fall and ski in the winter. In such cases, savings on hotel and restaurant bills might make a motor home a sound investment. But a motor home that stands unused much of the year can be an extravagance.

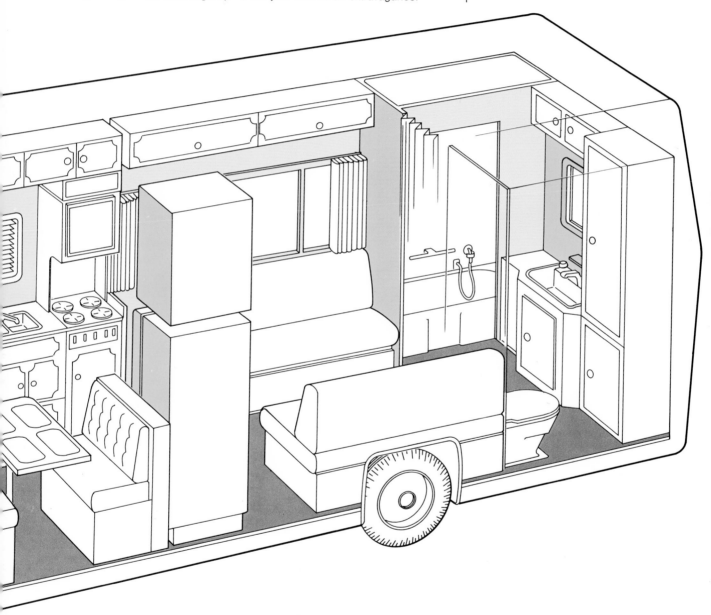

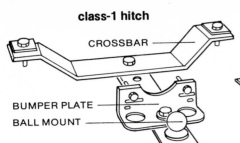

class-1 hitch

CROSSBAR

BUMPER PLATE

BALL MOUNT

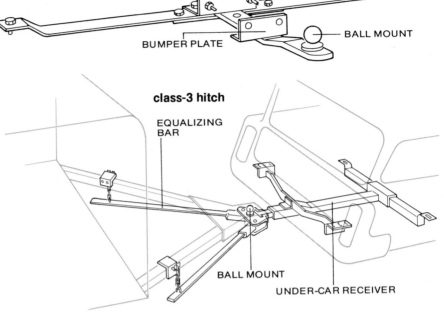

class-2 hitch

CROSSBAR

BALL MOUNT

BUMPER PLATE

class-3 hitch

EQUALIZING BAR

BALL MOUNT

UNDER-CAR RECEIVER

Use of the right hitch is vital to safe towing. The class-1 hitch is for light duty, such as towing a camping trailer with a maximum tongue weight of 200 pounds and a gross weight of 2,000 pounds. (For subcompact cars the top tongue weight is 100 pounds and the gross weight is 1,500 pounds.) Class-2 hitches are 300 pounds of tongue weight and 3,500 pounds gross weight. Class-3 hitches are also called load equalizers because they distribute the trailer's weight more evenly between the wheels of the trailer and those of the towing vehicle; they are designed for 550 to 1,200 pounds of tongue weight and for more than 3,500 pounds gross weight.

By means of a crossbar and a bumper plate, a hitch is welded or, preferably, bolted to the floorboard, trunk floor, bumper or, best of all, to the frame of the towing vehicle. A ball mount provides a seat for the trailer's tongue.

For heavy loads, an under-car receiver can be added to the car's frame behind the rear axle; this special apparatus distributes the weight better than a crossbar.

The three of them climbed into the trailer and, at Joel's direction, stood first in the front and then in the rear of the vehicle to check for sagging. If a trailer lists, the springs could be broken, or the chassis might have been bent out of alignment in an accident. The same would hold true for a truck camper or motor home.

Joel then dropped to the ground to examine the tires. He was satisfied that the treads were worn evenly and still had some mileage left in them. Next he asked the salesman for a hydraulic jack. He jacked up each side of the trailer in turn and spun the tires to make sure they were properly aligned. Then he took off the wheels to check the brakes and bearings. He noted that the brake linings were fairly thick and evenly worn and the bearings were smooth —without rough spots.

After Joel had replaced the wheels, the salesman gave a sigh of relief and was about to talk money. But before he could complete the first full sentence, Joel wrestled his ladder to the rig, then scrambled up it. "Always check the top and corner seams," he called down. "Looks okay." He bent down and sighted along the roof. "Roof's curve is good; no sunken spots to catch rain and cause leaks. Low spots would also be a dead giveaway that the frame is rotted." While on the ladder and then back on the ground Joel checked to make sure that the trim and fastenings of the trailer's aluminum skin were secured with rustproof screws.

Now he was ready to scrutinize the interior. Joel slid the windows open and closed, running his fingers around the door, peering into all the corners. He made certain that none of the interior fastenings had pulled loose and that the windows moved without binding. "Sometimes the trailer body will work away from the frame," he explained. "It's rare, but if you see evidence of it, find yourself another vehicle."

Next, Joel checked the interior and exterior lights and the water pump to make sure they operated properly on the trailer's 12-volt battery. Then he had the dealer plug the trailer into an outside 110-volt circuit, which would power the lights, refrigerator and water pump at campsites. "The refrigerator," he said, "also works on liquid propane gas when electricity is not available, and the stove and water heater work on gas exclusively."

After assuring himself that all appliances were functioning, he pulled a plastic bottle of children's bubble-making liquid from his bag. With a wink he said, "Inspect for gas leaks." He coated the junctions where the gas lines attached to the stove, refrigerator and water heater. "Escaping gas will cause a bubble to form," he said. He also checked to see that all the gas appliances had safety valves that prevent gas from escaping if the pilot light goes out—which happens regularly.

The couple hesitantly asked if he was finished. "All except the road test," he answered. The salesman, having anticipated this would come next, had already called for a tow car and Joel, Steve and Sylvia drove the rig around the parking lot, testing the brakes and listening for strange noises. Finally, Joel pronounced his verdict. "It's a beauty. But you knew that all along, didn't you?" Steve and he looked at each other and grinned broadly.

On the road

The open road beckons romantically toward fascinating places near and far. Now it's just a matter of getting there. But remember this: most RVs are considerably longer, higher and heavier than passenger cars. You must pay the proper respect to all that mass in motion. You should always check the pressure in the tires at the outset of a trip, because tires that are under- or overinflated can produce handling problems—causing an RV to ride roughly, bounce or swing wide on curves.

Don't set off on a long trip until you are sure that your rig is properly loaded. Overloading

---

WINTER STORAGE TIPS FOR THE RV

A garage is the best place to store an RV during the cold season. However, if none is available, find a high place with firm ground, but keep away from trees—branches could drop during winter storms. Remove snow from the roof as soon as possible. To protect the finish, wrap the RV in a plastic sheet —but loosely, so that it can breathe.

- ☐ Drain all plumbing. Add a cupful of antifreeze to toilets and drains.
- ☐ Remove and store all batteries in a warm place.
- ☐ Shut off the propane-gas tank.
- ☐ Remove all bedding and curtains.
- ☐ Clean the interior thoroughly.
- ☐ Shut tightly all windows and vents except one on a sheltered side; leave it slightly open for ventilation.
- ☐ Wax the exterior and smear grease on all exposed chrome.

---

can make the vehicle difficult to handle, cause engine and transmission breakdowns, or damage the suspension, wheels and tires. The manufacturer of the RV specifies the maximum load the vehicle is designed to carry, and you can make sure you are within the stipulated limits by having your rig weighed at a drive-on public scale. To find one, query your department of motor vehicles or look in the Yellow Pages under Weighers, Public; the charge will be about two dollars.

If your RV is a truck camper, van or motor home, a sticker near the driver's door will list the Gross Vehicle Weight Rating (GVWR) —the maximum permissible weight of the whole vehicle, fully loaded—and also a Gross Axle Weight Rating (GAWR) for each axle. To determine if you are within the GVWR, simply drive the loaded rig onto the scale with all passengers on board. Next, check to see that you are within the GAWR for the rear axle by pulling the front wheels off the scale. The load

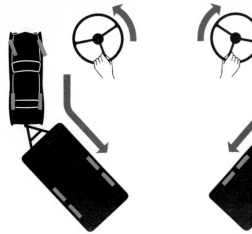

Backing up a trailer can be, at first, an unsettling maneuver for a motorist to master. You must learn to turn the steering wheel in the direction opposite to where you want the trailer to go.

A simple trick for overcoming resistance to this seemingly illogical maneuver is to place a hand at the bottom of the steering wheel whenever your car is in reverse. Then when you want to back the trailer to the right, move that hand to the right, which revolves the wheel counterclockwise *(left)*. To back the trailer to the left, move that hand to the left, or clockwise *(right)*.

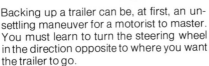

When pulling a trailer, always give yourself plenty of room, particularly for negotiating curves. Keep more toward the center of the lane than you would while driving a car. Before swinging around a curve, move more to the left so that the car and trailer describe a wide arc *(blue dotted line)*.

Be careful not to drift into the lane to your left. If you stay too close to the right-hand side of the road and cut a curve too sharply *(red dotted line)*, the trailer's right wheels will slip onto the shoulder or hit the curb —either of which could cause an accident.

being borne by the front axle can be determined by subtracting the scale's reading for the rear axle from the reading for the whole vehicle. Ideally, the loads on the rear and front axles should be in a proportion of 60 to 40.

For a trailer, the pertinent figures are the GVWR and the hitch, or tongue, weight (this is the load that rests on the hitch ball of the towing vehicle; it is usually 10 to 15 per cent of the GVWR). To ascertain that your trailer is under the GVWR, haul the unit onto the scale—taking care, of course, that the towing vehicle's wheels are not on the scale. For the hitch weight, move the trailer's wheels off the scale and unhitch the unit, leaving the tongue resting on its jack or dolly on the scale.

To avoid overloading, be cognizant of the weights of each of the articles you put in your RV *(box, opposite)*. Liquids are especially deceptive. A five-gallon can of gasoline means 35 more pounds while a spare 36-gallon tank of water adds 300 pounds. Take along only equipment that is essential and carry only the amount of food that is needed for each leg of the trip; additional supplies can be purchased along the way. Police sometimes make spot checks for overloaded RVs and it is much easier to pare down at home than on the road.

When packing things that will stay with you for the whole trip, place the heaviest items on the floor to help lower the center of gravity; this will yield greater stability on curves and in crosswinds. To keep the pots, pans and dishes from rattling around in the cupboards, stuff some rumpled newspaper around them. Pillows, sheets and towels can also be wadded into the dish cupboard. Containers for flour, sugar and other staples can be carried in the sink, where they cannot tip over or fall. Pans may ride in the oven only if surrounded by crumpled newspapers to keep the cookware from crashing around inside. Fragile items such as cameras and binoculars can be protected by wrapping them in towels and placing them under a blanket tucked into a bunk.

Even when you are only renting an RV, it should be taken out on short shakedown cruises before embarking on a long trip. Drive to an empty parking lot or a little-used road and practice the basics—starting, stopping, backing up, parking and turning around. Learn where all the outer edges and surfaces are located and double check brakes and lights. Maneuvering a trailer can be especially tricky *(opposite),* and it pays to practice in a convenient place before setting off on a journey.

A few minutes behind the wheel will teach you that an RV has certain special driving characteristics. Because of its weight it will have slow acceleration, especially when climbing hills. The RV will also take more time and space to stop and it demands special precautions when descending steep grades. Never rely solely on the brakes; before beginning the descent, slow down and drop into a lower gear —even with an automatic shift. When your foot is off the accelerator, the engine will help keep the vehicle from picking up momentum. Brakes that are constantly used down a long hill will "fade," losing some of their stopping power due to a build-up of heat. You can prevent this by applying them intermittently.

Even on level terrain, leave plenty of space between your rig and any vehicle ahead. On turnpikes, stay in the far right-hand lane, except when passing. Keep track of the traffic behind by regular glances in the rear-view mirrors, and on single-lane roads pull over at intervals to allow backed-up traffic to pass. If you carefully observe all these precautions and stay within the speed limits for trucks, you will find that your rig is neither difficult nor dangerous to drive, even if it is one of the largest specimens of this new breed of vehicle.

A GUIDE TO JUDGING THE LOAD

Since the gross weight of a recreational vehicle must not exceed a figure specified by the manufacturer *(page 311),* a driver loading up for a trip should know the weight of everything he is packing. The list below gives some of the more common equipment and supplies and their weight in pounds. It thus demonstrates how quickly familiar items add up to amazing poundage. A list of nearly 300 items and their weights may be obtained from The Recreational Vehicle Institute, 2720 Des Plaines Avenue, Des Plaines, Illinois 60018.

air mattress - 2	motorbike - 84 to 170
auto hand-vacuum - 5	oil, spare (10-qt. can) - 20
ax - 1 1/4	propane (20-lb.
backpack - 3	container) - 44
bat, ball, glove - 6	radio, portable - 6
bicycle - 24 to 33	rope (100 ft., 5/8") - 14
blanket - 3 1/4	scuba gear (with tank) - 71
boat, rubber (for 8) - 85	shovel, folding - 3
camera, movie - 4 to 8	sleeping bag (down) - 3 1/4
camp cot, aluminum - 7	sleeping bag (polyester) - 9
canoe, aluminum - 65 to 75	stool, folding - 2
canteen (2 qt.) - 1	stove, gas (2 burner) - 11
cookware set (8 pieces) - 15	suitcase (collapsible) - 2
cooler (8 gal.) - 9	table, folding - 8
dishes (set for 4) - 20 to 25	tableware (for 4) - 3 1/2
electric fan - 10	tackle box (large) - 8
fire extinguisher - 5 to 17	tarpaulin - 5
first-aid kit - 1 1/4	television, portable b/w - 20
guide book - 2	tent (large) - 37
insect spray - 1	tent (pup) - 6 1/2
iron, electric - 2 1/2 to 4	thermos (1 qt.) - 2
lantern - 6	tire iron - 4
life vest, adult - 2	toilet, portable - 4 1/4

THE CAR OF THE FUTURE

MAJOR OBJECTIVES FOR TOMORROW AND THE DAY AFTER

13

Tomorrow will solve today's problems—or so goes one of the optimistic tenets of our culture. If we start with this notion and give free rein to our imagination, we can assume that time and technology eventually will produce the ideal automobile. Who can say what will or won't happen in 50 years? Our current lives are full of gadgets beyond the wildest imaginings of our parents and grandparents. In 1940 the computer was merely a laboratory device, its practical applications the stuff of science fiction. By 1960 it was ubiquitous, and today a hand-held calculator has the same capability that an entire roomful of computing equipment had a little over 20 years ago.

We are standing, then, in front of Supercar, the best of all possible automobiles. It is swift, silent and inexpensive. It will bounce off a concrete abutment at 60 mph, leaving its occu-

pants shaken (and perhaps chastened) but uninjured, and continue on its way. Its non-polluting engine, about the size of a bread box, uses sunlight for fuel—even on cloudy days. When the engine wears out, replacement cost will be only $31.85 (in 1975 dollars, including federal, state and city taxes). Supercar's color can be changed electronically at the owner's whim with the touch of a dashboard button. Its on-board computer will do everything but empty the ash trays; and a low-cost option available next year will do that, too.

Supercar is whimsy, of course. But there is a down-to-earth reason for conjuring up the vision. Dedicated automotive designers carry around similar dreams in the backs of their heads. For them, Supercar is a target, something to strive for.

The ultimate real-world automobile will, naturally, be something substantially less. It will come as close to doing the things Supercar does as technology and the market allow. It may not be ideal, but in the light of driving problems as we know them it will represent the optimum set of solutions, i.e., those solutions that incorporate the best trade-off between costs and results.

How long we must wait for a real-world Supercar is anybody's guess. The realization depends on the discovery of new materials and techniques that do not exist today. But we have been on our way toward it ever since automobiles chugged over dirt and cobblestones.

Formulating a strategy for the future

To understand fully where automotive evolution is heading, we need to review the problems that are yet to be solved. For most of the automobile's history, changes and improvements were focused rather narrowly on performance, comforts and amenities. America's long and largely uncritical love affair with the automobile reached its peak in the 1950s and 1960s with baroque cars designed as much for ego gratification as for transportation. But within a few short years there have been some radical—and more realistic—changes in attitudes toward our basic unit of transportation.

We are looking increasingly to the automobile for its functional and practical virtues, as well as its glamour. The nation has come to recognize the vehicle's shortcomings as well as deleterious side effects, and in a remarkably short time has plunged into efforts to control them. A list of immediate concerns would have to include the following:

■ POLLUTION CONTROL. While there is a lot of debate over whether automobile-emission laws are trying to achieve too much in too short a time, the goal of clean exhausts is accepted as an important national priority. There are really two approaches to pollution control. One is to deal with the automobile engine itself on a national scale, as we have now begun to do; and the other involves limiting the number of automobiles—or outfitting them with extra controls—in densely populated areas where pollution is a serious problem. Until a reasonably pollution-free engine can be manufactured inexpensively enough to be standard on all cars, the second approach probably will be a part of the strategy.

■ FUEL CONSUMPTION. The job of controlling automobile emissions has exacerbated another important national problem, i.e., the rising cost of energy. Almost overnight, motorists who once accepted poor gas mileage as a concomitant of performance and comfort have begun to protest and grumble. Gasoline prices have risen notably in recent years and probably will continue to climb over the long run. The nation is being forced to use petroleum more wisely.

■ SAFETY. The most valuable resource wasted on the highways is human life. Several years ago Washington and Detroit agreed that something had to be done about rising death tolls —and, after that, the rising cost of nonlethal fender-bender accidents. Federal legislation already has brought about many improvements in vehicle safety, and in the future driving will be made even safer. But there remains some argument over how much of the effort will, or should, center on beefing up automobiles to make them more crash-resistant. The ESVs (experimental safety vehicles) built for the government by auto makers and other manufacturers in the early 1970s were designed to protect all passengers in 50-mph head-on crashes, 30-mph side collisions and 70-mph rollover accidents. They were massive tank-like vehicles, with passenger compartments buttressed like cathedrals, and womblike seats

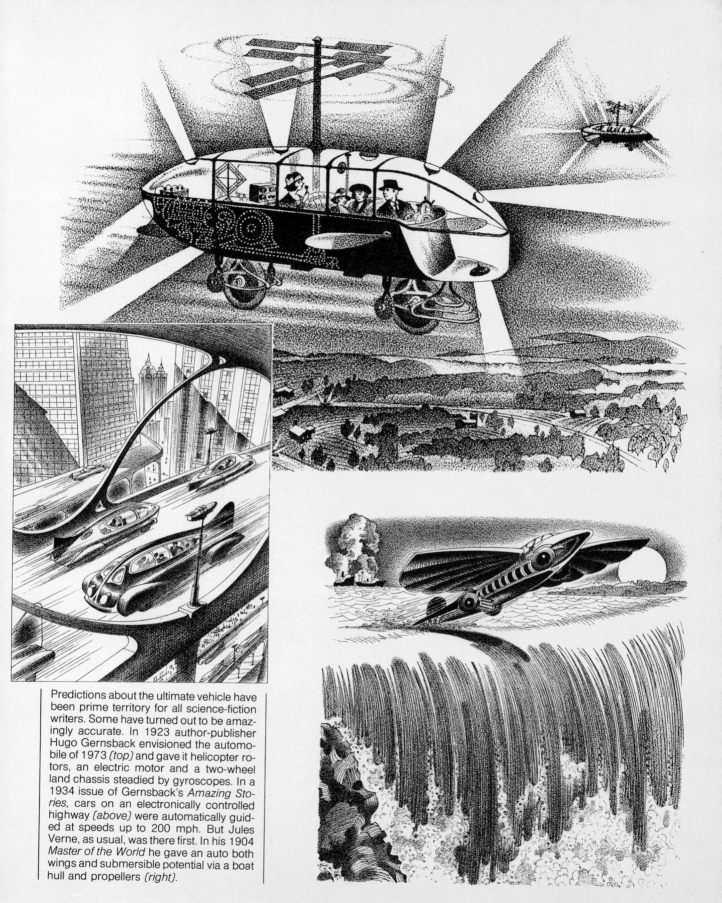

Predictions about the ultimate vehicle have been prime territory for all science-fiction writers. Some have turned out to be amazingly accurate. In 1923 author-publisher Hugo Gernsback envisioned the automobile of 1973 *(top)* and gave it helicopter rotors, an electric motor and a two-wheel land chassis steadied by gyroscopes. In a 1934 issue of Gernsback's *Amazing Stories*, cars on an electronically controlled highway *(above)* were automatically guided at speeds up to 200 mph. But Jules Verne, as usual, was there first. In his 1904 *Master of the World* he gave an auto both wings and submersible potential via a boat hull and propellers *(right)*.

with a variety of passive safety restraints.

Safe as they are, ESV-type cars are ruinous to any dreams of economy. A production model built along the same lines would weigh as much as a light truck but have no more interior room than an intermediate-sized two-door sedan. Gas consumption would, by best estimates, be eight or 10 miles per gallon. It's unlikely there will be a tank in your tomorrow.

Some of the concepts embodied in ESVs will appear—but only in forms that do not add dramatically to weight and cost. And generally improved steering, braking and other controls will make cars naturally safer.

The overall safety problem will be solved best by more attention to highway design and to better driving, though safety experts admit glumly that most people regard driving as a right rather than a privilege and resent attempts to impose limits or enforce stricter standards. Better roads do make a difference; the interstate system has a much better safety record than most of the highways it replaces. And even on ordinary roads safety structures can be made much less lethal to cars that collide with them, e.g., breakaway lampposts and road signs, improved guardrails and abutments faced with collapsible materials.

■ TRAFFIC CONGESTION. Federal laws have brought about emission controls and safer cars. But it will take more than laws to cope with traffic congestion, which is, after death tolls, the most pervasive automotive problem.

As a nation, we have grown accustomed to having personal mobility more or less on demand, and nothing yet has matched the automobile for providing both of the important elements: a personal environment and mobility. But personal mobility is being thwarted in many urban and suburban settings. As one of Detroit's leading engineers observes, "When you ride the subway during rush hour, you've got mobility—but it's not personal. On the street above, a man sitting in his automobile enjoys his personal environment. But if he's stalled in traffic, he hasn't got mobility."

Bringing about a happy reunion of personal environment and mobility will be one of the greatest challenges of the decades to come. Most transportation researchers—in government, academia and the auto industry alike —agree that some of the personal environment will be sacrificed in pursuit of mobility. In other words, there will be more emphasis on mass transit. But it appears evident that the automobile is too entrenched in our life style ever to yield entirely to public transportation.

By defining the problems that have to be solved, we have set up a rough framework of influences on automotive design for the years to come. However, it is not possible for a prognosticator to call all the shots, even for the car of the near future—say, 1980 to 1982. Automotive engineers and designers have prejudices and hopes of their own, as do government officials and auto buffs, and the outcome of these various influences is difficult to predict.

In any case, we can expect evolution rather than revolution for the short-term future. This is because the industry needs at least three years to take a new invention through prototype tests into mass production. Also, the industry likes to put new devices on a limited number of models at first to see if everything goes as it should—and whether the public will pay for them. Some amenities no doubt will be extra-cost options. On the other hand, certain high-priced items, such as air conditioners, that are now optional will become standard —or negative options, just as heaters are today. That is, if you don't want one, you have to so stipulate by special order to get the equipment omitted from the car.

The typical car of the early 1980s probably will be the equivalent of today's intermediate. Generally speaking, its exterior dimensions will be smaller than those of its current counterpart. It will not be smaller inside, and it may even be more spacious; but weight and length that contribute nothing to performance or safety will be on their way out. Plastics and lightweight alloys will replace some panels and interior structures, although steel will continue to be the main body material for many years.

The job of shrinking the car's bulk without compromising interior accommodations will come easiest at first to manufacturers with rotary engines. Every pound saved with the engine makes possible the saving of another pound in overall car weight—and a rotary can weigh scarcely half as much as a conventional engine of the same output, while taking up only a quarter of the space. In a car designed especially to take advantage of this compactness, the extra space constitutes a free gift of interior room, or of space for energy-absorbing bumpers or whatever.

Electronic marvels to come

Even if nothing else were to change, innovations in electronics over the next decade should dramatically transform the automobile and the art of driving it. The technology that has revolutionized consumer appliances has only begun to show up in the automobile; there are enormous areas of performance, design and safety that will benefit from the application of transistors, integrated circuits and small-computer technology. For the probabilities of 1980, a check list would include:

■ DIAGNOSTIC SENSORS. Linked to various parts of the car's engine and running gear, they will be connected to a print-out terminal or socket that can be hooked up to a computer. The result will be a quick reading on needed

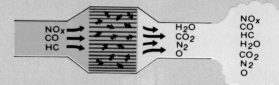

THE CATALYTIC CONVERTER

Designed to curb automotive pollution, the catalytic converter is a new wrinkle in an old technology. Industry has long capitalized on the ability of certain materials to stimulate chemical reactions while remaining unchanged themselves. The catalytic converter for cars uses noble metals such as platinum and palladium as catalysts or base metals such as copper, nickel and chromium. Reacting with the heat of the exhaust stream, they change most of the noxious combustion products into harmless or inert substances.

Two opposing chemical processes—reduction and oxidation—are needed to eliminate the three main automotive pollutants: oxides of nitrogen, carbon monoxide and hydrocarbons. Reduction strips oxygen atoms from oxides of nitrogen, compounds that contribute to smog, leaving elemental nitrogen and oxygen. Oxidation adds oxygen atoms both to carbon monoxide and to unburned hydrocarbons; as the exhaust passes over the catalyst, a molecule of poisonous carbon monoxide receives an additional oxygen atom and becomes essentially harmless carbon dioxide. At the same time, the hydrocarbons, which are the main ingredients of smog, combine with oxygen to become carbon dioxide and water vapor.

Catalysts, however, are sensitive to extreme temperature variations and can be ruined by a misfiring engine. They also are vulnerable to lead and other contaminants in gasoline.

The diagram above shows an idealized converter combining both oxidation and reduction reactions in a single canister. Oxides of nitrogen (NO_x), carbon monoxide (CO) and hydrocarbons (HC) pass through the catalyst and emerge as water vapor (H_2O), carbon dioxide (CO_2), nitrogen (N_2) and oxygen (O_2). In actual practice, reduction occurs first; then air is injected into the exhaust stream, providing oxygen for oxidation.

maintenance. This system will be an elaboration of one that a European manufacturer was offering in the early '70s.

■ COMPUTERIZED FUEL CONTROLS. Electronic fuel injection, already in use on some cars, or electronically controlled carburetion, will become standard. Computerized controls adjust fuel-air mixtures for best performance and least pollution.

■ ELECTRONIC IGNITION. The conventional mechanical distributor with its moving rotor and points will be replaced by solid-state components. This system, already used on many cars (page 41), will become standard. Among its advantages are greater reliability and more precise spark timing.

■ ANTISKID BRAKING. Tiny computers built into every brake system will sense impending wheel lock-up, and then will cause the brakes to be released and immediately reapplied—in a lightning-fast version of the stab braking that skilled drivers undertake in trying to avoid a skid on a slippery surface.

■ EXTERNAL OVERRIDES. Radar or microwave systems will warn drivers when they are following the car ahead too closely. And with the advent of fail-safe circuitry, they will also brake the car automatically if the driver fails to respond to the warning.

■ NEW INSTRUMENTATION. Advanced electronics will add some new and important information to that conveyed by today's standard dashboard light array. Wheel-mounted sensors could, for example, monitor tire pressures; others could inform the driver of low transmission fluid or high exhaust emissions.

Liquid-crystal dashboard panels—enlarged versions of the faces being used today in some electronic wristwatches—may be in wide production. Simple and reliable, they would give bright, clear readings, either in words or in digital figures, of all the information now conveyed through conventional dials, gauges and lights. Further, some information—speed, for example—might be projected onto the lower part of the windshield so that drivers would not have to take their eyes off the road.

The foregoing is not by any means an exhaustive list of likely electronic gadgets. Several manufacturers, for example, are experimenting with electronic devices that may prevent intoxicated persons from driving tomorrow's cars. One such drunk-discourager features a panel on the dash with a needle that moves back and forth after the driver turns the key. Before the ignition will function, the driver must turn the steering wheel just enough to keep the needle from swinging outside a designated area. He has from five to 10 seconds to complete the test, and may get a second or third chance; but if ultimately he fails, the car will not start.

A highly computerized car might also come with an elaborate brake-light system in the rear. Different brake-light colors would carry strong, unambiguous messages. Red would mean "driver stopping." Yellow, "foot off the accelerator—watch it." Green, "he's running; foot on the accelerator."

The radio may also figure in the automobile of the 1980s as a more utilitarian piece of equipment. Auto manufacturers are experimenting with a radio-alert system that uses the citizens' band wavelengths and warns drivers by means of roadside transmitters of changed highway conditions ahead. It works through the car radio, overriding normal broadcasting if the radio is turned on, and activating the radio if it is off. In another variation, motorists could use inexpensive transmitters in their cars to summon aid in the event of a breakdown or accident by calling in a report to nearby police cars or service centers.

For some people, the prospect of elaborate new gadgetry may appear to be more like a threat than a promise. "More things to go wrong," you might say—especially if you have recently paid a hefty repair bill for troubles that may not have been entirely solved. But a great deal of attention will be devoted in the coming years to making cars easier to maintain, despite their increasing complexity. More and more parts will be made into modular units —plug-in components that are easy to remove and replace. They could range from single instruments to entire accessory groups within the engine itself—for example, a combined carburetor-plus-distributor assembly.

The exact appearance of the 1980s car is, naturally, the stylist's secret. But design experts in Detroit are just about unanimous in proclaiming that it will be strongly influenced by aerodynamics. Its shape will be, according to some design engineers, more slippery.

Several years ago, the automobile companies renamed their styling sections; today, they are called design divisions. It was a change signifying a new emphasis on the functional. The car of the 1980s will reflect continuing efforts to adapt machine to man, rather than vice versa. Changes of this sort will not always be dramatic, but they will tend to eliminate the minor annoyances and deficiencies that are present to some degree in practically every automobile. Seats will give better support and will be more adjustable. Instruments will be positioned differently to make them more readable. Even the interior climate will be controlled: most windows will be permanently sealed, and improved air conditioners will keep the passenger compartment at a preselected year-round temperature. The car will be a more comfortable personal environment.

So far, we've been dealing with familiar vehicles and familiar concepts; it is not too hard,

HOW A BATTERY WORKS

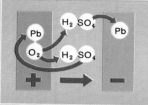 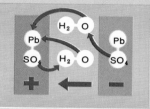

DISCHARGING   CHARGING

Power for an electric car, in its present stage of development, comes from the lead-acid battery design that provides electricity in your automobile. The schematic drawings above show a battery cell as it is discharging—that is, producing electricity chemically *(left)*—and as it is being recharged *(right)*, which reverses the reactions and returns the battery to its original chemical state. A standard 12-volt battery has six cells, each of which works the same way.

A battery cell has three basic components: positive plates made of lead peroxide (PbO_2), negative plates of pure lead (Pb), and a solution called electrolyte that contains water and sulfuric acid (H_2SO_4). When the cell is producing electricity, a chemical reaction takes place: the sulfuric acid reacts with the lead in both plates to form lead sulfate ($PbSO_4$). The interaction between the plates and the acid creates a flow of electric current *(straight arrow pointing right)*.

At the same time, however, the oxygen (O) from the positive plates joins the hydrogen (H) of the electrolyte to produce water (H_2O). As discharging continues, this manufactured water dilutes the electrolyte until eventually it halts the chemical reaction—and the production of electricity.

The cell must then be recharged. Electricity from an outside source reverses the discharging procedure *(straight arrow pointing left)*. The electricity breaks down the lead sulfate and water into their basic chemicals, which regroup into their original chemical structure. Now the cell can begin generating electricity again. Eventually, however, the chemically active materials erode and the battery can no longer accept a charge.

Recharging is slow and inconvenient. Some new battery designs, however, may yet make possible an efficient electric car *(pages 332-333)*.

after all, to peer a few years ahead. The car of the early 1980s represents the logical evolution from today's car. But what of the day after tomorrow — the car of 1990 or 2000, or even later?

Those shapes approaching us far down the highway are obscured and hazy. There is room in between for mirages; even the most sharp-eyed among us cannot fully trust his vision. J . B . S . Haldane, a British scientist, insisted in 1925 that men would live on the moon long before they learned how to split the atom.

We cannot say flatly with full confidence, "In 2000, cars will look like *this*, or go *that* fast." We cannot predict, for that matter, what an inventor will conceive next year that could radically alter our lives in 1990 or 2010.

We can, however, weigh probabilities. We know, generally, what the needs are: safe, clean, swift, reliable, cheap, convenient, flexible transportation. Also, as a general rule, inventions become mass-production reality only if there is a strong market demand and if the benefits that they offer can justify the cost of producing them.

With these caveats in mind, we can proceed to speculate about a central feature of the car of tomorrow: the engine. There is a popular assumption that the internal-combustion engine will someday be displaced by something better. The assumption may well be wrong, but the fact remains that never before have there been so many attractive-looking alternatives:
■ THE RANKINE-CYCLE ENGINE . If the name is unfamiliar, the most common version of this machine is not. William Rankine was a Scottish engineer and physicist who, more than a century ago, described in detail the thermodynamic cycle of vapor engines. Such engines are powered by heating a liquid beyond the boiling point and utilizing the energy of expanding gas. The steam engine, employing ordinary water as its working fluid, is by far the most fa-miliar example of the Rankine-cycle engine.

There is something satisfying about the idea that a power plant *(page 11)* that is even older than the industrial revolution could return to dominate transportation in the future. But the Rankine engine has much more to recommend it than nostalgia. Like other forms of external-combustion engines, it burns inexpensive low-grade fuels such as kerosene or fuel oil. And it produces fewer pollutants than the internal-combustion engine, since the fuel is not consumed in a series of explosions that yield many unwanted by-products.

The theoretical efficiency of the Rankine engine — meaning its ability to convert heat energy into useful power — is somewhat inferior to that of the internal-combustion engine. Nevertheless, in practice it appears to have the potential for becoming more efficient. The reason for this seeming paradox is that the internal-combustion engine can supply its maximum torque, or turning power, only at relatively high speeds. But the Rankine engine can produce its full measure of torque at low speed when power is most needed. The ability of the engine to deliver full power over a very broad range of speeds means that the Rankine could perform with only a simple transmission or perhaps none at all. A Rankine engine producing 168 horsepower can actually give the same propelling power as a 250-horsepower engine in a conventional car.

Rankine engines also should be more reliable. Their proponents say that practically the only attention needed would be periodic cleaning of the burner.

However, there is a long road between the prototypes now being tested — by a half dozen or more Rankine-engine companies — and the assembly lines of Detroit. At the present stage of development, water is the main candidate for a working fluid. But the steam engine is relatively bulky, because it requires a large heat-exchanger, or radiator, to condense the steam back into water. Furthermore, currently feasible designs fall short of the maximum theoretical efficiency for steam engines. To achieve the maximum efficiency, they would have to superheat the steam to temperatures upwards of 2,000° F. This is impractical because such temperatures would cause the engine's oils to break down into small droplets and lose their lubricating properties.

A lot of effort has gone into the quest for some working fluid other than water. Freon and benzene have been considered, and they possess some definite advantages: they vaporize at much lower temperatures and actually act as lubricants—thus eliminating the need for oil. But all of the alternative fluids tested so far fall short in one critical respect or another. They are either flammable or toxic or disintegrate under the demands made upon them. The ideal working fluid is not yet in sight; it could be discovered next week—or never.

■ THE ELECTRIC MOTOR. Like the steam car, the electric car is a long way from mass production. Nevertheless, electrics seem to stand a better chance of getting on the road sooner and in larger numbers, because they could fill a specific niche in the multicar market of tomorrow: that of a compact short-distance vehicle for urban traffic.

The theoretical advantages of the electric car are fairly well known. Such a vehicle could be quiet, dependable, simple to operate and nonpolluting. The last of these virtues needs some qualification, however. As part of our present energy system, a mass-produced electric car would create a multitude of new problems. The pollution that is not emitted by the car itself would result from power-generating stations necessary to charge its batteries—unless some tremendous new means of gener-

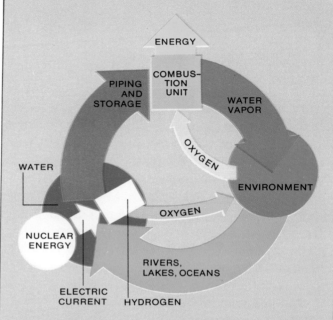

HYDROGEN: THE MOST EFFICIENT FUEL

The environmentally perfect energy cycle calls for a fuel that comes from water. The fuel is hydrogen, and because it is clean, abundant and theoretically cheap, it has attracted rising industrial and scientific interest as the fuel of the future.

The primary source of hydrogen is, of course, water. An electric current passed through water breaks the water down into hydrogen and oxygen. Ignited, the hydrogen burns cleanly in air, where it again combines with oxygen to form water vapor, its only major waste product. The vapor eventually passes through the environment and returns to water—and the cycle begins all over again.

Hydrogen can be as safe as other fuels, such as gasoline or natural gas, when it is handled with modern technological methods (the disastrous explosion of the dirigible *Hindenburg* in 1937 demonstrated only that hydrogen is dangerous when used for the wrong purposes).

But immense amounts of electricity will be required to produce hydrogen in the great quantities needed. Therefore, widespread use of hydrogen as a fuel awaits the perfection of clean nuclear electric power, or bountiful electrical production from such nonpolluting sources as geothermal and solar power.

ating energy is developed. What's more, it will be necessary to find some way around another wasteful step: the storage battery, where power is lost in the course of charging and discharging.

Ecology aside, one of the biggest technological problems is that batteries just don't pack enough power to make the electric car competitive in performance with gasoline-powered vehicles. Energy-producing sources are rated by two yardsticks: energy density, the total amount of energy a given unit of the source can hold; and power density, the total amount of power available at a given moment.

The common lead-acid battery has an energy-density rating of about 12 watt-hours per pound of its own weight, and a power-density rating of some 32 watts per pound. Some batteries that employ different materials—lithium and chlorine, for example, or zinc and air—have considerably higher ratings than the lead-acid battery. But none of them can match gasoline, which has between 600 and 1,500 times the energy density of a lead-acid battery and anywhere from 5 to 12 times the power density. As a result, electric vehicles are limited in range and speed—the more so in cold weather because batteries lose efficiency as the temperature drops.

One possible way of augmenting the battery is to use the hybrid vehicle, in which a small gasoline-powered engine turns a generator to keep the batteries charged. Because of its compact size and generally constant running speed, the engine would produce very little pollution and give good fuel economy. But a hybrid car, with its two separate power systems, would be much more complex and costly than a pure electric or gasoline-powered vehicle.

Meantime, there are ways around the limitations of the battery. In most urban settings, the low top speed and short range of an electric minicar might not be serious handicaps. Furthermore, over the next few years, lead-acid batteries can be expected to become more efficient—perhaps enough to push the electric into a slightly more reasonable performance category. And who knows? Maybe materials as yet undiscovered will make possible a battery that possesses energy and power densities competitive with those of gasoline.

■ THE GAS-TURBINE ENGINE. This power plant is another strong contender for the engine of the future, but today it has problems. The engine's high operating temperature requires that special, costly alloys be used in the combustion chambers. The turbines and complicated heat-exchangers needed to make the engine efficient also make it bulky. Nor is it free from pollution. Finally, automotive-type turbines tend to be inefficient in stop-and-go driving and under light loads—conditions that characterize much of the typical automobile's driving pattern.

But the turbine can use the same low-grade fuels as the Rankine-cycle engine. Researchers are striving to develop ceramic materials to take the place of expensive heat-resistant metal alloys. But for at least the time being, the gas-turbine engine will be used increasingly in trucks, where bulkiness is not such a serious drawback and where extra costs are offset by high efficiency at full-load conditions.

■ THE STIRLING-CYCLE ENGINE. A lesser-known alternative to present-day engines, the external-combustion Stirling-cycle engine utilizes a gas such as hydrogen or helium within a closed system; the gas is alternately heated and cooled to drive pistons up and down (page 327). The Stirling has all of the advantages of other external-combustion engines, plus a few extra ones. It is virtually noiseless and vibrationless, has few moving parts, and is extremely rugged and durable.

One excellent application might be in a hybrid electric car. However, the engine today is a complicated machine that requires costly metals and a sophisticated heat exchanger, and it is extremely expensive to build. Certainly the Stirling is farther from production than the steam, turbine or electric engines.

■ THE VERSATILE VETERAN. Despite the challenge that is being mounted by so many feisty competitors, the two kinds of internal-combustion engine in common use today—rotary and reciprocating—stand a better than even chance of being around well into the 21st Century. Beyond a reasonable doubt the reciprocating engine is the most improbable design of all: with its thousands of parts, wrenching forces and flailing masses of metal, it would seem at first glance a terrible way to generate power. Yet this engine sets the performance standards that all others must match or exceed. Some engineers argue that any further refinements of the reciprocating design are virtually impossible. But other engineers and inventors still continue to crop up with new improvements. One of the most remarkable recent examples is the stratified-charge system at right, which basically provides two different fuel-air mixtures to the engine at the same time, improving combustion and thereby expanding the possibilities for making the reciprocating engine cleaner and more efficient.

Engineers have only begun to refine the design of the Wankel rotary engine for the best performance, mileage and emission control. The rotary is, in fact, at about the same stage of development that the conventional engine was 30 or 40 years ago, and there is every reason to expect substantial improvements. Stratified charge, for example, may well prove to be achievable in the rotary at little extra cost and with no great increase in complexity. And some manufacturers are experimenting with a

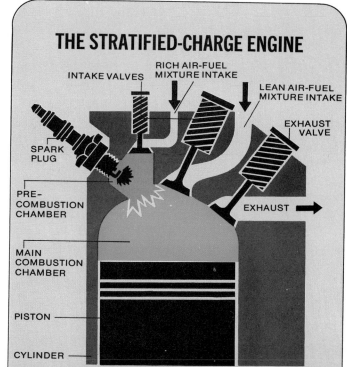

THE STRATIFIED-CHARGE ENGINE

Lean fuel-air mixtures create less pollution, since less pure fuel is being used. But they also tend to mean poor combustion. Enter the problem-solving stratified-charge engine, a modified piston design that has all the pollution-control benefits of lean mixtures and none of the drawbacks.

The trouble with lean mixtures is that, when the proportion of air to gasoline is too great, combustion does not spread evenly to all parts of the cylinder. In the stratified-charge engine a rich mixture is fed into a small chamber in the top part of the main combustion chamber. There it ignites with enough strength to burn the larger amount of lean mixture in the main chamber.

Theoretically, the drawbacks of this system are minor: slight penalties in horsepower per cubic inch of displacement and in fuel mileage. But with present V8 engines, the stratified-charge principle would further complicate an already complicated valve train.

Stratified charge may have a brighter future in the Wankel rotary engine, where it would not entail the addition of moving parts. The only change would be a subtle indentation in the rotor face to create the required combustion pattern (pages 24-25). If precisely the right shape can be found —a delicate, complex job—the result could be better performance with less pollution.

diesel rotary that could give good fuel mileage while holding down carbon-monoxide and hydrocarbon emissions.

Hydrogen as a fuel

As the 21st Century draws nearer, a major new source of energy may give the spark-ignited internal-combustion engine a new lease on life. The fuel is hydrogen, and it may become the basic fuel of tomorrow, making up for shrinking reserves of oil. The so-called hydrogen economy was sheer speculative fancy as recently as the early 1960s. Today, many scientists and energy experts regard it as plausible, if not downright inevitable.

Hydrogen is really the ecologically ideal fuel. It's the basic building block of all matter and can be extracted from the most abundant compound on the planet—water—by using electric current to separate it from oxygen. When hydrogen burns, it recombines with oxygen to form water vapor, completing a neat, clean and altogether perfect ecological cycle.

If electricity becomes cheaper and more efficient—possibly through nuclear power or perhaps solar and geothermal energy—the mass production of hydrogen can be equally cheap and efficient. Handling it in bulk is no longer any great trick; we have learned how to do so safely despite the hazards of the high pressures and super-cold temperatures (down to −423° F.) needed to liquefy it. Piping hydrogen over long distances should be no more difficult than handling natural gas and less expensive than transmitting the equivalent energy in electrical form.

Every spark-ignited engine, with some modifications, is capable of burning hydrogen, and the fuel's power density is competitive with that of gasoline. In an automobile, liquid hydrogen would require bulky storage tanks. But one possible alternative is storage in tanks filled with powdered metals called hydrides, which can absorb great amounts of this basic gas. A tankful stored in this manner would be far less dangerous than a tank of gasoline. It would release fuel in gaseous form when heated. At start-up this would be done by means of an electric heater powered by the car's battery; once the car was underway, the necessary heat would come from the engine itself.

Transportation, 2000 A.D.

Obviously there are innumerable possibilities for the years ahead, and the further ahead we look, the more they multiply. By the year 2000 we may be very close to Supercar indeed. New materials and techniques will have made the automobile into something bearing very little resemblance to today's cars. Bodies, for example, may be injection-molded of foam-plastic bubbles—cheap, sturdy units made like giant toys. All major mechanical components simply would be inserted into sockets or receptacles molded into the body-frame shell and could be replaced in minutes. Repairs to the body itself could be carried out easily: the plastic might be of the type that would pop back into shape when heated; or new panels could be fused into badly damaged areas. The basic materials would be strong enough to resist minor impacts, but structured so that they would collapse by stages in order to absorb the energy of high-speed collisions.

Some of the most important changes in driving are likely to take place outside the car. At times, the automobile might be transformed into a mass-transit unit. This is the aim of the proposed dual-mode highways (page 338)—automated highway systems that would have far more carrying capacity than today's biggest expressways. Cars would travel closer together and there would be no jam-ups, since cars would be fed into the system automatically.

A PROMISING NEW DEVELOPMENT IN PISTON ENGINES

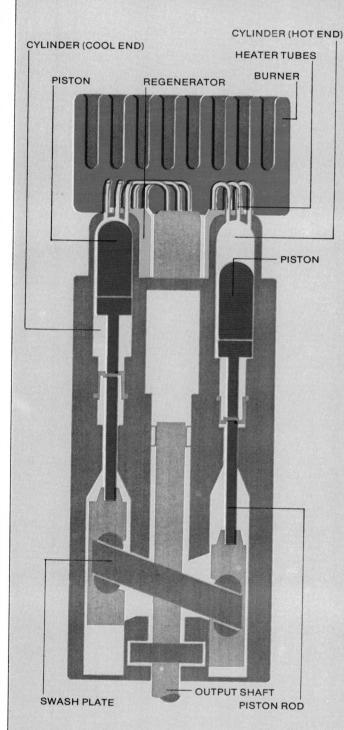

CYLINDER (COOL END)

CYLINDER (HOT END)

HEATER TUBES

PISTON

REGENERATOR

BURNER

PISTON

SWASH PLATE

OUTPUT SHAFT

PISTON ROD

Silence, smoothness, economy and low pollution are among the virtues of the Stirling engine, named for a Scottish churchman, Robert Stirling, who invented a crude prototype in 1816. Today's Stirling engine, being considered as a future alternative to gasoline-powered engines, produces power by the rapid expansion and contraction of a sealed-in gas—usually hydrogen or helium. The only fuel the engine needs is burned externally to provide heat for the expansion of the gas.

The promising design diagramed here uses four horizontal cylinders arranged in a square. Two of them can be seen in this cross section, which also shows the burner at the front of the engine and the output shaft at the rear. Each cylinder is divided by a close-fitting piston into a hot end in the front of the cylinder chamber and a cool end in the back of the chamber. All four cylinders are linked by tubing that connects the cool end of each cylinder with the hot end of an adjoining cylinder.

In this illustration, the gas flows back and forth between the cool end of the left cylinder and the hot end of the right cylinder. In going from hot (1,300° F.) to cool (175° F.), the gas passes from the heater tubes through first a regenerator that absorbs and stores heat and then through a cooler behind the piston (not shown) that further reduces its temperature. When the gas flows in the opposite direction, it regains heat in the regenerator and heater tubes.

The piston's cycle begins when heated gas enters the hot end of the cylinder. The hot gas expands and drives the piston back, compressing the gas in the cool end. As the piston continues on its power stroke, the compressed cool gas is forced into the hot end of the adjoining cylinder. At the same time, the piston is delivering power through piston rods connected to the swash plate, a disc mounted at an angle on the shaft. The piston forces the swash plate and shaft to rotate.

The rotation of the tilted swash plate also returns the piston for the next power stroke, forcing the spent gas out of the hot end as gas begins flowing back into the cool end.

These highways could be built wherever there is a heavy, regular traffic flow. Along suburban shopping routes or between office complexes and main residential areas, the automated limited-access highways could skim off the bulk of the traffic that now fumes, honks and snarls its way from place to place. Some planners envision even lengthier dual-mode operations—along interstate highways, for example, where driving today often is both headlong and tedious.

The practicality of dual-mode highways already has been demonstrated in test-scale facilities, and the federal Urban Mass Transit Administration hopes to have a full-sized one, using modified production cars, in operation by 1980. By the year 2000, dual-mode operations might be commonplace and widespread. In an extensive system, the electric car could really proliferate, even with modest improvement in battery performance. Its batteries could easily handle the relatively short hauls between its terminal points and the main highway; once on the dual-mode road, the electric car would pick up power from a control rail or, by induction, from a cable or rail buried beneath the road surface.

There also may be so-called public automobiles that supplement or replace privately owned ones, and we might see them appearing in some form much sooner—even in the 1980s. These would be simple, inexpensive, sturdy minicars, available to anyone with a driver's license. At first they would be stationed in convenient parking terminals near residential or office complexes. But the ultimate public automobile might be one that could be ordered with a phone call and would appear at the doorway by itself within minutes. It would be used as long as needed, driven either under manual control or directed to its destination by the regional traffic computer network, and then automatically returned to its garage or central station. The driver might pay for the service with a magnetic ticket or credit card, or his account might automatically be charged, as with today's phone bills.

Cars might also be able to fly by 2000 or thereabouts, using rotors, wings or some other device to provide lift. The most commonly imagined advantage of airborne automobiles is the unprecedented freedom of direction they offer, but they might also solve the problem of congestion on heavily traveled routes. When some interstate highways reach their full capacities, the next step might be to set up overhead flyways, with landing strips every 10 miles or so where airmobiles could take off and land on their way to and from local routes. Computer navigation systems, fully automatic, would keep traffic safely regulated. And computers could lessen or eliminate the need for the special skills and extensive training required of today's airplane pilots.

There even may be a demand for amphibious, submersible cars in the years after 2000. The ocean is the last great unexplored and unexploited frontier; its resources are going to be increasingly important to the world's growing population. If today's concepts of personal mobility still obtain several decades from now, people working or living on the ocean floor will want to be able to commute from dry land.

When it is not in the water or not flying, the car of the future probably will continue to use wheels. But here again there are alternatives. Air-cushion vehicles that float inches off the ground and do not require roads? Perhaps, although some way would have to be found to make present-day versions quieter and simpler. Magnetic levitation? This concept requires bulky and expensive equipment and today it looks feasible only for trains or other large vehicles. But tomorrow someone may discover a way to shrink the size of superconductive magnets and mass-produce all of the necessary parts for the levitating automobile.

Our broad transportation needs seem clear enough today, and the technology to solve them seems to be within the realm of possibility. But will our basic assumptions still apply in the year 2000? Perhaps the greatest change the future holds is a downgrading of the importance of the automobile. Although we tend to assume that the auto will continue to play a vital role in our world, a lot of work is being done on ways to minimize its use. Many residential communities—like the "new towns" of Reston, Virginia, and Columbia, Maryland—will be planned to substitute pedestrian and cycle traffic as much as possible, and cities will install more rapid-transit systems as well as moving sidewalks or other devices to carry people shorter distances. Increasingly sophisticated communications systems, such as two-way closed-circuit television hookups, may well obviate the need for some of the traveling we do today—going shopping, as one example.

On the other hand, the distant future may produce a kind of personal mobility that bears scarcely any resemblance to that of the automobile. Some far-off day we may whisk around the world or through space in antigravity machines. Most scientists think that such a dream-device contradicts the laws of physics—but the technocratic elite of the 19th Century scoffed at Jules Verne's "impossible" notions such as submarines and airships to the moon. Why not hope for a car supported by antigravity units and powered by a tiny engine that produces, say, a stream of electrons for propulsion? From what we know now, this supervehicle is not likely. But it is worth recalling that the greatest possible surprise would be a future without surprises.

A NEW TIRE FOR TOMORROW'S DRIVING

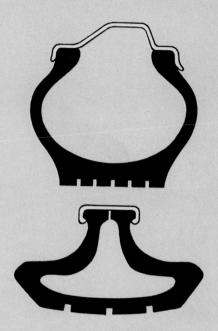

Cars of the future designed for use on high-speed roads may routinely travel at 100 miles an hour. Today's tires, however, were not designed for such speeds. One manufacturer has posed a solution by designing a differently shaped tire. Unlike the rounded contour of today *(top)*, the new design is triangular in cross section *(bottom)*.

In a rounded tire the air pressure exerts an outward force on the sidewalls. A puncture causes the tire to collapse abruptly, creating an emergency in which the car is difficult to control. The triangular tire exerts pressure downward, toward the road rather than toward the sidewalls. In addition, the tire's thick rubber casing holds less air to begin with. Following a puncture, the air does not flow out abruptly but escapes slowly as the thickened sides settle on the tread to form an all-rubber cushion on which the car can, if necessary, roll for more than 100 miles at cruising speeds before repairs are required. A special interior lubricant prevents friction from burning up the tire.

The triangular tires are about half the size of conventional models. This promises some additional safety dividends for tomorrow's car: space freed by the smaller wheels can be used to contain improved braking and suspension systems.

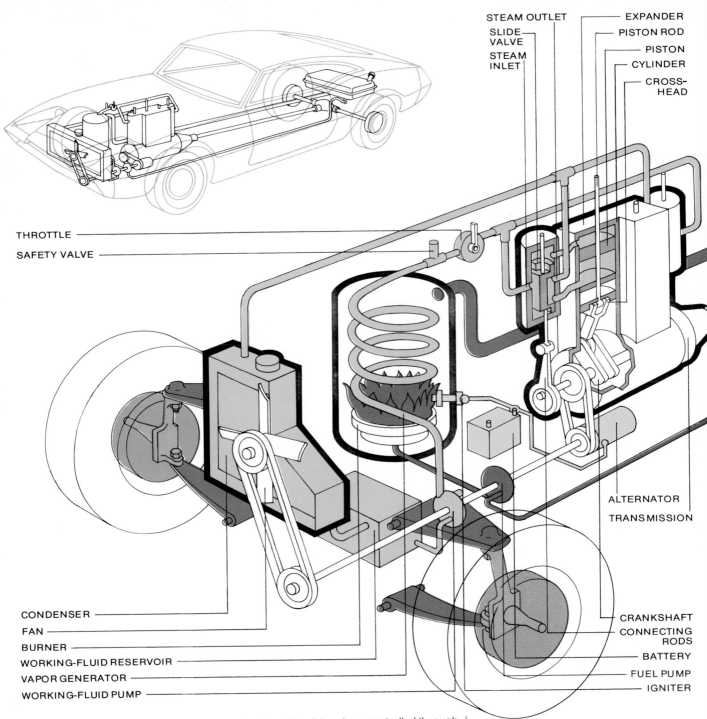

STEAM OUTLET

SLIDE VALVE

STEAM INLET

EXPANDER

PISTON ROD

PISTON

CYLINDER

CROSS-HEAD

THROTTLE

SAFETY VALVE

CONDENSER

FAN

BURNER

WORKING-FLUID RESERVOIR

VAPOR GENERATOR

WORKING-FLUID PUMP

ALTERNATOR

TRANSMISSION

CRANKSHAFT

CONNECTING RODS

BATTERY

FUEL PUMP

IGNITER

The Rankine cycle starts in the vapor generator. Fuel is pumped to a burner and ignited by a spark from a battery. The burner, much like that found in a home furnace, vaporizes the working fluid (currently water), which is stored in a reservoir and pumped into a coiled tube. Vapor under high pressure passes through the safety and throttle valves and is fed through the steam inlet into the expander—in this case a double-acting expander where power is provided for both the down and the up strokes of the piston. The slide valves, controlled through a linkage system from the crankshaft, feed vapor to each end of the cylinders alternately as the pistons complete their up and down strokes. The piston's power is transmitted to the crankshaft through a crosshead, which forms the junction between the piston rod and the connecting rod. Having done its work, the vapor is exhausted through the steam outlet and recirculated to the condenser, where it is cooled to liquid and recycled through the system.

PRINCIPLES OF THE STEAM CAR

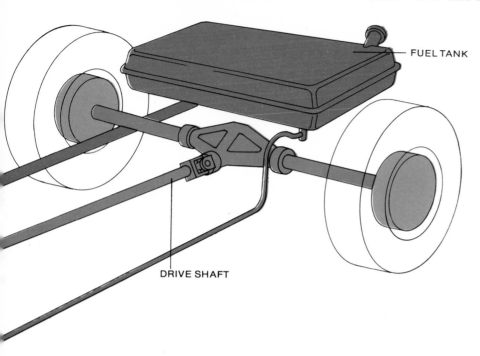

FUEL TANK

DRIVE SHAFT

Take the explosions out of an internal-combustion engine's cylinders, run them all together into a continuous, even-burning flame and you have external combustion. This is the principle of the steam, or Rankine cycle, engine—and the key reason for its desirability. Internal combustion, confined and violent, requires highly refined fuel and produces noxious pollutants. External combustion is as steady and quiet as an oven; kerosene or other cheap fuels will do nicely in it, and harmful pollutants are held to a minimum.

The basic technology of the steam engine has been greatly refined since it moved from the railroad locomotive into the horseless carriage in the days of the Stanley Steamer. The modern car's vapor system is sealed, so that water is continuously recirculated. Its vapor generator, or boiler, is of the monotube, or flash, type, in which a burner heats a relatively small amount of fluid fed through a coil of tubing. This does away with long warm-ups and the hazards of boiler explosions.

These features are not, however, entirely new in principle. The luxury Doble automobile, built in the 1920s, pioneered both of them. But technology has refined these advantages, making the engines more compact and less costly. The steam gener-

ator of the 100-horsepower Doble Standard F weighed 484 pounds; the generator for a 200-horsepower engine built recently by one American manufacturer weighed only 150 pounds. The Doble cost $10,000 in 1920; contemporary designers are shooting for the $3,000 to $4,000 range.

There are as many variations of the basic design as there are inventors and developers. The double-acting two-cylinder expander at left (an expander is an engine that utilizes the power of a compressed fluid) is reminiscent of the Doble's four-cylinder engine. But some designers prefer piston-, turbine- or even rotary-powered engines.

And water itself may someday be obsolete. As a working fluid, water has certain advantages—it is thermally stable, nontoxic, noncorrosive and cheap. But it needs a big condenser, and before the Rankine cycle can truly match the internal-combustion engine for compactness, its components as a package must be brought down in size. Like prospectors searching for gold, many Rankine designers are hunting feverishly for a suitable working fluid as an alternative—one that would vaporize at lower temperatures, serve as its own lubricant, be immune to freezing and remain chemically stable over a long operating lifetime.

PRINCIPLES OF THE ELECTRIC CAR

The electric automobile is clean and quiet, and a city full of electrics would be indisputably more pleasant than one full of gasoline-powered cars. But in the complex world of energy-pollution control, there is no free lunch. Somewhere, a plant must generate the electricity that is needed to power the cars, and there pollution will be produced.

Still, the power plant can be put miles away from the city, and hopefully its pollutants will be easier to control than the exhaust emissions of millions of cars. There are other advantages. The electric car is mechanically both simple and reliable: there is no carburetor and no transmission. The only dashboard instruments needed, other than the speedometer, are gauges to show the battery charge and the motor temperatures.

The big drawback of today's electrics, as illustrated below, is the huge batteries needed to produce reasonable speed over significant distances.

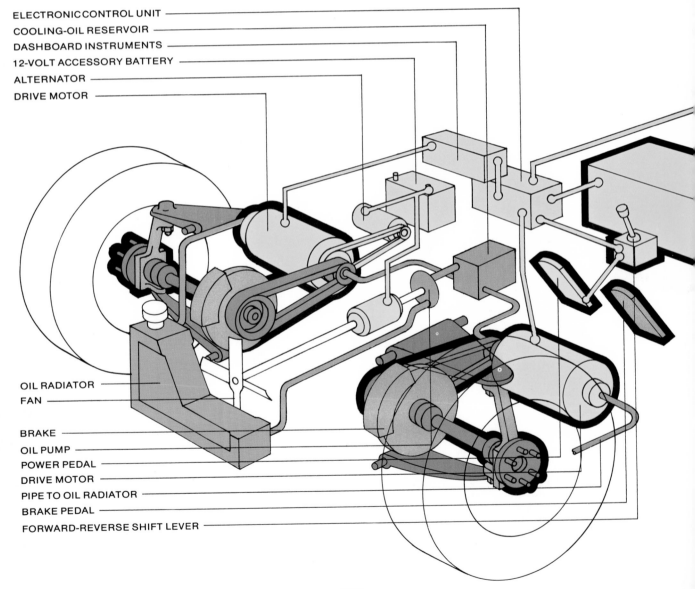

ELECTRONIC CONTROL UNIT
COOLING-OIL RESERVOIR
DASHBOARD INSTRUMENTS
12-VOLT ACCESSORY BATTERY
ALTERNATOR
DRIVE MOTOR

OIL RADIATOR
FAN

BRAKE
OIL PUMP
POWER PEDAL
DRIVE MOTOR
PIPE TO OIL RADIATOR
BRAKE PEDAL
FORWARD-REVERSE SHIFT LEVER

However, new battery technologies, still in the laboratory stage, hold the promise of someday shrinking battery size and weight. The present lead-acid battery *[page 321]* carries an energy-density rating—the measurement of the amount of energy it can deliver per pound of its own weight—of about 12 watt-hours. Experimental batteries have from six to 16 times this capacity, although some pose problems of heat and corrosion.

Still, a sophisticated new battery in itself would not necessarily create a flood of electric family cars. Even if there were enough power-generating capacity in the nation to support widespread electrification, fast recharging—in a time period comparable to filling a tank at a filling station—would require enormous investments in new facilities. Moreover, quick charging is less efficient than slow charging, which takes four to eight hours.

In the foreseeable future, the most likely use for electric vehicles appears confined to urban or suburban settings. There, a lightweight minibus or commuter car, with its short trips, low speed requirements and long rest periods, could be developed within the limits of electric-propulsion units already in the model stage. In fact some experts believe such vehicles will be on the roads soon.

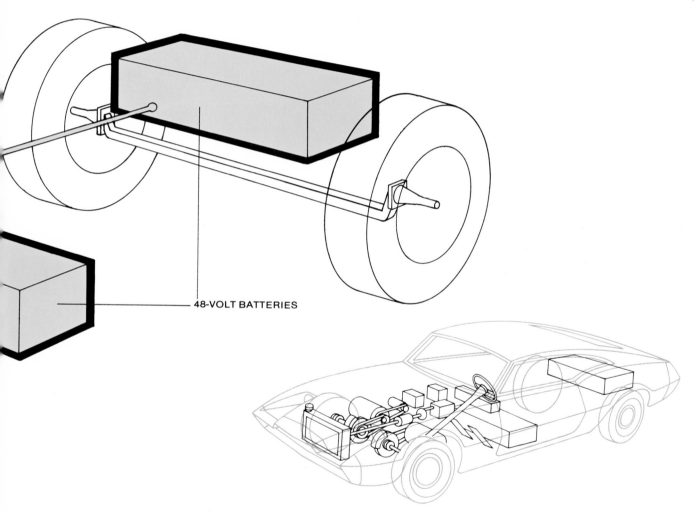

48-VOLT BATTERIES

The basic simplicity of an electric car is complicated only slightly by the devices needed to make it functional for everyday use. Electricity is fed from two 48-volt battery packs to an electronic control unit. When the power pedal (the accelerator in an ordinary car) is pressed, electricity is transmitted to a drive motor on each front wheel; the more power supplied, the faster the motors run. Since the motors are mounted at the drive wheels, there is no need for a transmission or other drive-train components. Only a simple shift lever is required to put the car in forward or reverse. The oil used to lubricate the motors also carries away heat generated by their operation. The heat is then dissipated in the oil radiator. An alternator, as in regular cars, charges a 12-volt battery that supplies electricity to operate lights and accessories.

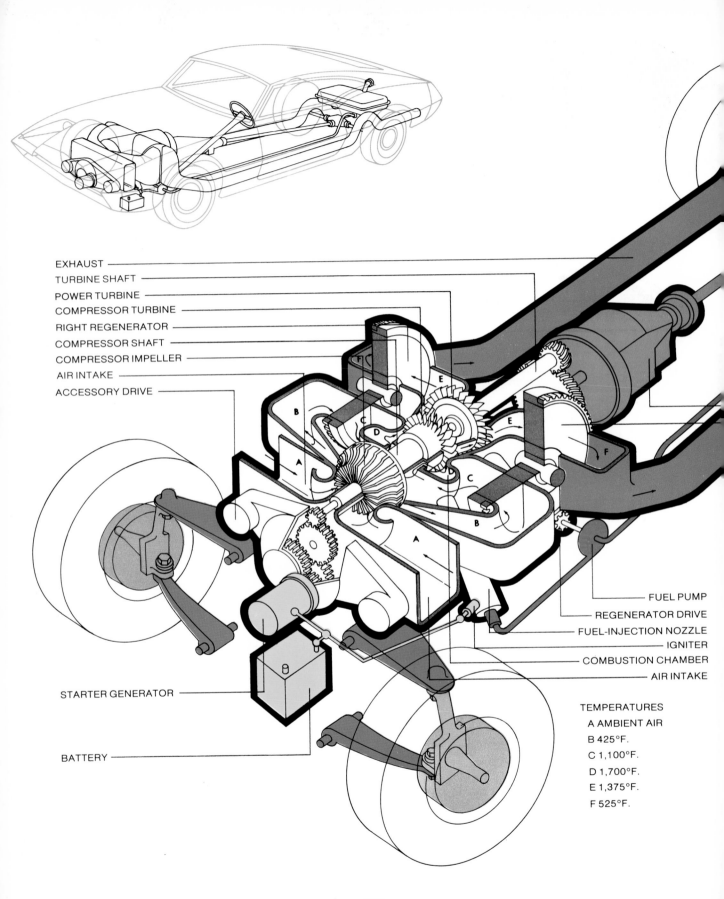

EXHAUST

TURBINE SHAFT

POWER TURBINE

COMPRESSOR TURBINE

RIGHT REGENERATOR

COMPRESSOR SHAFT

COMPRESSOR IMPELLER

AIR INTAKE

ACCESSORY DRIVE

FUEL PUMP

REGENERATOR DRIVE

FUEL-INJECTION NOZZLE

IGNITER

COMBUSTION CHAMBER

AIR INTAKE

STARTER GENERATOR

BATTERY

TEMPERATURES

A AMBIENT AIR

B 425°F.

C 1,100°F.

D 1,700°F.

E 1,375°F.

F 525°F.

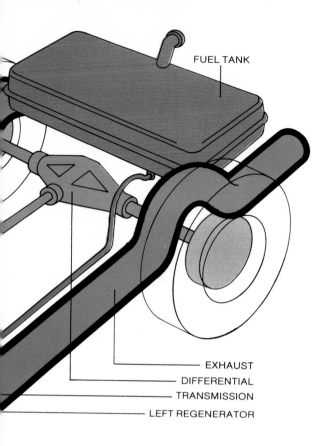

FUEL TANK

EXHAUST
DIFFERENTIAL
TRANSMISSION
LEFT REGENERATOR

PRINCIPLES OF THE GAS TURBINE

Descendant of the water wheel and cousin to the jet, the gas turbine has received more attention from major auto makers than any other alternative to the internal-combustion piston engine. Intensive research has taken it from a futuristic power plant to a point approaching general use in trucks and buses—and possibly in automobiles.

Although still in the development stage, today's automotive turbine is quiet and virtually vibrationless, basically simple and—by and large—a low polluter since combustion is highly efficient. Its maintenance requirements should be low, and it will burn almost any kind of fuel: gasoline, kerosene, coal gas or even, according to some of its proponents, peanut oil.

One of the biggest jobs development engineers have accomplished so far has been to adapt the turbine's rather narrow peak-performance range to the diverse requirements of the automobile. Turbines are high-speed engines; the compressor speeds in automotive models range from 30,000 to 90,000 revolutions per minute. When speeds drop much below these ranges, power output and efficiency fall off drastically. Therefore, a simple turbine needs a complex, multispeed transmission in order to provide reasonable acceleration.

Modern turbines like the one at left overcome the acceleration problem by using a free-turbine, or split-shaft, design. The exhaust from the compressor turbine drives the power turbine, which is on a separate shaft. Since the compressor turbine is free to spin at high speed, it can transfer full power to the power turbine at all times.

But there still are problems to be overcome. Turbines, combined with their necessarily large exhaust-heat regenerators, are both bulky and relatively heavy. Though simple in concept, they are expensive to build; the rotor blades must withstand high temperatures, and research so far has not turned up inexpensive alternatives to the costly metal alloys needed. Moreover, the split-shaft system introduces drawbacks of its own. Even in the most advanced configurations, the compressor turbine frequently will be running at high speeds while the car is decelerating or at a standstill, with adverse effects upon fuel economy.

The gas turbine's operating cycle begins at the compressor impeller where ambient air is drawn in through the air intakes *(points A on the diagram)* and compressed to a pressure of 50 to 75 pounds per square inch. Proceeding on a double path through the turbines, the air first is preheated to 425° F. at points B. Then it passes through the front halves of the two regenerators (shown with one quarter cut away), which store heat from the exhaust and further heat the air to 1,100° by the time it reaches points C. From there the air goes into the combustion chamber. Here, at points D, fuel is injected into the preheated air inside the chamber, ignites and the temperature instantaneously soars to 7,700°, expanding to drive both the compressor turbine and the power turbine. Passing through the turbines, the gases cool to 1,370° at points E. As they pass through the rear half of the regenerator, at points F, they drop to 525° before being released through the exhaust into the atmosphere.

A DESIGN FOR THE DAY AFTER TOMORROW

Few endeavors are more fallible than soothsaying, but the vehicle seen in different perspectives at right seems to stand at least a reasonable chance of coming into being. Based on concepts that seem both technically attainable and highly desirable, this design may represent the family car of the not-too-distant future. Within its plastic skin, sleek as a sea pebble, lie a host of conveniences —including an air conditioner contained entirely within the roof—that would make driving a pleasure even at speeds exceeding 100 mph. On ordinary highways, the car would be powered by a hydrogen-burning turbine engine; on dual-mode highways *(overleaf)* the car would extend a special guidance arm to pick up outside power for electric motors at each wheel. The driver—lounging in a seat that, in response to his body movements, stretches or shrinks for maximum support and accessibility to controls—would look out on the world through glass that darkens in bright light and through a periscope system providing a 360° perspective. At his right hand would be an electronic communications-and-control console that provides entertainment and traffic information —and even takes over the driving at times. At such moments, the driver could swivel his seat a full 180° to chat with the other passengers as his car whisks silently toward its destination.

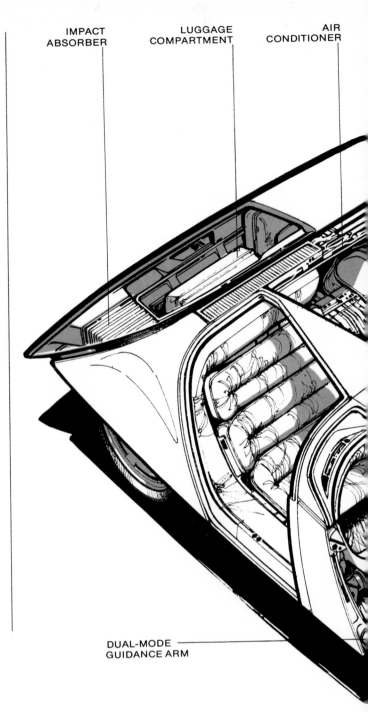

IMPACT ABSORBER · LUGGAGE COMPARTMENT · AIR CONDITIONER

DUAL-MODE GUIDANCE ARM

Safety will be at least as important a design consideration for the family car of the future as swiftness or comfort. To protect passengers in the event of a high-speed crash, the car would have such energy-absorbing features as a soft, multicellular radiator, massive hydraulic collision absorbers, a crash plate in the rear made of super-hard plastic glass windows that can bend 30° without breaking, and special channels along which the body's panels can compress and overlap when the car is hit from the front or rear. The seats would contain built-in restraining devices to grip the passengers the instant an impact occurs. And perhaps the car of the future will even include such safety features as computer-controlled airfoils to adjust for crosswinds and gyrostabilizers that would help prevent tumbling during an accident.

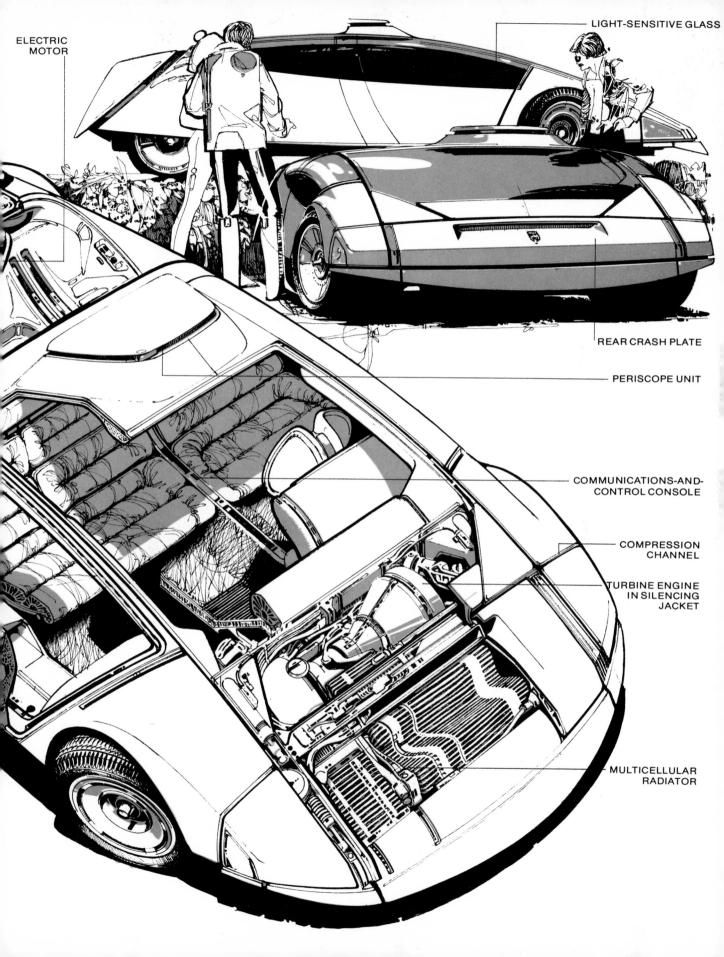

ELECTRIC
MOTOR

LIGHT-SENSITIVE GLASS

REAR CRASH PLATE

PERISCOPE UNIT

COMMUNICATIONS-AND-
CONTROL CONSOLE

COMPRESSION
CHANNEL

TURBINE ENGINE
IN SILENCING
JACKET

MULTICELLULAR
RADIATOR

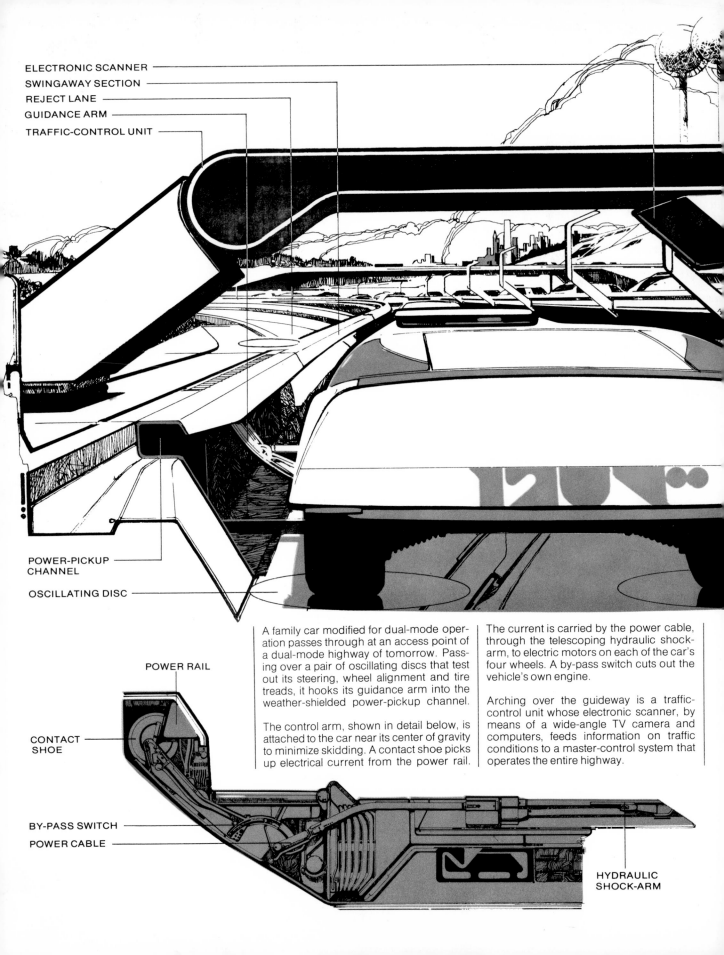

ELECTRONIC SCANNER

SWINGAWAY SECTION

REJECT LANE

GUIDANCE ARM

TRAFFIC-CONTROL UNIT

POWER-PICKUP
CHANNEL

OSCILLATING DISC

POWER RAIL

CONTACT
SHOE

BY-PASS SWITCH

POWER CABLE

HYDRAULIC
SHOCK-ARM

A family car modified for dual-mode operation passes through at an access point of a dual-mode highway of tomorrow. Passing over a pair of oscillating discs that test out its steering, wheel alignment and tire treads, it hooks its guidance arm into the weather-shielded power-pickup channel.

The control arm, shown in detail below, is attached to the car near its center of gravity to minimize skidding. A contact shoe picks up electrical current from the power rail.

The current is carried by the power cable, through the telescoping hydraulic shock-arm, to electric motors on each of the car's four wheels. A by-pass switch cuts out the vehicle's own engine.

Arching over the guideway is a traffic-control unit whose electronic scanner, by means of a wide-angle TV camera and computers, feeds information on traffic conditions to a master-control system that operates the entire highway.

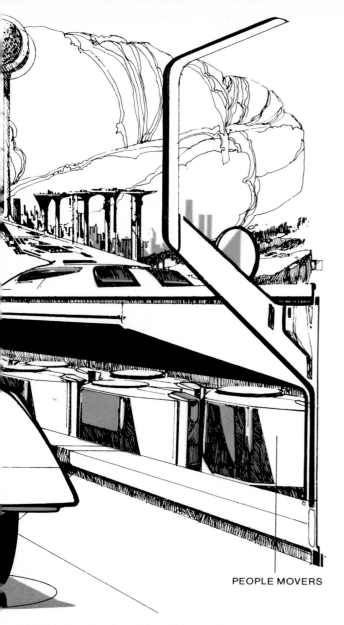

PEOPLE MOVERS

At left is the reject lane into which cars that do not qualify for guideway operation are detoured through swingaway sections of the guidance rail.

The design on the rear of the car is an electronically coded registration number. The guideway-control instruments record the car's code and deduct the highway toll charges from the driver's bank account. At right is a lane of compact "people-mover" capsules that whisk passengers along the highway to nearby destinations.

DUAL-MODE HIGHWAY SYSTEMS

Transportation experts have long been torn between the people-moving efficiency and the safety of rail systems as opposed to the door-to-door convenience of the automobile. The dual-mode system (DMS) is science's rebuttal to the assumption that you can't have it both ways. In a dual-mode system, vehicles would operate both as they do now, over ordinary highways, and also over special guideways by fully automatic control.

The DMS concept has been under close study for a couple of decades. The system pictured at left is the logical extension of a guideway designed in the late 1960s by Professor Dwight Baumann at Carnegie-Mellon University in Pittsburgh. It is the U.S. Department of Transportation's idea that such systems should be evolutionary, in order to make use of already existing facilities and equipment. The car shown at the access gate is a direct descendant of today's family car; it has been modified with a guidance arm that hooks into a power-pickup channel and with an electronic-guidance package. Each wheel has its own electric motor; when the car is not using its own power, it draws energy from the highway's power system.

The biggest advantage of computer-controlled dual-mode systems is that, theoretically, there need be no limits on speed, and headways between cars can be much closer. As a result, the capacity of each existing lane of highway is greatly increased. But that advantage carries the imperative that a variety of sensors be located at every entrance point to make sure that cars are mechanically up to snuff. Any car that shows signs of trouble would be denied access. (A DMS system could also be designed to accept faulty or unmodified cars; they would be shunted into large vanlike shells providing piggyback rides.)

Once a car has been whisked into the system, the driver would use a computer in his electronic-guidance package to dial a number advising the DMS master-control computer as to which exit he wants. When he arrives, he could simply drive off or he could stop, get out and direct the car's on-board computer to take the vehicle to another destination—a parking lot, perhaps, or even back to his starting point, where his wife could pick it up.

A 21ST CENTURY FLYING CAR

Still only a wild gleam in the eyes of uninhibited automotive engineers, the family car of the 21st Century could well be capable of tucking away its wheels and becoming airborne for high-speed, long-distance travel. The problems of creating such a car and the elaborate traffic-control system that it would require are enormous. But the scene at right is almost within the capabilities of existing technology and should be entirely feasible several decades hence.

Wingless flying cars would represent a further evolution of the dual-mode highway system depicted on the previous pages. This highway would now become a multimode system, with layers of superfast air-traffic lanes stacked over ground-traffic lanes. The air lanes could relieve 21st Century traffic congestion, leaving the highways to nonflyers content to lower their wheels and dawdle along at a mere 100 mph or so.

Passing through a U-shaped air-traffic control unit, a flying family car ascends on its aerodynamic lift panels and prepares to enter an air-traffic lane over the highway. Directly beneath, another car is about to fly over a grid of electronic sensors that will automatically identify the car and feed pertinent flight information into a traffic-flow computer. Television and radar systems in the tower at the top of one of the control-unit arms monitor air traffic for the flyway, where cars travel at speeds up to 250 mph and at altitudes up to 350 feet.

Several cars in the background, entering the take-off lane, accelerate toward a triangular abort plate set into the surface of the runway. If a car has not reached take-off speed when it passes over the plate, it is automatically shunted into an exit lane.

Off in the direction of the mushroom-shaped skyscrapers at the left rear can be seen the silhouette of another air-traffic control unit at the beginning of a landing lane. Here the flying cars can land and join surface traffic by hooking their control arms onto a guidance rail.

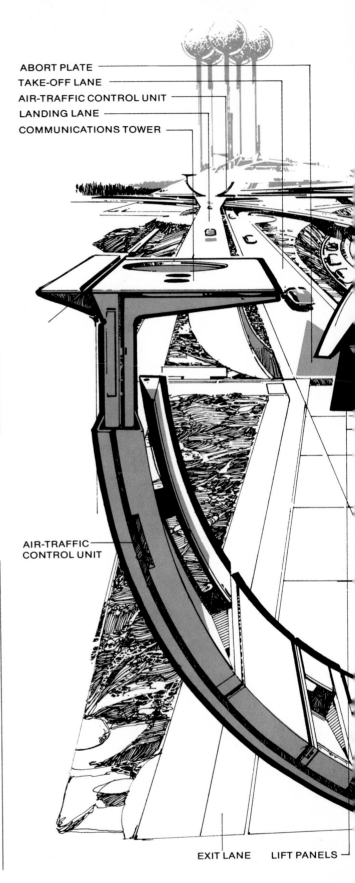

ABORT PLATE
TAKE-OFF LANE
AIR-TRAFFIC CONTROL UNIT
LANDING LANE
COMMUNICATIONS TOWER

AIR-TRAFFIC CONTROL UNIT

EXIT LANE   LIFT PANELS

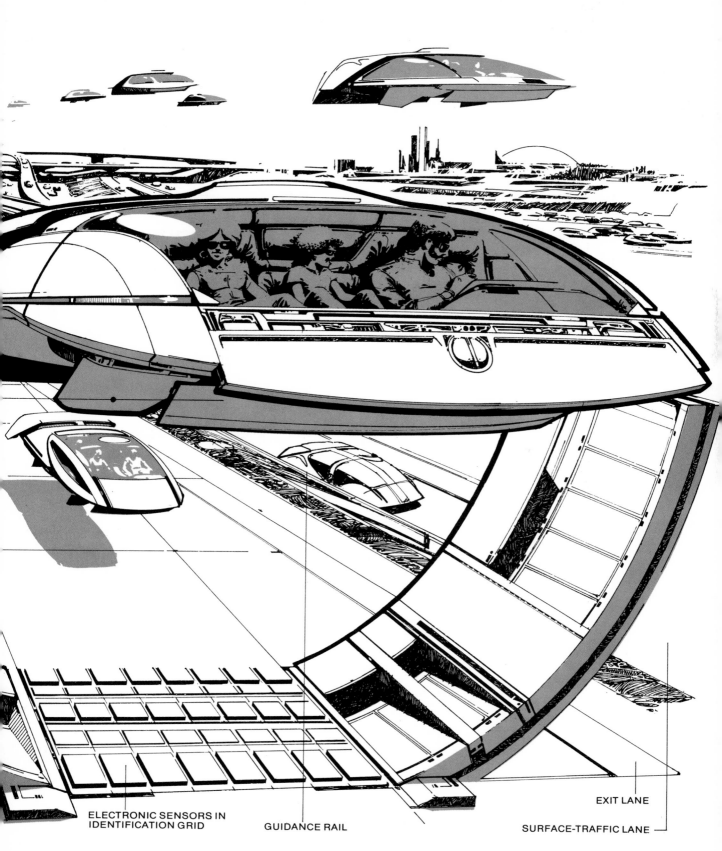

ELECTRONIC SENSORS IN
IDENTIFICATION GRID

GUIDANCE RAIL

EXIT LANE

SURFACE-TRAFFIC LANE

GLOSSARY

ACCELERATOR: Pedal that controls the amount of fuel and air entering the carburetor.

ACCELERATOR PUMP: Device in the carburetor that supplies additional gasoline when the accelerator is depressed quickly.

ADDITIVE: Chemical that is added in relatively small amounts to gasoline or oil to improve or correct some characteristic of the original product.

ADVANCING THE SPARK: Adjustment of ignition timing that causes a spark to occur earlier in a piston's cycle.

AIR CLEANER: Filter that removes dust from the air being drawn into a carburetor.

AIR INJECTION: Pollution-control system that mixes air (oxygen) with exhaust gases to consume unburned fuel.

AIR-FUEL RATIO: Proportion of air to gasoline in the fuel mixture that an engine uses in combustion.

ALIGNMENT: Process of positioning separate objects (such as wheels) into a correct relationship with each other.

ALTERNATING CURRENT (AC): Electric current that reverses its directional flow within a circuit at regular intervals.

ALTERNATOR: Generator that produces alternating current.

AMMETER: Instrument that measures, in amperes, the amount of electrical current flowing through a circuit.

AMPERE: Measuring unit that expresses the rate of electrical flow through a circuit.

AMPERE-HOUR CAPACITY: Measuring unit that expresses a battery's ability to deliver a specified amount of electrical current during a specified time period.

ANGLE PARKING: Positioning a car at an angle to a curb.

ANTIFREEZE: Chemical solution that lowers the freezing point of water; most such solutions, used as engine coolants, also raise the boiling point of water.

ANTIFREEZE HYDROMETER: Instrument for measuring the specific gravity of a coolant, and thus its antifreeze content.

ANTISTALL DASHPOT: Device that keeps an engine from stalling by preventing the throttle from closing too rapidly.

ARCING: Leaping of an electrical current across a gap between two conductors.

ARMATURE: Revolving part of electric devices such as a starter motor or generator.

AUTOMATIC CHOKE: Thermostatically operated device in a carburetor that controls the amount of air mixed with gasoline; in cold weather the choke aids starting by limiting the intake of air and thus providing a fuel mixture richer in gasoline.

AXLE SHAFT: Solid metal rod, extending from the differential, that transfers power to an automobile's drive wheel.

BAFFLE: Device that diverts or regulates the flow of liquids, gases or sound waves.

BALANCE: See *wheel balance*.

BALL BEARING: Bearing in which balls move inside two races. See also *race*.

BALL JOINT: Flexible joint that employs a ball-and-socket type of construction, such as that used in steering linkages.

BATTERY: Electrochemical device that produces and stores electricity.

BATTERY CHARGING: Process of restoring a battery's charge by passing an electric current through the battery.

BATTERY HYDROMETER: Instrument for measuring the specific gravity of a battery's electrolyte solution and thus its state of charge.

BATTERY POSTS: Round lead posts protruding from a battery to which the battery cables are attached. See also *negative terminal, positive terminal*.

BEARING: Any device or surface area that supports the moving parts of a machine.

BELTED-BIAS TIRE: Tire with the basic body structure of a bias-ply tire but that has an additional two or more layers (or belts) of material reinforced with steel or fabric between the body plies and the tread.

BELTS: Layers of material reinforced with steel or fabric within some tires that strengthen the tread and resist puncturing by sharp objects.

BIAS-PLY TIRE: Tire in which the reinforcing cords in the body plies run in alternating directions at an angle (or bias) to the center line of the tread.

BLEEDING THE BRAKES: Process of removing air from the brake lines of a hydraulic-brake system.

BOOSTER: Auxiliary device within a car system (such as the brakes or steering mechanism) that increases the force applied by the operator.

BORE: Diameter of an engine cylinder.

BRAKE: Device, usually employing friction, that slows and stops a wheel's motion. See also *disc brakes, dual brakes, hydraulic brake, power brakes*.

BRAKE BACKING-PLATE: Rigid steel plate, to which brake shoes are attached, that absorbs the braking force applied to those shoes.

BRAKE DRUM: Hardened-metal housing, attached to the wheel hub, against which the brake shoes apply pressure.

BRAKE FADE: Loss of braking power caused by excessive heat in drum-brake linings or disc-brake pads.

BRAKE FLUID: Special fluid used in a hydraulic-brake system.

BRAKE HORSEPOWER (BHP): Measurement of the actual horsepower delivered at the crankshaft of an engine.

BRAKE LINING: Friction-producing asbestos compound attached to the brake shoes that is pressed against the brake drum during braking.

BRAKE SHOES: Curved metal plates that hold the brake linings in a drum-brake system.

BREAKER ARM: Movable part within a distributor that holds one of the breaker points.

BREAKER POINTS: Pair of contacts within the distributor that open and close the primary ignition circuit.

BUSHING: Hollow cylindrical bearing for a shaft.

BUTTERFLY VALVE: Pivoting metal plate, resembling a butterfly's wings, that controls the flow of air or fuel mixture within a carburetor.

CAM: Curved projection on a shaft that moves another component as the shaft rotates.

CAMBER: Vertical wheel-alignment involving an outward (positive) or inward (negative) tilting of the tops of the wheels.

CAMSHAFT: Shaft that employs a number of cams, or lobes, which operate the valves and some of the other moving parts of an internal-combustion engine.

CAMSHAFT GEAR: Gear on the front of the camshaft that picks up power from the crankshaft to drive the camshaft.

CARBON: Black fuel residue, found on various parts of the engine, that is a by-product of combustion.

CARBON MONOXIDE: Colorless, odorless and highly toxic gas produced by incomplete combustion of gasoline hydrocarbons and always present in automobile exhaust.

CARBURETOR: Device that mixes gasoline with air in correct proportions for combustion.

CARBURETOR BARREL: Specially shaped tube in the carburetor where the air and gasoline are mixed.

CARBURETOR CIRCUITS: Various passages within a carburetor that provide the proper amount of fuel for various functions such as idling and accelerating.

CARBURETOR ICING: Formation of ice deposits in the carburetor during cool, humid weather.

CASTELLATED NUT: Nut with a series of radial grooves cut into one of its ends to receive a cotter pin, which prevents the nut from turning.

CASTER: Front-wheel alignment that tilts the kingpin or steering knuckle axis forward (positive) or backward (negative) to help return the wheels to a straight-ahead position after a turn.

CATALYTIC CONVERTER: Device that chemically reduces harmful emissions of automobile exhaust.

CELL: Separate compartment within a battery containing an element. See also *element*.

CELL CONNECTOR: Lead strap that connects the various cells in a battery.

CENTRIFUGAL ADVANCE: Device within the distributor that alters ignition timing through the action of centrifugal force as engine speed varies.

CENTRIFUGAL FORCE: Force that tends to impel a moving object away from the center of its rotation.

CHASSIS: Basic frame and suspension of an automobile (or sometimes the frame and all working parts) to which the body and fenders are attached.

CHOKE: Butterfly valve at the top of a carburetor that restricts the amount of entering air and thus enriches the fuel mixture.

CIRCUIT BREAKER: Protective switching device within an electrical circuit that can break the current flow if the current becomes excessive.

CLUTCH: Coupling device used to engage or disengage the flow of power from one moving part to another, such as from an engine to a transmission.

COIL: Device that increases battery voltage to the level needed to fire the spark plugs.

COIL SPRING: Suspension unit consisting of a spring-steel rod wound in a spiral shape.

COMBUSTION: Process by which an engine produces power by igniting a fuel mixture.

COMBUSTION CHAMBER: Area at the top of the cylinder above the piston head where the fuel mixture is ignited.

COMPRESSION: Process of reducing the volume within a cylinder and therefore increasing the pressure on a fuel mixture within that cylinder.

COMPRESSION GAUGE: Instrument used to test cylinder compression of an engine.

COMPRESSION RATIO: Proportion between the cylinder volume when the piston is at the bottom of its stroke and the cylinder volume when it is at the top of its stroke.

COMPRESSION TEST: Test of engine compression to ascertain the condition of valves, rings and cylinders.

CONDENSER: Device within the distributor that absorbs surges of electricity and prevents electrical arcing across the breaker points.

CONE CLUTCH: Clutch in which the moving, frictional surfaces are cone shaped.

CONNECTING ROD: Rigid metal link that transmits power between a piston and crankshaft.

CONSTANT-MESH GEARS: Gears that are always in working contact with each other.

CONSTANT-VELOCITY UNIVERSAL JOINT: Universal joint that transfers torque from a driving shaft to a driven shaft at an angle without any fluctuation of speed.

CONTACT POINTS: See *breaker points*.

COOLANT: Liquid used in the engine-cooling system; usually a mixture of water and antifreeze.

CORDS: Heavy, wound strands of reinforcing material (nylon, rayon, polyester) in the body of a tire.

COUNTERSHAFT: Shaft with a set of gears that connect the input and output shafts in the transmission.

CRANKCASE: Housing of the crankshaft within the engine.

CRANKSHAFT: Primary shaft in a piston engine that translates the reciprocating motion of the pistons into rotary motion.

CRANKSHAFT COUNTERWEIGHTS: Weights attached to the crankshaft that balance the reciprocating motion of the piston and rod assemblies.

CRANKSHAFT GEAR: Gear on the front of the crankshaft that drives the camshaft gear by means of a chain or belt.

CYLINDER: Hole in the engine block in which a piston moves and combustion takes place.

CYLINDER HEAD: Metal unit, bolted on top of the engine block, that covers the cylinders and forms the top of the combustion chamber.

DETONATION: Rapid, rattling combustion produced by low-octane gasoline igniting too violently; also called knocking.

DIAPHRAGM: Flexible wall separating two compartments.

DIESEL ENGINE: Internal-combustion engine that ignites fuel solely by means of the heat of highly compressed air within its cylinders.

DIESELING: Condition in which fuel continues to burn after the ignition has been turned off.

DIFFERENTIAL: Gear unit that allows the outside rear wheel to revolve faster than the inside rear wheel during a turn.

DIFFERENTIAL CASE: Steel unit in which the differential gears are located.

DIODE: Solid-state device that allows electrical current to flow in only one direction.

DIPSTICK: Removable, graduated metal rod used to indicate oil or fluid levels in the engine, automatic transmission and power-steering pump.

DIRECT CURRENT (DC): Electric current that flows in one direction only.

DIRECTIONAL STABILITY: Car's ability to continue moving in a straight line with a minimum of steering control.

DISC BRAKES: Braking system that employs a rotating steel disc and a caliper containing pads that pinch the disc to produce stopping friction.

DISC-BRAKE CALIPER: Mechanism that straddles a brake disc and contains the brake pads that pinch the disc.

DISCHARGE: Flow of electric current from a battery.

DISTRIBUTOR: Electrical switching device that controls the production and distribution of the high-voltage charges to the proper spark plugs in the correct sequence.

DISTRIBUTOR CAP: Insulated top of a distributor with a central input terminal for the coil wire and a series of output terminals for spark-plug cables.

DOWNSHIFT: Action of shifting a transmission to a lower gear.

DRIVE BELT: Any of several V-shaped belts that transfer power by means of pulleys from the crankshaft to various units such as the fan and power-steering pump.

DRIVE SHAFT: Heavy metal tube that transfers power from the transmission to the differential.

DUAL BRAKES: Braking system that provides two separate, independent hydraulic circuits for each pair of wheels.

DWELL ANGLE: Number of degrees the distributor cam rotates while the breaker points are closed.

DYNAMOMETER: Instrument for measuring the power output of an engine.

ELECTRICAL CIRCUIT: Complete path taken by electricity as it flows from a source to an electrical device, then back to the source through a ground.

ELECTRODES: Two conducting rods in a spark plug, separated by a gap across which the ignition spark leaps.

ELECTROLYTE: Mixture of sulfuric acid and water that conducts ions from one plate to another to help produce electricity in a battery.

ELECTROMAGNET: Magnetic device consisting of an iron bar surrounded by a coil of conducting wire: when current flows through the coil, the bar is magnetized.

ELEMENT: Battery unit consisting of positive and negative plates placed in an electrolyte-filled cell; there are six elements in a 12-volt battery.

ENGINE BLOCK: Main part of an internal-combustion engine, which contains the cylinders.

ETHYLENE GLYCOL: Chemical compound used in coolant solutions as a permanent antifreeze.

EVAPORATION CONTROL: Pollution-control system that employs a vapor separator to collect fumes from the fuel tank and a charcoal canister to store them for burning in the engine.

EXHAUST MANIFOLD: Pipe that connects the exhaust ports of the engine with the exhaust pipe.

EXHAUST PIPE: Pipe that connects the exhaust manifold to the muffler.

EXHAUST VALVE: Valve that opens to allow exhaust gases from the cylinder to pass to the exhaust manifold.

FEELER-GAUGE: Thin metal strip of a specified thickness or a round metal wire of a specified diameter used to check clearances between parts.

FIELD: Area encompassed by a magnetic force.

FILTER: Device or substance that removes foreign particles from air or from fluids.

FIREWALL: Metal partition that separates the passenger compartment from the engine compartment.

FIRING ORDER: Sequence in which the cylinders are ignited in an internal-combustion engine.

FLOAT BOWL: Chamber within a carburetor that holds a reservoir of gasoline, the level of which is regulated by a buoyant device controlling a needle valve.

FLOAT LEVEL: Height of the gasoline in the float bowl of the carburetor; also, the specified, correct level of fuel.

FLOODING: Condition of excess fuel in the cylinders that makes starting difficult or impossible.

FLUID COUPLING: Unit in which a flow of liquid is used to transmit engine torque to an automatic transmission.

FLYWHEEL: Heavy metal disc attached to the crankshaft that smooths out variations in torque and thus keeps the shaft turning at a near-constant speed.

FLYWHEEL RING-GEAR: Gear on the circumference of the flywheel that is engaged by the pinion gear of the starter motor.

FOUR-STROKE-CYCLE ENGINE: Engine that requires four strokes of each piston (intake, compression, ignition and exhaust) to complete its power-producing combustion cycle.

FUEL INJECTION: Carburetorless fuel system that sprays a programed amount of fuel into the intake manifold of an internal-combustion engine.

FUEL MIXTURE: Combination of gasoline and air used to power an engine.

FUEL PUMP: Device that draws gasoline from the tank and feeds it to the carburetor.

FUSE: Protective device in an electrical circuit that breaks the current flow when it becomes excessive.

GASKET: Material placed between mechanical parts to seal their connection.

GASOLINE: Volatile liquid-hydrocarbon fuel.

GENERATOR: Electromagnetic device that converts mechanical energy into electricity.

GOVERNOR: Mechanical device that automatically controls the speed of a rotating part.

GROSS AXLE-WEIGHT RATING (GAWR): Maximum amount of weight a given axle is designed to support.

GROSS VEHICLE-WEIGHT RATING (GVWR): Maximum total weight permissible for a fully loaded vehicle.

GROUND: Conducting body used as a common path for electrical circuits returning to the battery.

HORSEPOWER: Measurement of an engine's capacity to perform work; one horsepower is the unit of energy needed to lift 550 pounds a distance of one foot in one second.

HUB: Metal unit on which a wheel is mounted.

HYDRAULIC BRAKE: Brake that is activated by a fluid moving under pressure.

HYDRAULIC LIFTER: Valve lifter that uses hydraulic pressure from the engine's oil to keep it in proper adjustment with the camshaft and the push rod.

HYDROCARBON: Chemical compound of hydrogen and carbon; all petroleum fuels are composed of hydrocarbons.

HYDROMETER: Instrument for measuring specific gravities of liquids. See also *antifreeze hydrometer, battery hydrometer.*

HYDROPLANING: Driving phenomenon in which a car's tires ride up on a wedge of water and thereby lose contact with the road surface.

IDLE-CIRCUIT NOZZLE: Aperture through which the fuel from the idle circuit enters the carburetor barrel.

IDLE-MIXTURE SCREW: Controlling device that adjusts the idle-circuit nozzle to control the amount of fuel reaching the cylinders during idling.

IGNITION SYSTEM: Section of an automobile's electrical system that produces and distributes the sparks to ignite the fuel mixture in the cylinders.

IGNITION TIMING: Instant at which the spark plug ignites the fuel mixture.

IMPELLER: Finned rotor that pumps air or a fluid.

INDEPENDENT SUSPENSION: Suspension system that permits each wheel to move up and down independently of the action of the other wheels.

INJECTOR: Pump that squirts a programed amount of fuel into the intake manifold of an engine.

IN-LINE ENGINE: Internal-combustion engine in which the cylinders are arranged in a single row.

INPUT SHAFT: Shaft that delivers power to a mechanism.

INTAKE MANIFOLD: Pipe with tubes connecting the carburetor to the intake ports.

INTAKE VALVE: Valve that admits fuel mixture into the cylinder of an engine.

INTERNAL-COMBUSTION ENGINE: Engine that burns fuel inside its cylinders to produce power.

JET: Small opening that permits a controlled amount of fuel to enter a carburetor barrel.

KNOCKING: See *detonation.*

LEAF SPRING: Suspension device composed of several superimposed strips of spring steel, which is held to the frame at one end by a shackle.

LIMITED-SLIP DIFFERENTIAL: Differential unit that transfers more power to the drive wheel with the best traction.

LINKAGE: Any series of metal rods or levers that transmit motion from one unit to another.

LUBRICANT: Friction-reducing substance placed between moving parts.

MANIFOLD: Pipe that connects a series of outlets to a common opening. See also *exhaust manifold, intake manifold.*

MASTER CYLINDER: Unit in a hydraulic-brake system that forces brake fluid to the wheel cylinders.

MISFIRING: Failure of a fuel charge to ignite in a cylinder of an engine.

MOTOR: Power unit that transforms electrical energy into mechanical power.

MUFFLER: Chamber placed between the exhaust pipe and the tailpipe that quiets engine sounds and cools exhaust gases.

MULTIVISCOSITY OILS: Engine oils that have flow characteristics to provide adequate lubrication at both high and low temperatures.

NEGATIVE TERMINAL: Post in an automobile battery from which the electrons flow on their way to the positive post. See also *battery posts*.

OCTANE RATING: Number representing a particular gasoline's ability to resist detonation, determined by the quantity of antiknock substances blended into it.

ODOMETER: Instrument, set in the speedometer, that registers the total distance traveled by a vehicle.

OIL FILTER: Replaceable element that removes foreign particles from circulating oil.

OIL GALLERY: Pipes or bored passageways in an engine that carry oil from one area to another.

OIL PUMP: Mechanism that forces lubricating oil, under pressure, through the engine.

OSCILLOSCOPE: Electronic testing instrument that translates electrical-circuit performance into a pattern visible on a cathode-ray tube.

OUTPUT SHAFT: Any shaft that delivers power from within a mechanism; e.g., transmission output shaft.

OVERDRIVE: Gear designed into some manual transmissions that, when actuated, allows the drive shaft to turn faster than the crankshaft, resulting in higher speeds with less engine effort and lower fuel consumption.

OVERSTEER: Tendency of a car, when rounding a corner, to turn sharply with little steering input.

OXIDES OF NITROGEN: Exhaust gas formed by high combustion temperatures.

PAN: Metal reservoir bolted to the bottom of a crankcase or automatic transmission that holds oil or fluid.

PARKING BRAKE: Auxiliary mechanism that mechanically activates a vehicle's rear brakes for parking.

PCV: See *positive crankcase-ventilation*.

PENETRATING OIL: Special oil mixture that cuts through rust, used to loosen corroded fasteners.

PETROLEUM: Thick, flammable liquid of natural origin, consisting of various hydrocarbons, from which such products as gasoline, kerosene and lubricants are distilled.

PISTON: Part of the engine that moves inside the cylinder and transmits the force of combustion to the crankshaft through a connecting rod.

PISTON RINGS: Metallic bands that are fitted into grooves around a piston to provide a tight seal between the piston and the cylinder wall.

PITMAN ARM: Short metal rod attached to the steering box that transmits the turning force from the steering box to the steering-linkage system.

PLANETARY-GEAR SET: Gearing unit in an automatic transmission consisting of a sun gear, a planet gear and a ring gear, all of which are constantly meshed.

PLIES: Layers of rubber-coated cords that constitute the carcass of a tire.

PORT: Opening to the cylinder head; intake ports are conduits for fuel mixture, exhaust ports convey waste gases.

POSITIVE CRANKCASE-VENTILATION (PCV): A pollution-control system that uses engine suction to draw out gases from the crankcase and into the intake manifold for burning.

POSITIVE TERMINAL: Post in an automobile battery from which the current flows through a circuit on its path to the negative terminal. See also *battery posts*.

POWER BRAKES: System in which a booster mechanism, usually operated by engine vacuum, is engaged during braking to augment the force applied to the brake pedal.

POWER STEERING: System that uses a hydraulic-pressure booster to augment the driver's steering force.

PREIGNITION: Premature fuel-combustion within a cylinder.

PRIMARY CIRCUIT: Portion of the ignition system through which low-voltage battery current passes.

PRIMARY COIL-WINDING: Heavy-wire winding around the core of the coil that carries low-voltage current.

PUSHROD: Metal rod that connects a valve lifter to a rocker arm in an internal-combustion engine.

RACE: Inner surface of a bearing assembly in which the balls or rollers operate.

RACK-AND-PINION STEERING: Steering system, usually found on smaller cars, in which the input shaft (pinion) is geared directly to the output shaft (rack).

RADIAL TIRE: Tire in which the body cords run at right angles (radially) to the center line of the tread and that has two or more belts to strengthen the tread.

RADIATOR: Unit that dissipates engine-coolant heat to the outside air by passing the fluid through finned core-pipes.

RANKINE-CYCLE ENGINE: External-combustion engine that utilizes the energy of expanding gases (such as steam) to drive a piston or turbine.

RECIPROCATING ACTION: Back-and-forth movement, like the action of pistons inside cylinders.

RECIRCULATING-BALL STEERING BOX: Steering device in which a series of ball bearings follows a circular path through a worm gear to transmit turning motion and reduce friction.

RECTIFIER: Electronic device that changes alternating current into direct current.

REGULATOR: Electrical device that limits the alternator's output of current to a predetermined level.

RESISTOR: Device placed in an electrical circuit that reduces the flow of current.

RETARDING THE SPARK: Adjustment of ignition timing that causes a spark to occur later in a piston's cycle.

RING GEAR: Large gear that drives the differential carrier; or the outer gear in a planetary-gear set.

ROCKER ARM: Lever activated by a pushrod to open or close an engine valve.

ROCKER PANEL: Section of a car body between the front and rear wheel wells and beneath the doors.

ROCKER-PANEL MOLDINGS: Metal strips attached along the rocker panels to protect them from corrosion.

ROLLER BEARING: Bearing in which cylindrical rollers move between two races.

ROTARY ENGINE: Internal-combustion engine in which one or more three-sided rotors revolve in specially shaped chambers; in every revolution each side of the rotor performs all the functions of a four-stroke-cycle engine.

ROTOR: Revolving device that performs like a piston in a rotary engine; in the distributor it relays high-voltage current from the coil to the various spark-plug cables.

SEALED-BEAM HEADLIGHT: Standard automobile headlight lamp in which the lens, filament and reflector are parts of a single sealed unit.

SEALED BEARING: Permanently lubricated, closed bearing.

SEATING: Gradual wearing in of new moving parts so that they fit properly.

SECONDARY CIRCUIT: Part of the ignition system that carries the high-voltage current from the coil to the spark plugs.

SELECTOR FORKS: Devices that move the synchronizing rings in a transmission.

SHACKLE: Fastener that holds one end of a leaf spring to the automobile frame.

SHIMMY: Undesirable side-to-side motion of the wheels during driving.

SHOCK ABSORBER: Hydraulic mechanism that dampens oscillation in the suspension system.

SHORT, OR SHORT CIRCUIT: Electrical defect that results in the accidental grounding of a current before the circuit has been completed.

SHROUD: Metal or plastic hood within the engine compartment that guides the flow of cooling air drawn through the grill.

SKID: Sudden movement of a car, due to loss of tire traction, in which the driver loses control and the automobile slips sideways on the road.

SLUDGE: Thick sediment that develops as impurities mix with various liquids such as oil or water in automobile systems.

SNOW TIRE: Tire that has an open-tread pattern with deep grooves to provide extra traction for driving in soft snow.

SOLENOID: Electromagnetic device used to activate mechanical or electrical mechanisms.

SPARK: High-voltage electrical discharge that occurs when current moving through the spark plug jumps across the gap between the metal electrodes.

SPARK ADVANCE: See *advancing the spark.*

SPARK GAP: Distance between the center and side electrodes on a spark plug.

SPARK PLUG: Porcelain-insulated metal device that conducts high-voltage electricity across a gap between its two electrodes to ignite the fuel mixture.

SPARK-PLUG GAPPING: Adjusting a spark plug's side electrode to alter its distance from the center electrode.

SPECIFIC GRAVITY: Measuring ratio based on a comparison of the density of a standard substance (such as water) with that of another substance (such as coolant or electrolyte).

SPEEDOMETER: Instrument that measures the rotation of the transmission output shaft to indicate the car's forward speed.

SPINDLE: Shaft on which the front wheel of a car and its bearings are mounted.

SPIN-OUT: Skid in which all four wheels lose traction, causing the car to swing out of control and revolve from end to end.

STAB BRAKING: Emergency braking method in which the driver rapidly pumps the brake pedal with a series of sharp, brief stamps.

STABILIZER BAR: Transversely mounted spring-steel bar that controls and minimizes body lean or tipping during turns.

STATOR: Vaned ring in a torque converter that directs oil from the driven member back to the driving member.

STEAM ENGINE: See *Rankine-cycle engine.*

STEERING ARMS: Short metal rods that transmit turning motion from the tie rods to the steering knuckles.

STEERING BOX: Mechanism at the lower end of the steering column that translates the steering-wheel rotation into linear motion to turn the wheels.

STEERING KNUCKLE: Device that is pivoted by the steering mechanism, causing the wheels to turn.

STIRLING-CYCLE ENGINE: External-combustion engine that uses gas that is alternately heated and cooled within a closed system to drive pistons.

STRATIFIED-CHARGE ENGINE: Modification of the piston engine in which both lean and rich fuel mixtures are simultaneously supplied to each cylinder.

STROKE: Total distance a piston travels within a cylinder.

SUMP: See *pan.*

SYNCHROMESH TRANSMISSION: Manual transmission in which all gears are constantly meshed and ratios are selected by moving synchronizing rings.

SYNCHRONIZING RINGS: Devices in a synchromesh transmission that bring up the speed of the driven gear to that of the driving gear and lock the driven gear to the output shaft of the transmission.

TACHOMETER: Instrument that measures engine speed in revolutions per minute.

TAILPIPE: Section of the exhaust system from the muffler to the rear of the car.

THERMOSTAT: Device used to control the temperature of air, gas or liquid flowing through a system.

THICKNESS GAUGE: See *feeler-gauge.*

THROTTLE VALVE: Valve in the carburetor that regulates the amount of fuel mixture reaching the cylinders.

TIE ROD: Part of the steering linkage that connects the steering arm to the relay rod.

TIMING CHAIN: Chain that drives the camshaft by linking it to the crankshaft.

TIMING LIGHT: Stroboscopic light that is aimed at the timing marks on the crankshaft pulley or flywheel while timing the ignition of an engine.

TIMING MARKS: Marks on the crankshaft pulley or flywheel that correspond to the position of the piston in the first cylinder of an engine.

TIMING THE IGNITION: Tune-up procedure in which spark-plug firing is adjusted to occur at the correct instant of a given piston's cycle.

TIRE: See *belted-bias tire, bias-ply tire, radial tire.*

TIRE BEAD: Reinforced portion of a tire that holds the tire on the wheel rim.

TIRE CARCASS: Body of a tire, exclusive of the tread.

TIRE PLIES: See *plies.*

TIRE PROFILE: Ratio between a tire's tread-to-bead height and its sidewall-to-sidewall width.

TIRE ROTATION: Periodic repositioning of tires on different wheels to equalize irregular wear and prolong tread life.

TIRE SIDEWALL: Portion of a tire carcass between the tread and the bead.

TIRE TREAD: The part of a tire that contacts the road.

TOE-IN: Condition in which the distance between the front wheels of a car is less at their front than at their rear; front wheels normally are aligned to turn in a fraction of an inch.

TOE-OUT: Condition in which the distance between the front wheels of a car is greater at their front than at their rear; this turning out causes uneven tire wear.

TOP DEAD CENTER (TDC): Point at which a piston reaches the top of its travel in a cylinder.

TORQUE: Turning or twisting force.

TORQUE CONVERTER: Unit that transfers and multiplies engine torque in an automatic transmission.

TORQUE MULTIPLICATION: Process by which engine torque is increased.

TORQUE WRENCH: Wrench used to secure fasteners to a specified tension by measuring the torque being applied.

TORSION BAR: Steel rod that twists to provide spring action in a suspension system.

TRACK: Distance between either the two front wheels or the two rear wheels of a car.

TRANSMISSION: Gear unit that varies the relative speeds of the engine and the driving wheels to produce the proper amount of torque for different driving situations.

TREAD-WEAR INDICATORS: Horizontal bands molded into

a tire tread that appear across the tread grooves when only 1/16 of an inch of tread-rubber remains.

TUNE-UP: Process of checking, repairing and adjusting various components of the ignition and fuel systems to obtain maximum engine performance.

TURBINE ENGINE: Internal-combustion engine that utilizes burning gases to drive a turbine, or vaned wheel, which turns a drive shaft.

TWO-STROKE-CYCLE ENGINE: Engine that requires two strokes of each piston to complete its power-producing combustion cycle.

UNDERSTEER: Tendency of a car, when rounding a corner, to resist the turning forces applied by the driver and continue instead in a straight line.

UNIVERSAL JOINT: Flexible coupling between two rotating shafts that allows one shaft to be at an angle to the other.

V-TYPE ENGINE: Internal-combustion engine in which the cylinders are arranged in two banks at an angle to each other.

VACUUM: Condition inside a closed area (such as a pipe or chamber) in which the pressure of air or other gases present is less than the surrounding atmosphere.

VACUUM ADVANCE: Unit on the distributor that uses the intake-manifold vacuum to adjust the ignition timing.

VACUUM BOOSTER: Device that utilizes a vacuum to increase the force applied.

VACUUM PUMP: Pump that uses a diaphragm or a piston to produce a vacuum.

VALVE: Device used to open and close an aperture.

VALVE LIFTER: Device activated by the camshaft to move a pushrod, thus causing a valve to open and close.

VALVE PORT: Aperture in the cylinder head or engine block opened or closed by either an intake or exhaust valve.

VALVE SPRING: Coil spring used to keep a valve closed.

VALVE TRAIN: Engine valves and the parts that operate them.

VANE: Metal blade or plate jutting from a rotating unit that moves gas or liquid (as in a pump) or that is moved by gas or liquid (as in a turbine).

VAPOR LOCK: Vaporization of fuel within a fuel line that impedes its flow to the carburetor.

VAPORIZATION: Process in which a liquid (such as gasoline) is converted into a gas.

VARNISH: Deposits formed within an engine or carburetor by the breakdown of oil or gasoline.

VENTURI: Tapered constriction within the barrel of a carburetor that speeds up the flow of air and thus creates a partial vacuum that pulls in more fuel.

VISCOSITY: Measure of an oil's thickness and hence its inherent ability to flow.

VISCOSITY INDEX: Measure of an oil's ability to resist changes in viscosity when it becomes heated.

VOLT: Unit of electrical force that will move a current of one ampere through a resistance of one ohm.

VOLTMETER: Electrical instrument used to measure voltage in a circuit.

WANKEL ENGINE: Rotary engine, designed by German engineer Felix Wankel.

WATER JACKET: Passages in the engine block around the cylinder and valves through which coolant circulates.

WHEEL BALANCE: Distribution of weight within a wheel-and-tire assembly; a balanced wheel rotates without vibration.

WHEEL CYLINDER: Part of a hydraulic drum-brake system that transmits pressure from the master cylinder to cause the brake shoes to be moved.

WHEELBASE: Distance between the centers of the front and the rear wheels.

WORM GEAR: Spiral-shaped gear in the steering box used to engage and drive another gear.

WRIST PIN: Round steel pin inserted through a piston to which a connecting rod is fastened.

PICTURE CREDITS

The sources for the illustrations in this book are shown below. All illustrations by Arthur D. Gustafson except pages 8—Edward Frank. 11—The Bettmann Archive, Inc. 12—James Alexander. 16—Edward Frank. 58—Edward Frank. 61—Edward Frank, statistics from *1971 World Motor Vehicle Data*, Motor Vehicle Manufacturers Association of the United States, Inc., August 1972. 63—Edward Frank. 65—Statistics from *1972 Automobile Facts and Figures*, Motor Vehicle Manufacturers Association of the United States, Inc. 66—Frank Pagnato. 68—Edward Frank. 77—Base cost formula from *Consumer Reports*, April 1973. 80—Edward Frank. 88—*NADA Official Used Car Guide*, Eastern Edition, April 1973. 100—Jerome Kuhl. 104—Edward Frank. 107—Statistics from *Cost of Operating an Automobile*, U.S. Department of Transportation, April 1972. 108—Frank Pagnato, based on statistics from *Cost of Operating an Automobile*, U.S. Department of Transportation, April 1972. 114—Edward Frank. 116—Frank Pagnato, based on statistics from The National Safety Council. 126—Edward Frank. 128,131, 133,135—Nicholas Fasciano. 136—Frank Pagnato. 138 through 142—Nicholas Fasciano. 150,190,226,252—Edward Frank. 267—Nicholas Fasciano. 270—Edward Frank. 272—Jerome Kuhl. 274,275—Frank Pagnato, based on *How to Drive*, American Automobile Association, 1972. 277—Nicholas Fasciano. 280—Edward Frank. 281,282,283—Frank Pagnato. 284—Nicholas Fasciano. 286—Frank Pagnato. 291—Top to bottom: Nicholas Fasciano; Frank Pagnato; Nicholas Fasciano. 294—Edward Frank. 296,297—Edward Frank, based on *Recreational Vehicle Buyer's Guide*, Chevrolet Division, General Motors Corporation, 1973. 300 through 310—George V. Kelvin. 312—Frank Pagnato. 314—Edward Frank. 317—Top to bottom: Howard V. Brown from *Science and Invention* (May 1923) photographed by Christine E. Haycock from the science-fiction collection of Sam Moskowitz and redrawn by James Alexander; Leo Morey from *Amazing Stories* (August 1934) photographed by Christine E. Haycock from the science-fiction collection of Sam Moskowitz and redrawn by James Alexander; Frank R. Paul from *Amazing Stories* (February 1928) photographed by Christine E. Haycock from the science-fiction collection of Sam Moskowitz and redrawn by James Alexander. 319 through 325—Nicholas Fasciano. 327—Philips Research Laboratories, N. V. Philips, Eindhoven, The Netherlands, and redrawn by Nicholas Fasciano. 329—Industrie Pirelli and redrawn by Frank Pagnato. 330 through 335—Dan Todd. 336 through 341—Syd Mead.

BIBLIOGRAPHY

General

Allen, Willard A., *Know Your Car, Second Edition*. American Technical Society, 1971.

Denison, Merrill, *The Power to Go*. Doubleday, 1956.

Donovan, Frank R., *Wheels for a Nation*. Thomas Y. Crowell, 1965.

*Fales, E. D. Jr., *The Book of Expert Driving*. Hawthorne Books, 1970.

†Fales, E. D. Jr., and Neil Soderstrom, *How to Drive to Prevent Accidents*. Popular Science/E. P. Dutton, 1971.

Georgano, G. N., ed., *The Complete Encyclopedia of Motorcars: 1885 to the Present*. E. P. Dutton, 1968.

Gillespie, Paul, and Miriam T. Klipper, *No-Fault*. Praeger, 1972.

†Lee, Albert, *The IGO Guide to Best Buys in Used Cars, 1973 Edition*. Bantam Books, 1972.

Nevins, Allan, *Ford: The Times, the Man, the Company*. Charles Scribner's Sons, 1954.

*O'Connell, Jeffrey, *The Injury Industry and the Remedy of No-Fault Insurance*. Commerce Clearing House, 1971.

*Rae, John B., *The American Automobile*. University of Chicago Press, 1965.

Randall, Donald A., and Arthur P. Glickman, *The Great American Auto Repair Robbery*. Charterhouse, 1972.

Sports Illustrated Editors, *Sports Illustrated Book of Safe Driving*. J. B. Lippincott, 1962.

*Stapley, Ray, *The Car Owner's Handbook*. Doubleday, 1971.

*Till, Anthony, *What You Should Know Before You Have Your Car Repaired*. Sherbourne Press, 1970.

Technical

Ayers, Robert U., and Richard P. McKenna, *Alternatives to the Internal Combustion Engine: Impact on Environmental Quality*. Johns Hopkins University Press, 1972.

Blanchard, Harold F., and Ralph Ritchen, *Auto Engines and Electrical Systems, Fifth Edition*. Motor, 1970.

Crouse, William H., *Automotive Mechanics, Sixth Edition*. McGraw-Hill, 1970.

Day, Richard, *How to Service and Repair Your Own Car*. Popular Science/Harper & Row, 1973.

Goings, Leslie F., and Edward D. Spicer, *Automotive Maintenance and Troubleshooting, Fourth Edition*. American Technical Society, 1972.

Schofield, Miles, ed., *Motor Trend Basic Auto Repair Manual No. 4*. Petersen, 1972.

Stockel, Martin W., *Auto Mechanics Fundamentals*. Goodheart-Willcox, 1969.

Stockel, Martin W., *Auto Service and Repair*. Goodheart-Willcox, 1969.

Toboldt, William K., and Larry Johnson, eds., *Motor Service's Automotive Encyclopedia*. Goodheart-Willcox, 1972.

Weissler, Paul, ed., *Auto Repairs You Can Make*. Arco, 1971.

Periodicals

Automotive News, Marketing Services Inc., Detroit.

Car and Driver, Ziff-Davis Publishing Company, New York City.

Consumer Reports, Consumers Union, Mount Vernon, New York.

Motor Trend, Petersen Publishing Company, Los Angeles.

NADA Official Used Car Guide, National Automobile Dealers Used Car Guide Company, Washington, D.C.

Popular Mechanics, The Hearst Corporation, New York City.

Popular Science, Popular Science Publishing Company, New York City.

Other Publications

Accident Facts, 1972 Edition, National Safety Council.

Automobile Facts and Figures, 1972, Motor Vehicle Manufacturers Association of the United States.

Care and Service of Automobile Tires, Rubber Manufacturers Association, 1972.

Digest of Motor Laws, Fortieth Edition, American Automobile Association, 1973.

Hearings before the Subcommittee on Antitrust and Monopoly of the Committee on the Judiciary, United States Senate, Ninetieth Congress, Second Session, Automotive Repair Industry, U.S. Government Printing Office, 1969.

How to Drive, American Automobile Association, 1972.

Manual on Uniform Traffic Control Devices, Federal Highway Administration, U.S. Department of Transportation, 1971.

Motor Vehicle Crash Losses and Their Compensation in the United States, U.S. Department of Transportation, 1971.

Recreational Vehicle Facts and Trends, Recreational Vehicle Institute, 1973.

Tires: Their Selection and Care, F. C. Brenner, U.S. Department of Commerce, 1971.

Transportation Systems Technology: A Twenty-Year Outlook, George Kovatch, John B. Barber, Robert F. Casey, and George Zames, Office of the Secretary of Transportation, 1971.

World Motor Vehicle Data, 1971, Motor Vehicle Manufacturers Association of the United States, 1972.

* Also available in paperback   † Available only in paperback

ACKNOWLEDGMENTS

For their valuable assistance and contributions in the preparation of this book, the editors are particularly indebted to: George E. Brown, General Service Manager, American Motors Corporation, Detroit; M. R. Mutcher, Regional Public Relations Manager, Ford Motor Company, New York City; C. James Stickford, Manager, Eastern News Bureau, Chrysler Corporation, New York City; and Harry A. Turton and William B. Winters, Public Relations Staff, General Motors Corporation, New York City. They also wish to express their gratitude to: A. P. Aquilino, President, Manhattan Ford, Lincoln-Mercury, Inc., New York City; Gordon M. Baird, Staff Assistant, Service Section, General Motors Corporation, Detroit; Charles G. Barta, Technical Service Manager, S. C. Johnson & Son, Inc., Racine, Wisconsin; Stewart Baumgardner, President, Colorado Leisure Products, Inc., Broomfield, Colorado; Dr. Lees Booth, Senior Vice President, National Consumer Finance Association, Washington, D.C.; Philip Borelli Jr., Philbors Camperland, Hempstead, New York; William P. Boyer, Design Executive, Advanced Vehicles Design Center, Ford Motor Company, Dearborn, Michigan; James Bradley, Librarian, Automotive History Collection, Detroit Public Library, Detroit; Richard Burkhard, Manager of Quality Assurance, Globe-Union Inc., Milwaukee; B. H. Cason, Service Technical Support Assistant Manager, American Motors Corporation, Detroit; Mary M. Cattie, Librarian, Automotive Reference Collection, Philadelphia Free Library, Philadelphia; Robert J. Cerullo, Vice President, Vins Motor Service Corporation, Brooklyn, New York; J. H. Coyner, Advertising Manager, Delco-Remy Division, General Motors Corporation, Anderson, Indiana; Alice Critchley, Librarian, Automotive Information Council, New York City; Tom Decker, Maxon's Trailer World, Union, New Jersey; John T. Doran, Traffic Officer, California Highway Patrol, Indio, California; George Dunning, Store Manager, The Goodyear Tire & Rubber Company, New York City; W. Paul DuPré, Public Relations Director, Recreational Vehicle Institute, Des Plaines, Illinois; Peter Earl, Eastern Regional Public Relations Manager, The Goodyear Tire & Rubber Company, New York City; Dave Edwards, President, G. H. Meiser & Company, Blue Island, Illinois; Dorothy G. Emery, Ford Motor Company, New York City; Douglas C. Evans, Field Service Manager, Customer Service Division, Ford Motor Company, White Plains, New York; Herbert S. Fuhrman, President, National Institute for Automotive Service Excellence, Washington, D.C.; Morris G. Garter, Manager, Highway Safety Planning and Programs, Ford Motor Company, Dearborn, Michigan; Milton Goldish, President, Milton Manufacturing Company, Chicago; Alfred Haggerty, Insurance Information Institute, New York City; Joel Hamilton, Englewood, New Jersey; D. M. Hanley, Service Research Shop Supervisor, American Motors Corporation, Detroit; D. E. Helf, Product Reliability Manager, United Delco Division, General Motors Corporation, Detroit; David A. Herbert, Technical Service Representative for Automotive Products, Marshall Research and Development Laboratory, E. I. duPont de Nemours & Co., Philadelphia; Stanley Hopper, Vice President, Valley Tow-Rite, A Division of the Scott & Fetzer Company, Lodi, California; M. J. Horan, Product Coordinator, American Petroleum Institute, Washington, D.C.; G. J. Irwin, Supervisor, Technical Service, U.S. Automotive Sales and Service, Chrysler Corporation, Detroit; Ed Jurist, The Vintage Car Store, Nyack, New York; Robert H. Kastengren, Executive Vice President, Runzheimer and Company, Inc., Rochester, Wisconsin; Donald Keen, Director of Public Relations, Rubber Manufacturers Association, New York City; Kenneth Kingsley, Manufacturers Hanover Trust Company, New York City; James H. Lawrence, Director, National Automobile Dealers Used Car Guide Company, Washington, D.C.; J. J. Layton, Service Technical Support Manager, American Motors Corporation, Detroit; Leo Levine, General Manager, Public Relations, Mercedes-Benz of North America, Montvale, New Jersey; L. E. Loeffler, Marketing Manager, Philips Laboratories, North American Philips Corporation, Briarcliff Manor, New York; Eugene L. Malice, President, Mid-County Buick, Inc., Brooklyn, New York; Dr. Craig Marks, Technical Assistant to the Vice President of Engineering, General Motors Corporation, Warren, Michigan; Samuel L. Marshall, The Marshall Motor Company, Cleveland; James B. McCormick, Assistant Vice President and Manager, Loss Prevention Department, Liberty Mutual Insurance Companies, Boston; Paul Michel, Service Manager, Manhattan Ford, Lincoln-Mercury, Inc., New York City; Gale S. Molovinsky, Attorney, National Automobile Dealers Association, Washington, D.C.; John Pohanka, Pohanka Oldsmobile, Marlow Heights, Maryland; Joseph E. Ripley, Assistant to the Director, Tire Development, The Goodyear Tire & Rubber Company, Akron, Ohio; Stanley S. Roe, Manager, Statistics Department, Motor Vehicle Manufacturers Association of the U.S., Inc., Detroit; Asa Sharp, Tire Development, The Goodyear Tire & Rubber Company, Akron, Ohio; Don Sorum, Sales Manager for Mass Marketing, Valley Tow-Rite, A Division of the Scott & Fetzer Company, Lodi, California; W. M. Spreitzer, Head, Transportation and Urban Analysis Department, General Motors Corporation, Warren, Michigan; Dr. E. H. Wallace, Chief, Tire Division, National Highway Traffic Safety Administration, U.S. Department of Transportation, Washington, D.C.; Richard G. Wiliford, Public Relations Manager for Automotive Department, Sears Roebuck & Company, Chicago; Frank J. Winchell, Vice President of Engineering, General Motors Corporation, Warren, Michigan; H. W. Wynn, Service Training Specialist, United Delco Division, General Motors Corporation, Detroit; Sam Yaksich Jr., Director, Traffic Engineering & Safety, American Automobile Association, Washington, D.C.; James A. Young, Automotive Trade Practices Manager, The Council of Better Business Bureaus, Inc., Washington, D.C.

INDEX